Electricity Restructuring in the United States
Markets and Policy from the 1978 Energy Act to the Present

The electric utility industry in the United States is technologically complex, and its structure as a classic network industry makes it intricate in business terms as well, so deregulation of such a complicated industry was a particularly detailed process. Steve Isser provides a detailed and comprehensive analysis of the history of the transformation of this complex industry from the 1978 Energy Policy Act to the present, covering the economic, legal, regulatory, and political issues and controversies in the transition from regulated utilities to competitive electricity markets. The book is a multidisciplinary study that includes a comprehensive review of the economic literature on electricity markets, the political environment of electricity policy making, administrative and regulatory rule making, and the federal case law that restrained state and federal regulation of electricity. Dr. Isser offers a valuable case study of the pitfalls and problems associated with the deregulation of a complex network industry.

Steve Isser, PhD, JD, is the president of Energy Law & Economics, Inc. His work has been published in *Mathematical Modeling, Review of Policy Research*, and *Public Utility Fortnightly*, as well as two books on oil economics and politics.

Electricity Restructuring in the United States

Markets and Policy from the 1978 Energy Act to the Present

STEVE ISSER

Energy Law & Economics, Inc.

CAMBRIDGE
UNIVERSITY PRESS

CAMBRIDGE
UNIVERSITY PRESS

University Printing House, Cambridge CB2 8BS, United Kingdom

One Liberty Plaza, 20th Floor, New York, NY 10006, USA

477 Williamstown Road, Port Melbourne, VIC 3207, Australia

314-321, 3rd Floor, Plot 3, Splendor Forum, Jasola District Centre, New Delhi - 110025, India

79 Anson Road, #06-04/06, Singapore 079906

Cambridge University Press is part of the University of Cambridge.

It furthers the University's mission by disseminating knowledge in the pursuit of education, learning and research at the highest international levels of excellence.

www.cambridge.org
Information on this title: www.cambridge.org/9781107498228

© Steve Isser 2015

First published 2015
First paperback edition 2019

A catalogue record for this publication is available from the British Library

ISBN 978-1-107-10078-7 Hardback
ISBN 978-1-107-49822-8 Paperback

To My "Pack," and the memory of its departed members, and my wife Rhonda, the heart and soul of the Pack

Contents

Tables

Figures

Acronyms

AC	Alternating Current
AEP	American Electric Power
AGC	Automatic Generation Control
ALJ	Administrative Law Judge
ANWR	Artic National Wildlife Refuge
APPA	American Public Power Association
ATC	Available Transmission Capacity
BACT	Best Available Control Technology
CAA	Clean Air Act
CAFE	Corporate Average Fuel Economy
CAIR	Clean Air Interstate Rule
CAISO	California Independent System Operator
CDWR	California Department of Water Resources
CEC	California Energy Commission
CFTC	Commodities Futures Trading Commission
Com Ed	Commonwealth Edison
Con Ed	Consolidated Edison of New York
CONE	Cost of New Entry
CPUC	California Public Utility Commission
CSW	Central and SouthWest Corporation
CTC	Competitive Transition Charge
DC	Direct Current
DOE	Department of Energy
DOJ	Department of Justice
DSM	Demand Side Management

EDF	Environmental Defense Fund
EEI	Edison Electric Institute
EPAct	Energy Policy Act
EPRI	Electric Power Research Institute
ERCOT	Electric Reliability Council of Texas
ERO	Electric Reliability Organization
FCM	Forward Capacity Market
FERC	Federal Energy Regulatory Commission
FPA	Federal Power Act
FPC	Federal Power Commission
FTC	Federal Trade Commission
FTR	Financial Transmission Right
HHI	Herfindahl-Hirschman Index
ICAP	Installed Capacity
ICE	Intercontinental Exchange
IOU	Investor Owned Utilites
IPP	Independent Power Producer
IRP	Integrated Resource Planning
ISO	Independent System Operator
ISO-NE	Independent System Operator–New England
LaaR	Load Acting As a Resource
LECG	Law and Economics Group
LMP	Locational Marginal Prices
LSE	Load Serving Entity
MAPP	MidContinent Area Power Pool
MISO	Midwest Independent System Operator
NAAQS	National Ambient Air Quality Standards
NARUC	National Association of Regulatory Utility Commissioners
NEPA	National Environmental Policy Act
NEPOOL	New England Power Pool
NERC	North American Electric Reliability Corporation (formerly Council)
NIETC	National Interest Electric Transmission Corridor
NIMBY	Not In My Back Yard
NO_x	Nitrous Oxides
NOPR	Notice of Proposed Rule making
NRDC	Natural Resources Defense Council
NSPS	New Source Performance Standards
NSR	New Source Review

NYISO	New York Independent System Operator
NYMEX	New York Mercantile Exchange
NYPP	New York Power Pool
OASIS	Open Access Same-time Information System
OATT	Open Access Transmisson Tariff
PJM	Pennsylvania–New Jersey–Maryland Interconnection
$PM_{2.5}$	Small Particulate Matter (under 2.5 microns)
POLR	Provider of Last Resort
PPA	Purchased Power Agreement
PSD	Prevention of Significant Deterioration
PUHCA	Public Utilities Holding Company Act of 1935
PURPA	Public Utility Regulatory Policies Act of 1978
QF	Qualifying Facility
REP	Retail Electric Provider
RPM	Reliability Pricing Model
RTG	Regional Transmission Group
RTO	Regional Transmission Organization
SCADA	Supervisory Control and Data Acquisition
SCED	Security Constrained Economic Dispatch
SIP	State Implementation Plans
SO_2	Sulfur Dioxide
SPP	Southwest Power Pool
TLR	Transmisson Loading Relief
Transco	Transmission Company
TTC	Total Transmisson Capability
VoLL	Value of Lost Load
WSCC	Western Systems Coordinating Council
WSPP	Western Systems Power Pool

Energy Terminology

Barrel	Standard measure for Crude Oil, there are 42 gallons per barrel
Btu	British Thermal Unit (measure of energy)
kW	Kilowatt (measure of capacity)
kWh	Kilowatt-hour (measure of energy)
Mcf	Thousand cubic feet
MMBtu	Million Btu
MW	Megawatt (1000 kW)
MWh	Megawatt-hour

Energy Conversion Rates

Coal	20.1 million Btu per ton (varies per type of coal)
Crude oil	5.850 million Btu per barrel
Electricity	3,412 Btu per kWh
Natural gas	1.022 million Btu per Mcf
Residual fuel oil	6.287 million Btu per barrel

Introduction

Since all models are wrong the scientist cannot obtain a "correct" one by excessive elaboration. On the contrary following William of Occam he should seek an economical description of natural phenomena. Just as the ability to devise simple but evocative models is the signature of the great scientist so overelaboration and overparameterization is often the mark of mediocrity.

Since all models are wrong the scientist must be alert to what is importantly wrong. It is inappropriate to be concerned about mice when there are tigers abroad.
— George E. P. Box, "Science and Statistics," *Journal of the American Statistical Association* 71 (December 1976): 792

This book evolved out of what was originally planned as a one-volume work on the evolution of U.S. energy policy since the 1980s. It quickly became apparent that the topic was simply too complex to be contained in one book, so the project has morphed into a number of books. This book covers electricity restructuring in the United States from 1978 to the present.[1] The second book will cover oil and natural gas deregulation through the peak oil issue and shale gas development. The third book will focus on the future of energy, from global warming to new technologies. Since I plan to cover topics such as smart grid, renewable energy, and carbon markets in the future, I've given them cursory coverage in this volume.

---

[1] As opposed to deregulation, because what has become evident is that the electricity regulation has changed, but there are no unregulated electricity markets, nor will there be in the foreseeable future.

This book was written with academic rigor, but my intended audience are people who do things, not merely write about what others have done: energy lawyers, judges, consultants, regulatory commissioners, and their senior staff who want a deeper understanding of the industry. I have tried to tone down the more esoteric economic and legal concepts and banished many details to footnotes where the curious reader can go for guidance to the relevant legal cases and monographs.

This book is an economic/business history, and a case study of the complexities of transitioning from one regulatory regime to another, more diverse regulatory regime. History matters because one cannot understand the evolution of political decisions such as the passage of the Federal Power Act and the Energy Policy Acts of 1978 and 1992, nor how they shaped regulatory policy, investment decisions, and market outcomes, simply by the application of public choice models. Geography, technology, and politics caused different regions to have different incentives to welcome or resist restructuring and different means to encourage or resist its imposition. Federalism, ideology, and happenstance were as important in determining outcomes as the visible hand of politics and the invisible hand of the market. Regulatory choices determined market outcomes, since the set of rules and incentives that shaped the markets were the products of legislation and regulatory decisions. Market outcomes in turn influenced legislation and regulatory decisions, as economic actors invested resources into obtaining favorable decisions in the political and regulatory arenas.

This work is an unapologetic economic policy history that is more focused on description than theory. There has been a long-term trend in economics (and more recently political science) to denigrate qualitative analysis. Descriptive evidence is often given the pejorative name "anecdote." Ironically, this term has been used both ways, as "the plural of anecdote is data"[2] and "the plural of anecdote is not data."[3] To this observer, the confusion simply reveals a prejudice toward data that are quantifiable and easily organized into data matrices amenable to statistical manipulation. Anecdotes tend to be messy. Anecdotes that are simple observations are of limited value, but I would suggest that "anecdote"

---

[2] This phrase was coined by Raymond Wolfinger in 1969, but first appeared in print in Nelson W. Polsby, "Where Do You Get Your Ideas?" *PS: Political Science and Politics* 26 (1993): 83–87, http://blog.revolutionanalytics.com/2011/04/the-plural-of-anecdote-is-data-after-all.html (last visited May 1, 2012).

[3] This phrase has frequently been attributed to both Roger Brinner and George Stigler, but I cannot find a definitive source for its origins.

also applies to what are referred to as case studies, frequently created and applied by business professors, and economic histories, which unfortunately have fallen out of favor in the economics profession.[4] An economic history could be characterized as a more complete and thoroughly researched case study.[5] The value of economic history is that it allows economic theory and econometric results to be reviewed in light of their correspondence with reality. A good descriptive study will reveal nuances missed by theory and left out of econometric studies.

I value the insights to be gleaned from academic economists (and strained out of reports by consulting economists), but this is not an economic analysis of electricity markets.[6] I am interested in the economic debates as they pertain to policymaking, and the consequences of adopting a specific economic conclusion or recommendation. So my focus is not on economic theory, but the adoption of theory to political positions, regulatory decision making, and actual market design and operation. In this context, I am less interested in the validity of economic models than their influence on politics and policymakers and how these economic models were transformed into operational concepts. There is quite a leap from equations in a paper to the complex software models and detailed market rules embedded in an electricity market.

One problem with the economists' approach to restructuring was the tendency to dismiss the institutional environment and the restrictions created by technological limitations and requirements, which had an important influence on the actual outcome of economic policy change.[7] Markets

---

4 This trend has been proceeding for a few decades. Donald McCloskey, "Does the Past Have Use Economics?" *Journal of Economic History* (1976): 434–61. White claims there is still a place for economic history apart from Cliometrics; Euguene White, "The Past and Future of Economic History in Economics," *Quarterly Review of Economics and Finance* 36 (1996): 61–72. An interesting article uses geology, not physics, as the paradigm for economic history; Larry Neal, "A Shocking View of Economic History," *Journal of Economic History* 60 (June 2000): 317–34.

5 I always thought business history was economic history, but it seems there is a serious intellectual divide between the two. I confess to being more of a business historian if those distinctions have meaning. Naomi Lamoreaux, Daniel Raff, and Peter Temin, "New Economic Approaches to the Study of Business History," *Business and Economic History* 26 (Fall 1997): 57–79. Case studies tend to be snapshots, focused on a single issue or strategy, while an economic or business history will range over a longer period or wider scope of issues.

6 I recommend Steven Stoft, *Power System Economics: Designing Markets for Electricity* (New York, IEEE Press and Wiley-Interscience, 2002) as an accessible introduction to electricity economics.

7 Paul Joskow, "Regulation and Deregulation after 25 Years: Lessons Learned for Research in Industrial Organization," *Review of Industrial Organization* 26 (2005): 176–77.

are created by and operate within a complex legal structure. Depending on the type of goods and transactions, tort, property, and contract law principles may apply. Depending on the market structure and the perceived existence of externalities, competition and environmental regulations may impact the transaction. There may be overlapping legal jurisdictions, federal, state, and local, that have authority over different aspects of a transaction. There may also be written and unwritten standards of behavior created by customary practice and industry associations.

Complex market/institutional systems such as the electricity industry tend to be characterized by path dependence and lock-in on multiple levels. Path dependence occurs when initial conditions are followed by a series of contingent (or chance) events whose influence on the path taken is larger than that of the initial conditions themselves. Contingency in organizational life can take many shapes (e.g., unexpected encounters, trial-and-errors leading to unattended consequences).[8] In a path-dependent pattern, selection processes during a critical juncture period are marked by contingency. Once a path has been contingently selected, various mechanisms can lead to its self-reinforcement, such as positive network externalities, increasing returns, sunk costs, or adaptive expectations. It becomes progressively more difficult to return to the initial point at which multiple alternatives were still available. Features of self-reinforcement are very common in organizational life.[9] A mechanism that decreases the relative attractiveness of alternatives will lock in one of the possible outcomes if no exogenous shock disturbs the system. Lock-in is a hard-to-escape situation. Because paths are selected contingently, lock-in can happen on any path. Path dependence potentially leads to a large diversity of outcomes owing to the stochastic nature of the underlying process.[10]

Path dependence is also the basis of a theory of institutional change. Institutions are seen as 'carriers of history' that maintain existing

---

[8] Jean-Philippe Vergne and Rodolphe Durand, "The Missing Link Between the Theory and Empirics of Path Dependence; Conceptual Clarification, Testability Issue, and Methodological Implications," *Journal of Management Studies* (2010): 741–43.

[9] W. Brian Arthur, "Competing Technologies, Increasing Returns, and Lock-In By Historical Events," *Economic Journal* 99 (1989): 126–28; Paul Pierson, "Increasing Returns, Path Dependence, and the Study of Politics," *American Political Science Review* 94 (2000): 263–66.

[10] Scott Page, "Path Dependence," *Quarterly Journal of Political Science* 1 (2006): 90; Jean-Philippe Vergne and Rodolphe Durand, "The Missing Link between the Theory and Empirics of Path Dependence: Conceptual Clarification, Testability Issue, and Methodological Implications," *Journal of Management Studies* (2010): 743.

behavioral norms and cultural patterns throughout time. Institutions are the humanly devised constraints that structure human interaction. They are made up of formal constraints (e.g., rules, laws, constitutions), informal constraints (e.g., norms, conventions, codes of conduct), and their enforcement characteristics. Together they define the incentive structure of societies and economies. When it is costly to transact, then institutions matter.[11] Specific path processes are caused by limited rationality on the one hand and high transaction costs for changing institutional systems on the other. Institutional perspectives understand "institutions" as enduring entities that cannot be changed instantaneously or easily. Repeated patterns of investment in human or material resources lead to routine creation and asset specificity, which both introduce stickiness at the governance level and prevent subsequent adjustment. Organizations that thrive within a given institutional matrix have a stake in perpetuating the "rules of the game" that favor their own survival, even when such rules are globally inefficient, thereby hampering institutional change. Path dependence provides an explanation for the "inefficiency of history" that results from the stickiness of institutions. Institutions create reliability of expectations, and ongoing applicability raises an interest in their perpetuation. Change is bounded until something erodes or swamps the mechanisms of reproduction that generate institutional continuity.[12]

Law is a key institution, and both the law, its interpretation and implementation by regulatory agencies, and review by courts impact economic actors. Laws, rules, and regulations are not created in a policy vacuum by disinterested technocrats pursuing an optimal solution. There is a complex interplay of interest groups, ideologically driven actors,[13] and

---

[11] Douglass North, "Economic Performance though Time," *American Economic Review* (1994): 360.

[12] Douglass North, *Institutions, Institutional Change and Economic Performance* (Cambridge, Cambridge University Press, 1990); Paul Pierson, "Increasing Returns, Path Dependence, and the Study of Politics," *American Political Science Review* 94 (2000): 262; James Mahoney, "Path Dependence in Historical Sociology," *Theory and Society* 29 (2000): 510–16; Paul David, "Why Are Institutions the 'Carriers of History': Path Dependence and the Evolution of Conventions, Organizations and Institutions," *Structural Change and Economic Dynamics* 5(1994): 217–19.

[13] Joseph Kalt and Mark Zupan. "Capture and Ideology in the Economic Theory of Politics," *American Economic Review* 74 (June 1984): 279–300; Steve Isser, *The Economics and Politics of the United States Oil Industry, 1920–1990: Profits, Populism, and Petroleum* (New York, Garland Publishing, 1996): 423–35; Lawrence Grossback, Sean Nicholson-Crotty, and David Peterson, "Ideology and Learning in Policy Diffusion," *American Politics Research* 31 (2003): 1–25.

self-selected bureaucrats[14] who often have their own vision of the public good. While regulatory agencies are constrained by procedural rules,[15] and potential intervention by both Congress[16] and the executive branch,[17] in practice they have a great deal of discretion because of the cost of oversight.[18] Judicial oversight also acts to limit agency discretion,[19] and although it is shaped by political considerations,[20] it is also constrained by doctrine laid down by the Supreme Court.[21]

There can be little doubt that path dependence is an important phenomenon in law. Some evidence of this is that the convergence of legal systems is much slower than the convergence of technology and economic institutions. The modem law is full of vestiges of early law. The more heavily the judges rely on precedent, the more likely is current doctrine to be determined by history. Courts' early resolutions of legal issues become locked in and resistant to change. Thus, the order in which cases arrive in the courts can significantly affect the specific legal doctrine that ultimately results. This inflexibility can lead to inefficiency when legal rules fail to respond to changing underlying conditions. Legislators are not constrained by precedent, but their ability to innovate is limited by the inertia built into the legislative process. The Constitution makes it

---

[14] Sue Frank and Gregory Lewis, "Government Employees: Working Hard or Hardly Working," *American Review of Public Administration* 34 (March 2004): 36–51; Sanjay Pandey and Edmund Stazyk, "Antecedents and Correlates of Public Service Motivation," in James L. Perry and Annie Hondeghem, eds., *Motivation in Public Management: The Call of Public Service* (Oxford, Oxford University Press 2008), 80–98.

[15] Lisa Bressman, "Procedures as Politics in Administrative Law," 107 *Columbia Law Review* 1749 (2007).

[16] Jack Beermann, "The Turn Toward Congress in Administrative Law," 89 *Boston University Law Review* 727 (2009).

[17] Gary Coglianese, "Presidential Control of Administrative Agencies: A Debate Over Law or Politics?" 12 *Journal of Constitutional Law* 637 (2010); Lisa Bressman and Michael Vandenbergh, "Inside the Administrative State: A Critical Look at the Practice of Presidential Control," 105 *Michigan Law Review* 47 (2006).

[18] Mathew McCubbins and Thomas Schwartz, "Congressional Oversight Overlooked: Police Patrols versus Fire Alarms," *American Journal Political Science* 28 (February 1984): 165–79.

[19] Thomas Merrill, "Article III, Agency Adjudication, and the Origins of the Appellate Review Model of Administrative Law," 111 *Columbia Law Review* 939–1003 (June 2011).

[20] Thomas Miles and Cass Sunstein, "The Real World of Arbitrariness Review," 75 *University of Chicago Law Review* 761 (2008).

[21] *Chevron U.S.A., Inc. v. Natural Resources Defense Council, Inc.*, 467 U.S. 837 (1984). *See also* Evan Criddle, "Chevron's Consensus," 88 *Boston University Law Review* 1271 (2009); Kenneth Bamberger and Peter Strauss, "Chevron's Two Steps," 95 *Virginia Law Review* 611 (2009).

difficult to enact statutory law, but once enacted, it is, by the same token, difficult to change. The Constitution, being difficult to amend, is itself a potent source of path dependence.[22]

The concept of path dependence and the associated framework of analysis are anchored in the quest to integrate historicity into economics. Path dependence is an important concept for an economic historian, because the economy is embedded in society, which in turn is shaped by its history.[23] It had become evident to some within the field that trying to understand economic history through the assiduous application of ahistorical concepts and tools was a fool's errand. While some mathematical processes do converge to a stable equilibrium, real history does not. Exogenous shocks are a central motor of change, and history is marked by critical junctures in which old routines lose their force and possibilities emerge for new paths, revolution, and wholesale transformation. History proceeds as both punctuated equilibria and as an incremental accumulation of evolutionary changes. When the institution, or technology, legal regime, or behavioral norm has become deeply embedded in numerous activities throughout the economy, an exogenous shock may be required to disrupt the status quo. In other cases, changes in technology and social attitudes over time may erode the stability of the current equilibrium to the extent that incremental change may move society and the economy to a more efficient equilibrium. A great deal of human ingenuity is devoted to trying to cope with "mistakes" and to assure that their more pernicious effects will be moderated, if not abated altogether. This is done ex post, by contriving technological fixes, by creating temporary task forces to handle emergencies, and by sustained efforts at reforming long-standing institutions.[24]

In energy policy in general, and the restructuring of the energy industries in particular, path dependence, exogenous shocks, and adaptive incrementalism have all played a role, at different times and in different

---

[22] Richard Posner, "Past-Dependency, Pragmatism, and Critique of History in Adjudication and Legal Scholarship," 67 *University of Chicago Law Review* 584 (2000); Oona Hathaway, "Path Dependence in the Law: The Course and Pattern of Legal Change in a Common Law System," 86 *Iowa Law Review* 105 (2001).

[23] A system whose evolution exhibits characteristic of path dependency may be more suited to the case study method. Andrew Bennett and Colin Elman, "Complex Causal Relations and Case Study Methods; the Example of Path Dependence," *Political Analysis* 14 (2006): 250–67.

[24] Paul David, "Path Dependence, Its Critics and the Quest for 'Historical Economics'," in Geoffrey Hodgson, ed., *The Evolution of Economic Institutions: A Critical Reader* (Cheltenham, UK, Edward Elgar, 2007): 134–35.

forms. The shape of natural gas and electricity regulation was determined by a stream of jurisprudence that goes back to English common law and *Munn v. Illinois*,[25] delineating the power of the state to control the activities of industries endowed with a "public interest."[26] However, the Great Depression, an exogenous shock to the economy, created the impetus to overturn the status quo and motivate New Deal regulation.[27] Along with the evolution of law and regulatory policy, energy technologies also exhibited path dependence, and the dominance of the pressurized water reactor in the nuclear power industry[28] would result in a serious of misfortunate investments that helped create the climate for deregulation of conventional electricity regulation. The impact of imprudence decisions concerning nuclear power plants was bounded by state court and Supreme Court decisions.[29] The rise of the environmental movement would result in environmental laws and air pollution regulations that would determine the relative economic viability of different generation technologies, while political forces would contort the implementation of those regulations, aided again by court decisions that limited the impact of some regulations.

Other exogenous shocks, such as the Arab Oil Embargo of 1973, and the subsequence rise and then collapse of oil prices, would shake the energy regulatory regime to its core. Developing a new regulatory regime would be an incremental process in natural gas and electricity, but a revolutionary process in oil, where the U.S. market was almost completely deregulated and tied to the world market (oil pipelines remained regulated, but not crude oil or product sales) over a few years. While some

---

[25] *Munn v. Illinois*, 94 U.S. 113 (1876).
[26] Walton Hamilton, "Affectation With Public Interest," 39 *Yale Law Journal* 1089 (1930); Thomas McGraw, "Regulation in America: A Review Article," *Business History Review* 49 (1975); 160–62; Harry Scheiber, "The Road to Munn: Eminent Domain and the Concept of Public Purpose in the State Courts," *Perspectives in American History* 5 (1971): 329–402; Herbert Hovenkamp, "Regulatory Conflict in the Gilded Age: Federalism and the Railroad Problem," 97 *Yale Law Journal* 1017 (1988).
[27] Daniel Gifford, "The New Deal Regulatory Model: A History of Criticisms and Refinements," 68 *Minnesota Law Review* 299 (1993); William Emmons III, "Franklin D. Roosevelt, Electric Utilities, and the Power of Competition," *Journal of Economic History* 54 (1993): 880–907.
[28] Robin Cowan, "Nuclear Power Reactors; A Study in Technological Lock-in," *Journal of Economic History* 50 (1990): 541–67.
[29] Roger Colton, "Excess Capacity: A Case Study in Ratemaking Theory and Application," 20 *Tulsa Law Journal* 402 (1984); Jonathan A. Lesser, "The Used and Useful Test: Implications for a Restructured Electricity Industry," 23 *Energy Law Journal* 349 (2002).

observers might claim that the path taken to the eventual restructuring of natural gas was irrelevant, given that the final outcome – deregulation of production at the federal level and restructuring of pipelines and distribution regulation – was inevitable, the path taken had important implications for the shape of electricity restructuring.

The Creation of the Electricity Regulatory Regime

The structure of the utility industry evolved during the twentieth century from one composed of many small private and municipal electric power companies to large private utilities that integrated electricity generation, transmission and distribution, and sales. These private utilities were created by the merger of small companies or by their absorption by a private utility. This process continued with larger utilities often combining under holding companies. Municipal and cooperative utilities reemerged in the 1930s, when the federal government joined the electric power industry as a wholesale supplier, mainly through the development of large hydroelectric sites. Federal participation spurred the growth of other publicly and cooperatively owned utilities by offering them the preferential sale of lower-priced federally generated power, as well as federal low-interest loans and other technical assistance.[30]

During the early 1930s, two developments impeded state public utility commissions (PUCs) from effectively regulating electricity and natural gas rates of Investor owned utilities (IOUs) operating in their states. The *Attleboro* case held that the Dormant Commerce Clause precluded states from regulating interstate wholesale sales of electricity and natural gas, and created a gap between state and federal regulation of electricity.[31] *Attleboro* prevented states from regulating the prices that retail utilities paid for power they purchased at wholesale, allowing utilities to circumvent cost-based state regulation. The second development was the emergence of multistate holding companies, which, because of their size and complexity, defied effective regulation by the states. *Attleboro* allowed these holding companies to shift costs among subsidiaries through price discrimination in the sale of wholesale electricity.

A 1928 investigation by the Federal Trade Commission (FTC) led to hearings by the House Committee on Interstate and Foreign Commerce

---

[30] EIA, *The Changing Structure of the Electric Power Industry, 1970–1991* (1991): 3–4.
[31] *Pub. Util. Comm'n of Rhode Island v. Attleboro Steam & Electric Co.*, 273 U.S. 83, 89 (1927).

and the Senate Committee on Interstate Commerce between 1933 and 1935, resulting in the two-part Public Utility Act of 1935,[32] which included both the Public Utility Holding Company Act (PUHCA)[33] and the Federal Power Act (FPA), Part II of the Public Utility Act. The FPA gave federal authorities jurisdiction over interstate electricity transactions. The prices of transmission service (wheeling) and wholesale trades of power between utilities have been regulated by the Federal Power Commission (FPC) or its successor agency, the Federal Energy Regulatory Commission (FERC), since 1935.

PUHCA reshaped the industry by limiting the operations of the holding company system to a single integrated public utility system.[34] Between 1938 and 1955, 214 holding companies controlling 922 electric and gas utilities and more than 1,000 nonutility companies were reduced to 25 holding companies with 171 electric and gas subsidiaries and 137 nonutility subsidiaries, and nearly $13 billion in assets were divested in the process. The effective result was to reduce holding companies to one integrated gas or electric system with only functionally related subsidiaries.[35] The vertically integrated, investor-owned utility, primarily operating within one state, became the fundamental economic unit of the industry.[36]

The FPA extended regulation not only to the transmission of electricity in interstate commerce but also to the sale of wholesale electric energy that entered interstate commerce. Jurisdiction over local distribution and intrastate transmission was left with the states.[37] The FPC was

[32] See 49 Stat. 803 (1935).

[33] 15 U.S. Code §§79 *et seq.* (repealed in 2005). Also known as the Wheeler-Rayburn Act. PUHCA gave the Securities and Exchange Commission broad authority over the structure, finances, and operations of public utility holding companies.

[34] 49 Stat. at 820.

[35] Robert L. Bradley, Jr. "The Origins of Political Electricity: Market Failure or Political Opportunism?" *Energy Law Journal* 17 (1996): 59, 86.

[36] Attempts to break the status quo and move to a more efficient electricity network during the 1920s in the Northeast (Superpower) and Pennsylvania (Giant Power) failed to gain traction, despite large potential gains in trade, estimated to be as high as 40 percent of total costs. While there were large efficiency gains to be obtained, the difficulty of making the political side payments, as well as ideological objections to centralized control, thwarted these attempts at industry rationalization. This illustrates how once the status quo is entrenched, movement to a pareto superior point may be difficult or impossible. William Hausman and John Neufeld, "The Economics of Electricity Networks and the Evolution of the U.S. Electric Utility Industry, 1882–1935," *Business and Economic History On-line* 2 (2004): 20–24; DeGraaf , "Corporate Liberalism and Electric Power System Planning in the 1920s," *Business History Review* 64 (1990): 1–31.

[37] Wholesale electricity markets as well as transmission are regulated by FERC, except for the Electric Reliability Council of Texas (ERCOT), which is connected to the two main national grids only through direct current (DC) ties, and thus falls under the exclusive

empowered to set "just and reasonable" rates.[38] The FPC was also directed to promote and encourage interconnections between and within defined regions to assure an abundant supply of electric energy throughout the United States.

The Road to Restructuring

The vertically integrated IOUs defined the status quo after World War II until the 1970s. While the government-owned Tennessee Valley Authority and Bonneville Power Administration provided low-cost power for development of their regions, rural cooperatives exploited tax advantages to maintain their independence, and a few municipal utilities persisted, the IOUs dominated the industry. The combination of PUCHA, certificates of convenience and necessity, and incremental improvements in efficiency in generation and transmission due to both technological progress and economies of scale reinforced their economic position. Sheltered from potential competition and buffered from regulatory pressure by declining costs and thus rates, utility management lived the proverbial "comfortable life."

Long-lived fixed investments, such as large generation plants and transmission and distribution systems, may create regulatory inertia even in the face of changes in technology that modify the competitive nature of the industry. Once these investments are made, the lower marginal cost of production from sunk generation investment created a barrier to the entry of newer, more efficient technologies that must cover both capital and operating costs to profitably enter. In the case of transmission and distribution networks, the geographical structure of these fixed investments determined the locational economics of potential entry into generation and provided the means to hinder new entrants. Regulatory mandates (serving native load, prudent investment standards, and reliability requirements) helped lock in integrated systems. It required organized pressure to overcome the status quo and accelerate the transition to a more competitive regime.

One factor that helped lock in this regulatory regime was the economic theory of natural monopoly. An industry with large fixed investments and

---

jurisdiction of the Public Utility Commission of Texas (PUCT). This was less a legal than a political conclusion, as until recently the political power of Texas congressional representatives counseled against FERC attempting to extend its jurisdiction to ERCOT. However, the 2005 Energy Policy Act formalized the Texas exemption from federal regulation.

[38] See FPA § 202(a).

increasing returns to scale characterizes the classic notion of a natural monopoly. A natural monopoly arises from two sources: economies of scale and economies of scope. Economies of scale exist when the average cost of production decreases as output expands. The most prevalent source of economies of scale is fixed costs that must be incurred no matter how many units of output are produced. Economies of scale are relative to the size of the market, since a large enough market can permit entry of numerous large plants and remain workably competitive. Economies of scope occur when several goods are produced with shared equipment or common facilities that make it less expensive to produce them together than producing them separately.[39] With economies of scope, allocating costs to various products becomes somewhat arbitrary. Portions of the electricity industry have exhibited economics of both scale and scope at times, as well as economies of "coordination," that is, efficiencies generated by reduced transactions costs through vertical integration.

As long as regulators and policymakers accepted this paradigm of a vertically integrated electric utility as a natural monopoly, there was little pressure to allow or encourage competition. Public power advocates offered public ownership, not competition, as an alternative to regulation. PUCs focused on the rate base, supervision and control of costs, and the structure of rates. While there were concerns with issues such as optimal pricing, marginal cost pricing, regulatory lag, and excess investment, these concerns were more theoretical than practical as long as rates kept declining or at least did not rise.[40]

However, a series of exogenous shocks disrupted this serene equilibrium. Regulatory miscues in the natural gas industry resulted in supply constraints of one fossil fuel used for generation, disruptions in the world oil market and the resulting escalation of oil prices dramatically raised the cost of fuel oil, and air pollution regulations raised the cost of high-sulfur fuel oil and bituminous coal. Misplaced optimism in, and incompetent contracting for, nuclear power plants resulted in cost escalation that translated to additional pressure on electricity rates and utility profits. Exhaustion of economics of scale in conventional steam power plants ended the downward trend in generation costs, while the gradual development of gas turbines positioned a potentially disruptive technology

---

[39] Kenneth Train, *Optimal Regulation: The Economic Theory of Natural Monopoly* (Cambridge, MA, MIT Press, 1991): 5–12.

[40] Alfred Kahn, *The Economics of Regulation: Principles and Institutions, Volume II* (New York, John Wiley & Sons, 1970); Richard Schmalensee, *The Control of Natural Monopolies* (Lexington, Lexington Books, 1979).

on the horizon. State PUCs, reacting to an environment of inflation and escalating utility rates, placed increased pressure on utility management. Environmental activists, consumer advocates, and policy entrepreneurs at both the state and federal levels supported energy efficiency measures and pressed for the implementation of resource planning, threatening the steady growth in demand for electricity that allowed management mistakes to be buried in an ever growing rate base and increased sales over which to spread these costs.

There were four fundamental influences that lead to restructuring of the electricity industry: ideology, technology, economics, and interest groups. All four factors were historically contingent, as the various ideologies that contested to shape policy were embedded in American political history, technological change altered the economic model of the industry while interest groups shifted in identity and position, both with respect to their self-interest and their ability to leverage resources and ideologically based arguments.

Ideology in this context includes both the political zeitgeist and the currents of intellectual discourse among academics, consultants, and policymakers. There are multiple streams of political ideology in American history, achieving dominance in different time periods. However, even an ideology that seemed to have lost the battle for hearts and minds can influence politics and policy. Populism,[41] which has its roots in Jeffersonian democracy, reached its apex in the nineteenth century, yet the language and themes of the Populist movement echo throughout the twentieth century and even in the platitudes of the Tea Party. Suspicion of big business permeated regulatory policy, which made protection of consumers and small business a priority.[42] Progressivism, in its multitude of currents and causes,[43] morphed into post–World War II liberalism, and then back into "progressivism" once again, with its confidence in government

---

[41] Charles Postel, *The Populist Vision* (New York, Oxford University Press, 2007); Lawrence Goodwyn, *Democratic Promise: The Populist Moment in America* (New York, Oxford University Press, 1976); Norman Pollack, *The Populist Response to Industrial America: Midwestern Populist Thought* (Cambridge, MA, Harvard University Press, 1962).

[42] Robert Rabin, "Federal Regulation in Historical Perspective," *Stanford Law Review* 38 (1986): 1189–1326.

[43] Elizabeth Sanders, "Rediscovering the Progressive Era," *Ohio State Law Journal* 72 (2011): 1281–94; Daniel Rodgers, "In Search of Progressivism," *Reviews in American History* (December 1982): 113–32; Robert H. Wiebe, *The Search for Order, 1877–1920* (New York, Hill and Wang, 1967); Richard Hofstadter, *The Age of Reform* (New York, Knopf, 1955).

action.[44] Pro-business and pro-property conservatism waned and waxed, bursting forth under Ronald Reagan, retreating, and then morphing under the leadership of Newt Gingrich and more recently with the ascendance of the Congressional Republicans.[45]

Technological change in a number of areas impacted electricity markets. The development of gas turbines, and especially combined-cycle gas-fired power plants, challenged the traditional model of ever increasing economies of scale in generation. The rapid development of computing technology made it feasible to coordinate large-scale electricity transactions in real time and to solve highly complex, multi-goal optimization models. Information technology also allowed greater control of energy consumption by consumers, shifting the load off peak hours. Appliances, air conditioning, insulation and motors, responding to both prices and regulatory mandates, exhibited dramatic efficiency improvements. Improvements in environmental control technology changed the relative costs of using different fuels, while improvements in exploration technology impacted the cost and availability of various fossil fuels.

Economics provided the intellectual "cover" for electricity restructuring to proceed. The Chicago school of economics suggested that regulation was driven by a desire to obtain rents,[46] and the public-choice approach explained regulation as the product of self-interested groups.[47] Capture theory cast doubt on whether regulators could be trusted to

[44] Gary Gerstle, "The Protean Character of American Liberalism" *American Historical Review* (October 1994): 1043–73; Kevin Mattson, *When America Was Great: The Fighting Faith of Postwar Liberalism* (New York, Routledge, 2004); David Plotke, *Building a Democratic Political Order: Reshaping American Liberalism in the 1930s and 1940s* (Cambridge, Cambridge University Press, 1996).

[45] Pau Edward Gottfried, *Conservatism in America: Making Sense of the American Right* (New York, Palgrave McMillan, 2007); Donald Critchlow, *The Conservative Ascendancy: How the GOP Right Made Political History* (Cambridge, MA, Harvard University Press, 2007).

[46] George Stigler, "The Theory of Economic Regulation," *Bell Journal of Economics and Management Science* 2 (1971): 1–21; Richard Posner, "Theories of Economic Regulation," *Bell Journal of Economics and Management Science* 5 (1974): 335–58; Sam Peltzman, "Toward a More General Theory of Regulation," *Journal of Law and Economics* 19 (1976): 210–40.

[47] Interest group theory had gained prominence in the 1950s with works by V. O. Key and Douglas Adair, culminating with Theodore Lowi's *The End of Liberalism* in 1969. William Nelson, "The Growth of Distrust: The Emergence of Hostility toward Government Regulation of the Economy," 25 *Hofstra Law Review* 1 (1996). Public-choice theory provided a "scientific" veneer to interest group theory, as well as explanations for bureaucratic behavior that cast doubt on the efficacy of regulations. Dennis Mueller, *Public Choice III* (Cambridge, Cambridge University Press, 2003).

pursue the public interest,[48] while other scholars questioned whether regulated entities manipulated their rate base through excessive investment. Contestability theory raised the prospect that some "natural monopolies" could be constrained by market forces if entry and exit were sufficiently feasible.[49] If electricity was no longer a natural monopoly, and bureaucrats were "captured" or empire builders, then deregulation became a viable alternative.

Interest groups, especially economically motivated groups with deep pockets to influence politicians, played an important role in electricity restructuring. The prompting of interest groups, from Enron to industrial consumers, provided the fuel for the engine of deregulation. Contributions provided access and at times influenced representatives and regulators,[50] but their influence depended on the interest group's importance to politicians' constituents. As Ken Lay discovered, much to his chagrin, those large campaign contributions have value only as long as your demands coincide with the zeitgeist and political currents – when you become an embarrassment, your name quickly disappears from Beltway contact files.[51] Cooperative and municipal electric companies, with limited resources, were important players in the electricity restructuring debates because they were often influential in local politics. Large industrial users used the threat of exporting jobs as much as campaign contributions to exert pressure on policymakers. IOUs, with strong local support in many states, often fought a fierce rear-guard action to preserve the status quo.

---

[48] Marver H. Bernstein, *Regulating Business by Independent Commission* (Princeton, NJ, Princeton University Press, 1955).

[49] William J. Baumol, "Contestable Markets: An Uprising in the Theory of Industry Structure," *American Economic Review* 72 (1982): 7–15; Elizabeth E. Bailey and William J. Baumol, "Deregulation and the Theory of Contestable Markets," *Yale Journal on Regulation* 1 (1984): 111.

[50] Lynda W. Powell, "The Influence of Campaign Contributions on Legislative Policy." *The Forum* 11 (2013): 339–55; Rui J. P. de Figueiredo, Jr. and Geoff Edwards, "Does Private Money Buy Public Policy: Campaign Contributions and Regulatory Outcomes in Telecommunications," *Journal of Economics & Management Strategy* 16 (2007): 547–76. In polite circles one talks about "purchasing access." It is far less expensive to purchase access and to make friends and influence people at the state level, especially smaller states that may have only a few large industrial firms and one or two major investor-owned utilities.

[51] Jim Drunkard, "Contacts Between Enron, Bush Cabinet Detailed," *USA Today*, January 14, 2002, at http://www.usatoday.com/money/energy/2002-01-14-enron.htm, last visited on May 1, 2012; Frank Pellegrini, "Bush's Enron Problem," *Time*, January 10, 2002, at http://www.time.com/time/nation/article/0,8599,192920,00.html, last visited on May 1, 2012.

The structure of federalism, the happenstance of nuclear power invest-ment and qualifying facility contracts (created by the 1978 Energy Policy Act as almost an afterthought), and changes in generation technology created a patchwork pattern of opportunities to promote electricity mar-kets. State politics would both promote and hinder efforts to promote retail electricity markets and extend wholesale markets. The inability of Congress to form a coherent vision for national electricity policy would create a power vacuum that the FERC filled with varying success, con-strained by both political pressure and court decisions.

While there has been a flood of energy policy studies and numer-ous executive branch policy proposals, these have had little impact on actual policy other than as symbolic gestures. The reality is that Congress pretty much ignores the best-laid plans of the executive branch and policy savants. Once a bill hits the committee process, and then the floor of the House and Senate, followed by often acrimonious conference committee negotiations, whatever coherence that might have been existed in the orig-inal proposal has long since fled the scene. Congress does pass measures, but these are usually disjointed, piecemeal policy proposals. It would be easy to blame the structure of our government as established by the Con-stitution, or to decry the lack of statesmanship in Congress, but the truth is more complex. In the case of energy policy, there are numerous factors that come into play: geography, economics, environmental impacts, and ideology. The importance of energy production varied between states, not only with regard to how much energy they produced but, in the case of California, the relative importance of energy production to the state's economy. Oil and natural gas production were concentrated in a few states, primarily Texas, Oklahoma, and Louisiana. Coal was also concentrated in a few states: West Virginia, Kentucky, Illinois, Montana, Wyoming, and Utah. The environmental impacts of burning fossil fuel, especially coal, often fell on neighboring states. Only a few industries consume enough electricity for it to compose more than a tiny fraction of input costs, but these industries tended to be dominated by large compa-nies that were effective lobbyists. Intra-fuel competition split the energy industries, but cross-fuel mergers internalized some of those conflicts.

Ideology added another layer of complexity to legislative negotiations over energy issues. Free-market supporters wanted decontrol, but many Congressmen retained traditional anti–big business attitudes. The oil companies, as a result of the Standard Oil aura and huge profits after the 1974 Oil Embargo, were the lightning rod for populist animosity, but anti-business animus impacted all the energy industries because large corporations were required to make the massive investments needed to develop coal mines, large generating plants, and transmission and distribution networks. Progressives wanted to deregulate, but only if consumers obtained the benefit of lower prices. Environmentalists wanted pollution to be controlled, but were also driven by symbolic issues like arctic and offshore oil drilling. Since energy bills in Congress tended to be omnibus affairs, prompted by the perception of a "crisis," negotiations over federal regulation of electricity were often held captive to other energy squabbles. There was also a fundamental problem: constituents wanted plentiful, cheap energy.

The structure of the electricity industry made developing a legislative solution more complicated than for natural gas deregulation. Since the gas pipelines were primarily interstate in nature (outside of Texas and Louisiana), deregulating gas was a federal issue and could proceed more or less independently of state actors. Due to PUCHA, the primary economic unit in the electricity industry was the vertically integrated utility that either operated in one state or, when owned by a holding company, consisted of linked adjacent vertical utilities. A change in the status quo would mean a serious diminishment of the role of state PUCs, and the power and prestige associated with running those agencies. States with cheap electricity saw it as a weapon for economic development and did not want interstate transmission and participation in power pools that might reduce this advantage. Other states simply wanted to maintain their relative independence from FERC dictates.

This meant that even when Congress could finally agree on legislation, it failed to grant FERC the comprehensive authority to restructure the national grid. The 1978 Act allowed experimentation with cogeneration and some new technologies but failed to provide a significant increase in authority. The 1992 Act provide FERC with more latitude, but the agency still had to depend on cajoling states and utilities into participating in markets absent the ability to coerce or order cooperation. The 2005 Act expanded FERC's authority over reliability issues, but FERC still lacks the authority to rationalize the transmission of electricity in interstate commerce, eight decades after the Federal Power Act of 1935.

Restructuring was a slow, meandering process, with bursts of activity separated by periods of retrenchment. Regions with higher electricity rates, driven by state politics and pressure from industrial customers, were most likely to push for restructuring at the state level. Areas where power pools were already operating made the quickest transition to wholesale electricity competition. States with low electricity rates and/or politically entrenched vertically integrated utilities fought any efforts to deregulate their utilities or provide out-of-state customers with access to low-cost generation. In the end, most regions experienced some sort of restructuring, from complete disaggregation (separating generation, transmission and distribution, and retail sales) to partially opening up integrated utility service areas to third-party generators.

The history of electricity restructuring fits the "muddling through" model of policymaking, where policymakers rely on the record of past experience with small policy steps to predict the consequences of similar incremental steps going forward, instead of trying to implement some comprehensive plan.[52] While the failure of Congress to enact a cohesive vision of electricity restructuring is one explanation for this approach, the sheer complexity of the task also counseled caution by regulators. This was the pattern seen in electricity restructuring, as the exception proved the wisdom of this approach. California got into trouble when it tried to make a great leap forward, building a market almost from scratch without taking incremental steps toward integration of the state's utilities. The reason "muddling" is often the best strategy is that comprehensive plans formed by consultants and academics assume the capability to implement those plans as a seamless whole. However, capabilities are often created and enhanced by experience, and "muddling through" builds up the human capital required to realize the idealized plan. Most of the successful electricity markets gradually coalesced from power pools, and the FERC developed its policies by hit-and-miss over three decades.[53]

Muddling through ties in well with Paul David's advice to maximize policy optionality. Preserving options, for a longer period than impatient market agents would wish, is the generic wisdom that history has to offer to public policymakers where positive feedback processes are likely to be preponderant over negative feedbacks. The "first best" public policy role in these matters may be the improvement of the informational state in which choices can be made by private parties and government agencies. The more history matters, the more worthwhile it is to invest in being

---

[52] Charles Lindblom, "The Science of 'Muddling Through'," *Public Administration Review* 19 (1959): 79–88; Charles Lindblom, "Still Muddling, Not Yet Through," *Public Administration Review* 39 (1979): 517–26.

[53] While it is not the intent of this book, a fruitful avenue of exploration might be to apply the "garbage can and the new institutionalism" to the analysis of FERC policy over the past two decades. See Johan Olsen, "Garbage Cans, New Institutionalism, and the Study of Politics," *American Political Science Review* 95 (March 2001): 193.

better informed before leaping.[54] Mudding through allows policymakers to accumulate information and experience before making irrevocable investments or decisions. It is easier to make incremental changes, and borrow ideas (and object lessons) from the successes and failures of others, than to create new institutions from scratch. A "muddling through" model will not satisfy those who prefer grand, all-encompassing theories of economics and politics, but to echo Joe Friday: "All we want are the facts, ma'am."[55]

---

[54] Paul David, "Path Dependence, Its Critics and the Quest for 'Historical Economics'," in Geoffrey Hodgson, ed., *The Evolution of Economic Institutions: A Critical Reader* (Cheltenham, Edward Elgar, 2007), 137–38.

[55] http://www.snopes.com/radiotv/tv/dragnet.asp.

I

The Regulated Electricity Industry

The Era of Stability

The electricity industry combines three interrelated processes to deliver power to final customers: power *generation* at the wholesale level, which is sent over high voltage *transmission* lines from power plants to local *distribution* networks that reduce voltage levels and send power to retail customers. Customers connect at various voltage levels, some at transmission voltages,[1] and at different levels of distribution voltages. Transmission and distribution are generally considered to be natural monopolies, and even under partial or total deregulation, these services are still provided by regulated entities.

The utility segments of the electric power industry were predominantly owned by the private sector in the United States. However, a large number of utilities were owned by federal government agencies, local government units, or organized as cooperatives. At the end of 1992, at the dawn of deregulation, there were 262 investor-owned utilities (79 percent of utility electricity generation), 2,017 publicly owned utilities (8 percent of electricity generation), 943 cooperatives (5 percent of electricity generation),[2] and 10 federally owned facilities (8 percent of electricity generation).[3]

---

[1] The delineation between transmission and distribution has important legal ramifications with respect to the division of authority between FERC and state regulators, but it is a bit of an ad hoc process. Generally the separation is by voltage, as well as function. The distribution system is generally considered to be involved only in the delivery of power to final customers, and not transmission of power between different distribution systems.

[2] Most cooperatives are local distribution companies, which often band together to jointly own a generation and transmission (G&T) cooperative to provide power and transmit it to the local cooperatives.

[3] EIA, *Financial Impacts of Nonutility Power Purchases on Investor-Owned Electric Utilities* (June 1994): 8. The two major federal power companies – the Tennessee Valley

The birth of the electricity industry can be traced back to the afternoon of September 4, 1882, when electric lights in the Wall Street offices of Drexel, Morgan & Co. were switched on for the first time. Power was supplied from a generator situated several blocks away in the Edison Electric Illuminating Company's Pearl Street station. The key to Thomas Edison's ultimate success was that, along with inventing a practical incandescent lightbulb, he conceived and developed an entire system for generating and delivering electric current from a central station to homes and businesses. By the end of the year Edison had constructed or licensed more than 150 central stations around the country, and within eight years Edison and his competitors had installed more than 1,000 stations. Twenty years later, in 1902, there were 3,620 electric light and power stations in operation in the United States.[4]

The early electric utilities were exclusively urban phenomena whose prime business was providing lighting services to central business and residential districts. They spread only gradually to immediately surrounding and suburban areas. The need to run distribution lines over (or under) city streets necessitated the acquisition of municipal franchises, which entangled the companies intimately in local (and sometimes state-level) political affairs. In the early 1900s, there was loose regulation, and many cities had multiple providers. New York City had six electric companies in 1887 and Chicago had forty-five in 1907. Electric firms paid local governments a typical franchise fee of 5 percent of revenue and soon became an important source of local government revenue. Multiple local franchises were a conscious policy to regulate through competition. Franchises typically were not exclusive and often were granted for limited time periods. Electric generators at this time were relatively small and easy to operate, so that commercial or industrial customers could install plants on their own premises, while firms such as street railway companies and ice manufacturers sold their excess self-generated electricity in competition with central stations.[5]

Authority and the Bonneville Power Administration – are both based around federally funded dams built for flood control and regional development.

4 William Hausman and John Neufeld, "The Structure and Profitability of the US Electric Utility Industry at Turn of Century," *Business History* 32 (1990): 225.

5 William Hausman and John Neufeld, "The Structure and Profitability of the US Electric Utility Industry at Turn of Century," *Business History* 32 (1990): 225–26; A.H. Barnett, Keith A. Reutter, and Henry Thompson, "The First Step in Restructuring the US Electric Industry," *Energy Economics* 27 (2005): 226; Mark Granovetter and Patrick McGuire, "The Making of an Industry: Electricity in the United States," in Michel Callon, ed., *The Laws of the Markets* (London, Blackwell Publishers, 1988): 153–61.

The introduction of alternating current (promoted enthusiastically by George Westinghouse) permitted higher transmission voltages, expanding the range of transmission and providing a means to bring hydroelectric generation to urban markets. The prospects for alternating current were enhanced with the development of electric motors and metering devices. Edison vigorously resisted alternating current, but lost the battle of the systems, and Edison General Electric merged Thomson-Houston to form General Electric in 1892. Technological advances such as transformers allowed exploitation of economies of scale, and larger firms began to absorb their weaker competitors or drive them out of business.[6]

As electricity networks grew in scope, state regulation, based on existing procedures used to regulate railroads, began to replace franchises granted by municipalities. Since each city had an independent franchising authority, electric firms trying to expand found multiple negotiations and differing fees both costly and burdensome. Local control of electric utilities was also riddled with corruption. The industry, led by Samuel Insull of Chicago Commonwealth Edison and members of the National Electric Light Association, later the Edison Electric Institute, called for state regulation. The first state to implement a public service commission was Massachusetts in 1889, followed by Virginia in 1902. By 1912, there were eighteen states with PUCs.[7] The number of PUCs reached thirty-eight by 1922, and they became almost universal by the 1930s. State monopolies ended franchise fees for local governments. Uniform accounting rules were established, and regulatory commissions were provided detailed records of all operating expenses. PUCs set utility rates at a level that enabled the regulated utility to cover its operating expenses and receive a "fair" return on the value of its capital facilities. What constituted a fair return depended on the utility's capital cost, which in turn depended on the amount invested in facilities. States began to require a "Certificate of Convenience and Necessity" for new facilities before accepting investments into utility rate bases. This requirement also protected the regulated utility's monopoly because such certification was unavailable to a competitor who wanted to offer utility service to the same service area.[8]

---

[6] Hausman and Neufeld, "The Structure and Profitability of the US Electric Utility Industry at Turn of Century," 226.

[7] This includes Public Service Commissions or other variations on the names of regulatory agencies with similar authority over utility rates.

[8] William J. Hausman and John L. Neufeld, "The Market for Capital and the Origins of State Regulation of Electric Utilities in the United States," *Journal of Economic History*

Certification requirements resulted in the dominance of the vertically integrated (generation, transmission, and distribution in one entity), but primarily localized, electricity utility. Adjacent utilities might interconnect but not integrate their operations. State regulation meant that any facility built by a utility in one state that provided substantial benefits to a utility in another state would struggle to garner regulatory approval. This biased investments toward facilities that primarily served the integrated utility, even if it would have been more efficient to establish an interconnected network across utilities. Under state regulation, a firm could hold on to its service area even if serving it inefficiently, which increased its bargaining power when selling out to a larger company. Thus, the system of state regulation created an environment that discouraged the growth of electricity networks that were jointly owned and increased the barriers to unified ownership of an expanded electricity network. Although the number of privately owned utilities declined substantially, there were still 1,627 of them in 1932.[9]

Holding companies by the late 1920s had consolidated a substantial portion of the nation's electric utilities into a relatively small number of large systems (only parts of which were physically interconnected). Electric utility holding companies acquired control of electric utilities simply by purchasing the utility's stock. This method of acquiring control avoided many of the legal obstacles to outright acquisition of the utility. Several of the holding companies arose out of the financial practices of the major electrical manufacturers, which accepted the securities of electric utilities as payment for equipment. The equipment manufacturers created subsidiaries to hold the securities issued by their customers and to convert these into cash by then issuing their own securities. Electric Bond

---

47 (Dec. 2002): 1050–73; A.H. Barnett, Keith A. Reutter, and Henry Thompson, "The First Step in Restructuring the US Electric Industry," *Energy Economics* 27 (2005): 226; Christopher Knittel, "The Adoption of State Electricity Regulation: The Role Of Interest Groups," *Journal of Industrial Economics* 54 (2006): 206–07. The last states to establish commissions were Alaska (1960), Iowa (1963), Minnesota (1975), Texas (1975), and South Dakota (1976). State laws generally followed the models of the New York, Wisconsin, and California laws. In general, commissioners are appointed by the governor, with terms longer than those of elected officials, to insulate them from political pressure. The commissions' decision-making functions are quasi-judicial in nature, operating under rules of civil procedure. Robert Swartwout, "Current Utility Regulatory Practice From a Historical Perspective," *Natural Resource Journal* 32 (Spring 1992): 300–01.

9 William J. Hausman and John L. Neufeld, "The Economics of Electricity Networks and the Evolution of the U.S. Electric Utility Industry, 1882–1935," *Business and Economic History On-line* 2 (2004): 16–18, at http://www.thebhc.org/publications/BEHonline/2004/HausmanNeufeld.pdf.

& Share, for example. was created as a subsidiary of General Electric in 1905. A number of other holding companies evolved from firms that originally were in the business of providing management and engineering consulting services, including Stone & Webster and the H.L. Doherty (Cities Service) group. By 1930, 90 percent of all operating companies in electricity were ultimately controlled by nineteen holding companies. The largest holding company controlled more than 19 percent of private electricity generation in the United States, and the six largest controlled more than 70 percent. The holding companies developed technical and managerial expertise in the business of operating electric utilities, which led to standardization and more professional management of the electric utilities. Holding companies facilitated the consolidation of the industry by enabling member companies to take advantage of potential economies of scale in financing, in the creation of regional networks, or in the provision of engineering services. However, the holding companies took advantage of their special ability to exploit state regulation to the detriment of electricity consumers. Because legitimate operating costs were, under regulation, passed on to the utility's customers, the holding companies had an incentive to inflate service charges to subsidiaries.[10]

An FTC investigation, beginning in 1928, uncovered a number of financial excesses. The Great Crash in 1929 and the Depression that followed produced a major shift in the American political climate. With the onset of the Great Depression in 1929, and in light of public anger against big business, breaking the "money trusts" gained popular support. Highly leveraged holding companies that managed to stay solvent during the prosperous 1920s collapsed after the stock market crash because they could not service their debt. Between 1929 and 1936, fifty-three holding companies went into bankruptcy or receivership. The anti–big business sentiment was fueled by the collapse of the Insull Group, the third-largest utility group with combined assets of $2.5 billion, the biggest business failure the United States had experienced. In 1931, the highly leveraged Insull Group could no longer service its debt following a sharp drop in its electricity-based revenues. In June 1932, Samuel Insull resigned from all the eighty-five directorships and eleven presidential posts he held and fled

[10] Hausman and Neufeld, "The Economics of Electricity Networks and the Evolution of the U.S. Electric Utility Industry, 1882–1935," 18–19; Hausman and Neufeld, "The Structure and Profitability of the US Electric Utility Industry at Turn of Century," 227–28; Eugene Kandel, Konstantin Kosenko, Randall Morck, and Yishay Yafeh, *Business Groups in the United States: A Revised History of Corporate Ownership, Pyramids and Regulation, 1930–1950*, NBER Working Paper 19691 (Dec. 2013): 12.

to Europe, leaving hundreds of thousands of creditors and shareholders with nearly worthless claims.[11]

Relations between the Roosevelt administration and the public utility industry had never been cordial. Early on, tensions centered on the Tennessee Valley Authority Act, enacted in May 1933. To Roosevelt, the Tennessee Valley Authority embodied the transformative possibilities of modern government. To the public utility companies, government production and distribution of cheap power threatened to undercut private production. In July 1934, Roosevelt signed an executive order creating the National Power Policy Committee, chaired by Secretary of the Interior Harold Ickes and housed within the Public Works Administration. Benjamin Cohen was appointed legal counsel to the National Power Policy Committee due to his reputation for legislative draftsmanship and his experience with the securities legislation of 1933 and 1934. Cohen drafted a holding company bill, but rather than eliminating holding companies, Cohen's proposal sought to regulate and restrict the use of the holding company form. Cohen's recognition of the economies of scale that stem from some holding company arrangements differed sharply from the Brandeisian liberals, who opposed bigness as a matter of principle.[12]

Roosevelt's State of the Union message, calling for the abolition of holding companies, was delivered on January 4. Lawyers at the FPC had been working on a bill using taxation to make holding companies an unattractive form of corporate organization. Lawyers at the Justice Department were taking a similar approach. Critics of the holding companies included Rep. Sam Rayburn (D-Texas), chairman of the powerful Interstate Commerce Committee. A February meeting at the White House considered the approach that should be taken. Roosevelt preferred the elimination of the holding companies, or at least to send a strong message to the utilities industry. In the end, the conferees decided to accept Cohen's overall approach but to add language condemning holding company abuses and to include a provision allowing the Securities and Exchange Commission (SEC) to compel the dissolution of holding companies unless it could be shown that a particular operating company

[11] Kandel, Kosenko, Morck, and Yafeh, *Business Groups in the United States*, 14; Richard Cudahy and William Henderson "From Insull to Enron: Corporate (Re)Regulation After the Rise and Fall of Two Energy Icons," 26 *Energy Law Journal* 35, 39–55 (2005); Paul Mahoney, "The Public Utility Pyramids," 41 *Journal of Legal Studies* 37 (2012).

[12] William Lasser, *Benjamin V. Cohen, Architect of the New Deal* (New Haven, Yale University Press, 2002): 110–17; Joseph Lash, *Dealers and Dreamers: A New Look at the New Deal* (New York, Doubleday, 1988): 194–95.

cannot be operated as an independent system without the loss of substantial economies. This "death penalty provision" soon came to dominate the debate over the public utility holding company bill.[13]

Roosevelt also ordered Cohen to include the water act amendments (expanding FPC authority) as section II of the bill. The FPC had originally been created under the Water Power Act of 1920 to regulate hydroelectric companies. After a final revision by the Justice Department, the Wheeler-Rayburn bill was introduced into both houses of Congress. The legislation was the most bitterly contested of the New Deal. Utility executives regarded the bill as a declaration of war. The power industry lobbyists were led by Wendell Willkie, chairman of the Commonwealth & Southern Electric Company and, six years later, the Republican nominee for president of the United States. Armed with a war chest of millions of dollars, their public relations firms bombarded Congress and the public with pamphlets, letters, and advertisements designed to discredit the legislation and the president. Their lobbyists swarmed over Capitol Hill, buying votes and threatening legislators. Roosevelt stood firm, due to his need for the support of Western progressives, who were adamant that the holding companies be dissolved. During the summer of 1935, the House removed the death sentence from its version of the bill. However, Senator Hugo Black of Alabama compelled numerous utility executives to appear before a special committee on lobbying and subpoenaed their correspondence. The committee discovered various abuses and misrepresentations. This provided the impetus to get the bill out of conference with a compromise that restricted holding company activities.[14]

Title I of the Public Utility Act of 1935 is PUHCA. A holding company under PUHCA is an enterprise that directly or indirectly owns 10 percent or more of stock in a public utility company. Section 11b (the "Death Sentence Clause") of PUHCA abolishes all holding companies that were more than twice removed from their operating subsidiaries. All electric and natural gas holding companies were required to register with the SEC. By January 1, 1940, every holding company was to dissolve. The only exceptions were cases where the FPC issued a finding that a holding company was necessary to the continued operation of an existing integrated

[13] Lasser, *Benjamin V. Cohen, Architect of the New Deal*, 110, 117–19; Lash, *Dealers and Dreamers: A New Look at the New Deal*, 196–97.
[14] Cudahy and Henderson "From Insull to Enron: Corporate (Re)Regulation After the Rise and Fall of Two Energy Icons," 75–77; Lasser, *Benjamin V. Cohen, Architect of the New Deal*, 119–26; Lash, *Dealers and Dreamers: A New Look at the New Deal*, 200–214.

multistate or international supply system. Appeals to the Supreme Court were finally resolved in 1946, as the Court ruled in favor of the SEC.[15] A study of the impact of the PUHCA found that the stand-alone or independent firms formed by the breakup of the holding companies were more productive and profitable, grew faster, and paid more dividends than firms affiliated with holding companies. The only advantage of the holding companies seemed to be in minimizing tax obligations or charging higher prices to consumers.[16]

The FPA is Title II of the Public Utility Act of 1935. The original proposal for the FPA included a provision to oversee and encourage the development of new integrated utility networks. Utilities would be compelled to provide transmission services in response to any reasonable request at reasonable rates, and the FPC was given the power to order a public utility to make additions and extensions to its facilities and to establish physical connection with other facilities. The proposal faced stiff opposition, especially from state regulators. The final version of the law reiterated that the regulatory powers of the FPC extended only to areas not subject to state jurisdiction.[17] The Commission was to encourage the interconnection of power systems, but it could compel such actions only in times of emergency or when an application was made to interconnect, provided that such interconnection did not impair existing service. The Commission had no jurisdiction over power plants, other than hydroelectric plants, nor over the construction of transmission lines. Jurisdiction was extended to the sale of power by a public utility in interstate commerce, to mergers, acquisitions, and transfers of assets, most aspects of international commerce in electric energy, and accounting rules.[18]

Although the FPC was granted authority over interstate transactions, the state PUCs remained the key actors in electricity regulation. Traditional electric public utility regulation was based around balancing the revenue requirements of the utility and encouraging the public interest. Utility rates and revenues were determined on the basis of average costs of

---

[15] *American Power & Light Co. v. SEC*, 329 US 90 (1946); *North American Co. v. SEC*, 327 US 686 (1946).

[16] Francisco Perez-Gonzalez, "Organizational Form and Firm Performance: Evidence from the 'Death Sentence' Clause of the Public Utility Act of 1935," Working Paper, April 2014.

[17] Hausman and Neufeld, "The Economics of Electricity Networks and the Evolution of the U.S. Electric Utility Industry, 1882–1935," 26–28.

[18] John Miller, "A Needed Reform of the Organization and Regulation of the Interstate Electric Power Industry," *Fordham Law Review* 38 (1970): 638–39.

service. Grants of exclusive service area franchises to electric utilities were predicated on a mandate to provide service for anyone requesting it and a "fair" rate structure based on the cost of service to each class of customer. Utility rate setting required calculating a rate base, the eligible asset base upon which the utility could recover capital charges, based on an allowed rate of return on equity and the utility's cost of debt. Determining the rate of return required an evaluation of comparable returns on similar electric and nonelectric companies. Utility investment decisions, which increased the amount of capital eligible for a rate of return and debt that must be serviced, were subject to *ex ante* judgments with regard to necessity and ex post judgments of whether they were "used and useful."[19]

The formal hearing structure for setting public utility prices is generally similar from one state to the next. The utility commission first seeks to determine the capital stock that will be included in the firm's rate base. The rate base is usually based on the original cost of assets, net of depreciation, used to provide service, adjusted for write offs of imprudent capital and the additional of regulatory or other assets. The rate of return is generally based upon the actual capital structure, the cost of debt and the allowed return on capital, adjusted for tax impacts. Rules specify the items which may and may not be included in the rate.

Determination of operating costs was usually based on actual costs during a historic 12 month period – the "test year." Actual costs were often adjusted to account for known and measurable events occurring after the test year, and in some jurisdiction were normalized to account for economic and weather impacts on demand in the test year.

Typically, cost of service is determined through a quasi-judicial adversary process in which the utility, regulatory staff, often a state funded consumer advocate, and various customer and public interest intervenors

---

[19] Commission skepticism about the validity of utility investments was acerbated by an economics article that received wide circulation, Harvey Averch and Leland L. Johnson, "Behavior of the Firm Under Regulatory Constraint," *American Economic Review* 52 (Dec. 1962): 1053–1069. The authors postulated that, if the allowed rate of return is greater than the regulated utility's cost of capital, the regulated utility will inefficiently substitute capital for labor to increase their rate base. This became widely known as the Averch-Johnson effect. Tests of the Averch-Johnson effect have yielded mixed results, and it cannot be considered conclusive. Paul L. Joskow, "Regulation and Deregulation After 25 Years: Lessons Learned for Research in Industrial Organization," *Review of Industrial Organization* (2005): 188; Stephen M. Law, "Assessing Evidence for the Averch-Johnson-Wellisz Effect for Regulated Utilities," Working Paper, 2008, at http://www.unb.ca/fredericton/arts/departments/economics/acea/pdfs/2008_3.pdf (last visited June 2, 2011); Donald Vitaliano and Gregory Stella, "A Frontier Approach to Testing the Averch-Johnson Hypothesis," *International Journal of the Economics of Business* 16 (2009): 347–363.

submit voluminous expert testimony and exhibits. The utility will file a large, complex set of documents of testimony and exhibits of executives and outside experts. Intervenors will respond with their own expert testimony. The influence of intervenors depends on their resources (industrial customers tend to be better financed) and political impact. Hearings will be held and arcane issues will be discussed. Utility regulation at the state level is generally slanted toward the utility, since they can focus far more resources on rate cases than are available to most PUCs. PUCs in most states have small staffs, with limited experience and technical, economic, legal and financial expertise. The best and the brightest staff often flee low state salaries after they garner a few years of experience for the more lucrative private sector, usually the utility companies and their corporate law firms. Even the PUCs with the largest staffs and budgets often must allocate that expertise to numerous rate proceedings for local electric, gas, and telephone utilities.[20]

Finally, the commissioners will make a decision with insufficient time to absorb more than a fraction of the details of the dispute put before them. A regulatory commission will often split the difference on many issues, as the mass of materials can overwhelm a regulatory staff, as it often involves technical minutia (for example, what is the proper rate of depreciation for wooden distribution line poles). Commissioners will use the flexibility to disallow costs, set a rate of return and arbitrarily assign joint costs to customer groups to develop a politically acceptable rate structure that can survive a court challenge. The participants will often formulate a settlement agreement, negotiating in the shadow of the commission, to steer the commission's final decision toward their jointly preferred outcome.[21]

---

[20] Information asymmetries between the utility and PUC affect the rate proceeding initiation decisions of each party. More astute PUCs are better able to assess the validity of any utility claims that they are under-earning and that rate increases are required. Utilities are less likely to initiate reviews that call for rate increases when PUCs have better information about the utility. Regulatory agencies with more experienced commissioners, with larger staffs and with the ability to observe other agencies' related rate rulings on the same utility, all tended to implement more frequent rate reductions and provide smaller rate increases. Firms with more experience with the rate making process tended to obtain better results. Adam Fremeth and Guy Holburn, "Information Asymmetries and Regulatory Decision Costs: Evidence From Electric Utility Rate Reviews 1980–2000," *Journal of Law, Economics & Organization* 28 (2012): 127–162; Jean-Philippe Bonardi, Guy Holburn & Richard Vanden Bergh, "Nonmarket Strategy Performance: Evidence From U.S. Electric Utilities," *Academy of Management Journal* 49 (2006): 1209–1228.

[21] A commission is not obligated to accept even an unanimous settlement. However, a settlement that is generally accepted provides the framework for a decision that is less likely

Once a state commission approved the utility's revenue requirements, the rate structure, or allocation of the revenue requirement among customers, must be resolved to develop customer rates schedules.[22] The test year levels of costs, revenues and sales is used to calculate rates for various customers. The revenue requirement is assigned to different customer classes, and converted into rates by customer class on a per customer (fixed charge), kW (demand charge) and kWh (energy charge). The general principle in almost all state statutes governing ratemaking for classes of customers has been cost causation, and most laws governing rate regulations include some sort of nondiscrimination clause, to protect consumers from paying more than their "fair" share of costs. These rates would remain at assigned levels until the next rate case (there might be a fuel charge pass through to account for volatility in fuel costs).

If the utility sold more power than presumed under the rate calculations, or reduced costs below test year levels, it could receive additional profits until the next rate case reset rates. This tendency for rates to lag behind changes in costs or revenues is referred to as "regulatory lag." Regulatory lag provided both an incentive to increase efficiency, but also to encourage demand growth. As long as costs continued to decline, regulators felt no pressure to squeeze every last cent from utilities that were delivering consistent improvements. Regulators rarely reduced rates when actual profits exceed the target rate of return.[23]

Regulators often circumvented the standard nondiscrimination clauses that required cost based ratemaking for all customer classes, cross-subsidizing residential customers by imposing higher costs on industrial and commercial customers. Regulators would encourage or require utility companies to expand their service areas to include new residential and industrial developments, paying for this expansion through higher rates

---

to incite objections expressed through either political pressure or a petition to a court. Experienced practitioners did not present regulatory agencies with proposals that would be obviously unacceptable, had characteristics which could embarrass the commission in future cases, or would be violative of established precedent. Alan Buchmann and Robert Tongren, "Nonunanimous Settlements of Public Utility Rate Cases: A Response," 113 *Yale Journal on Regulation* 337, 340–342 (Winter 1996). For a general overview of the use of settlements in utility proceedings, see Joseph Doucet and Stephen Littlechild, "Negotiated Settlements: The Development of Economic and Legal Thinking," CWPE 0622 and EPRG 0604 (September 2006).

22   Paul Joskow, The Determination of the Allowed Rate of Return in a Formal Regulatory Hearing, *Bell Journal of Economics* 3 (1972): 632–644.

23   Paul Joskow, "Pricing Decisions of Regulated Firms: A Behavioral Approach." *Bell Journal of Economics* 4 (1973): 118–140.

on existing customers. Regulators traditionally turned a blind eye to rates that provide preferential treatment to new industry, or to prevent existing industries from resorting to cogeneration. For example, many interruptible rate programs that looked onerous on paper were implemented with a "nudge nudge, wink wink"[24] agreement, allowing utilities to provide discounts that met the nondiscrimination requirement without actually using the option to require industrial customers to shed load. Regulators also cross-subsidized low income customers through lifeline rates and other measures.[25]

These policies were encouraged by declining costs of generation due to technological advances and economies of scale. This trend allowed utility regulators to grant subsidies at no political cost, since as long as subsidies were limited to a small proportion of overall costs, they would go unnoticed as other ratepayers faced constant or declining rates. Policies that encouraged increased consumption lowered the average cost of power as the lower costs of new, more efficient generation units were averaged with the costs of older generation units. In some cases, utilities would employ declining block rates, with the customer's incremental cost declining as consumption rose. Low inflation and expansion of service territories (it's less expensive to build wires infrastructure to serve suburban developments than to "infill" in urban areas) kept the cost of transmission and distribution assets from rising rapidly, so as not to counterbalance the savings on the generation side.

The electric power industry and its customers benefitted from a decline in inflation-adjusted electric rates for almost a half century, from the 1920's until about 1970. The long decline in rates was due largely to improved technology that increased the thermal efficiency of fossil fuel steam generation. The new technology exploited engineering economies of scale available from the utilization of larger, high pressure boilers, improved turbine design and high voltage transmission. These economies of scale could reduce average costs if the larger units could be utilized at a high capacity rate, allowing higher capital costs to be spread over a larger output. Steady growth in demand allowed new technologies to be introduced gradually and eased the problem of planning an optimum investment mix.

---

[24] *Monty Python's Flying Circus*, third episode, "How to Recognize Different Types of Trees From Quite a Long Way Away" written by Eric Idle, broadcast on BBC One, in 1969.

[25] Gary D. Allison, "Imprudent Power Construction Projects: The Malaise of Traditional Public Utility Policies," 13 *Hofstra Law Review* 507, 513–517 (1985).

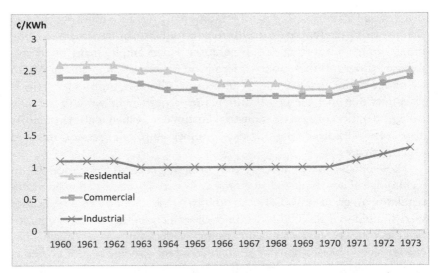

FIGURE I.I. Nominal Electricity Prices 1960–1973. *Source*: EIA, *Annual Energy Review 2010*, Table 8.10. Average Retail Prices of Electricity, 1960–2010.

Nominal prices are more important than real prices for short-term regulatory policies. Consumers, other than sophisticated industrial customers, are usually unaware except in a vague fashion whether real prices are rising or declining, but they can easily note whether nominal prices have changed. Consumers saw electricity prices gradually declining until 1970, and then begin to rise, but didn't realize that real prices had dramatically declined since 1960, by 35% by 1970, and continued to decline slowly for all but industrial customers in the beginning of the "energy crisis." While most of the technological efficiency improvements from big, modern power plants were exhausted by 1960 or so, these newer plants continued to replace older, less efficient generators throughout the decade.

The maximum thermal efficiency of pulverized coal power plants improved from 8% in 1900 to 40% in 1960.[26] Much of this improvement was due to advances in boiler technology. The overall thermal efficiency of a steam generation cycle increases with the temperature and pressure of the steam, the thermal efficiency of the boiler, and the efficiency of the turbine. By the late 1950s, a steam temperature threshold of 1,000°F was reached. In response, steam pressure steadily increased until 1970. The

[26] Thermal efficiency = energy value of net electricity produced/energy value of fuel.

size of coal fired plants also steadily increased until the early 1970s, when the average plant was 591 MW, and the largest plants were 1300 MW. This reflected increased economies of scale with higher pressure units, for example, supercritical plants (operating above 705°F and 3212 psi, where there is no phase transition from water to steam, but only a decrease in density) were less costly per kW for plants above 500 MW capacity. Other design changes that led to large increases in thermal efficiency had become standard by the early 1960s.[27] Operations and maintenance costs also showed a steady decline until 1970, due to single boiler designs, automatic controls and improved instrumentation.[28]

Since 1980, however, the maximum thermal efficiency of new coal plants in the U.S. declined slightly to less than 38%.[29] The decline in new plant performance was due to the demise of higher-efficiency supercritical plants. During the late 1960s and early 1970s, boiler tubes on supercritical units started to experience metal fatigue and creep, and scale deposits from boiler walls induced greater corrosion and erosion damage. As a result, the availability of these plants dropped and they became more costly to operate.[30] By the early 1980s, supercritical boiler technology was essentially abandoned in the U.S.[31]

By the late 1960s, the explosive growth in energy consumption stretched the capabilities of many utility companies. Utilities plan up to a decade in advance, because of the long lead times to build generation, transmission and distribution systems. Even before the advent of environmental regulation, a large coal plant could still take 5 or 6 years from planning to completion. The utility industry was also vulnerable to lags in investment by its input suppliers, as coal mining companies needed to develop new mines, railroads to expand coal transportation capacity, and natural gas companies had to extend gas pipelines into new

---

[27] Paul Joskow and Nancy Rose, "The Effects of Technological Change, Experience, and Environmental Regulation on the Construction Cost of Coal-Burning Generating Units," *Rand Journal of Economics* 16 (Spring 1985): 3–4.

[28] James McNerney, Jessika Trancik and J. Doyne Farmer, "Historical Costs of Coal-Fired Electricity and Implications for the Future," *Energy Policy* 39 (2011): 3045.

[29] Sonia Hey and Edward Rubin, "A Centurial History of Technological Change and Learning Curves for Pulverized Coal-Fired Utility Boilers," *Energy* 32 (2007): 1997–98. Current plant designs typically have thermodynamic limit efficiencies around 46%. The operational efficiencies of the boiler, turbine, generator, and other components reduce the efficiency achievable in practice.

[30] Hey and Rubin, "A Centurial History of Technological Change and Learning Curves," at 1998, 2001.

[31] Joskow and Rose, "The Effects of Technological Change, Experience, and Environmental Regulations," at 4–5, 23.

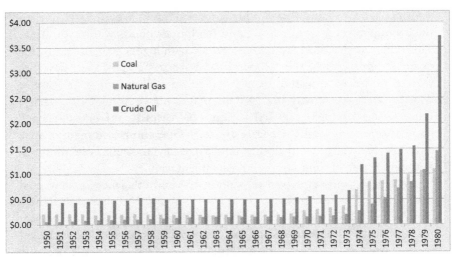

FIGURE I.2. Fuel Prices 1950–1980 ($ per million Btu). *Source*: EIA, *Annual Energy Review 2010*, Table 8.2b.

regions. As long as demand growth was steady and predictable, this could be handled, but rapidly accelerating demand resulted in reliability issues and short-term shortages.

During the 1960s, some utilities became increasingly dependent on diesel and fuel oil on the margin. The low price of oil, and even lower prices of fuel oil used to fire steam boilers,[32] made oil fired units economically competitive. Oil and gas fired units could be added more quickly than coal units, and with constraints on natural gas constricting supply, fuel oil seemed a safer alternative. Distortions in the natural gas market due to regulation drove up the price of natural gas and resulted in shortages in certain areas. With the passage of the Environmental Protection Act in 1969, and the Clean Air Act Amendments of 1970 and again in 1977, low sulfur oil and natural gas became favored fuels in many regions. However, natural gas shortages and the oil embargo of 1973 which triggered a dramatic increase in oil prices, limited the move from coal.

---

[32] Since gasoline and aviation fuels were premium products, refineries sold residual fuel oil for a discount relative to the price of petroleum. As refinery technology improved, allowing greater yield of high value products per barrel, the supply of residual oil gradually declined. In 1949, 24% of refinery products by barrel were residual fuel oil. This ratio declined to around 15% between 1960 to 1980, then dropped to 9% by 1983, and is down to only about 3% of refinery products today. Percentages derived from data in Table 5.11 Petroleum Products Supplied by Type, 1949–2010, EIA, *Annual Energy Review 2010*, October 19, 2011.

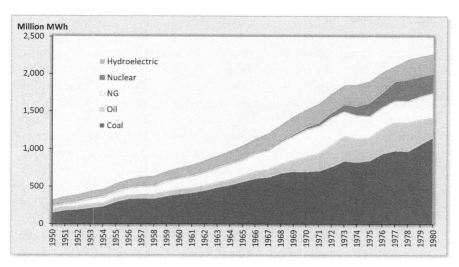

FIGURE 1.3. Net Generation By Fuel. *Source*: EIA, *Annual Energy Review*, 2010, Table 8.2b.

Rising Costs Sink All Boats

Utilities were whipsawed between the rapid inflation of the early 1970s, combined with fuels shortages and oil price spikes, and the recessions of 1974–1975 and 1980–1983. The precipitous rise in oil prices in the 1970s were soon accompanied by an increase in natural gas prices. Rising fuel prices meant higher electricity prices, which, combined with stagnant economic demand, meant that many utilities suddenly found themselves with excess capacity and commitments to expensive and redundant infrastructure investments.

The unexpected sharp drop in the growth of electricity demand in the mid-1970's took the electricity industry by surprise. The average annual rate of growth in demand for electricity declined from 7.3 percent from 1960 through 1973 to 2.2 percent from 1973 through 1982. This slower growth of electricity demand would become a permanent trend. This development occurred while the industry was implementing an expansion program geared to meet historical growth rates. When companies realized that planned growth wasn't going to materialize, they cancelled projects, writing off sunk investment costs. Between 1974 and 1978, 184 large generation plants (250 MW or greater) were canceled, representing over 155,000 MW of new capacity, or about one-quarter of all electric capacity. Eighty of these units were nuclear plants (accounting for almost 90,000 MW) and eighty-four were coal-fired units (51,000 MW).[33]

Along with cancellations, power plants under construction were almost universally delayed after 1974. Of the 189 electric power plants put in operation between January 1974 and December 1978, 149 experienced delays averaging 17 months. Plants under construction in the late 1970s experienced even longer delays, as 267 of the 330 plants projected to come on line experienced delays averaging 40 months by 1990. Factors contributing to plant cancellation and delays included financing problems, regulatory hurdles, construction roadblocks and special problems with nuclear power design, which were exacerbated by the blowback after the Three Mile Island meltdown.[34] Given the high interest rates experienced throughout the decade, these delays added considerable expense to new generation construction. Carrying charges (in the form of dividends on equity and interest on debt) for construction work in progress increased significantly. Interest rates on Moody's Aaa rating bonds rose from 4.5% in 1965, to 8.6% in 1974, 9.5% in 1979 and exceeded 14% in 1981, staying in double digits until 1986.[35] Utilities were hit with a double whammy, they had taken on large capital investments with demand drastically declining and the costs of servicing capital rising to unprecedented levels.

The inflation of the 1970s also hit utilities. While some of the cost increases can be attributed to environmental standards, the real cost per kW for coal plants doubled from the late 1960s to the late 1970s, and scrubbers and cooling towers were only responsible for about 20% of this increase in cost.[36] Rising costs meant increased resistance to new investment from consumer groups and regulators responding to general discontent with rising energy prices.

The straw that would break the back of many utility companies was their flirtation with nuclear power. Utilities purchased a new, unproven technology without shifting the risk to the vendors of nuclear plants, exposing themselves to huge liabilities. The earliest nuclear projects, managed by the reactor vendors, were contracted for on a fixed-price

---

[33] GAO, *Electric Powerplant Cancellations and Delays*, Report to the Congress (December 8, 1980): 6.

[34] GAO, *Electric Powerplant Cancellations and Delays*, 11–20.

[35] *Economic Report of the President*, 2012, Table B–73. Bond yields and interest rates, 1940–2011.

[36] Joskow and Rose, "The Effects of Technological Change, Experience, and Environmental Regulation," 21–22.

(turnkey) basis. The first initial plants built in the 1960s had been offered by Westinghouse and General Electric under turnkey contracts at prices below cost to entice utilities into investing in the new technology. Thirteen plants were sold on this basis, as the two companies wanted to rapidly climb the learning curve and preempt competing nuclear technologies.[37] The majority of utilities relied on vendors and contractors to provide the nuclear steam system as well as plant engineering and construction on a cost-plus basis.[38] This was clearly imprudent for a new, unproven technology.

Unrealistic expectations of cost savings from scaling up from the experience with a few small initial nuclear power plants encouraged in a boom in nuclear plant construction. Reactors were ordered based on the claims of manufacturers that the next, bigger generation would achieve enormous cost reductions. In 1968, the largest light water reactor that had been operating for a year or more was 200 MW, while the mean size of reactors ordered that year was 926 MW. With only two companies building plants, a rapid increase in orders escalated costs for major components and strained the limited supply of qualified labor.[39]

However, attempts to blame the rise on costs on regulation and environmental opposition are off the mark. From 1968 to 1976, nuclear plant construction costs increased by less than other steam power plants, but both accelerated at a higher rate than general inflation.[40] During the 1970s, despite the proliferation of nominal regulations, the appearance of tighter federal regulation of nuclear power in the 1970s was somewhat illusory. By the time the Nuclear Regulatory Agency geared up its monitoring and enforcement activities in the late 1970s, most of the nuclear plants built in the US were close to completion.[41]

---

[37] Robin Cowan, "Nuclear Power Reactors: A Study in Technological Lock-in," *Journal of Economic History* 50 (Sept. 1990): 564–565. Those contracts, for plants ordered between 1965–67, ranged between $70–$105/kW, except for one outlier at $200/kW. Nine non-turnkey plants ordered in 1966 ranged from $150–400/kW. The seventeen non-turnkey plants ordered in 1967 had costs ranging from $200–580/kW. William Mooz, *Cost Analysis of Light Water Reactor Power Plants*, Rand for the DOE, R-2304-DOE (June 1978): 59.

[38] Mark J. McCabe, "Principals, Agents, and the Learning Curve: The Case of Steam-Electric Power Plant Design and Construction," *Journal of Industrial Economics* 44 (December 1996): 360–361.

[39] Robin Cowan, "Nuclear Power Reactors: A Study in Technological Lock-in," at 566, nt 70.

[40] William Mooz, *Cost Analysis of Light Water Reactor Power Plants*, at 57.

[41] Richard W. England and Eric P. Mitchell, "Federal Regulation and Environmental Impact of the U.S. Nuclear Power Industry, 1974–1984," *Natural Resources Journal* 30 (Summer 1990): 540–542.

The impacts weren't uniform across utilities and projects. Investment costs of nuclear power plants completed in the 1980s ranged from about $1,300 to over $6,000 per kW. Reasons for this wide variation include differences in project management, regulatory approach, site-related factors, plant design, and regulatory accounting allowances. Projects with high costs were those which experienced difficulties with construction management and regulatory procedures. These factors led to extended construction schedules up to about fourteen years, with associated interest charges on project financing. Low-cost projects with construction periods of five to six years reflected efficient project management by experienced companies who completed the detailed design and resolved regulatory issues before the start of construction.[42]

A series of accidents at U.S. nuclear plants, culminating in the incident at Three Mile Island in 1979, led to additional safety retrofits for nuclear plants, further escalating the costs of units under construction, while instigating opposition to nuclear power. Nuclear plants, once completed, had unplanned outage times, and operations and escalating maintenance costs.[43] As a result, between 1972 and 1992 construction on more than 115 nuclear power plants was eventually abandoned and losses reached more than $42 billion.[44]

Many states instituted prudency reviews to examine the costs of nuclear power plants as a result of large cost overruns.[45] Frequently, the utility would be unable to recover the full cost of the plant. Virtually all regulatory cost disallowances occurred between 1984–1991, with over fifty separate disallowances on thirty-seven different generating units, for a total of $19.1 billion in disallowed costs. Twenty-six of these units

---

[42] P.M.S. Jones and G. Woite, "Cost of Nuclear and Conventional Baseload Electricity Generation," *IAEA Bulletin*, 3 (1990): 18–23.

[43] Richard J. Pierce, "The Regulatory Treatment of Mistakes in Retrospect: Canceled Plants and Excess Capacity," 132 *U. Pennsylvania Law Review* 497 (1984). There is some evidence that the forcing of the Light Water Reactor, by Admiral Rickover, and then by General Electric and Westinghouse, resulted in an inferior design that was more vulnerable to safety problems and less reliable, becoming dominant in the American nuclear power market. Cowan, "Nuclear Power Reactors: A Study in Technological Lock-in," 546–547.

[44] Ralph Cavanagh, "Least-Cost Planning Imperatives for Electric Utilities and Their Regulators," 5 *Harvard Environmental Law Review* 299, 302 (1988); Charles M. Studness, "The Big Squeeze: 1992 Electric Utility Financial Results," *Public Utility Fortnightly* (June 1, 1993): 79.

[45] Between 1945 and 1975, there were fewer than a dozen prudence cases reported. Robert E. Burns et al., *The Prudent Investment Test in the 1980s* (Columbus, Ohio, National Regulatory Research Institute, April 1985).

were nuclear plants, with the eleven non-nuclear plants accounting for only $782 million in disallowances.[46]

Shareholders challenged the constitutionality of the prudency reviews, but the Supreme Court, in *Duquesne*[47] upheld a Pennsylvania Supreme Court decision that a state statute precluded utility rates from reflecting either a return on or a return of any investment in a cancelled nuclear power plant. While "the Constitution protects utilities from being limited to a charge for their property serving the public which is so 'unjust' as to be confiscatory", if the total effect of the rate order cannot be said to be unreasonable, judicial inquiry is at an end. The Court rejected the suggestion that the prudent investment rule should be adopted as the constitutional standard for regulatory disallowances.[48] The decision in *Duquesne* affirmed the *Hope* end-result test,[49] and made investments in nuclear energy even more risky, as regulators could use their discretion to disallow costs.[50]

While utility executives and many academics claimed that opportunistic behavior by state regulators stifled investment in new generation during the 1980s,[51] the empirical evidence doesn't support that conclusion.

---

[46] Thomas Lyon and John Mayo, "Regulatory Opportunism and Investment Behavior: Evidence From the U.S. Electric Utility Industry," *Rand Journal of Economics* 36 (Autumn 2005): 642.

[47] *Duquesne Light Co. v. Barasch et al.*, 488 U.S. 299 (1989).

[48] *Duquesne Light Co. v. Barasch et al.*, 488 U.S. 299, 308, 315 (1989).

[49] *FPC v. Hope Natural Gas Co.*, 320 U.S. 591 (1944).

Under the statutory standard of "just and reasonable" it is the result reached not the method employed which is controlling. It is not theory but the impact of the rate order which counts. If the total effect of the rate order cannot be said to be unjust and unreasonable, judicial inquiry under the Act is at an end. The fact that the method employed to reach that result may contain infirmities is not then important. Moreover, the Commission's order does not become suspect by reason of the fact that it is challenged. It is the product of expert judgment which carries a presumption of validity. And he who would upset the rate order under the Act carries the heavy burden of making a convincing showing that it is invalid because it is unjust and unreasonable in its consequences. [citations omitted]

Id. at 602.

[50] The *Duquesne* case signaled the Court's acceptance of commission oversight. Richard J. Pierce, "Public Utility Regulatory Takings: Should the Judiciary Attempt To Police the Political Institutions?" 77 *Georgetown Law Journal* 2031 (1989); Richard J. Pierce, "The Regulatory Treatment of Mistakes in Retrospect."

[51] Typical of the conventional wisdom:

The massive disallowances of utility investments in nuclear power plants dramatically changed utility incentives. The high perceived risk of future disallowances reversed utilities' incentives to overinvest, and made utilities extremely reluctant to build new

Utilities that suffered a regulatory cost disallowance did subsequently invest less, but other utilities in the same state show no significant reduction in investment, indicating that disallowances were interpreted as punishment of company-specific managerial excess. Regulatory cost disallowances appear to have had "reputational spillovers" only for utilities planning to serve as operators of nuclear power plants under construction. This may have reflected regulatory opportunism or just as plausibly, a rational reconsideration by utility management of the wisdom of their involvement with a sophisticated technology that might make demands that exceeded their managerial capabilities.[52]

Average cost based ratemaking creates significant financial risk during periods of rapid changes in inflation or energy demand. The same regulatory lag that benefited utilities during flush times exposed them to eroding real revenues and rising operating costs during the 1970s. Rising fuel and other operating costs paid from a steady or declining revenue stream could result in declining or negative net revenues. The average adjustment lag was about nine months, due to PUCs granting interim rate relief during lengthy proceedings.[53] While most utilities were able to request a rate case, these proceedings often take six to twelve months or longer to complete, and there is a limit to a PUC's patience with numerous rate case requests.

The cost of attracting capital rose dramatically, partially due to increased risks of regulatory disallowances, though a larger impact was due to the impact of inflation on nominal interest rates, followed by Federal Reserve Chairman's Paul Volcker's tight monetary policy of the early 1980s. The combination of disallowances, regulatory lag and high financing charges put severe financial pressure on many utilities. The ratio of market to book value declined from 1.23 in 1970 to 0.68 in 1975 and 0.65 in 1980, before rebounding back to 1.33 in 1990. By the mid-1980s,

---

power plants. Shareholders are not compensated for this risk through the allowed rate of return. Disallowances also place utility managers' jobs in jeopardy. As a result, utilities now systematically underestimate future demand to justify *not* building new generating capacity. The unwillingness of utilities to invest in new power plants created a void that must be filled with a new industry structure and new forms of government oversight.

Bernard S. Black and Richard J. Pierce, Jr., "The Choice Between Markets and Central Planning in Regulating the U.S. Electricity Industry," 93 *Columbia Law Review* 1339, 1346 (1993).

[52] Lyon and Mayo, "Regulatory Opportunism and Investment Behavior," at 630.

[53] Emeka Nwaeze, "Public Utility Regulation in the U.S. and Asymmetric Return Responses to Positive and Negative Abnormal Earnings," *Multinational Finance Journal* 2 (1998): 273.

completion or cancellation of the ongoing construction activity removed financial uncertainty from many utilities. Lower inflation and lower fossil fuel prices reduced operating costs, and lessened resistance to rate increases needed to finance new construction. Nominal interest rates, while still high relative to historical levels, fell below the double digit level of the early 1980s. A procedure to permit all or part of the construction work in progress to be included in the rate base was adopted by FERC to alleviate financial hardships. States also began to permit the inclusion of construction work in progress in the rate base.[54]

The escalation in electricity rates brought pressure on utilities from their largest customers.[55] Manufacturing plants account for the lion's share of electricity purchases by the industrial sector, and in that group a few industries dominate electricity consumption. The top 5 percent of electricity consuming firms consume about 70 percent of all industrial electricity and electricity represents a much higher share of their overall input costs. Rising real electricity prices encouraged the migration of electricity-intensive manufacturing activity to areas served by utilities with cheaper electricity. Large purchasers of electricity also had greater opportunities and incentives to reduce their costs by managing load factors (ratio of average to peak demand), self-generating, taking high-voltage power, and accepting curtailable or interruptible power.[56]

One method used by utilities to circumvent pressure against capacity additions, and criticism of investments in "surplus" generation capacity, was to increase the size and frequency of electricity sales and purchases to other utilities. Coordination transactions, short-term purchases and sales of electricity engaged in by interconnected integrated utilities, allowed selling utilities to obtain additional revenues from power plants while retaining the capacity to ensure reliability. Purchasing utilities could buy power when the price was below their cost of generating additional electricity, reducing their average cost of generation. Wholesale requirements transactions accounted for about 10 percent of IOU generation and 5 percent of IOU revenues in the 1980s.[57]

[54] EIA, *Financial Impacts of Nonutility Power Purchases on Investor-Owned Electric Utilities* (June 1994): 7–8.

[55] Industrial purchasers accounted for 47 percent of retail electricity sales in 1960, 40 percent in 1980 and 30 percent in 2000. Table 8.9 Electricity End Use, 1949–2010, EIA, *Annual Energy Review 2010* (October 19, 2011).

[56] Steven J. Davis, Cheryl Grim, John Haltiwanger and Mary Streitwieser, *Electricity Pricing to U.S. Manufacturing Plants, 1963–2000* (January 21, 2008): 18, 24–25.

[57] J. A. Bouknight, Jr., and David B. Raskin, "Planning for Wholesale Customer Loads in a Competitive Environment: The Obligation to Provide Wholesale Service under the

These two trends, a small group of energy intensive large industrial companies focused on reducing electricity costs, and an increased volume of inter-utility transactions, would begin to erode the traditional regulated electricity model. Change would be gradual, because viable alternatives were simply not available in the 1970s and 1980s. Oil was expensive, and utilities were discouraged from consuming it to reduce oil imports. Burning natural gas in utility boilers was prohibited in the 1970s. And while nuclear plants under construction were gradually completed and brought on line throughout the 1980s, no new plants were constructed.

A number of overlapping trends gradually eroded the institutional foundations of the energy status quo and created economic pressure and incentives for change. Deregulation of natural gas created a surplus that could now be used to fire new generation technologies. The collapse of the world oil market in 1986 supported the deflationary trend in the energy markets. Implementation of the new environmental legislation meant higher costs for Eastern coal and limited market penetration by less expensive Western coal. By the early 1990s it was possible for independent generators to exploit new gas fired technologies to compete with the vertically integrated IOUs. The promise of cheaper electricity would in turn mobilize actors to pressure FERC and then Congress to permit entry into existing markets by these new companies.

Federal Power Act," 8 *Energy Law Journal* 237 (1987); Paul Joskow, "Regulatory Failure, Regulatory Reform, and Structural Change in the Electrical Power Industry," *Brookings Papers: Microeconomics 1989*, 132.

2

The EPA Steps In

From the perspective of the energy industry, air pollution regulation has been the most important aspect of environmental regulation, with cooling water requirements a distant second. Rules governing heat discharge into rivers and lakes primarily impacted large power plants through the additional expense of building cooling towers as an alternative to direct discharge. Air pollution regulations have had a tremendous impact on coal generation, due to sulfur dioxide (SO_2) and particulate emission restrictions, and to a lesser extent on gas turbines, because of nitrous oxide (NO_x) restrictions. Differential treatment of new and grandfathered coal-fired generation plants distorted investment patterns for decades and encouraged the continued operation of relatively inefficient plants well past their expected lives. From the perspective of electricity deregulation, the most important impact of air pollution regulation was the increase in cost of coal-fired generation and the barriers to siting coal plants, opening opportunities for the new, gas-fired technologies to gain market share.

The issues surrounding the evasion of the air pollution regulations by coal plants were generally too arcane to garner public and media attention, so lobbying contests between environmental groups and industry groups determined policy outcomes. Support for the environment has been more an aspirational goal than a high priority for the public. Although the public overwhelmingly supports strict environmental standards and regulation, environmental concerns are never high salience issues comparable to the economy and foreign policy.[1] There is a lack

[1] Everett Ladd and Karlyn Bowman, "Public Opinion on the Environment," *Resources* 123 (1996): 5. For example, in a 1996 poll, the environment ranked fourteenth of fifteen

of public opinion data on the environment before 1970 for the simple reason that pollsters did not see it as an important issue. There was a brief jump in public interest in environmental issues in 1970, after which interest in environmental protection declined and remained stagnant into the 1980s before rising to record levels between 1987 and 1991, descending again in the years that followed. Public concern with the environment is conditioned by the business cycle, rising during periods of prosperity and falling when times turn hard.[2]

The federal government's first major role in the regulation of air pollution came with the passage of the Federal Air Pollution Act of 1955. The Air Pollution Control Act appropriated $25 million over five years for a program to fund federal air pollution studies and provide technical assistance to state and local agencies. This began the explosion of federal funding that created an independent source of expertise on health effects of pollution. Federal support for cancer research underwrote the development of new techniques and tools for understanding the chronic effects of pollution and toxic chemicals. The National Cancer Institute played a central role in the development of a key tool for studying chronic harms from pollution – the long-term rodent bioassay for identifying carcinogens. The National Science Foundation became a major supporter of basic research across a range of life science disciplines, from molecular biology and genetics to plant biology, ecology, and systematic biology. The new researchers who emerged in the 1960s generally operated without professional and financial linkages to industry.[3]

The Clean Air Act (CAA) of 1963 was the culmination of a two-year-long congressional battle. The act created a complex multistage process that maintained the primacy of state and local authority over air pollution control. Federal involvement in enforcement actions was mandated

---

national problems in importance. In an open-ended survey, the environment did not make a list of the most important problems facing the country. *Id.*

[2] Jon Agnone, "Amplifying Public Opinion: The Policy Impact of the U.S. Environmental Movement," *Social Forces* 85(4) (June 2007): 1600, 1609; Deborah Lynn Guber, "Up and Down with Ecology Revisited: The Stability of Public Attitudes towards Environmental Spending, 1973–1998," *33rd Annual Meeting of the Northeast Political Science Association*, Philadelphia, Pennsylvania (November 8–10, 2001): 6–8, 13. This contrasted with the perception among academics and environmental activists of an eminent environmental crisis. See Cary Coglianese, "Social Movements, Law, and Society: The Institutionalization of the Environmental Movement," 150 *University of Pennsylvania Law Review* 85, 91 (2001).

[3] Joe Greene Conley II, *Environmentalism Contained: A History of Corporate Response to the New Environmentalism* (Ph.D. Diss., Princeton University, November 2006): 22–38.

only when notice was received from a designated local official that an air pollution problem had arisen.[4] States and municipalities showed little enthusiasm for the abatement procedure authorized under the 1963 law until a four-day air pollution inversion in New York City, blamed for the death of an estimated 168 people, focused renewed attention on air pollution. On January 30, 1967, President Johnson called for major new air pollution legislation. As Chairman of the Senate Air and Water Pollution Subcommittee of the Public Works Committee, Senator Edmund Muskie was the principal architect of the new legislation.[5] President Johnson signed the Air Quality Act of 1967 in November. It established a formal air quality management process but provided no penalties for states that failed to comply.[6]

The growing weight of evidence that industrial pollution was endangering public health gradually led to a shift in public opinion. The public blamed a handful of industries, including the steel, chemical, and energy industries, for the nation's environmental degradation. The national media helped solidify the linkage of industry with pollution problems. A blowout at a Union Oil platform on January 29, 1969 caused a major oil spill off the coast of Santa Barbara and provided a steady stream of images of oil-soaked beaches and devastated wildlife. The June 22, 1969 conflagration of an oil slick and debris on the Cuyahoga River in Cleveland also attracted national media attention, with stories on the blaze appearing in both *Time* and *National Geographic*. *Time*, which misleadingly ran a photo from a more severe blaze in 1952, helped make the event a symbol of the nation's environmental crisis.[7]

The 1960s and 1970s saw the growth and resurgence of older environmental organizations and the creation of new environmental organizations, particularly those that specialized in litigation. A successful

---

[4] Bruce M. Kramer, "The 1970 Clean Air Amendments: Federalism in Action or Inaction," 6 *Texas Tech Law Review* 47, 50–54 (1974); John Bachman, "Will the Circle Be Unbroken: A History of the U.S. National Ambient Air Quality Standards," *Journal of the Air & Waste Management Association* 57 (June 2007): 662.

[5] Arnold W. Reitze, Jr., "Overview and Critique: a Century of Air Pollution Control Law: What's Worked; What's Failed; What Might Work," 21 *Environmental Law* 1549, 1558 (1991).

[6] Bachman, "Will the Circle Be Unbroken," 664.

[7] Joe Greene Conley II, *Environmentalism Contained: A History of Corporate Response to the New Environmentalism*, 64–65. See Jonathan H. Adler, "Fables of the Cuyahoga: Reconstructing a History of Environmental Protection," 14 *Fordham Environmental Law Journal* 89 (2002) for a history of the Cuyahoga's unfortunate tendency toward spontaneous combustion and its subsequent elevation into national mythology.

lawsuit against the spraying of pesticides on Long Island brought together a group of scientists and lawyers to create the Environmental Defense Fund (EDF) in 1967.[8] Other new environmental groups included the Natural Resources Defense Council (NRDC), the Friends of the Earth, Environmental Action, and Greenpeace. Groups that had previously emphasized nature preservation, such as the Sierra Club, Wilderness Society, and the National Audubon Society, worked together with the new environmental groups toward a common cause of environmental protection.[9]

In 1969, Congress passed the National Environmental Policy Act (NEPA). NEPA was primarily a symbolic piece of legislation, stating the congressional intent to declare a national environmental policy, but without going into specifics. NEPA established a Council on Environmental Quality in the executive branch and institutionalized the tradition of writing environmental impact statements for proposed legislation and rulemakings.[10]

Senator Gaylord Nelson saw a linkage in both the audience and the methods of the student protests against the Vietnam War. He conceived the idea of a national teach-in on the environment that eventually turned into a coordinated series of events held across the country on Earth Day in 1970. Eight protest events were recorded in conjunction with the first Earth Day. Seven of these events focused on air pollution, the largest involving 2,000 people protesting against automobile pollution in front of General Motors' New York City offices.[11]

President Nixon saw the rising concern about the environment as an opportunity, and in December 1969, he appointed a White House committee to consider a separate environmental agency. Nixon also made the environment a theme in his State of the Union Address. On July 9 of the following year, President Nixon submitted to Congress Reorganization Plan No. 3 of 1970 to establish a new environmental agency. The

---

8 Philip Shabecoff, *A Fierce Green Fire: The American Environmental Movement*, rev. ed. (Washington, DC, Island Press, 2003): 93–96.
9 Shabecoff, *A Fierce Green Fire*, at 109–13; Cary Coglianese, "Institutionalization of the Environmental Movement," 150 *University of Pennsylvania Law Review* 85, 91–94, 99–102 (2001); Erik Johnson, "Changing Issue Representation Among Major United States Environmental Movement Organizations," *Rural Sociology* 71 (March 2006): 132–54.
10 National Environmental Policy Act of 1969, Pub. L. No. 91–190, 83 Stat. 852.
11 Jon Agnone, "Amplifying Public Opinion: The Policy Impact of the U.S. Environmental Movement," at 1602; Cary Coglianese, "Social Movements, Law, and Society, at 85, 91.

Environment Protection Agency (EPA) was founded on December 2, 1970.[12] It was charged with protecting public health and safeguarding the natural environment. Over the course of a decade, the EPA grew from a budget of $455 million and a staff of 6,000 in 1970 to a budget of $5.6 billion and a staff of 13,000 in 1980.[13]

EPA coordinates and submits major rules for review by federal agencies as well as for public comment. The rulemaking process provides formal avenues for intervention. Interest groups meet with agency policymakers, lobby the Congress and the executive branch, and, when all else fails, resort to litigation. Key industrial actors include the American Petroleum Institute, Edison Electric Institute (EEI), Motor Vehicle Manufacturers Association, American Iron and Steel Institute, the National Mining Association, and the Business Roundtable along with company lobbyists and lawyers. However, well-organized environmental groups such as the EDF, NRDC, the Sierra Club, and the American Lung Association have been effective counterbalances to industry lobbyists. In the 1970s, environmental groups added scientists and lawyers to their staffs, who interacted regularly with industry and government experts. In 1969, there were only two full-time environmental lobbyists; by 1975, twelve major environmental organizations employed forty lobbyists. Environmental groups also influenced public opinion through education and grassroots campaigns.[14]

---

[12] The EPA merged fifteen function units from different departments and organizations, including air quality with the National Air Pollution Control Administration (HEW) and the Air Quality Advisory Board; solid waste with the Bureau of Solid Waste Management (HEW); drinking water with the Bureau of Water Hygiene (HEW); pesticide tolerance functions under the Federal Food, Drug and Cosmetic Act (HEW) and pesticide regulation and registration (Department of Agriculture); and water quality with the Federal Water Quality Administration and the Water Pollution Control Advisory Board (Department of the Interior). Xin Liu, *The U.S. Environmental Protection Agency: A Historical Perspective on Its Role in Environmental Protection* (Ph.D. Diss., Ludwig-Maximilians-Universität, München, 2010): 23–24.

[13] Coglianese, "Social Movements, Law, and Society," at 98; Liu, *The U.S. Environmental Protection Agency*, at 21.

[14] Liu, *The U.S. Environmental Protection Agency*, at 93. Former EPA Administrator William Reilly points out that lobbyists often use indirect channels to influence policy:

I was continually amazed that the kinds of contacts and information that EPA was restricted in having, at least ex parte, other than on the record with notes taken and memoranda prepared and acknowledgments in the record, went on unconstrained by these rules all the time with people in the Executive Office of the President. It was not uncommon in my time to get back comments from the Office of Management and Budget or the Competitiveness Council that incorporated verbatim lobbyist documents that we had seen from trade associations three or four months before on particular matters of

An "iron triangle" relationship soon developed between the environmental interest groups, the EPA staff, and congressional committee staffs. Self-selection by EPA staff members resulted in a certain amount of zealotry inside the EPA, balanced by the need to balance political pressures emanating from the White House and the rest of Congress. Environmental groups used dissatisfaction with the agency, and inevitable political compromises in the rulemaking process, as an antagonist to raise money and get more members. The agency tacitly encouraged environmental groups to sue for objectives it was trying to accomplish but lacked the political leverage to implement. As long as the Democrats controlled Congress, the relevant Congressional committees also pushed the agency toward more stringent regulation.[15]

The Nixon administration sponsored a bill that provided for more extensive federal air pollution regulatory power. Given the perceived intensity of environmental issues after Earth Day, politicians found themselves in a race to the top, proposing increasingly stringent clean air legislation. The supervisory powers of the EPA were expanded in the House bill. The Senate version provided for direct federal enforcement of air pollution regulations. After resolving differences between the Senate and House versions, the Clean Air Act Amendments of 1970 were passed and signed into law on New Year's Eve.[16]

The 1970 CAA amendments established the fundamental structure of air quality management regulation, the Air Quality Management system. The air quality system relies on National Ambient Air Quality Standards (NAAQS), based on an estimate of undesirable health and environmental effects of pollution. Section 109 specified that the EPA administrator propose NAAQS for each pollutant for which air quality criteria had been issued. After public comment, the administrator was required to establish

---

concern in legislative or regulatory policy. That had a very demoralizing effect on EPA. Finally, as this sort of thing came to the attention of Congressman Waxman and others, it resulted in unpleasant but very well publicized hearings.

William K. Reilly: Oral History Interview, EPA 202-K-95-002, September 1995, at http://www.epa.gov/history/publications/print/reilly.htm (last visited May 5, 2011). See also Mathew McCubbins, Rogers Noll, and Barry Weingast, "Administrative Procedures as Instruments of Political Control," *Journal of Law, Economics and Organization* 3 (1987): 262–63.

[15] *William D. Ruckelshaus: Oral History Interview*, at http://www.epa.gov/history/publications/print/ruck.htm, last visited February 15, 2011.

[16] John Bachman, "Will the Circle Be Unbroken: A History of the U.S. National Ambient Air Quality Standards," *Journal of the Air & Waste Management Association* 57 (June 2007): 665–66; Bruce M. Kramer, "The 1970 Clean Air Amendments: Federalism in Action or Inaction," *6 Texas Tech Law Review* 47, 58–65 (1974).

each standard. At the time of enactment, criteria had been issued for five pollutants: particulate matter, SO_2, oxidants, hydrocarbons, and carbon monoxide. NO_x was the only additional pollutant to be added during the EPA's first decade. The 1970 amendments specified two kinds of standards: Primary NAAQS, to protect the public health, and Secondary NAAQS, to protect the public welfare. New pollution sources may be subject to controls based on best available control technology (BACT).[17]

The EPA was required to establish NAAQS that were sufficient "to protect the public health" with "an adequate margin of safety."[18] The courts made it clear that the EPA was to do this regardless of cost.[19] The states had primary responsibility to develop State Implementation Plans (SIPs) to attain the standards by specified dates. The EPA reviewed SIPs and could impose sanctions for failure to submit an adequate plan. EPA regulations required the states to enforce the standards, but the EPA became the primary enforcement agency by default.[20] Federal approval of SIPs combined with federal enforcement authority limited the ability of local economic interests to circumvent environmental regulations through influence in state politics.

The 1970 CAA Amendments set tight deadlines for SIP development, review, and approval. SIPs needed to achieve attainment three years after plan approval, generally by 1975, unless granted an extension. It soon became clear that many states could not meet the 1975 deadlines.[21] The hurried pace of initial rulemakings also led to procedural shortcuts that did not withstand judicial scrutiny. Various courts required the EPA to disclose for comment the data and methodology relied on in formulating the proposed rules, to provide detailed statements of its reasoning, to respond to comments, and to afford opportunity for cross-examination of witnesses. These procedural innovations were designed to ensure that

---

[17] Bachman, "Will the Circle Be Unbroken," at 654, 666–67.

[18] Clean Air Act 5 109(b)(l), 42 U.S.C. 6 7409(b)(l) (1988).

[19] *See Lead Indus. Ass'n v. EPA*, 647 F.2d 1130, 1148–51 (D.C. Cir.), *cert. denied*, 449 U.S. 1042 (1980): "The legislative history of the Act also shows the Administrator may not consider economic and technological feasibility in setting air quality standards; the absence of any provision requiring consideration of these factors was no accident; it was the result of a deliberate decision by Congress to subordinate such concerns to the achievement of health goals." *Lead Industries* at 1149. *See also Union Elec. Co. v. EPA*, 427 U.S. 246, 257 (1976) (These requirements are of a "technology-forcing character" and are expressly designed to force regulated sources to develop pollution control devices that might at the time appear to be economically or technologically infeasible; citation omitted). These decisions were affirmed in *Whitman v. American Trucking*, 531 U. S. 457, 465–71 (2001).

[20] Kramer, "The 1970 Clean Air Amendments: Federalism in Action or Inaction," 69–71.

[21] Bachman, "Will the Circle Be Unbroken," 675.

the agency had taken a "hard look" at all affected interests before acting, and provided a record to facilitate judicial review.[22] The EPA responded by adopting a more formal regulation development process and stricter administrative procedures. The EPA made the information and technical methodologies it relied on publicly available, and the preambles to the proposed and final rules provided detailed explanations of EPA's decisions.[23] The EPA would respond to all "significant" comments on the proposal before issuance of a final rule.[24] While this slowed the pace of rulemaking, it also reduced the probability of remand or reversal under the inevitable judicial review.

The EPA originally established uniform NAAQS that only required states to prevent emission concentrations from rising above applicable secondary standards. The Sierra Club appealed this decision to the DC District Court of Appeals, which ruled that the EPA had to reject SIPs that did not prevent the significant degradation of air quality.[25] The EPA replaced uniform NAAQS with a more complex set of standards based on each region's actual air quality. The EPA established three classes of air quality areas: Class I applied to pristine areas; Class II applied to areas of moderate growth; and Class III applied to areas with significant pollution. Areas designated as Class III were only required to meet the NAAQS. New Source Performance Standards (NSPS) reviews were required for any major new source of pollutants. All new or modified sources were required to meet an emissions limit equivalent to the level of emissions reduction achieved by the application of BACT.[26]

Electric utilities dependent on coal generation, and the coal industry, were united against the Clean Air Act. Ambient air quality standards for

---

[22] Robert Glicksman and Christopher H. Schroeder, "EPA and the Courts: Twenty Years of Law and Politics," *Law and Contemporary Problems* 54 (1991): 268.

[23] Under the Administrative Procedures Act, codified at 5 U.S.C. § 551–559, general notice of proposed rulemaking (NOPR) shall be published in the Federal Register. 5 U.S.C. § 553(b). The agency shall give interested persons an opportunity to participate in the rulemaking through submission of written data, views, or arguments. After consideration of the relevant matter presented, the agency shall incorporate in the rules adopted a concise general statement of their basis and purpose. 5 U.S.C. § 553(c). The general procedure is to issue a NOPR that describes the reason and a preliminary proposal for the proposed rule, a round of comments, issuance of a final rule, a round of petitions requesting changes and modifications, and often issuance of additional orders incorporating modifications or explaining why the agency has rejected such requests.

[24] Bachman, "Will the Circle Be Unbroken," 673–74.

[25] *Sierra Club v. Ruckelshaus*, 344 F. Supp. 253 (DC Cir. 1972), atf'd per curiam sub nom. *Fri v. Sierra Club*, 412 U.S. 541 (1973).

[26] Mathew McCubbins, Rogers Noll, and Barry Weingast, "Structure and Process, Politics and Policy: Administrative Arrangements And The Political Control Of Agencies," 75 *Virginia Law Review* 431, 450–53 (1989).

particulates and SO_2 would require development and adoption of new pollution control equipment. This raised the cost of electricity relative to power generated from natural gas, resulting in a split in the energy industry. The American Gas Association launched a public relations campaign touting the environmental advantage of "clean" natural gas in 1971.[27] While regulations restraining fuel switching would curtail gas industry lobbying in the 1970s, the opportunity to raise a rival's costs would put the natural gas industry on the opposite side of the environmental fence from the coal industry and its utility allies in subsequent decades.[28]

Under the mandate of the 1970 CAA Amendments, the EPA established NSPS for stationary sources, setting the SO_2 ceiling at 1.2 lb/million Btu for new generation plants. Bituminous coal would need to contain 0.5–0.7% sulfur by weight to meet this standard without emission control equipment.[29] The only coal with sulfur content low enough to meet this standard was from open pit mines in the Power River Basin of Northwestern Wyoming and Eastern Montana.

The CAA Amendments of 1977 addressed a number of issues that had arisen since 1970, including the attainment deadlines for the NAAQS, vehicle emission standards, and prevention of significant deterioration (PSD). The 1977 Amendments required that the EPA review all existing criteria and standards by 1980 and every five years thereafter. It established the Clean Air Scientific Advisory Committee to recommend new

---

[27] Conley, *Environmentalism Contained: A History of Corporate Response to the New Environmentalism*, at 88–92.

[28] However, the natural gas industry was split. Some of the natural gas producers were major oil companies that opposed stricter standards on automobile emissions (which could lower gasoline demand and/or raise refinery costs). This required that at times they might work with other industry groups to weaken emission standards, but they also cut deals to soften automobile emission standards at the expense of other sources of pollution.

[29] The oxygen in SO_2 is equal in weight to sulfur, so that if all the sulfur is combusted, the weight of SO_2 will be double that of the sulfur in the original coal. There are two types of sulfur in coal: pyritic and organic. Pyrite (FeS_2) is much heavier than carbon, so crushing and washing the coal with water will remove up to 50% of the pyritic sulfur. Organic sulfur is chemically bound to the coal and cannot be removed by washing. Flue gas desulfurization, or "scrubbing," works by a reaction between calcium carbonate (limestone) and sulfur dioxide to produce calcium sulfite: $CaCO_3 + SO_2 \rightarrow CaSO_3$. In wet scrubbing, limestone is slurried in water. Oxification of the calcium sulfite gives anhydrous calcium sulfate, $CaSO_4$, which can be transformed to gypsum by exposure to water. Dry scrubber systems use lime (CaO) as the reagent in a spray dryer system that achieved lower removal rates (70–80% initially, but now up to 94%), compared to wet scrubbers (initially 90%, now as high as 99%). Edward Rubin, Sonia Yeh, David Hounshell, and Margaret Taylor, "Experience Curves for Power Plant Emission Control Technologies," *International Journal of Energy Technology and Policy* 2 (2004): 56.

standards or revision of existing standards as appropriate. It required that the EPA establish a primary standard for NO_x unless the administrator found it unnecessary based on scientific criteria.[30]

Under the 1977 CAA Amendments, all "new sources" must install BACT that has been "adequately demonstrated."[31] This was accomplished by changing the language in the 1970 CAA Amendments from requiring the use of the "best system of emission reduction" to the "best *technological* system of continuous emission reduction." The ceiling rate of emissions per million Btu was replaced by a percentage of sulfur reduction requirements.[32] New sources in nonattainment areas had to install equipment to reach the lowest achievable emissions rate.[33] Proposed regulations were promulgated on September 19, 1978, and that date controlled the determination of a "new source."[34]

The PSD provisions that had been adopted in response to *Sierra Club v. Ruckelshaus* were further strengthened in the 1977 Amendments. Senator Muskie used the carrot of relaxed auto industry emission standards to garner support for more stringent PSD provisions. The PSD program was designed to maintain the air quality of areas of the country with air quality better than the NAAQS.[35] Classification of additional areas as Class III was severely limited. In PSD areas, major new sources of pollution were required to install BACT. The permit seeker had to submit an environmental impact statement and to participate in a "new source review" procedure.[36]

These provisions worked to reduce the South and West's advantages in attracting new factories and power plants to smaller cities with higher levels of ambient air quality. The industrial cities and states realized that PSD created a mobility barrier to new industry and became ardent supporters. Since existing facilities were unaffected by the provisions, only those businesses planning to relocate or build new facilities in the South

---

[30] Bachman, "Will the Circle Be Unbroken," 677–78.

[31] CAA §165(a)(4), 42 U.S.C. §7475(a)(4).

[32] Peter Navarro, "The 1977 Clean Air Act Amendments: Energy, Environmental, Economic, and Distributional Impacts," *Public Policy* 29 (1981): 127–28.

[33] CAA §173(a)(2), 42 U.S.C. §7503(a)(2).

[34] Arnold W. Reitze, Jr., "Overview and Critique: a Century of Air Pollution Control Law: What's Worked; What's Failed; What Might Work," 21 *Environmental Law* 1597 (1991).

[35] Pashigian, "Environmental Regulation: Whose Self-Interests Are Being Protected?" at 556.

[36] Navarro, "The 1977 Clean Air Act Amendments: Energy, Environmental, Economic, and Distributional Impacts," at 129–30.

and West had strong incentives to support the weakening of PSD.[37] These provisions also discouraged building power plants in remote regions, such as mine-mouth low-sulfur coal plants, and wheeling the power to high pollution regions. Plants burning low-sulfur coal would have to install scrubbers that removed 70% of sulfur emissions (high-sulfur coal-burning plants had to remove 90% of sulfur emissions).[38] The EPA planning office had proposed to lower the SO_2 emission ceiling, which would allow western generators to employ limited scrubbing to meet this standard. Under pressure from Senate Majority Leader Robert Byrd (D-WV), the EPA required plants burning western coal to employ dry scrubbing technology (an unproven technology).[39]

The 1977 CAA Amendments illustrate what Bruce Yandle has called "bootleggers and Baptists," the combination of idealists and self-interested actors in coalitions supporting public interested legislation that advantages private interest groups.[40] Environmentalists played the role of Baptists, garnering public support for their secular religious views[41] and creating support for environmental regulation, despite the costs it imposes on the public. Industry groups and local jurisdictions were the bootleggers, using those regulations to "raise rival's costs."[42]

---

[37] R. Shep Melnick, *Regulation and the Courts: The Case of the Clean Air Act* Washington, DC, Brookings, 1983): 98–100; Bruce A. Ackerman and William T. Hassler, "Beyond the New Deal: Coal and the Clean Air Act," 89 *Yale Law Journal* 1466, 1504–10 (1980). See the discussion in *United States v. City of Painesville*, 644 F.2d 1186, 1192 (6th Cir. 1981), *cert. denied*, 454 U.S. 894 (1981).

[38] Melnick, *Regulation and the Courts: The Case of the Clean Air Act*, 80–82. Scrubbers were estimated to add about 15% to the capacity cost of a new coal-fired power plant in 1980. Paul Joskow and Nancy Rose, "The Effects of Technological Change, Experience, and Environmental Regulation on the Construction Cost of Coal-Burning Generating Units," *Rand Journal of Economics* 16 (Spring 1985): 20.

[39] Ackerman and Hassler, "Beyond the New Deal: Coal and the Clean Air Act," 1548–54.

[40] Bruce Yandle, "Bootleggers and Baptists-The Education of a Regulatory Economist," *Regulation* (May/June 1983): 12–16.

Bootleggers, you will remember, support Sunday closing laws that shut down all the local bars and liquor stores. Baptists support the same laws and lobby vigorously for them. Both parties gain, while the regulators are content because the law is easy to administer.

Id. at 13.

[41] Robert H. Nelson, "Environmental Religion: A Theological Critique," 55 *Case Western Reserve Law Review* 51 (2004).

[42] Steven Salop and David Scheffman, "Raising Rivals' Cost," *American Economic Review* 73 (May 1983): 267–71. See Ackerman and Hassler, "Beyond the New Deal: Coal and the Clean Air Act," 1498–1500.

When Congress enacted the CAA Amendments of 1970, it exempted power plants constructed prior to the publication of EPA's regulations (on August 17, 1971) from having to meet the legislated emission standards. These exempt plants produced a disproportionate share of utilities' sulfur dioxide and nitrogen oxide emissions. These old plants still had to meet NAAQS requirements, but they were able to do so through the installation of tall smokestacks that reduced local concentrations of SO_2 and, perversely, increased acid rain downwind from the plant.[43] In 1970, there were only two smokestacks higher than 500 feet. By 1985, there were more than 180, with 23 more than 1,000 feet in height. Plants would vent multiple boiler exhaust streams to a smokestack, increasing the exhaust gas temperature and the height of the stack plume. However, the Fifth Circuit ruled that the EPA could not allow the use of dispersion techniques in lieu of emission reductions.[44] The 1977 CAA Amendments addressed this issue, and EPA regulations limited smokestacks to 250 percent of the facility's height after 1982.[45]

A contentious issue with these grandfathered coal plants was the point at which modifications designed to modernize their operations and extend their life resulted in the application of PSD rules requiring BACT to be installed. EPA had limited PSD review to only major modifications, those which increased the potential emissions of any regulated air pollutant by 250 tons per year for a stationary source.[46] The court in *Alabama Power* found that the EPA did have discretion to exempt activities on grounds of *de minimis* or administrative necessity, but could not limit the application of PSD review to modifications to facilities above a threshold quantity of emissions.[47] After the *Alabama Power* decision, the EPA issued revised PSD and nonattainment rules, defining a "major modification" as any physical or operational change "that would result in a significant net emissions increase," taking into account offsets within a facility. The modification rules exempted an increase in hours of

[43] Melnick, *Regulation and the Courts: The Case of the Clean Air Act*, 115–26.

[44] *National Resources Defense Council v. Environmental Protection Agency*, 489 F.2d 390 (5th Cir. 1974).

[45] Arnold W. Reitze, Jr., "Overview and Critique: a Century of Air Pollution Control Law: What's Worked; What's Failed; What Might Work," 21 *Environmental Law* 1549, 1597–99 (1991).

[46] Approximately 5 MW at 75% capacity.

[47] *Alabama Power Co. v. Costle.* 636 F.2d 323, 360–61, 399–400 (D.C. Cir. 1979).

operation or in production rates from the definition of physical or operational change.[48]

One reason the EPA failed to consider economic instruments as part of its pollution control strategy was the lack of interest in Congress. Despite the support of President Nixon, agency officials, numerous economists, the National Academy of Sciences, the National Association of Manufacturers, and even some environmental groups for a tax on sulfur dioxide, both the House and Senate Committees dealing with environmental legislation completely rejected this approach.[49] A sulfur tax would fall primarily on Eastern coal. The EPA did attempt to employ some limited market-based approaches to environmental regulation through its bubble, offset, and netting policies. Offsets allow new sources in nonattainment areas if firms obtain emission reductions that equal or exceed the emissions from that new source. The offset program was included in the 1977 CAA Amendments and was eventually strengthened to require a net reduction in overall emissions.[50]

In 1981, the Reagan administration took office with an agenda to roll back environmental regulation. Reagan appointed Anne Gorsuch as the director of the EPA. Gorsuch was a telecommunications lawyer whose primary qualifications were ideological conformity and powerful friends. Gorsuch and her inner circle of administrators immediately set about reducing the EPA's regulatory presence. During Gorsuch's twenty-two months at the EPA, enforcement referrals to the Justice Department were cut in half and the agency's budget was cut by more than 20 percent. Gorsuch initiated a purge of careerists at the EPA, firing almost every previous presidential appointee on staff. A scandal involving mismanagement of Superfund money ignited a backlash that resulted in her resignation in early March 1983, and more than thirty other senior EPA appointees were shown the door.[51] James Baker, President Reagan's Chief of Staff, engineered the return of William Ruckelshaus, the agency's first

[48] Jonathan Nash and Richard Revesz, "Grandfathering and Environmental Regulation: The Law and Economics of New Source Review," 101 *Northwestern University Law Review* 1677, 1688–89 (2007).

[49] Melnick, *Regulation and the Courts: The Case of the Clean Air Act*, at 149–51.

[50] Thor Ketzback, *The Evolution of Offsets and the Dawn of Emissions Trading Markets* (LLM Thesis, DePaul College of Law, 1997): 5–9.

[51] Richard N. L. Andrews, *Managing the Environment, Managing Ourselves: A History of American Environmental Policy* (New Haven, Yale University Press, 1999): 258–60; Kevin Hillstrom, *U.S. Environmental Policy and Politics: A Documentary History* (Washington, DC, CQ Press, 2010): 478–79.

director, as an exercise in political damage control. Ruckelshaus was able to restore morale at the agency, quiet the media firestorm, and reassure the Reagan people that he would not bring in staff antagonistic to the administration.[52]

The Reagan administration misread the tea leaves, confusing general discontent with regulation with dislike of environmental regulation. Business groups had conducted lobbying campaigns against environmental regulation since the "energy crisis" of the early 1970s. By 1980, affected industries had raised awareness that there were costs to environmental regulation, which needed to be balanced against economic goals. However, business interests failed to achieve major revisions of the Clean Air Act or prevent the passage of new environmental legislation. The salience of environmental problems had declined, but the public commitment to protecting environmental quality remained strong.[53]

Acid rain gradually emerged as a serious political issue because of pressures from environmental groups, Northeastern states, and Canadian objections to cross-border pollution. Numerous acid rain bills were proposed by Western and Northeastern senators and representatives during the 1980s. Midwestern and Appalachian high-sulfur coal-producing states generally opposed any new acid rain controls. Acid rain legislation was blocked in the House by John Dingell (D-MI), who became chairman of the House Energy and Commerce Committee in 1981. His main concern was that legislation amending the Clean Air Act would likely tighten auto emission standards. In the Senate, legislation was blocked by Robert Byrd.[54]

President George H. W. Bush was determined to fulfill a campaign pledge to beef up the 1970 Clean Air Act and took a hands-on role in pushing proposed Clean Air Act amendments through Congress. He was greatly aided in these efforts by new Senate majority leader George Mitchell (D-ME), who replaced Byrd. Senator Max Baucus (D-MT) became chairman of the Environmental Protection Subcommittee of the Committee on Environment and Public Works. The full committee, under

---

[52] William D. Ruckelshaus: Oral History Interview, at http://www.epa.gov/history/publications/print/ruck.htm (last visited February 15, 2011).

[53] Joe Greene Conley II, "Environmentalism Contained: A History of Corporate Response to the New Environmentalism" (Ph.D. Diss., Princeton University, November 2006): 144–50.

[54] Paul Joskow and Richard Schmalensee, "The Political Economy of Market-Based Environmental Policy: The U.S. Acid Rain Program," 41 *Journal of Law and Economics* 37, 45–48 (1998).

his leadership, pushed strongly for more stringent pollution standards. Of the Committee's sixteen members, seven were from New England, New York, and New Jersey, the states most impacted by acid rain, and four members were from the Rocky Mountains States. The bill passed by large majorities in both houses, and Bush signed the 1990 Clean Air Act Amendments into law on November 15, 1990.[55]

Some environmental groups, such as EDF, had begun to support the use of market-based incentives as alternatives to conventional regulation. Market-based approaches, such as emissions trading, promised to lower the costs of achieving environmental goals.[56] EDF's president, Fred Krupp, argued in favor of these approaches because he claimed Americans do not want to choose "between improving our economic well-being and preserving our health and natural resources." The EPA staff developed the acid rain elements of the 1990 CAA Amendments. William Reilly credited the pollution trading rights concept to Resources For the Future. The Council of Economic Advisors, especially Robert Hahn, provided legitimacy within the executive branch.[57]

Title IV of the 1990 CAA Amendments, Acid Deposition Control, created a new program to reduce sulfur dioxide emissions from electric power plants. Congress set the cap on SO_2 emissions and established a trading program to be managed by EPA. The Acid Rain Program began in 1995, and the SO_2 cap-and-trade program currently affects more than 3,500 generation units. The Acid Rain Program set a long-term cap on SO_2 emissions at 9 million tons, to be reached by 2010. This represented a reduction in SO_2 emissions of 42 percent from 1990.[58]

The first phase of SO_2 reductions was implemented in 1995 (through 1999). During Phase I, the 263 dirtiest generating units (known as "Table A" units specified in the Act) were required to reduce their emissions by roughly 3.5 million tons per year. In Phase II, all fossil-fueled plants with capacity greater than 25 MW – more than 2,000 units – became

---

[55] Hillstrom, *U.S. Environmental Policy and Politics: A Documentary*, 481; Gary C. Bryner, *Blue Skies, Green Politics, The Clean Air Act of 1990* (1993): 85; Richard E. Cohen, *Washington at Work: Back Rooms and Clean Air* 18 (Boston, Allyn and Bacon, 1995).

[56] Tom Tietenberg, "Cap-and-Trade: The Evolution of an Economic Idea," *Agricultural and Resource Economics Review* 39 (October 2010): 1–7.

[57] *William K. Reilly: Oral History Interview*, EPA 202-K-95–002, September 1995, at http://www.epa.gov/history/publications/print/reilly.htm (last visited May 5, 2011).

[58] Edward Rubin, Sonia Yeh, David Hounshell, and Margaret Taylor, "Experience Curves for Power Plant Emission Control Technologies," *International Journal of Energy Technology and Policy* 2 (2004): 59.

subject to the national cap on aggregate annual SO_2 emissions.[59] Units affected only after the year 2000 could voluntarily opt in during Phase 1. This provision allowed owners of Table A units to substitute less costly emission reductions from opt-in units for more expensive reductions at other units, as opt-in sources that reduced emissions before 1995 received allowances above their actual emissions.[60]

During Phase II, each utility-generating unit was allocated a specific number of SO_2 allowances. During Phase II, utilities could buy or sell allowances or bank allowances for future use. The statute contained more than thirty individual exceptions to the Phase II allowance allocation. The first category of provisions generally shifted allowances from relatively dirty states to clean states. The second category of allocation rules were narrowly tailored special interest provisions benefiting individual states or individual utilities, some clearly the work of influential legislators.[61] The rules reduced allocations for dirty coal plants by far more than for other facilities. This partially reflected the balance of power shifting to Western states, but also a decision by Midwestern and Appalachian states to trade stricter standards five years down the road for additional Phase I allowances.[62]

The critical compliance element of the SO_2 program was a requirement for each regulated source to have sufficient allowances in its account to offset its annual SO_2 emissions. The penalty was statutorily set in 1990 at \$2,000/ton of SO_2, indexed for inflation, and it reached \$3,152 per ton for the 2006 compliance year. Compliance rates averaged more than 99 percent. There were few legal challenges to the rules the EPA issued and none delayed the implementation of the cap-and-trade program. One reason was the legislation required the EPA to reduce allocations on a pro-rata basis if total allocations exceeded the Phase II cap. This made lobbying for special allocations a zero-sum game, where other actors had a vested interest in opposing exceptions. The law also provided that if the rules were delayed, every source would have to meet a specific emission limit without the flexibility of trading. This reduced the

---

[59] Dallas Burtraw et al., "The Costs and Benefits of Reducing Acid Rain," RFF DP 97–31-REV (September 1997): 9; Joskow and Schmalensee, "The Political Economy of Market-Based Environmental Policy," 41.

[60] Juan-Pablo Montero, "Voluntary Compliance with Market-Based Environmental Policy: Evidence from the U.S. Acid Rain Program," *Journal of Political Economy* 107 (1999): 999–1005.

[61] Joskow and Schmalensee, "The Political Economy of Market-Based Environmental Policy," 55–58.

[62] Id. at 63.

incentive to engage in litigation designed to delay implementation (and delay expenditures for emission reduction).[63]

For many utilities in the Midwest, the cheapest SO_2 control strategy involved switching to Powder River Basin low-sulfur coal. However, some state legislatures and PUCs, at the behest of local coal interests, prevented utilities from switching and encouraged them to build scrubbers, as state regulators preapproved scrubber installations. The ability to pass costs on to consumers reduced the incentive to minimize costs of pollution control by trading allowances. These state actions were in addition to a one-time subsidy for scrubbing built into the Clean Air Act. Utilities that scrub got an extra 3.5 million permits, worth about $1 billion.[64]

The price of SO_2 allowances was much lower than forecasted: early predictions ranged from $290 to $410 per ton for Phase I and from $580 to $815 per ton for Phase II. However, evidence from actual contracts negotiated before the onset of Phase I suggested an implicit price of $50 per ton of SO_2, suggesting that market actors knew those estimates were exaggerated.[65] The sulfur premium rose as railroads adjusted rates, discriminating between Table A and other coal-burning plants.[66] The first annual allowance auction, in March 1993, cleared at a price of $131 per ton.[67] Even as the more stringent Phase II requirements became effective in 2000, prices remained below the $200 per ton mark until the end of 2003 when the proposed Clean Air Interstate Rule (CAIR) raised concerns of more stringent regulation.[68] Prices rose in 2004 and reached $1,000 per ton at times in 2005 before falling back to the $400–500 range in 2007. A subsequent court challenge to CAIR brought down allowance prices,

[63] Sam Napolitano et al., "The U.S. Acid Rain Program: Key Insights from the Design, Operation, and Assessment of a Cap-and-Trade Program," *Electricity Journal* 20 (August/September 2007): 50–51.

[64] Paul Sotkiewicz and Lynne Holt, "Public Utility Commission Regulation and Cost-Effectiveness of Title IV: Lessons for CAIR," *Electricity Journal* (October 2005): 74–75; Bernard Black and Richard Pierce, Jr., "The Choice Between Markets and Central Planning in Regulating the U.S. Electricity Industry," 93 *Columbia Law Review* 1339, 1395–96 (1993).

[65] Ian Lange and Allen S. Bellas, "The 1990 Clean Air Act and the Implicit Price of Sulfur in Coal," *The B.E. Journal of Economic Analysis & Policy* 7 (2007), at http://www.bepress.com/bejeap/vol7/iss1/art41.

[66] Busse and Keohane estimated a $4 per ton premium to Table A plants for Power River Coal. Meghan R. Busse and Nathaniel O. Keohane, "Market Effects of Environmental Regulation: Coal, Railroads, and the 1990 Clean Air Act" (March 13, 2007).

[67] A. Denny Ellerman and Juan-Pablo Montero, "The Declining Trend in Sulfur Dioxide Emissions: Implications for Allowance Prices," *Journal of Environmental Economics and Management* 36 (1998): 27.

[68] EPA, "Allowance Markets Assessment: A Closer Look at the Two Biggest Price Changes in the Federal SO_2 and NO_x Allowance Markets," White Paper (April 23, 2009): 2.

but natural gas price spikes, which made coal generation and associated emissions allowances more valuable, kept prices above historical levels.[69] Allowance prices fell to $61 per ton in 2009 when natural gas prices tumbled.[70]

Factors contributing to lower costs of abatement include lower transportation costs for low-sulfur coal (attributed to railroad deregulation),[71] productivity increases in coal production, cheaper-than-expected installation and operation costs for scrubbers, and boiler adaptations to allow mixing of high- and low-sulfur coal. Average production costs for Powder River Basin coal declined by 64 percent between 1985 and 2000, as a result of capital investment in excavation equipment.[72] Competition among coal suppliers led to the virtual elimination of unwashed coal, and the removal of pyritic sulfur reduced sulfur content of high-sulfur coals. Declining low-sulfur coal prices and rail rates were the main factor for emissions reductions until 1994, as about half of emissions reductions in Phase I were due to coal switching and mixing.[73] In Phase II, the primary contributor to lower SO_2 emissions was a shift from coal generation to natural-gas-fired combined cycle units in the Atlantic states, New England, and East South Central region.[74]

Technological advances in scrubber production reduced their costs and improved their effectiveness. Before 1980, scrubber systems were unreliable. By 1995, wet scrubber systems were more reliable than the plants they serviced. Wet scrubbers could reliably remove 95–99 percent

[69] Dallas Burtraw et al., "Price Discovery in Emissions Permit Auctions," RFF DP 10–32 (June 2010): 3.

[70] EPA, "Acid Rain and Related Programs; 2009 Emission, Compliance, and Market Analyses" (September 2010).

[71] Ellerman and Montero, "The Declining Trend in Sulfur Dioxide Emissions," 30.

[72] Shelby Gerking and Stephen Hamilton, "What Explains the Increased Utilization of Powder River Basin Coal in Electric Power Generation," *American Journal of Agricultural Economics* 90 (November 2008): 933–950, 935.

[73] Denny Ellerman and Florence Dubroeucq, "Sources of Emission Reductions: Evidence for US SO_2 Emissions 1985–2002," Cambridge Working Papers in Economics, CWPE 0429 (2004): 13; Dallas Burtraw and Karen Palmer, "The Paparazzi Take a Look at a Living Legend: The SO_2 Cap-and-Trade Program for Power Plants in the United States," RFF, DP03–15 (April 2003): 14–15; Lauraine Chestnut and David Mills, "A Fresh Look at the Benefits and Costs of the US Acid Rain Program," *Journal of Environmental Management* 77 (2005): 255. Among Phase I units, fuel switching and blending accounted for about 2.8 million of the 4.9 million ton reduction in SO_2 emissions. Scrubbers accounted for almost 1.4 million tons of reduced emissions. EIA, *The Effects of Title IV of the Clean Air Act Amendments of 1990 on Electric Utilities: An Update* (March 1997): 5.

[74] Ellerman and Dubroeucq, "Sources of Emission Reductions," 14–15, 18–19.

of the SO_2 while dry scrubbers often achieved greater than 90 percent SO_2 removal on low-sulfur coals. Capital costs were reduced by more than 30 percent, and operating and maintenance costs fell to half of that for pre-1990 wet scrubbers.[75] However, scrubber manufacturers engaged in price discrimination, charging coal plants higher prices based on the distance of the plant from Powder River Basin coal mines.[76]

The NO_x provisions of the Acid Rain Program set rate limits to achieve a 2 million ton reduction in NO_x relative to projected 2000 emissions levels. The first phase of the NO_x program applied primarily to larger coal-fired units, and was expanded to cover smaller sources starting in 2000.[77] However, the 1990 CAA Amendments did not specify an overall cap on NO_x emissions and there was no trading program in effect for NO_x.[78] The primary means of reducing NO_x emissions from power plants were selective catalytic reduction (SCR) systems, which inject ammonia into the flue gas stream, producing nitrogen and water.[79]

One impact of trading programs was to allow utilities to exploit economies of scale in emission reduction. In Phase II of the Acid Rain Program, the quartile of plants with the largest emissions reduced emissions by 73 percent and the smallest quartile by 10 percent. Transaction and administrative costs are far lower in cap-and-trade programs than in traditional rate-based standards. The costs of transactions declined rapidly as emissions brokers charged $3 to $10 per allowance to carry out trades in 1995, but less than 20 cents per allowance traded in 2005. Governmental administration costs are lower because the role of the government regulator shifts from evaluating and approving technologies to monitoring emissions and enforcing compliance. Technology allows monitoring to be automated and checked against electricity production and sales data, to identify potential fraud. In Phase I of the Acid Rain

---

[75] EIA, "The Effects of Title IV of the Clean Air Act Amendments of 1990 on Electric Utilities: An Update" (March 1997): 9–10; Rubin et al., "Experience Curves for Power Plant Emission Control Technologies," 61–62.

[76] Grischa Perino, "Price Discrimination Based on Downstream Regulation: Evidence from the Market for SO2 Scrubbers," Centre for Competition Policy Working Paper 10-9 (July 9, 2010): 19.

[77] Bryan Hubbel, Richard Crune, Dale Evars, and Jeff Cohen, "Regulation and Progress Under the 1990 Clean Air Act Amendments," *Review of Environmental Economics and Policy* 4 (2010): 134.

[78] EPA, *NO_x Reductions Under Phase II of the Acid Rain Program* at http://www.epa .gov/airmarkets/progsregs/arp/nox.html (last visited May 21, 2011).

[79] Costs of SCR also declined from $90/kW in 1989 to about $60/kW by 1996. Rubin et al., "Experience Curves for Power Plant Emission Control Technologies," 64.

Program, only 150 people were needed to operate the program, out of the approximately 15,000 people working on air pollution control.[80]

The grandfathering of existing coal plants had allowed them to avoid major expenditures for control equipment for decades. In developing regulations following the 1977 Clean Air Act Amendments, EPA assumed that utilities would continue to replace most plants at the end of their traditional thirty- to forty-year service life.[81] Members of EPA's policy analysis staff noted the trend toward power plant life extension and suggested that all power plants over thirty years of age could be required to achieve the NSPS and the PSD program provisions.[82] Had this policy been followed, SO_2 emissions would have been reduced by almost 60 percent in 1995.[83] By the late 1990s, new coal plants were rarely economic relative to combined-cycle plants. However, most existing coal plants were cheaper to operate than the fully loaded cost of a new combined-cycle plant.[84]

In 1997, the EPA announced it was investigating potentially widespread noncompliance with New Source Review (NSR) program requirements. The EPA's authority to challenge life-extending investments of power plants had been confirmed by the Seventh Circuit in 1990.[85] The EPA said it would take appropriate enforcement actions if it found noncompliance. In 1998, the EPA issued a notice to modify its NSR proposal. In response to the 1998 notice, a number of electric utilities

---

[80] Byron Swift, "U.S. Emissions Trading: Myths, Realities, and Opportunities," *Natural Resources & Environment* (Summer 2005): 7–8.

[81] Estimates of the cost of extending the life of a coal-fired plant ranged from $89 to $230 per kW compared to a cost of $1,300 per kW (in 1990) for building a new coal-fired plant. GAO, *Older Plants' Impact on Reliability and Air Quality* (September 1990): 14; E. S. Rubin et al., "Integrated Environmental Modeling of Coal-Fired Power Systems," *Journal of Air & Waste Management Association* 47 (1997): 1180. In 2010, there were still 106,000 MW of coal generation that was forty years or older (i.e., "grandfathered") still in operation.

[82] James DeMocker, Judith Greenwald, and Paul Schwengel, "Extended Lifetimes for Coal-fired Power Plants: Effect Upon Air Quality," *Public Utilities Fortnightly* (March 20, 1986): 30–37.

[83] Garth Heutel, "Plant Vintages, Grandfathering, and Environmental Policy," *Journal of Environmental Economics and Management* 61 (2011): 37.

[84] Frank Ackerman et al., "Grandfathering and Coal Plant Emissions: the Cost of Cleaning up the Clean Air Act," *Energy Policy* 27 (1999): 933–34.

[85] *Wisconsin Electric Power Co. v. Reilly*, 893 F.2d 901, 905–06 (7th Cir. 1990). The EPA had challenged Wisconsin Electric Power's investments to extend the life of a large coal-fired plant, concluding that the project would subject the plant to both NSPS and PSD requirements. Wisconsin Electric challenged the EPA's interpretation, but the Appeals Court found that the "massive" overhaul of the existing unit was not routine. *Id* at 909, 911–13.

voluntarily proposed programs to achieve further utility emission reductions.[86] In November 1999, the Justice Department, on behalf of EPA, brought legal actions against dozens of coal-fired power plants controlled by American Electric Power (AEP), FirstEnergy, Illinois Power, Southern Indiana Gas & Electric, Cinergy, the Southern Company, and Tampa Electric, charging that these companies undertook major modifications at their power plants without installing required emissions control equipment. In December 2000, the EPA added Duke Energy to the list of companies being sued.[87] The EPA entered into settlement agreements with Tampa Electric, PSEG Fossil, ALCOA, Virginia Electric and Power, and Wisconsin Electric Power.[88]

The election of President George W. Bush in 2000 gave a green light to continued "maintenance" of aging coal plants. Bush's first EPA administrator, Christine Whitman, had a reputation as a moderate and was trusted by many environmental groups. Whitman said she had to fight "tooth and nail" to prevent Vice President Dick Cheney's task force from handing over the job of reforming NSR to the Energy Department. Whitman agreed that the exception for routine maintenance and repair needed to be clarified, but not in a way that undercut the ongoing Clinton-era lawsuits. Whitman wanted to work a political trade, eliminating the NSR in return for support of Bush's 2002 "Clear Skies" initiative, which outlined a market-based approach to reducing emissions. Clear Skies went nowhere as there was no reason for industry to embrace even modest pollution control when the vice president was pushing to change the rules.[89]

Haley Barbour, a former Republican Party chairman who was a lobbyist for electric power companies, sent a memorandum to Cheney laying down a challenge. "The question is whether environmental policy still prevails over energy policy with Bush-Cheney, as it did with Clinton-Gore." As Republican National Committee chairman from 1993 to 1997, Barbour had helped the party gain control of Congress and had been one of its most prodigious fundraisers. At Barbour's urging, a handful of

[86] EEI, "New Source Review: a History," (2001) at http://www.eei.org/industry_issues/environment/air/New_Source_Review/NSR_history.pdf (last visited May 22, 2011).

[87] Makram B. Jaber, "Utility Settlements in New Source Review Lawsuits," *Natural Resources & Environment* 18 (Winter 2004): 22.

[88] EPA, *Wisconsin Electric Power Company (WEPCO) Clean Air Act Civil Settlement April 2003*, Docket No. 05-CE-113.

[89] Christopher Drew and Richard Oppel, Jr., "Air War – Remaking Energy Policy; How Power Lobby Won Battle of Pollution Control at E.P.A.," *New York Times*, March 6, 2004; Jo Becker and Barton Gellman, "Angler: The Cheney Vice Presidency," *Washington Post*, June 27, 2007, A01.

coal-burning utilities (Southern Company, TXU, FirstEnergy, Duke Energy, Progress Energy, and the Salt River Project) formed their own lobbying group in the spring of 2001. The six utility companies and their employees made more than $10 million in political donations over five years, nearly three-fourths of that going to Republicans. Southern and its employees account for nearly $4 million of the total.[90] Jeffrey Holmstead, who had represented electric utility groups at Latham and Watkins, became EPA Assistant Administrator for Air and Radiation, where he would steer the implementation of air pollution policy.[91]

In May 2001, Cheney's Energy Task Force recommended that the EPA reassess the air quality rules that were the basis of lawsuits against nine electric utilities. Whitman publicly advised defendant utilities to stall any NSR settlement discussions with the government until new rules were unveiled by Bush's EPA.[92] An EPA report, released in June 2002, found that the NSR program was having an adverse impact on investment in both electric generation capacity and energy efficiency at existing coal plants.[93]

The final rule, published in October 2003, was written at the direction of the White House, and exempted from NSR changes that cost 20 percent or less of the replacement value of the unit, even if they result in a significant net increase in emissions.[94] It allowed some of the nation's dirtiest plants to make major modifications without installing new pollution controls. Whitman announced her resignation, saying she wanted to spend more time with her family. But the real reason was the new

---

[90] Drew and Oppel, Jr., "Air War – Remaking Energy Policy."

[91] http://www.polluterwatch.com/blog/jeffrey-holmstead-coal-industrys-mercury-lobbyist-report (last visited March 26, 2012).

[92] William S. Eubanks II, "The Clean Air Act's New Source Review Program: Beneficial to Public Health or Merely a Smoke-And-Mirrors Scheme?" *Journal of Land, Resources & Environmental Law* 29 (2009): 368–69. FirstEnergy's President Anthony Alexander, Dominion's VP Thomas Farrell, Southern's VP Stephen Wakefield, and Cinergy's Chairman Jim Rogers were all asked to participate on the Energy Department Transition Team. These and other utilities made $4.8 million in campaign contributions to Bush and the Republican National Committee for election campaigns in 2000. *Id.* at p. 368.

[93] EPA, "New Source Review: Report to the President" (June 2002): 17. However, the report did not examine the costs and benefits of forcing these units to reduce emissions. Given the growing glut in electricity generation baseload capacity in 2002, shutting down many of these plants would have had little impact on electricity prices but a substantial impact on SO_2 and particulate emissions.

[94] Jonathan Nash and Richard Revesz, "Grandfathering and Environmental Regulation: The Law and Economics of New Source Review," 101 *Northwestern University Law Review* 1677, 1697–98 (2007); *Equipment Replacement Provision of the Routine Maintenance, Repair and Replacement Exclusion*, 68 FR 61,248, 61,270 (October 27, 2003); 70 FR 33,838 (June 10, 2005).

rule.[95] In light of the rule changes, the EPA announced in November that it would be dropping many of the lawsuits against coal-fired power plants.[96]

Feeding this aggressive stance toward nonenforcement of environmental regulations was a decline in public concern about the environment. The number of Americans in 2004 willing to prioritize protection of the environment over the economy (49 percent) was the lowest since Gallup's first query on the subject in 1984.[97] The Great Recession that began at the end of 2007 strengthened this trend, as support for the environment receded as the unemployment rate escalated.[98] While the environment might be an important "swing" issue for independents and moderate Republicans, the potential for partisan defection among Republican identifiers is low.[99]

The DC Court sided with environmental groups in holding that the EPA's 20 percent rule violated section 111(a)(4) of the Clean Air Act and ordered it vacated. Congress's use of the word "any" in defining a "modification" meant that all types of "physical changes" are covered.[100] The Supreme Court ruled that the EPA could use a net emissions increase standard to determine whether a PSD modification has occurred.[101] This meant that modifications that increased total emissions from a plant would trigger PSD requirements.

EPA issued new, stricter NAAQS for ozone and particulate matter in 1997 after fifteen years of delay, in light of new evidence revealing

---

[95] Jo Becker and Barton Gellman, "Angler: The Cheney Vice Presidency."

[96] Colin Provost, Brian Gerber, and Mark Pickup, "Enforcement Dynamics in Federal Air Pollution Policy," Paper Presented at the Meeting of the European Consortium of Political Research, Pisa, Italy, September 6–8, 2007, 14–15. However, the Department of Justice (DOJ) continued to press with litigation against companies charged with violating the major modification provisions of the CAA. Ohio Edison settled for $1.1 billion and Illinois Power agreed to a $500 million settlement in 2005. AEP agreed to spend more than $4.6 billion to comply with a consent degree in 2007. Shi-Ling Hsu, "The Real Problem With New Source Review," *Environmental Law Reporter* 36 (2006): 10095, fn. 3,4; EPA, *United States et al. v. American Electric Power Information Sheet*, at http://www.epa.gov/compliance/resources/cases/civil/caa/americanelectricpower-infosht.pdf (last visited May 26, 2011).

[97] Christopher J. Bosso and Deborah Lynn Guber, "Maintaining Presence: Environmental Advocacy and the Permanent Campaign," in N. J. Vig and M. E. Kraft, eds., *Environmental Policy: New Directions for the Twenty First Century* (Washington, DC, CQ Press, 2006): 81–83.

[98] Matthew Kahn and Matthew Kotchen, "Environmental Concern and the Business Cycle: The Chilling Effect of Recession," National Bureau of Economic Research, Working Paper 16241 (July 2010).

[99] Deborah Lynn Guber, "Voting Preferences and the Environment in the American Electorate," *Society and Natural Resources* (2001): 461–63.

[100] *New York v. EPA*, 443 F.3d 880, 890 (D.C. Cir. 2006), *cert. denied*, 127 S. Ct. 2127 (2007).

[101] *Environmental Defense v. Duke Energy Corporation*, 127 S. Ct. 1423, 1430–34 (2007).

increased morbidity due to ozone and particulate matter measuring under 2.5 microns in diameter ($PM_{2.5}$). In October 1994, a federal district court ordered EPA to review and, if necessary, revise the current NAAQS for particulates by January 31, 1997.[102] A challenge to the new NAAQS reached the Supreme Court in October 2000. The Supreme Court ruled unanimously in February 2001 that the CAA does not allow EPA to consider costs in setting NAAQS.[103] The Court acknowledged that EPA and the states could continue to take costs into account in implementing the standards.[104] These tighter standards for ozone and $PM_{2.5}$ created new challenges for many urban areas due to the contribution of upwind sources to downwind nonattainment.

The Ozone Transport Commission NO_x Budget Program began in 1999 with eight states plus the District of Columbia. This program was then replaced by the NO_x Budget Trading Program (NBP) in 2003. The EPA NO_x SIP Call, finalized in 1998, expanded this program to cover twenty eastern states, and required a 65 percent reduction from a 1995 baseline. The NBP was a market-based cap-and-trade program for power plants and other large combustion sources in the eastern United States. Compliance with the NO_x SIP Call was scheduled to begin on May 1, 2003, but litigation delayed full implementation for a year. The EPA distributed NO_x allowances to each state, and the states allocated these allowances to sources in their jurisdictions. Sources could buy, sell, and bank allowances. The NBP was replaced by the CAIR NO_x Ozone season trading program, which went into effect May 1, 2009.[105]

With the implementation of the Acid Rain Program, the NO_x Sip Call, and CAIR, the importance of NSR faded almost into irrelevance. The primary effect of forcing coal plants into adding scrubbers is to continue the use of high-sulfur coal, whereas requirements to reduce

[102] Mark R. Powell, "The 1987 Revision of the NAAQS for Particulate Matter and the 1993 Decision Not to Revise the NAAQS for Ozone: Two Case Studies in EPA's Use of Science," Resources for the Future, Discussion Paper 97–07, March 1997): 1–6; *American Lung Assoc. v. Browner*, 884 F.Supp. 345 (DCD Az. 1994).

[103] *Whitman v. Am. Trucking Ass'ns, Inc.*, 531 U.S. 457, 471 (2001) ("The text of § 109(b), interpreted in its statutory and historical context and with appreciation for its importance to the CAA as a whole, unambiguously bars cost considerations from the NAAQS-setting process, and thus ends the matter for us as well as the EPA.").

[104] *Id. at* 467.

[105] EPA, "Clean Air Markets: Highlights," at http://www.epa.gov/airmarkets/progress/NBP_4.html (last visited May 23, 2011); EPA, *Finding of Significant Contribution and Rulemaking for Certain States in the Ozone Transport Assessment Group Region for Purposes of Reducing Regional Transport of Ozone*, 63 FR 57,356 (October 27, 1998).

overall emissions under a cap-and-trade regime encourages substitution of low-sulfur coal.[106]

It is easy to berate environmental policy for lacking economic rationality as long as you ignore the complex political and regulatory forces that shaped pollution control. The original legislation was deliberately technology forcing, in part because of the tendency of industry to "cry wolf" and overestimate the cost of compliance. Environmentalists remain suspicious of economists bearing cost-benefit models, as these were susceptible to political manipulation. During the Clinton years, economics had a diminished role at the EPA, despite requirements for benefit-cost analysis that resulted in EPA performing more applied economic analysis.[107] However, these analyses were rarely forwarded to Administrator Carol Browner during her eight-year tenure. The substantive role of economic analysis in the development and review of EPA regulations was abandoned by the Agency in 1995. Browner and Vice-President Al Gore were skeptical of the application of benefit-cost analysis to environmental policy, although Browner did support economic analysis to improve cost-effectiveness of EPA regulations.[108] However, this removed a powerful tool to constrain the second Bush administration from weakening environmental regulations. By emasculating the role of cost-benefit in

---

[106] David A. Evans et al., "Modeling the Effects of Changes in New Source Review on National SO_2 and NO_x Emissions from Electricity-Generating Units," Resources For the Future, RFF DP 07–01 (March 2007).

[107] Since 1978, federal regulatory agencies had been required to conduct economic analyses for regulations with expected annual costs greater than $100 million. First established under the Carter administration through Executive Order No. 12044, these Regulatory Impact Analyses were required under Reagan Executive Orders 12291 and 12498. Shortly after taking office in 1993, President Clinton revoked the Reagan orders, replacing them with Executive Order 12866, Regulatory Planning and Review. The Clinton order required only that benefits *justify* costs. Executive Order 12866 also mandated selection of cost-effective regulatory alternatives such as user fees and marketable permits. John Graham, Paul Noe, and Elizabeth Branch, "Managing the Regulatory State: The Experience of the Bush Administration," 33 *Fordham Urban Law Journal* 101, 106–13 (2006); Sheila Cavanagh, Robert Hahn, and Robert Stavins, "National Environmental Policy During the Clinton Years," Resources for the Future, Discussion Paper 01–38 (September 2001): 4–6. Despite numerous assertions that economic reviews would slow the pace of rulemaking, the small proportion of rules – less than 4 percent – that were subject to Executive Order 12866 were implemented as quickly as other EPA rules. However, of the "economically significant" rules issued by EPA, 75 percent were challenged at some point after they were promulgated. Stephen M. Johns, "Ossification's Demise? An Empirical Analysis of EPA Rulemaking From 2001–2005," 38 *Environmental Law* 467, 470 (2008).

[108] Cavanagh, Hahn, and Stavins, "National Environmental Policy During the Clinton Years," 8–9.

developing environmental regulations, environmentalists removed a barrier to political rule making.

Environmental regulations, especially air pollution emission controls, gradually shifted the electricity generation playing field toward the new gas-fired technologies. However, it was not until natural-gas-fired generation was able to exploit the Acid Rain program to enter markets that air pollution controls had a real impact on electricity markets. For most of the 1980s and 1990s, coal generation steadily increased its share of fossil-fired generation, despite the increasing burden of air pollution regulation. This was due to the lagged effect of investment decisions made in the 1970s, when electricity demand was expect to continue to grow, and oil and natural gas supplies were uncertain and prices were escalating.

While coal generation capacity growth leveled off by 1990, as planned units were completed, coal generation steadily increased, increasing from 1.57 billion MWh in 1990 to 2 billion MWh in 2007, while capacity increased by only 7 percent. This was due to the replacement of older units with new, more efficient baseload units, but also to upgrades to coal generators that were grandfathered. The percent of coal generation that came from plants with scrubbers increased only from 23 percent in 1990 to 33 percent in 2005.[109] However, the primary reason for coal's continued dominance was that it was still cheaper than natural gas in many regions where it was the primary fuel for baseload electricity generation. In the West North Central region, closer to the Power River Basin, gas failed to make any inroads. Along the eastern seaboard, where coal was more expensive due to transportation costs, environmental regulations were enough to tip the balance toward natural gas. In areas like the Midwest and the South, coal held its own, but natural gas was the fuel of choice for new generation.

[109] EIA, *Electricity Industry Reports*, various years.

3

The Rise and Fall of Demand-Side Management

The second force reshaping the electricity industry was the change in energy consumption patterns, especially electricity, due to responses to prices, changes in the structure of the economy, and government policy to encourage efficiency and conservation.

The rise of energy efficiency as a policy objective dates back to the 1970s, when increasing electricity demand, higher capital costs, and rising electricity prices led to heightened public awareness of the need to moderate energy use. Energy conservation and energy efficiency[1] were first brought to public consciousness as an outgrowth of the environmental movement in the early 1970s.[2] These ideas became mainstream thought after the first oil crisis, as the Ford Foundation Energy Policy Project incorporated some of these concepts, especially the decoupling of

---

[1] The two terms are often confused: energy conservation is generally used in reference to reducing energy consumption with a concurrent reduction in energy services; energy efficiency is associated with reducing the quantity of energy used to produce the same quantity of energy services, usually by substituting capital or employing new technology.

[2] The Club of Rome study, *The Limits to Growth*, provided doomsday scenarios of the exhaustion of natural resources, although these results were a result of poorly constructed models that lacked price-driven feedback loops that would have constrained consumption. Donela H. Meadows, Dennis L. Meadows, Jorgen Randers, and William W. Behrens III, *The Limits to Growth: A Report for the Club of Rome's Project on the Predicament of Mankind* (New York, Signet, 1972). Other works published during this time period that were influential included: Paul Ehrlich, *The Population Bomb* (New York, Ballantine, 1968); E.F. Schumacher, *Small is Beautiful: Economics as If People Mattered* (London, Blond and Briggs, 1973); Herman E. Daly, *Toward a Steady-State Economy* (San Francisco, W.H. Freeman, 1973); Amory Lovins, "Energy Strategy: The Road Not Taken?" *Foreign Affairs* 55 (October 1976): 65–96.

energy consumption and economic growth.[3] The publication of *Energy Future* by the Harvard Business School,[4] while it contained little original thought or research, completed the legitimatization of energy efficiency as an alternative strategy to constant expansion of energy production and consumption.

Three laws passed in the 1970s laid the groundwork for the various demand reduction and load management strategies that collectively became known as demand-side management (DSM). These were the Energy Policy and Conservation Act of 1975, the Energy Conservation and Production Act of 1976, and the National Energy Conservation Policy Act of 1978.[5]

The Energy Policy and Conservation Act established a wide range of energy conservation programs, including fuel economy standards for passenger cars and light trucks and the Corporate Average Fuel Economy (CAFE) standards, with the goal of doubling new car fuel economy by model year 1985. CAFE standards applied to passenger cars and light trucks (gross vehicle weight less than 8,500 lbs) on a fleet-wide basis for each manufacturer.[6]

The Energy Conservation Policy Act created a federally authorized national conservation program, which expanded programs started by the Energy Conservation and Production Act.[7] The Act provided grants for low-income families, secondary financing and loan insurance for energy conservation improvements, grants to state and local governments for energy conservation, energy performance standards for federal buildings, and support for state energy conservation plans. It established test

---

[3] Energy Policy Project of the Ford Foundation, *A Time to Choose: America's Energy Future* (Cambridge, Ballinger, 1974). The report was strongly influenced by S. David Freeman, who had been chosen to as the director of the Energy Policy Project.

[4] Robert Stobaugh and Daniel Yergin, eds., *Energy Future: Report of the Energy Project at the Harvard Business School* (New York, Random House, 1979). What was odd about this report is the editors had no special expertise in energy issues. Dr. Yergin's expertise was in international relations, not economics, as his first book was *Shattered Peace: The Origins of the Cold War and the National Security State* (Boston, Houghton Mifflin, 1977). He cleverly employed his notoriety from *Energy Future* into writing *The Prize*, a popular history of the world oil industry, and the development of an energy consulting firm with a strong marketing flair, Cambridge Energy Research Associates. Professor Stobaugh was a management professor who specialized in international business but had written a couple of guides to petrochemical manufacturing and marketing.

[5] Part of the National Energy Act of 1978. The National Energy Conservation Policy Act, Pub. L. No. 95–619, 92 Stat 3206 (1978).

[6] American Gas Foundation, "Public Policy and Real Energy Efficiency" (October 2005): 1.

[7] P.L. 94–385, 90 Stat. 1125 (1976).

procedures and energy efficiency standards for thirteen types of appliances, including refrigerators, freezers, water heaters, room and central air conditioners, furnaces, ovens, and clothes dryers. The Act also authorized the Department of Energy (DOE) to prescribe test procedures and labeling requirements with respect to electric motors, pumps, and other industrial equipment. The development of efficiency standards was highly politicized from the outset. DOE received more than 1,800 comments totaling 40,000 pages after publishing the Notice of Proposed Rulemaking (NOPR) on Energy Performance Standards for New Buildings in 1979. With an unreceptive administration and opposition from some manufacturers, standards for residential appliances were never finalized.[8]

A number of states also turned to appliance energy consumption standards to cut the growth in energy demand. California led the way under Governor Ronald Reagan. A 1974 Act gave the California Energy Commission (CEC) the authority to set appliance standards. In 1976, the state of New York created standards for several residential and commercial products. Several other states quickly followed suit, including Florida, Connecticut, and Massachusetts.[9] The proliferation of varying state standards led many manufacturers to support passage of the 1987 National Appliance Energy Conservation Act. The Appliance Conservation Act established national standards for twelve categories of household appliances. The first standards – for refrigerators, freezers, water heaters, and room air conditioners – took effect in 1990. Further discussions between manufacturers and energy efficiency advocates led to amendments creating standards for other appliances such as washers, dryers, and dishwashers.[10]

The Public Utility Regulatory Policies Act of 1978 (PURPA) also encouraged state commission to implement DSM measures. PURPA's Titles I and III encourage retail regulatory bodies to encourage conservation of energy, efficiency of use of resources by utilities, and equitable rates to consumers. Section 111(d) of the Act required each state regulatory authority and nonregulated utility to consider the use of rates

---

[8] American Gas Foundation, "Public Policy and Real Energy Efficiency," 80–81.

[9] Steve Nadel and David Goldstein, "Appliance and Equipment Efficiency Standards: History, Impacts, Current Status, and Future Directions," American Council for an Energy Efficient Economy (ACEEE) (1996).

[10] Kenneth Gillingham, Richard G. Newell, and Karen Palmer, "Retrospective Examination of Demand-Side Energy Efficiency Policies," Resources for the Future, RFF DP 04–19 REV (September 2004): 7–8; American Gas Foundation, "Public Policy and Real Energy Efficiency," 15–16.

that would reflect the costs of service, and the use of load management techniques.[11] However, there was no enforcement mechanism or firm requirement to adopt these standards.

The PURPA marginal cost pricing standards were generally opposed by industrial and commercial customers and the utilities, but supported by environmental and consumer groups. As the cost of building new plants became greater than the embedded costs of existing plants, marginal cost-based pricing would result in utilities collecting more than their required revenue. The solution, according to consumer groups, was to use Ramsey pricing rules and set rates below, but close to, marginal costs where demand was elastic and set rates well below marginal costs where demand was inelastic. Environmental groups also supported this approach, hoping that these rates would decrease the demand for new plants. Industrial users recognized the possibility that their competitive position could be harmed if their state adopted rate reforms while other states did not. Many utilities opposed these new pricing initiatives because the use of marginal cost-based pricing would make future revenues more uncertain. Commissioners exposed to greater political pressure from utilities and industrial customers were more likely to reject the cost-of-service standard.[12]

State regulators, starting in the early 1970s, in reaction to rising electricity costs, had begun to increasingly scrutinize the cost-effectiveness of new capacity investments brought before them by regulated utilities. In the late 1970s and early 1980s, state regulators began disallowing significant portions of the costs of nuclear power plant construction projects as imprudently incurred excess costs.[13] These proceedings encouraged regulators to play a more active role in overseeing planning decisions by utilities.

California and Wisconsin pioneered prescribing utility efficiency measures. In California, the combination of a progressive governor, Jerry Brown, and desperation due to declining reserve margins, motivated utility efficiency measures. An activist California Public Utility Commission (CPUC), with the support of the governor, began pressuring the utilities to finance energy efficiency measures to slow load growth, and punished

---

[11] 16 U.S.C. § 2621(d).

[12] Clifford Nowell and John Tschirhart, "The Public Utility Regulatory Act and Regulatory Behavior," *Journal of Regulatory Economics* 2 (1990): 21–36.

[13] Joseph Eto, "The Past, Present, and Future of U.S. Utility Demand-Side Management Programs," LBNL-39931 (December 1996): 6.

laggards in rate cases. The CPUC introduced decoupling of utility revenues and load in 1981, and the utilities responded by dramatically expanding efficiency programs.[14] Wisconsin made a more explicit commitment to efficiency as part of utility planning with the adoption of the Power Plant Siting Act of 1975. The law established a planning process that required twenty-year load forecasts and the evaluation of alternative sources of electricity. After 1986, the Public Service Commission explicitly incorporated demand-side resources as part of resource planning.[15]

The term "integrated resource planning" (IRP) was coined by Jon Wellinghoff and Cynthia Mitchell in an article describing Nevada's new utility planning model.[16] It was then popularized, with the help of a small DOE program, by Clark Gellings at the Electric Power Research Institute (EPRI). The hiring of Gellings by EPRI put the stamp of industry legitimacy on the concept of DSM. Gellings argued that utilities should manage consumption by influencing customer behavior. However, there is an important distinction between managing demand to allow for more efficient provision of electricity (usually by peak shaving to improve the load factor of low cost generation units) and reducing consumption of electricity through increased end-use efficiency. While the two strategies are not mutually exclusive, they have different impacts on utility costs and revenues and can interact in ways that reduce short- or long-term benefits of either strategy considered exclusively. Through such venues as the National Association of Regulatory Utility Commissioners (NARUC), the concept spread among state regulatory commissions and became common practice toward the end of the 1980s.[17]

IRP, also known as least-cost planning, is a process in which utilities consider a broad range of resource options to meet the future energy needs of their customers. These resource options include new transmission capacity, new generation, and demand-side management. IRP put DSM on equal footing with capital investments, and often as a first priority if social externalities were included in the social cost-benefit calculation.

---

[14] Richard F. Hirsh, *Power Loss: The Origins of Deregulation and Restructuring in the American Electric Utility System* (Cambridge, MA, MIT Press, 1999): 179–83.

[15] Id., at 183–86.

[16] Jon B. Wellinghoff and Cynthia K. Mitchell, "A Model for Statewide Integrated Utility Resource Planning," *Public Utilities Fortnightly* 116 (August 8, 1985): 19–26. Wellinghoff was the first head of the Office of Consumer Advocate, created in 1981, and he wrote draft legislation that required utilities to use least-cost planning techniques, which became the Nevada Utility Resource Planning Act of 1983. Hirsh, *Power Loss*, 196–97.

[17] Hirsh, *Power Loss*, 190–200.

The DSM programs considered under IRP were often known as "resource acquisition" programs because they were expected to meet the demand for energy services at a lower cost than that of acquiring generation services.[18] Least-cost planning advocates argued that, in view of the utilities' obligation to serve at lowest cost, utilities should pursue demand-side options whenever these options were less expensive than supply-side alternatives. States and utilities took an active role in promoting energy efficiency as a cost-saving tool for avoiding expensive power plant construction.[19]

The first utility energy efficiency programs in the 1970s were information and loan programs, designed to educate consumers and businesses about the cost-effectiveness of energy efficiency measures and to provide subsidized financing for efficiency investments. Utilities gradually learned that education alone produced limited energy savings, and most consumers were not interested in subsidized loans. Financial incentive programs such as cash rebates given to consumers who purchased designated energy-efficient equipment proved to be more effective.[20] During the 1980s, these utility-operated residential programs gradually expanded to small and then to large commercial and industrial customers. Customers were provided with technical assistance, information, and financial incentives to purchase or invest in energy-efficient building materials, equipment, or appliances. Other incentives employed in these programs included free installation of energy-efficient technologies.[21] Direct installation programs were more expensive than rebates and were usually limited to targeted low-income customers, often at the bequest of the regulatory commission.

Market transformation strategies attempted to influence the market for particular types of equipment or energy services. Demonstration projects, training programs, and informational activities were combined with financial incentives to establish a technology or technique as a norm and substantially increase market penetration rates. Market transformation

---

[18] Gillingham et al., "Retrospective Examination of Demand-Side Energy Efficiency Policies," 15–16.

[19] Donald D. Gilligan, "Energy Efficiency Program Planning Workbook," US DOE, EERE (December 2002): 13; Eto, "The Past, Present, and Future of U.S. Utility Demand-Side Management Programs," 7.

[20] Rebate programs, such as incentives for purchasing more efficient appliances, raised the question of "free-riding," as many people who received the rebates would have purchased the equipment anyway.

[21] Carl Blumstein, Charles Goldman, and Galen Barbose, "Who Should Administer Energy-Efficiency Programs?" LBNL (August 2003): 2; Eto, "The Past, Present, and Future of U.S. Utility Demand-Side Management Programs," 2.

efforts include encouraging retailers, distributors, contractors, and builders to change their business models to promote energy efficiency, as well as targeted education and training efforts at decision points such as the replacement of existing appliances or equipment and the remodeling of buildings.[22]

The IRP bidding programs offered opportunities to new types of companies that could develop, engineer, finance, and implement resource acquisition projects. Specialized, full-service energy service companies emerged in the late 1970s to provide utility programs with manpower and systems. Entrepreneurs jumped into the business while controls companies transferred their expertise to energy service business units. Energy service companies tended to focus on large commercial and industrial customers, where a single project could yield larger energy savings at lower costs due to economies of scale and smaller transactions costs. By the early 1990s, energy services had become a real industry.[23]

Utilities used DSM bidding programs in which energy efficiency service providers bid prices for blocks of energy and/or demand savings as part of a competitive resource solicitation to obtain demand-side resources. Due to concerns from energy service companies that DSM bidding programs often involved high transaction costs for bid preparation, lengthy periods for contract negotiation, and limited access to program funds, the concept of a "standard offer" was developed. A standard offer program included a standardized contract and program rules. Qualified participants could apply on a first-come, first-served basis and received posted prices for delivered energy savings subject to measurement and verification protocols.[24]

The late 1980s saw a growing number of states adopt IRP regulations, with the consequence that utility DSM budgets grew rapidly. Utility spending on DSM tripled, rising from $900 million in 1989 to $2.7 billion in 1993 and 1994. In 1990, more than 14 million residential, 125,000 commercial, and 37,500 industrial customers nationwide were involved in DSM programs run by more than a thousand utilities. Utilities in the states of California, Washington, New Jersey, Rhode Island, Maine, Massachusetts, Minnesota, and Oregon led the way. Energy

[22] Blumstein, Goldman, and Barbose, "Who Should Administer Energy-Efficiency Programs?" 3.
[23] Donald D. Gilligan, "Energy Efficiency Program Planning Workbook," 13–14.
[24] Steven Schiller, Charles Goldman, and Brian Henderson, "Public Benefit Charge Funded Performance Contracting Programs – Survey and Guidelines," LBNL (August 2000): 1–2.

efficiency savings increased from 32 billion kWh and 6,900 MW in 1992 to nearly 60 billion kWh and more than 14,200 MW in 1996.[25]

DSM programs presented some unique regulatory rate issues. Traditional rate-of-return regulation discouraged utilities from pursuing DSM programs because utilities lost revenue from reduced sales. It became common practice to allow utilities to recover costs for DSM programs through annual adjustments to rates, and to decouple net revenue from sales. Some states created separate financial incentives for the delivery of superior DSM programs, including a percentage adder on the money spent on DSM, a bonus based on the quantity of energy or capacity saved by a DSM programs, or a bonus based on a percentage of the value of the net avoided cost associated with a DSM program. A handful of utilities, primarily in the northeast and in the west, doubled and tripled their DSM budgets in response to new ratemaking procedures.[26]

There is some disagreement concerning the overall effectiveness of DSM in the 1980s and 1990s. Overall energy intensity of the U.S. economy has declined about 1 percent per year on average for the past 200 years. The rate of energy intensity reduction accelerated to 2 percent per year in the United States between 1973 and 2003, although it is hard to separate autonomous improvements from responses to price spikes in the 1970s. On the other hand, there is strong evidence that much of the improvement in household energy consumption was driven primarily by efficiency standards along with labeling and incentive schemes.[27]

A number of DSM studies in the 1990s produced estimates of "negawatt" costs in the range of 2 to 4 cents per kWh.[28] Negawatt cost refers to the full life cycle cost per kWh saved due to a DSM program, including all of the costs of running the DSM program and installing

---

[25] Ned Raynolds and Richard Cowart, "The Contribution of Energy Efficiency to the Reliability of the U.S. Electric System," ASE White Paper (2000): 3, 7.

[26] Eto, "The Past, Present, and Future of U.S. Utility Demand-Side Management Programs," 9–10.

[27] Howard Geller and Sophie Attali, "The Experience with Energy Efficiency Policies and Programmes in IEA Countries," International Energy Agency (August 2005): 9–12.

[28] Martin Kushler, Dan York, and Patti Witte, "Five Years In: An Examination of the First Half-Decade of Public Benefits Energy Efficiency Policies," ACEEE (April 2004): 30; Reynolds and Cowart, "The Contribution of Energy Efficiency to the Reliability of the U.S. Electric System," 4; Eto, "The Past, Present, and Future of U.S. Utility Demand-Side Management Programs," 9–10; EIA, "U.S. Electric Utility Demand-Side Management: Trends and Analysis 1997"; Gillingham et al., "Retrospective Examination of Demand-Side Energy Efficiency Policies," 26–29; Geller and Attali, "The Experience With Energy Efficiency Policies and Programmes in IEA Countries," 19. All costs adjusted to 2002 dollars.

the equipment. The true cost to utilities of purchasing negawatts may be underestimated in DSM studies because of the unaccounted-for effects of free riders, underreporting of all relevant costs, and optimistic assumptions of energy savings. On the other side of the coin, energy savings from commercial DSM programs were underreported, based on the observation that reported year-to-year decreases in commercial DSM savings were unrealistic, unless DSM program activity ceases and performance of installed equipment quickly deteriorates.[29]

Studies of appliance standards effectiveness have found substantial benefits. Mandated appliance standards were criticized as unlikely to lead to significant energy savings or to be cost-effective because energy efficiency improvements, by reducing the effective cost of energy services, would lead to increased demand. This effect has become known in the literature as the "rebound" effect. The magnitude of the rebound effect is unlikely to be significant. Increased efficiency may lower the cost of energy per service, but this will not necessarily increase utilization of the appliance. A more efficient refrigerator or freezer is not going to be opened more often, nor will efficient washing machines lead to multiple cleaning of the same clothes. More efficient air conditioners are unlikely to result in large differences in thermostat settings, except for low-income individuals who face income constraints. The other impact will be through the income effect, which increases the consumption of all goods, not just energy. Another skeptical argument postulates that the negative impacts of appliance standards are more likely to fall on lower-income households. Empirical studies have cast doubt on the rebound effect, while other studies have refuted the contention that appliance standards are regressive.[30]

---

[29] Gillingham et al., "Retrospective Examination of Demand-Side Energy Efficiency Policies," 30–31. Geller and Attali, "The Experience With Energy Efficiency Policies and Programmes in IEA Countries," 12. Another factor accounting for the divergence among analysts is the question of how to discount the value of efficiency savings over time. Discount rates used in energy efficiency studies vary, with most analysts using a real discount rate of 4–8 percent. While market decisions show that people demand a 6 percent annual return on risky investments such as corporate stocks, they also show that people accept much lower returns on safe investments such as U.S. Treasury Bills and corporate bonds, which generate long-term real yields between 1 percent and 2 percent per year. Richard B. Howarth, "Against High Interest Rates," Working Paper (March 2004): 4, citing A. Sandmo, "Discount Rates for Public Investment under Uncertainty," *International Economic Review* 13 (June 1972): 287–302.

[30] Gillingham et al., "Retrospective Examination of Demand-Side Energy Efficiency Policies," 12–13; Geller and Attali, "The Experience With Energy Efficiency Policies and Programmes in IEA Countries," 5–6. Studies suggest that the rebound effect is less than

Market research has shown that the increased cost of more efficient products predicted in advance of the adoption of standards was often overstated. In the case of refrigerators, the average retail price actually declined after appliance efficiency standards took effect in both the European Union and the United States. Once forced to improve energy efficiency, manufacturers figured out less costly ways of meeting the standards. The actual average energy efficiency of new appliances has exceeded the minimum required by the standard, sometimes by a significant amount. Standards stimulated a broader shift in the efficiency of manufacturer offerings, and not merely removal of the least efficient products from the market. Standards create a level playing field, where no manufacturer is punished for investing in improving efficiency relative to investing in other attributes that might have greater competitive value.[31] However, an arbitrary constraint on consumption choices such as standards imposes welfare losses on consumers that are not captured by these calculations.

As IRP gained momentum, the move toward retail competition, or "retail wheeling," as it was called then, also strengthened. Most of the states that had been leaders in applying IRP moved toward initiatives to restructure their gas and electric utilities in order to promote wholesale and retail competition or "customer choice." By 2000, a total of twenty-three states and the District of Columbia had passed some sort of electric industry restructuring policy. As attention of state PUCs shifted to retail competition, the deregulatory process stopped IRP and DSM programs in their tracks. In the new regulatory environment, price caps and greater reliance on markets for setting electricity prices created strong incentives for utilities to cut costs and provided fewer incentives to spend money on DSM programs. Utility DSM spending declined more than 50 percent by 1999.[32]

---

10 percent for residential appliances, residential lighting and commercial lighting, and less than 20 percent for industrial process uses. For residential space heating and cooling it's probably in the 10–30 percent range. The economy wide impact on increased energy consumption from reduced energy expenditures is around 1–2 percent.

[31] Geller and Attali, "The Experience With Energy Efficiency Policies and Programmes in IEA Countries," 21; Stephen Meyers, James McMahon, and Michael McNeil, "Realized and Prospective Impacts of U.S. Energy Efficiency Standards for Residential Appliances: 2004 Update," LBNL (May 2005): 26, 31.

[32] Energy efficiency spending in the United States reached a low point of $918 million in 1997, a drop of almost 50 percent compared to 1993 spending. Spending then rebounded to $1.1 billion in 2000. D. York and M. Kushler, "State Scorecard on Utility and Public Benefits Energy Efficiency Programs: An Update," ACEEE (2002).

As DSM spending plummeted in the mid- to late 1990s, states recognized that deregulation was the leading cause and began establishing mechanisms to stem the decline. Where the utilities were vertically integrated monopolies, regulators simply ordered the utilities to include program costs in the utilities' rates. After restructuring, there was concern that customers might avoid the charges for DSM and other programs by switching from the incumbent utility to a new competing supplier. This problem was addressed by creating "non-bypassable" charges, public benefit funds, system benefit charges, or, in Texas, the system benefits fund. These new charges fund energy efficiency programs, renewable energy programs, and programs to assist low-income families to pay their energy bills. They are typically a per-kWh charge on the state-regulated electricity distribution system. These charges are considered competitively neutral in terms of both wholesale and retail competition.[33]

Over the past thirty years, the energy efficiency of the U.S. economy has improved remarkably. Energy efficiency and conservation activities from 1973 through 1991 curbed the pre-1973 growth trend in annual primary energy use by about 18 percent.[34] Energy intensity – the amount of energy it takes to produce one dollar of goods – has been cut by more than half, from 9,130 Btu in 1970 to 4,320 in 2003. Roughly half of the reduction in energy intensity can be attributed to energy efficiency improvements, while the rest is the result of structural changes in the economy, such as changes in the product mix and shifting energy-intensive manufacturing to offshore locations.[35]

The decline in intensity from 1960 to 1980 was predominantly owing to changes in industrial composition, but after 1980 the importance of this factor wanes in comparison to improvements in the efficiency of energy use. Most of the energy savings come from reduced energy use associated with residential and commercial buildings. Estimates suggest roughly 30 percent of total energy savings is attributable to federal appliance standards and 15 percent to DSM programs.[36] Appliance standards, building codes, Energy Star programs, government research and development, and

[33] Blumstein, Goldman, and Barbose, "Who Should Administer Energy-Efficiency Programs?" 3.
[34] Fred Sissine, "Energy Efficiency: Budget, Oil Conservation, and Electricity Conservation Issues," Congressional Research Service (August 22, 2005): 3.
[35] National Association of Manufacturers, "Efficiency and Innovation In U.S. Manufacturing Energy Use" (2005): 3.
[36] Gillingham et al., "Retrospective Examination of Demand-Side Energy Efficiency Policies," 59–70.

utility DSM all contributed to reducing energy consumption.[37] The other important source of energy demand reduction is associated with vehicle stocks, reflecting the impact of CAFE regulations. Forced technical change has been far more important than price-induced technical change.[38]

The effect of reduced electricity demand growth for the industry was to institutionalize the slower growth trend of the 1970s. While energy costs steadily declined in real terms from the early 1980s to 2000, electricity growth only rebounded from 2.2 percent a year in the high-cost 1970s to 2.8 percent a year. The failure of electricity growth to recover to expected levels created a capacity glut as coal and nuclear plants that had begun construction in the 1970s, even with many delayed and canceled, came on line in the 1980s. Average capacity margins (equal to the percentage by which total summer capacity exceeds peak demand) exceeded 20 percent in the early part of the 1990s and did not fall to "normal" levels until the end of the decade. This glut was reflected in low-capacity factors (the percent of potential generation actually produced) for coal plants, which are primarily built to service baseload and to operate at high-capacity factors. In 1990, the capacity factor for coal plants was only 60 percent, rebounding to 71 percent in 2002, as growth in demand combined finally absorbed the glut in capacity.[39]

---

[37] Maximilian Auffhammer and Alan Sanstad, "Energy Efficiency in the Residential and Commercial Sectors," Resources for the Future (January, 2011): 5–12.

[38] Ian Sue Wing, "Explaining the Declining Energy Intensity of the U.S. Economy" (2007): 25–30.

[39] EIA, *Electric Power Annual*, various issues.

4

Congress Acts, Investors React

The third factor setting the stage for change in the electricity industry was the 1978 Energy Policy Act. While it created an environment for experimentation with independent power, it was the establishment of bad contracts that raised electricity rates that would help create incentives for deregulation. The Act also had an important indirect impact: by initiating the deregulation of the natural gas market, it provided the infrastructure to support new natural-gas-fired generation.

The Carter administration attempted to deal with the perceived "energy crisis" with a comprehensive proposal to deregulate natural gas, encourage conservation, and tax energy consumption and imports. A contentious political debate that lasted more than a year resulted in a congressional conference committee working out compromises motivated by fatigue.[1] The Energy Policy Act included the Power Plant and Industrial Fuel Use Act, PURPA, and the Natural Gas Policy Act.

PURPA created a new category of power plants – "qualifying facilities" (QFs). QFs included power plants that burned renewable fuels or employed renewable energy sources and cogeneration plants that met efficiency thresholds. Section 201 of PURPA generally defined a qualifying small power production facility as one using only biomass, waste, and/or renewable resources as a primary energy source, with a capacity no greater than 80 MW. A cogeneration facility was a facility that produced both electricity and steam or some other useful form of energy. There was no size limit for qualifying cogeneration facilities. A QF must

[1] Richard Corrigan and Dick Kirschten, "The Energy Plan–What Has Congress Wrought?" *National Journal* (November 14, 1978): 1760–68.

be owned by a person not primarily engaged in the generation or sale of electric power. Nonutility generation before 1978 was typically undertaken to meet demands of major industry groups such as the paper, chemical, mining, and oil refining. Most of the power was produced through cogeneration, and the electricity was for the producers' own use. Utilities purchased surplus power at wholesale power rates and charged retail rates for backup power and additional charges for transmission and distribution capacity.

Section 210 of PURPA established a rule requiring electric utilities to interconnect with and purchase power from any facility meeting the criteria for a QF under the Act. Qualified cogenerators of any size, and renewable energy small producers under 30 MW, were exempt from both PUHCA and the FPA, while small producers from 30 MW to 80 MW were exempt from PUHCA. Cogenerators must meet certain non-electricity production and overall efficiency standards.[2] FERC held that electric utilities, public utility holding companies, or subsidiaries of either can own up to 50 percent of the entity that owns the qualifying facilities.[3]

A key to the successful passage of the cogeneration and small renewable energy producer provisions was the lobbying efforts of Wheelabrator-Frye Corporation. Wheelabrator was a developer of waste-to-energy facilities, and saw an opportunity to expand its market by improving the economics of its projects through better terms from sales of electricity to utilities. Wheelabrator hired the law firm of Van Ness, Feldman, and Sutcliffe, which had excellent Washington connections, to lobby for selected provisions. Van Ness managed to extend the exemption from PUHCA to small power producers. Van Ness, along with Senator Durkin of New Hampshire, a supporter of small power production, was also able

---

[2] For a topping-cycle cogeneration facility (waste heat from the generator used for process heat or other purposes) for which any of the energy input is natural gas or oil, the useful power output plus one-half the useful thermal energy output of the facility must be at least 42.5 percent of the energy input of natural gas and oil to the facility. However, if the useful thermal energy output is less than 15 percent of total energy output, the power output plus one-half the useful thermal energy must be at least 45 percent of the total energy input. *Small Power Production and Cogeneration Facilities–Qualifying Status*, FERC SR 1977–1981 ¶ 30,134 (1980), at 30,948–49. Efficiency standards were not applied to bottom-cycling plants, where a turbine utilized waste heat streams to generate electricity. Efficiency is determined by dividing the net energy produced (kWh = 3413 Btu) by the energy content of the fuel used to produce electricity and useful thermal energy.

[3] *Small Power Production and Cogeneration Facilities–Qualifying Status*, FERC SR 1977–1981 ¶ 30,134, 30,953 (1980).

to base the payment by utilities for surplus electricity on total avoided cost rather than incremental (i.e., operating) avoided cost. While incremental cost was not defined in the final bill, the conference report noted that full avoided cost was the conferees' intent. The author of the report, Ross Ain, would become the FERC associate general counsel in 1979, writing the interpretation that was incorporated in FERC regulations governing avoided costs.[4]

In 1980, FERC specified how the price for QF power was to be determined. The agency established general ratemaking principles in its rules but delegated their implementation to the state regulatory commissions.[5] The rule defined "avoided costs" as the costs to an electric utility of energy or capacity, or both, which the electric utility would generate or construct itself or purchase from another source. It included both the fixed and operating costs that could be avoided by obtaining energy or capacity from QFs. If a purchase from a QF permitted the utility to avoid the addition of new capacity, then the avoided cost of this new capacity should be used.[6]

A challenge to PURPA's constitutional legitimacy was denied in *FERC v. Mississippi*.[7] The Supreme Court not only upheld PURPA but implicitly provided permission for the federal government to extend its authority to intrastate electricity transactions:

We agree with appellants that it is difficult to conceive of a more basic element of interstate commerce than electric energy, a product used in virtually every home and every commercial or manufacturing facility. No State relies solely on its own resources in this respect. Indeed, the utilities involved in this very case, Mississippi Power & Light Company and Mississippi Power Company, sell their retail customers power that is generated in part beyond Mississippi's borders, and offer reciprocal services to utilities in other States. The intrastate activities of these utilities, although regulated by the Mississippi Public Service Commission, bring them within the reach of Congress' power over interstate commerce.[8] [citations omitted]

In *American Paper Institute v. AEP*, the Supreme Court held that FERC had the authority to require payments up to the full avoided cost. The

---

[4] Richard F. Hirsh, *Power Loss: The Origins of Deregulation and Restructuring in the American Electric Utility System* (Cambridge, MA, MIT Press, 1999): 81–88.
[5] *Small Power Production and Cogeneration Facilities; Regulations Implementing Section 210 of the Public Utility Regulatory Policies Act of 1978*, Order No. 69, FERC SR 1977–1981 ¶ 30,128 (1980).
[6] FERC SR 1977–1981 ¶ 30,128 at 30,865–66.
[7] 456 U.S. 742 (1982).
[8] 456 U.S. 742 at 757 (1982).

Commission noted that ratepayers and the nation as a whole would benefit from the decreased reliance on scarce fossil fuels and the more efficient use of energy. Under these circumstances it was not unreasonable for the Commission to prescribe the maximum rate authorized by PURPA.[9]

QFs could exploit highly leverage financing structures unavailable to conventional utilities. Utilities were required to purchase power from QFs, and rates were exempt from state regulation. FERC's decision to establish full avoided cost as the default price if a QF and utility could not agree on a price schedule gave the QF leverage in negotiations. A long-term purchased power agreement (PPA) provided guaranteed cash flow that enabled QF developers to obtain financing. Investors could leverage a small amount of equity, since they could use the PPAs as collateral for loans. Nonutilities were able to finance projects with high debt/equity ratios, with the percentage of debt in the capital structure often ranging between 80 percent and 90 percent. Sale-leaseback agreements allowed for 100 percent debt financing once the nonutility plant became operational. The potential advantage of highly leveraged project financing may have been partially offset by the higher cost of borrowing for nonutilities, since this financing was usually done on a nonrecourse basis, with the project as security.[10]

In addition, the Energy Tax Act of 1978 gave a 10 percent tax credit to businesses, including QFs, that installed certain classes of energy equipment after September 1978 until the end of 1982. Tax credits for renewable energy were extended through 1985 with the passage of the Windfall Profits Tax Act of 1980, and included a 10 percent credit for cogenerators. The 1981 Economic Recovery Tax Act allowed a five-year depreciation of wind turbines. These provisions encourage the development of investment vehicles designed to exploit tax shields.[11]

While a few states, such as New Hampshire and Vermont, established avoided cost rates on a statewide basis, most states determined avoided costs utility by utility. California became the key state for the expansion of independent power producers (IPPs), owing to a regulatory environment that was friendly to cogenerators and small producers,

9 *American Paper Institute v. AEP*, 461 U.S. 402, 406, 415–17 (1983).
10 EIA, *The Changing Structure of the Electric Power Industry 1970–1991* (March 1993): 28.
11 An initial burst in wind power, which reached an installed capacity of 183 MW in 1983, soon receded as generous renewable tax credits and QF rates dissipated. The average wind farm had a capacity of 5.8 MW. Investor Responsibility Research Center, "Survey of Non-Utility Electric Power Producers," July 11, 1984.

rapid economic growth that created a growing market, and physical and regulatory constraints that increased costs of adding new capacity. In January 1982, the CPUC ordered utilities to offer one of five power purchase contracts, or standard offers, with prices based on the short-run avoided cost of fuel and capacity payments. US Windpower won regulatory approval in 1982 for a contract with costs above avoided costs in the early years and lower costs in later years. This contract became the template for a new standard offer with fixed prices based on a ten year forecast of full avoided costs, after which price would be based on short-run avoided costs. The contracts offered in 1983 and 1984 assumed continual increases in the cost of electricity, even though fuel prices had already begun to decline. The result was a response to these standard offers that far exceeded the expectations of regulators and utility managers.[12]

The escalating fixed contracts made investment in QFs almost riskless. Since an investor could sign a standard offer without a financial commitment, and had five years to complete the project, these contracts became zero-cost options to build. If energy prices rise, making a project uneconomical, the investor could walk away. However, if fuel prices declined, the project had a guaranteed revenue stream. The CPUC realized that they had engendered a potential capacity glut and suspended these offers in 1985, issuing a new standard offer that was less attractive to investors. But the damage had already been done, with 15,000 MW of contracts signed.[13]

High-priced states such as New York, the New England states, New Jersey, and Pennsylvania also embraced PURPA requirements with enthusiasm. Many state PUCs and legislatures greatly overestimated long-run avoided costs, thus forcing utilities to buy huge amounts of overpriced power. When utilities entered into long-term PPAs, they assumed financial risks, with payment agreements (in particular capacity payments) viewed as being analogous to off-balance sheet debt by bond-rating agencies. When power purchases by a utility exceeded 10 percent of their capacity or total sales, bond-rating agencies added some portion of the fixed payment obligations to the utility's existing debt to compute its total long-term debt liability.[14] This resulted in an additional, "hidden" cost to purchases of power from QFs.

[12] Hirsh, *Power Loss*, 95–97.
[13] Hirsh, *Power Loss*, 98.
[14] EIA, *Financial Impacts of Nonutility Power Purchases on Investor-Owned Electric Utilities* (June 1994): 1–2. Section 712 of the Energy Policy Act of 1992 addressed this issue by requiring state regulatory authorities to consider whether the long-term power

Over time, utilities convinced regulators that competitive bidding was a more effective means of setting avoided costs for purchasing QF power than arbitrary avoided cost calculations. In 1984, Central Maine Power and the Maine Public Service Commission became the first to put competitive bidding into practice. The commission set avoided cost rates for QFs based on the cost of a nuclear power plant, which resulted in offers to supply more power than Central Maine needed.[15] After 1984, utilities or public utility commissions in twenty-seven states adopted or developed competitive bidding systems, and as of December 1989, competitive bidding solicitations were conducted in nineteen states.[16]

By the late 1980s, FERC had become concerned with the rates provided to QFs in some states and issued a prospective order in April 1988, holding that in light of changes that had occurred since 1980, states thereafter could not impose a rate for QF sales to utilities in excess of avoided cost.[17] However, FERC stayed this prospective order a few months later, pending completion of a then-pending rulemaking proceeding.[18] FERC finally ruled on the issue in January 1995, declaring that a statute that could require an electric utility to purchase power at a rate above avoided cost was preempted by PURPA.[19] However, the Commission also "grandfathered" QF contracts where the avoided cost issue could have been raised.[20]

PURPA spurred the sale of nonutility power to the U.S. electric utilities. Sales to IOUs increased from 28.3 million MWhs in 1985 to 164 million MWhs in 1992, or almost 6 percent of the electricity generated for sale to end-use consumers. Cogenerator QFs accounted for about 60 percent of U.S. nonutility electricity-generating capacity, and other small power producers accounted for 15 percent. Most nonutility generating capacity was in the manufacturing sector of the economy. The chemical industry (25 percent of nonutility capacity), the paper industry (18 percent), and petroleum refining (8 percent) were the chief beneficiaries of the QF

---

purchase agreements by the investor-owned utilities (from nonutility generators) would increase or decrease the utilities' cost of capital.

[15] EIA, *The Changing Structure of the Electric Power Industry 1970–1991*, 27.

[16] GAO, *Electricity Supply: The Effect of Competitive Power Purchases Are Not Yet Certain* (August 23, 1990): 13.

[17] *Orange & Rockland Utils., Inc.*, 43 FERC ¶ 61,067, *reh'g denied*, 43 FERC ¶ 61,546 (1988).

[18] *Orange & Rockland Utils., Inc.*, 43 FERC ¶ 61,547, *reh'g denied*, 44 FERC ¶ 61,273 (1988).

[19] *Connecticut Light & Power Co.*, 70 FERC ¶ 61,012 (1995).

[20] *Connecticut Light & Power Co.*, 71 FERC ¶ 61,035 (1995).

rules.[21] All three industries are characterized by steady and predictable thermal loads, which allowed operation of cogeneration facilities at high levels of utilization.

The success of PURPA generators created the perception that economies of scale in generation had been supplanted by new technologies. This was partially the result of problems building large power plants, but also because of the ability of small combustion turbines to exploit low natural gas prices. The success of cogeneration facilities had less import for utility structure, since the population of favorable locations would eventually be exhausted. However, the creation of so-called PURPA machines – power plants with a contrived thermal application masquerading as a cogeneration facility – suggested that independent power projects were becoming economic without the need for a thermal energy revenue stream.[22] PURPA had little direct impact on gas turbine development as the primary customers for these generators were the traditional utilities and their need for flexible generation to meet peak loads.

PURPA did create a constituency of independent power suppliers who promoted state and federal policies to expand opportunities for independent power.[23] Some utilities, with experience with negotiating PPAs and a track record working with small power producers, became more receptive to reliance on third-party supplies as a less risky alternative to building major new generating facilities. Other utilities saw an opportunity to spin off subsidiaries to supply generation to utilities outside of their traditional service territories and without traditional cost-of-service constraints.

The decline in the price and the increased availability of natural gas due to deregulation made natural gas a more attractive fuel for electricity generation during a period when there were significant advances made in turbine and power plant design. The early 1960s saw the beginning of

[21] EIA, *The Changing Structure of the Electric Power Industry 1970–1991*, 5–7, 87; EIA, *Financial Statistics of Major U.S. Investor-Owned Electric Utilities 1992* (December 1993): 49; EIA, *Electric Power Annual 1992* (January 1994): 119.

[22] FERC SR 1988–1998 ¶ 32,456, *Regulations Governing Independent Power Producers* (March 16, 1988). A common example of a PURPA machine is a combined-cycle power station with a greenhouse tacked on the back. Extraction steam is used to heat the greenhouse. The greenhouse operated only because of the requirement for useful thermal energy output. The cogenerator sold the steam at a loss as the price of getting the benefits of QF status. *Id.* at 32,117, ft 112, 113.

[23] Michael Russo, "Institutions, Exchange Relations, and the Emergence of New Fields: Regulatory Policies and Independent Power Production in America, 1978–1992," *Administrative Science Quarterly* 46 (2001): 61.

gas turbine "packages" for power generation when GE and Westinghouse engineers were able to standardize designs. To win over customers from traditional steam turbine or reciprocating engine equipment, manufacturers offered fully assembled packages, which included turbines, compressors, generators, and auxiliary equipment. Standardization allowed for multiple sales with little redesign for each order, easing the engineering burden and lowering costs. Advances in cooling and improvements in turbine materials allowed manufacturers to increase their firing and rotor inlet temperatures and improve efficiencies. The fast startup times of gas turbines allowed them to ramp up quickly during demand peaks, making them better suited for that role than steam-driven turbines. Despite efficiencies of only around 25 percent, the market for combustion turbines rapidly expanded in the late 1960s and early 1970s.[24]

The first gas turbine installed in an electric utility applied in a combined-cycle (gas turbine and steam boiler) power system was a 3.5 MW gas turbine that used the energy from the turbine exhaust gas to heat feed water for a 35 MW conventional steam unit in 1949. Most combined-cycle power generation systems installed during the 1950s and early 1960s were basically adaptations of conventional steam plants, with the gas turbine exhaust gas serving as combustion air for the boiler, raising the efficiency of the combined cycle by 5–6 percent compared to a similar conventional steam plant. Heat recovery combined cycles, which recovered the heat in the gas turbine exhaust gas using finned tubes, entered service in 1959. In the 1970s and 1980s, heat recovery for feed water preheating became a mature technology. Material enhancements and cooling evolutions were the main gas turbine improvements that would increase operating efficiencies over the next three decades. An increase in firing temperature made possible through improved metals and coatings and metal surface cooling techniques provided more efficient turbine operation, and better heat exchangers improved utilization of exhaust heat.[25] The GE Frame 7F gas turbine marked the beginning of a period of rapid market expansion, successive product launches, and intensified technological competition. The 147 MW power output of the Frame 7F was almost double that of GE's previous vintage of large gas turbines. A new combined cycle utilizing the Frame 7F was

---

[24] Darian Unger and Howard Herzog, "Comparative Study on Energy R&D Performance: Gas Turbine Case Study," MIT Energy Laboratory (August 1998).

[25] David L. Chase, "Combined-Cycle Development Evolution and Future," GE Power Systems (April 2001): 5–9.

larger and more efficient than competitive systems offered by Westing-house, ABB, and Siemens. The first GE Frame 7F turbine combined cycle was installed in Virginia Power's Chesterfield power plant, completed in 1990.[26] These larger combined-cycle systems, although they had signif-icantly higher capital costs, could achieve net plant efficiencies around 45 percent, compared to 30–35 percent for a state-of-the-art combustion turbine.[27] Since coal plants were limited to a net efficiency of less than 40 percent, this gave combined-cycle plants a competitive advantage if gas prices were close to coal prices.

Natural gas had no particulate or sulfur dioxide issues, and improve-ments in combustion turbines reduced NO_x emissions. The 1987 repeal of the Fuel Use Act, which prohibited construction of new gas and oil-fired boilers, allowed merchant generators to use gas as their primary fuel. Combustion turbines could be built in eighteen months in increments of 100–200 megawatts, while combined-cycle plants could be built in twenty-four to thirty months, compared to the six-to-eight years neces-sary to develop a coal-fired plant.[28]

Technological advances continued during the 1990s, resulting in incre-mental improvements in a number of areas of plant design. A triple pressure reheat cycle became the industry standard for achieving higher efficiency. With higher gas exhaust temperatures from the combustion turbines, the steam boiler pressure steadily increased. In warm weather, a combined-cycle plant may lose as much as 10–15 percent of its rated output because of higher ambient air temperature. Inlet air cooling, evaporative cooling, refrigeration cooling, and/or moisture injection

---

[26] Anna Bergek et al., "Technological Capabilities and Late Shakeouts: Industrial Dynamics in the Advanced Gas Turbine Industry, 1987–2002," *Industrial and Corporate Change* (2009): 353–54.

[27] The 1989 EPRI Technical Assessment Guide provided the following values for the heat rate of an Advanced Combine Cycle Unit:

Full Load	7,514 Btu/kWh	45.4% efficiency
75% Load	7,885 Btu/kWh	43.3% efficiency
50% Load	8,860 Btu/kWh	35.5% efficiency
25% Load	11,860 Btu/kWh	28.8% efficiency

Note the importance of capacity factor to unit efficiency; if run at 100% as a baseload unit, it was highly efficient, but if only run for a few hours a day, the fuel costs (and the capital cost per kWh) would be much higher. Edward Kahn, Steven Stoft, Chris Marnay, and Douglas Berman, "Contracts For Dispatchable Power: Economic Implications for the Competitive Bidding Market," LBNL (October 1990): 1-12–1-15.

[28] "Natural Gas for Electric Generation: Realizing the Potential," Prepared for the INGAA Foundation by Washington International Energy Group (May 1994): 17.

provided power output enhancement, though at a cost in operating efficiency.[29]

One factor that slowed the adoption of new combustion turbines was the emergence of reliability problems stemming from the rush to increase the size and operating efficiency of these plants. In the mid-1990s, the problems of reliability, which had plagued combustion turbine technology before 1986, returned with a vengeance, and all the major manufacturers had to devote significant efforts to problem solving. Although these problems were addressed, and newer generations of turbines were developed, the market remained soft until the end of the decade.[30]

The larger combustion turbines allowed combine-cycle plants to exploit economies of scale in steam boiler size and pressure. Most of the aeroderivative combustion turbines[31] and older combustion turbine units were used for peaking. Peaking units frequently ramp electricity output up and down (cycling), leading to greater maintenance needs, more rapid performance degradation, and shorter life for turbines. The larger combustion turbines were reliable as long as they could be used as part of baseload combined-cycle generation plants.[32]

Construction of independent generation plants began in earnest in the late 1980s, as independent generators sold power to utilities wary of committing to new construction and directly to large industrials when they could bypass the local utility's monopoly franchise. By 1992, there were almost 44,000 MW of QF facilities on the ground, and another 13,000 MW of independent power plants. Most of the purchasing utilities were located in high-cost areas. Demand risk was allocated to buyers, with price rising when capacity factors fell. A study of power contracts during the 1990–1993 period found that natural gas plants were clearly more economic than coal.[33] A key element of these contracts was dispatchability, as utilities wanted to be able to dispatch these resources similar to

---

[29] Ram Narula, Martin Massy, and Jyoti Singh, "Design Considerations for Combined Cycle Plants for the Deregulated Market – An EPC Contractor's Perspective," IGTI ASME Turbo Expo 2002, Amsterdam, June 3, 2002.

[30] Bergek et al., "Technological Capabilities and Late Shakeouts: Industrial Dynamics in the Advanced Gas Turbine Industry, 1987–2002," 356–58.

[31] Small combustion turbines were basically jet engines adapted for power generation. They were more efficient but also more expensive and less reliable than the heavy-frame combustion turbines developed specifically for power generation.

[32] Jun Ishii, "Technology Adoption and Regulatory Regimes: Gas Turbine Electricity Generators from 1980 to 2001," Center for the Study of Energy Markets, CSEM WP 128 (March 2004): 25–28.

[33] G. A. Comnes, T. N. Belden, and E. P. Kahn, "The Price of Electricity from Private Power Producers, Stage II: Expansion of Sample and Preliminary Statistical Analysis," LBNL, LBL-36054 (February 1995): 15–18.

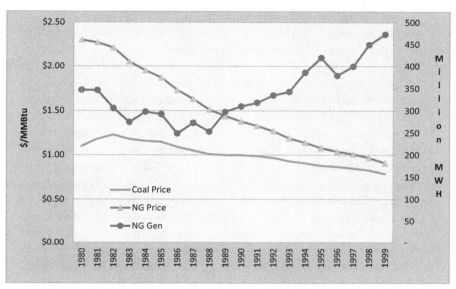

FIGURE 4.1. Natural Gas Generation. *Source*: EIA, *Annual Energy Review 2010*, Table 8.10. Average Retail Prices of Electricity, 1960–2010.

the way they operated their own plants. Explicit linkage of bidding with the utility's resource planning process became common practice.

Access to transmission emerged as a key element for projects located outside a utility's service area. This put the developer into a quandary: locate within the service area and you may face a monopsony buyer who can pressure you into accepting lower prices; locate elsewhere and you have to negotiate long-term transmission rights, sometimes across multiple utility service areas.[34] Buyers had to arrange for transmission or wheeling service if the transaction required use of a third utility's transmission system. FERC's jurisdiction regulated the rates charged for transmission service, but it couldn't order a utility to provide such service.[35]

[34] Edward Kahn, Steven Stoft, Chris Marnay, and Douglas Berman, "Contracts for Dispatchable Power: Economic Implications for the Competitive Bidding Market," LBL-29447 (1990): 1-1, 1-2.

[35] Jim Rossi, "Redeeming Judicial Review: The Hard Look Doctrine and Federal Regulatory Efforts to Restructure the Electricity Utility Industry," 1994 *Wisconsin Law Review* 763, 783 (1994). Section 211 of the FPA barred FERC from requiring wholesale wheeling service unless such order would reasonably preserve existing competitive relationships. This section was added to the FPA by PURPA. The Second Circuit held that wheeling could not be ordered solely on the basis of the public interest and the enhancement of competition. *New York Elec. & Gas Corp. v. FERC*, 638 F.2d 388, 401–02 (2d Cir. 1980), *cert. denied*, 454 U.S. 821 (1981).

This limited transmission arrangements to voluntary agreements, subject to the transmission utility's whims, with only the threat of antitrust sanction as a weapon to encourage cooperation.

However, the situation was not as bleak as it seemed at first glance. The political power of municipal utilities and cooperatives had forced some cracks in the IOU monopoly over power wheeling. Prior to 1979, many municipal utilities had obtained limited permission to wheel power on IOU transmission systems. Their success was unanticipated fallout from nuclear projects. In a compromise between public and private power proponents, the Atomic Energy Act of 1954 endorsed development of nuclear generating plants by the IOUs but required the Atomic Energy Commission (later the Nuclear Regulatory Commission) to consider antitrust issues in its licensing procedures. In 30 of the 100 construction permits issued by the Nuclear Regulatory Commission during the 1960s and 1970s, the agency imposed conditions to relieve alleged anticompetitive activities by licensees. These typically took the form of allowing municipal systems within the IOU's service area some participation in the nuclear project (e.g., partial ownership), including transmission access. The result was that these IOUs had to publish a transmission tariff, which subsequently served as a wedge to obtain more extensive access.[36]

Municipal power companies obtained additional wheeling rights from antitrust suits brought under the Sherman Act. In *Otter Tail*,[37] the most prominent of these cases, the Supreme Court found that the Otter Tail Power Company used its monopoly over transmission to impede municipalities within its retail area from establishing viable distribution companies when their contracts with Otter Tail expired. The Court found that electric power companies were subject to the antitrust laws, but there was no authority granted the Commission under the FPA to order wheeling of power, as common carrier provisions were deleted from the final act.[38] However, when a transmission utility blocks a distribution utility in its service area from accessing power from third parties, the Commission must order the utility to provide transmission services when such action is "necessary or appropriate in the public interest."[39] Courts ordered

---

[36] Linda Cohen, Stephen Peck, Paroma Sanyal, and Carl Weinberg, *Retrospective Report on California's Electricity Crisis*, California Energy Commission, PIER Project Report, CEC-500-2006-021, January 2004, pp. 6–7.

[37] *Otter Tail Power Co. v. United States*, 410 U.S. 366 (1973).

[38] 410 U.S. 366, 373–75 (1973).

[39] 410 U.S. 366, 373 (1973).

wheeling services in a series of subsequent cases, but only as a remedy for anticompetitive practices.

PURPA created a group of independent power producers that would lobby for more access to electricity markets, but their emergence was merely one of many trends converging toward the opening of electricity markets. IRP provided incentives for utilities to sign PPAs with independent power, while regulatory pressure encouraged utilities to pursue cost-saving measures such as bulk wholesale purchases. The gradual development of combustion turbine technology provided a viable alternative to central station, "natural monopoly" generation. However, to take the next step, it was necessary to provide the rationalization for disrupting the regulatory status quo. Enter the economists.

5

The Economists Are Coming, the Economists Are Coming

Deregulation swept through Washington in the 1970s. The convergence of a number of intellectual, political, and economic developments, beginning in the late 1970s and continuing through the 1980s, caused a radical revision of the traditional view of natural monopoly. These developments included: (1) revisionist views on the origin of state utility regulation;[1] (2) theoretical and empirical challenges to the natural monopoly view of many industries;[2] (3) incentive failures under rate-of-return regulation; and (4) the worldwide economic failure of government utility ownership and regulation, which weakened political opposition to reform.[3]

The first wave of regulatory reform was driven as much by intellectual currents as by interest group politics. There had been a broad consensus among economists since the early 1970s, if not before, that the original paradigm of active government regulation made no sense applied to industries without natural monopoly features – such as trucking and airlines.

---

[1] Harold Demsetz, "Why Regulate Utilities," Journal of *Law* and Economics 11 (April 1968): 55–56; Walter J. Primeaux, "The Monopoly Market in Electric Utilities," in Almarin Phillips, ed., *Promoting Competition in Regulated Markets* (Washington, DC, Brookings Institution, 1975): 175–200; George Priest, "The Origins of Utility Regulation and the 'Theories of Regulation' Debate," *Journal of Law and Economics* 36 (1993): 289–323.

[2] George J. Stigler and Claire Friedland, "What Can Regulators Regulate? The Case of Electricity," 5 *Journal of Law and Economics* 1 (October 1962); George J. Stigler, "The Theory of Economic Regulation," *Bell Journal of Economics* 2 (Spring 1971): 3–21; Richard A. Posner, "Theories of Economic Regulation," *Bell Journal of Economics* 5 (Autumn 1984): 335–58.

[3] Vernon L. Smith, "Regulatory Reform in the Electric Power Industry," *Regulation* 19 (1996): 33–47.

This broad consensus was eventually translated to key White House staffers in the Ford and Carter administrations, as well as congressional staffs. Policy elites and their economic advisers began to call for greater competition in regulated industries, most prominently in the transportation sector.[4] An ideological consensus developed among policy elites that the risks of regulatory failure were greater than the risks of market failure associated with competition. The combination of "regulatory capture"[5] and economic rent-seeking theories[6] generated skepticism regarding the motivations behind and the value of economic regulation. The theory of contestable markets provided a justification for more limited regulation of natural monopolies.[7]

Economists influenced the regulatory debate through their presence in the Office of Management and Budget, the General Accounting Office, the Congressional Budget Office, the FTC, the Department of Energy, the Federal Communications Commission, and other regulatory agencies. The fact that everyone engaged in shaping regulatory policy found it necessary to obtain some sort of economic blessing for their policy preferences suggests that economic reasoning had acquired legitimacy as a method for resolving policy disputes. Economics shaped the regulatory agenda by defining the language of discourse and the set of acceptable arguments. While the balance of political power determined which policies were implemented, the ubiquitous presence of economists set limits to the rapacity of interest group demands.[8]

---

[4] Martha Derthick and Paul J. Quirk, *The Politics of Deregulation* (Washington, DC, Brookings Institute, 1985); Roger G. Noll and Bruce M. Owen, eds., *The Political Economy of Deregulation: Interest Groups in the Regulatory Process* (Washington, DC, American Enterprise Institute, 1983); Richard H. K. Vietor, *Contrived Competition: Regulation and Deregulation in America* (Cambridge, MA, Harvard University Press, 1994).

[5] Thomas McGraw, *Prophets of Regulation: Charles Francis Adams, Louis D. Brandeis, James M. Landis, Alfred E. Kahn* (Cambridge, MA, Harvard University Press, 1984), 153–221.

[6] Anne O. Krueger, "The Political Economy of the Rent Seeking Society," *American Economic Review* 64 (June 1974): 291–94; Gordon Tullock, "The Welfare Costs of Tariffs, Monopolies, and Theft," reprinted in James Buchanan, Robert Tollison, and Gordon Tullock, eds., *Toward A Theory of the Rent-Seeking Society* (College Station, Texas A&M University Press, 1980): 39–50; Fred McChesney, "Rent Extraction and Rent Creation in the Economic Theory of Regulation," *Journal of Legal Studies* 16 (1987): 101–09.

[7] William J. Baumol et al., *Contestable Markets and the Theory of Industry Structure* (New York, Harcourt Brace Jovanovich, 1982); Elizabeth E. Bailey, "Contestability and the Design of Regulatory and Antitrust Policy," *American Economic Review* 71 (May 1981): 178–83; Elizabeth E. Bailey and William J. Baumol, "Deregulation and the Theory of Contestable Markets," 1 *Yale Journal on Regulation* 111 (1984).

[8] Steve Isser, *Economics and Politics of the Oil Industry: 1920–1990* (New York, Garland Press, 1996): 428–29.

The political influence of economists was felt in the rush toward deregulation. Electricity restructuring was partially a product of the zeitgeist of deregulation, which reached its apex in the Carter administration. The driving force behind deregulation was economics transmuted by political actors, with most of the "one-handed" nuances removed. While the Reagan administration added an ideological tint to the deregulation debate, the technocratic logic was embedded in federal policymaking during the 1970s. Gerald Ford began the deregulation movement, appointing pro-deregulation commissioners and convincing Congress to partially deregulate railroads and oil and gas. Ford received support for airline deregulation from Democratic Senator Ted Kennedy.[9] Jimmy Carter picked up where Ford left off. He lifted most of the remaining regulations on oil and gas, and he revolutionized the transportation industry by eliminating controls on airlines, railroads, and trucking companies. Carter signed the Air Cargo Deregulation Act on November 9, 1977, and the Airline Deregulation Act of 1978 in October of that year. In July 1980, Carter signed the Motor Carrier Act, partially deregulating the trucking industry. Carter submitted a bill to further deregulate the railroads in 1979, and signed the Staggers Rail Act on October 14, 1980.[10]

The key element in the acceptance of deregulation was the emergence of Neopopulism as a force in American politics. Neopopulist ideology initiated with the consumer movement of the late 1960s, and bloomed into full force during the energy debates of the 1970s. The primary difference between Neopopulism and New Deal Liberalism was the attitude toward containing the power of the corporation. Traditional liberals called for increased authority of government over business, requiring a more centralized and powerful bureaucracy. Neopopulists opposed attempts to centralize regulatory authority in the executive branch, preferring a decentralized system that allowed them access to policymakers. They wanted consumers, taxpayers, and environmentalists to have the same influence over public policy as business did.[11]

---

[9] Kennedy convinced one of the prominent proponents of deregulation, Harvard law professor Stephen Breyer, to join his staff in August 1974. Justice Breyer has been a consistent supporter of deregulation from the bench, demonstrating that economic deregulation has never been simply a liberal versus conservative political issue in either Congress or the Courts.

[10] Andrew Craink, "Ford, Carter, and Deregulation in the 1970s," *Journal on Telecommunications & High Technology Law* 5 (2007): 421–37.

[11] David Vogel, "The Public-Interest Movement and the American Reform Tradition," *Political Science Quarterly* (Winter 1980–81): 616–27.

In the 1970s, a coalition of Liberals and Neopopulists would dominate congressional energy policy, choosing oil and natural gas price controls as a solution to the "energy crisis." Neopopulists at first welcomed the concentration of authority in agencies open to interest group influence, but eventually became skeptical of the efficacy of regulation by agency fiat. The collapse of support for price controls in the late 1970s was a result of the defection of Neopopulists such as Bill Bradley, Paul Tsongas, and John Dingell, who had become disillusioned with governmental interference in the market and accepted the need for prices to provide necessary incentives.[12] However, Neopopulists did not necessarily accept the dictates of the free market; they were just skeptical that regulatory agencies could be trusted to manage industries for the benefit of consumers.

A solution that promised to curtail what was perceived as wasteful industry practices and provide consumers with lower prices was irresistible to Neopopulists. The gains from increased efficiency were an important source of political support, owing to the perception that consumers could get "something for nothing." Consumer groups were important participants in the deregulation debates, trading their support for guaranteed benefits for consumers. Environmental interest groups for the most part stayed on the sidelines, allowing consumer groups to develop coalitions with large industrial users and potential industry entrants to split these projected gains. The promises by economists that markets would provide savings to consumers were essential to the political coalition in favor of deregulation.

The language and concepts of economics are frequently employed as part of the rhetoric of economic regulation. Unfortunately, many noneconomists and some economists use these terms promiscuously, without understanding or at least referencing the caveats that should accompany them. For example, an "efficient market" is a relative term, as there are no perfectly competitive or efficient markets in existence. This is why, when pressed on the issue, many economists resort to "workably competitive"[13] as shorthand for about as competitive and efficient as you can reasonably expect in a real-world context.

---

[12] *CQ Weekly Report* (October 25, 1980): 3208.

[13] The classic article is John Maurice Clark, "Toward a Concept of Workable Competition," *American Economic Review* 30 (1940): 241–56. The concept has fallen out of favor among American economists, as there is no mention in the Handbook(s) of Industrial Organization, because it was originally associated with the concept of monopolistic competition. Today it is used more as a term of art referring to quasi-competitive markets that approximate a competitive solution to the extent that there are limited potential gains from additional regulation.

In the real world, there are numerous reasons why economic efficiency is impossible. First, anyone who has studied economics knows that practically every postulate behind the proofs of the theoretical possibility of an optimal state of the economy (Arrow-McKenzie-Debreu general equilibrium) is violated in practice.[14] A general equilibrium requires each market to be in equilibrium with no market power or strategic behavior, increasing returns, and so on, and with rational, utility-maximizing consumers all making perfect intertemporal decisions with full and accurate information. In this best of all possible worlds, price equals short-run marginal costs, equals long-run marginal costs, and welfare is maximized.[15]

The "Theory of the Second Best"[16] pointed out the difficulty of a piecemeal, or individual market, solution to the problem. If there is a constraint or distortion that prevents one market from reaching an optimal solution, one can no longer assume that the rest of the economy is at its optimal point. This could be due to market power, government regulation, or any other distortion that is not amenable to market correction. Nor can one assume countervailing distortions (i.e., two wrongs can make a right) will balance out. Once we allow for endogenous technological change under uncertainty, we cannot even define the conditions for an efficient allocation of resources. In practical situations we do not know the necessary and sufficient conditions for achieving an economy-wide, first-best allocation of resources.[17]

The problem of achieving an efficient allocation over the economy is even more complicated. Real markets are never in equilibrium because input prices, tastes, and technology constantly change. Since this is happening in every market, and these markets are interlinked (either producing inputs for other markets, buying the outputs of markets, and/or

---

[14] Bryan Caplan points out the difference between a valid argument, where the conclusion follows from the assumptions, and a sound argument, which is a valid argument where all the assumptions are true. Bryan Caplan, "From Friedman to Whittman: The Transformation of Chicago Political Economy," *Economic Journal Watch* 2 (April 2005): 8. My contention is that economic theories are usually valid arguments but rarely sound arguments.

[15] My apologies to sophisticated readers, but for the sake of brevity I've chosen to oversimplify some concepts.

[16] R. G. Lipsey and Kevin Lancaster, "The General Theory of Second Best," *Review of Economic Studies* 24 (1956): 11–32.

[17] Richard G. Lipsey, "Reflections on the General Theory of Second Best at Its Golden Jubilee," Presented to the 62nd Congress of the International Institute of Public Finance (2007): 7. Lipsey and Lancaster felt that a second best optimum was as unlikely to be achieved as a first best optimum. *Id.* at 8–9.

competing for the expenditures of consumers facing income constraints), the economy will always be in a constant state of flux. (It would require a mythical Walrasian auctioneer to clear markets continuously, much like Maxwell's Demon sorting molecules). Throw in additional complications like market power, due to concentration from economies of scale[18] or mergers and acquisitions or barriers to entry,[19] strategic behavior,[20] asymmetric information,[21] deception,[22] coordination,[23] and various limits to rational behavior by both consumers and managers,[24] and the likelihood of any market being in short- or long-run equilibrium is highly unlikely. Economic models require care when generalizing to actual economic actors and markets. It is our models that are simple, not the world.[25]

One solution is simply to reformulate the economic model to internalize many sources of inefficiency.[26] This is the core of the Chicago School approach to economics: markets do work, and imperfections are generally bad modeling, not distortions or irrational behavior that lead to inefficient markets. That is, the economy is efficient given these imperfections,

[18] Paul Joskow, "Regulation of Natural Monopoly," in Mitchell Polinsky and Steven Shavell, eds., *Handbook of Law and Economics, Volume 2* (Amsterdam, Elsevier, 2007): 1227–1348.

[19] David Scheffman and Mary Coleman, "Quantitative Analyses of Potential Competitive Effects from a Merger," *George Mason Law Review* 12 (2003): 319.

[20] Jeffrey Perloff, Larry Karp, and Amos Golan, *Estimating Market Power and Strategies* (Cambridge, Cambridge University Press, 2007).

[21] George Akerlof, "The Market for 'Lemons': Quality Uncertainty and the Market Mechanism," *Quarterly Journal of Economics* (1970): 488–500; Michael Spence, "Signaling in Retrospect and the Informational Structure of Markets," *American Economic Review* 92 (June 2002): 434–59.

[22] Paul Milgrom, "What the Seller Won't Tell You: Persuasion and Disclosure in Markets," *Journal of Economic Perspectives* 22 (Spring 2008): 115–31; Xavier Gabaix and David Laibson, "Shrouded Attributes, Consumer Myopia, and Information Suppression in Competitive Markets," *Quarterly Journal of Economics* 121 (May 2006): 505–40.

[23] Joseph Farrell and Paul Klemperer, "Coordination and Lock-In: Competition With Switching Costs and Network Effects," in Mark Armstrong and Robert Porter, eds., *Handbook of Industrial Organization, Volume 3* (Amsterdam, North-Holland, 2007): 1967–2143.

[24] Robert Shiller, "From Efficient Markets Theory to Behavioral Finance," *Journal of Economic Perspectives* 17 (Winter 2003): 83–104; Wolfgang Pesendorfer, "Behavioral Economics Comes of Age: A Review Essay on Advances in Behavioral Economics," *Journal of Economic Literature* 64 (September 2006): 712–21.

[25] Emanuel Derman and Paul Wilmott, "The Financial Modelers' Manifesto," January 7, 2009.

[26] George Stigler and Gary Becker, "De Gustibus Non Est Disputandum," *American Economic Review* 67 (March 1977): 76–90; Gary Becker, "Irrational Behavior and Economic Theory," *Journal of Political Economy* 70 (February 1962): 1–13.

not in spite of them.[27] Taken to extremes, this approach can result in Panglossian economics, but in judicious doses it counsels against assuming the policymaker can successfully intervene in a market just because an imperfection has been identified.

Once you accept that economic models[28] are incapable of accurately describing the real world and providing determinate predictions, you can glean the real value of models, their insights into market behavior. Markets do allow the coordination of numerous actors, creating and disseminating information that leads to more efficient behavior by those actors. They do clear, more or less, in many cases using inventories to balance out mistakes by actors each period. Companies compete through exploitation of technology to reduce costs and increase value, while consumers invest in information to make better decisions. Markets provide a decentralized mechanism for organizing economic behavior, and the invisible hand moves actors to better positions much of the time. To paraphrase Churchill, markets are the worst form of organizing economic behavior except all those other forms that have been tried from time to time.

The limits of economic modeling should be kept in mind when examining the role of economists in the electricity restructuring policy debate. Economists provided the arguments for electricity "deregulation," the blueprints for the new markets, and the rationale for practically every argument over electricity for the last two decades (from stranded costs to ameliorating market power). Understanding electricity restructuring requires examination of not just the various economic models of

---

[27] The misinterpretation of the Coase theorem exemplifies the Chicago approach. Stigler put forth an interpretation of Coase that in the absence of transaction costs, the allocation of resources is independent of the initial assignment of property rights. So that whether the polluter pays or the victim suffers, the market will efficiently allocate liability and damage. Coase's actual point was to note that when the situation *does* have high transactions costs, then it *does* matter where the liability for pollution is placed. Nor will simply taxing the polluter necessarily result in the efficient solution. There is no "right" answer; it becomes a difficult empirical question. Deirde McClosky, "The Good Old Coase Theorem and the Good Old Chicago School: A Comment on Zerbe and Medema," in Steven G. Medema, ed., *Coasean Economics* (Boston, Kluwer, 1992), 239–48.

[28] I use the term "model" rather than "theory," because theory implies a scientific "certainty" that is absent from economics. The term "physics envy" has been used in the social science and business literatures to characterize the desire to develop universal theories from a limited set of postulates. Economics may be closer to disciplines such as evolutionary biology, ecology, and meteorology than physics. This is a reflection of the dynamic, nonstationary, and ultimately human aspect of economic interactions. Andrew W. Lo and Mark T. Mueller, "WARNING: Physics Envy May Be Hazardous to Your Wealth!" Available at SSRN: http://ssrn.com/abstract=1563882 or http://dx.doi.org/10.2139/ssrn.1563882 (March 19, 2010): 65.

electricity markets but the biases and self-interest of the economists putting forth these theories. The battle of the experts has been a major part of electricity (and energy) policymaking for three decades.[29]

Economists and lobbyists pushing to deregulate markets because it would increase efficiency were engaging in an act of faith as much as analysis, with little empirical evidence to support their arguments. In some cases, such as oil price caps and natural gas rate regulation, government-driven market distortions were so egregious that faith in a market solution was justified. In the case of electricity, there was good reason to question whether deregulation, at least in the short run, was as beneficial as claimed by its proponents.

Academic economists had an indirect effect on electricity restructuring, with the exception being those professors who acted as consultants or became involved with the new electricity markets.[30] This is because academic papers tend to be inaccessible to those the academy, and most are rarely read at all. About one-quarter of economics articles have never been cited,[31] and a larger number are cited infrequently. Only 146 papers out of tens of thousands published between 1997 and 2006 received at least 500 citations, and many of these were papers dealing with econometric techniques that would be routinely cited in empirical research.[32] Note that of those 146 articles, none dealt with energy, and only a few with regulation, all critical of the economics and politics

---

[29] There has always been a market for expert witnesses in rate cases, but the stakes are lower, the issues are simpler, and the temptations to err from the path of righteous, or at least intellectual rigor are fewer. I had a small role in the Pennsylvania and New Jersey restructuring proceedings as a consultant for Hagler Bailly, and a larger role as a lawyer/economist/lobbyist in proceedings before the Public Utility Commission of Texas and legislation before the Texas legislature. So I have firsthand experience with the "tricks of the trade."

[30] Publications by consulting academics require educated skepticism, since their consulting income can often exceed their academic salaries. The American Economic Review recently established a policy requiring authors to reveal any financial interest or funding for research submitted for publication. "American Economic Association Adopts Extensions to Principles for Author Disclosure of Conflict of Interest," January 5, 2012 at http://www.aeaweb.org/PDF_files/PR/AEA_Adopts_Extensions_to_Principles_for_Author_Disclosure_01-05-12.pdf, last visited June 2, 2012. Few other journals follow this policy, so it is difficult to ascertain if an author has a financial interest in the results of his paper.

[31] David Laband and Robert Tollison, "Dry Holes in Economic Research," *Kyklos* 56 (2003): 161–74.

[32] E. Han Kim, Adair Morse, and Luigi Zingales, "What Has Mattered to Economics Since 1970," *Journal of Economic Perspectives* 20 (Fall 2006): 189–202. With the proliferation of "plug and play" econometric software packages, it is routine to cite seminal articles as justification for application of a technique the researcher may have simply chosen from a menu of options.

of government intervention in the economy.[33] A study of the ten most cited papers in energy-related journals found the top papers had between forty-two and sixty-eight citations. Seven of the ten papers were related to climate change.[34]

So how did economic theory manage to infiltrate public policy debates on electricity deregulation? There are a number of avenues for transmitting energy economics into the popular arena. There are a few literate economists who can write accessible articles and books, both for the general public and in industry journals. The key journals in energy have been the *Energy Law Journal*, the *Energy Journal*, *Public Utility Fortnightly*, and, specific to electricity, *The Electricity Journal*. Interested parties such as consultants and lawyers translate economic concepts for policymakers (often the path for knowledge dissemination is academic to consultant, to lawyer/lobbyist, to policymaker). A third channel is through journalists and popular writers, although they tend to be indicators of the salience of an issue more than initiators of debates. Engineers, especially those in the industry, often brought a tinge of realism to these debates, as they pointed out the physical limitations of transmission systems and the limited flexibility of generation technology.

The result was a cacophony of voices pushing various positions and oversimplifying complex issues. The two key terms that were tossed around promiscuously were "efficiency" and "markets." Efficiency is the economist's mantra, but it is a platonic ideal, the product of perfect markets that do not exist in the real world. It also means something different to an engineer, who is more focused on optimizing physical output from a given set of resources and technology, not choosing the economically optimal set of inputs and outputs. Markets are a means to efficiency, but too often are referred to not as mechanisms for organizing economic activity but as an end in and of themselves. These terms have influence outside the profession where they seem to promise certainty. I have always found it amusing in hearings to listen to a non-economist speak of the importance of a "market solution" as if it were a magic talisman.

---

[33] These articles were: George Stigler, "Theory of Economic Regulation"; Sam Peltzman, "Toward a More General Theory of Regulation," *Journal of Law and Economics* 19 (1976): 211–40; Gary Becker, "A Theory of Competition Among Pressure Groups for Political Influence," *Quarterly Journal of Economics* 26 (1983): 371–400; Ann Krueger, "The Political Economic of the Rent-Seeking Society."

[34] Richard Tol and John Weyant, "Energy Economics' Most Influential Papers," *Energy Economics* 28 (2006): 405–09.

A good example of the gap between economic theory and practice was the application of marginal cost pricing to electricity regulation. Application of marginal cost theory to utility pricing can be traced back to the turn of the century, when the difference between short-run variable costs (cost of generating power) and long-run costs (cost of building the system to meet the peak demand) became a concern of engineers. The engineering approach focused on the proper allocation of costs; when the economists began to address the issue, they were worried about the proper structure of incentives that would minimize costs.[35] Marginal cost pricing in electricity gained popularity in the 1970s as electricity rates began to rise, and the cost of building new capacity rose above the average cost of existing facilities. Time of use pricing (paying more during peak hours) requires customers to pay the true short-run cost of electricity. Baseload generation is less expensive than peak load generation, and line losses increase with the volume of electricity transmitted. The electricity system is designed to meet peak demand, so capacity charges based on the consumer's contribution to peak demand was a solution to assigning capital costs.[36] Consumers who used more electricity were forcing the utility to add new capacity. Marginal cost pricing seemed an obvious way of assigning the cost of new capacity and to weigh it against alternatives such as DSM. However, it was a more complex undertaking than most regulators and economists realized.[37] The attempt to approximate the long-run cost of

---

[35] William J. Hausman and John L. Neufeld, "Time-of-Day Pricing in the U.S. Electric Power Industry at the Turn of the Century," *Rand Journal of Economics* 15 (Spring 1984): 116–26; William J. Hausman and John L. Neufeld, "Engineers and Economists: Historical Perspectives on the Pricing of Electricity," *Technology and Culture* 30 (January 1989): 83–104.

[36] Alfred Kahn, *The Economics of Regulation: Principles and Institutions* New York, John Wiley & Sons, 1970): 87–122. Utilities often set a demand charge based on the customer's overall peak demand, not the customer's demand at the time of the system's peak demand. One reason was that it was relatively simple to design an electric meter that measured the customers' total and peak consumption (but not when it occurred) to be read manually once a month. For this reason, time-of-day rates and peak demand charges were usually restricted to large industrial customers for whom the cost of the more sophisticated meter, and eventually the associated telemetry, were relatively small compared to the value of the electricity consumed. With the advent of "smart" meters it has become feasible to extend time-of-use and peak load pricing to all customers.

[37] Paul J. Joskow, "Regulatory Failure, Regulatory Reform, and Structural Change in the Electric Power Industry," *Brooking Papers on Economic Activity: Microeconomics* (1989): 169–74. One problem is that the optimal economic rate structure will recover the utility's revenue requirement only by accident, necessitating a mechanism to make up shortfalls or return surpluses to customers, raising a new set of economic, regulatory, and political issues.

electricity in a hypothetical competitive market would run afoul of the problem of projecting fuel costs, new-generation technology, and changes in load shapes over time.

The observation that economies of scale had been exhausted in power generation created the rationale for electricity deregulation.[38] If the optimal generator is small relative to the load it would serve, then there was no natural monopoly in generation, and competition should be more efficient than continued regulation of electricity generation. While there was general consensus that economies in scale in generation had been exhausted, there was more doubt whether cost complementarities between different stages of the electric industry persisted. If cost complementarities do not exist, vertical integration did not reduce the cost of electric supply, and divesting generation from transmission and distribution would not increase costs.[39] Path dependence suggests that there should be cost complementarities, because historically investment decisions in generation, transmission, and distribution in an integrated utility were coordinated.[40] This coordination was not always just to provide power at least cost but also to satisfy regulatory and political constraints (for example, providing infrastructure to encourage economic development in certain areas of

[38] L. W. Weiss, "Antitrust in the Electric Power Industry," in Almarin Phillips, editor, *Promoting Competition in Regulated Markets* (Washington, DC, Brookings, 1975); Laurits Christensen and William Greene, "Economies of Scale in U.S. Electric Power Generation," *Journal of Political Economy* 84 (1976): 655–76; David Huettner and John Landon, "Electric Utilities: Scale Economies and Diseconomies," *Southern Economic Journal* 44 (1977): 883–912.

[39] J. Stephen Henderson, "Cost Estimation for Vertically Integrated Firms: The Cost of Electricity," in M. A. Crew, ed., *Analyzing the Impact of Regulatory Change in Public Utilities* (Lexington, Lexington Books, 1985): 75–94; David Kaserman and John Mayo, "The Measurement of Vertical Economies and the Efficient Structure of the Electric Utility Industry," *Journal of Industrial Economics* 39 (September 1991): 483–502; Keith Gilsdorf, "Vertical Integration Efficiencies and Electric Utilities: A Cost Complementarity Perspective," *Quarterly Review of Economics and Finance* 34 (Fall 1994): 261–82; Herbert Thompson et al., "Economies of Scale and Vertical Integration in the Investor-Owned Electric Utility Industry," NRRI 96–05 (January 1996); Paul Hayashi, James Yeoung-Jia Goo, and William Chamberlain, "Vertical Economies: The Case of U.S. Electric Utility Industry, 1983–87," *Southern Economic Journal* 63 (1997): 710.

[40] Recent studies have found a statistically significant and substantial cost savings associated with vertical integration, together with a smaller cost saving associated with the horizontal integration of generation. Pablo Arocena, David Saal, and Tim Coelli, "Measuring Economies of Horizontal and Vertical Integration in the US Electric Power Industry: How Costly Is Unbundling?" Working Paper RP 0917, Aston Business School (June 2009); Roland Meyer, "Benchmarking Economies of Vertical Integration in U.S. Electricity Supply: An Application of DEA," Jacobs University Bremen (October 17, 2010).

the utility's territory). While the proper market signals should result in efficient generation investment and location decisions over the long run, there could be short-term costs of divesting generation from transmission.

The first wave of electricity deregulation articles and books arrived in the late 1970s and early 1980s.[41] Initially, there were two conceptual problems to overcome: the shift from theory to actually modeling deregulation and its impacts; and the practical problem of designing real markets, including the technical problem of information gathering and processing required to settle numerous transactions and maintain reliability. Multiple area dispatching production costing models that could account for purchases from neighboring utilities and the associated transaction cost and impact on transmission utilization were not generally used by utilities in the 1980s, let alone by policy analysts. A model developed by General Electric was only used on a sporadic basis by a small number of utilities, because the data requirements were so extensive.[42]

There were both technical and political reasons why electricity markets presented more difficulties than did other deregulated markets. Electricity must be consumed when produced. While there are some storage technologies, such as pumped hydroelectric, the high cost and exhaustion of suitable sites has pretty much prevented the construction of new pump storage facilities for decades. Other technologies such as batteries, flywheels, and Compressed Air Energy Storage have proven too costly to be provided on a utility-level scale. Thus, unlike natural gas with the tremendous storage capabilities of pipelines and storage caverns, an electricity

---

[41] James Fairman and John Scott, "Transmission, Power Pools, and Competition in the Electric Utility Industry," 28 *Hastings Law Journal* 1159 (May 1977); Matthew Cohen, "Efficiency and Competition in the Electric Power Industry," 88 *Yale Law Journal* 1511 (1979); EEI, "Deregulation of Electric Utilities: A Survey of Major Concepts and Issues" (July 1981); Joe Pace and John Landon, "Introducing Competition into the Electric Utility Industry: An Economic Appraisal," 3 *Energy Law Journal* 1 (1982); William Berry, "The Case for Competition in the Electric Utility Industry," *Public Utilities Fortnightly* 110 (September 1982): 12–20; DOE, "Integration of Electric Power: A Framework for Analysis, A Draft Discussion Paper, Phase 2 Report" (September 1982), prepared by MIT; NPS Energy Management, "Alternative Models of Electric Power Deregulation," EEI (May 1982); CBO, "Promoting Efficiency in the Electricity Sector" (November, 1982); Paul Joskow and Richard Schmalansee, *Markets for Power: An Analysis of Electrical Utility Deregulation* (Cambridge, MA, MIT Press, 1983); Fred Schweppe, Michael Caramanis, Richard Tabors, and Roger Bohn, *Spot Pricing of Electricity* (Boston, Kluwer, 1988).

[42] Peter Blair, *The Role of Analytical Models: Issues and Frontiers*, Energy Modeling Forum WP 10.2 (March 1991): 3. GE's Multi-Area Production Simulation (MAPS) is still utilized today, although advances in computation and availability of data permits far more sophisticated modeling than two decades ago.

market must constantly clear in real time. Reliability requires the proper mix of generation to fine-tune generation to match load on a continuous basis.

On the supply side, sufficient fast-response reserves must be available to meet most contingencies because the ramp rates of generators are limited. Continuous power availability depends on the provision and payment for sufficient reserves to reduce the probability of system failure. This is a classic free-rider problem as each customer prefers that others provide and pay for reliability, as what each customer pays for reserves has little effect on its own access to power. Without regulatory intervention and engineering command-and-control, markets for reserves are bound to be inefficient or even to collapse. These considerations extend beyond daily operating reserves to the general problem of ensuring adequate supply resources, including both generation and transmission capacity.[43]

Politically, one method of balancing supply and demand was off the table: involuntarily terminating customers if demand was excessive relative to supply. Theoretically, if every customer had a reservation price (i.e., a cost at which they would be willing to be temporarily blacked out rather than pay for electricity), and could be switched off when market prices exceeded that level, an electricity market could work perfectly with limited supervision (voltage control would still be required because there is a quality component to electricity: if current fluctuates too much, it can damage equipment). However, while this may become a technical possibility in the next decade or two, with advanced meters and remote-disconnect switches, it was certainly impossible to implement in the 1980s and 1990s. It is also unlikely that any PUC would approve mandatory disconnects due to price spikes for residential or even small commercial customers. Therefore, most electric demand will remain highly inelastic in the very short run.

The practical complexity of deregulating electricity markets lead most deregulation advocates to coalesce around five common elements: (1) severing ownership of electricity generation and "wires" (transmission and distribution infrastructure); (2) deregulating the price of wholesale generation; (3) removing entry barriers in generation; (4) creating a separately

---

43 Hung-po Chao, Shmuel Oren, and Robert Wilson, "Restructured Electricity Markets: Reevaluation of Vertical Integration and Unbundling," in Fereidoon P. Sioshansi, ed., *Competitive Electricity Markets: Design, Implementation, Performance* (Amsterdam, Elsevier, 2008): 36–37.

owned, regional transmission system (a government-owned or -franchised monopoly) that had an obligation to coordinate operations and planning in the region; and (5) continued regulation of local distribution systems. The primary disagreement revolved around whether the wholesale electricity market should rely on bilateral contracting or spot market sales using centralized dispatch to minimize cost.[44]

Harvard, led by William Hogan, was the center of advocacy for locational marginal pricing (LMP) by the end of the 1980s. Hogan was a professor of public policy and management at the John F. Kennedy School of Government and a director at Putnam, Hayes & Bartlett, from 1980 to 1999.[45] Putnam, LECG, Hagler Bailly, the Brattle Group, Tabors, Caramanis and Associates, and NERA[46] would play key roles in influencing the federal and state debates over deregulation of electricity.[47] Hogan was also a major participant in the Harvard Electricity Policy Group, which provided a forum for the analysis and discussion of electricity policy issues.

The nodal pricing approach was first put forth by Fred Schweppe, Michael Caramanis, Richard Tabors, and Roger Bohn[48] and championed by Hogan, Scott Harvey,[49] and Susan Pope,[50] among others. A node is where electricity is either supplied to the network from a generator or withdrawn from the network at a point of connection with a distribution system or large customer. The operator runs auction markets for energy and uses the submitted bids by load and offers by generators to conduct security-constrained economic dispatch (SCED). The difference between these markets and economic dispatch under regulation is that

---

[44] See Roger Bohn, Richard Tabors, Bennett Golub, and Fred Schweppe, *Deregulating the Electric Utility Industry*, MIT Energy Laboratory Technical Report, MIT-EL82-003 (January 1982).

[45] He then moved to the Law and Economics Group (LECG).

[46] National Economic Research Associates.

[47] PHB would merge with Hagler Bailly in 1999, and the new company was purchased by PA Consulting in December 2000. LECG merged with SMART Business Advisory & Consulting, LLC in 2010, but a term loan assumed in the merger sunk the new company and it was liquidated in 2011. See http://finance.yahoo.com/news/LECG-Provides-Update-on-State-iw-3429020450.html?x=0&.v=1.

[48] Schweppe et al., *Spot Pricing of Electricity*. Schweppe was a professor of electrical engineering at MIT from 1966 until his death in 1988. Bohn pursued an academic career in operations research, but was also a principal with Tabors, Caramanis and Associates in the 1990s.

[49] Putnam, 1987–1998, then LECG. After LECG imploded, he moved to FTI Consulting in 2011.

[50] Putnam, 1988–1998, then LECG. After LECG imploded, she moved to FTI Consulting in 2011.

regulated companies in a tight pool submitted marginal cost data to the operator instead of price offers, and load was generally independent of price. Owing to thermal and other constraints, transmission lines have maximum loads they can carry; when that limit is met, generation has to be shifted between generators to restrict the loading on that line, increasing total system costs. The model solves for congestion as the shadow prices at each node (i.e., the increased cost to the whole system of supplying one more MW of power at a withdrawing node). When there is no congestion, all nodes have the same price, but when some lines are congested, the cost of congestion is the differences in price between nodes. While this is a nonlinear programming problem, the bids were required to be submitted in a stepwise linear form, approximating a bid curve, to convert the problem into a linear programming problem and allow it to be solved in real time (and with confidence that the model will converge to a solution). It was the "security-constrained" part of SCED that made this problem far more intractable in the real world than in theory.

Transferring theoretical concepts to operational constructs was not a simple task. It is one thing to write an article with a three- or four-node model to demonstrate the efficiency of locational marginal pricing; it is quite another to write the software and develop the system monitoring, communications, and information-processing capability to identify, measure, and then solve a real-world model with hundreds or even thousands of nodes every fifteen or, as has become common, five minutes. Electricity industry restructuring is a never-ending, evolving, multi-objective, politically oriented process. A restructured electricity industry can be thought of as a complex system characterized by interactions between centralized and decentralized human decision-making processes, automatic control systems, and the physical processes of the energy conversion chain. In practice, theory can only provide limited guidance in terms of designing the way in which a restructured electricity industry will operate.[51]

There were a number of key issues that had to be resolved to develop a fully functioning wholesale electricity spot market. First, matching generation to load on a continuous basis presented an administrative nightmare of constantly changing offers and bids as new demand and price information became available to participants. Second, congestion in transmission had to be modeled, the resulting constraints honored during dispatch,

---

[51] S. R. Thorncraft, H. R. Outhred, and D. J. Clements, "Heuristics to Assist in Overcoming the Complexity of a Restructured Electricity Industry," IEEE PES General Meeting, Montreal, Canada (June 18–22, 2006).

and the costs of congestion allocated to participants. Third, to minimize total costs, generation had to be optimally dispatched and these dispatch instructions had to be constantly updated and communicated as conditions changed, taking into account transmission constraints and the ability of generation units to ramp (the rate at which they can increase or decrease generation). Fourth, the system required constant monitoring to detect and react to contingencies (such as a generator unexpectedly going offline or a transmission line failing), and reserves maintained to allow rapid response to events that threatened reliability of the grid. Fifth, the market had to be designed to discourage gaming by participants manipulating bids or loads.

A fundamental question in using equilibrium models to analyze electricity markets is whether they are reasonable models of industry behavior. In some cases, the underlying assumptions about knowledge, profit maximization, and rationality may not be consistent with observed behavior. There are also a large number of economic modeling assumptions made in equilibrium models. Given all of these assumptions, it is likely that the models are not capable of exact predictions of market prices and outcomes. These models are useful for a sensitivity analysis of the general effect of changes in market rules or market structure.[52] However, policymakers often failed to understand that policy conclusions to be made from these studies should be considered suggestive, not determinative.

Economists and consultants were both guilty of understating the difficulties and oversimplifying the complexity of building real-world electricity markets. This in turn encouraged politicians to support overly ambitious timelines for restructuring markets, resulting in software and market structures that contained serious design flaws. At best, this meant numerous software iterations, as market flaws were identified and desired functionality was added to stakeholder and regulator wish lists. The worst case scenario was the California market meltdown, where poor market design, rushed implementation, and a "perfect storm" of events lead to an economic disaster.

---

[52] Ross Baldick, "Computing the Electricity Market Equilibrium: Uses of Market Equilibrium Models," Power Systems Conference and Exposition, IEEE (2006): 6.

6

The Energy Policy Act of 1992

FERC had been moving toward opening up transmission access for independent power producers since the mid-1980s, with the blessing of the Reagan and Bush administrations, but proceeded cautiously due to a lack of authority to require transmission providers to allow access by third parties. The passage of the Energy Policy Act of 1992 (EPAct 1992), with its open-access provisions and the increased freedom of action for IPPs, gave new impetus to FERC actions to open up wholesale markets.

Prior to EPAct 1992, FERC had no authority to order utilities to provide transmission service or to require utilities to build power plants or transmission facilities to provide wholesale power or transmission service. As a result, regulatory authority for utility investments, operating costs, and prices lay primarily with individual state regulatory agencies. However, in practice, FERC used its discretionary authority to encourage open access. FERC imposed open-access transmission terms as a condition to approval of "market-based" rates under its general rate regulation authority, contained in sections 205 and 206 of the FPA. FERC initiated this policy with a flexible pricing experiment in bulk power transactions known as the Southwest Experiment.[1] Four utility companies proposed in December 1983 to conduct a two-year experiment to see whether competition could develop in a market in two bulk power commodities:

---

[1] Under this experiment, utilities made transmission service available more openly to competitors, and in return had pricing flexibility to sustain this competitive market. *See Public Service Company of New Mexico, et al.*, Opinion No. 203, "Opinion and Order Finding Experimental Rate to Be Just and Reasonable and Accepting Rate for Filing." 25 FERC ¶ 61,469 (1983), *reh'g denied*, 27 FERC ¶ 61,154 (1984) (Opinion No. 203-A).

economy energy and block energy. The utilities would make transmission services available for trading among them in the two commodities, and the Commission would allow pricing flexibility for these transactions and permit the utilities to retain some portion of the profits from sales.[2]

The Western Systems Power Pool (WSPP) experiment took the concept of wholesale bulk power markets a step further. WSPP proposed to permit flexible pricing not only for bulk power sales but also for transmission service. The WSPP Experiment involved utilities in ten states with approximately 12 percent (82,000 MW) of the total electric generating capacity of the United States. Membership was opened to all utilities connected to the existing members. Energy prices were to be capped based on the costs of the highest-cost participant. The WSPP Agreement provided for transmission service on a voluntary basis, at the cost of new transmission. The WSPP would utilize an "electronic bulletin board," a computer to facilitate the daily exchange of buy and sell quotes among Participants.[3]

Pacific Gas & Electric (PG&E), on behalf of the other WSPP participants, petitioned FERC in 1991 to allow the Pool to operate permanently. FERC had expressed uneasiness over the possibility that sellers of services under the Pool Agreement could wield market power, especially with regard to the WSPP's transmission-dependent utilities. FERC specifically requested that the Pool address issues of transmission access and market power. In response, the WSPP application proposed the so-called Exhibit C transmission principles, requiring member utilities to provide transmission services to other members on reasonable terms. On April 23, 1991, FERC accepted the WSPP's application with major modifications. While Exhibit C did not go far enough in opening access to transmission lines, FERC noted that ordering more stringent transmission access requirements would jeopardize the continued existence of the Pool because of its members' opposition to such commitments. Accordingly, the Commission developed and published uniform energy and transmission rate ceilings.[4]

---

[2] *Public Service Company of New Mexico, et al.*, 25 FERC ¶ 61,469, at 62,029-30 (1983).
[3] *Pacific Gas & Elec. Co.*, 38 FERC ¶ 61,242, 61,781–83 (1987).
[4] *Environmental Action et al. v. FERC*, 996 F.2d 401, 405–10 (D.C. Cir 1993). The Court found that "the flexible pricing that fosters trading among the members of the Pool also permits price discrimination, especially against captive utilities. Yet given the benefits of this trading, the limited number of captive members, and the provisions for monitoring transactions and remedying any abuses of market power, we do not find that the Commission acted arbitrarily when it approved the use of flexible prices, despite their admitted risks." *Id*. at 411.

FERC also used its merger approval authority to develop transmission policy on a case-by-case basis. FERC began this process in the 1980s, requiring access to transmission as a mechanism to alleviate potential market power concerns.[5] FERC consistently imposed "open access" transmission terms as a condition to its approval of mergers under section 203 of the FPA. In *Utah Power & Light*,[6] FERC specifically conditioned merger approval on opening transmission. FERC required that the merged utility wheel power for competitors in order to remedy the merger's likely adverse effect on competition.[7] Similar conditions were imposed on the merged utility in *Northeast Utilities Service Co.*[8] In the rehearing of *Northeast Utilities*, the Commission detailed the incremental-cost approach for recovery of transmission expansion costs. Only those costs that are additional to those required to satisfy native load requirements can be assigned to the third party requesting service.[9]

The courts confirmed FERC's authority over wholesale transactions, requiring that state regulation of the purchasing utility respect FERC-approved "filed rates." The "filed rate" doctrine, which had been implied in *Montana-Dakota Utilities*,[10] was set forth formally in *Hall*[11] and

---

[5] GAO, *Electricity Supply: Regulating Utility Holding Companies in a Changing Electric Industry* 4 (1992) (noting that more than fifty-three utilities were merged or acquired between 1980 and 1991).

[6] *Utah Power & Light Company, et al.*, Opinion No. 318, 45 FERC ¶ 61,095 (1988), *order on reh'g*, Opinion No. 318-A, 47 FERC ¶ 61,209 (1989) *order on reh'g*, Opinion No. 318-B , 48 FERC ¶ 61,035 (1989), *aff'd in relevant part sub nom. Environmental Action Inc., et al. v. FERC*, 939 F.2d 1057 (D.C. Cir. 1991), *order on remand*, 57 FERC ¶ 61,363 (1991) (merger of Pacific Power & Light and Utah Power & Light into Pacificorp, a holding company).

[7] *Utah Power & Light*, 47 FERC ¶ 61,209, 61,282 (1989).

[8] *Northeast Utilities Service Company (Re Public Service Company of New Hampshire)*, Opinion No. 364-A, 58 FERC ¶ 61,070, *reh'g denied*, Opinion No. 364-B, 59 FERC ¶ 61,042, *order granting motion to vacate and dismissing request for rehearing*, 59 FERC ¶ 61,089 (1992), *affirmed in relevant part sub nom. Northeast Utilities Service Company v. FERC*, 993 F. 2d 937 (1st Cir. 1993) (Northeast combined with bankrupt Public Service of New Hampshire), *affirmed, Northeast Utilities Service Co. v. FERC*, 55 F. 3d 686 (1st Cir. 1993).

[9] *Northeast Utilities Service Company*, 58 FERC ¶ 61,070, 61,200–07 (1992). This approach was upheld by the First Circuit, *Northeast Utilities v. FERC*, 993 F.2d 937, 955 (1st Cir. 1993).

[10] *Montana-Dakota Utilities v. Northwestern Public Service Co.*, 341 U.S. 246 (1951).

[11] *Arkansas Louisiana Gas Co. v. Hall*, 453 U.S. 571, 581–82 (1981) ("But under the filed rate doctrine, the Commission alone is empowered to make that judgment and until it has done so, no rate other than the one on file may be charged.... The court below, like the state court in *Kalo Brick*, has consequently usurped a function that Congress has assigned to a federal regulatory body. This the Supremacy Clause will not permit.")

confirmed in *Natahala*.[12] The FPA preempted any state commission investigation into wholesale rates, as the FPA gave exclusive jurisdiction to the FPC, leaving no room for state action. The Supreme Court also made it clear that "States may not alter FERC-ordered allocations of power by substituting their own determinations of what would be just and fair. FERC-mandated allocations of power are binding on the States, and States must treat those allocations as fair and reasonable when determining retail rates."[13]

These decisions opened the way for utilities to purchase power from power pools and in bilateral arrangements, secure in the knowledge that as long as they followed FERC tariffs, they could pass those costs along at the retail level. It also prevented state commissions from imposing their judgment of the proper allocation of joint costs of power pools or integrated utility systems in setting retail rates, forcing subsidization of in-state consumers at the expense of utility shareholders or customers in other jurisdictions. Utilities still had to perform due diligence to ensure that those power purchases were economic, since a state commission retained the power to rule a purchase to be imprudent, even at a FERC-approved price, if lower-cost power could be obtained elsewhere.[14] While regulators allow utilities to earn a return on their investments in plants they own, utilities were not allowed to earn a return on power purchased from nonutility generators, with the costs generally passed directly to consumers. This limited utilities' incentives to rely on purchased power to situations where they considered building generation too risky of an alternative.

While FERC was establishing policy through adjudication, it also engaged in rulemaking efforts to encourage competition. In 1985, FERC initiated proceedings to investigate how its regulatory policies ought to reflect the changes in the bulk power marketplace.[15] In 1986, President Reagan nominated Martha Hesse to be chairman of FERC. Hesse was a

---

[12] *Nantahala Power & Light v. Thornburg*, 476 U.S. 953, 962 (1986) ("This Court has held that the filed rate doctrine applies not only to the federal-court review at issue in *Montana-Dakota*, but also to decisions of state courts. In this application, the doctrine is not a rule of administrative law designed to ensure that federal courts respect the decisions of federal administrative agencies, but a matter of enforcing the Supremacy Clause.")

[13] *Miss. Power & Light Co. v. Miss. ex rel. Moore*, 487 U.S. 354, 371 (1988).

[14] *Nantahala*, 476 U.S. at 971 (1986).

[15] Donald F. Santa, Jr. and Clifford S. Sikora, "Open Access and Transition Costs: Will the Electric Industry Transition Track the Natural Gas Industry Restructuring?" *Energy Law Journal* 15 (Spring 1994): 273, 292–95.

DOE official, and her candidacy was supported by Energy Secretary John Herrington. Together with two other commissioners – Charles Stalon, an economist, and C. M. Naeve, an attorney – Hesse laid the groundwork for bringing more competition into the electric power industry. Her staffers held a series of public inquiries into issues concerning the generation and transmission of wholesale electric power.[16] On September 4, 1987, twelve electric utility chief executive officers sent a letter to all five FERC commissioners to endorse Chairman Hesse's effort to craft rules bringing more competition into the wholesale electric power industry.[17] Within a few weeks, the utilities that signed that letter formed an ad hoc coalition called the Utility Working Group. They were opposed to complete decontrol but welcomed the opportunity to obtain additional revenues from sales of surplus power.[18]

In 1988, FERC issued a series of NOPRs addressing concerns raised in the earlier conferences and leading to the development of standards for approving market-based generation sales on a case-by-case basis. The rulemakings addressed competitive bidding,[19] avoided costs,[20] and IPPs.[21] FERC had become concerned that many utilities had adopted a very conservative strategy with respect to building new capacity. The Commission felt that it had an obligation to create a regulatory environment that ensured that needed capacity investments would be made in a timely and efficient manner. The Commission recognized that its cost of service rules and other regulations placed onerous burdens on IPPs, discouraging entry and development of new power plants. Cost-of-service regulation was fundamentally incompatible with IPPs who lack market power. Regulatory burdens include the administrative costs of complying with regulations, delays inherent in the regulatory process, and interference with the firm's decision-making. Traditional cost-based regulation policies discouraged investment by passing on to ratepayers much or

---

[16] John Howes, "The Politics of Electric Power Deregulation," *Regulation* (Winter 1992): 17–20.

[17] The utilities included Consumers Power, Duke Power, Baltimore Gas and Electric, General Public Utilities, New England Electric, Eastern Utilities Associates, Boston Edison, Nevada Power, Public Service of New Mexico, Arizona Public Service, and Entergy. They were subsequently joined by PG&E.

[18] *Id.*

[19] *Regulations Governing Bidding Programs*, NOPR, FERC Stats. & Regs. ¶ 32,455 (1988), 53 FR 9324 (March 22, 1988).

[20] *Administrative Determination of Full Avoided Costs, Sales of Power to Qualifying Facilities, and Interconnection Facilities*, FERC Stats. & Regs. ¶ 32,457 (1988), 53 FR 9331 (March 22, 1988).

[21] *Regulations Governing Independent Power Producers*, NOPR, FERC Stats. & Regs. 1988–1998 ¶ 32,456 (1988), 53 FR 9,327 (March 22, 1988).

all of the gains from innovative technology and efficient production. In setting rates for short-term purchases, the Commission allowed departures from seller's costs, accepting rates that recovered incremental costs plus equitable sharing of the trade gains, usually capped at 50 percent. The adders provided an incentive for sellers to make power available. The Commission began accepting rate filings for voluntary coordination transactions.[22]

In January 1989, the Office of Technology Assessment (OTA) issued a report in response to a request from the House Committee on Energy and Commerce to evaluate the technical feasibility of increased competition in the electric utility industry. The OTA report found no specific reason why competition could not be made to work. However, the OTA warned that insufficient analysis had been done to determine whether benefits outweigh costs. Five scenarios were presented, ranging from the status quo to complete disaggregation into generation, transmission, and distribution functions.[23]

A new coalition, formed in September 1990, urged Congress to amend PUHCA. The coalition included the Utility Working Group, the IPP Working Group, the Cogeneration and Independent Power Producers Coalition of America, the Natural Gas Alliance for the Generation of Electricity, the National Independent Energy Producers, and the Ad Hoc Committee for a Competitive Electric Supply System (a group of industrial consumers). The coalition urged Congress and the administration to support a change to PUHCA to lift restrictions on the ability of utilities and IPPs to locate their facilities where they might be needed. The group could not agree on whether PUHCA legislation should include transmission.[24]

Industrial customers started to advocate for electric industry restructuring in the early 1990s in states where average utility rates were high due to the costs of nuclear units and QF contracts. These customers pointed out that if they could obtain generation directly from new gas-fired combined-cycle units, they might be able to obtain power for 3–4 cents per kWh, not the 5–8 cents per kWh they were currently paying. High electricity prices were discouraging location of heavy industry in some states, which prompted measures to lower costs to industry to

---

[22] *Regulations Governing Independent Power Producers*, NOPR, FERC Stats. & Regs. ¶ 32,456, 32,106–08.

[23] OTA, *Electric Power Wheeling and Dealing: Technological Considerations for Increasing Competition* (May 1989).

[24] John Howes, "The Politics of Electric Power Deregulation," *Regulation* (Winter 1992): 17–20.

prevent the loss of manufacturing employment.[25] These high prices also encouraged a growing chorus of voices calling for deregulation of the bulk power market, encouraged by the apparent success of deregulation efforts in other industries.[26] The smaller group of observers counseling caution were generally ignored.[27]

The Bush administration initially made noises about developing a new energy strategy based around environmental concerns, but Bush's credibility was limited given his close ties with the Texas oil industry. However, when Iraq President Saddam Hussein, on August 1, 1990, invaded Kuwait, world oil prices shot up and Congress was suddenly amenable to a new energy bill. The proposed White House energy blueprint called for stimulating domestic oil production, including drilling in the Arctic National Wildlife Refuge (ANWR) and consolidation of nuclear licensing procedures. The administration proposal would also eliminate FERC as an independent commission and fold it into DOE as the Natural Gas and Electricity Administration, headed by a presidential appointee whose nomination would be subject to Senate confirmation. The idea for shutting down the Commission came from Vice President Dan Quayle's Council on Competitiveness. Wholesale generators would be exempted from the PUHCA provisions, permitting businesses to own or invest in generating plants in more than one geographic area. However, state regulators would have to approve certain transactions between a utility and its subsidiary. PURPA's exemption for power produced from geothermal, solar, wind, or waste sources would no longer be limited to plants of less than 80 megawatts in states that require a competitive bidding process for utility electricity purchases.[28]

The plan did not receive overwhelming applause on the Hill. Environmentalists criticized it as a "drain America first" policy, with no provisions for increasing conservation. In the Senate, Energy and Natural Resources Committee chairman Bennett Johnston (D-LA), working with the committee's ranking Republican, Malcolm Wallop, put together a bill

---

[25] "Washington State, Spurred by Big Industrials, Eyes Retail Wheeling," *Electric Utility Week*, December 26, 1994, 1.

[26] Richard Pierce, "A Proposal to Deregulate the Market For Bulk Power," 72 *Virginia Law Review* 1183, 1185 (October 1986).

[27] Paul Joskow and Richard Schmalensee, *Markets For Power: An Analysis of Electric Utility Deregulation*; Benjamin Holden, "Total Deregulation in Electricity Sector Would Hurt Customers, a Report Says," *Wall Street Journal*, August 4, 1995, B4.

[28] Steve Isser, *The Economics and Politics of the Oil Industry: 1920–1990: Profits, Populism and Petroleum* (New York, Garland Publishing, 1996): 173–74.

combining drilling in ANWR with higher CAFE standards. The Committee's Democrats opposed many of the Johnston-Wallop bill's provisions, including the opening of the Alaska wildlife refuge to drilling and easing regulation of the nuclear industry. The bill was reported 17–3 after a final markup session on May 23, adding provisions deregulating the wholesale electricity business.[29]

Philip Sharp (D-IN), chairman of the Energy Subcommittee of the House Energy and Power Committee, began hearings on energy policy. However, with the end of the Iraq war, energy quickly faded as a hot-button issue, and the Subcommittee on Energy and Power did not begin to mark up legislation until the middle of July 1991. The subcommittee voted out a bill that included electricity generation deregulation, with provisions to protect consumers and to require free access to transmission networks. The bill exempted wholesale power producers from PUHCA and provided FERC with the authority to order utilities to give independent producers access to their transmission lines. The bill provided that federal regulators review power sales by new wholesale producers to ensure they would not hurt consumers. Another provision banned utilities from building an affiliated, independent power plant and then selling the electricity to itself. The House bill that passed on May 19, 2002, included the Sharp electricity deregulation provisions.[30]

The electricity provisions became a contest between proponents of deregulation and retail wheeling, including the Electricity Consumers Resource Council[31] and environmental and consumer groups, and the defenders of the status quo, the investor-owned utilities, represented by the EEI, and a new lobby organization, the Electric Reliability Coalition.

The Johnston bill was derailed by a filibuster over the issues of Alaska oil drilling, electric utility deregulation, and CAFE standards.[32] Johnston tried again in January 1992, offering a trimmed-down version of the

---

[29] Isser, *The Economics and Politics of the Oil Industry*, 174–75.
[30] *CQ Weekly Report* (February 9, 1991); *CQ Weekly Report* (August 3, 1991); *CQ Weekly Report* (October 12, 1991), *CQ Weekly Report* (May 23, May 30, 1992).
[31] ELCON, founded in 1976, provided a voice for energy-consuming industries to publically push their positions, while members lobbied behind the scenes at regulatory commission, state legislatures, and FERC. The financial resources of large industrial companies, and their relatively small numbers that prevented "free riding," gave them a disproportionate voice in the political process. The threat of plant closures and subsequent job losses was a powerful club to use against state politicians and even members of the House of Representatives.
[32] *National Journal* (July 27, 1991): 1893; *National Journal* (November 9, 1991): 2767; *CQ Weekly Report* (November 2, 1991).

energy bill, discarding the proposals to open ANWR to drilling and to increase CAFE standards. Conservation and energy efficiency sections were strengthened and environmental protections were restored. The revised bill passed the Senate on February 19, but the only major accomplishment of the bill was the deregulation of wholesale electric power generation. A coalition of utilities vigorously opposed the proposal but received little support in the Senate. An amendment to protect consumers from self-dealing passed, under which utilities could only buy power from an independent affiliate if state regulators approved. Other provisions included exempting wholesale electricity generators from PUHCA, allowing utilities to operate independent wholesale plants outside their service territories, and encouraging independent producers to operate generating plants.[33]

The major point of contention in the conference negotiations was the lack of guaranteed access by producers to electric transmission systems in the Senate version. Malcolm Wallop, a key author of the Senate bill, was the chief opponent of mandatory transmission access. Wallop said the House transmission proposal would ride roughshod over private utilities and "envisions making FERC the electric utility czar." Environmental groups supported these changes, believing competition would open up opportunities for renewable-energy producers. Sharp and Johnston cleared the way for the deal by directing their key staff aides to draft a comprehensive proposal. The House accepted the Senate provision to let utilities buy power from independent affiliates as long as state regulators approve the deals. Conferees also agreed to a new provision that would permit utility holding companies to build plants overseas. After a month of haggling, the conference finally came up with a final product on October 1. Tax incentives for conservation, renewable energy, and alternative fuel cars survived the conference, as well as relief for independent oil and gas producers. The conference report flew through both the House and Senate, and was signed by the President on October 24, ending an eighteen-month odyssey.[34]

The new law empowered FERC to order any "transmitting utility" to provide transmission for wholesale electricity transactions whenever

---

[33] Isser, *The Economics and Politics of the Oil Industry: 1920–1990*, 175; Donald Santa and Patricia Beneke, "Federal Natural Gas Policy and the Energy Policy Act of 1992," *Energy Law Journal* 14 (1993): 10–11.

[34] Isser, *The Economics and Politics of the Oil Industry: 1920–1990*, 175–77; Santa and Beneke, "Federal Natural Gas Policy and the Energy Policy Act of 1992," 11–12.

the requested transmission can be provided consistent with maintaining reliability and would be in the public interest. The definition of "transmitting utility" includes "any electric utility, qualifying cogeneration facility, qualifying small power production facility, or Federal power marketing agency which owns or operates electric power transmission facilities which are used for the sale of electric energy at wholesale."[35] FERC could compel a transmission provider to enlarge its transmission capacity where existing capacity is inadequate to provide the requested service. FERC was prohibited from requiring retail transmission to an ultimate consumer of electricity or conditioning any regulatory approval on agreeing to provide retail wheeling.[36]

As amended, section 212 of the FPA required FERC to set rates, charges, terms, and conditions for wholesale transmission service that permit the transmitting utility to recover all costs "incurred in connection with the transmission services and necessary associated services," including "any benefits to the transmission system of providing the transmission service, and the costs of any enlargement of transmission facilities." Rates shall "promote the economically efficient transmission and generation of electricity." The cost causation principle should be used to allocate costs.[37]

A new category of utility was created: Exempt Wholesale Generators (EWGs). EWG eligibility was restricted to "persons" (including an affiliate of an electric utility) who are exclusively in the business of owning or operating power generation facilities and selling electric power at wholesale. An EWG was not an "electric utility company" under the PUHCA. In addition, an EWG was deemed not to be "primarily engaged in the generation or sale of electric power" for purposes of the FPA. An EWG is, however, a "public utility" within the definition of the FPA, and is subject to regulation of rates and charges for sales of electricity or leased capacity, tariff requirements, and information reporting.[38]

FERC authority to require the wheeling of power from these new independent wholesale generators was the next step toward establishing wholesale electricity markets. PURPA had allowed independent power

---

[35] 16 U.S.C. § 796(23).

[36] 16 U.S.C. § 824k(h).

[37] *Id.*

[38] Jeffrey D. Watkiss and Douglas W. Smith, "The Energy Policy Act of 1992 – A Watershed for Competition in the Wholesale Power Market," 10 *Yale Journal on Regulation* 447, 464–68 (Summer 1993).

developers to build plants, but restrictions on QFs basically limited them to either cogeneration facilities (which were limited by the population of customers with substantial thermal loads) and fringe plants that were a substitute for IOU generation under state IRPs. EWGs would build merchant plants that competed on price against incumbent IOUs.

7

Jump into the Power Pool

The North American Electric Reliability Corporation (NERC)[1] was formed after the 1965 Northeast blackout.[2] It was a voluntary organization whose mission was to ensure that the bulk power system in North America is reliable, adequate, and secure. Ten Regional Reliability Councils were established on the basis of the physical design of transmission systems and historic cooperation among various utilities.[3] The Reliability Councils established an obvious framework for the evolution of power pools, since the type of coordination that would increase reliability, especially planning transmission to allow access to external reserves in emergency situations, was also conducive to more routine energy transactions.

---

[1] Originally called the North American Electric Reliability Council.
[2] The Great Northeast Blackout of 1965 affected more than 80,000 square miles and 30 million customers from Buffalo to the eastern border of New Hampshire and from New York City to Ontario.
[3] The ten original councils were:

> East Central Area Reliability Coordination Agreement (ECAR)
> Electric Reliability Council of Texas (ERCOT)
> Florida Reliability Coordinating Council (FRCC)
> Mid-Atlantic Area Council (MAAC)
> Mid-America Interconnected Network (MAIN)
> Mid-Continent Area Power Pool (MAPP)
> Northeast Power Coordinating Council (NPCC)
> Southeastern Electric Reliability Council (SERC)
> Southwest Power Pool (SPP)
> Western Systems Coordinating Council (WSCC)

The FERC's predecessor, the FPC, had actively encouraged utilities to form power pools. The FPA, as a matter of general policy, held that power pooling arrangements were in the public interest. As of 1970, there were twenty-two formal power pools nationally, which had 60 percent of the nation's generating capacity.[4] Section 202(a) of the FPA directed the Commission to divide the country into regional districts for the voluntary interconnection and coordination of facilities for the generation, transmission, and sale of electric energy. In enacting this section, Congress was "confident that enlightened self-interest will lead the utilities to cooperate . . . in bringing about the economies which can alone be secured through . . . planned coordination."[5]

An effective pooling agreement must coordinate all major design, construction, and operating decisions of the contracting utilities, while dividing the gains of trade among the various participants in a mutually satisfactory manner. Cost-of-service regulation of utility rates reduced the incentive for firms to enter into cost-saving pooling contracts, because regulators confiscated most of the increased profits achieved through pooling. Regulators and courts frequently complicated the negotiating process by mandating that all utilities in a region be allowed to participate in the pooling arrangement, including smaller firms that had little to contribute in terms of transmission or generation to provide cost savings to other members.[6]

Agreements not to compete were common in pooling contracts, because each party to the agreement was generally unwilling to risk losing part of its market to other participants. While the FPC was not formally bound by the antitrust laws, the agency's duty to regulate in the public interest required it to consider the possible anticompetitive consequences of a proposed pooling agreement. The FPC should determine whether the cost savings from the pooling contract would outweigh the adverse effects of any anticompetitive restrictions.[7] However, the decision in *Central Iowa Power Coop v. FERC* showed that the court would accept FERC rulings that allowed reasonable restrictions in pooling agreements.[8]

[4] GAO, *Problems in Planning and Constructing Transmission Lines Which Interconnect Utilities* (June 9, 1977): 10.

[5] *Central Iowa Power Coop v. FERC*, 606 F.2d 1156 (D.C. Cir. 1979) *citing* S. Rep. No. 621, 74th Cong., 1st Sess. 49 (1935).

[6] Richard Pierce, "A Proposal to Deregulate the Market for Bulk Power," 72 *Virginia Law Review* 1183, 1195–96 (October 1986).

[7] *City of Huntingburg v. FPC*, 498 F.2d 778, 783, 788–89 (D.C. Cir. 1974).

[8] *Central Iowa Power Coop v. FERC*, 606 F.2d 1156 (D.C. Cir. 1979).

In the 1980s, there were two types of tight power pools: contractual pools between different companies, and holding company power pools. Centrally dispatched pools accounted for about one-third of installed generating capacity in the United States in 1989. The four major contractual pools were the Michigan Electric Coordinated System, New England Power Pool (NEPOOL), New York Power Pool (NYPP), and the Pennsylvania New Jersey-Maryland Interconnection (PJM). The Great Northeast Blackout of 1965 had prompted the Northeast's power companies to form power pools to ensure a dependable supply of electricity. The five large holding company pools were the Allegheny Power System, American Electric Power System, Middle South Utilities (renamed Entergy), Southern Company, and Texas Utilities Company (renamed TXU). Among the centrally dispatched pools, all but NYPP utilized centralized unit commitment. Brokered pools provided a managed market for power, using auction markets or electronic bulletin boards to facilitate market transactions among their members. Brokered pools did not engage in centralized dispatch. Brokered pools included the WSPP, the MidContinent Area Power Pool (MAPP), and the Florida Coordinating Group.[9]

These pools gradually solved many of the technical problems that needed to be addressed to make centralized spot markets a reality. The most important issue was extending coordinated operation from a single utility control area across a region with multiple, interconnected utility systems, independent generators, and other entities. A control area is a geographic region with a control center responsible for operating the power system within that area. System control consists of the control area operator functions that schedule generating units, transmission resources, and transactions before the fact and monitor and control transmission resources and some generating units in real time to maintain reliability. This service can also include after-the-fact accounting and billing.[10]

Control center equipment and procedures are typically organized into three somewhat overlapping systems that are generally integrated in an energy management system (EMS). The Automatic Generation Control (AGC) system coordinates the power output of generators, the supervisory control and data acquisition (SCADA) system monitors and controls

[9] FERC, Office of Electric Power Regulation, *Power Pooling in the United States* (Washington, DC, December 1981); Richard Gilbert, Edward Kahn, and Matthew White, "Coordination in the Wholesale Market: Where Does It Work?" *Electricity Journal* (October 1993): 52–53.

[10] Eric Hirst and Brendan Kirby, "Unbundling Generation and Transmission Services for Competitive Electricity Markets," ORNL for NRRI (January 1998): 5.

transmission line equipment and generator voltages, and the unit dispatch software monitors and evaluates system security and performance and dispatches generation units. Unit dispatch software was designed to minimize generation costs subject to reliability constraints. Telemetry is used to transmit data and commands to and from the various components of the interconnected grid system and the control center. A State Estimator program gathers all available telemetry data on the system and gives a real-time picture of system status. Control centers must ensure that generating units will be ready when needed to follow the daily load cycle (accounting for ramping constraints), that the transmission system is capable of carrying the loads, and that backup generating capacity is available in case of equipment failure.

Transmission networks can be viewed as consisting of combinations of nodes ("buses") and links between the nodes ("flowgates"). Transmission lines can be direct current (DC) or alternating current (AC). Power in North America is largely generated and delivered via AC systems. Power system frequency is the number of sine wave cycles that the alternating current completes each second. In North America, the power system frequency is 60 cycles per second, or 60 hertz (Hz) (most of the world uses 50 Hz). Electrical current flows proportionally through the conducting paths in inverse proportion to the paths' resistance. The resistance of a transmission or distribution line will be a function of the line's length and thickness. Through the interactions of Kirchoff's laws,[11] a line limitation affects every other power flow in an AC network. Power flows in networks follow Kirchhoff's laws and cannot be directly controlled. Therefore, it is impossible for a buyer or seller of electricity to specify the route the electric power follows.

Power generation, load, and flow in an AC system are divided into both active and reactive power components. Active power is measured in watts while reactive power is measured in volt ampere reactive (Var).[12] Reactive power supports the magnetic and electric fields necessary to operate the power system equipment. Reactive power is never consumed but is constantly exchanged (at twice system frequency) between devices that produce reactive power and those that store reactive power. Voltage can

[11] Kirchhoff's Current Law: The sum of all the currents flowing into and out of any one point in an electrical circuit equals zero.
Kirchhoff's Voltage Law: The sum of all the voltage rises and voltage drops around any closed path in an electrical circuit equals zero.
[12] Together, active power and reactive power equal the total or complex power. This total flow (the product of voltage and current) has units of volts-amperes (VA).

be affected by both active and reactive power loads, and the interaction between the two is critical in determining limits on real power flows.[13] During peak load conditions, generators are usually operated to supply reactive power to the grid to help maintain adequate voltage levels. During light load conditions, generators may be used to absorb excess reactive power from the grid to prevent voltages from becoming too high.[14]

The thermal capacity of a transmission line sets an upper limit on the flow of power on that line. Owing to electrical resistance of the conductors (the wires, usually made of stranded aluminum woven around a core of stranded steel to provides structural strength), a small portion of transmitted power is converted into heat. If the power flow is too large, the wire will expand and eventually sag too close to the ground, causing a short circuit. Every transmission line is designed to carry a certain maximum amount of electric current, which, if exceeded for an extended period, could damage the transmission line. A normal rating is the level of power flow that the line can carry continuously. An emergency rating is usually defined as the levels of power flow the line can carry for a limited period of time.[15]

Even when power flows do not approach the thermal limits of the system and transmission lines appear to have excess capacity, other factors can constrain the transfer capacity. Reactive power must be taken into account when calculating thermal limits on transmission links. In an AC transmission system, the voltage is maintained at nearly same average level at all points in the system. To induce power to flow from one point to another, there must be a "phase difference" between the alternating voltage at the point of generation and the load. However, this phase difference cannot become too large without threatening voltage collapse. Stability limits on power lines specify a maximum power flow. Thermal limits dominate over shorter transmission lines; at intermediate distances the limits are related to voltage drop; and beyond roughly 300–350 miles, stability limits dominate.[16]

[13] "EPRI Power System Dynamics Tutorial," July 2009.

[14] Jack Casazza and Frank Delea, *Understanding Electric Power Systems: An Overview of Technology, the Marketplace and Government Regulation*, 2nd Ed. (Hoboken, IEEE Press and John Wiley & Sons, 2010): 39–44.

[15] Casazza and Delea, *Understanding Electric Power Systems*, 98–99.

[16] Kenneth Costello, Robert Burns, and Youssef Hegazy, "Overview of Issues Relating to the Retail Wheeling of Electricity," NRRI 94–09 (May 1994): 60–61; Eric Hirst and Brendan Kirby, "Unbundling Generation and Transmission Services for Competitive Electricity Markets," ORNL/CON-454 (January 1998): 42–47.

A key task of the control area operator is to prevent overloading of transmission lines, accounting for both power flows and reactive power. This was traditionally performed using generation shift factors, which express the change in flow on a particular flowgate that results from increasing generation at a node. Shift factors are meaningful only when considered in source-sink pairs, because power injected at one location must be matched by power removed at another location. Generation shift factors are used to identify which generator pairs can influence a particular flowgate.[17] A nodal model automatically solves for the optimal set of shift factors.

Transactions were initially scheduled by local utility control authorities who monitored actual interchange flowing over the tie lines. Utilities monitored the power flowing across interconnection lines to record power transactions for accounting purposes and to enable their control centers to make corrective actions in order to balance the area's total generation requirements. The difference between the total required generation (i.e., real-time load) and actual generation is called the area control error. AGC is used to adjust generator output to regulate area control error. The information needed to implement AGC includes tie line flows, system frequency, and capability of generating units on line. As attempts are made to adjust the area control error for each area, errors inevitably accumulate because the actions of generators differ from what was instructed; thus the term "uninstructed deviations." Consistent errors in one direction or the other, along with unexpected changes in demand, give rise to frequency drift, which must be corrected with frequency regulation.

Large central generators are driven by prime movers, which may be steam or hydro turbines. Under steady-state operation of a generator, the net mechanical torque supplied by a prime mover is equal to the net electrical torque. Mechanical torque generated by a prime mover can only be changed with some time delay, due to the mechanics of the machine. As a utility's system load varies throughout a day, there will be imbalances between the mechanical power input and the electrical power output. As a result, changes in system frequency will occur continuously. System frequency is maintained close to the nominal value of 60 Hz to prevent damage to rotating equipment. Large steam turbines are especially vulnerable to off-speed operation, and the units will be tripped as

---

[17] Ian Dobson et al., "Electric Power Transfer Capability: Concepts, Applications, Sensitivity and Uncertainty," Power Systems Engineering Research Center, Publication 01–34 (November 2001): 22.

soon as abnormal frequencies are sensed by over/under-frequency relays. One effect of poorer-quality frequency regulation is that the frequency excursions around the nominal frequency become greater, and last for longer periods, increasing the potential for generation unit tripping and even cascading failures.[18]

Electricity systems rely on ancillary services to provide protection against inevitable errors and contingencies. Operators attempt to maintain system frequency at 60 Hz using various types of ancillary services to balance generation and load. The key ancillary services are Regulation, Spinning Reserves, and Nonspinning Reserves. Most generators have automatic control systems that sense local frequency deviations and respond in a sub-minute time frame to increase or decrease generator output in response, without signals from a control authority. Regulation is the use of online generating units equipped with governors and AGC that can change output quickly in response to control authority signals to balance fluctuations in customer loads and unintended deviations in generation. Spinning Reserve is the use of generating equipment that is online and synchronized to the grid that can begin to increase output immediately and be fully available within ten minutes to correct for generation load imbalances. Loads under the control of the system operator can also provide this service. Nonspinning Reserve is comprised of generating equipment and interruptible load that can be fully available and synchronized with the grid within ten or thirty minutes.

In general, nonutility generators (NUGs) did not follow the stringent operating guidelines adopted by virtually all electric utilities. Permitting access by numerous NUGs to transmission systems increased the number of transactions to be monitored, and thus the complexity of maintaining coordinated control of the interconnected bulk transmission system.[19]

By the end of the 1980s, there were more than 140 control areas. Because most systems were interconnected with neighboring utilities, each control area had to match its load to its own internal generation plus power exports (or interchanges to other control areas) less power imports. Utilities also belong to an interconnected network. There are three such networks in the United States: the Eastern Interconnection (which extends nearly to the Rocky Mountains), the Texas Interconnection,

---

[18] John Grainer and Stan Lee, "Identification, Definition and Evaluation of Potential Impacts Facing the U.S. Electric Utility Industry Over the Next Decade," for Los Alamos National Laboratory (November 26, 1994): 32.

[19] Grainer and Lee, "Identification, Definition and Evaluation of Potential Impacts," 18–19.

and the Western Systems Coordinating Council (WSCC). These interconnections extend into Canada, which has a fourth system, the Hydro Quebec System. Within each interconnection, all connected generators must be synchronized. There were about ninety-nine control areas in the Eastern Interconnection, thirty-four in the WSCC, and ten in the Texas Interconnected System. Because of interconnection, each control area must satisfy more stringent requirements for generation control, frequency control, and tie line flows than would be needed for an isolated system. Connections between networks are accomplished through DC interties to avoid synchronization problems.[20]

Within an interconnection, inertia due to the mechanical torque from a larger number of generators can provide additional time to resolve contingencies that require immediate action to restore frequency by bringing on additional generation and/or shedding load. When a major generation unit (or transmission line from a generator) trips, the effect is to lower system frequency. The frequency decline is initially arrested because many electrical loads (e.g., motors) are frequency responsive; that is, their demand varies with system frequency. Once the frequency decline exceeds the deadband of the generator governors, the governors sense the frequency decline and open valves on the steam turbines, which rapidly increases generator output. After a few more seconds, generator output declines slightly because the higher steam flow through the turbine is not matched by the steam flow from the boiler to the turbine. At this point, operating reserves, in response to AGC signals from the control center, hopefully kick in and increase generation to match load, restoring system frequency.[21]

Centrally dispatched pools became "super" control centers, working with each utility's control area to coordinate their activities. Over time, as pools became tighter, these central dispatch controls gradually superseded the activities of local control areas, treating the pool as one big control area. Independent generators operating in these control areas were required to coordinate with the pool's control center and implement load frequency controls.

Ancillary services were produced by traditional utilities as part of the bundled electricity product they provide to their customers. They were also joint products of the overall design of power plants, optimized to

---

[20] OTA, "Electric Power Wheeling and Dealing: Technological Considerations for Increasing Competition" (May 1989): 36–38.

[21] Eric Hirst and Brendan Kirby, "Unbundling Generation and Transmission Services for Competitive Electricity Markets," ORNL/CON-454, Oak Ridge National Laboratory for NRRI (January 1998): 29.

meet all of the technical specifications (including voltage control and dispatch flexibility) at minimum total cost. So determining costs attributable to voltage control, or the flexibility to provide other ancillary services separate from the costs attributable to real-power production, required some arbitrary assumptions. Determining the cost of these services would also require calculation of opportunity costs (for example, to provide some ancillary services, a generation unit may have to operate at less than full capacity, which might affect heat rates as well as the net costs from having to run another unit to supply additional output) and increased operations and maintenance costs from frequent changes in output.[22] Once pool control centers spanned multiple utility control areas, ancillary services gradually became products purchased in markets, allowing payments to suppliers of these services and a means to allocate costs between utilities, and eventually among all market participants.

The need for coordination over a larger region led to recognition that there must be a system operator coordinating use of the transmission system, which also implied control of the dispatch, at least at the margin. This is because adjusting dispatch of generation units is the principal means of affecting the flow of power on the grid. Available capacity on transmission systems is difficult to determine because it depends on changing factors, such as the mix of generators and load, as well as the interaction between transmission flows, known as loop flow.[23] Engineering power flow models are used to determine the available transmission capacity (ATC) of a transmission interface based on a variety of assumptions about system conditions and reliability. The rights to use the ATC over a contract path from a set of injection points to one or more withdrawal points on the network can be sold or assigned to generators or loads, assuring that sold/purchased power can be delivered.

---

[22] Hirst and Kirby, "Unbundling Generation and Transmission Services," 19–22.

[23] Loop flow not only raises technical issues but also creates a problem in assigning transmission costs and revenues.

In general, utilities transact with one another based on a contract path concept. For pricing purposes, parties assume that power flows are confined to a specified sequence of interconnected utilities that are located on a designated contract path. However, in reality, power flows are rarely confined to a designated contract path. Rather, power flows over multiple parallel paths that may be owned by several utilities that are not on the contract path. The actual power flow is controlled by the laws of physics that cause power being transmitted from one utility to another to travel along multiple parallel paths and divide itself among those paths along the lines of least resistance. This parallel path flow is sometimes called loop flow.

Indiana Michigan Power Company, 64 FERC ¶ 61,184, 62,545 (1993).

The economic power granted the system operator through control of dispatch in turn suggested that the system operator should be independent of the participating utilities. This independent system operator (ISO) would be providing a service, but would not be competing in the energy market. An ISO with no economic interest in which generator is dispatched, or the cost of transmission and associated congestion, other than minimizing total cost and maintaining reliability, lacks the economic incentive that an integrated utility would have to manipulate ATC calculations to favor its own generation. The question then became whether the ISO should be completely independent from the spot market, which would be organized in a power exchange that was strictly separated from the activities of the ISO. The ISO would focus only on reliability and not receive any bidding information, perform any economic dispatch, or determine any spot market prices.[24] However, separating economic dispatch from reliability redispatch was fraught with complications because it required constant iteration from one subsystem to another (remember, SCED solved for economic dispatch given reliability constraints).

Developments in transmission and coordination technology had led to increased interconnection between independent IOUs, with joint planning and operation of facilities owned and operated by proximate utilities. Short-term purchases and sales of electricity by interconnected integrated utilities provided additional resources for reliability and to exploit opportunities for both parties to lower costs. These wholesale transactions gradually expanded to include longer-term purchase and sale contracts to take advantage of surplus generation stemming from unexpected declines in demand growth. However, state regulators were reluctant to allow utilities to use these contracts to meet capacity requirements for reliability.[25]

Despite the advantages of strong pools, in terms of operating efficiencies and reliability, most regions never progressed further than informal arrangements. The reasons for reluctance to engage in pooling included the reduction of the scope of managerial control due to participation in a pool. Many utilities expressed strong reservations about centralized dispatch and felt that most of the benefits could be obtained with more

---

[24] William Hogan, "A Wholesale Pool Spot Market Must Be Administered by the Independent System Operator: Avoiding the Separation Fallacy," *Electricity Journal* (December 1995): 26–28.

[25] FERC, Office of Economic Policy, *Regulating Independent Power Producers: A Policy Analysis* (Oct. 13, 1987): 4–5; Wilbur C. Earley, "FERC Regulation of Bulk Power Coordination Transactions," FERC Working Paper (July 1984); and *Notice of Inquiry Re Regulation of Electricity Sales-far-Resale and Transmission Service*, 31 FERC ¶ 61,376 (1985).

informal cooperation. The appropriation of potential benefits by regulators reduced any incentive senior management might have to relinquish managerial control.[26]

Regional transmission groups (RTGs) were coalitions of transmission-owning and transmission-using entities in an identified geographic region, which adopted voluntary terms of transmission access and expansion. A number of utilities had voiced concerns that formation of RTGs would violate the antitrust laws. The Department of Justice expressed support for the use of RTGs as a means of encouraging efficient planning and use of the transmission system, alleviating concerns that these organizations might raise antitrust issues.[27]

During the final stages of congressional consideration of the Energy Policy Act there was support for legislation that would encourage RTGs, but the legislative clock ran out before a bill could be finalized. FERC issued a policy statement in response to this congressional interest, in which it formally stated its approval of RTGs and set out some guidance for their formation. The Commission believed that RTGs could be vehicles for promoting competition in generation. RTGs could provide mechanisms for encouraging negotiated agreements and resolving transmission issues and reduce the need for litigation before the Commission. As a voluntary association of transmission owners, users, and others with differing interests, an RTG could not insulate transmission utility members from proceedings under FPA section 211. However, the Commission promised an appropriate degree of deference to decisions of RTGs, depending on the degree to which an RTG agreement mitigated the market power of transmission owners and provided for fair decision making.[28] FERC approved a number of RTG agreements, including the Northwest Regional Transmission Association,[29] the Southwest Regional Transmission Association,[30] and the Mid-Continent Area Power Pool.[31]

---

[26] Mathew W. White, "Dynamic Efficiency and the Regulated Firm: Empirical Evidence," (January 2005): 20–21.

[27] Jade Alice Eaton, "Recent United States Department of Justice Actions in the Electric Utility Industry," *Connecticut Journal of International Law* 9 (Summer 1994): 865–866. See also James R. Atwood, "Antitrust, Joint Ventures, and Electric Utility Restructuring: RTGS and POOLCOS," 64 *Antitrust L.J.* 323 (Winter 1996).

[28] *Policy Statement Regarding Regional Transmission Groups*, FERC Stats. & Regs. ¶ 30,976, 30,869–72 FR 41,626 (August 5, 1993) (RTG Policy Statement).

[29] *Northwest Regional Transmission Association*, 69 FERC ¶ 61,099, *order on reh'g*, 69 FERC ¶ 61,352 (1994), *order on compliance filing*, 71 FERC ¶ 61,158 (1995), *order approving*, 71 FERC ¶ 61,397 (1995).

[30] *Southwest Regional Transmission Association*, 69 FERC ¶ 61,100 (1994).

[31] *Mid-Continent Area Power Pool*, 76 FERC ¶ 61,261 (1996).

The Commission initiated a notice of inquiry on alternative power-pooling institutions in 1994. A major focus of this inquiry was on power pooling to facilitate short-term transactions. FERC envisioned power pools operating spot markets while RTGs would focus on long-term and regional transmission planning. Anticipating the development of ISOs, FERC noted that the same institution could perform both functions.[32]

The initial impact of EPAct 1992 was to open up electricity markets for IPPs and utilities wishing to establish unregulated subsidiaries to generate and sell power. Many utilities began to issue request for proposals for power purchases as new suppliers provided a credible alternative to generation investment. Wholesale power bids fell as low as 3 cents per kWh on long-term contracts, based on low natural gas prices.[33] The Commission began to formulate policies to deal with the brave new world of power pools, NUGs, and EWGs. Utilities had begun to sell excess generation in bilateral deals and in power pools, but needed "rules of the road" that defined permissible prices in lieu of directly regulated rates. It was too complicated and time consuming to go to FERC every time a utility wanted to sell surplus power to a wholesale customer in order to determine a "just and reasonable" rate for the transaction.[34]

---

[32] *Inquiry Concerning Alternative Power Pooling Institutions Under the Federal Power Act*, FERC Stats. & Regs. ¶ 35,529, 35,715 (1994), 59 FR 54851 (November 2, 1994).

[33] Olof S. Nelson and Roger W. Sant, "Two IPP Points of View," *Public Utilities Fortnightly* (June 1, 1993): 62, 63; Charles M. Studness, "Estimating The Financial Cost of Utility Regulation," *Public Utilities Fortnightly* (November 1993).

[34] The phrase "just and reasonable," as determined by a string of Supreme Court decisions, provided the Commission with considerable discretion in exercising its judgment. There are some bounds to the Commission's discretion, as the lowest reasonable rate is one that is not confiscatory in the constitutional sense. *FPC v. Natural Gas Pipeline Co. et al.*, 315 U.S. 575, 585 (1942). However, the Supreme Court has refrained from otherwise defining what reasonable rates are:

The Constitution does not bind rate-making bodies to the service of any single formula or combination of formulas. Agencies to whom this legislative power has been delegated are free, within the ambit of their statutory authority, to make the pragmatic adjustments which may be called for by particular circumstances. Once a fair hearing has been given, proper findings made and other statutory requirements satisfied, the courts cannot intervene in the absence of a clear showing that the limits of due process have been overstepped.

Id. at 586.

There is a presumption in favor of cost-based ratemaking. "The [Natural Gas] Act was patterned after earlier regulatory statutes that applied to traditional public utilities and transportation companies, and that provided for setting rates equal to such companies' costs of service plus a reasonable rate of return." *Mobil Oil Corp. v. FPC et al.*, 417 U.S. 283, 301 (1974). Because the NGA and the FPA are similar in text and structure,

FERC had begun experimenting with rates for wholesale electricity transactions as early as 1983. In *Ocean State*, the Commission set forth its general approach to market transactions. The Commission can rely on market-oriented pricing for determining whether a rate is just and reasonable when a workably competitive market exists, or when the seller does not possess significant market power. A seller lacks significant market power if the seller is unable to increase prices by restricting supply or by denying the customer access to alternative sellers. Lack of market power is the key prerequisite for allowing market-oriented pricing.[35] Despite the assertion that the decision applied only to the specific circumstances presented by *Ocean State*, Commissioner Charles Trabandt pointed out that the decision established a new market pricing policy. The majority had adopted "marginal cost" pricing as the new ratemaking approach under the FPA, modeling it on the avoided cost methodology in section 210 of PURPA for qualifying facilities.[36] Trabandt prophetically asserted the need for adequate monitoring to ensure prompt Commission action if market forces are inadequate to constrain rates.[37]

The legal basis for relying on market-based rates was established in the Commission's natural gas proceedings. As long as FERC exercised its authority to assure that a market rate was just and reasonable, the Commission may rely on market-based prices in lieu of cost-of-service regulation to assure a "just and reasonable" result. However, the Commission must confirm that either there is no market power or that it has established a mechanism to monitor and check market power.[38] Where there is a competitive market, the Commission may rely on market-based rates in electricity markets.[39]

Once the Commission committed itself to permitting some sort of market-based ratemaking, it faced the requirement that it develop a

---

they are interpreted consistently. *Transmission Access Policy Study Group v. FERC*, 225 F. 3d 667, 686 (D.C. Cir. 2000) ("We have repeatedly recognized the similarity of the two statutes and held that they should be interpreted consistently.").

[35] *Ocean State Power*, 44 FERC ¶ 61,261, 61,979 (1988).

[36] *Ocean State Power*, 44 FERC ¶ 61,261, 61,988–89 (1988).

[37] *Ocean State Power*, 44 FERC ¶ 61,261, 61,993 (1988).

[38] *Farmers Union Central Exchange v. FERC*, 734 F.2d 1486, 1509–10 (D.C. Cir. 1984) (Market-based rates require that the regulatory scheme monitor to see if market forces result in competitive prices and check rates if they do not); *Tejas Power Corp. v. FERC*, 908 F.2d 998, 1004 (D.C. Cir. 1990) ("In a competitive market, where neither buyer nor seller has significant market power, it is rational to assume that the terms of their voluntary exchange are reasonable, and specifically to infer that the price is close to marginal cost, such that the seller makes only a normal return on its investment"); *Elizabethtown Gas Co. v. FERC*, 10 F.3d 866, 870 (1993).

[39] *Louisiana Energy and Power Authority v. FERC*, 141 F.3d 364, 365 (1998).

methodology for analyzing market power. At first, the Commission seemed uncertain, relying on an "I know it when I see it" approach:

> Our primary concern in a market power analysis is that customers have genuine alternatives to buying the seller's product. There are various methods of analyzing market power such as HHI determinations, market shares, concentration ratios, share of total generation capacity in the region, and potential entry by utility and nonutility generators. However, we do not believe that any one type of evidence is sufficient for this analysis, and we will not rely on any mechanical market share analysis to determine whether a firm has market power.[40]

The Commission required evidence as to whether the seller was a dominant firm in generation in the relevant market; whether the seller controlled transmission facilities that could be used by the buyer to reach alternative generation suppliers; and whether the seller was able to erect other barriers to entry.[41]

The FERC's increased willingness to accept competitive procurement was encouraged by the DOJ, which urged the FERC to approve negotiated rates rather than to impose rates for wholesale bulk power where purchasers have competitive alternatives. DOJ encouraged FERC to reconsider a decision it had reached disapproving a wholesale power contract because the DOJ Antitrust Department felt that eighty proposals totaling 2,697 MW from seventy-four generating units constituted a competitive market for a 30 MW purchase proposal.[42]

As long as market-based sales were on the margin, it really did not matter if FERC developed internal capabilities to analyze, monitor, and intervene in market transactions. However, as electricity markets developed, the lack of economic expertise inside of FERC would leave the agency incapable of dealing with the radically new environment. Sales of surplus electricity from and to IOUs where the bulk of generation and sales were executed under cost-based regulation could have little impact on prices and consumers. In organized electricity markets, any divergence from "just and reasonable" prices could have large impacts because a market price applied to all sales.

---

[40] *Public Service Company of Indiana, Inc.*, 51 FERC ¶ 61,367, 62,205 (1990).
[41] *Pacific Gas and Electric Company*, 53 FERC ¶ 61,145, 61,501 (1990).
[42] Eaton, "Recent United States Department of Justice Actions in the Electric Utility Industry," 858–59.

8

What Hath FERC Wrought?

The Clinton administration was provided with an opportunity to choose four commissioners in 1993 and chose a group of pro-competition candidates. The issue was more ideological than party oriented, as incumbent utilities often contributed to Republican candidates while pro-competition interests ranged from the hard right to Democratic Party supporters. Elizabeth Moler, the one incumbent since 1988, was named chair. Moler was championed by Senator Bennett Johnston (D-LA), chairman of the Senate Energy Committee.[1] The four new commissioners were Bill Massey,[2] Donald Santa,[3] James Hoecker,[4] and Vicky Bailey.[5] While

[1] Moler was senior counsel to the Senate Energy and Natural Resources Committee. She joined the Committee staff in 1976. Moler received her B.A. from the American University and her J.D. from George Washington University. James R. Pierobon, "The Well Soon Could Run Dry for Texas Representation on the FERC," *Houston Chronicle*, May 15, 1988, at http://www.chron.com/CDA/archives/archive.mpl/1988-543377/the-well-soon-could-run-dry-for-texas-representati.html.

[2] Massey served on the Clinton/Gore transition team for the Energy Department, and was a partner in the law firm of Mitchell, Williams, Selig, Gates & Woodyard. He was previously chief counsel and legislative director on the staff of Senator Dale Bumpers (D-AR). He held a B.A. from Oachita Baptist University, a J.D. from the University of Arkansas, and LLM from Georgetown University.

[3] Santa was counsel to the Senate Committee on Energy and Natural Resources since 1989. He was previously an attorney with Van Ness, Feldman, Sutcliffe & Curtis, and with Andrews & Kurth. Santa was a graduate of Duke University and of the Columbia University School of Law.

[4] Hoecker served as an attorney with FERC from 1979 to 1988. Of counsel to Jones, Day, Reavis & Pogue, Hoecker had a Ph.D. in History from the University of Kentucky and J.D. from the University of Wisconsin.

[5] Bailey was a commissioner of the Indiana Utility Regulatory Commission and served on the executive committee of NARUC. She was a graduate of Purdue University.

all five had regulatory experience, none had a background in economics, finance, or engineering.

FERC soon dealt with a number of transmission issues that would eventually coalesce into a more cohesive policy to implement the mandate of the EPAct 1992. These orders would provide an impetus to the formation of ISO led centralized electricity markets.

Historically, the Commission had permitted transmission rates to be calculated using the embedded cost of the integrated grid, including the rolled-in costs of any new facilities or upgrades. Rates were set on a "postage stamp" basis over a utility's transmission service area. Postage stamp rates do not vary based on the length of transmission provided. When a utility added new capacity to relieve a transmission constraint, the utility could charge a third party a rate based on the incremental cost of expansion. In situations in which a utility chose not to add new capacity, the Commission allowed the utility the option of charging a third party a rate based on opportunity costs (the increase in the utility's cost of servicing its native load when the utility accommodates a third-party request for transmission service) capped at the incremental cost of expansion. A utility could also charge for the costs associated with interconnecting a particular customer or building a line to the utility's transmission system.[6]

The Commission needed to revisit its transmission rate methodology in light of the EPAct 1992. Rates for transmission service had to meet the requirements of section 212(a) of the FPA, added by the Act. Such rates must allow the transmitting utility to recover all costs of providing transmission service, promote economically efficient transmission and generation of electricity, and be just and reasonable and not unduly discriminatory.[7]

In October 1993, FERC issued a proposed order under section 211, requiring Florida Power & Light to provide network transmission service under nondiscriminatory rates to the Florida Municipal Power Agency. This was the first time the Commission addressed a request for transmission service under sections 211 and 212 subsequent to the passage of EPAct 1992, and the Commission was aware that the order in this proceeding could establish binding precedent on these issues. FERC interpreted the public interest language of section 212 to require that service must be provided so long as the transmitting utility is fully and fairly

---

[6] FERC Stats. & Regs. ¶ 35,024, 35,162–63.
[7] FERC Stats. & Regs. ¶ 35,024, 35,164.

compensated and there is no unreasonable impairment of reliability. Florida Power's rates for this service must not be unduly discriminatory when compared to transmission rates for Florida Power's other customers.[8] This was the first step in imposing on the electricity industry the "comparability" standard FERC had adopted in the natural gas context.[9]

FERC clarified its new focus on discrimination in transmission rates and services. As a result of the emergence of nontraditional suppliers, undue discrimination had changed from discrimination in the treatment of different utility customers to discrimination in the rates and services the utility offered to third parties. An open-access tariff that is not unduly discriminatory or anticompetitive should offer third parties access on the same or comparable basis, and under the same or comparable terms and conditions, as the transmission provider's use of its system.[10] The Commission also held that it could not find any newly filed merger consistent with the public interest if the merging public utilities did not offer comparable transmission services to third parties. Comparable transmission access should, in general, adequately mitigate transmission market power.[11]

The Commission, after reviewing comments, issued a transmission rate policy statement in October 1994.[12] FERC formulated five principles to guide approval of pricing for both firm and non-firm transmission services:

1. *Transmission Pricing Must Meet the Traditional Revenue Requirement.* A utility must allocate costs in a manner that reflects the costs of providing transmission service.
2. *Transmission Pricing Must Reflect Comparability.* Any new transmission pricing proposal must meet the comparability standard.
3. *Transmission Pricing Should Promote Economic Efficiency.* Transmission pricing should promote efficient expansion of transmission

---

[8] *Florida Power & Light Co.*, 65 FERC ¶ 61,125, 61,612–15 (1993).

[9] *ANR Pipeline Co.*, 56 FERC ¶ 61,293, at 62,205 (1991) (requiring pipeline to offer natural gas transportation service customers transportation service comparable to firm sales customers).

[10] *American Electric Power Service Corporation*, 67 FERC ¶ 61,168, 61,490 (1994).

[11] *El Paso Electric Company and Central and Southwest Services Inc.*, 68 FERC ¶ 61,181 61,914–15 (1994), *dismissed*, 72 FERC ¶ 61,292 (1995).

[12] *Inquiry Concerning the Commission's Pricing Policy for Transmission Services Provided by Public Utilities Under the Federal Power Act; Policy Statement*, FERC Stats. & Regs. ¶ 31,005 (1994), 59 FR 55031 (November 3, 1994).

capacity, location of new generators, and allocation of constrained capacity through appropriate market clearing mechanisms, and efficient dispatch of generation. To the extent practicable, transmission rates should reflect marginal costs.

4. *Transmission Pricing Should Promote Fairness.* Existing wholesale, retail, and transmission customers should not pay for the costs of providing transmission services to third parties, and third-party transmission customers should not subsidize existing customers.

5. *Transmission Pricing Should Be Practical.* A user should be able to calculate how much it will be charged for transmission service. Complex pricing proposals should be balanced by efficiency gains or other advantages produced by such complexity.[13]

In the spring of 1995, the Commission issued a NOPR concerning open-access transmission and stranded cost recovery[14] (which became known as the mega-NOPR) and issued a NOPR on information systems in December.[15] The Commission had come to realize that its section 211 authority alone was not enough to eliminate undue discrimination. The significant time delays involved in filing a request for bilateral service under section 211 placed the transmission customer at a severe competitive disadvantage. It was an inadequate procedural substitute for service under a filed nondiscriminatory open access tariff. The Commission was also reacting to a growing volume of competitive electricity sales, creating pressure to permit wholesale customers access to third-party suppliers. Competitive bidding for new generation resources since 1984 resulted in more than 350 projects selected to supply 20,000 MW, and 126 were online producing almost 7,800 MW of power. Electricity consumers were demanding access to newer, lower-cost generation resources.[16]

In the year after the proposed rules were issued, the pace of competitive changes in the electric utility industry continued to accelerate. By April

---

[13] FERC Stats. & Regs. ¶ 31,005, 31,141–44.

[14] *Promoting Wholesale Competition Through Open-Access Non-Discriminatory Transmission Service by Public Utilities and Recovery of Stranded Costs by Public Utilities and Transmitting Utilities, Notice of Proposed Rulemaking and Supplemental Notice of Proposed Rulemaking,* FERC Stats. & Regs. ¶ 32,514 (1995), 60 FR 17662 (April 7, 1995). Previously, FERC had addressed stranded costs in *Recovery of Stranded Costs by Public Utilities and Transmitting Utilities,* FERC Stats. & Regs. ¶ 32,507 (1994), 59 FR 35274 (July 11, 1994), as well as the Transmission Pricing Policy Statement, RTG Policy Statement and the Pooling Notice of Inquiry.

[15] Real-Time Information Networks and Standards of Conduct, Notice of Proposed Rulemaking, FERC Stats. & Regs. ¶ 32,516 (1995), 60 FR 66182 (December 21, 1995).

[16] FERC Stats. & Regs. ¶ 32,514, 33,069–75.

1996, 106 of the approximately 166 public utilities that owned, controlled, or operated transmission facilities used in interstate commerce filed some form of wholesale open-access tariff. Numerous states were considering retail customer choice programs or other utility-restructuring alternatives. In response to these changes, and after extensive hearings (including 20,000 pages of comments), the FERC adopted two major sets of rules in 1996: Order 888[17] and Order 889.[18]

Order 888 required all transmission owners to file with FERC pro forma nondiscriminatory open-access transmission tariffs (OATTs) that transmission service customers could rely on to define the terms and conditions of transmission services. Order 888 specified the types of transmission services that must be made available, the maximum prices that can be charged for these services, the definition of ATC and how it should be allocated when there is excess demand for transmission, the specification of ancillary services that transmission owners must provide, requirements for reforms to power-pooling arrangements to comply with Order 888, and provisions for stranded cost recovery.

The Commission required functional unbundling of wholesale services. A utility must state separate rates for wholesale generation, transmission, and ancillary services and rely on the same electronic information network as its transmission customers. Functional unbundling also required a code of conduct, and the requirement to separate employees involved in transmission functions from those involved in wholesale power merchant functions. Adoption of this code of conduct was discussed in detail in Order 889. FERC was not prepared to require corporate unbundling absent evidence that functional unbundling would not work.[19]

The Commission noted that its authority under sections 205 and 206 of the FPA permitted it only to require public utilities to file open-access

---

[17] *Promoting Wholesale Competition Through Open Access Non-discriminatory Transmission Services by Public Utilities; Recovery of Stranded Costs by Public Utilities and Transmitting Utilities*, Order No. 888, FERC Stats. & Regs. ¶ 31,036 (1996), 61 FR 21540 (May 10, 1996), *order on reh'g*, Order No. 888-A, FERC Stats. & Regs. ¶ 31,048 (1997), 62 FR 12274 (March 14, 1997), *order on reh'g*, Order No. 888-B, 81 FERC ¶ 61,248 (1997), *order on reh'g*, Order No. 888-C, 82 FERC ¶ 61,046 (1998), *aff'd in relevant part sub nom. Transmission Access Policy Study Group v. FERC*, 225 F.3d 667 (D.C. Cir. 2000), *aff'd sub nom. New York v. FERC*, 535 U.S. 1 (2002).

[18] *See Open Access Same-Time Information System and Standards of Conduct*, Order No. 889, FERC Stats. & Regs. ¶ 31,035 at 31,588–91 (1996), 61 FR 21,737 (April 24 1996), *order on reh'g*, Order No. 889-A, FERC Stats. & Regs. ¶ 31,049 (1997), 62 FR 12484 (March 4, 1997), *order on reh'g*, Order No. 889-B, 81 FERC ¶ 61,253 (1997), *order on reh'g*, Order No. 889-C, 82 FERC ¶ 61,046 (1998).

[19] Order 888 at 31,654–56.

tariffs. However, FERC established a reciprocity requirement that called for municipal power authorities or federal power marketing administrations that receive transmission service under a FERC jurisdictional tariff to offer the same access to other transmission service customers.[20]

The Commission determined in Order 888 that it must address stranded costs. FERC limited the opportunity to seek stranded cost recovery under the Rule primarily to two discrete situations: (1) costs associated with customers under wholesale requirements contracts executed on or before July 11, 1994 ("existing wholesale requirements contracts") that do not contain an explicit stranded cost provision; and (2) costs associated with retail-turned-wholesale customers. Order 888 provided an opportunity to recover stranded costs from a departing customer if the utility could demonstrate that it incurred costs to provide service to the customer based on a reasonable expectation of continuing service beyond the contract term.[21]

Firm transmission customers, including network customers, were allowed to retain their rights to firm capacity even if they did not use that capacity, since they had paid for the option to use that capacity. Firm transmission customers remain obligated to pay the utility a reservation charge that covered the utility's fixed costs associated with the reserved capacity. The utility was free to schedule and sell any unscheduled firm point-to-point transmission capacity on a non-firm basis. Where a transmission customer retained capacity to block entry, relief was available under section 206 of the FPA.[22]

The Commission concluded that all firm transmission customers, upon the expiration of their contracts or when their contracts become subject to renewal or rollover, should have the right to continue to take firm transmission service. The contract must have been for a term of at least one year and the existing customer must match a rate offered, including contract length, by another potential customer. This right of first refusal was an ongoing right that could be exercised at the end of all firm contract terms.[23] Utilities could reserve existing transmission capacity needed for reasonably forecasted native load growth and network transmission customer load growth. However, reserved capacity that was not currently needed must be posted on the Open Access Same-time Information System

---

[20] Order 888 at 31,691.
[21] Order 888-A at 30,346–48.
[22] Order 888 at 31,693.
[23] Order 888 at 31,665.

(OASIS) and made available until such time as it is actually needed and used.[24]

FERC required that six ancillary services be provided or offered to transmission customers:[25]

1. *Scheduling, System Control, and Dispatch Service* (Transmission Provider must provide and Transmission Customer must purchase from Transmission Provider);[26]

2. *Reactive Supply and Voltage Control from Generation Sources Service* (Transmission Provider must provide and Transmission Customer must purchase from Transmission Provider);[27]

3. *Regulation and Frequency Response Service* (Transmission Provider must offer only to Transmission Customers serving load in the Transmission Provider's control area and Transmission Customers must acquire, from the Transmission Provider, a third party, or self-supply);[28]

4. *Energy Imbalance Service* (Transmission Provider must offer only to Transmission Customers serving load in Transmission Provider's control area and Transmission Customers must acquire);[29]

5. *Operating Reserve – Spinning Reserve Service* (Transmission Provider must offer only to Transmission Customers serving load in Transmission Provider's control area and Transmission Customers must acquire);[30]

---

[24] Order 888 at 31,694.
[25] Order 888 at 31,703–04. FERC adopted NERC's recommendations for definitions and descriptions with modifications.
[26] Order 888 at 31,706.
[27] The Commission accepted NERC's identification of two ways of supplying reactive power and controlling voltage. One is to install facilities, usually capacitors, as part of the transmission system. Costs of these facilities were considered part of the cost of basic transmission service. The second is to use generating facilities to supply reactive power and voltage control, which was considered to be an ancillary service that must be unbundled from basic transmission service. Because customers have some control over reactive power requirements, the Commission required that reactive supply and voltage control service be offered as a discrete service, and to the extent feasible, charged for on the basis of the amount required. Order 888 at 31,706–07.
[28] Order 888 at 31,707.
[29] Order 888 at 31,708. The transmission customer's service agreement with the transmission provider should identify the party responsible for supplying real power loss. If a transmission provider does not charge for transmission used to supply losses for its own wholesale power sales and purchases, it may not charge others for these losses. Order 888 at 31,709.
[30] Order 888 at 31,708.

6. *Operating Reserve – Supplemental Reserve Service* (Transmission Provider must offer only to Transmission Customers serving load in Transmission Provider's control area and Transmission Customers must acquire).[31]

The obligation to plan for power restoration capability is a system control area function that rests with the operator of the control area. Therefore, there was no reason to require a transmission provider to provide black start capability[32] to transmission customers. Restoration planning and contracting for black start services is intrinsic to basic transmission service and included in its cost.[33]

Order 888 directly addressed power pools, ISOs, or other coordination arrangements, requiring removal of preferential transmission access and pricing provisions from agreements. The filing of open-access tariffs by the public utility members of a power pool was not sufficient to cure undue discrimination in transmission in a power pool. Although the Commission did not require power pools to form an ISO, FERC suggested that ISOs might be an effective means for providing comparable access through operational unbundling.[34] An ISO, acting as a control area operator, was considered a transmission operator subject to FERC jurisdiction, and as such, the ISO's operating standards and procedures must be approved by the Commission.

The Commission also established rules for public utility holding companies that were not part of power pools, moving their operations closer to that of a unified system. Holding company member utilities were required to file a single system-wide pro forma tariff permitting transmission service across the entire holding company system at a single price.[35] This prevented these companies from using multiple transmission tariffs to create barriers to entry, since even with comparable tariffs, the subsidiaries would be paying each other for transmission services, allowing cross-subsidization while blocking potential competition.

---

[31] Supplemental reserve is available within a short period (usually ten minutes). Order 888 at 31,708.

[32] When the system goes down, generators need to be able to supply auxiliary energy to restart their facilities, usually from batteries or small diesel generators on site. Once a few "Black Start" generators are up and running, the control area operator powers up other generators to restore the electrical system to full capability.

[33] Order 888 at 31,711–12.

[34] Order 888 at 31,726–27.

[35] Order 888 at 31,728.

FERC developed a pro forma OATT that included specific terms and conditions. The Commission intended to foster broad access across multiple systems under standardized terms and conditions by requiring a standardized tariff. The tariff provided for deviations where it could be demonstrated that unique practices in a geographic region required modifications to tariff provisions. Establishment of a general template reduced transactions costs for independent power producers and power marketers operating in multiple regions. It also simplified FERC's oversight task.

The most complicated tariff issue that Order 888 tried to resolve was the interplay between control of transmission capacity and the allocation of transmission costs. Utilities wanted to reserve capacity for the current and future requirements of their native load customers, who they had an obligation to serve, but charge third parties a similar rate for short-term transmission capacity, an inferior product. Customers wanted to reserve the right to short-term firm service during peak periods while avoiding paying the long-term costs of the system. The Final Rule pro forma tariff provided that reservations for short-term firm point-to-point service (less than one year) would be conditional until one day before the commencement of daily service, one week before the commencement of weekly service, and one month before the commencement of monthly service.[36]

Order 889, issued at the same time as Order 888, required each public utility or its agent (e.g., a power pool) that owns, controls, or operates facilities used for the transmission of electric energy in interstate commerce to create or participate in an OASIS. This system must provide information, by electronic means, regarding available transmission capacity, prices, and other information that will enable transmission service customers to obtain open access nondiscriminatory transmission service in a time frame necessary to support power transactions. Entities subject to this rule were to have a basic OASIS in operation by November 1, 1996.[37]

Order 889 also required public utilities to implement standards of conduct to functionally separate transmission and unregulated wholesale power merchant functions to prevent preferential access to information about the transmission network. Utilities must also make the same terms (e.g., service price discounts) available to third parties as they do to their wholesale power marketing affiliates. All discounts provided

[36] Order 888 at 31,746.
[37] Order 889 at 31,590–91.

to any transmission customer must be posted within twenty-four hours after the agreement is entered. The standards of conduct required that transmission-related information must be made available to all customers through OASIS postings available at the same time and on an equal basis. Transmission providers were required to post prices and a summary of the terms and conditions of transmission products. Employees of transmission providers and any affiliates were prohibited from disclosing (or obtaining) nonpublic transmission-related information through communications not posted on the OASIS. In addition, transmission providers were required to provide a downloadable file of their complete tariffs. Transmission providers were required to post on the OASIS information about all ancillary services provided or offered to customers.[38]

The proposed regulations defined the paths for which ATC and total transmission capability (TTC) must be posted. A transmission path becomes a "posted path" in one of three ways. First, ATC and TTC must be posted for any path between two control areas. Second, posting is required for any path for which transmission service has been denied, curtailed, or subject to interruption in the last twelve months. Finally, transmission customers can request that ATC and TTC be posted for other transmission paths. Since formal methods to calculate ATC and TTC did not exist, the Commission deferred to NERC regarding the development of a consistent, industry-wide method of calculation, subject to FERC approval. Planning studies of the transmission network performed by the transmission provider would be posted on the OASIS, as well as the details of the calculations of ATC and TTC. This information can be voluminous, so final transmission studies would be made available on request in electronic format. A list of available studies was to be posted on the OASIS.[39]

OASIS became operational on January 3, 1997, and reached 167 transmission providers. It was developed on an accelerated schedule, going from concept in August 1995 to an operational network of computers seventeen months later. OASIS was one of the first large-scale uses of the Internet for business-to-business commerce across North America. It was designed through an open, consensus-based process with representation from both users and providers. Not surprisingly, there were numerous complaints by customers that the systems did not provide reliable information, problems with the computer-to-computer protocols and

[38] Order 889 at 31,603, 31,609.
[39] Order 889 at 31,604–08.

graphical displays, and inconsistencies among transmission providers, some of whom were less than cooperative in assisting OASIS customers. Inadequate Internet provider services and database software running on the OASIS node servers resulted in computer and communication delays. The volume of customer and provider interactions slowed the response time of some nodes and even crippled several nodes in the first two months of operation. Upgrades were made to larger and faster computers, but node performance continued to be a cause for concern.[40] As Internet and computer technology advanced, many of these issues were resolved.

OASIS-related business practice implementation details were left for transmission providers to determine. This flexibility resulted in significant variation among business practices across OASIS nodes.[41] The Commission responded to complaints about transmission provider operation of OASIS with a new rulemaking to implement a set of uniform business practices to improve interactions between transmission providers and customers. The proposed business practices were divided between mandatory standards and voluntary best-practice guides. Industry proposals, accompanied by public comment, evolved into the NOPR, and the final rule. The Commission adopted the set of business practices in Order 636, issued in February 2000.[42]

A number of petitions for review of Orders 888 and 889 were consolidated and transferred to the DC circuit court. The DC Circuit, acknowledging the precedent set by *Associated Gas Distributors*,[43] and relying on *Chevron*[44] deference to FERC's interpretation of FPA §§ 205 and 206, found that the Commission had the authority to require open access as a generic remedy to prevent undue discrimination.[45] The Supreme Court tacitly accepted the Appellate Court's decision.[46] The Court affirmed FERC's jurisdiction to order unbundling of wholesale transactions, as

---

[40] Commercial Practices Working Group and OASIS How Working Group, "Industry Report to the Federal Energy Regulatory Commission on the Future of OASIS," October 31, 1997.

[41] *Open Access Same-Time Information System and Standards of Conduct, Notice of Proposed Rulemaking*, FERC Stats. & Regs. ¶ 32,539, 33,607–08 (1999), 64 FR 5206 (February 3, 1999).

[42] *Open Access Same-Time Information System and Standards of Conduct*, Order 636, FERC Stats. & Regs. ¶ 31,093, 31,398–99 (2000), 65 FR 17370 (March 31, 2000).

[43] *Associated Gas Distributors v. FERC*, 824 F.2d 981, 998 (D.C. Cir. 1987).

[44] *Chevron U.S.A. Inc. v. Natural Resources Defense Council*, 467 U.S. 837 (1984).

[45] *Transmission Access Policy Study Group v. FERC*, 225 F.3d 667, 686–87 (D.C. Cir. 2000).

[46] *New York et al. v. FERC*, 531 U.S. 1, 16 (2002).

well as to regulate the unbundled transmissions of electricity retailers.[47] The majority opinion held that if FERC were to investigate and make findings concerning undue discrimination in the retail electricity market, § 206 of the FPA would require FERC to provide a remedy for that discrimination.[48] Justice Thomas, joined by Scalia and Kennedy, went further, suggesting that FERC should be required to engage in reasoned decision making to determine whether there is undue discrimination with respect to transmission associated with retail bundled sales, and if so, what remedy is appropriate.[49]

Shortly after the adoption of Order 888, NERC recognized that contract path scheduling created incentives to overload the electric network system. In early 1997, NERC formed a Security Coordinator Subcommittee in response to numerous transmission line overloads in the Eastern Interconnection caused largely by parallel flows. NERC adopted transmission loading relief (TLR) protocols to protect the physical integrity of the grid when contracted flows exceeded transmission capacity. In essence, NERC created an ad hoc administrative unscheduling system to counteract the effects of the FERC-mandated scheduling system.[50]

TLR protocols relieve congestion in a hierarchical fashion. If a transmission-owning utility is forced to call a TLR event, the holders of non-firm transmission service rights are curtailed first, followed by holders of firm transmission service. Thus, a utility calling a TLR event essentially voids the purchase/sale contract involved in the wheeling transaction. Aggregate data collected by NERC indicated that most TLR events were called in the Midwestern and Mid-Atlantic portions of the Eastern Interconnect.[51] The TLR rules were inefficient, easily gamed, and exposed customers to paying unnecessarily high prices for electricity under transmission congestion conditions.[52]

NERC asked that the Commission address the interrelationship of the proposed TLR procedures with the pro forma OATT. The Commission

[47] *New York et al. v. FERC*, 531 U.S. 1, 23–24 (2002).

[48] *New York et al. v. FERC*, 531 U.S. 1, 27 (2002).

[49] *New York et al. v. FERC*, 531 U.S. 1, 41–42 (2002). In effect, the most conservative members of the Court were inviting FERC to extend its authority to retail electricity sales.

[50] William Hogan, "Electricity Market Restructuring: Reforms of Reforms," paper presented at the 20th Annual Conference, Center for Research in Regulated Industries (May 25, 2001): 8.

[51] Seth Blumsack, "Network Topologies and Transmission Investment Under Electric-Industry Restructuring" (Ph.D. Diss., Carnegie Mellon University, 2006): 14–15.

[52] Fernando Alvarado and Rajesh Rajaraman, "The Best Game in Town: NERC's TLR Rules," IEEE Winter Meeting, 1999, Tutorial on Game Theory.

concluded that the TLR procedures were being used for routine congestion management, and approaches to curtailment should be developed
concurrently with procedures to avoid curtailment through redispatch.
The Commission required filing of both interim TLR procedures and
interim redispatch solutions by March 1, 1999.[53] The Commission also
encouraged innovative market approaches to avoid constraints and/or
ensure that curtailment is accomplished in an efficient and nondiscriminatory manner. NERC's TLR Procedure was further revised in 1999,[54]
2000,[55] and 2005.[56] In October 2005, the Commission approved Version 1.[57] On November 30, 2006, the Commission conditionally accepted
NERC's revised Version 3 TLR Procedure.[58] No matter how much they
were adjusted, TLRs remained an inferior solution to a real congestion
management system.

One immediate impact of Order 888 was a sudden jump in merger
applications, as utilities maneuvered to restructure themselves for the
coming competitive market place. After Order 888 was issued, more
than forty applications were filed for Commission approval of proposed
mergers, including a number of electric and natural gas company mergers. The FERC responded by revising its merger policy guidelines in 1996,
incorporating the Federal Trade Commission/Department of Justice 1992
Horizontal Merger Guidelines into its merger policy.[59] The Commission's merger policy was further updated in 2000, but without significant
changes in its methodology for determining market power in its merger
analysis.[60]

A number of trends in electricity markets soon made the measures incorporated in Order 888 inadequate to deal with emerging
wholesale and retail electricity markets. Between August 1997 and
January 2000, generating facilities representing approximately 50,000
MW of generating capacity were sold by utilities, and an additional

[53] *North American Electric Reliability Council*, 85 FERC ¶ 61,353 (1998), *reh'g denied*,
     87 FERC ¶ 61,161 (1999).
[54] *North American Electric Reliability Council*, 88 FERC ¶ 61,046 (1999); *North American
     Electric Reliability Council*, 89 FERC ¶ 61,031 (1999).
[55] *North American Electric Reliability Council*, 91 FERC ¶ 61,122 (2000).
[56] *North American Electric Reliability Council*, 110 FERC ¶ 61,388 (2005).
[57] *North American Electric Reliability Council*, 113 FERC ¶ 61,013 (2005).
[58] *North American Electric Reliability Council*, 113 FERC ¶ 61,248 (2006).
[59] *Inquiry Concerning the Commission's Merger Policy Under the Federal Power Act:
     Policy Statement*, Order No. 592, FERC Stats. & Regs. ¶ 31,044 (1996), 61 FR 68,595
     (1996), *reconsideration denied*, Order No. 592-A, 79 FERC ¶ 61,321 (1997), 62 FR 33,
     34 (1997) (Policy Statement).
[60] *Revised Filing Requirements Under Part 33 of the Commission's Regulations*, Order
     No. 642, FERC Statutes and Regulations ¶ 31,111 (2000), 65 FR 70,983 (2000).

30,000 MW was offered for sale – more than 10 percent of U.S. generating capacity. There was significant growth in the volume of trading, and particularly in the number of marketers, in the wholesale electricity market.

FERC initially responded to the growing volume of electricity transactions by development of a market-based pricing policy in which FERC routinely required wholesale transmission access as a condition to approval of market-based rates. FERC then announced that for sales from new generating capacity, there was no need for the Commission to focus on whether the seller had market power in generation, as long as the seller demonstrated that it did not have transmission market power and did not control other barriers to entry. The prospect of entry by other suppliers would check the seller's ability to sustain monopoly prices. However, sales from existing capacity would still have to pass a more stringent test.[61] The Commission granted market-based rate authority to more than 800 entities, of which nearly 500 were power marketers (including more than 100 marketers affiliated with IOUs).[62]

The extension of the filed rate doctrine to market-based rates[63] would become a serious problem as power pools morphed into centralized electricity markets and independent power proliferated. FERC based market-based rate authority on simplistic analyses of sales on the margin, and simply was not prepared to analyze the operation of electricity markets. Granting market-based rates would block application of the Clayton Act or the Sherman Act. *Keogh* established the principle that a filed rate precluded the right to private antitrust action.[64] Subsequent cases affirmed

[61] *Kansas City Power & Light Co.*, 67 FERC ¶ 61,183, 61,552–53 (1994).

[62] *Regional Transmission Organizations*, Order No. 2000, FERC Stats. & Regs. ¶ 31,089, 30,997 (1999), 65 FR 809 (January 6, 2000).

[63] *Town of Norwood, Mass. v. New England Power Co.*, 202 F.3d 408, 419 (1st Cir. 2000) (It is the *filing* of the tariffs, and not any affirmative approval or scrutiny by the agency, that triggers the filed rate doctrine); *Utilimax.com, Inc. v. PPL Energy Plus, LLC*, 378 F.3d 303, 306 (3rd Cir. 2004) (Under the filed rate doctrine, a plaintiff may not sue the supplier of electricity based on rates that, though alleged to be the result of anticompetitive conduct, were filed with the federal agency responsible for overseeing such rates.); *Public Utility District No. 1 of Snohomish County v. Dynegy Power Marketing, Inc.*, 384 F.3d 756, 762 (9th Cir. 2004) (FERC approved tariffs that governed the California wholesale electricity markets. Therefore, if the prices in those markets were not just and reasonable or if the defendants sold electricity in violation of the filed tariffs, Snohomish's only option is to seek a remedy before FERC.); *Texas Commercial Energy v. TXU Energy*, Inc., 413 F.3d 503, 509 (5th Cir. 2005) (PUCT's oversight over the market is sufficient to conclude that the BES energy rates are "filed" within the meaning of the filed rate doctrine.).

[64] *Keogh v. Chicago & N.W. Ry. Co.*, 260 U.S. 156, 163 (1922).

that holding,[65] and despite some misgivings, the Supreme Court refused to overturn it.[66]

Price spikes in the Midwest soon exposed FERC's lack of preparation for the new market environment. From June 22 to June 24, more than twenty Midwestern and Canadian nuclear and coal units were down either due to planned maintenance or forced outages caused by a storm. During this period, unexpected hot weather hit the Midwest and the eastern United States. As a result, demand was higher than the level of all available generation. Some market participants had bought call options for energy at low prices around $50/MWh, and when prices rose to much higher levels, those parties exercised their option contracts to meet their needs. Unfortunately, some of the option sellers failed to meet their contract obligations to provide physical capacity or generation. On June 25, prices hit the limit of $1,500/MW as a result of the loss of a FirstEnergy nuclear plant caused by tornado damage. When the news spread, participants who expected prices to increase to much higher levels rushed to buy as much power as they could. Springfield announced that it would not perform on its options, which led prices to increase sharply to $7,500/MWh in real-time trading and $4,900/MWh for prescheduled power, compared with an average price for the summer of approximately $40/MWh. These severe price spikes caused several utilities to spend tens of millions of dollars on replacement power. Customers were initially unaffected by the price run-up because retail rates were regulated in the Midwestern states, but the costs would eventually be rolled into rates.[67]

This experience led to calls for price caps, allegations of market power, and a questioning of the effectiveness of open-access transmission and wholesale electric competition. A report by the Commission's Staff concluded that the unusually high price levels were caused by a combination of factors, particularly above-average generation outages, unseasonably hot temperatures, storm-related transmission outages, transmission constraints, poor communication of price signals, contract defaults, and inexperience in dealing with competitive markets.[68]

---

[65] *Wah Chang v. Duke Energy Trading and Marketing, LLC*, 507 F.3d 1222, 1225–26 (9th Cir. 2007).

[66] *Square D Co. v. Niagara Frontier Tariff Bureau, Inc.*, 476 U.S. 409 (1986); *MCI Telecommunications Corp. v. AT & T Co.*, 512 U.S. 218, 234 (1994).

[67] Mohammad Shahidehpour and Muwaffaq Alomoush, *Restructured Electrical Power Systems: Operation, Trading, and Volatility* (New York, Marcel Dekker, Inc., 2001): 290–91.

[68] *Staff Report to the Federal Energy Regulatory Commission on the Causes of Wholesale Electric Pricing Abnormalities in the Midwest During June 1998* (Sept. 22, 1998) (Staff Price Spike Report).

FERC also had to deal with complaints from newly independent affiliates and independent power producers that incumbent utilities were using control of their grid to discriminate in favor of their own generation. Distribution companies claimed they were being blocked from access to third-party generation.[69] A key issue was the calculation of ATC. Capacity benefit margin is transmission capability reserved by load serving entities (LSEs) to ensure access to electricity to supply captive load. NERC has broad guidelines for calculating capacity benefit margin, but left the calculations to the discretion of LSEs.[70] Capacity benefit margin was a key component in the computation of ATC. ATC indicates how much additional transmission capability is available. The greater the ATC along a transmission path, the more power can be shipped to potential customers.[71]

FERC required transmission owners to calculate ATC continuously for their transmission paths and to post this information on their OASIS. FERC lacked the resources to effectively monitor ATC calculations and relied on market participants to initiate and prosecute challenges to incumbent transmission owners. Transmission providers manipulated ATC and "native-load preference," creating entry barriers for competitive wholesale suppliers. Transmission providers had an incentive to favor their own regulated units (additional revenues meant additional profits until the next rate case, and conversely, if outside supply exposed some generation units as uneconomic, there could be a "used and useful question") as well as "independent affiliates" (transmission employees know the profits flow up to the holding company, and holding company executives have indirect authority over their bosses).

The combination of TLR calls and the ability to override the transmission limit settings provided flexibility in adjusting dispatch and flows over the transmission provider's system. Compliance relied on self-enforcement of the rules in Order 888 and subsequent regulatory rulings, but evidence of rule violations was difficult to assemble and verify. Requests for firm service were frequently rejected a day ahead, when there would be a large amount of capacity available the next day. This allowed transmission to remain available for the provider's affiliated generation taking non-firm service, and foreclosed competing generators as

---

[69] *Aquila Power Corporation v. Entergy Services.* FERC Docket No. EL98-36-000.
[70] Narasimha Rao and Richard Tabors, "Transmission Markets: Stretching the Rules for Fun and Profit," *Electricity Journal* (June 2000): 22.
[71] *Order Clarifying Methodology for Computing Available Transmission Capability,* 88 FERC ¶ 61,099.

traders would have committed that capacity to other markets. Suspicious TLR calls also seemed to block entry by competing generation to certain markets.[72]

NERC attempted to fashion reliability requirements to fit a more competitive electric power industry. Various NERC committees considered ways to improve the tracking of power transactions, identify the network impacts of transactions, and reflect the actual flow of power over the network when making reservations for transmission service.[73] However, NERC still represented the interests of its utility members. A FERC staffer circulated a memo pointing out the difficulty of obtaining NERC data to check for price manipulation. The response to a request for supply and demand data for the price spikes of June 1998 was limited by NERC to one week of data. Although seventy-six utilities, regional councils, and other entities had real access to data, a request by FERC for access to real data on generation and transmission was denied. Data for examining the price spikes of the last week in July 1999 did not arrive at FERC until December 1999, mostly in hardcopy format. Conversely, a middle-of-the-night reliability event that affected a relatively small number of people got NERC to produce a quick and thorough analysis by more than fifty people. NERC's attitude was that FERC should let the experts at NERC sift through and analyze the data and provide information to FERC. FERC did not have NERC's staff or capabilities to evaluate data, and, by implication, FERC should not develop such capabilities.[74] It would take more shocks to the system to motivate the Commission to put its foot down and regulate instead of conciliate.

---

[72] Narasimha Rao and Richard Tabors, "Transmission Markets: Stretching the Rules for Fun and Profit," *Electricity Journal* (June 2000): 23–25.

[73] Order 888-A at 30,195.

[74] Ron Rattey, *Open Memorandum, To FERC Staff*, June 2, 2000, at http://www.mresearch.com/pdfs/202.pdf (last visited June 25, 2011). The memo was widely circulated among FERC staff, and soon leaked out, creating pressure on senior executives at FERC to take more forceful action. NERA's June 2000 *Global Energy Regulation* cited a June 19, 2000, *Natural Gas Intelligence* mention of the memo, at http://www.nera.com/extImage/4019.pdf.

9

Reorganization on the Eve of Deregulation

At the end of 1992, vertically integrated, investor-owned utilities (IOUs) dominated the industry. The makeup of this traditional sector was split between 262 IOUs[1] (79 percent of utility electricity generation), 2,017 publicly owned utilities[2] (8 percent of electricity generation), 943 cooperatives[3] (5 percent of electricity generation), and 10 federally owned facilities[4] (8 percent of electricity generation).

[1] Actual control of the industry was far more centralized because about one-quarter of these utility operating companies were subsidiaries of nine electric utility holding companies regulated under PUHCA. The registered utility holding companies were: Allegheny Power System, Inc., AEP, Central and South West Corp. (CSW), Eastern Utilities Associates, General Public Utilities Corp., Middle South Utilities (Entergy), New England Electric System (NEES), Northeast Utilities, and The Southern Company. By 1999, additional major holding companies included Alliant Energy, Ameren, CINergy, Conectiv, New Century Energies, and PECO Energy.

[2] Local, municipal, state, and regional public power systems range from tiny municipal distribution companies to the Power Authority of the State of New York. Municipal systems are usually run by the local city council or an independent board elected by voters or appointed by city officials. Other public systems are typically run by public utility districts (PUDs), irrigation districts, or special state authorities. Many public systems are involved only in retail power distribution.

[3] Rural electric cooperatives are owned by their members, each of whom has one vote in the election of a board of directors. Congress created the Rural Electrification Administration in 1935 and subsequently gave it broad lending authority to stimulate rural electricity use. Cooperatives have access to low-cost government-sponsored financing through the Rural Electrification Administration, the Federal Financing Bank, and the Bank for Cooperatives. Most cooperatives are small distribution companies that purchase their power from generation and transmission cooperatives. The generation and transmission cooperatives tend to be owned by their member distribution cooperatives. Both government and cooperative utilities receive implicit subsidies owing to exemption from taxation and access to below-market cost of capital.

[4] The federal government is primarily a wholesaler of electric power produced at federally owned hydroelectric facilities operated by the Bureau of Reclamation and the U.S.

TABLE 9.1. *Selected Electric Utility Data by Ownership, 1992*

Type of Utility	Number	Number of Consumers (Millions)	Capacity (GW)	Net Electricity Generation (1000 GWH)	Electricity Sales (1000 GWH)
Investor Owned	262	85.8	573.0	2,214	2,112
Publicly Owned	2,017	15.5	76.5	231	395
Federal	10	0.0	66.1	225	49
Cooperative	943	12.0	26.1	127	207
Total	3,232	113.3	741.7	2,797	2,763

Source: EIA, *Financial Impacts of Nonutility Power Purchases on Investor-Owned Electric Utilities* (June 1994): 9, table 3.

The privately owned utilities began diverging in their business strategies in the 1980s, which led to fissures in their former opposition to competitive markets. Dissatisfaction with the results of traditional rate-of-return regulation in a slow-growth environment led some companies to see deregulation as an opportunity, rather than a threat. A majority of IOUs began to diversify their business interests by investing revenues in potentially more profitable business ventures outside the electric utility business. Most of this investment was in related industries, such as coal mining, telecommunications, oil and gas extraction, natural gas production and distribution, and steam and air conditioning supply.[5] Salomon Brothers found that 58 of the 100 utilities it followed diversified or intended to diversify, including 24 that formed holding companies during the decade. As one means of implementing their new business strategies, utilities adopted a variety of financial restructuring measures

Army Corps of Engineers. Power is marketed through five federal marketing agencies: Bonneville Power Administration, Western Area Power Administration, Southeastern Power Administration, Southwestern Power Administration, and Alaska Power Administration. The Tennessee Valley Authority is an independent government corporation. Federal power systems are required to give preference in the sale of their output to other publicly owned systems and to rural electric cooperatives. Bonneville, the Tennessee Valley Authority, and the Western Area Power Administration control most of federal power supplies. Federal power preference sales to government-owned utilities and cooperatives were valued between $1.6 billion and $2.0 billion measured at market prices. Most of the below-market sales went to Bonneville and western area customers.

[5] Tomas Jandik and Anil Makhija, "Can Diversification Create Value? Evidence from the Electric Utility Industry," *Financial Management* (Spring 2005): 14.

TABLE 9.2. *Electric Capacity Data (MW)*

	1998	2003	2012
Integrated Utilities	686,692	547,249	644,358
Independent Power Producers	34,675	329,049	389,349
Cogenerators	54,502	64,871	70,753
Total	775,868	948,446	1,104,459

Source: EIA, *Electric power Annual 2012* (December 2013): table 4.4.

designed to improve their operational and financial flexibility. Some firms even proposed some form of vertical disaggregation, although state regulators were not receptive to proposals from IOUs.[6]

One factor driving IOUs toward acceptance of deregulation was the improvement in their financial health by the end of the decade. With most of the excess capacity build-out completed, and the investments embedded in their rate base or written off, the ratio of expenditures to internal funds returned to historical levels. Regulatory lag and a slow adjustment to a new low-inflation environment meant that the realized regulated return on equity increased in real terms even as it declined in nominal value. The markets responded by raising the ratio of the market price to book price from 66 percent in 1974 to 146 percent in 1992.[7] This meant that CEOs had plenty of cash to play with, owing to both reduced capital expenditures and debt service requirements, but limited opportunities for investment in traditional utility functions.

Between 1980 and 1992, utility diversification created excess value, but benefits to diversification of utilities significantly diminished following partial deregulation of the industry after 1992.[8] Deregulation would not have reduced profits outside the industry, but the best opportunities in

---

[6] OTA, *Electric Power Wheeling and Dealing: Technological Considerations for Increasing Competition* (May 1989): 47–49. Some utilities went a little crazy, entering businesses that were far removed from the electricity business. Potomac Electric Power leased Boeing 747s to KLM and Singapore Airlines. FPL Group acquired Colonial Penn Group, an insurance company. Pacific Lighting Corp bought a chain of drug stores. Jandik and Makhija, "Can Diversification Create Value? Evidence from the Electric Utility Industry," 10.

[7] OTA, *Electric Power Wheeling and Dealing: Technological Considerations for Increasing Competition*, at 51–53; EIA, *Financial Impacts of Nonutility Power Purchases on Investor-Owned Electric Utilities* (June 1994): 20–21.

[8] Jandik and Makhija, "Can Diversification Create Value? Evidence From the Electric Utility Industry," 20–23.

the deregulated sector were soon exhausted. The performance of utility holding companies after 1992 raised doubts about management's ability to use surplus funds outside of the regulated business. Regulated utility subsidiaries outperformed the utility holding company every year, with an average 10.8 percent ROE compared to 9 percent for the consolidated company.[9] Financial markets responded to the threat of deregulation by shifting the focus of value from book value to earnings potential in a competitive market.[10] Reflecting the value of earnings, the stock prices of utilities with low costs, especially those utilities with excess capacity, outperformed those of higher-cost utilities after 1992.[11]

This encouraged a merger wave, as efficient managers were able to purchase underperforming utility holding companies, while less efficient management shifted resources from diversification to acquisitions of assets they knew how to manage. Cash-rich utilities looked to both expand and optimize their mix of assets in preparation for the new regulatory regime. A flood of deals was announced during the 1995–1997 period, paralleling state restructuring proceedings. Some IOUs pursued "convergence" mergers with natural-gas companies. However, there is little evidence that these mergers created value. The owners of the acquired companies benefited, but acquiring companies experienced significantly negative abnormal returns, and the post-merger market performance of the merged companies was significantly worse relative to a benchmark portfolio of electric utilities. Active bidders, those who acquired more than one target, had the worst post-merger performance.[12] One reason was that merger efficiencies were difficult to obtain. Mergers of distribution systems resulted in target firms' post-merger efficiency declining, while acquiring firms recorded little or no efficiency gains. Nor did the merger of adjacent utilities create significant efficiencies.[13] It would seem

[9] Leonard Hyman, "Ten Years of Electricity Restructuring: A Financial Postmortem," *Public Utilities Fortnightly* (November 15, 2003): 10–15.

[10] Walter G. Blacconiere, Marilyn F. Johnson, and Mark S. Johnson, "Market Valuation and Deregulation of Electric Utilities," *Journal of Accounting and Economics* 29 (2000): 231–60.

[11] David Besanko, Julia D'Souza, and S. Ramu Thiagarajan, "The Effect of Wholesale Market Deregulation on Shareholder Wealth in the Electric Power Industry," 44 *Journal of Law and Economics* 65, 80–87 (April 2001).

[12] John Becker-Blease, Lawrence Goldberg, and Fred Kaen, "Post Deregulation Restructuring of the Electric Power Industry: Value Creation or Value Destruction?" Working Paper (February 26, 2004).

[13] John Kwoka and Michael Pollitt, "Industry Restructuring, Mergers, and Efficiency: Evidence from Electric Power," CWPE 0725 & EPRG 0708 (April 2007).

that, at least in the short and medium run, utility systems were so self-contained that mergers allowed little opportunities for cost savings.

FERC has jurisdiction over all mergers of electric utility companies that fall under the FPA.[14] Until the repeal of PUCHA, most major mergers also fell under Securities and Exchange Commission (SEC) jurisdiction. The SEC generally deferred to FERC on the question of market power. The SEC reasoned that the expertise and technical ability for resolving anticompetitive issues lied principally with FERC. The DC Circuit agreed that the SEC may "watchfully defer" to proceedings held before another agency.[15]

Pursuant to section 203(a) of the FPA, a merger is to be approved if the Commission finds that it "will be consistent with the public interest."[16] Under section 203(b), the Commission may grant any application "upon such terms and conditions as it finds necessary or appropriate to secure the maintenance of adequate service and proper coordination in the public interest of facilities subject to the jurisdiction of the Commission."[17] The Applicants are required to fully disclose all material facts and carry the burden of showing affirmatively that the merger is compatible with the public interest.[18]

The Commission had been analyzing proposed mergers for almost thirty years by examining six factors that were set forth in *Commonwealth Edison Company*:[19]

1. the effect of the proposed action on the Applicants' operating costs and rate levels;
2. the contemplated accounting treatment;
3. the reasonableness of the purchase price;
4. whether the acquiring utility has coerced the target utility into acceptance of the merger;
5. the effect of the proposed merger on the existing competitive situation;
6. whether the consolidation will impair effective regulation either by the Commission or the appropriate state regulatory authority.

---

[14] 16 U.S.C. Section 824a.
[15] *City of Holyoke Gas & Elec. Dept. v. SEC*, 972 F. 2d 358, 363–64 (D.C. Cir 1992).
[16] 16 U.S.C. §824b(a) (1982).
[17] 16 U.S.C. §824b(b) (1982).
[18] *Pacific Power & Light Co. v. FPC*, 111 F.2d 1014, 1017 (9th Cir. 1940).
[19] 36 FPC 927 (1966), *aff'd sub nom. Utility Users League v. FPC*, 394 F. 2d 16 (7th Cir. 1968), *cert. denied*, 393 U.S. 953 (1968).

TABLE 9.3. *Major Utility Mergers and Acquisitions*
(Target value > $1 billion)

Partners		New Name	Year
Pacific Power & Light	Utah Power & Light	*PacifiCorp**	1989
Iowa Public Service	Iowa Power	*Midwest Resources*	1990
UtiliCorp	WestPlains Energy	*UtiliCorp*	1991
Iowa Electric L&P	Iowa Southern Utilities	*IES Industries*	1991
Kansas Power & Light	Kansas Gas & Electric	Western Resources	1992
Northeast Utilities	Public Service of NH	Northeast Utilities	1992
Entergy	Gulf States Utilities	Entergy	1993
PSI Resources	Cincinnati Gas & Electric	*CINergy*	1994
Midwest Resources	Iowa-Illinois Gas & Electric	MidAmerican Energy	1995
Duke Power	PanEnergy (NG)	Duke Energy	1997
Houston Industries	NorAm Energy (NG)	*Reliant*	1997
Ohio Edison	Centerior Energy	FirstEnergy	1997
Texas Utilities	Enserch (NG)	Texas Utilities	1997
Public Service of Co.	Southwestern Public Service	*New Century Energies*	1997
Puget Sound P&L	Washington Energy (NG)	Puget Sound Energy	1997
Tampa Electric	Peoples Gas	TECO Energy	1997
PG&E Energy	US Generating Co.	PG&E Energy	1997
PG&E Energy	Valero Energy (NG)	PG&E Energy	1997
Union Electric	CIPSCO	Ameren	1997
Louisville Gas & Electric	Kentucky Utilities	*LG&E Energy*	1998
Delmarva Power & Light	Atlantic Energy	*Conectiv*	1998
Long Island Lighting	Brooklyn Union Gas	*KeySpan Energy*	1998
Wisconsin Power & Light	IES Industries/ Interstate Power Co. (IPL)	Alliant Energy	1998
SDG&E	Pacific Enterprises (NG)	Sempra Energy	1998
Consumers Energy	Continental Natural Gas	CMS Energy	1998

(continued)

TABLE 9.3. *(continued)*

Partners		New Name	Year
AEP	Equitable Resources (NG)	AEP	1998
Duke Power	Union Pacific Fuels (NG)	Duke Energy	1999
Boston Edison	Commonwealth Energy	NSTAR	1999
Consolidated Edison	Orange and Rockland	Consolidated Edison	1999
MidAmerican Energy	CalEnergy	MidAmerican Energy	1999
Sierra Pacific Resources	Nevada Power	Sierra Pacific Resources	1999
Dominion Resources	Consolidated Natural Gas	Dominion Resources	2000
AEP	Central & South West	AEP	2000
Wisconsin Electric	Wisconsin Gas	Wisconsin Energy	2000
Northern States Power	New Century Energies	XCEL Energy	2000
National Grid Group	New England Electric System	National Grid USA	2000
Wisconsin Electric Power	Wisconsin Natural Gas	WE Energies	2000
NYSEG	Connecticut NG	*Energy East*	2000
Energy East	Central Maine Power	*Energy East*	2000
Carolina Power & Light	Florida Power	*Progress Energy*	2000
Commonwealth Ed	PECO	Exelon	2000
Dynegy	Illinova	Dynegy	2000
FirstEnergy	General Public Utilities	FirstEnergy	2001
AES	IPALCO	AES	2001
UtiliCorp	Aquila	*Aquila*	2002
National Grid USA	Niagara Mohawk	National Grid USA	2002
Detroit Edison	Michigan Consolidated Gas	DTE Energy	2002
Exelon	Sithe North America	Exelon	2002
Potomac Electric	Conectiv	PEPCO Holdings	2002
Energy East	Rochester Gas & Electric	*Energy East*	2002

Partners		New Name	Year
Ameren	Cilcorp	Ameren	2003
Ameren	Illinois Power	Ameren	2004
Public Service of NM	Texas-New Mexico Power	PNM Resources	2005
Duke Energy	Cinergy	Duke Energy	2006
MidAmerican	PacifiCorp	MidAmerican	2006
National Grid USA	KeySpan Energy	National Grid USA	2007
WPS Resources	Peoples Energy (NG)	Integrys	2007
Aquila	GreatPlains Energy	GreatPlains Energy	2008
Iberdrola SA	Energy East	Iberdrola USA	2008
PPL	LG&E Energy	PPL	2010
RRI	Mirant	GenOn	2010
First Energy	Allegheny Energy	First Energy	2011
AES	Dayton Power & Light	AES	2011
Northeast Utilities	NSTAR	Northeast Utilities	2011
Exelon	Constellation Energy	Exelon	2012
Duke Energy	Progress Energy	Duke Energy	2012
Exelon	Pepco	Exelon	2014
Wisconsin Energy	Inegrys Energy Group	Wisconsin Energy	2015

* Companies in italics were later merger targets.

Source: http://www.publicpower.org/aboutpublic/index.cfm?ItemNumber=2729&sn .ItemNumber=2691; various company websites.

FERC issued Order 592 in December 1996, updating its merger review procedures. The Commission proposed to take into account three factors in analyzing proposed mergers: the effect on competition, the effect on rates, and the effect on regulation.[20] FERC adopted the Department of Justice/Federal Trade Commission Merger Guidelines[21] as the analytical framework for analyzing the effect on competition. A market in the Guidelines is defined as a geographic area in which a hypothetical

---

[20] *Inquiry Concerning the Commission's Merger Policy Under the Federal Power Act: Policy Statement*, Order No. 592, FERC SR ¶ 31,044, 30,111 (1996).

[21] U.S. Department of Justice and Federal Trade Commission, *Horizontal Merger Guidelines*, issued April 2, 1992, 57 FR 41,552 (1992).

profit-maximizing firm that was the only seller in that area likely would impose at least a "small but significant and nontransitory" increase in price. Participants include firms currently producing or selling in the market's geographic area as well as other firms that would enter the market in response to a price increase without incurring significant sunk costs of entry and exit. In evaluating horizontal mergers, both the post-merger market concentration and the increase in concentration resulting from the merger are examined. There was an implicit safe harbor for markets with a post-Merger Herfindahl-Hirschman Index (HHI)[22] below 1000. A post-Merger HHI between 1000 and 1800 represents markets that are moderately concentrated, and an increase in the HHI of more than 100 points raises significant competitive concerns. HHIs above 1800 reflect markets that are considered highly concentrated. Mergers producing an increase in the HHI of more than 50 points in highly concentrated markets raise significant competitive concerns.[23]

In the past, the Commission analyzed three products: non-firm energy, short-term capacity (firm energy), and long-term capacity. Evaluating long-term capacity markets included the effect of a merger on barriers to entry into those markets. The Commission made a tentative stab at recognizing the complexity of electricity markets in its delivered price test, used to delineate geographic markets and potential suppliers. Potential supply depends on the flows on a transmission system, which can be very different under different supply and demand conditions, such as peak and off-peak periods. The analysis should treat these periods separately and separate geographic markets should be defined for each period.[24] However, this analysis reflected the markets of the 1990s, where utilities were making sales of surplus electricity under fairly well defined contracts, not bidding into auction markets on an hourly or daily basis.

---

[22] The HHI is calculated by summing the squares of the individual market shares of all the participants. So if ten firms each have 10% of the market, the HHI would be 1000; if one firm has 50% and 5 firms had 10%, the HHI would be 3000. The HHI accounts for both the number and size of competitors.

[23] U.S. Department of Justice and Federal Trade Commission, *Horizontal Merger Guidelines*, Section 1, Market Definition, Measurement and Concentration. While the FTC often considered increased efficiency as a mitigating factor, the low demand elasticity for electricity meant that it was unlikely that any conceivable efficiency from a merger would be sufficient to reduce prices to final consumers in light of the increase in market power. See Alan Fisher, Frederick Johnson, and Robert Lande, "Price Effects of Horizontal Mergers," 77 *California Law Review* 777, 801–09 (1989).

[24] Order No. 592, at 30,130–33.

The Commission eliminated the requirement that applicants submit cost-benefit analyses of mergers, replacing it with a requirement that applicants propose rate protection for customers. FERC encouraged parties to engage in a pre-filing consensus-building effort that would result in a filing that includes appropriate rate protection. When parties failed to reach an agreement, the Commission could approve a merger after a hearing or on the basis of parties' filings.[25]

In response to the merger wave of the late 1990s, FERC went back to the drawing board and revised its merger policy. The Commission adopted a Final Rule on new merger guidelines in November 2000. The Final Rule affirmed the Commission's screening approach to mergers that may raise horizontal competitive concerns and set forth guidelines for vertical competitive analysis. The Final Rule also addressed the use of computer simulation models in merger analysis. The FTC staff recommended that the Commission expand its data requirements in order to match more closely the Merger Guidelines. The competitive effects of horizontal and vertical mergers were best analyzed with documents, interviews, and data from a variety of sources. In the FTC staff's view, depending on a merging firm to supply its own analysis might not produce reliable information. Therefore, assessments from third parties would be important, including documents from industry trade associations, depositions of third-party executives and consultants, financial analysts' reports, consultants' reports on competitive conditions in the industry, and documents and interviews with suppliers and customers. The Commission's response was that this information could be obtained from merger applicants (through, e.g., a technical conference) or it will be raised in the intervention process.[26]

The FTC Staff also argued that because electricity cannot be stored in large quantities and supply and demand conditions within short time intervals may be independent of each other, there may be a need to

---

[25] *Inquiry Concerning the Commission's Merger Policy Under the Federal Power Act: Policy Statement*, Order No. 592, FERC Stats. & Regs. ¶ 31,044 (1996), 61 FR 68,595 (Dec. 30, 1996), *reconsideration denied*, Order No. 592-A, 79 FERC ¶ 61,321 (1997), 62 FR 33,340 (June 19, 1997) (Merger Policy Statement).

[26] *Revised Filing Requirements Under Part 33 of the Commission's Regulations*, Order No. 642, FERC Stats. & Regs. ¶ 31,111, 31,880–81 (2000), 65 FR 70,983 (November 28, 2000), *order on reh'g*, Order No. 642-A, 94 FERC ¶ 61,289 (2001), 66 FR 16,121 (March 23, 2001). There were studies that suggested that the FERC approach would underestimate the actual extent of market power. See Severin Borenstein, James Bushnell, and Steven Stoft, "The Competitive Effects of Transmission Capacity in a Deregulated Electricity Market," *Rand Journal of Economics* 31 (Summer 2000): 320.

define electricity sales during individual hours as separate product markets. FERC responded by requiring merger applicants to use load levels, not time of day. FERC included spinning and non-spinning reserves and imbalance energy markets among the products to be analyzed.[27]

However, neither the FTC nor FERC addressed the potential for gaming in the new electricity auction markets, where actors engage in repeated interactions. There is an extensive literature on collusion in repeated games and various strategies to block entry and encourage cooperation among bidders. Most of the original work in this area was done in the 1980s and 1990s and was known to industrial organization economists.[28]

The antitrust laws limited the authority of both the FTC and the DOJ to challenge anticompetitive conduct stemming from the structure of regulated markets. Joel Klein, head of the DOJ's Antitrust Division under the Clinton administration, noted that "[t]he antitrust laws provide ample authority for the Justice Department to challenge anticompetitive conduct of various sorts, but we cannot challenge market structure itself. In other words, to whatever extent restructured electric power markets are too highly concentrated to yield pricing at or near competitive levels, the antitrust laws provide no remedy." The DOJ Antitrust Division suggested in testimony before the House Judiciary Committee in June 1997 that Congress might want to look into providing authority to order divestiture in any federal restructuring legislation. DOJ also suggested that the Commission undertake a comprehensive study of market power in a restructured electric power industry. Klein noted that there was little experience with fully restructured electricity markets in actual operation. A competitive analysis based on assumptions may make it more difficult to carry a burden of proof in court, where empirically based fact finding is clearly favored.[29]

---

[27] *Order No. 642*, FERC Stats. & Regs. ¶ 31,111, 31,883–84.

[28] Reviews of game theory, auction theory, and applications to market structure and market power were available in articles and textbooks by the mid-1990s. Preston McAfee and John McMillan, "Auctions and Bidding," *Journal of Economic Literature* 25 (June 1987): 699–738; Jean Tirole, *The Theory of Industrial Organization* (Cambridge, MA, MIT Press, 1988); Paul Milgram, "Auctions and Bidding: A Primer," *Journal of Economic Perspectives* 3 (Summer 1989): 3–22; David Kreps, *Game Theory and Economic Modeling* (Oxford, Oxford University Press, 1990); Dennis W. Carlton and Jeffrey M. Perloff, *Modern Industrial Organization* (Glenview, IL, Scott Foresman/Little Brown, 1990); Preston McAfee and John McMillan, "Competition and Game Theory," *Journal of Marketing Research* 33 (August 1996); 263–67.

[29] Joel I. Klein, "Making the Transition from Regulation to Competition: Thinking about Merger Policy during the Process of Electric Power Restructuring," FERC Distinguished

Utilities also began creating competitive generation affiliates, purchasing generation assets in other jurisdictions, and often financing those purchases with generation divested in their home territory. At least thirty-two utility companies created independent subsidiaries to own power generation assets. The utilities most likely to diversify into power production were those who had experience and competence running a variety of power plants, especially the older steam plants most likely to be divested. Utilities that were divesting large quantities of generation in one market had surplus human capital that could be used to operate generation assets in other markets. These may have encouraged the "swapping" of generation assets among IOU parent companies.[30] Between 1998 and 2002, about 100,000 MW of generation assets were divested as part of restructuring proceedings or voluntarily by utilities in areas undergoing restructuring. Of that capacity, 84,000 MW ended up in the hands of utility generation affiliates.[31] This capacity was split between coal plants and older natural-gas-fired steam turbine plants that tended to be relatively inefficient but provided brownfield sites with access to natural-gas supplies. This often meant the site, as the potential location of a new combined-cycle plant, had as much or more value than the old gas-fired plant did.[32]

Utility companies also reacted to potential and actual deregulation through changes in corporate financial strategy. Policies that decreased earnings stability, or increased competition and threatened market share, lowered debt levels. Firms with a larger industrial customer base, and thus likely to face competition, and utilities whose state encouraged divestiture of generation assets or had policies that encouraged competition, and hence increased market uncertainty, reduced leverage. Overall, regulatory risk and market uncertainty were associated with a 28 percent

Speaker Series (January 21, 1998). *See United States v. Grinnell Corp.*, 384 U.S. 563, 570–71 (1966) (The offense of monopoly under §2 of the Sherman Act has two elements: (1) the possession of monopoly power in the relevant market; and (2) the willful acquisition or maintenance of that power as distinguished from growth or development as a consequence of a superior product, business acumen, or historic accident.)

30 Jun Ishii, "From Investor-Owned Utility to Independent Power Producer," CSEM WP 108 (January 2006): 23–25.

31 Paul L. Joskow, "The Difficult Transition to Competitive Electricity Markets in the U.S.," CEEPR (May 2003), table 1.

32 EIA, *The Changing Structure of the Electric Power Industry 1999: Mergers and Other Corporate Combinations* (December 1999), 46.

TABLE 9.4. *Ten Largest IOUs Divesting*
Generation Assets, 1999

Utility	Capacity (Gigawatts)
Dominion Resources (Virginia Power)	13.3
Unicom (Commonwealth Edison)	11.0
Pacific Gas & Electric Corp.	10.8
Southern California Edison	10.4
Consolidated Edison	7.0
General Public Utilities System	6.9
Potomac Electric Power Co.	6.0
Niagara Mohawk Power	5.3
Illinois Power	4.7
Duquesne Light	4.4
Total Capacity	79.8

Source: EIA, *The Changing Structure of the Electric Power*
Industry 1999: Mergers and Other Corporate Combinations
(December 1999), 46.

TABLE 9.5. *Leading Purchasers of Recently*
Divested Utility Generation

Company	Capacity (Gigawatts)
1. Dominion Generation*	13.3
2. Edison Mission Energy*	11.7
3. NRG Energy*	6.9
4. Southern Energy*	6.6
5. Sithe Energies	6.3
6. AES	6.1
7. Orion Holdings*	5.4
8. Allegheny Energy Generation*	4.1
9. PG&E Generating/U.S. Generating*	4.1
10. Illinova Generation*	3.8
11. Reliant*	3.8
12. Duke Energy*	2.7
13. PPL Global*	2.7
14. FPL Group*	2.4
15. KeySpan Energy*	2.1
Total Capacity	81.6

* Affiliates of traditional utilities.
Source: EIA, *The Changing Structure of the Electric Power*
Industry 1999: Mergers and Other Corporate Combinations
"Divestiture Action and Analysis" (April 1999).

decline in leverage. Two factors that encouraged leverage were ownership by large holding companies – providing greater access to internal capital markets – and vertical integration, which provided some protection against competitive forces.[33]

---

[33] Paroma Sanyal and Laarni Bulan, "Regulatory Risk, Market Uncertainties, and Firm Financing Choices: Evidence from US Electricity Market Restructuring," *Quarterly Review of Economics and Finance* 51 (2011): 248–68.

10

The Emergence of Independent Power Producers

EPAct 1992 prompted a number of firms that had been involved in developing qualifying facilities under PURPA to become developers of independent generation projects. This trend was supported by Order 888 and the movement toward retail competition. In states where the incumbent utility divested its generation, the wires company might still need to purchase electricity to serve its captive customers, and where there was retail competition, new entrants selling at retail needed sources of electricity supplies. The advent of centralized electricity markets provided the opportunity to sell power directly to the market without the need to negotiate a long-term contract, allowing a developer to use a mix of instruments to obtain revenues, including sales of ancillary services in these markets.

The companies listed in Table 10.1 were primarily engaged in selling power from cogeneration facilities under long-term contracts as PURPA QFs. The opportunity to sell power from divested generation and new gas-fired plants tempted many of these companies into aggressive expansion campaigns, and a number of these companies "crashed and burned." Private equity funds took advantage of the resulting bargains, buying up assets and companies, looking more to flip assets than build energy companies. Shifting markets and fuel prices have kept the generation sector in turmoil, even though investors have grown more cautious.

AES was the most successful of the true independents. Roger Sant and Dennis Bakke founded Applied Energy Systems in 1981.[1] Sant was a

---

[1] Roger Sant received a B.S. from Brigham Young University and an MBA in 1960 from Harvard. Dennis Bakke was a 1970 Harvard MBA.

TABLE 10.1. *Largest Private Power Producers in the United States, 1995*

	MW
Mission Energy*	3,463
Enron Development	2,638
AES	2,316
Sithe Energies	2,045
U.S. Gen./InterGen	1,909
Southern Electric Intl. (Mirant)*	1,615
CMS Generation*	1,455
Cogen Technologies	1,364
Cogentrix Energy	996
NRG Energy*	982
Dominion Energy*	872
California Energy	835
Wheelabrator	727
GE Capital	715
Energy Initiatives	633

* Affiliates of traditional utilities

political appointee in the Nixon and Ford administrations, as the Assistant Administrator for Energy Conservation and Environment in the Federal Energy Administration, and Bakke served as Sant's deputy. The two had been instrumental in drafting preliminary versions of PURPA. Following government service, they moved on to the Mellon Institute's Energy Productivity Center, where they came up with the idea of starting their own company. AES initially focused on energy conservation consulting and developing cogeneration projects at manufacturing plants. From 1981 to 1985, they sought alliances from ARCO, IBM, and Bechtel. While they were never able to formalize these relationships, these contacts led to financing for a Texas plant in December 1983. AES Deepwater is a 143 MW petroleum coke–fired cogeneration plant located in Pasadena, Texas, on the Houston Ship Channel. Power from the plant was sold to Houston Lighting and Power as a QF, the steam sold to ARCO for refinery use, and ARCO supplied the petroleum coke.[2]

The Deepwater plant established the pattern employed by AES (and a number of other firms) to finance expansion. To mitigate risk, AES treated each plant as a separate project and financed it through non-recursive

[2] Robert M. Grant, "Case 17: AES Corporation: Rewriting the Rules of Management," in R.M. Grant, *Contemporary Strategy Analysis*, 4th ed. (Malden, MA, Blackwell Publishing, 2002).

TABLE 10.2. *Largest Independent Power Producers in the United States, 2012*[a]

	MW
Exelon[b]	35,413
Calpine	28,155
NRG[c]	23,585
GenOn Energy (RRI and Mirant)	22,061
First Energy[d]	18,316
LS Power[e]	14,900
Luminant	13,772
International Power/GDF Suez[f]	13,261
PSEG	13,060
Dynegy	11,596
PPL Energy Supply	10,508
Dominion Resource[g]	9,157
NextEra Energy Resources[h]	8,038
Duke Energy[i]	7,553
Edison Energy Group[j]	7,361
AES[k]	6,902

[a] Capacity derived from Form 10-K Annual Reports unless otherwise noted.
[b] Exelon controlled another 5,025 MW of capacity through long-term contracts. Exelon also has 735 MW of wind. Constellation also had 147 MW of wind and solar. Constellation merged with Exelon in March 2012.
[c] NRG also has 450 MW of wind and 95 MW of solar.
[d] FirstEnergy also has 1,182 MW of pumped storage and 376 MW of wind. FirstEnergy's regulated subsidiaries have 2,936 MW of generation.
[e] http://www.lspower.com/newsArchives.htm. Estimated from announced acquisitions, asset sales and development plans.
[f] http://www.iprplc-gdfsuez.com/our-company/assets.aspx. The number is for North America.
[g] This excludes generation owned by Virginia Power.
[h] This excludes 8,569 MW of wind generation and generation controlled by the integrated subsidiary Florida Power & Light.
[i] Duke renewables had 772 MW, and Duke's regulated subsidiaries in Carolina, Ohio, and Indiana had 27,397 MW of generation capacity.
[j] Edison also had 428 MW of merchant wind, 1,011 MW of contracted power, and 1,444 MW of contracted wind.
[k] Integrated subsidiaries IPL and Dayton control an additional 7,516 MW of generation. AES also has 1,132 MW of wind generation in the United States.

financing from local banks and other lending institutions. AES projects had long-term contracts indexed to inflation, currency fluctuations, and other specified risks. The company used its QF PPAs as collateral to raise additional funds. This allowed the company to leverage small amounts of investment funds into substantial equity positions, and management fees provided steady cash flow.

Buoyed by its success, the company changed its name from Applied Energy Sources to AES and became a publicly traded company. Sant assumed the position of company chairman, while Bakke became the firm's president and CEO. AES experienced success with its initial strategy, but Sant and Bakke began to question the future viability of the U.S. cogeneration market as the most lucrative opportunities had been exhausted. In the early 1990s, AES began expanding into China, India, and several other thriving power markets. By 1995, the firm was spending an estimated 85 percent of its venture capital abroad. The company's shift to the developing world was a response to three factors: higher electricity demand growth, less stringent environmental and siting regulations, and lower tax rates.

In 1999, AES purchased Cilcorp and acquired California-based NewEnergy in July 1999. In March 2001, the firm acquired Indiana-based IPALCO Enterprises (owner of Indianapolis Power & Light Company with 3,370 MW of capacity) for $3 billion. As part of its regulatory approval to acquire IPALCO, AES was required to divest Cilcorp.[3]

Revenues increased steadily from 1996 to 2000, from $835 million to $6,691 million, and net income from $125 million to $641 million. Total assets exploded, from $3.6 billion to $31 billion (on paper), but much of this was backed by nonrecourse loans, which increased to $12.2 billion, compared to only $4.8 billion of equity and $4.6 billion of other debt.[4] AES faced a grave financial crisis in 2001 when it suffered three major shocks. The first was the Californian power crisis, which threatened to halt deregulation in the U.S. electricity sector. The Argentina financial crisis led to its six businesses in Argentina going into default, and problems in Brazil further hurt South American operations. The bankruptcy of its 3,000 MW Drax plant in the United Kingdom was the final blow. In eighteen months, the company lost around 90 percent of its stock value, from $70 a share in September 2000 to below $4 in February 2002. Book equity declined from $5.5 billion in 2001 to negative $340 million in 2002. The sharp decline in AES's market value made it increasingly difficult for AES to access the capital markets.[5]

---

[3] http://www.fundinguniverse.com/company-histories/AES-Corporation-Company-History .html (last visited June 20, 2011); AES, *10-K Annual Report, 2005*, 8; AES, *10-K Annual Report*, 2001, 10.

[4] AES, *10-K Annual Report, 2000*, 22–23.

[5] AES, *10-K Annual Report, 2001*, 35–36; AES, *10-K Annual Report, 2002*, 35; Robert M. Grant, "Case 17: AES Corporation: Rewriting the Rules of Management."

AES completed a $2.1 billion refinancing and sold off AES NewEnergy, Cilcorp, generation businesses in Africa, Bangladesh, and Pakistan, and ownership interests in Oman and Qatar. The company took $2.3 billion in asset impairments associated with several large utility and generation businesses.[6] By 2005, the company had recovered, as cost cutting and stabilization of its Latin American markets reversed the collapse. The company was back on a growth track by 2010, with $16.6 billion in revenues. However, net income has stagnated, averaging less than $500 million a year since 2006. This has been partially due to large write-offs from impairment losses to domestic plants and some foreign operations. While total assets had increased to $40 billion, equity reached $7.6 billion, finally exceeding the level experienced before the 2001 shock.[7] In 2011, AES acquired DPL (the parent company of Dayton Power & Light). Dayton operates more than 3,800 MW of generation, of which 2,800 MW are coal fired.[8]

Calpine also had its origins in PURPA, as it was founded in 1984 by Peter Cartwright, four of his coworkers, and the Electrowatt corporation.[9] The name "Calpine" was derived from the company's California location and alpine, a reference to the Zürich home base of Electrowatt. The firm initially provided management services to independent power generation companies, but like AES, soon became a power plant developer. In 1996, Calpine had interests in fifteen power generation facilities with an aggregate capacity of a little more than 1,000 MW, almost half of which was geothermal power. Growth had been achieved through a conservative strategy similar to AES, with financing based on take-and-pay power and/or steam sales agreements generally having terms of twenty or thirty years.[10]

Starting in 1994, Cartwright shifted Calpine's financial strategy from project finance with nonrecourse debt to corporate debt, trying to obtain a first-mover advantage in restructured markets. The key decision in this change in strategic direction was the Pasadena Power Plant. Responding

---

[6] AES, *10-K Annual Report*, 2002, 3–4; AES, *2002 Annual Report*, 37.

[7] AES, *10-K Annual Report*, 2013, 115.

[8] Chris Nicholson, "AES to Buy Ohio Utility for $3.5 Billion," *New York Times*, April 20, 2011, at http://dealbook.nytimes.com/2011/04/20/aes-to-buy-ohio-utility-dpl-in-4-7-billion-deal/ (last visited September 19, 2011).

[9] http://www.referenceforbusiness.com/biography/A-E/Cartwright-Peter-1930.html (last visited September 20, 2011). Cartwright spent twenty years with General Electric, working in nuclear plant construction, project management, and new business development, and five more with Gibbs and Hill as an engineering consultant.

[10] Calpine, *10-K Annual Report*, 1996, 2.

to a request for bids by Phillips Petroleum for a twenty-year fixed-price contract on 90 MW of power in 1996, Calpine won the bid but then proceeded to build a 240 MW combined-cycle plant and sell the other 150 MW to the Texas market. The $152 million project loan, the first loan to a primarily merchant power plant, was oversubscribed.[11] This signaled to market participants that the financial markets would finance nonrecourse projects on the strength of forecasted market revenues.

Calpine's strategy was built around developing the capability of building standardized combined-cycle plants at lower cost than its competitors, exploiting learning-curve efficiencies in construction and operation to reduce life-cycle costs. Calpine would manage construction instead of relying on outside general contractors, allowing more control over projects and eliminating the contractor's margin. An in-house maintenance group reduced operations and maintenance costs, and standardization of design allowed the company to have a single inventory of spare parts for the entire fleet of power plants. Gas purchases could be centralized, hedged, and arbitraged over a wide geographic expanse. Management saw a five-year window in which they could garner the best sites, get their plants on the ground, and exploit higher electricity market prices before the more efficient plants drove down market prices. Because there were only two domestic major producers of high-efficiency gas turbines – Siemens-Westinghouse and General Electric – Calpine moved to tie up their output by placing orders for sixty turbines to be delivered by 2002 at a cost of $3 billion.[12]

Calpine's reason for moving from project finance to corporate finance revolved around the desire to operate their plants as part of a system, and to avoid the delays intrinsic to project finance and the need for separate negotiations for each plant. With only fifty or so banks in the project loan market, and each bank with limits on exposure to a single customer, financing a $6 billion project portfolio would be a difficult proposition. Also, typical project finance terms would place a large cash flow burden on the company. For example, a $300 million plant would receive 100 percent construction financing for two years, but Calpine would have to repay $150 million once the plant was complete. The other $150 million would convert to a nonrecourse loan, to be paid back in three years,

[11] Benjamin Esty and Michael Kane, "Calpine Corporation: The Evolution from Project to Corporate Finance," Harvard Business School Case 9–201–098 (January 21, 2003): 4–5.

[12] Id., 5–6.

swallowing the cash flow from the plant and requiring refinancing at the end of the loan's life. The banks would have a lien on the plant and control over cash flows, and only residual cash flows after expenses would be available to Calpine.

Calpine developed a third financing option, a revolving construction facility. A new subsidiary borrowed $1 billion in a secured revolving construction facility with a four-year maturity. This loan was secured by the plants under construction. Once the initial plants were completed, the funds repaid could be re-borrowed to finance additional plants.[13]

The expansion program was in full swing in 2000, and in early 2001 Calpine had 5,850 MW of capacity, 14,000 MW under construction, and 15,000 MW under development.[14]

Cartwright's scheme came crashing to a sudden halt by the end of 2001, as the collapse of Enron, the end of windfall revenues from California, and a crushing debt burden squeezed the company. The shift from long-term contracts to market prices, as only 60 percent of capacity was under contract, meant that revenues were impacted by declining electricity prices. Calpine completed projects under construction, leaving the company with 26,500 MW of capacity and 5,500 MW under construction by March 2005.[15] Almost all this capacity was gas-fired combined-cycle units. Calpine replaced its chief executive and its chief financial officer as it struggled with a court ruling that restricted its ability to buy fuel for its plants.[16] In December 2005, the company filed for bankruptcy protection.[17] Coming out of bankruptcy in 2008, Calpine reduced its consolidated debt to $10.5 billion, while the extension of debt maturities meant that Calpine did not need to refinance more than $2 billion of corporate debt from 2017 to 2023 in any given year.[18] Calpine still had 26,000 MW of capacity in 2014, following the sale of 3,500 MW to LS Power.[19]

---

[13] Id., 7–10.
[14] Calpine, *10-K Annual Report, 2000*, 4–8.
[15] Calpine, *10-K Annual Report, 2001*, 3; Calpine, *10-K Annual Report, 2004*, 13.
[16] "Energy Producer Changes Its Top Executives," *Reuters*, November 30, 2005, at http://www.nytimes.com/2005/11/30/business/30calpine.html?ref=calpinecorporation (last visited September 19, 2011).
[17] Leonard Anderson and Michael Erman, "Calpine Files for Bankruptcy Protection," *Reuters*, December 21, 2005 at http://www.usatoday.com/money/industries/energy/2005-12-21-calpine-bankruptcy_x.htm (last visited September 19, 2011).
[18] Calpine, *10-K Annual Report, 2011*.
[19] Calpine Agrees to Sell Six Southeast Power Plants for $1.57 Billion," *Business Wire*, April 14, 2014, at http://www.businesswire.com/news/home/20140418005217/

Where Calpine was an object lesson in the perils of an aggressive investment campaign, Dynegy paralleled Enron, in that it became seduced by energy trading. Dynegy began as Natural Gas Clearinghouse (NGC) in 1984, a marketing arm jointly owned by six pipeline companies, Morgan Stanley, and the law firm Akin Gump. Morgan Stanley bought out Transco and Akin Gump in 1985 and recruited Chuck Watson to head up the company.[20] By the beginning of the 1990s, as margins on sales of natural gas fell, Watson responded by expanding NGC into gathering, processing, storing, and marketing natural gas, as well as other fuel oils. Trident NGL was acquired by NGC in March 1995, creating a natural gas powerhouse with annual revenue of $3.4 billion.[21] The merger also took the company public, and the name was changed to NGC Corporation. Chevron Corporation then merged its Houston gas business unit with the NGC Corporation. NGC had set up a marketing concept it called the "energy store," under which utilities and industrial customers could buy natural gas, gas liquids, crude oil, and electricity. NGC would buy and resell nearly all of the natural gas, natural gas liquids, and electricity produced by Chevron.[22]

NGC expanded its foothold in electricity marketing by acquiring Destec Energy,[23] along with twenty gas-fired plants with about 1,800 MW of capacity. About two-thirds of this capacity was tied up in long-term QF contracts to utilities. In November 1997, NGC, in a partnership with NRG, acquired a gas-fired power generating facility in Los Angeles, and additional California generation plants in 1998. NGC became the

---

en/Calpine-Agrees-Sell-Southeast-Power-Plants-1.57#.U-03GGdOWUk (last visited August 14, 2014).

[20] Neil Weinberg and Daniel Fisher, "Power Player," *Forbes*, December 24, 2001, at http://www.forbes.com/forbes/2001/1224/052.html (last visited September 22, 2011).

[21] "Natural Gas Clearinghouse to Buy Trident NGL," *New York Times*, October 25, 1994, at http://www.nytimes.com/1994/10/25/business/company-news-natural-gas-clearinghouse-to-buy-trident-ngl.html?scp=1&sq=Natural%20Gas%20Clearinghouse%20&st=Search (last visited September 21, 2011).

[22] Agis Salpukas, "In Deal, Chevron Passes Some Operations to NGC," *New York Times*, January 23, 1996, at http://www.nytimes.com/1996/01/23/business/in-deal-chevron-passes-some-operations-to-ngc.html?scp=12&sq=Natural%20Gas%20Clearinghouse&st=Search (last visited September 21, 2011).

[23] Destec Energy was another PURPA child, but from the steam customer side. Destec, founded in 1989, was a subsidiary of Dow Chemical. Destec developed cogeneration plants for steam sales to other companies and marketed electricity from Dow's cogeneration facilities. At http://www.fundinguniverse.com/company-histories/destec-energy-inc-history/ (last visited June 8, 2012).

lead party on fuel procurement, power marketing, and asset management, while NRG operated the facilities.[24]

By 1998, the company was well on its way to morphing from a natural gas marketing company to one based on energy trading. Dynegy (renamed by Watson in 1997) began building a portfolio of merchant generation capacity in select markets across the country. Merchant generation capacity offered the greatest flexibility in executing a strategy of developing an integrated gas and power marketing and power generation business. Dynegy purchased Illinois Power in February 2000 in a complex deal valued at about $4 billion. After the deal, Dynegy had interests in power plants with more than 14,000 MW of capacity, natural gas sales of more than 10 billion cubic feet per day, and more than 1.4 million retail customers. The combined company had more than $12 billion in assets. By the end of 2000, Dynegy was one of the largest energy companies in the United States, and poised to make the Fortune 50 list. Revenues approached $28 billion.[25]

Dynegy agreed to acquire Enron as it was on the verge of collapse at the end of 2001. As part of the deal, Dynegy would give Enron a cash infusion of $1.5 billion, to buy Northern Natural Gas pipeline, and an additional $1 billion when the deal closed. Dynegy would take on Enron's $12.8 billion debt load, but not the off–balance sheet debt.[26] Dynegy's $1.5 billion investment gave it the right to keep the pipeline even if the deal was aborted. On November 19, Enron filed quarterly financials that revealed an obligation to repay $690 million within a week, and that Enron had $1 billion less in cash on hand than it had stated. On November 28, three credit agencies downgraded Enron to junk status, and Watson killed the deal.[27]

While trading accounted for a smaller proportion of Dynegy revenues, the company had engaged in some of the same behavior as Enron had. Two former executives would plead guilty, and a third would be convicted, of disguising a $300 million loan as a natural gas contract in

---

[24] NGC, *Form 10-Q*, September 1997; NGC, *Form 10-K*, 1997, 24.

[25] Dynegy, *Form 10-K*, *1998*, 3; Dynegy, *Form 8-K*, February 2, 2000; Dynegy, *Form 10-K*, *2000*, 12.

[26] Richard Oppel Jr. and Andrew Sorkin, "Dynegy Is Said to Be Near to Acquiring Enron for $8 Billion," *New York Times*, November 8, 2001, at http://www.nytimes.com/2001/11/08/business/dynegy-is-said-to-be-near-to-acquiring-enron-for-8-billion.html?ref=dynegyinc (last visited September 21, 2011).

[27] Neil Weinberg and Daniel Fisher, "Power Player," *Forbes*, December 24, 2001, at http://www.forbes.com/forbes/2001/1224/052.html (last visited September 22, 2011).

2001 in order to book it as cash flow.[28] Dynegy admitted doing sham energy trades with CMS Energy aimed at pumping up revenue and volume. Dynegy was also stung by an SEC probe and questions about its role in California's power crisis. Dynegy settled a civil lawsuit brought by regulators that accused the company of using off–balance sheet partnerships and bogus trades to hide its true financial condition from investors. Watson would resign in the wake of these events.[29] Dynegy would eventually settle shareholder suits for $468 million in 2005.[30]

Dynegy appointed a former Duke Energy executive, Bruce Williamson, with twenty years of experience in energy and finance, as its president and chief executive. Faced with a credit crisis, the company began shedding assets. Dynergy sold its UK gas storage business and disposed of its of European communications business and its global liquids business.[31] The biggest moves were the sale of Northern Natural Gas pipeline to MidAmerican Energy Holdings, and of Illinois Power to Ameren.[32] Dynegy purchased Sithe Energies and Sithe/Independence Power Partners from Exelon in January 2005 and sold its natural-gas processing business, leaving Dynegy as an electricity generating company with power plants in twelve states.[33] Dynegy completed a merger agreement with LS Entities, part of the LS Power Group, a privately held power plant investor, in April 2007. Dynegy then sold eight power plants and its

[28] David Teather, "Former Dynegy Executive Jailed for 25 Years after $300m Fraud," *The Guardian*, March 26, 2004, at http://www.guardian.co.uk/business/2004/mar/26/corporatefraud (last visited September 21, 2011).

[29] "Watson Resigns Amid Dynegy Trading Scandal," *Houston Business Journal*, May 28, 2002, at http://www.bizjournals.com/houston/stories/2002/05/27/daily1.html (last visited September 22, 2011). A comparison of Dynegy's 2001 10-K with its 2002 10-K reveals the extent to which revenues and income were misstated. Restated revenues for 2001 declined from $42 billion to just less than $9 billion, and net income from $650 million in 2002, the company had losses of $2.7 billion.

[30] "Ex-Dynegy Execs Settle Fraud Case," *Los Angeles Times*, October 2, 2007 at http://articles.latimes.com/2007/oct/02/business/fi-wrap2.s2 (last visited September 22, 2011).

[31] Dynegy, *Form 10-K, 2002*, 40.

[32] "Dynegy Staves Off Bankruptcy with Sale of Pipeline," *New York Times*, August 17, 2002, at http://www.nytimes.com/2002/08/17/business/company-news-dynegy-staves-off-bankruptcy-with-sale-of-pipeline.html?ref=dynegyinc (last visited September 21, 2011); "Ameren Agrees to Buy Illinois Utility from Dynegy," *New York Times*, February 4, 2004, at http://www.nytimes.com/2004/02/04/business/company-news-ameren-agrees-to-buy-illinois-utility-from-dynegy.html?ref=dynegyinc (last visited September 21, 2011).

[33] Dynegy, *Form 10-K, 2006*, F-18; "Big Energy Mergers in U.S. and Canada," *Bloomberg News*, August 3, 2005, at http://www.nytimes.com/2005/08/03/business/worldbusiness/03energy.html?ref=dynegyinc (last visited September 21, 2011).

interest in the Sandy Creek Project to LS Power on December 1, 2009, ending the collaboration between the companies.[34]

Dynegy teetered on the brink of insolvency for years, barely meeting its debt obligations. Despite sales of assets and termination of numerous obligations, the company lost almost $1.4 billion between 2005 and 2010.[35] Dynegy had been trying to sell itself since 2008, but a series of maneuvers between Blackstone, Seneca Capital, and Carl Icahn kept the company from finalizing any deal.[36] Icahn engineered a complex restructuring deal that attempted to hide coal assets from creditors, but the court-appointed bankruptcy examiner concluded that the conveyance was a fraudulent transfer and a breach of duty by the board of directors. In June 2012, a New York judge approved a deal that resolved more than $2.5 billion in claims.[37] The newly reorganized Dynegy still had 13,000 MW in operation at the end of 2013.[38]

While each of the companies that pursued aggressive expansion plans ran into financial difficulties, a number of privately held independent power producers were successful with more modest and measured expansion programs. Tenaska, an employee-owned company started in 1987, has coal, natural gas, and alternative energy projects throughout the United States, with 2010 revenues of almost $10 billion. A Tenaska affiliate ranks in the top ten natural gas marketers in North America. Tenaska's power marketing affiliate develops power supply solutions for customers and managed 20,000 MW in 2010. Tenaska Capital Management is the manager of stand-alone private equity funds with $4.4 billion invested in energy and power assets.[39]

---

[34] Dynegy, *Form 10-K, 2007*, 39–40; Dynegy, *Form 10-K, 2009*, 42.

[35] Dynegy Inc., *Form 10-K, 2010*, 41.

[36] Michael de la Merced, "Blackstone to Pay $4.7 Billion for Dynegy," *New York Times*, August 14, 2010, at http://www.nytimes.com/2010/08/14/business/14dynegy .html?ref=dynegyinc (last visited September 21, 2011); Steven M. Davidoff, "A Free-for-All at Dynegy," *New York Times*, November 16, 2010, at http://dealbook.nytimes .com/2010/11/16/a-free-for-all-over-dynegy/?ref=dynegyinc (last visited September 21, 2011).

[37] Matt Wirz, "Icahn-Dynegy Plant Gets Test: Loan Sale Will Gauge Investor Confidence in Contested Reorganization Proposal," *Wall Street Journal*, July 29, 2011, at http://online .wsj.com/article/SB10001424053111903635604576474633861309582.html, (last visited, September 21, 2011); Stephen Lubben, "Dynegy Bankruptcy Examiner Finds Fraudulent Transfer," *DealB%k*, March 9, 2012, at http://dealbook.nytimes.com/ 2012/03/09/dynegy-bankruptcy-examiner-finds-fraudulent-transfer/ (last visited June 7, 2012); Kelsey Butler, "Dynegy Deal Involving More Than $2.5B in Claims OK'd," *The Deal Pipeline*, June 6, 2012, at http://www.thedeal.com/content/restructuring/ dynegy-deal-involving-more-than-25b-in-claims-okd.php (last visited June 7, 2012).

[38] Dynegy Inc., *Form 10-K, 2013*, at 5.

[39] http://www.tenaska.com/page.aspx?id=6&pid=2.

LS Power Development, LLC was founded in 1990 and is based in New York City. LS Power raised $1.2 billion in 2005 for its first private equity vehicle, and raised $3 billion in 2007.[40] Various funds have invested $28 billion in power projects since the firm's inception, and the company now controls more than 32,000 MW of generation.[41]

Some of the smaller independents were bought up by utilities and equity funds, but a few have managed to remain independent. Sithe Energies, Inc. was founded in 1984, headquartered in New York City. Sithe Energies was owned by Compagnie Generale des Eaux (61.3 percent), Marubeni Corporation (27.6 percent), and its two other founders (11.1 percent). Sithe was an independent energy producer engaged in the development construction, ownership, and operation of nonutility electric generating facilities. Sithe was acquired by Exelon on November 2003,[42] then flipped to Dynegy in 2004.

Founded in 1982 by Robert W. Carter, Panda Energy has developed, financed, constructed, and operated large-scale energy facilities both domestically and internationally. The creation of the company was a direct result of the passage of PURPA. The Carter family has owned a controlling stake in the company, making Panda Energy a family business. The company has raised more than $6 billion to develop and build 9,000 MW of capacity. Panda Energy has diversified into wrestling, purchasing Total Nonstop Action Wrestling in 2002, and appointing Dixie Carter as president.

Sempra Energy Partners and Carlyle/Riverstone formed a new group called Topaz Power Partners in 2004 to oversee the acquisition of ten Texas power plants, including a 632 MW coal-fired plant formerly owned by AEP. Financing was obtained from a consortium comprised of Citigroup, JP Morgan Chase, and Goldman Sachs. Partnering with an outside investment firm such as Carlyle/Riverstone allowed Sempra to mitigate its own financial risk.[43]

Despite a few important start-up companies, the majority of the independent power producers that replaced IOUs in wholesale electricity markets have been subsidiaries of parent companies that also own IOUs in

---

[40] "LS Power Announces Final Closing of LS Power Equity Partners II at $3.085 Billion," *Business Wire*, May 22, 2007, at http://findarticles.com/p/articles/mi_moEIN/is_2007_May_22/ai_n27247099/ (last visited, Sept. 24, 2011).

[41] http://www.lspower.com/about.htm.

[42] http://phx.corporate-ir.net/phoenix.zhtml?c=124298&p=irol-newsArticle_Print&ID=570360 (last visited February 9, 2015).

[43] Al Senia, "Invasion of the Asset Snatcher," *ENERGYBIZ Magazine*, November/December 2004, 32.

other states. When many utilities reorganized in anticipation of deregulation, they transferred operations personnel to their unregulated subsidiary, maintaining their corporate plant valuation and operational human capital. Utility subsidiaries were more likely to purchase divested generation units because they had more experience with older technologies, which aided in proper valuation of assets, and could manage operations and maintenance costs and reduce the probability of outages. IOUs often divested in their home territory, then acquired similar assets in other regions. Parents of IPP subsidiaries accounted for 55 percent of all divested generation capacity, providing large immediate cash flows for the IOU parent company to finance IPP investments.[44] However, experienced utility managers often made the same mistakes their entrepreneurial cousins did.

NRG Energy, Inc. (NRG) is one of the leading participants in the independent power generation industry. NRG was established in 1989 as a wholly owned subsidiary by Northern States Power Company. NRG had 2,650 MW of generation at the end of 1997, and operational responsibility for an additional 5,374 MW.[45] NRG began a substantial acquisition campaign in 1998 and continued to grow through acquisitions in 1999 and 2000, purchasing plants from Niagara Mohawk, Montaup Electric, San Diego Gas and Electric, Consolidated Edison, Rochester Gas and Electric, and Connecticut Light & Power. In March 2000, Cajun Electric Power Cooperative's facilities were acquired in a competitive bidding process following a Chapter 11 bankruptcy filing. NRG made numerous other purchase agreements in 2000 and continued its frantic purchasing program in 2001, picking up projects and properties in Missouri, Texas, Delaware, and Oklahoma. In November 2001, NRG Energy signed agreements to acquire or lease 2,500 MW of coal-fired generation from FirstEnergy Corporation. At the end of 2001, NRG had a net ownership interest of 24,357 MW, with 19,077 MW in the United States.[46]

This rapid expansion program raised both operating revenues and debt exposure. Operating revenue rose from a mere $104 million in 1996 to $3 billion in 2001. However, long-term debt rose from $212 million to

[44] Jun Ishii, "From Investor-owned Utility to Independent Power Producer," Center for the Study of Energy Markets, CSEM WP 108, January 2006, 4–5.

[45] NRG Energy, *Form 10-K*, 1997, 3.

[46] NRG Energy, *Form 10-K*, 1998, 6–8; NRG Energy, *Form 10-K*, 1999, at 3; NRG Energy, *Form 10-K*, 2000, 4–16; NRG Energy, *Form 10-K*, 2001, 1, 8–9.

$8.3 billion.[47] The company spent $8.2 billion on acquisitions between 1999 and 2001, had another $1.6 billion committed to the FirstEnergy acquisition, and estimated capital expenditures for project development over the 2002–2006 period of $7.5 billion.[48] By the end of 2002, even after remedial measures, NRG debt had reached $9.4 billion.[49]

In 2002, NRG Energy entered into discussions with its creditors in anticipation of a comprehensive restructuring. Xcel sold $500 million in stock in July to avert a default by NRG, and NRG sold power plants in Hungary and the Czech Republic.[50] Despite these measures, NRG failed to make interest and/or principal payments resulting in cross-defaults of numerous nonrecourse and limited-recourse debt instruments. NRG also recorded asset impairment charges of $3.1 billion, related to operating projects and projects under construction that NRG Energy stopped funding. In 2003, Xcel Energy made payments to NRG of $752 million for the benefit of NRG Energy's creditors, and took a $2 billion write-off for NRG.[51] NRG Energy filed for Chapter 11 bankruptcy reorganization on May 14, 2003. Xcel Energy relinquished its ownership interest, and NRG became an independent public company upon its emergence from bankruptcy. NRG eliminated approximately $5.2 billion of corporate debt and $1.3 billion of additional claims by distributing equity and cash among unsecured creditors.[52]

The reorganized NRG was soon back to its aggressive expansion strategy. By the end of 2005, the company had added 7,600 MW of domestic capacity and was pursuing deals to add still more generation. In December 2005, NRG acquired Dynegy's 50 percent of their jointly owned 1,800 MW of generation in California. On February 2, 2006, NRG acquired Texas Genco for $6.1 billion and the assumption of $2.7 billion

---

[47] NRG Energy, *Form 10-K*, 2001, 29.

[48] NRG Energy, *Form 10-K*, 2001, 31–41.

[49] NRG Energy, *Form 10-K*, 2002, 3.

[50] XCEL Energy Will Sell Stock to Save Subsidiary," *New York Times*, July 27, 2002, at http://www.nytimes.com/2002/07/27/business/company-news-xcel-energy-will-sell-stock-to-save-subsidiary.html?ref=nrgenergyinc (last visited September 21, 2011); "NRG in a Deal to Sell Some European Energy Operations," *New York Times*, September 12, 2002, at http://www.nytimes.com/2002/09/12/business/company-news-nrg-in-a-deal-to-sell-some-european-energy-operations.html?ref=nrgenergyinc (last visited September 21, 2011).

[51] NRG Energy, *Form 10-K*, 2002, 4–5; NRG Energy, *Form 10-K*, 2003, 3; "NRG Says Chapter 11 Bankruptcy Filing Is Possible," *New York Times*, November 9, 2002 at http://www.nytimes.com/2002/11/09/business/company-news-nrg-says-chapter-11-bankruptcy-filing-is-possible.html?ref=nrgenergyinc (last visited September 21, 2011).

[52] NRG Energy, *Form 10-K*, 2004, 2.

of outstanding debt. During 2006, NRG began retreating internationally, focusing its attentions on the domestic electricity markets. The company began to focus on growth opportunities through expansion of its existing generating capacity through plant improvements and repowering, and through development of new generating capacity at its brownfield sites. In May 2009, NRG acquired the Texas electric retail business operation of Reliant Energy and added Austin-based Green Mountain Energy, the nation's leading competitive provider of clean energy and carbon offset products, in November 2010. By the end of 2011, NRG had a generation portfolio with capacity of 25,135 MW, with all but 1,000 MW in the United States.[53] In December 2012, NRG added GenOn Energy (Mirant) for $1.7 billion, then picked up Edison Mission for $2.6 billion in 2013, giving the company 46,000 MW of total generation capacity. The company also invested heavily in new wind and solar and added Energy Curtailment Specialists, a demand response company in 2013, thus covering almost every area of the electricity industry.[54]

Mirant was another utility subsidiary that pursued an aggressive expansion strategy only to run afoul of a hostile market. Mirant began its corporate existence in 1981 as Southern Electric International, a small consulting division of Southern Company that provided engineering and technical services. After EPAct 1992 Southern Electric ventured into global markets. By the end of 2000, Mirant owned or controlled more than 17,400 MWs of electric generating capacity around the world, with approximately another 9,000 MWs under development. Mirant also controlled access to 3.7 billion cubic feet per day of natural gas production, as well as gas transportation and storage. Mirant was 80 percent owned by Southern Company, which distributed to its stockholders its interest in Mirant in 2001.[55]

On December 19, 2000, Mirant closed the acquisition of PEPCO's generation assets in Maryland and Virginia. Along with the PEPCO acquisition, Mirant was engaged in a major construction and development program. The rapid expansion of Mirant was reflected in operating

53 NRG Energy, *Form 10-K, 2005*, 6–7; NRG Energy, *Form 10-K, 2006*, 6–7; NRG Energy, *Form 10-K, 2009*, 9, 76; NRG Energy, *Form 10-K, 2010*, 21; NRG Energy, *Form 10-K, 2011*, 9, 93.
54 Jim Polson and Mark Chediak, "NRG Energy to Buy Edison Mission Energy for $2.64 Billion," *Bloomberg News*, October 18, 2013, at http://www.bloomberg.com/news/2013-10-18/nrg-energy-agrees-to-purchase-edison-mission-energy.html (last visited August 29, 2014); NRG Energy, *Form 10-K, 2013*, 9, 23–26.
55 Mirant, *Form 10-K, 2000*, at 4.

revenues, which jumped from $2.27 billion in 1999 to $13.3 billion in 2000 and $31.5 billion in 2001. Unfortunately, these inflated revenues were primarily the product of the same fraudulent accounting that some of its rivals had employed. Restated operating revenues were $4 billion for 2000 and $8.5 billion in 2001.[56]

As of December 31, 2002, Mirant owned or controlled through operating agreements more than 21,800 MW of capacity, but had a $2.3 billion loss from continuing operations. Mirant had $1.7 billion in scheduled debt maturities during 2003, and did not have sufficient liquidity to repay debt maturities as they came due. The sale of investments in the United Kingdom, Germany, China, and other countries was used to reduce debt, along with the cancelation of purchase or sale of seventy turbines. Mirant scaled back its commodity trading activities to reduce the impact on liquidity and credit positions. Despite these efforts, in July 2003, Mirant filed voluntary petitions for relief under Chapter 11. Mirant emerged from bankruptcy protection on January 3, 2006. Mirant sued Southern in 2005, saying that Southern had saddled the company with crippling debt before spinning it off. Southern settled for $202 million. In the third quarter of 2006, Mirant auctioned off Philippine businesses and some U.S. natural gas–fired assets, garnering $5.1 billion, of which $4 billion was used for stock repurchases, reflecting a poor investment environment in the power business. The result of divestiture activities was to create a smaller, more financially stable Mirant. At the end of 2007, Mirant owned or leased 10,280 MW of electric generating capacity.[57] On December 3, 2010, Mirant and Reliant Resources merged, with the new company named GenOn Energy, Inc.[58]

In June 1999, the Texas legislature adopted an electric restructuring law in order to allow retail electric competition with respect to all customer classes beginning in January 2002. In response to this legislation, CenterPoint, formerly Reliant Energy, adopted a business separation plan. Under the plan, Reliant Resources Inc. was incorporated in Delaware in August 2000, and CenterPoint transferred all of its unregulated businesses to Reliant. Reliant completed an IPO of approximately 20 percent of common stock in May 2001 and received net proceeds

---

[56] Mirant, *Form 10-K, 2000*, at 8–10; Mirant, *Form 10-K, 2001*, at 24; Mirant, *Form 10-K, 2002*, at F-3.

[57] Mirant, *Form 10-K, 2002*, 3, 36, F-8; Mirant, *Form 10-K, 2006*, 6; Mirant, *Form 10-K, 2007*, 5; Mirant, *Form 10-K, 2008*, 5.

[58] GenOn Energy, *Form 10-K, 2011*, 1.

of $1.7 billion. Reliant purchased Orion Power Holdings[59] in February 2002 for $2.9 billion, in effect swapping out Texas generation for generation in other regions. In February 2003, Reliant signed a share purchase agreement to sell its European energy operations for $1.2 billion. As of December 31, 2004, Reliant owned, had an interest in, or leased fifty generation facilities with capacity of 18,737 MW in six regions of the United States. Still, despite $10 billion in revenue, Reliant struggled to turn a profit, as net losses from 2002 to 2006 totaled $2.6 billion. Some of these losses stemmed from the California crisis, as Reliant recorded charges of close to $400 million relating to various settlements. The company also had a goodwill impairment charge of $985 million in 2003, stemming from its overpayment for Orion Power. The most consistently profitable group was its Texas retail energy operations, profiting from consumer inertia. The company began disinvesting, shedding hydropower plants in 2004 and selling three New York plants.[60]

Record heat and Hurricane Ike were a double blow to Reliant's retail operations, along with a failure to adequately hedge against high electricity costs caused by congestion in Houston and skyrocketing natural gas prices. Due to heavy retail losses, Reliant terminated its $300 million retail working capital facility agreement with Merrill Lynch in December 2008. Merrill Lynch contended that Reliant violated the credit sleeve and reimbursement agreement and filed an action seeking a judgment declaring an event of default. Reliant was faced with a credit crisis, as it would either have to post cash for outstanding letters of credit and/or post collateral for new retail supply and hedging transactions. Reliant exited the commercial and industrial portions of its retail energy business to reduce its collateral posting obligations. In February 2009, Reliant sold its Texas retail business to NRG. The litigation with Merrill was dismissed concurrent with the sale. Reliant became a pure generation play.[61]

After the 1996 deregulation of California's electricity market, PG&E set up the National Energy Group in 1998 to administer pipelines and power plants, as well as to trade gas and electricity. The company had more than 600 miles of pipelines and 23 power plants, mainly in the

---

[59] Founded in March 1998, Orion Power was a joint venture of Baltimore Gas and Electric and Goldman Sachs. Orion purchased seven generating plants located in Ohio and Pennsylvania from Duquesne Light, as well as Columbia Electric Corporation, a power generation company. Orion Power Holdings, *Form 10-K*, *2000*.

[60] Reliant Resources, *Form 10-K*, *2002*; Reliant Resources, *Form 10-K*, *2003*, 6; Reliant Resources, *Form 10-K*, *2006*, 18–19; Reliant Resources, *Form 10-K*, *2006*, 36, F-159.

[61] Reliant Resources, *Form 10-K*, *2008*, 1; Reliant Resources, *Form 10-K*, *2009*, 3.

Northwest. Its Energy Trading group swapped billions of dollars' worth of power and natural gas. National Energy Group lost $3.4 billion in 2002 and had $7.6 billion in assets and $9 billion in liabilities.[62] National Energy sold off numerous assets, and ceased operations in 2005.[63]

Edison Mission Energy was another utility subsidiary with a grandiose vision that imploded. Edison Mission was one of the first deregulated utility subsidiaries, beginning its acquisition binge in the late 1980s. Edison Mission expanded into Australia and New Zealand, Spain, England, Germany, and Indonesia before selling off its foreign properties in 2004. Edison Mission had slightly more than 10,000 MW of capacity at the end of 2011, with the bulk of it in older coal-fired plants (7,000 MW) in PJM.[64] Edison Mission transferred control of an 1,880 MW coal facility back to GE Capital to avoid additional investments in pollution equipment. Edison Mission also said it would shut down two coal-fired power plants in Chicago by 2014. S&P lowered its credit rating on Edison Mission to CCC+ from B−, noting the company faced greater refinancing risk in 2013 with reduced cash flow prospects from its coal-fueled assets.[65]

CMS Energy, the parent of Consumers' Power, wowed Wall Street in the 1990s by going global and expanding into almost every part of the energy industry. However, its rise and fall rivaled that of Dynegy. CEO William McCormick Jr. rescued CMS from the verge of bankruptcy after it built a $4 billion nuclear plant that never opened. He managed to convert that to a gas cogeneration plant and expanded the company into fields like interstate gas pipelines and oil exploration. McCormick resigned after the company disclosed sham electricity trades. CMS, which had a loss of $545 million in 2001, had inflated revenue by 28 percent over two years. CMS cooperated with investigations of the trades by the SEC, the Commodities Futures Trading Commission (CFTC), and U.S. attorneys.[66] The sham trades, which inflated revenues by $5.2 billion in

---

[62] Carolyn Said, "Power Unit is Bankrupt: PG&E Plans to Abandon National Energy Group," *SFGate*, July 9, 2003, at http://www.sfgate.com/cgi-bin/article.cgi?f=/c/a/2003/07/09/BU197233.DTL#ixzz1xGjrLmF3 (last visited June 8, 2012).

[63] http://www.negt.com/ (last visited August 30, 2014).

[64] Edison International, *Form 10-K 2011*, 13, 25.

[65] "Edison Unit Can't Finance Pa. Homer City Coal Plant Upgrade," *Reuters*, March 2, 2012, at http://www.reuters.com/article/2012/03/02/utilities-edisoninternational-homercity-idUSL2E8E22JS20120302 (last visited June 8, 2012).

[66] "Chief of CMS Energy Says He Is Resigning," *New York Times*, May 25, 2002, at http://www.nytimes.com/2002/05/25/business/chief-of-cms-energy-says-he-is-resigning.html?ref=cmsenergycorporation (last visited September 21, 2011).

2000 and 2001, resulted in the company shutting down its Marketing Services and Trading unit, and selling off its natural gas and electricity contracts in 2003. The suits were settled for $200 million in 2007.[67] As debt woes mounted, the company moved to sell off 3.6 billion in assets, including foreign assets, the Panhandle natural gas pipeline, and its wholesale natural gas trading book.[68] CMS Energy has 1,135 MW of generation while the regulated subsidiary, Consumers Energy, has a little more than 6,000 MW of capacity.[69]

Power marketers help integrate these new independent producers into nascent wholesale markets. Enron was the leader and pioneer, introducing financial derivatives to the electricity markets. Electricity derivatives allow hedging, which potentially reduced risk for both producers and consumers. Derivatives allow for the creation of multi-period electricity supply contracts and provided instruments that could insure against weather events and changes in input prices, such as natural gas. Unfortunately, the financial shenanigans at Enron have obscured the company's role in modernizing the U.S. energy industries.

Kenneth Lay became chief executive of Houston Natural Gas in 1984. Houston Natural Gas was purchased by InterNorth, a natural gas pipeline company headquartered in Omaha, Nebraska, in May 1985. The takeover of Houston Natural Gas was largely the brainchild of Lay. Working with Michael Milken, Lay helped structure the deal as a leveraged buyout relying heavily on junk bond finance.[70] Houston Natural Gas had purchased the Transwestern pipeline and the Florida Gas pipeline. Combined with InterNorth, the new company would have 37,000 miles of pipe and annual revenues around $10 billion. Lay became the president of the new company a year later, renamed Enron, and based in Houston, Texas.[71]

---

[67] "Utility Settles Lawsuit," *New York Times*, January 6, 2007 at http://query.nytimes .com/gst/fullpage.html?res=9D05E4D61430F935A35752C0A9619C8B63ref= cmsenergycorporation (last visited September 23, 2011).

[68] "CMS Energy Selling Some Assets Outside of the U.S.," *New York Times*, October 27, 2001, at http://www.nytimes.com/2001/10/27/business/company-news-cms-energy-selling-some-assets-outside-of-the-us.html?ref=cmsenergycorporation (last visited September 23, 2011).; Andrew Sorkin, "Southern Union and Insurer Unit to Acquire CMS Gas Pipeline" *New York Times*, December 23, 2002, at http://www. nytimes.com/2002/12/23/business/southern-union-and-insurer-unit-to-acquire-cms-gas-pipeline.html?ref=cmsenergycorporation (last visited September 23, 2011).

[69] CMS Energy, *Form 10-K 2013*, 17, 24.

[70] Christopher Culp and Steve Hanke, "Empire of the Sun: An Economic Interpretation of Enron's Energy Business," *Policy Analysis* 470 (February 20, 2003): 5.

[71] Robert Bryce, *Pipe Dreams: Greed, Ego and the Death of Enron* (New York, PublicAffairs, 2002): 31–33.

In 1989, Jeff Skilling, who was working at McKinsey as an Enron consultant, realized that there was plenty of natural gas available, and there was plenty of demand from new utilities that wanted to burn gas to make electricity, but there was no intermediary that could aggregate and balance the gas supplies coming from producers with the demand coming from consumers. Skilling called his idea the Gas Bank. Gas users liked it because they would be able to predict fuel costs over multiyear terms. In less than two weeks Skilling and Vice Chairman Rich Kinder lined up multiyear contracts for a billion dollars' worth of gas. Initially, Enron depended on the spot market, as producers did not want to sell at the prevailing low prices. Within two years, Enron had signed contracts with thirty-five producers and more than fifty gas customers. Enron also developed a supply of gas from its subsidiary, Enron Oil and Gas, and could guarantee delivery to gas consumers over long periods of time. Enron would then sell the gas through the Gas Bank. Skilling also came up with the idea of providing financing to natural gas producers in return for supply contracts. On August 1, 1990, Skilling became chairman and chief executive officer of the newly created Enron Finance Corp.[72]

Employing both internal gas reserves and its widespread pipelines and concurrent knowledge of the natural gas markets, Enron gradually accepted the role of market maker who could take positions as a buyer and seller to close gaps between supply and demand over a wide geographic area. Enron was engaged in the development of a derivatives market in gas in which Enron would provide its customers with various price risk management solutions, forward contracts, and option contracts. Given that the company was already selling physical "futures" in its contracts, the next logical step was to develop financial futures and hedges to balance its portfolio of physical obligations. The company paired with a New York bank, Bankers Trust, which had derivatives expertise. In 1991, having developed an in-house derivatives-trading capability, Enron dissolved the partnership. Bankers Trust remained in the natural gas futures business, along with Morgan Stanley and AIG Financial.[73]

In 1990, the New York Mercantile Exchange (NYMEX) began trading futures based on delivery of gas to the Henry Hub, a major gas depot in Louisiana where fourteen different intra- and interstate gas pipelines come together. With the NYMEX's published prices, traders were given

---

[72] Bryce, *Pipe Dreams: Greed, Ego and the Death of Enron*, 54–55; Kurt Eichenwald, *Conspiracy of Fools* (New York, Broadway Books, 2005): 43–45.

[73] Loren Fox, *Enron: The Rise and Fall* (Hoboken, John Wiley & Sons, 2003): 24–28.

TABLE 10.3. *Top Ten Wholesale Power Marketers, 1998*

Company	GWHs	Market Shares
Enron Power Marketing	161.2	19.3%
Southern Co. Energy Marketing*	66.3	7.9%
Electric Clearing House	51.4	6.2%
Aquila Energy (UtiliCorp)*	43.7	5.2%
LG&E Energy Marketing*	41.7	5.0%
Entergy Power Marketing*	38.2	4.6%
Duke Energy Trading and Marketing*	31.7	3.8%
PG&E Energy Trading*	30.4	3.7%
Statoil Energy Trading	29.6	3.5%
PacifiCorp Power Marketing*	27.4	3.3%
All Others	328.4	37.5%
Total	850.0	100.0%

* Affiliates of traditional utilities.
Source: EEI, *Edison Times* (December 1998).

a reliable market index that they could then use to establish prices for all kinds of gas contracts. NYMEX provided Enron and other natural gas marketers a source of derivatives on an organized futures exchange to balance out their risk portfolios. The NYMEX Henry Hub index became the anchor price for deals everywhere but the West Coast. Enron piggy-backed on the index by offering four hubs along its pipeline system for delivery, and adjusting prices accordingly at those points. Enron gradu-ally evolved from a physical to financial trading company, and by 1992 Enron was the largest marketer of gas in North America, selling nearly 5.6 billion cubic feet daily.[74]

In 1993, Enron obtained a power marketer license from the FERC and set up a team of power traders. In June 1994, Enron North America executed its first electricity trade. Enron soon became the leading marketer in what was still a small market, selling 7.8 million MWhs in 1995. After Enron acquired Portland General Electric in 1997, Enron started to engage in trades based on the spark spread (the spread between natural gas prices and the price of electricity that could be generated by a typical gas-fired power plant from that gas). Enron also began selling weather derivatives. Enron supported the Rio global warming agreement in 1992 and urged U.S. participation in the Kyoto Treaty in 1997 because the

[74] *Id.*, 29–30.

company saw a business opportunity in global trading of CO_2 emission permits.[75]

By 1999, the four largest players in electricity trading were Enron, Southern Company, Utilicorp, and Entergy. PacifiCorp and Louisville Gas and Electric had dropped out because of trading losses. NGC, Aquila, Duke Energy, and other gas traders also entered electricity trading. Energy trading became the new "hot" business opportunity, as Enron, Dynegy, Duke, Reliant, and El Paso poured millions into their trading operations. Companies like CMS Energy and Calpine joined the party.[76]

The CFTC oversees on-exchange trading of energy-related futures and options contracts based on crude oil, natural gas, heating oil, propane, gasoline, and coal. The overwhelming majority of on-exchange transactions were executed on NYMEX.[77] Electricity trading through an exchange started for the first time in March 1996, when electricity futures were traded on the NYMEX. Electricity options were started on NYMEX in April 1996. NYMEX reported that in 1998, more than 80 million futures contracts were traded.[78] These financial trades allow generators, power marketers, and customers to hedge or buy insurance against unexpected changes in prices. Financial trades can either be over-the-counter trades where specified contracts are traded openly or negotiated privately by the counterparties.

The CFTC did not regulate trading of energy products on spot markets or forward markets, due to a ruling by Wendy Gramm, then chairman of the CFTC and wife of Senator Phil Gramm. Enron, along with eight other companies, such as Mobil, Exxon, BP, J.P. Morgan, and Chase Manhattan, lobbied Dr. Gramm for an exemption from regulatory oversight on energy derivatives contracts. Of the nine companies writing letters of support for the rule change, Enron gave the largest contributions to Phil Gramm's campaign fund. Wendy Gramm then joined the Enron board

---

[75] *Id.*, 68, 110.

[76] Greg Hassell, "Energy Trading Fast, Furious And Lucrative," *Houston Chronicle*, May 20, 2001, at http://www.chron.com/default/article/Energy-trading-fast-furious-and-lucrative-2020246.php (last visited September 1, 2011).

[77] Other key commodity exchanges were the Chicago Board of Trade (CBOT), the Chicago Mercantile Exchange (CME), and the Minneapolis Grain Exchange (MGE).

[78] Mohammad Shahidehpour and Muwaffaq Alomoush, Restructured Electrical Power Systems: Operation, Trading, and Volatility (New York, Marcel Dekker, Inc., 2001): 250; "Staff Report to the Federal Energy Regulatory Commission on the Causes of Wholesale Electric Pricing Abnormalities in the Midwest during June 1998" (September 22, 1998).

after her tenure at the CFTC.[79] The rule was written into law with the passage in 2000 of the Commodity Futures Modernization Act.[80] Senator Phil Gramm ensured that the legislation included a complete exclusion for energy-trading companies from financial or disclosure requirements for portfolios of OTC derivative securities.[81] The bill amended the Commodity Exchange Act to exempt two types of markets for contracts based on energy products from much of the CFTC's oversight. The first type was bilateral trades between sophisticated entities such as regulated banks and well-capitalized companies. The second type was electronic multilateral trades among eligible commercial entities that have an ability to either make or take delivery of the underlying commodity, or dealers that regularly provide hedging services to those entities. Other types of bilateral energy trades that were unregulated by virtue of statutory exclusions were forward contracts and swap contracts.[82]

On November 29, 1999 Enron Corporation launched EnronOnline, an electronic trading platform which allowed no-cost transactions and real-time pricing information for approximately 850 commodities including electricity and natural gas. Unlike every other commodities-trading exchange, which match buyers and sellers in "many-to-many" trading exchanges, EnronOnline was designed and operated as a "one-to-many" platform, allowing buyers and sellers to trade only with Enron. EnronOnline reflected the company's ambitions but also the lack of alternative market makers during the first days of electricity markets. To conduct a trade with Enron on EnronOnline, a trader simply clicked on either the offer or the bid price, depending on whether the trader wished to buy or sell at Enron's posted price, and the trade was executed. As a market maker and counterparty on one side of every trade, Enron had the opportunity to influence price signals in electricity and natural gas markets.

[79] Public Citizen, *Blind Faith: How Deregulation and Enron's Influence Over Government Looted Billions From Americans*, December 2001, 10. Dr. Gramm would receive almost $1 million in compensation from Enron over the next eight years. *Id*. at p. 15.

[80] Commodity Futures Modernization Act of 2000, Pub. L. No. 106–554, 114 Stat. 2763 (2000).

[81] William Bratton, "Does Corporate Law Protect the Interest of Shareholders and Other Stakeholders? Enron and the Dark Side of Shareholder Value," 76 *Tulane Law Review* 1275, 1280 (June 2002); Minority Staff, Committee on Government Reform, U.S. House of Representatives, "How Lax Regulation and Inadequate Oversight Contributed to the Enron Collapse," 107th Congress, February 7, 2002.

[82] Statement of Hon. James E. Newsome, Chairman of the Commodities Futures Trading Commission, in *The Effect of the Bankruptcy of Enron on the Functioning of Energy Markets*, Hearing before the Subcommittee On Energy and Air Quality, 107th Congress, 2nd Session, February 13, 2002, 45–46.

EnronOnline soon triggered new automated competitors. In March 2000, BP Amoco, Royal Dutch/Shell, Goldman Sachs, and other companies formed Intercontinental Exchange (ICE), an Internet market for trading energy and other commodities. Power marketers Aquila, AEP, Duke Energy, Reliant, and Mirant later joined ICE. ICE purchased three regulated futures exchanges, built its own clearinghouse, and invested in its own compliance operations. ICE Futures US, a subsidiary formerly called the New York Board of Trade, has long been monitored by the CFTC. ICE purchased the International Petroleum Exchange in London in 2001. The ICE trading network allows traders with at least $100 million in assets to conduct OTC swaps. ICE now handles about a tenth of all OTC swaps involving natural gas and electricity.[83] In September 2000, Dynegy, Williams Companies, Texas Utilities, and other companies created TradeSpark, another online exchange.[84]

Enron's revenues increased by $10 billion from 1998 to 1999, and by $60 billion (to $100 billion) from 1999 to 2000. Enron's spectacular revenue growth stemmed from the fact that when it effected a transaction, it followed the energy industry practice of booking the entire contract sale price as a revenue, instead of booking only its commission, and the cost of filling those contracts as costs of goods sold. Meanwhile, net after-tax income rose by only $1 billion in 1998, and then by only $500 million in each of 1999 and 2000. Entrance barriers into energy trading were low, and as time went on, Enron had to deal with dozens of competitors who hired away its employees to compete in this business, undercutting its profit margins. The California energy crisis and resulting high electricity prices provided extraordinary returns to all traders in that market, but as California's prices dropped back to normal, shrinking trading returns became more apparent.[85]

While competition cut margins, the disadvantage of being the counterparty for every trade was the requirement for sufficient liquidity to float commodities to meet the company's trading obligations. Borrowing

---

[83] Diana Henriques, "After Facing Scrutiny, Commodities Trading Accepts Regulations," *New York Times*, July 25, 2008, at http://www.nytimes.com/2008/07/25/business /worldbusiness/25ice.html?scp=17&sq=Natural%20Gas%20Clearinghouse&st= Search (last visited September 21, 2011).

[84] Fox, *Enron: The Rise and Fall*, 234–35.

[85] William Bratton, "Does Corporate Law Protect the Interest of Shareholders and Other Stakeholders? Enron and the Dark Side of Shareholder Value," *Tulane Law Review* 76 (June 2002): 1275, 1299–1300; Stuart L. Gillan and John D. Martin, "Financial Engineering, Corporate Governance, and the Collapse of Enron," Center for Corporate Governance (November 6, 2002): 6–7.

large sums of cash on a short-term basis required sufficient real cash flow to cover interest payments (not paper earnings from mark-to-market accounting). It was also necessary to maintain a high credit rating to maintain the confidence of counterparties to each trade. When that confidence collapsed, so did Enron's trading business. UBS Warburg acquired Enron's trading group and platform, and even though it renamed it UBS Warburg Energy, the staff was almost all Enron employees.[86] Enron's implosion left most of its intellectual capital intact, and Enron employees would become omnipresent among energy firms.

---

[86] Kristen Hays, "UBS Warburg Launches Trading Business Acquired From Enron," *Associated Press*, February 12, 2002, at http://www.highbeam.com/doc/1P1-50176302.html (last visited September 23, 2011).

11

The Politics of Electricity Deregulation

There was a lot of confusion about the meaning of deregulation and competition. Wholesale competition appealed to distribution utilities, trapped inside the transmission systems of surrounding IOUs, and IOUs with surplus power to sell. Retail wheeling was primarily retail competition limited to large customers, many at the transmission level, who wanted to purchase power from third parties and require their local utility to "wheel" that power to their facilities. This required some sort of open access to transmission lines, similar to common-carrier status in the natural gas and oil pipelines. Utilities objected to both the loss of a significant portion of their customer base to competitive bypass and the requirement that they operate their transmission system for the benefit of third parties.

The expansion of wholesale markets set IOUs against rural electric cooperatives and public power groups, and their respective trade associations, the EEI, the National Rural Electric Cooperative Association, and the American Public Power Association (APPA). The IOUs saw the smaller utilities as captive customers and did not want them shopping for cheaper power and be forced to supply transmission services to wheel that power.

However, these same groups became allies in contesting retail wheeling, because it threatened to "cherry pick" their best customers, driving up costs to their remaining customer base. The rural electric cooperatives and municipalities who fought hard to gain access to competitive wholesale supply sources closed ranks with the IOUs to oppose opening the transmission grid to retail customers. Consumer groups opposed retail wheeling because it could raise costs for small consumers, and it endangered programs that subsidized low-income customers. Environmentalists opposed retail wheeling for the threat it presented to DSM and energy efficiency programs, and because competing on cost would create pressure to relax environmental regulation.[1] While many IOUs opposed retail wheeling, they also began to see it as inevitable, given the political pressure building for permitting more competition.[2]

The driving force behind deregulatory efforts were industrial consumers, who saw the opportunity to bypass integrated utilities as they did in the natural gas markets, buying electricity from low-cost independent generators fueled by natural gas. Deregulation would also allow them to avoid the charges imposed to finance DSM programs and the politically popular cost shifting that required them to subsidize low-income and other residential consumers. Quantity discounts in the form of declining-block tariffs were a well-known feature of retail electricity pricing and a contentious topic in ratemaking proceedings. They are driven by supply costs, which fall by more than half in moving from smaller to bigger purchasers. This pattern provided a clear cost-based rationale for quantity discounts. Marginal prices were nearly identical to marginal costs before the mid-1970s, a trend that continued for larger industrial customers through 2000. Among smaller manufacturing customers, after 1981, marginal supply costs exceeded marginal prices by 10 percent or more, reflecting favorable treatment of smaller firms.[3]

The onset of rising real electricity prices in 1973 encouraged the migration of electricity-intensive manufacturing activity to areas served by utilities with cheaper electricity. Bigger purchasers also had greater opportunity and incentive to reduce price per kWh by managing load factors (ratio of average to peak demand), taking high-voltage power, responding to peak-load pricing incentives, and accepting interruptible power.[4] A manufacturer can respond to higher electricity tariffs by taking steps to reduce power requirements per unit of output or by taking steps to lower the per-kWh cost of supplying its power (or both). Plants that pay relatively high electricity prices compared to other plants in the same industry

[1] Kenneth W. Costello, Robert E. Burns, and Youssef Hegazy, "Overview of Issues Relating to the Retail Wheeling of Electricity," NRRI 94–09 (May 1994): 24, fn. 43.

[2] Costello, Burns, and Hegazy, "Overview of Issues Relating to the Retail Wheeling of Electricity," 24, fn. 44, citing "Survey: Two-Thirds of Utility Execs Consider Retail Wheeling Inevitable," *Electric Power Daily*, January 12, 1994, 3. The survey was based on responses from 285 senior utility managers.

[3] Steven J. Davis, Cheryl Grim, John Haltiwanger, and Mary Streitwieser, "Electricity Pricing to U.S. Manufacturing Plants, 1963–2000" (April 2009): 2–5.

[4] Davis et al., "Electricity Pricing to U.S. Manufacturing Plants, 1963–2000," 15–16.

tend to have a high value of output per kWh. Plants that use electricity-intensive production technology are more likely to increase output per kWh as prices rise.[5]

While industrial customers lobbied for deregulation, they saw it as a much narrower issue of retail wheeling, similar to natural gas. ELCON objected to the wide spread in electricity prices, both between states and within states, owing to the fragmented structure of regulated electric utilities. Industries wanted the opportunity to engage in retail wheeling in order to exploit those price differences and obtain the lowest-cost electricity.[6] They wanted to contract for low-cost electricity and require the owner of the transmission grid to act as a common carrier in order to gain access to this power. While they gave lip service to market efficiency, their real interest was reducing their cost of power. The problem of stranded investment was proposed to be alleviated by provision of adequate notice, but no more than five years. ELCON suggested that the alternative was plant relocations, investments in cogeneration, or other measures that would have similar impacts in terms of shifting costs to other consumers.[7]

Advocates of deregulation formed a plethora of corporate front groups and coalitions, including the Alliance for Competitive Electricity,[8] Citizens for State Power, Electric Utilities Shareholders' Alliances, the Alliance for Power Privatization, and the Coalition for Customer Choice in Electricity. The campaign was coordinated by Americans for Affordable Electricity, whose members included the Ford Motor Company, Enron, and various utilities. Americans for Affordable Electricity raised millions of dollars for lobbying and advertising, spending $4 million a year on top of what its members spent. Member companies and groups also donated the time of their public relations, legal, policy, and lobbying personnel.[9]

---

[5] Steven Davis, Cheryl Grim, and John Haltiwanger, "Productivity Dispersion and Input Prices: the Case of Electricity," U.S. Bureau of the Census, Center for Economic Studies, CES 08–33 (September 2008).

[6] John Anderson, "The Competitive Sourcing of Retail Electricity: An Idea Whose Time Has (Finally) Come," presented at the Utility Director's Workshop, Williamsburg, VA, September 10, 1993, 8.

[7] Id., 11.

[8] Founding members include Central Maine Power, Detroit Edison, Duke Energy, Entergy, GPU, New Century Energies, NEES, Public Service of New Mexico, PSEG, and SCE. *Restructuring Today*, March 27, 1998.

[9] Sharon Beder, "The Electricity Deregulation Con Game," Center for Media and Democracy, at http://www.prwatch.org/prwissues/2003Q3/dereg.html (last visited March 19, 2010). Also Ruth Conniff, "Power Companies Use Sham 'Grassroot' Groups in Push

The leading advocate for deregulated markets, other than industrial customers, was Enron. Enron's interest was not exactly benign, but neither was it the nefarious corporation suggested by many in the media and among public interest groups. In the early 1990s, Enron pursued a strategy of deregulation along with opposition to regulated, centralized auction markets. Enron's business was arbitrage, which required open markets but also a lack of transparency that made its services valuable; in transparent, efficient markets prices are obvious to all participants and arbitrage is relatively costless. So Enron opposed a national grid and wanted bilateral contracting markets instead of a central spot market.[10] Terms of bilateral contracts are generally unpublished, and services like *Platt's* can only provide a sampling of terms, so a sophisticated contracting party like Enron has a significant negotiating advantage.

Political campaign donations helped Enron play a major role in the deregulation campaign. Enron donated just under $6 million to election campaigns beginning with the 1989–90 election cycle. It contributed to the campaigns of 71 senators and 188 House representatives. It became the sixth-highest contributor during the 1994 election cycle and by 2000 was the top contributor of all corporations in the energy/natural resources sector. Enron also spent millions lobbying Congress, the White House, and federal agencies. Like the EEI, Enron drew its lobbyists from both the Republican and Democrat parties. By the late 1990s, it employed more than 150 people on state and federal government affairs in Washington, DC.[11] Enron spent more than $2 million on lobbying in 2000, including a stable of lobbyists and consultants such as former Christian Coalition head Ralph Reed, FERC Chairwoman Elizabeth Moler, Marc Racicot, the new Republican National Committee chairman, and Jack Quinn, former White House counsel to President Clinton.[12] Enron was the largest patron

---

for Deregulation," first published in the *Progressive*, reprinted at http://www.monitor .net/monitor/9707a/wattage.html (last visited June 10, 2012).

[10] Catherine Abbott and Jeffrey Skilling, "Untitled Draft Presentation on Competitive Market Models," Enron Gas Services (1993).

[11] Sharon Beder, "The Electricity Deregulation Con Game," Center for Media and Democracy, at http://www.prwatch.org/prissues/2003Q3/dereg.html (last visited March 19, 2010). Kenneth Lay made direct use of his political connections at times, for example when he asked Governor George W. Bush to call Pennsylvania Governor Tom Ridge to help Enron crack into the regulated Pennsylvania electricity market. Robert Scheer, "Connect the Enron Dots to Bush," *The Nation*, December 24, 2001, at http://www .thenation.com/article/connect-enron-dots-bush (last visited June 23, 2011).

[12] John Dunbar, Robert Moore, and Mary Jo Sylwester, "Enron Top Brass Accused of Dumping Stock Were Big Political Donors," Center for Public Integrity, January 9,

of George W. Bush's political career. A frequent flier on Enron corporate jets, Bush received $774,100 from Enron management and the company, including $312,500 for his campaigns for governor. Lay reportedly is the only executive who got a private audience with Vice President Cheney to discuss energy policy.[13]

Enron was also a major campaign contributor at the state level, as well as spending millions on lobbying. Enron spent $548,526 in Texas on state candidates in 1998 and 2000, $438,155 in California, $149,549 in Oregon, $142,750 in Florida, and smaller amounts in dozens of other states.[14] However, except for Texas, where Enron had a home court advantage, and Oregon, where the company made a large political investment to protect its investment in Portland General Electric, these efforts had minimal impact. Local utilities simply had far more resources at their disposal and decades of entrenched political network connections. The real force for deregulation in most states were industries with substantial local employment and the financial resources and political capital to counter utility lobbying.

Wholesale power producers also supported retail competition, which would allow them to reach new customers. They found ways within the existing regulatory structure to bypass the local utility and sell power to large customers, but they wanted easier access to new markets. Cities, often in league with large companies with plants located in their jurisdiction, used the threat of municipalization to force suppliers to cut rates. State commissions in high-cost states such as New York began allowing some industrial facilities to bypass their utilities and buy power directly, setting compensation for stranded assets at levels far below the level requested by the affected utility.[15]

These actions encouraged incumbent utilities to engage in new tactics to head off the threat of retail bypass by their large customers. In Illinois, Commonwealth Edison (Com Ed) won legislative permission, over PUC opposition, to create an unregulated subsidiary to provide

2002, at http://projects.publicintegrity.org/report.aspx?aid=221 (last visited June 27, 2011).

[13] Pratap Chatterjee, "Enron: Pulling the Plug on the Global Power Broker," CorpWatch, December 17, 2001, available at http://www.commondreams.org/views01/1217-04.htm (last visited June 23, 2011).

[14] Table in *USA Today*, January 27, 2002, from the National Institute on Money in State Politics, at http://www.usatoday.com/money/energy/2002-01-28-enron-chart.htm (last visited June 27, 2011).

[15] Peter Navarro, "Electric Utilities: The Argument," *Harvard Business Review* (January–February 1996): 122.

electricity-related services to large customers. Niagara Mohawk, facing a threat that as many as 100 of its largest customers would switch to self-generation, obtained regulatory approval to lower the rates it charged to these customers.[16] One effect was to reduce the resistance of high-cost utilities to deregulation, as they either saw opportunities to diversify or reduce their exposure to losses from retail competition (i.e., lower rates to industrial customers required shifting costs to the rest of one's rate base; once these rates were approved, the loss of those industrial customers had a smaller impact on net revenues).

The argument was made, with little analysis, that retail competition was necessary to ensure competitive wholesale markets. It was argued that competitive wholesale markets would not work if distribution utilities remained regulated purchasing agents in a deregulated wholesale market. The obvious but misleading parallel was long-distance telephony. Of course, the individual customers would be primarily large industrial consumers, as no one really understood how competition would play out at the retail distribution level.

Their arguments were supported by a spate of studies showing huge savings from electricity restructuring, combined with a general misinterpretation of the British experience (and other foreign markets) with deregulation as a model for U.S. states. A report released by Citizens for a Sound Economy estimated that consumers could initially save between $9.50 and $18 per month, with long-run declines in consumer electric bills of 40 percent.[17] A study sponsored by the American Gas Association estimated that electricity prices in a deregulated generation market with retail competition would drop by an average of 14 percent by 2015, with price declines of about 25 percent in high-cost states such as California,

---

[16] Bernard S. Black and Richard J. Pierce, Jr., "The Choice Between Markets and Central Planning in Regulating the U.S. Electricity Industry," 93 *Columbia Law Review* 1339, 1352–53 (1993).

[17] Michael Maloney, Robert McCormick, and Robert Sauer, "Customer Choice, Customer Value: An Analysis of Retail Competition in America's Electric Industry" (Washington, DC: Citizens for a Sound Economy Foundation, 1996). Citizens for a Sound Economy was established in 1984 by David Koch and Charles Koch of Koch Industries. Citizens for a Sound Economy received almost $5 million from various Koch foundations between 1986 and 1990, and David Koch and several Koch Industries employees serve as directors. Dan Morgan, "Think Tanks: Corporations' Quiet Weapon," *Washington Post*, January 29, 2000, A1, at http://www.washingtonpost.com/ac2/wp-dyn?pagename=article&node=&contentId=A46598-2000Jan28; http://www.endgame.org/corpcon2.html#CitizensforaSoundEconomy (last visited July 25, 2010).

New England, and the Mid-Atlantic region.[18] DOE's Energy Information Administration (EIA) was more circumspect, finding that retail prices for electricity could be lower on average by as much as 6–13 percent within two years. However, if policymakers mandated full recovery of stranded costs, there would be little difference between competitive and regulated prices in the short term.[19]

Electricity industries had already been restructured in a number of other countries – including Sweden, Norway, Spain, Argentina, Chile, New Zealand, Canada (Alberta), parts of Australia, and the United Kingdom (England and Wales). U.S. regulators tended to point to the success of the UK market, with only limited understanding of the operations of the UK market and the differences between the UK and the bifurcated U.S. markets.

The British Electricity Act of 1989 set out dramatic structural changes that went into effect on March 31, 1990. Under the new structure the former public-sector, Central Electricity Generating Board operations were transferred to four successor companies. The high-voltage transmission system was owned and operated by the National Grid Company. Nuclear power remained in the hands of a government-owned company, which would act as a price taker. The coal-, oil-, and gas-powered stations were divided between National Power and PowerGen, who controlled 75–80 percent of capacity and were essentially a duopoly with the ability to set price. Initially, most electricity sales were covered by cost-based contracts that hedged the pool price, so that a generator would not affect its short-run revenues by raising its bids. As excess capacity was absorbed, prices started to increase significantly.[20]

In the United Kingdom, all electricity supply was required to flow through a centralized spot market known as the Pool. The NGC then procured power from the Pool by arranging all supply bids from lowest to highest bid and setting price at the marginal bid that made supply equal to "need." Regulatory oversight was the responsibility of the Office of

---

[18] "AGA Study Forecasts Average 14 Percent Drop In Electricity Prices by 2015 In A Deregulated Generation Market," *Foster Electric Report* (August 9, 1998), 24.

[19] EIA, *Electricity Prices in a Competitive Environment: Marginal Cost Pricing of Generation Services and Financial Status of Electric Utilities* (August 1997): xii–xiv.

[20] Richard Green and David Newbery, "Competition in the British Electricity Spot Market," *Journal of Political Economy* 100 (1992): 929–30, 946. Green and Newbery had warned of the potential for market power, as did Niles-Henrik March von der Fehr and David Harbor, "Spot Market Competition in the UK Electricity Industry," *Economic Journal* 103 (1993): 531–46.

Electricity Regulation. Concerns about the level and volatility of prices led to several investigations and threats of referral to the Monopolies and Mergers Commission (which had the authority to break up the companies) until a 1994 agreement was reached in which price caps were instituted and generation was to be divested by each of the two companies.[21]

Privatization and restructuring delivered substantial improvements in efficiency. After the first five years, costs were 6 percent lower, labor productivity doubled, real fuel costs per unit generated fell dramatically (even in the publicly owned nuclear company), and substantial new investment occurred at considerably lower unit cost than before privatization. However, problems with the Pool led to a redesign of the British market in 1998. The Pool was replaced by New Electricity Trading Arrangements (NETA). Under NETA, each plant was self-dispatched, and bilateral contracts were used to balance supplies with demand. The Balancing Mechanism, a pay-as-bid auction, resolved the residual imbalances of parties that failed to self-balance. Just before NETA went into effect, the two power companies decided to divest generation so as to be permitted to purchase retail companies. With the new buyers keen to improve the returns on their purchases by increasing plant output, the duopoly equilibrium was no longer sustainable and prices collapsed before NETA went live.[22]

The lesson to be learned from the British electricity market was that there was no lesson to be learned; it was an ongoing experiment in a very different institutional environment than the United States. Unlike most of the countries that had deregulated their electricity markets, institutional considerations made it impossible to engage in comprehensive deregulation in the United States. Only three states had markets large enough to potentially combine wholesale and retail deregulation, and California and New York imported significant quantities of power. In most cases, the combination of numerous state regulatory commissions, integrated utilities, municipal utilities, and electric cooperatives meant market design was driven by political compromise as much as technical clarity.

The problem with the presumption of huge savings from retail deregulation was that they could only come by replacing older, less efficient generation units with new, highly efficient units. While this was socially beneficial, these efficiency savings destroyed the value of existing assets

[21] Frank Wolak and Robert Patrick, "The Impact of Market Rules and Market Structure on the Price Determination Process in the England and Wales Electricity Market," POWER Working Paper (February, 1997): 13–14.

[22] David Newbery, "Electricity Liberalisation in Britain: The Quest for a Satisfactory Wholesale Market Design," *Energy Journal* 26 (2005): 43–70.

financed under the expectation of regulated cost recovery. Utility stockholders would lose the difference between the book value of the expensive plants and contracts and their lower value in the emerging competitive markets (the stranded costs) unless compensated. Generally, the largest component of positive stranded costs, where they existed, was attributable to nuclear power plants, with the second-largest component coming from QF contracts. If utilities received 100 percent reimbursement for stranded costs, there would be little short-term savings from restructuring because the savings from more efficient generation would be used to pay for stranded assets until their book value was paid off. Since this result was politically unacceptable, some combination of paying less than 100 percent recovery of stranded costs and legislating an up-front rate reduction when retail competition was established was employed. Typically, state legislatures provided 5–15 percent initial rate reductions, as part of their restructuring legislation. These reductions were made possible by declining fuel costs and improved generator efficiency (since the least efficient plants were usually the oldest plants and therefore would be gradually retired in any case). Once the mandated rate reductions expired, customers found themselves exposed to the vagaries of market forces.

FERC responded to the problem of stranded costs by essentially mandating full recovery, diverging from its actions during natural gas deregulation. The primary reason for this approach was that the stranded costs that fell under FERC's purview were a small fraction of the total stranded cost exposure.[23] This allowed FERC to take a position that reduced the opposition of integrated utilities to measures that opened electricity markets without engendering a consumer backlash. The real battles over stranded costs took place at the state level.

The general structure of restructuring plans included a competitive transition charge (CTC), which funded the recovery of stranded costs, the wires (transmission and distribution) charge, and an energy cost the incumbent utility would charge customers who chose to purchase from the utility. The incumbent utility was often designated the provider of last resort (POLR), to ensure that all customers had access to electricity. Incumbent utilities wanted state commissions to use a low projected

---

[23] John Burritt McArthur, "The Irreconcilable Differences Between FERC's Natural Gas and Electricity Stranded Cost Treatments," *Buffalo Law Review* 46 (Winter, 1998): 71–122. A Resource Data International study suggested that only $10.4 billion of $114 billion in potential stranded investment was associated with wholesale transactions, similar in magnitude to the costs stranded by open-access transportation of natural gas. Order 888 at 31,787.

electricity price as the basis for the POLR, because this maximized the estimated stranded costs (based on the difference between the projected electricity price and the cost of uneconomic generation units). They were happy to commit to charging a low POLR price conditional on receiving a higher CTC. A low POLR price created a barrier to competitive entry. The result was often the battle of the dispatch models, with consultants projecting different future electricity prices depending on the identity of their clients.

The alternative to forecasting stranded costs was to order the divestiture of generation assets, and stranded costs were calculated as the difference between book value and the revenue received from the sale of the generation assets. This seemed to be a more "exact" method, although it did require a more drastic restructuring process, establishing a completely independent generation market.[24] The driving force behind restructuring was low natural gas prices, and selling assets during a period of low natural gas prices ensured a relatively low price for those assets and high stranded costs. With prices for assets reflecting low natural gas prices, there was little downside risk for purchasers but large upside potential. With a stranded cost calculation, a future true-up could protect consumers from excessive stranded cost payments, but once assets were sold, there was no recourse for correcting a bad bargain.

Estimates of industry-wide stranded costs varied from $10 billion to $500 billion, with the most oft-cited estimates in the $100–200 billion range.[25] The Energy Information Administration suggested a reasonable competitive scenario would result in stranded costs could range between about $72 and $169 billion (1995 dollars), with costs rising

---

[24] Massachusetts and New York states required that generation capacity be divested as a condition for stranded cost recovery. California required divestiture of a large portion (50%) of generation assets. Divestiture sales generally occurred at prices above the book value of the generating facilities. The premiums over book values ranged from 19% to 253%. A variant on divestiture was to require dominant firms to sell portions of their generation capacity as contracts that buyers can bid into the market in competition with the incumbents. Comments of the Staff of the FTC, *Before the Alabama Public Service Commission Docket No. 26427 Restructuring in the Electric Utility Industry* (January 8, 1999): 17, n. 27.

[25] EIA, *The Changing Structure of the Electric Power Industry: An Update* (December 1996); CBO, *Electric Utilities: Deregulation and Stranded Costs* (October 1998): 15–17. The CBO report cited three independent estimates: Lester Baxter and Eric Hirst, "Estimating Potential Stranded Commitments for U.S. Investor-Owned Electric Utilities," ORNL/CON-406 (January 1995) ($72–104 billion), Resource Data International, "Power Markets in the U.S." (1996) ($122 billion), and A. Hackett, J. Cohen, and S. Abbott, "Moody's Calculates Little Change in Potential Stranded Investments" (1996) ($136 billion).

to $400 billion under an intense competition scenario.[26] These estimates were inflated by low natural gas prices and strategic exaggeration as utilities wanted to create an aura of financial peril to improve their negotiating position.

Utility consultants tried to portray the issue as one of economic efficiency and legal rights[27] rather than as a political question of how to distribute the costs of a socially desirable transition in market structure. Ostensibly, the recovery of stranded costs reflected states accepting their obligations under the "regulatory compact," in lieu of being forced to honor their agreements by the courts. The problem with this explanation is that no such "regulatory compact" existed in regulatory law (at least since the Supreme Court overturned the *Smyth v. Ames*[28] line of reasoning), as it was an invention of consultants hired by utilities to protect their interests. Alfred Kahn first presented this position in a *Wall Street Journal* piece in 1985:

The essential basis of public-utility regulation is an implicit bargain between consumers and investors that, in exchange for a monopoly franchise, the company accepts the strict legal obligation to serve all customers on reasonable terms. This means that shareholders accept a return on investment equivalent only to something like the market cost of capital – the minimum that investors must see a reasonable prospect of earning if they are to put up the necessary funds – along with the duty conscientiously to anticipate the future needs of the public and to make whatever investments may be necessary in order to meet them efficiently.[29]

The first mention of a regulatory compact that could be found in a court case is a concurrence in a 1988 DC Circuit case.[30] However, nothing in the case law has ever suggested that a regulatory compact exists, or supersedes

---

[26] EIA, *Electricity Prices in a Competitive Environment: Marginal Cost Pricing of Generation Services and Financial Status of Electric Utilities* (August 1997): xiv.

[27] William J. Baumol and J. Gregory Sidak, "Stranded Costs," 18 *Harvard Journal of Law & Public Policy* 837 (Summer 1995); J. Gregory Sidak and Daniel Spulber, *Deregulatory Takings and the Regulatory Contract* (Cambridge, Cambridge University Press, 1998).

[28] 169 U.S. 466 (1898).

[29] Alfred E. Kahn, "Who Should Pay for Power-Plant Duds?" *Wall Street Journal*, August 15, 1985. Kahn, who had been a leading scholar and regulator, became a special consultant to NERA.

[30] Starr concurring:

The utility business represents a compact of sorts; a monopoly on service in a particular geographical area (coupled with state-conferred rights of eminent domain or condemnation) is granted to the utility in exchange for a regime of intensive regulation, including price regulation, quite alien to the free market.... Each party to the compact gets something in the bargain. As a general rule, utility investors are provided a level of stability in earnings and value less likely to be attained in the unregulated or moderately regulated sector; in turn, ratepayers are afforded universal, non-discriminatory service

Supreme Court precedents governing the constitutional limitations on ratemaking.[31]

Financial investors understood the politics of ratemaking and assumed that some of those costs would be borne by shareholders, depending on the source of stranded costs. Investors assigned a higher probability to recovery of mandated costs such as QF contracts than for uneconomic assets that were the result of utility business decisions.[32]

States that engaged in deregulation usually included a side payment to the incumbent utilities to purchase their acquiescence to these dramatic changes. Utilities threw considerable resources into lobbying to recover sunk costs, and providing some compensation for potential losses reduced their opposition to restructuring and retail competition. Stranded costs permitted regulators to buy off the utilities by offering them a discount on the book value of potentially stranded assets. The utility received cost certainty and freedom from capricious regulatory judgments of "used and useful" and arguments over the proper return on equity. Book losses could be used as tax shields against future net income. One motivation for utilities to take this deal was that the markets had already discounted

and protection from monopolistic profits through political control over an economic enterprise.

Jersey Cent. Power & Light Co. v. FERC, 810 F. 2d 1168, 1188 (DC Cir 1988).
    The term "Regulatory Bargain" appears in 1983, citing a 1980 ICC case, with regard to whether a carrier could uphold its part of the regulatory bargain – that is, it would perform the operation as proposed. *Steere Tank Lines, Inc. v. Interstate Commerce Commission*, 703 F.2nd 927, 930 fn 4 (5th Cir. 1983).
    The reason that there is no "Regulatory Compact" in the case law is due to the line of Supreme Court cases from *Hope* to *Duquesne*, delineating the authority of the regulatory agency over the rates of a regulated utility:

... Without analyzing rate cases in detail, it may be safely generalized that the due process clause never has been held by this Court to require a commission to fix rates on the present reproduction value of something no one would presently want to reproduce, or on the historical valuation of a property whose history and current financial statements showed the value no longer to exist, or on an investment after it has vanished, even if once prudently made, or to maintain the credit of a concern whose securities already are impaired. The due process clause has been applied to prevent governmental destruction of existing economic values. It has not and cannot be applied to insure values or to restore values that have been lost by the operation of economic forces.

Market Street Railway Co. v. Railroad Commission of California et al., 324 U.S. 548, 567 (1945).

[31] This view is shared by a number of scholars who examined the issue. See, for example, Jim Chen, "The Death of the Regulatory Compact: Adjusting Prices and Expectations in the Law of Regulated Industries," 67 *Ohio State Law Journal* 1265 (2006).

[32] Julia D'Souza and John Jacob, "Electric Utility Stranded Costs: Valuation and Disclosure Issues," *Journal of Accounting Research* 39 (December 2001): 495–96.

utility stocks in anticipation of write-offs stemming from deregulation.[33] Therefore, accepting a regulatory bargain that formalized these write-offs placed no onus on management, while establishing a basis for future revenue growth. Utility executives could blame regulators for losses due to deregulation and claim credit for future gains.

In many cases the stranded costs were securitized, taking them out of the rate base. This lowered the annualized cost of writing off these assets because the utility no longer earned a return after taxes, nor paid property and other taxes on those assets. The result is that consumers were levied a lower payment, which reflected the cost of financing a lump-sum payoff. Assets in a rate base can have cost of 20 cent or more per dollar of book value, owing to the impact of various taxes and fees, as well as return on capital. Securitization can cut those costs substantially, especially in the low-interest-rate environment that was experienced in the late 1990s (interest rates on corporate bonds had fallen to their lowest level since the late 1960s).

In low-cost states, the fear that low-cost generation might benefit other regions while increasing in-state average costs made regulators reluctant to support any changes. However, the availability of profitable export markets for power in some cases encouraged legislative and regulatory decisions to consider competition. Although "domestic" consumers might potentially stand to lose if their own rates rose if their utility sold power to neighboring high-price states, excessive capacity reduced that potential impact relative to the gains in trade, which could be shared with home state consumers. This explains early consideration and decisions to adopt retail competition by state legislatures in low-cost states such as Montana and Oklahoma.[34]

On the other hand, some states acted to protect their monopoly utilities from competition. In Florida, the state supreme court interpreted a state power plant siting statute to limit plant siting to Florida utilities

---

[33] John L. Domagalski, Agustin J. Ros, and Philip R. O'Connor, "Another Look at What's Driving Utility Stock Prices," *Public Utilities Fortnightly* 135 (January 15, 1997): 42–44.

Utilities with low marginal costs experienced a more favorable stock price reaction than utilities with high marginal costs to the events that presaged passage of the 1992 Act. This cost advantage effect was significantly pronounced for utilities with excess capacity. Investors expected that only marginal cost advantages of incumbent utilities would be valuable in the post deregulation market.

See David Besanko, Julia D'Souza, and S. Ramu Thiagarajan, "The Effect of Wholesale Market Deregulation on Shareholder Wealth in the Electric Power Industry," *Journal of Law and Economics* 44 (April 2001): 67–68.

[34] Amy W. Ando and Karen L. Palmer, "Getting on the Map: The Political Economy of State-Level Electricity Restructuring," RFF 8–19-REV (May 1998): 25.

or suppliers who have contracts with Florida residents.[35] The result was to close Florida's wholesale power market to merchant power plants. Taking their cue from Florida's success in blocking the development of wholesale power supply, other state and local governments, particularly in the South, imposed moratoria on merchant power plants.[36]

Most of the states that had been leaders in applying IRP adopted initiatives to restructure their gas and electric utilities in order to promote wholesale and retail competition or "customer choice."[37] The New York Public Service Commission issued its Opinion and Order on the Transition to Competition in December 1994.[38] After New Hampshire in May 1996 became the first state to enact restructuring legislation, it was quickly followed by Rhode Island and California. California was an early leader with issuance of the CPUC's "Blue Book," but Connecticut, Massachusetts, and Maryland quickly responded to the California example.[39] In 1997, Pennsylvania, Oklahoma, Montana, Maine, Nevada, New Jersey, and Illinois followed suit.[40] Arizona, Connecticut, and Virginia joined the crowd in 1998,[41] Arkansas, Delaware, Maryland, New Mexico, Oregon, Ohio, and Texas in 1999,[42] and Michigan in

---

[35] *Tampa Elec. Co. v. Garcia*, 767 So. 2d 428, 435 (Fla. 2000) (holding that state's power plant siting statute "was not intended to authorize the determination of need for a proposed power plant output that is not fully committed to use by Florida customers who purchase electrical power at retail rates").

[36] Jim Rossi, "The Electric Deregulation Fiasco: Looking to Regulatory Federalism to Promote a Balance Between Markets and the Provision of Public Goods," *Michigan Law Review* 100 (2002): 1768, 1785; Jeffery S. Dennis, "Federalism, Electric Industry Restructuring, and the Dormant Commerce Clause: Tampa Electric Co. v. Garcia and State Restrictions on the Development of Merchant Power Plants," *Natural Resources Journal* 43 (Spring 2003): 620–21.

[37] One reason was a growing recognition that IRP was resulting in expensive demand management programs that might not be cost effective. Alfred Kahn, "Environmentalists Hijack the Utility Regulators," *Wall Street Journal*, August 7, 1991, A10.

[38] *In re Competitive Opportunities Regarding Electric Service*, No. 94 -E-0952 (N.Y. Pub. Serv. Comm'n, December 22, 1994).

[39] Barbara R. Alexander, "Part One: An Analysis of Residential Energy Markets in Georgia, Massachusetts, Ohio, New York and Texas," at http://neaap.ncat.org/experts/PartOnePDF.pdf (last visited June 17, 2011); Roger Bergstrom, Christi Cao, and Tommie Tolbert, "Key Aspects of Electric Restructuring Supplemental Volume II: the State Summaries 2003 Updates," Florida Public Service Commission, Office of Market Monitoring and Strategic Analysis (July 2003): 31–32; EIA, *Status of Electricity Restructuring by State*, at http://www.eia.gov/electricity/policies/restructuring/restructure_elect .html (last visited June 17, 2011).

[40] EIA, *Status of Electricity Restructuring by State*.

[41] "Current Status Summery For Deregulation in All US States," *Power Economics* (November 30, 1999): 16; EIA, *Status of Electricity Restructuring by State*.

[42] "With Summer Lull in Washington, State Restructuring Presses Ahead," *Inside FERC*, August 25, 1997, 1; EIA, *Status of Electricity Restructuring by State*.

2000, but momentum toward retail competition began to slow as most of the high-cost states had already initiated programs.[43] All states with deregulation laws, with the exception of New Hampshire, allowed utilities to recover most of their stranded costs.[44]

The first few states to implement retail competition programs also required their utilities to divest their generating capacity through an auction process (e.g., California, Massachusetts, New York, Maine, Connecticut, and Rhode Island).[45] Other states that implemented retail competition programs permitted the utilities under their jurisdiction to retain the bulk of their generating assets and to move them into separate unregulated wholesale power affiliates within a holding company structure (e.g., Pennsylvania, Illinois, Maryland, Ohio, Texas, and New Jersey). A few utilities in these states chose voluntarily to divest their generating assets.[46]

Nearly two-dozen states proceeded to consider implementation of wholesale and retail competition reforms, although only about a dozen states proceeded very far with the restructuring of their electricity industries. These states included California, five of the six New England states, New York, Pennsylvania, New Jersey, Maryland, Michigan, and Illinois. Most of these "pioneer states" shared many attributes with California: high retail rates, excess generating capacity, expensive nuclear plants and QF contracts, and angry industrial customers. Nearly 100,000 MW of utility generating capacity was divested from 1997 through 2000.[47] The state reform initiatives proceeded with no new federal mandates or obligations.

Deregulation in Texas was the national experience in miniature. Since the Texas grid was regulated by the Public Utility Commission of Texas

---

[43] "State by State: Where Deregulation Currently Stands Across the Country," *Wall Street Journal*, September 14, 1998, R6; "Electric Restructuring: Second Wave, Second Thoughts; Hurdles Loom in 10 States Eyeing Deregulation" *Public Utilities Fortnightly* (November 15, 1998): 54.

[44] Benjamin A. Holden, "Electric-Deregulation Machine Starts to Pick Up Steam," *Wall Street Journal*, July 14, 1997, B4; EIA, *Status of Electricity Restructuring by state.*

[45] Bergstrom, Cao and Tolbert, "Key Aspects of Electric Restructuring Supplemental Volume II: the State Summaries 2003 Updates," 14; EIA, *Status of Electricity Restructuring by State.*

[46] Paul L. Joskow, "The Difficult Transition to Competitive Electricity Markets in the U.S.," CEEPR (May 2003): 18.

[47] Divestitures mandated by state regulatory authorities had adverse effects on the efficiency of the stand-alone distribution companies, measured by both operating costs and total costs. These effects were both large and significant. Utilities that undertook divestitures that were not the result of mandates did not experience adverse effects on efficiency. John Kwoka, Sanem Ozturk, and Michael Pollitt, "Divestiture Policy and Operating Efficiency in U.S. Electric Power Distribution," EPRG Working Paper 0819 (July 2008).

TABLE 11.1. *State Retail Competition*

State	First Year	Full Retail Access	Default Rates	Rate Cap Period
Connecticut	2000	2000	Regulation	1996–2006
DC	2001	2001	Auction	1999–2007
Illinois	1999			
Maine	2000	2000	Auction	None
Maryland	2000	2000	Auction	1999–2006
Massachusetts	1998	1998	Market	1999–2005
New Jersey	1999	1999	Auction	1999–2003
New York	2001	2001	Market	None
Ohio	2001	2001	Regulation	1999–2008
Pennsylvania	1999	2000	Regulation	1999–2010
Texas	2002	2002	Market	1999–2007

Source: Seth Blumsack and Dimitri Perekhodtsev, "International Experience with Retail Competition and Pricing," in Joan Evans and Lester C. Hunt, eds., *International Handbook on the Economics of Energy* (Cheltenham, Edward Elgar Publishing, February 2008): 18.

TABLE 11.2. *Average Natural Gas Prices for Electric Power Generation (per million Btu)*

1991–99	$2.40
2000–02	$4.12
2003–04	$5.68
2005–08	$7.82
2009–12	$4.49

Source: EIA, *Electric Power Annual*, Various Issues.

(PUCT),[48] not FERC, the Texas legislature could deregulate the wholesale and retail markets in tandem. In 1995, Senate Bill 373 was passed, requiring utilities to provide unbundled transmission service on a nondiscriminatory basis and to establish an ISO. Restructuring legislation, Senate Bill 7, was enacted in June 1999 to allow retail competition by January 2002 in the Electric Reliability Council of Texas (ERCOT) market. Rates would be frozen for three years, followed by a 6 percent reduction for residential and small commercial consumers. This would remain the "price to beat"

---

[48] Texas was the last state to authorize a public utility commission. In 1975, the Texas legislature passed the Public Utility Regulation Act, formally granting the PUCT regulatory powers. The legislature adopted the traditional ratemaking principles employed by most state commissions and FERC. PUCT, *Volume II, The Scope of Competition in the Electric Industry in Texas*, January 1997, II–10.

for five years or until utilities lost 40 percent of their consumers to competition. All net, verifiable, nonmitigated stranded costs were recovered, and securitization was allowed as a recovery mechanism. Utilities were required to unbundle, into separate or affiliate companies, their generation, distribution and transmission, and retail operations. Utilities were limited to owning and controlling no more than 20 percent of installed generation capacity in ERCOT. Municipals and cooperatives were not affected by the law, unless they choose to open their territories to competition. A competitive bidding process designated the POLRs for each consumer class.

The real problem was that the rush by states to deregulate electric utilities was based on a faulty assumption, that natural gas prices would remain as low as they were during the glut that followed natural gas price decontrol. Low natural gas prices, combined with highly efficient combined-cycle gas turbines, meant that new plants could undercut conventional generation. It was this expectation that fueled the desire to break up IOUs and allow new plants to access utility customers, and provided the impetus for a boom in independent power plant construction. When gas prices rose, everyone found out that "there ain't no such thing as easy money."

12

The Creation of Wholesale
Electricity Markets

The requirement in Order 888 that the public utility members of tight pools file reformed power pooling agreements no later than December 31, 1996 encouraged some entities to file proposals with FERC to create ISOs. Establishment of an ISO was one option for a power pool agreement to meet the requirements for open, nondiscriminatory membership. The key ISO principles put forth by the Commission in Order 888 addressing power pools included:

- *ISO governance should be structured in a fair and nondiscriminatory manner.* An ISO should be independent of market participants. The ISO's rules should prevent control, and appearance of control, of decision making by any class of participants.
- *An ISO and its employees should have no financial interest in the economic performance of any power market participant.* Transmission owners need to be able to hold the ISO accountable in its fiduciary role but should not be able to dictate day-to-day operational matters.
- *An ISO should provide open access to the transmission system pursuant to a single, unbundled, grid-wide tariff.* The portion of the transmission grid operated by a single ISO should be as large as possible, and the ISO should schedule all transmission.
- *An ISO should have the primary responsibility in ensuring short-term reliability of grid operations.* An ISO should oversee all maintenance of the transmission facilities under its control. The ISO should be responsible for developing and implementing curtailment policies to ensure the security of the system.

- *An ISO should have control over the operation of interconnected transmission facilities within its region.*
- *An ISO should identify constraints on the system and be able to take operational actions to relieve those constraints.* The ISO may need to exercise operational control over generation facilities in order to regulate the power system. An ISO will provide, or cause to be provided, ancillary services.
- *An ISO should make transmission system information publicly available on a timely basis via an electronic information network.*[1]

A number of ISO proposals – California ISO (CAISO),[2] PJM ISO (PJM),[3] ISO New England (ISO-NE),[4] the New York ISO (NYISO),[5] and the Midwest ISO (MISO)[6] – were accepted by the Commission, and these organizations (except for MISO) began operation, with various degrees of success (the California meltdown would not become apparent until 2000). In addition, the Texas Commission ordered an ISO for ERCOT that became the first established ISO in the United States.[7] The PJM, New England, and New York ISOs were established on the platform of existing tight power pools. ERCOT had existed as a loose power pool. In contrast, the establishment of the California ISO was the direct result of a state government mandate. MISO was the product of voluntary actions by utilities in the region, and the lack of a well-organized predecessor explains its convoluted evolution.

For the most part, these markets gradually evolved from a loose power pool to highly coordinated markets. The establishment of formal power pools, and then the mandate of FERC's Orders 888 and 890, shifted control area responsibilities to a central authority. Once the ISO was established, it would run a balancing market that would clear the residual supply and demand in the region, but most trades were either internal

---

[1] Order 888, 31,730–32.
[2] *Pacific Gas & Electric Company, et al.*, 77 FERC ¶ 61,204 (1996), *order on reh'g*, ¶ 81 FERC 61,122 (1997).
[3] *Pennsylvania-New Jersey-Maryland Interconnection, et al.*, 81 FERC ¶ 61,257 (1997), *order on reh'g and clarification*, 92 FERC ¶ 61,282 (2000).
[4] *New England Power Pool*, 79 FERC ¶ 61,374 (1997), *order on reh'g*, 85 FERC ¶ 61,242 (1998).
[5] *Central Hudson Gas & Electric Corporation, et al.*, 83 FERC ¶ 61,352 (1998), *order on reh'g*, 87 FERC ¶ 61,135 (1999).
[6] *Midwest Independent Transmission System Operator, et al.*, 84 FERC ¶ 61,231 (1998), *order on reconsideration*, 85 FERC ¶ 61,250 (1998), *order on reh'g*, 85 FERC ¶ 61,372 (1998).
[7] See 16 Texas Administrative Code § 23.67(p).

(the utility "selling" generation to its distribution function) or between generators and customers (often small utilities with insufficient generation to meet their demand) through bilateral contracting. Over time, these arrangements would coalesce into more formal electricity markets, encouraged by FERC rulings and guidance. State-level restructuring, by opening markets to independent generators, and allowing customers to contract for power, accelerated this development.

PJM began in 1927 when three utilities, realizing the benefits and efficiencies possible by interconnecting to share their generating resources, formed the world's first continuing power pool. Additional utilities joined in 1956, 1965, and 1981. Throughout this time, PJM was operated by a department of one member utility. In 1962, PJM installed its first online computer to control generation. PJM completed its first Energy Management System (EMS) in 1968. The EMS is the information technology system that makes it possible to monitor transmission grid operations in real time. PJM began the transition to an independent, neutral organization in 1993 when the PJM Interconnection Association was formed to administer the power pool.[8]

On July 24, 1996, nine of the ten members of PJM[9] submitted a filing for a proposed comprehensive restructuring of the PJM pool. The proposal provided for a regional market for wholesale electricity and related services, and for transmission service on a pool-wide basis under a single transmission tariff. The market would be operated by an ISO that would coordinate day-to-day control area operations and administer the transmission service.[10] Philadelphia Electric Co. (PECO) filed an alternative PJM restructuring proposal. PECO proposed a wholesale energy market, called the Power Exchange, and a regional transmission tariff that would be administered by the ISO.[11] The Commission rejected both proposals as failing to meet the Commission's ISO principles. Both proposed ISOs fail to comport with the ISO governance principle because the proposed governance structure precluded meaningful representation by non-PJM stakeholders, nor did the proposals ensure the financial independence of ISO employees. The proposals fell short in numerous other aspects, relating

---

[8] *See* PJM History, at http://www.pjm.com/about-pjm/who-we-are/pjm-history.aspx (last visited August 21, 2011).

[9] Atlantic City Electric, Baltimore Gas and Electric, Delmarva Power & Light, Jersey Central Power & Light, Metropolitan Edison, Pennsylvania Electric, Pennsylvania Power & Light (PP&L), Potomac Electric Power, and Public Service Electric and Gas (PSEG).

[10] *Atlantic City Electric Company, et al.*, 76 FERC ¶ 61,306, 62,511 (1996).

[11] *Atlantic City Electric Company, et al.*, 76 FERC ¶ 61,306, 62,512 (1996).

to transmission rates, control of transmission facilities, and congestion management.[12]

An Order 888 Compliance Filing was submitted in December 1996, with supplemental materials presenting alternative approaches to certain issues proposed by PECO and the Supporting Companies. In November 1997, FERC conditionally accepted a modified PJM proposal, to become effective January 1, 1998, subject to revisions.[13] The Filing established an ISO as an independent body to administer the PJM Transmission Tariff, operate the spot energy market, and approve a regional transmission expansion plan. An independent board would be responsible for supervision and oversight of the day-to-day operations. The PJM Operating Agreement also called for the formation of a Members Committee, on the basis of the following sectors: Generation Owners, Other Suppliers, Transmission Owners, Electric Distributors, and End-Use Customers. All transmission services would be subject to a single rate based on the costs of the individual utility's transmission system where the point of delivery is located. LMP would be adopted for calculating and recovering the costs of transmission congestion. Every firm point-to-point and network service under the PJM Transmission Tariff would be awarded fixed transmission rights. The Commission directed PJM to implement PECO's transmission congestion pricing proposal, and to implement Supporting Companies' proposal with respect to options dealing with all other issues.[14]

The Commission suggested that a multi-settlement system, utilizing both the day-ahead and real-time markets, could provide a mechanism for addressing the risks of uncertain congestion charges. Such a system would allow market participants to commit and obtain commitments to energy prices and transmission congestion charges in advance of real-time dispatch. A multi-settlement system proposal would permit each transmission customer to inform the ISO of the maximum price (including the congestion charge) it is willing to pay. In developing the day-ahead schedule, the ISO would schedule only those transmission customers that are

---

[12] *Atlantic City Electric Company, et al.*, 77 FERC ¶ 61,148, 61,573–80 (1996).

[13] *Pennsylvania-New Jersey-Maryland Interconnection, et al.*, 81 FERC ¶ 61,257 (1997). See also *PJM*, 84 FERC 61,051 (1998) (accepting the revised PJM Transmission Tariff, PJM Operating Agreement, PJM Reliability Assurance Agreement, and Transmission Owners Agreement); *PJM*, 84 FERC ¶ 61,224 (1998) (accepting revisions to give all market participants the opportunity to schedule deliveries or receipts of spot market energy on an hour-ahead basis); *PJM*, 86 FERC ¶ 61,015 (1999) (accepting the proposal to provide redispatch service as an alternative to TLR curtailment procedures).

[14] *PJM*, 81 FERC ¶ 61,257, 62, 234–35, 62,253–54 (1997).

willing to pay the applicable market clearing prices.[15] The Commission also approved market-based rates for sales of energy and certain ancillary services in PJM.[16]

LMP proved to be a superior option to an alternative zonal pricing approach, which, implemented in April 1997, proved to be fundamentally inconsistent with a competitive market. The zonal pricing system allowed market participants the flexibility to choose between bilateral transactions and spot purchases, but did not simultaneously present them with the costs of their choices. The circumstances created a false impression that savings of $10 per MWh or more could be achieved simply by converting a spot transaction into a bilateral schedule. Faced with this perverse pricing incentive, market participants responded naturally by scheduling more bilateral transactions than the transmission system could accommodate. Locational pricing was also applied by PJM for managing interregional transmission loading relief. In addition, the anecdotal evidence suggested that investments in new generation and transmission were being considered with careful attention to the effects of system congestion, as intended.[17]

The success of the PJM market encouraged additional utilities to apply for membership. They included Allegheny Power in 2002, Com Edison, AEP, and Dayton Power & Light in 2004, and Duquesne Light and Dominion Power in 2005. In 2011, American Transmission Systems, the transmission affiliate of FirstEnergy, and Cleveland Public Power were integrated into PJM.

Although New York was similar to California in that it established an electric market in a single state, there were some significant differences. When the New York utilities sold their power plants, with the exception of Consolidated Edison (Con Ed), they entered into power purchase agreements to buy that power back. New York primarily imports power from Quebec Hydroelectric, which has a tremendous amount of surplus capacity and does not experience the same variability of water flow as is typical in the Western United States. New York also has a public power entity, which can act as a backstop to the market. In New York, transmission constraints were primarily limited to New York City and Long Island.

[15]   *PJM*, 81 FERC ¶ 61,257, 62, 257–58 (1997).
[16]   *Atlantic City Electric Co., et al.*, 86 FERC ¶ 61,248, 61,902 (1999).
[17]   William Hogan, *Getting the Prices Right in PJM: Analysis and Summary: April 1998 through March 1999, The First Anniversary of Full Locational Pricing* (April 2, 1999): 7.

The NYISO grew out of the NYPP, which had controlled the New York transmission system and the real-time dispatch of the generating units in the state since the 1960s. The NYPP was created after the Great Northeast Blackout of 1965, and was owned by the member utilities in New York (seven investor-owned utilities[18] and the New York Power Authority). The Power Pool was structured as a tight power pool, but did not centralize unit commitment and dispatch, unlike NEPOOL and PJM. Units were only dispatched to balance supply and demand after the individual utilities decided which units they would commit to meet the loads of their own customers. NYPP carried out many of the reliability functions normally performed by a control area operator, such as balancing electric system supply and demand in real time, maintaining voltage, monitoring contingencies, managing operating reserves, and dispatching generation. NYPP provided a forum for arranging short-term trades among utilities and allocated the benefits of these trades based on a "split-savings" price formula.[19]

On January 31, 1997, the Member Systems filed with the Commission a conditional proposal to establish an ISO and form a fully competitive wholesale electricity market in New York. In December 1997, the Member Systems submitted an additional supplemental filing that provided for location-based marginal pricing with three-part bids, day-ahead and real-time markets, transmission congestion contracts, a New York State Reliability Council to establish reliability standards for the bulk power system, and an independent ISO board. The Commission conditionally approved the ISO and the new market.[20] Tariff issues, market rules, and a request for market-based rates were approved in January 1999. Market-based rate approval, similar to PJM, revolved around meeting the 20 percent market share threshold, as well as a proposed market-monitoring plan.[21]

NEPOOL was initially organized in 1971 and has more than 130 members. NEPOOL operated the central dispatch of virtually all of the

---

[18] Central Hudson Gas & Electric Corporation, Consolidated Edison Company of New York, Inc., Long Island Lighting Company, New York State Electric & Gas Corporation, Niagara Mohawk Power Corporation, Orange and Rockland Utilities, Inc., and Rochester Gas and Electric Corporation.

[19] Susan Tierney and Edward Kahn, "Cost-benefit Analysis of the New York Independent System Operator: The Initial Years," Analysis Group (March 2007): 6–7.

[20] *Central Hudson Gas & Electric Corporation, et al.*, 83 FERC ¶ 61,352, 63,405–6 (1998).

[21] *Central Hudson Gas & Electric Corporation, et al.*, 86 FERC ¶ 61,062, 61,235–36 (1999), *order on reh'g*, 88 FERC ¶ 61,138 (1999).

generation and transmission facilities in New England as a single control area. As the control area operator, NEPOOL assumed responsibility for the minute-to-minute operation of the region's bulk power system, including regulating system frequency, maintaining system voltage, managing interchange between NEPOOL and neighboring power systems, dispatching NEPOOL generating capacity, managing the NEPOOL transmission system, and coordinating daily transmission and generation outages. NEPOOL also provided operational planning services in support of central dispatch (e.g., coordination of annual generator maintenance schedules, transmission facility outage scheduling, administration of bilateral contracts between NEPOOL Participants and non-NEPOOL entities, and short-term and long-term load forecasting).[22]

NEPOOL filed a comprehensive restructuring proposal on December 31, 1996, in response to the Order 888 deadline, with supplements in 1997. The Commission accepted for filing the NEPOOL proposal and made it effective on March 1, 1997. NEPOOL proposed to transfer operational control of the New England bulk power system to the new ISO. The Commission accepted a negotiated arrangement, leaving market rules primarily under the control of NEPOOL committees.[23] On July 1, 1997, ISO-NE was activated.

NEPOOL also proposed that network loads and resources in NEPOOL would be integrated over nine local utility systems after a five-year transition period. A single postage stamp rate would be assessed regardless of the number of transmission systems involved in providing a service. The NEPOOL Tariff also offered nonfirm point-to-point transmission for Through and Out Service, in which power is transported across, or exported from, the pool. The Commission ordered continuation of point-to-point transmission service despite the availability of network service.[24]

NEPOOL proposed the unbundling of electric services in the NEPOOL control area and the development of competitive wholesale markets for capacity and energy.[25] The energy market would be a residual market. Each participant settles through the market the net difference between its energy produced and consumed. The energy market also allowed LSEs to submit bids reflecting the price at which they are willing to reduce

[22] *New England Power Pool*, 79 FERC ¶ 61,374, 62,576 (1997).
[23] *New England Power Pool*, 79 FERC ¶ 61,374, 62,585 (1997).
[24] *New England Power Pool*, 83 FERC ¶ 61,045, 61,230-31 (1998).
[25] *New England Power Pool*, 85 FERC ¶ 61,379, 61,457 (1998), *reh'g denied*, 95 FERC ¶ 61,074 (2001).

load. Each participant is required to bid any capacity that has not been self-scheduled. NEPOOL proposed a one-settlement system where scheduled quantities are settled at real-time prices. At least every five minutes, the ISO calculates a market-clearing price for energy. The price at settlement is the weighted average of these five-minute clearing prices over the hour. NEPOOL would also operate markets for Installed and Operable Capability.[26] The NEPOOL Tariff provided that, until January 1, 2000, each transmission customer would pay an "uplift charge" reflecting a pro rata share of redispatch costs incurred as a result of transmission constraints. The interim congestion management proposal would continue in effect as a default method unless the NEPOOL Management Committee agreed to an alternative method.[27] The additional expense of redispatch to clear congestion would be uplifted on a pro rata basis to all loads.[28]

The single settlement proposal was problematic, as the ISO's consultants pointed out. The single settlement system planned at NEPOOL would allow for gaming of the market that could circumvent the requirement to bid all uncommitted capacity into the market. A generator could nominally comply with the requirement by submitting a bid, but then fail to follow the ISO's dispatch instructions in real time to produce the energy consistent with its day-ahead bid. To replace the unproduced energy, more expensive energy would need to be dispatched, which would increase the real-time energy price. A multi-settlement system was not vulnerable to these strategies because prices are locked in a day ahead, removing the temptation to game the real-time market.[29] The Commission agreed and required NEPOOL and the ISO to develop plans for implementation of a multi-settlement system and to submit the plans with a revised congestion management plan.[30]

The Commission granted NEPOOL's request for market-based rates in the ISO-administered markets. The Commission directed NEPOOL to expand its mitigation measures to require bidding into the energy market at the seller's marginal cost. This mitigation measure would limit the bids of sellers found by the ISO to have market power, but it did not cap prices. Sellers should be permitted to receive market-clearing prices, even

[26] *New England Power Pool*, 85 FERC ¶ 61,379, 62,459–60 (1998).
[27] *New England Power Pool*, 83 FERC ¶ 61,045, 61,236–37 (1998).
[28] *New England Power Pool*, 85 FERC ¶ 61,379, 62,461 (1998).
[29] Peter Cramton and Robert Wilson, *A Review of ISO New England's Proposed Market Rules*, Exhibit A, ISO-NE filing, September 9, 1998.
[30] *New England Power Pool*, 85 FERC ¶ 61,379, 62,462 (1998).

if the prices exceed bids. The Commission continued to employ its 20 percent market share threshold, along with examination of HHIs. FERC rejected studies by intervenors demonstrating the potential for strategic behavior, relying on market monitoring to prevent the exercise of market power.[31]

ERCOT is the only major wholesale electricity market that is not under FERC jurisdiction. On or about August 26, 1935, solely to avoid becoming subject to FPC Jurisdiction, certain Texas utilities elected to isolate their properties from interstate commerce. During World War II, these and other intrastate utilities interconnected their grids, forming the Texas Interconnected System. In 1970, members of the Texas Interconnected System as well as municipalities and rural electric cooperatives, all operating on an exclusively intrastate basis, formed ERCOT, a regional electric reliability council reporting to NERC. In 1981, the Interconnected System transferred all its operating functions to ERCOT.[32]

The autonomous nature of ERCOT was challenged in the 1970s when a group of Oklahoma utilities filed an action asserting PUHCA noncompliance by CSW, because its Oklahoma subsidiaries lacked electrical connections to its Texas subsidiaries. CSW tried to interconnect on the night of May 4, 1976, known as the "midnight connection," to subject ERCOT to federal jurisdiction and then petition the FPC to order interconnection to the Southwest Power Pool (SPP). The FPC held CSW's constituent utilities to be "public utilities" subject to federal jurisdiction due to their interstate connection, but found that the other ERCOT utilities, which had disconnected shortly after the midnight connection, could not be subjected to federal regulation. The PUCT then ordered CSW to disconnect its Texas utilities from Oklahoma. On July 28, 1980, both CSW and the other ERCOT utilities submitted an Offer of Settlement, agreeing on an asynchronous DC interconnection to Oklahoma because the power flows over a direct-current link could be controlled. FERC accepted the settlement offer.[33]

---

[31] *New England Power Pool*, 85 FERC ¶ 61,379, 62,472–78 (1998).

[32] Jared Fleisher, "ERCOT's Jurisdictional Status: A Legal History and Contemporary Appraisal," 3 *Texas Journal of Oil, Gas, and Energy Law* 5, 11–12 (2008).

[33] Id., 13–17. EPAct 2005 eliminated the potential application of section 211 of the FPA to ERCOT utilities by defining the term "transmitting utility" to include only those entities that "own, operate, or control facilities used for the transmission of electric energy (a) in interstate commerce and (b) for the sale of electric energy at wholesale." 16 U.S.C. § 796, as amended by EPA 2005, Pub L. No. 109–58, section 1291, 119 Stat. 594, 984 (2005).

In 1995, the Texas legislature, in Senate Bill 373, exempted power marketers and EWGs from being regulated as utilities, but they were authorized to sell only wholesale electric power in Texas. Utilities that owned or operated transmission facilities must provide wholesale transmission access at rates, terms, and conditions comparable to their own use of their system. The PUCT could require utilities (including municipal utilities) to provide access to transmission services to another utility, a QF, an EWG, or power marketer. In 1996, PUCT employed its rulemaking authority under the 1995 amendments to make ERCOT the ISO for Texas.[34]

Unlike California and the northeast states, high electricity prices were not a motivating force behind the creation of the Texas electricity market. Electricity prices were 10–15% lower than the national average, with industrial customers receiving the greatest discount.[35] Deregulation was primarily an insider's game, between the industrials who wanted competition, utilities that wanted protection from financial risks of deregulation, and Enron, which wanted to open up a business opportunity on its home turf.

Enron played a significant role in Texas deregulation, owing to long-standing investments in political influence. Ken Lay had developed a reputation for ruthlessness, using his money and influence to punish state legislators who opposed his company's interests. In Texas, Enron spent $5.8 million between 1998 and 2000 funding state politicians. The company also spent as much as $4.8 million on Texas lobbying. It used its political influence to overcome the resistance of the existing regulated utilities in Texas.[36] A longtime supporter of the Bush clan, Lay became a close advisor to George W. Bush and a key source of funds for his first gubernatorial campaign in 1994.[37] Bush then appointed Pat Wood

---

[34] PUCT, *Volume II, The Scope of Competition in the Electric Industry in Texas* (Jan. 1997): II-23.

[35] UEIA, *State Energy Price and Expenditure Report*, 1995.

[36] Sharon Beder, "The Electricity Deregulation Con Game," *Center for Media and Democracy*, at http://www.prwatch.org/prwissues/2003Q3/dereg.html (last visited March 19, 2010); Kevin McCoy, "Enron's Contribution Trail Reads Like U.S. Road Map," *USA Today*, January 27, 2002, at http://www.usatoday.com/money/covers/2002-01-28-enron-states.htm (last visited June 27, 2011).

[37] Lay's ties to George W. Bush began with his father, former President George H. W. Bush, who was also a recipient of Enron/Lay's financial largesse. Lay remained a key supporter for George W. Bush as he ran for president. Pratap Chatterjee, "George W. Bush Gets Layed: The Mutually Beneficial Relationship between Enron CEO Ken Lay and the Republican Contender," *CorpWatch*, July 20, 2000, at http://www.corpwatch.org/article.php?id=462 (last visited June 23, 2011).

III from Port Arthur, a Harvard law graduate with a bachelor's degree in engineering from Texas A&M, to the PUCT. Wood began his public career on the staff of the FERC, serving as legal advisor to Commissioner Jerry Langdon from 1991 until 1993. Lay endorsed Wood for the PUCT job in a letter to Bush in 1994. After four months on the Commission, Bush made Wood the chairman of the PUCT. Wood said that his orders from Bush were clear: "Get us to a market."[38]

Enron stepped up its lobbying campaign, buying statewide television and billboard ads hawking competition. Enron funded front groups, such as Texans for Affordable Energy, to stimulate a grassroots call for deregulation. As Enron made inroads with legislators, the IOUs began to see the writing on the wall. Chairman Wood sweetened the deal for the IOUs by suggesting that they might be allowed to recover stranded costs. When the 1999 legislative session rolled around, the big utilities were finally on board. Two bills were introduced in the 1999 session, House Bill 349 (proposed by Dallas Democrat and lawyer Steve Wolens) and Senate Bill 7 (by Waco Republican dentist David Sibley). Some sources claimed industry lobbyists wrote most of the text. Wolens vociferously denied these allegations, claiming he wrote the bill with Pat Wood and, to a lesser extent, Sibley. The Wolens/Sibley plan would freeze electricity rates for five years. At the end of the freeze period, prices would be cut by 5 percent, and then competition would begin. Utilities would be split into three distinct functions: generation, wires, and retail sales. TXU officials vehemently opposed the proposal and vowed that they would fight the deregulation bills if they were forced to sell capacity.[39]

Large industrials have always had a disproportionate political influence in Texas, and they demonstrated their power by killing an amendment that would have spread the cost of stranded costs on the basis of consumption.[40] The eventual demise of the amendment ensured that

---

[38] "FERC," *National Journal*, June 23, 2001, 2020; Nate Blakeslee, "Naked Emperors and Wet Rats: As Enron Goes Under, Texas Pols Scramble for Cover," *Texas Observer*, February 15, 2002 at http://www.texasobserver.org/article.php?aid=557 (last visited June 23, 2011).

[39] Jeff Mandell, "Capitol Offenses: De-Reg or Not De-Reg," *The Texas Observer*, April 2, 1999, at http://www.texasobserver.org/article.php?aid=1017 (last visited June 9, 2011).

[40] "Political Intelligence: Act for Peace," *Texas Observer*, May 28, 1999, at http://www.texasobserver.org/article.php?aid=1205 (last visited June 9, 2011). The major chemical and refinery companies, approximately fifty of the largest energy consumers in Texas, were represented by the Texas Industrial Energy Consumers, organized by a lawyer at Mayer, Day, Caldwell & Keeton, which later merged with Andrews Kurth. See Petition by Commission Staff for a Review of the Rates of Centerpoint Energy Houston Electric,

stranded costs would be allocated on the basis of peak demand, which large industrial customers can reduce easier than residential consumers can. Governor Bush signed SB 7 on June 18, 1999. The Texas Chemical Council hailed the signing of the bill, as the larger companies with cogeneration facilities would be able to sell their surplus electricity for extra revenues.[41]

As a consequence of Senate Bill 373, the PUC adopted a policy of postage stamp pricing for transmission services. The embedded costs of owning and operating each utility's transmission system are pooled and divided among the utilities that serve loads. Seventy percent of the costs were allocated among transmission customers on the basis of load, and 30 percent on the basis of megawatt-miles of transmitted power.[42] In 1999, the Commission adopted new rules that allocated transmission costs 100 percent based on peak demand.[43] Postage stamp pricing and socialization of transmission costs across ERCOT removed political barriers to transmission expansion, as it avoided the cost allocation conflicts that have stalled transmission projects in other jurisdictions. Chairman Wood warned in early 2001 that a shortage of transmission lines and power plants could complicate the transition to deregulation. ERCOT, in a report filed in 2001, identified six areas of the state that would require more transmission construction.[44] The PUCT encouraged an aggressive transmission construction program to overcome these constraints on the eve of deregulation. Eight of nine major construction projects were completed by December 2002.[45]

LLC Pursuant to PURA § 36.151 Before SOAH, (July 31, 2006): 1, ft 3. The Texas Coalition for Competitive Electricity (TCCE) was represented by the same lawyers, with many of the same members, lobbying under a different name.

[41] There was about 10,000 MW of cogeneration capacity in place before 2000, almost two-thirds in chemical processing facilities, one-third in oil refineries, and 640 MW in various other industries. After 2000, another 6,000 MW was installed, often as third-party plants built by IPPs, led by Calpine.

[42] *Regional Transmission Proceeding to Establish Postage Stamp Rate and Statewide Load flow Pursuant to Subt. Rule 23.57,* Docket No. 15840, Order (August 11, 1997), p. 2.

[43] Subst. Rule. 25.192(b). Transmission rates were assigned to each distribution service provider based on its average load during the ERCOT coincident peak demand hour for the months of June, July, August, and September.

[44] Steering Committee of Cities Served by Oncor & The Texas Coalition for Affordable Power, "The Story of ERCOT: The Grid Operator, Power Market & Prices Under Texas Electric Deregulation," February 2011, 28.

[45] FERC Staff, *Investigation of Bulk Power Markets: ERCOT (Texas)* (November 1, 2000): 4–17.

On July 31, 2001, ERCOT consolidated its existing ten control areas into a single control area. Wholesale power sales began to operate under new guidelines, including centralized power scheduling and the procurement of ancillary services. Commercial functions, including the acquisition of meter data and the profiling of electrical consumption, were transferred to ERCOT, and there was statewide registration of retail premises to facilitate the switching of customers between competitive electricity providers.[46] Utilities were limited to owning and controlling no more than 20 percent of installed generation capacity within ERCOT. The statute prohibited wire companies from selling electricity or other competitive energy services. Rates were frozen from 1999 through 2002, when competition would start. During the period when rates were frozen, excess earnings were applied to write down stranded costs. SB 7 also provided funds for energy efficiency[47] and a system benefit fund to help low-income ratepayers.[48]

Deregulation in Texas resulted in reorganization. Texas Utilities became TXU, the holding company for Oncor (wires), TXU generation (renamed Luminant), and TXU Retail (renamed TXU Energy). Houston Light and Power became CenterPoint (wires), Reliant Energy (retail), and its generation was spun off in July 2004 to Texas Genco (an entity owned by a consortium of private equity firms) for approximately $3.7 billion. Texas Genco was then flipped to NRG for $8.8 billion a year later. The jump in value can be traced to the rise in natural gas prices from $6 to $12 per MMBtu over this period, which increased the market price of electricity and profit margins for generators with coal and nuclear capacity. HL&P ratepayers were still on the hook for $2.3 billion in stranded costs.[49]

---

[46] Steering Committee of Cities, "The Story of ERCOT," 24.

[47] Tex. Util. Code (PURA) §39.905 required electric utilities (wires companies and non-ERCOT IOUs) to achieve energy savings of at least 10% of the utility's annual growth in demand in Texas by January 1, 2004.

[48] PURA § 39.903. The purpose of the fund was to compensate school districts for loss of property taxes, provide a discount for low-income consumers, and fund a targeted low-income energy efficiency program. In subsequent legislation the system benefit fund was repealed as a dedicated fund and made part of the general revenue fund. PUCT, *The Scope of Competition in the Electric Industry in Texas* (January 2001): 31–32. Starting in FY 2006, the legislature refused to fund the 10% low-income discount, diverting SBF funds to general revenue. PUCT, *Scope of Competition in Electric Markets in Texas* (January 2007): 47.

[49] PUCT, *Electricity Pricing in Competitive Retail Markets in Texas*, Legislative Report (March 3, 2006): 14–16; Loren Steffy, "Deregulation Helps Buyout Firms, If Not the Ratepayers," *Houston Chronicle*, October 4, 2005, at http://www.chron.com/business/

TXU would be purchased by private equity firms Kohlberg Kravis Roberts, Texas Pacific Group Capital, and Goldman Sachs in a leveraged buyout in 2007, and renamed Energy Future Holdings. The CEO of TXU, John Wilder, received almost $280 million due to change of control clauses in his contract.[50] The total cost of the acquisition was almost $47 billion, financed with $8 billion of equity investment and $39 billion of debt.[51] The transaction was greased through $11 million in advertising and $6 million in lobbying expenses.[52] The deal soon turned sour as projected electricity prices in ERCOT, due to declining natural gas prices, fell well below the levels required to meet debt service requirements.[53] Energy Future Holdings restructured its debt a few times in a bid to buy time, paying close to $1 billion in fees, as well as higher interest rates to shift maturity dates.[54] Despite these steps, the company declared bankruptcy in 2014.[55]

Texas established a price to beat, which set electricity rates for incumbent retail providers. The rate was in effect from January 1, 2002 until December 31, 2006.[56] The wires companies were also permitted to charge a fee to recover their stranded costs, which were finalized in true-up proceedings in 2004.[57] The average rate was 6 percent less than the average rates charged as of January 1, 1999. During the first three years, the price to beat was the only price that could be charged by an affiliated retailer

energy/article/Steffy-Deregulation-helps-buyout-firms-if-not-1941914.php (last visited September 1, 2011).

[50] Loren Steffy, "Deregulation's Value Can Be Found in CEO's Pockets," *Houston Chronicle*, September 7, 2007, at http://www.chron.com/default/article/Deregulation-s-value-can-be-found-in-CEO-s-pockets-1794007.php (last visited September 1, 2011). The driving force behind the deal was the expectation of higher natural gas prices, which would increase the value of TXU's 8,100 MW of lignite and nuclear generation, plus the three proposed coal plants.

[51] TXU Corp., *Proxy Statement Pursuant to Section 14(a) of the Securities Exchange Act of 1934* (July 24, 2007).

[52] "TXU's Takeover Lobby Cost About $17 Million," *Lobby Watch*, August 14, 2007.

[53] FitchRatings, *Corporates: Energy Future Holdings Corp.*, at 5.

[54] Naureen Malik and Katy Burne, "Utility Revamps Debt to Aid Survival," *Wall Street Journal*, April 4, 2011, at http://online.wsj.com/article/SB10001424052748703806304576236443466187996.html (last visited September 15, 2011).

[55] Mike Spector, Emily Glazer, and Rebecca Smith, "Energy Future Holdings Files for Bankruptcy: Chapter 11 Filing by Texas Power Firm, Formerly TXU, Is Among the Biggest Ever," *Wall Street Journal On-line*, April 29, 2014 at http://online.wsj.com/news/articles/SB10001424052702304163604579531283352498074 (last visited August 15, 2014).

[56] PURA § 39.202.

[57] PUCT, *Scope of Competition in Electric Markets in Texas* (January 2007): 10–11.

in the incumbent utility's service area. Other retailers could enter and bid customers away, knowing the affiliated retailer could not match their prices. During the last two years of the five-year period, the affiliated retailer was capped by the price to beat, but could offer lower prices.[58] ERCOT performs functions in the retail market that were performed by the LSEs in other states that introduced retail competition. ERCOT acts as a neutral third party to perform settlement functions for the retail market. ERCOT also serves as the registration agent for all retail transactions. Customer switch requests, move-in and move-out requests, and monthly electricity usage data flow through ERCOT.[59]

The combination of an emerging electricity market with growing demand and old plants with high operating costs made Texas an attractive destination for new merchant power plants. Low gas prices made combined-cycle gas plants competitive against older gas-fired facilities and new nuclear and coal plants. Deregulation coincided with an unprecedented power plant construction boom, adding 24,680 MW of new capacity between 2000 and 2004.[60] The combination of excess capacity and new transmission provided a buffer for the new market from design flaws.

An unintended consequence of deregulation was the creation of the largest demand response market in the United States. Traditionally, utilities provided "interruptible service" tariffs to generally large industrial customers. In return for the right to interrupt a customer, the utility offered interruptible service customers a discounted rate, usually a reduction in firm demand charges. Before restructuring, the ERCOT utilities reported 3,125 MW of interruptible load in ERCOT, but it was rarely called: for example, in 1999, only 52 MW was curtailed during peak hours.[61] To pave the way for retail choice, all tariffs (including interruptible rates) offered by IOUs in ERCOT were terminated. Faced with the loss of these lucrative discounts, industrial customers lobbied for eligibility to provide ten-minute spinning ("responsive") reserves, and were able to obtain 25 percent of the 2,300 MW responsive reserve market for Load acting as Resources (LaaRs). LaaR requirements included at least 1

[58] PURA § 39.202(a).
[59] PUCT, *Scope of Competition in Electric Markets in Texas* (January 2003): 19.
[60] PUCT, 1998, 1999, 2000, "Annual Update on Activities in the ERCOT Wholesale Electricity Market," Project No. 19616; *New Electric Generating Plants in Texas Since 1995*, December 31, 2010.
[61] PUCT Market Oversight Division, *2000 Annual Update of Generating Electric Utility Data*, Project No. 22209 (December 2000): 4.

MW of interruptible load, with the telemetry to respond to a command to drop load within ten minutes and armed with an under-frequency relay that would immediately drop load if system frequency fell below 59.7 Hz. In 2003, LaaRs became eligible to supply 50 percent of responsive reserves.[62]

On November 1, 2000, the ERCOT filed its Protocols, and the PUCT approved them on April 11, 2001, and on rehearing on June 4, 2001. The PUCT required a generation bid cap of $1,000/MWh (and $1,000/MW for ancillary services) as a backup stop against the possible exercise of market power, to expire in July 2003. All scheduling of energy or bidding for ancillary services must be done through a Qualified Scheduling Entity. A Scheduling Entity had to meet credit requirements to ensure that it could pay for the ERCOT services it used. Initially, Scheduling Entity were required to submit balanced schedules in terms of loads and their corresponding resources, but this requirement was eventually relaxed. ERCOT compared the sum of these schedules to its own load forecasts, to determine balancing energy and ancillary services requirements. If submitted schedules result in congestion of the transmission system, ERCOT redispatched system resources out of merit order to resolve the congestion.[63]

When ERCOT began operation, the costs for relieving congestion were "uplifted" based on the market participant's load share. The PUCT required ERCOT to switch to a direct cost assignment methodology, including local congestion costs.[64]

However, 95 percent of transactions continued to be bilateral contracts between generators and retail electric providers (REPs) or unregulated distribution companies. While this provided a buffer against the impact of price spikes in the spot market, it also led to a thin, inefficient spot market. Price spikes during a three-day winter storm in February 2003 raised concerns of market manipulation.[65] The PUCT, following

---

[62] ERCOT Board of Directors, *Minutes of December 8, 2001 Meeting*; ERCOT Technical Advisory Committee, *Minutes, November 8, 2001 Meeting*; *2004 ERCOT Methodologies for Determining Ancillary Service Requirements, Proposal for Board Approval* (November 18, 2003).

[63] *Petition of the Electric Reliability Council of Texas for Approval of the ERCOT Protocols*, Docket No. 23220, *Order on Rehearing* (June 4, 2001): 13–14. Note that the rationale was to avoid using the balancing market, ensuring a thin spot market: "The intent of this requirement is to preclude QSEs from relying on the ERCOT-administered balancing energy market as part of their resource portfolios, except to cover any underestimated energy needs." *Id.*

[64] PUCT, *Scope of Competition in Electric Markets in Texas* (January 2003): 49–50.

[65] PUCT, *Scope of Competition in Electric Markets in Texas* (January 2005): 32.

an investigation, concluded that a wholesale market strategy known as "hockey stick" bidding was partially responsible for the price disruptions. The price spikes resulted from one market participant's offering a *single* MW at $990.[66] A Modified Competitive Solution Method was implemented. It precluded hockey stick bids from setting the market price by establishing a lower market price, at the price level at which 95 percent of the bid stack is exhausted. Market participants bidding above that level were paid as bid. The PUCT required the disclosure of market offers in excess of $300/MWh.[67]

Problems with operations under the zonal system resulted in increasing support to switching to a nodal/zonal system. The PUCT held hearings on this proposal in 2002, and adopted a rule in 2005 directing ERCOT to implement a nodal market design. The original cost-benefit study estimated a cost to ERCOT from $55 million to $70 million.[68] The development of a nodal market ran into software snags, partially as a result of poor management, as well as demands from municipals and cooperatives to incorporate their special status and grandfather their existing contracts into the software design. The first nodal budget of $263 million was based on a start date in January 2009. In May 2008, ERCOT officials announced an indefinite delay in the nodal project, because a vendor had failed to deliver the required software. The nodal market began operation in December 2010, with a final cost of $561 million.[69]

[66] Hockey stick bidding occurs when a generator bids the incremental output of a unit at a very high price, reasoning that the loss of the net income from a few MW not being dispatched in most periods would be recovered by raising prices during the few hours when that last increment of generation was required to balance the market.

[67] *Report of the Electric Reliability Council of Texas to the PUCT Regarding Implementation of the ERCOT Protocols*, Docket No. 24770, Order (August 22, 2003): 4–5, 11; *Rulemaking on Pricing Safeguards for ERCOT-Operated Wholesale Markets*, Project No. 27917, Order Adopting New § 25.502 (December 20, 2004): 12, 21–24.

[68] Tabors, Caramanis & Associates and KEMA Consulting, Inc., "Market Restructuring Cost-Benefit Analysis, Final Report" (November 30, 2004): 5–22.

[69] PUCT, *Scope of Competition in Electric Markets in Texas* (January 2009): 2; Steering Committee of Cities, "The Story of ERCOT," 73; PUCT, *Scope of Competition in Electricity Markets in Texas*, Legislative Report (January 2011): 23–24.

13

Pushing Markets – Order 2000

The Midwest and Southwest electricity markets did not evolve out of tight power pools or state legislative action; they gradually coalesced under pressure from FERC. While Order 888 was the primary motivation for New England and PJM to take the final step from pool to formal market, Order 2000 was the impetus that encouraged the creation of the Midwest and Southwest markets.

In January 2000, in response to numerous comments that Order 888 had not been sufficient to alleviate discrimination and implement competitive markets, the Commission issued Order 2000.[1] FERC, in Order 2000, wanted all transmission owning entities, including nonpublic utility entities, to place their transmission facilities under the control of appropriate Regional Transmission Organizations (RTOs) in a timely manner. The Order established minimum characteristics and functions for RTOs and a collaborative process by which public and nonpublic transmission-owning utilities, in consultation with state officials, would consider and develop RTOs. Although this was stated as a voluntary approach, the Commission held out the threat of further regulatory steps if the industry failed to form RTOs.[2]

---

[1] Regional Transmission Organizations, Order No. 2000, FERC Stats. & Regs. ¶ 31,089 (1999), 65 FR 809 (January 6, 2000), *order on reh'g*, Order No. 2000-A, FERC Stats. & Regs ¶ 31,092 (2000), 65 FR 12,088 (February 25, 2000), *petitions for review dismissed, Public Utility District No. 1 of Snohomish County, Washington v. FERC*, 272 F.3d 607 (D.C. Cir. 2001).

[2] Order 2000 at 30,993.

The Commission's sense of urgency was fueled by a number of trends. The increased use of TLR procedures was an indication that the increased and different use of the transmission system was stressing the grid. Price spikes in the Midwest wholesale electric market in June 1998 raised concerns about the adequacy of transmission infrastructure and management. The secretary of the Energy Advisory Board Task Force on Electric System Reliability published its final report on September 29, 1998. The Task Force found that traditional reliability institutions and processes needed to be modified to ensure that reliability was maintained in a competitively neutral fashion. Because bulk power systems are regional in nature, they should be operated more reliably and efficiently when coordinated over large geographic areas.[3]

The Commission found that when utilities control monopoly transmission facilities and also have power-marketing interests, they have poor incentives to provide quality transmission service to their power-marketing competitors. Transmission service problems related to discriminatory conduct were impeding competitive wholesale power markets. Some instances of discrimination may be undetectable in a nontransparent market, and others are hard to identify with certainty after the fact. The Commission expressed concern that functional unbundling may not be an appropriate long-term regulatory solution. Mistrust of IOUs by market participants inhibited participation in the market, and may harm reliability.[4]

The Commission had also realized that the movement toward establishing ISOs had exhausted its momentum after the conversion of the tight power pools and the two state-legislated markets. After more than two years of effort, the proponents of an ISO in the Pacific Northwest and Rocky Mountain regions ended their efforts. Members of the MAPP failed to achieve consensus for establishing a long-planned ISO, although some of the utilities involved in that effort began discussions on a proposed Midwest ISO. In the Southwest, proponents of the Desert STAR ISO were not able to reach an agreement after more than two years of discussion. Reasons for the failure to form voluntary, multistate ISOs included cost shifting, disagreements about sharing transmission revenues among transmission owners, and concerns about the loss of rights embedded in existing transmission agreements.[5]

[3] Order 2000 at 30,998–99.
[4] Order 2000 at 30,004–05, 30,114–17.
[5] Order 2000 at 31,002.

However, the Commission was not prepared to go beyond a voluntary approach, despite urging by some parties,[6] although it was willing to apply carrots and sticks to prompt utilities to join RTOs. FERC maintained that it possessed both general and specific authority to advance voluntary RTO formation, as well as the authority to order RTO participation to remedy undue discrimination or anticompetitive effects where supported by the record.[7] The Commission provided favorable ratemaking treatments for utilities who assumed the risks of the transition to a new structure. While RTO participation would not be required in order to retain or obtain market-based rate authorization for wholesale power sales, the burden of proof would be shifted to the applicant in the absence of RTO participation. Similarly, with merger applications, a showing would be required that the merger was in the public interest without RTO participation.[8]

The Commission focused on ratemaking to eliminate practices that might facilitate discrimination, but also because of a growing concern about inadequate investment in transmission. RTOs should develop ratemaking practices that eliminate regional rate pancaking (piling up separate charges for moving power across different transmission provider service areas), manage congestion, internalize parallel path flows, and provide incentives for transmission-owning utilities to operate and invest in their systems efficiently. The Commission encouraged RTOs to develop and propose innovative ratemaking practices, particularly with respect to incentives. The Commission added regulatory text regarding performance-based ratemaking, which identified a list of innovative transmission rate treatments.[9]

The Commission addressed but did not have a solution for the concerns of states with low-cost power that an RTO would result in this power being sold out of state, consequently increasing local electricity

---

[6] Joint comments filed by APPA, ELCON, TAPS, and TDU Systems argued that the FPA gave the Commission legal authority to require participation by public utilities in properly structured and configured RTOs. Order 2000 at 31,039–40. Major opponents of mandatory participation included EEI, United Illuminating, Southern Company, Duke, First Energy, NYPP, Indianapolis P&L, FP&L, Detroit Edison, and the Florida and Alabama Commissions. Order 2000 at 31,041.

[7] Order 2000 at 31,043. The Court of Appeals agreed that Commission's language passed muster as encouragement to voluntary participation and not coercive actions to mandate participation in RTOs. *PUD No.1 Snohomish County v. FERC*, 272 F.3d 607, 614–16 (D.C. Cir 2001).

[8] Order 2000 at 31,034.

[9] Order 2000 at 31,170–73.

costs. Among the state commissions expressing apprehension about the potential impact of RTOS were South Carolina and Alabama. The Commission did note that states without retail competition could still order their utilities to sell low-cost power in-state and export only higher-cost power.[10]

Despite Order 2000, a number of utilities gave only lip service to forming RTOs in their filings. The Commission rejected Southern Company's initial filings, which proposed a GridCo that would only provide new transmission services, excluding all of the Southern Company's existing transmission services, and ordered it to file a report on efforts to join neighboring utilities in an RTO for the Southeast. A scope limited to regional nonpublic utilities with whom Southern had memorandums of understanding, while an improvement over the company's original proposal, fell far short of the regional RTO the Commission had in mind.[11] Eventually, Southern Company would join with Entergy as well as some cooperatives and nonpublic utilities and file the SeTrans RTO proposal in June 2002.[12] Carolina Power, Duke Energy, and South Carolina Electric and Gas filed their GridSouth proposal in October 2000. Like the SeTrans proposal, this RTO would gradually fade away.[13] A similar fate awaited a Florida RTO proposal[14] and Western RTO proposals.[15]

The development of the Midwest ISO (MISO) market was more convoluted, because there was no tight power pool to serve as precedent. Two states in the region required utilities either to participate in a Commission-approved ISO (Illinois and Wisconsin) or to sell their transmission assets to an independent transmission company that would operate under a regional ISO (Wisconsin). Ohio also enacted legislation requiring its electric utilities to join or establish regional transmission entities.[16] Approximately twenty-five Midwest transmission-owning utilities met over a two-year period. In April and May 1998, a number of major utilities signed on to the MISO proposal.[17]

---

[10]   Order 2000 at 31,209–10.
[11]   *Southern Company Services, Inc.,* 94 FERC ¶ 61,271 (2001), *reh'g denied,* 95 FERC ¶ 61,172 (2001).
[12]   *Cleco Power LLC et al.,* 101 FERC ¶ 61,008 (2002).
[13]   *Carolina Power & Light Company et al.,* 94 FERC ¶ 61,273 (2001).
[14]   *GridFlorida, LLC,* 94 FERC ¶ 61,363 (2001).
[15]   *Avista Corporation et al.,* 95 FERC ¶ 61,114 (2001); *Avista Corporation et al.,* 100 FERC ¶ 61,274 (2002); *Avista Corporation et al.,* 100 FERC ¶ 61,297 (2002); *Arizona Public Service Company et al.,* 101 FERC ¶ 61,033 (2002).
[16]   Order 2000 at 31,000.
[17]   *Midwest Independent Transmission System Operator et al.,* 84 FERC ¶ 61,231, 61,239 (1998). The original signatories include Cinergy, Commonwealth Edison, Illinois Power,

Concurrently with the Midwest ISO filings, a group of companies (the Alliance Companies[18]) filed on June 3, 1999, to form a Transmission Company (Transco) or an ISO. The Commission rejected a proposal to allow the companies to control 25 percent of the voting stock of the proposed Transco and other impediments to Transco independence.[19] The Alliance companies made further changes to meet the independence requirements of Order 2000, and addressed the scope issues with the announcement that Dayton Power and Light and Northern Indiana Public Service would join. The Commission accepted the modified proposal, subject to clarifications.[20] Commissioner Massey dissented on the grounds that "[a]n organization shaped more or less like a snake that stretches from the Great Lakes to the Mid-Atlantic does not satisfy the scope and configuration characteristic."[21]

The Midwest ISO's primary responsibilities included ensuring reliability of the transmission system and administering a single system-wide transmission tariff. The proposed MISO Tariff provided for network transmission service based on the cost of transmission facilities in the service area in which the loads are located. MISO would prevent curtailment of firm service by purchasing redispatch services from generators. The proposed process was cumbersome as extensive communication was necessary between the ISO, users, and generators to synchronize multiple redispatch requests.[22] The RTO proceedings provided the opportunity to move toward a more comprehensive organization. Midwest state commissions were unanimous in their support of a single RTO. Meanwhile, MISO had expanded its membership to meet the requirement that it serve an appropriate region, by adding major utilities such as Indianapolis Power and Light, Minnesota Power, and UtiliCorp.[23]

MISO increased its authority over transmission facilities, including exclusive authority over interchange schedules and dispatch. While local control area operators would still have some responsibility for certain

Wisconsin Electric Power, Union Electric, Louisville Gas & Electric and Kentucky Utilities. Additional members include Alliant, Allegheny Energy and Duquesne Light, Alliant Corporation, Central Illinois Public Service, Interstate Power, and IES Utilities.

[18] AEP, Consumers Energy, Detroit Edison Company (DTE), FirstEnergy, and Virginia Electric and Power.

[19] *Alliance Companies,* 89 FERC ¶ 61,928, 61,580–82 (1999).

[20] *Alliance Companies,* 94 FERC ¶ 61,070 (1999), *reh'g denied,* 95 FERC ¶ 61,182 (2001).

[21] *Alliance Companies,* 94 FERC ¶ 61,070, 61,330–31 (1999).

[22] *Midwest Independent Transmission System Operator et al.,* 84 FERC ¶ 61,231, 61,162–64, 61,240 (1998).

[23] *Midwest Independent Transmission System Operator et al.,* 97 FERC ¶ 61,326, 62,503–06 (1998).

control area functions, the MISO would have superseding authority to ensure short-term reliability. However, MISO would not operate as a control area, nor did it provide ancillary services; rather, it would merely help secure these services for customers from third parties. MISO's proposal for a real-time balancing market provided that customers could avoid imbalance charges by staying "in balance" through the use of bilateral schedules arranged with third-party providers. MISO would make available a posting system where the buy and sell quotes could be posted. MISO and its stakeholders were developing a Day Two proposal for congestion management based on real-time locational pricing.[24]

The Commission agreed that a larger Midwest ISO with fewer gaps than the one proposed would have significant additional reliability and competitive benefits. However, the Commission chose to encourage voluntary arrangements among industry participants rather than mandate membership.[25] The Commission directed the Alliance Companies to explore an accommodation with MISO, which was approved as an RTO. This decision was motivated by both appeals by the state commissions in the region and lack of progress in eliminating seams between the MISO, the Alliance, and PJM.[26]

The convoluted MISO proceeding encouraged some members to explore other options. The Commission accepted a Settlement Agreement that allowed Illinois Power, Ameren, and Com Ed to withdraw from MISO.[27] Ameren, FirstEnergy, and NIPSCO moved to form an independent transmission operator, GridAmerica LLC, which would then join MISO. AEP and Com Ed decided to form a transmission company and join PJM. Dayton and Virginia Electric Power also stated their intent to join PJM. The Commission expressed concern about these choices as it pertained to internalizing loop flow and other operational issues, as well as rate pancaking resulting from the gerrymandered scope of both RTOs.[28] The Commission's concerns would prove to be well grounded.

SPP was a nonprofit corporation, headquartered in Little Rock, Arkansas, covering all or part of the states of Arkansas, Kansas, Louisiana,

---

[24] *Midwest Independent Transmission System Operator et al.*, 97 FERC ¶ 61,326, 62,509–22 (1998).

[25] *Midwest Independent Transmission System Operator et al.*, 84 FERC ¶ 61,231, 61,245 (1998).

[26] *Alliance Companies*, 97 FERC ¶ 61,327, 62,529–31 (2001).

[27] *Illinois Power Company et al.*, 95 FERC ¶ 61,183 (2001), *reh'g denied*, 95 FERC ¶ 61,026 (2001) (*Illinois Power*).

[28] *Alliance Companies*, 100 FERC ¶ 61,137 (2002), *reh'g denied and clarification*, 103 FERC ¶ 61,274 (2003).

Mississippi, Missouri, New Mexico, Oklahoma, and Texas. SPP's members included thirteen IOUs, seven municipal systems, eight generation and transmission cooperatives, three state authorities, one federal power-marketing agency, one wholesale generator, and seventeen power marketers. In 1968, SPP became a regional reliability council within NERC and began administering regional transmission service on June 1, 1998.[29] Entergy was formerly an SPP member but withdrew from membership in 1997. Entergy rejoined SPP as an associate member in September 2000 but remained a member of the Southeastern Electric Reliability Council.[30]

On December 30, 1999, SPP filed a proposal for recognition as ISO and RTO. The Commission rejected the filing for failing to provide the RTO with operational authority for all transmission facilities under its control, failure to provide sufficient detail on transmission pricing, lack of an energy imbalance service and a real-time balancing market, concerns about the independence of the proposed ISO's board of directors, and inadequate geographical scope.[31] A second attempt was rejected because the Commission found that SPP's regional configuration was inadequate.[32] In October 2000, SPP submitted a proposal in partnership with Entergy, but the Commission refused to approve the scope and configuration of the SPP/Entergy RTO.[33] SPP and Entergy each submitted a filing on May 25, 2001, reporting on progress made to expand their RTOs, but the Commission again rejected the RTO filings.[34] Finally, owing to both revisions and Commission exhaustion, SPP came up with a filing in October 2003 that was acceptable to the Commission, with some conditions. SPP proposed a phased implementation of a comprehensive strategic plan that included market-based congestion management, in addition to a real-time, offer-based energy market to calculate the price of imbalance energy. The real-time market would determine nodal prices and include central dispatch instructions to resources. The real-time

---

[29] *Southwest Power Pool, Inc.*, 82 FERC ¶ 61,267, *order deferring effective date*, 82 FERC ¶ 61,285 (1998). SPP members include: AEP (Public Service Company of Oklahoma, Southwestern Electric Power Company); Aquila, Cleco Power LLC, Kansas City Power & Light, Oklahoma Gas and Electric Services, Southwestern Public Service Company, Westar Energy-Western Resources, Inc. and Kansas Gas & Electric Company, and Sunflower Electric Power Corporation.

[30] *Southwest Power Pool, Inc.*, 96 FERC ¶ 61,062, 61,248 (2001).

[31] *Southwest Power Pool, Inc.*, 91 FERC ¶ 61,137 at 61,523–30.

[32] *Southwest Power Pool, Inc.*, 91 FERC ¶ 61,137 at 61,350 (2000).

[33] *Southwest Power Pool, Inc.*, 94 FERC ¶ 61,359 (2001), *reh'g denied and clarification*, 95 FERC ¶ 61,431 (2001).

[34] *Southwest Power Pool, Inc.*, 96 FERC ¶ 61,062, 61,247 (2001).

market would be integrated with SPP's current congestion management system, using TLR while providing alternative redispatch options. SPP also committed to establishing competitive ancillary service markets.[35] The Commission authorized the SPP RTO as of October 1, 2004.[36]

On January 4, 2006, SPP filed its plan to implement a real-time energy imbalance market and establish a market monitoring and market power mitigation plan. The Commission conditionally accepted the SPP's filing and permitted it to become effective October 1, subject to changes.[37] SPP calculated locational imbalance prices (LIPs) at each node and issued dispatch instructions every five minutes. SPP defined the LIP as the marginal cost of serving load at a specific location as calculated by the economic dispatch algorithm.[38] The Commission approved the February 1, 2007 date for the opening of the imbalance market.[39]

SPP finally moved to adopt the dominant multi-settlement/LMP market design when it filed tariff revisions to implement the SPP Integrated Marketplace in February 2012. SPP had begun work on the design of the new market in 2010 and requested an effective date of March 1, 2014 for the new market. SPP endeavored to model its Integrated Marketplace on those successfully operating in other markets, modified to address regional differences. SPP will function as the Reliability Coordinator, Balancing Authority, Transmission Service Provider, Planning Coordinator, Reserve Sharing Group Administrator, and Market Operator.[40]

[35] *Southwest Power Pool, Inc.*, 106 FERC ¶ 61,110 at 116–22, 146 (2004), *order on reh'g*, 109 FERC ¶ 61,010 (2004).
[36] *Southwest Power Pool, Inc.*, 109 FERC ¶ 61,009 (2004), *order on reh'g*, 110 FERC ¶ 61,137 (2005).
[37] *Southwest Power Pool, Inc.*, 114 FERC ¶ 61,289 at 1–3 (2006).
[38] *Southwest Power Pool, Inc.*, 114 FERC ¶ 61,289 at 58–62 (2006).
[39] *Southwest Power Pool, Inc.*, 118 FERC ¶ 61,055 (2007).
[40] *Southwest Power Pool, Inc.*, 141 FERC ¶ 61,048 (2012); *r'hrg and clarification*, 142 FERC ¶ 61,025 (2013).

14

Great Expectations

The California electricity fiasco was used as a poster child for the failure of electricity deregulation by many of its opponents, but it really reflected the twin problems of political market design and overambitious implementation scheduling. The market design was a "camel,"[1] a mishmash of concepts driven by compromise between competing interests, based on faulty assumptions and hastily enacted. While a "perfect storm" triggered the collapse of the California market, its dysfunction made some sort of crisis inevitable.

In the midst of the recession of the early 1990s, which hit California especially hard, large industrial consumers revolted against the high electricity prices. The cost of generation service in regulated prices was 6 to 7 cents/Kwh (exclusive of transmission and distribution costs) while the wholesale energy price was about 2.5 cents/kWh. This was a result of CPUC decisions designed to financially stabilize the three major utilities by allowing higher returns on capital. The CPUC added insult to injury when, to help QFs acquire financing, it required utilities to negotiate long-term QF contracts at prices based on estimates of long-run avoided cost, locking in large amounts of overpriced power for decades. By 1985, QF capacity exceeded 15,000 MW. Fortunately, most of these contracts reverted to short-run avoided costs by 1993, but the damage was done, piling excessive purchase costs on top of excessive returns on

---

[1] "A camel is a horse designed by a committee." The phrase has been attributed to *Vogue* magazine, July 1958, to Sir Alec Issigonis, and also to University of Wisconsin philosophy professor Lester Hunt. http://en.wikipedia.org/wiki/Design_by_committee.

utility capital.[2] Industrial customers in the state began to agitate for the right to buy power directly in the wholesale market and to pay the utilities only for the costs of T&D service. They were supported by independent power producers and energy marketers.[3]

Dan Fessler was the president of the CPUC during the initial period of deregulation. Fessler was a UC Davis contracts law professor who had no particular background in energy issues,[4] but he did boast a conservative ideology and the friendship of the state's First Lady Gale Wilson. That was enough to make him Wilson's choice as president of the CPUC in 1991. Fessler looked to the electric power deregulation in Britain for inspiration. Fessler went on a junket to England, sponsored and paid for by the California Council for Environmental and Economic Balance, headed by former Southern California Edison (SCE) president Michael Peevey. Fessler was especially taken with his meeting with Stephen Littlechild, head of the UK's Office of Electric Regulation.[5]

Commissioners Jesse Knight and Norm Shumway, both appointees of Governor Pete Wilson, were the key retail wheeling champions within the CPUC. They were frustrated with the myriad of balancing accounts and rate adjustment mechanisms with which they had to contend as part of the ratemaking process. They became increasingly perplexed about the utility resource planning process. The move toward greater reliance on the marketplace to make supply decisions was clearly in line with the free-market ideology of the Republican governor.[6] Although disagreeing at times with the methods of implementation, Commissioner Gregory Conlon

---

[2] Division of Strategic Planning, California Public Utilities Commission, *California's Electric Services Industry: Perspectives on the Past, Strategies for the Future* (San Francisco: California Public Utilities Commission, February 1993) ("Yellow Book"): 51–56.

[3] *Yellow Book*, 82–84.

[4] Fessler actually boasted of his lack of knowledge:

> In 1991 I accepted a challenge from Pete Wilson to take leave from the UC faculty and serve a six-year term on the California Public Utilities Commission. The fact that I had no involvement with, or experience in, the energy, telecommunications, water and transport mandates of that Commission made me the ideal candidate.

> http://www.wyopipeline.com/information/presentations/2004/Daniel%20W.%20Fessler %20Remarks.htm (last visited August 10, 2010).

[5] Bill Bradley, "Master of Disaster: How Pete Wilson's Energy Chief Short-Circuited the California Grid," *LA Weekly*, February 22, 2001, at http://www.laweekly.com/ 2001-02-22/news/master-of-disaster/ (last visited June 11, 2012).

[6] Mark Stout, "Comparative Power Analysis of the California Electric Utility Industry Deregulation Process" (MS Thesis, University of California at Berkeley, May 25, 1997): 26–27.

shared Fessler's dedication to market-oriented reform of the state's electric utility industry.[7] The other commissioner, Patricia Eckert, along with Shumway, left by early 1995, to be replaced by former banker Henry Duque and attorney Josiah Neeper.

In September 1992, the CPUC directed its Division of Strategic Planning to undertake a comprehensive review of the electricity industry. The CPUC staff report, also referred to as the "Yellow Book,"[8] was released in February 1993. High prices were blamed on the existing system of regulated vertically integrated monopolies, the high costs of nuclear power plants,[9] and expensive long-term QF contracts. There was broad agreement that the existing industry structure and regulatory system were seriously broken and needed to be fundamentally reformed.

The study identified and evaluated four future regulatory strategies, three of which modified the regulatory model, but the fourth would restructure the industry through a competitive market for electricity, including divestiture of generation by the state's three major electric investor-owned utilities. The newly formed utilities would become common-carrier transmission and distribution companies and provide open, nondiscriminatory access.[10]

On April 20, 1994, the CPUC issued a controversial order (the "Blue Book") stating that it would institute retail wheeling in the state, for large electricity consumers by 1996, and for residential consumers by 2002.[11] Customers would have the choice of continuing to receive bundled service from the utility. The utility would provide transmission and distribution services on a nondiscriminatory basis to direct-access

---

[7] Charles David Jacobson, "Expecting the Unexpected: Networks, Markets, and the Failure of Electric Utility Restructuring in California," *Business and Economic History Online* (2004): 14–15, at http://www.thebhc.org/publications/BEHonline/2004/Jacobson .pdf.

[8] CPUC, "California's Electric Services Industry: Perspectives on the Past, Strategies for the Future" (February 1993).

[9] PG&E's infatuation with nuclear power in a state that is prone to dramatic seismic events began in 1957, and the company constructed one of the first private nuclear power plants in the United States. By 1968, PG&E, SCE, and San Diego Gas & Electric (SDG&E) were all involved in nuclear power plant construction. *Yellow Book*, 36–39.

[10] *Yellow Book*, 5–6.

[11] *Order Instituting Rulemaking on the Commission's Proposed Policies Governing Restructuring California's Electric Services Industry and Reforming Regulation; Order Instituting Investigation on the Commission's Proposed Policies Governing Restructuring California's Electric Services Industry and Reforming Regulation; Order Instituting Rulemaking and Order Instituting Investigation*, R.94-0-031, I.94-04-032 (Cal. Pub. Util. Comm'n, April 20, 1994) (*"Blue Book"*).

consumers. Traditional cost-of-service regulation would be replaced with performance-based regulation for the regulated portions of the industry.

The Blue Book embraced two competing strategies for the future structure of the California electric power industry. One was a bilateral retail wheeling structure, and the other was a United Kingdom–style transmission pool. Under a bilateral retail wheeling, utilities would continue to be vertically integrated but would have to compete for the demand of their native load customers. The Blue Book approved of the United Kingdom's spot market, known as the Pool, because its half-hourly price signals served as a guide to consumer decisions about energy services and generator decisions about constructing new plants, as well as providing for economic dispatch of the existing generation sources.[12] In the United Kingdom, the creation of the Pool was accompanied by the complete separation of ownership of generation, transmission, and distribution. This was not proposed by the Blue Book, despite lobbying by the California Large Energy Consumers Association for a transmission company to operate the grid.[13] The Blue Book did not specify how new generation for utility service customers would be acquired, or how resource adequacy could be maintained in a bifurcated market.[14]

Two weeks later, on May 3, 1994, the chairs of the State Assembly Natural Resource Committee and Utilities and Commerce Committee informed the CPUC president that at least eleven state statutes would need to be repealed or amended prior to the implementation of the order. The legislature expressed clear disapproval of the CPUC's action. On August 31, 1994, the legislature passed Assembly Concurrent Resolution 143, establishing a Joint Oversight Committee to ensure that the legislature was consulted on electric restructuring proposals.[15]

California's well-funded interest groups then spent the next four years arguing about exactly how this reform vision would be implemented. The state's large industrial and agricultural customers came down firmly on the side of radical restructuring. They strongly supported direct access

---

[12] *Blue Book*, 25.

[13] Arthur J. O'Donnell, *Soul of the Grid: A Cultural Biography of the California Independent System Operator* (Lincoln, NE, I Universe, 2003): 15.

[14] James Bushnell and Carl Blumstein, "A Reader's Guide to the Blue Book: Issues in California's Electric Industry Restructuring and Regulatory Reform," POWER (June 1994): 7–8.

[15] Letter from Gwen Moore, Chair of Assembly Utilities and Commerce and Byron D. Sher, Chair of Assembly Natural Resource Committee, to Daniel Wm. Fessler, President, California Public Utility Commission (May 3, 1994), cited in James D. Elliott, "Electric Utility Regulation Reform in New York: Economic Competitiveness at the Expense of the Environment?" 13 *Pace Environmental Law Review* 281, 283, fn 3.

and vertical disintegration, and many of them opposed full recovery of stranded costs. The state's two largest consumer advocacy groups also opposed full recovery of stranded costs and strongly emphasized the need for a comprehensive strategy for aggregating small consumers.[16]

Big energy consumers did not like the idea of an electricity pool, complaining it would give the utilities too much control over the market. Big users pressed state officials to let them negotiate directly with suppliers as part of any deregulation plan. PG&E, the largest of the utilities, generally sided with the manufacturers, as did Enron.[17] During the restructuring hearings and negotiations, both at the CPUC and in the legislature, the discussion centered on preventing the large utilities from dominating the new market(s). Edison International's (parent company of SCE) unregulated affiliates had a strong presence in the California QF market. Sempra Energy (the parent corporation of SDG&E) presented potential conflicts for independent generators in southern California.

Enron was a key supporter of deregulation, constantly drumming the message that deregulation would save billions for California consumers. In June 1994, Jeffrey Skilling promised California "enormous" savings if companies like his could compete for the state's utility customers, tossing out a figure of $8.9 billion a year. However, its influence did not come from campaign contributions, but from lobbyists and experts. By 1998, Enron was paying nearly $500,000 for lobbyists working the legislature and CPUC. Enron was the only company other than the utilities that had the resources and motivation to send lawyers and experts to thousands of working groups and hearings. The companies that would later dominate the California market – Reliant Energy, Duke Energy, and Mirant – did not hire lobbyists or begin giving campaign contributions until after 1997, when they bought divested power plants.[18]

The independent producers that spent resources on lobbying during the restructuring proceedings of 1995–96 were primarily Californian companies. Big electricity users formed Californians for Competitive Electricity to lobby for deregulation. Consumer and environmental groups

---

[16] Peter Navarro, "Electric Utilities: The Argument," *Harvard Business Review* (January–February 1996): 118–19.

[17] Ron Russell, "Dim Bulbs: Greedy Out-of-State Profiteers Make Easy Targets, but the Real Villains of California's Energy Debacle Are the Ones under the State Capitol Dome," *San Francisco Weekly*, March 7, 2001, at http://www.sfweekly.com/sanfrancisco/dim-bulbs/Content?oid=2141079 (last visited August 10, 2010).

[18] Nancy Vogel, "Enron Vision Proved Costly to Firm, State," *Los Angeles Times*, January 28, 2002, at http://articles.latimes.com/2002/jan/28/local/me-enronca28 (last visited June 10, 2012).

were not powerless, at least in terms of financial resources.[19] The three major utilities, however, could bring far more political pressure to bear on the CPUC and the legislature than other interest groups could. The three utilities would spend almost $4 million lobbying during 1995–96. PG&E and SCE would spend $18.7 million on lobbying and campaign contributions between 1995 and 2000, and an additional $35 million to defeat Proposition 9.[20]

SCE was worried about the prospect of losing $9 billion in stranded investment. Edison International was run by John Bryson,[21] whose political connections would prove valuable in the battle over deregulation. In early 1995, SCE was positioned as an anti-restructuring, don't-rock-the-boat utility. As restructuring came to be viewed as inevitable, SCE decided it needed to control the process. SCE pushed for a Poolco in the belief that it would be easier to collect stranded cost surcharges from one centralized power pool. SCE lobbied the CPUC intensely, focusing on ensuring stranded cost recovery and preventing forced divestiture of generation.[22]

The CPUC proceeded to flesh out its initial proposals. Extensive public hearings were held with testimony submitted by hundreds of individuals and organizations. On May 24, 1995, the CPUC issued majority and minority policy preference statements. The majority preference was to create an independent system operator that would operate a day-ahead electricity auction market and arrange the necessary transmission access for all bids meeting the pool price. The CPUC's proposal embraced both Poolco and full recovery of stranded costs. Rather than require the spin-off or divestiture of generating assets, the CPUC decided to wait and see if the problems of market concentration and price fixing emerged. The minority preference was for bilateral contracting to begin immediately.

---

[19] Stout, "Comparative Power Analysis of the California Electric Utility Industry Deregulation Process," 53–58.

[20] Proposition 9 was an initiative put on the ballot in 1998, which would have changed the terms of AB 1890 to stop stranded costs charges for nuclear power plants, require a 20% (instead of a 10%) reduction in charges to electricity customers, and not allow utilities to charge customers extra fees to pay for the bonds that were sold to help pay for the rate reduction. See http://www.environmentcalifornia.org/reports/energy/energy-program-reports/california39s-biggest-utilities-victims-of-deregulation-or-victors-money-spent-by-pg-e-and-edison-to-enact-and-protect-deregulation-1995-2002 (last visited August 10, 2010).

[21] Bryson, fresh out of Yale Law School, cofounded the NRDC in 1970, then served as chairman of the California Water Resources Control Board and was president of the CPUC from 1979 to 1982. http://www.forbes.com/2001/05/03/bryson.html (last visited August 10, 2010).

[22] Peter Navarro, "Electric Utilities: The Argument," 119.

The minority felt that the operator's role did not need to include the dispatch of generation except as necessary for system balance or stability. Multiple competing operators of the transmission grid might be more desirable than a single operator. Enron was the chief supporter of this approach, carried by Commissioner Jesse Knight.[23]

A broad coalition formed in opposition to the CPUC's proposal, threatening its political viability. Led by the California Manufacturers Association (CMA), the group included the Sierra Club, consumer advocates, EDF, the California Retailers Association, and the Agricultural Energy Consumers Association. The group sent a letter to CPUC President Fessler attacking the proposal to establish a pool that would function as an independent system operator. The coalition argued that the plan placed alternative-energy providers at a disadvantage, would trigger cuts in energy efficiency services and programs aimed at low-income users, and pass on artificially high rates to residential and business users.[24]

In the spring of 1995, SCE and the manufacturers were at such loggerheads that deregulation almost foundered just as Wilson was getting ready to run for president. To get things back on track, the governor directed two aides – George Dunn, his chief of staff, and Philip Romero, his chief economist – to convene negotiations with the major parties. The participants included lobbyists and lawyers for Edison, the California Large Energy Consumers Association, CMA, and the Independent Energy Producers Association. CMA's energy committee was able to get retailers and agricultural groups on board. Consumer groups were not invited. SCE was the only utility directly involved. The backroom provision deemed essential to win SCE's support required an agreement that any deregulation plan ensure that the utilities be reimbursed for their stranded costs. The manufacturers, in turn, insisted on the divided structure, with the ISO only able to make short-term purchases for reliability. Despite the opposition of the CEC to the divided market, politics triumphed over rational market design.[25]

[23] Carl Blumstein, L.S. Friedman, and R.J. Green, "The History of Electricity Restructuring in California," CSEM (August 2002): 8–9; Nancy Vogel, "Enron Vision Proved Costly to Firm, State."

[24] Patrick Lee, "Group Forms to Oppose PUC Pool Proposal Energy: Broad Coalition Says Effort to Deregulate Electricity Industry 'Sticks It to Everyone.'" *Los Angeles Times*, August 9, 1995, at http://articles.latimes.com/1995-08-09/business/fi-33282_1_broad-coalition (last visited June 10, 2012).

[25] Ron Russell, "Dim Bulbs"; Arthur J. O'Donnell, *Soul of the Grid*, 18–19; Mark Stout, "Comparative Power Analysis of the California Electric Utility Industry Deregulation Process," 41–42, 110, 138.

In September 1995, the CPUC received a Memorandum of Understanding that conveyed the joint recommendations of SCE, the CMA, the California Large Energy Consumers Association, and the independent energy producers. The Memorandum suggested two different entities, a spot market run by a new entity called the Power Exchange, operating in parallel with an ISO scheduling transmission activities.[26]

The December 1995 Policy Decision[27] planned for all electricity to be provided through the spot market except for customers who chose to obtain electricity by direct access to generators and aggregators through bilateral contracts. Utilities would have to purchase their requirements on the spot market. This policy decision was based on concerns voiced particularly by Enron and other market participants that the IOUs would use their market power to keep wholesale prices down, a desire for a transparent market price to assist in the process of paying off stranded costs, and bad experiences with long-term utility contracts.[28] Customers could obtain long-run price stability by entering into financial hedging contracts with third parties.

The CPUC Policy Decision Order chose the Power Exchange and ISO option.[29] The ISO would have the responsibility of coordinating the daily scheduling and dispatch activities of all market participants. The ISO would be limited to day-ahead scheduling and hourly redispatch to make sure the system is in balance. The Policy Decision also evidenced

---

[26] *Memorandum of Understanding on Joint Recommendations Among California Manufacturers Association, California Large Energy Consumers Association, Independent Energy Producers, Californians for Competitive Electricity and Southern California Edison Company, Order Instituting Rulemaking on the Commission's Proposed Policies Governing Restructuring California's Electric Service Industry and Reforming Regulation,* R.94-04-031, filed September 14, 1995.

[27] *Order Instituting Rulemaking on the Commission's Proposed Policies Governing Restructuring California's Electric Services Industry and Reforming Regulation.* Decision 95-12-063 (December 20, 1995) as modified by D.96-01-009 (January 10, 1996) (*Policy Decision Order*).

[28] Attorney General Bill Lockyer, State of California, "Attorney General's Energy White Paper: A Law Enforcement Perspective on the California Energy Crisis" (April 2004): 16.

[29] The Commission all but stated that political pressure was the reason for this decision:

Because the new market framework must at its conception have the support and confidence of market participants, and because the separate entities will function similarly to and bring the same benefits as a structure which combines the two, we are convinced that these potential problems are best resolved by requiring that the functions of the ISO and the pool be vested in separate entities.

Policy Decision Order at 28.

substantial concern about the potential for abuse of market power in the new market, particularly in transmission and in the centralized spot market. SCE and PG&E were required to file plans within ninety days for the voluntary divestiture of at least 50 percent of their fossil-fueled generating assets. The CPUC provided a financial incentive in the form of modestly higher stranded asset allowances.[30] Restructured operations were to begin on January 1, 1998.

The series of proposals had a stunning financial impact on the state's electric utilities. When California's regulators began developing their deregulatory reform proposals at the end of 1993, California's three investor-owned electric utilities had a combined market value of more than $30 billion. This value plummeted more than $12 billion over the ensuing six months as the plan was developed and formal industry restructuring proceedings commenced. In January 1996, the California Commission affirmed its plan. In response, PG&E announced write-downs in March 1996 and saw its stock value fall more than $1 billion in a single day.[31]

At this point, attention turned to the state legislature. The utilities and industrial users wanted their gains locked in by law, not subject to bureaucratic whim. At the same time, lawmakers' willingness to get into the act was fueled by campaign contributions flowing from a host of powerful interests.[32] Waiving numerous rules, lawmakers initiated the bill in a conference committee composed of three members from each chamber. The job of championing the bill to codify the PUC's actions fell to state Senator Jim Brulte, the bill's official sponsor, but state Senator Steve Peace (D-El Cajon), chair of the Senate Energy, Utilities and Communication Committee, provided the leadership throughout the process.[33] The template was based on the CPUC's December 1995 Decision.[34]

---

[30] *Policy Decision Order* at 97.

[31] Matthew W. White, "Power Struggles: Explaining Deregulatory Reforms in Electricity Markets," *Brookings Papers: Microeconomics* 1996, 209.

[32] Russell, "Dim Bulbs."

[33] Peace was an actor, writer, and producer of the film, *Attack of the Killer Tomatoes*, and a series of sequels, before he went into politics. Peace and Brulte both received substantial contributions from the IOUs. David Takashima, who had been Peace's chief of staff in the 1980s before working as a lobbyist for SCE, returned to work for Peace and helped shape the deregulation bill. Takashima then left to be director of government affairs for PG&E. Sharon Beder, "The Electricity Deregulation Con Game, Center for Media and Democracy," *PR Watch* 10(3) at http://www.prwatch.org/prwissues/2003Q3/dereg .html (last visited March 19, 2010).

[34] Stout, "Comparative Power Analysis of the California Electric Utility Industry Deregulation Process," 152.

Rather than encouraging the usual behind-the-scenes negotiations of competing bills put forth by different interest groups, Peace held marathon public sessions in which all stakeholders had to work on a single bill together, often into the wee hours of the morning. During eighteen days in August 1996, dubbed the "Steve Peace death march" for his propensity to keep negotiators at the table late into the night, the fine points of the energy law were hashed out. He became notorious for his caustic style, including a penchant for banishing contentious parties from the hearing room with orders to settle their differences or not come back.[35]

The large manufacturers and utilities accounted for the majority of the people in the hearing room. A key witness before the Committee was Ann Cohn, senior legal counsel for Edison International. Ms. Cohn wrote the first draft of the bill and brought it to the Committee for consideration. The governor's office offered help with technical drafting. Power marketers such as Enron were absent when their issues came up. Groups that opposed the bill without participating also were ineffective.[36]

Rank-and-file lawmakers relied heavily on six legislators, and few members of either house knew what was in the bill or understood it. Historically, utilities were a pretty boring topic, and legislators were happy to delegate to anyone willing to do the hard work of mastering the details. Given that interested groups had already voiced their positions in the CPUC proceeding, it was more a matter of negotiating around the edges than try to develop a more comprehensive plan. The legislature had little wiggle room in drafting the law, because the governor was breathing down their necks not to change what the CPUC had approved. Wilson had sent a letter to federal regulators in July 1996, declaring he would oppose any legislation that altered the CPUC's basic framework.[37] The bill, officially designated AB 1890, passed with no dissenting votes on August 31, 1996, and Governor Wilson signed it shortly thereafter.[38]

---

[35] Christian Berthelsen, "Genesis of State's Energy Fiasco / String of Bad Decisions on Deregulation Could End Up Costing Consumers $40 Billion," *San Francisco Chronicle*, December 31, 2000, at http://www.sfgate.com/news/article/Genesis-Of-State-s-Energy-Fiasco-String-of-bad-3302201.php (last visited June 10, 2012); Russell, "Dim Bulbs."

[36] Stout, "Comparative Power Analysis of the California Electric Utility Industry Deregulation Process," 43, 154, 157. There was limited public involvement because it was too esoteric a topic to obtain press coverage. Id., 45.

[37] Christian Berthelsen, "Genesis Of State's Energy"; Russell, "Dim Bulbs."

[38] A.B. 1890 was signed into law on September 23, 1996. See A.B. 1890, 1996 Leg. (Ca. 1996).

The bill mandated a 10 percent rate cut during the four-year transition period that allowed for stranded asset cost recovery through a CTC. The bill guaranteed a second 10 percent rate cut in 2002, after the bulk of the utilities' $28.5 billion in stranded costs was paid off.[39] As part of the provisions Peace helped engineer, environmentalists got $540 million in subsidies for renewable energy.[40] The CPUC supported a renewable portfolio standard approach. The legislature rejected this approach in favor of a program to support existing and new renewable energy projects during the four-year transition period beginning January 1998.[41] Other pork barrel deals included $200 million in price breaks for targeted consumers, including the Bay Area Rapid Transit District, the University of California, and even chicken farmers in the San Joaquin Valley. CTC exemptions for irrigation districts were provided. Divested power plants had to retain the original staff for two years and unions were promised $100 million for retraining and severance benefits for any workers laid off.[42] There were provisions for low-income consumers, energy efficiency, resource diversity concerns, and other factors.

The three utilities sold off 18,350 MW of generation with a book value of $1.8 billion for $3.3 billion. The utilities were to receive compensation for their remaining stranded costs from a non-bypassable fee. Retail customers of the utilities would pay for these stranded costs through the difference between the competitive market price and the applicable 1996 rate. Once the accounts were paid up, retail rates would be deregulated. The plan depended on the 1996 rate exceeding the average market price by a reasonable margin. In the CPUC planning

---

[39] A.B. 1890.

[40] AB1890 drew critical support from the nation's two leading environmental groups, NRDC and EDF. NRDC's Ralph Cavanagh helped get some $500 million in solar and conservation funding into AB1890. Cavanagh said he supported AB1890 because of the subsidies for renewables and conservation, and because he favored competition. However, Cavanagh had a long apprenticeship with John Bryson. Harvey Wasserman, "Power Play," *Salon*, October 27, 1998, at http://www.salon.com/news/1998/10/27newsb.html (last visited August 10, 2010). A staff member at the CPUC gives some credit to NRDC's insider strategy, noting that Cavanagh was influential in making sure that public purpose programs stayed on the plate. Mark Stout, "Comparative Power Analysis of the California Electric Utility Industry Deregulation Process," 48.

[41] Blumstein, Friedman, and Green, "The History of Electricity Restructuring in California," 12.

[42] Russell, "Dim Bulbs"; Stout, "Comparative Power Analysis of the California Electric Utility Industry Deregulation Process," 116.

documents, the AB 1890 hearings, and the bill itself, this assumption was unquestioned.[43]

A newly created nonprofit California ISO was responsible for managing the transmission network. David Freeman was hired to create the CAISO from scratch. There was no preexisting organization in California that could gradually shift responsibility for scheduling and transmission from local control areas to a central ISO. Utility personnel dominated technical decision making simply because when it came to questions of reliability, few people outside the large IOUs had any experience with transmission planning and operations. Market design decisions, which to some extent were ignored by the legislature and CPUC, were made on the fly. Stanford economist Robert Wilson triumphed over consumer advocate Eric Woychick on the issue of the single price auction. Duke Engineering and Services was given the contract to be project manager, with Asea Brown Boveri (ABB) awarded the assignment of developing the dispatch software and data management infrastructure. Coopers Lybrand was the project manager for the California Power Exchange (CalPX), with Om/Hand-el of Norway writing the exchange software to handle bidding, settlement, and billing. The large customers and power marketers' insistence on a firm demarcation between the CalPX and CAISO hindered coordination between the two entities. The two market systems had incompatible designs, bundled data differently, and could not be coordinated for market simulations.[44]

On March 31, 1997, SCE, SDG&E and PG&E, and the Trustee for the CAISO and the CalPX tendered several filings to implement Phase II of the comprehensive restructuring of the California electric marketplace. The March 31 submissions included the ISO filing, consisting of the ISO organizational and governance documents, the ISO's Operating Agreement and Tariff, the Transmission Control Agreement, and other materials required by the FERC. The filings also included a Pro Forma Transmission Owner's Tariff jointly tendered by the utilities.[45] The size and frequency of the CAISO and CalPX filings made it virtually

---

[43] Linda Cohen, Stephen Peck, Paroma Sanyal, and Carl Weinberg, "Retrospective Report on California's Electricity Crisis," California Energy Commission, PIER Project Report, CEC-500-2006-021 (January 2004): 27.

[44] Arthur J. O'Donnell, *Soul of the Grid*, at 34–42.

[45] *Pacific Gas and Electric et al.*, 80 FERC ¶ 61,128 (1997). The ISO/PX Trustee made these filings, rather than the ISO and PX Governing Boards, which were not yet in existence.

impossible for third parties to provide meaningful comments and for FERC to engage in an adequate review of the filings prior to the expected commencement of CAISO and CalPX operations.

The CalPX operated an hour-by-hour spot market, in which generators could sell and retailers could buy power. By 7 AM each day, generators and retailers submitted a separate schedule of up to fifteen price-quantity pairs for each hour of the following day. These schedules were assembled into demand and supply curves, and the market-clearing price and quantity were given by their intersection. To ensure that the market was liquid, the investor-owned utilities were required to meet the demands of their native loads in the CalPX. The CalPX provided schedules to the ISO by 10 AM on the day prior to the dispatch day. Other Scheduling Coordinators, representing bilateral transactions, submitted their balanced schedules to CAISO in a similar manner. These schedules also included Participants' Ancillary Services Bids and Schedule Adjustment Bids (for interzonal transmission congestion).

CAISO had three primary tasks: congestion management, ancillary services, and real-time energy balancing. The CAISO had to manage the balancing energy market to ensure that supply and demand were balanced in real time. Generators provided supplemental energy bids for increasing (incremental or INC bids) or decreasing (decremental, or DEC bids) their output into the energy balancing market. The CAISO would keep demand in line with generation by calling on the cheapest bids to increase or decrease output. The most expensive bid (if extra energy was required) or cheapest offer (if there was a surplus of power) set the balancing energy market-clearing price in each ten-minute period. A market participant whose delivery or consumption of power deviated from its final schedule was charged, or paid, the energy price for the hour in question. The CAISO did not institute penalties for imbalances, providing incentives for parties to deliberately mis-schedule whenever it was economically advantageous to do so.[46]

For purposes of pricing and definition of delivery location, California was divided into pricing zones and scheduling points. There were three major pricing zones in California: SP15 in the south, NP15 in the north, and ZP26 in the center of the state. Scheduling points were the points of receipt and delivery for energy sold by or purchased by traders in the

---

[46] James G. Kritikson, "California Electric Market Primer," prepared for the CalPX Board of Governors (February 2000): 3–4.

CalPX market that make or take delivery outside of the ISO controlled grid. Typically, a scheduling point is one of the major substations or switchyards on the electrical grid that interconnects the thirteen western states, British Columbia, and Baja, Mexico (the Western-Interconnect). Traders wishing to sell or buy in the CalPX market from remote locations arranged to make or take delivery of their energy at these points. A price was calculated in the CalPX Day-Ahead market for each zone and scheduling point, for each hour of the delivery day. If any of the transmission paths between the active zones (NP15, SP15, and ZP26) or between any of the scheduling points and one of the active zones were congested, there would be a different price at these two locations.

Hydroelectric facilities constitute a significant part of the resources available to serve demand in the Pacific Northwest and Northern California. Electricity demand in the Pacific Northwest peaks in the winter months, while Northern California, Southern California, and the Inland Southwest all experience electricity demand peaks during the summer months. Under most conditions, utilities can transport electricity from the Northwest into Southern California either by the DC Pacific Intertie, which directly connects the two regions, or by using a combination of AC lines. AC lines also connect Southern California with the Southwest. Congestion occurs during the spring when demand for hydroelectric energy from the Pacific Northwest exceeds north-south transfer capacity. Peak summer periods are also frequently characterized by congestion along various transmission paths.[47]

In California, the lines between the north and the south of the state, known as Path 15, are frequently congested. The CPUC, unlike the PUCT in Texas, did not make relieving this constraint through additional investment a priority before opening the market. The CAISO also had to deal with intrazonal congestion, where a local constraint on the system required redispatch of generation. The solution was to buy from or sell to the generator (or load) affected and pass on the cost to the load in the zone (uplift). In some cases, when a particular generator had to frequently operate to relieve congestion, to prevent them from exercising market power, they were required to sign Reliability Must Run (RMR) contracts that compensated on a cost-plus or other regulated basis.

---

[47]　Elizabeth M. Bailey, "The Geographic Expanse of the Market for Wholesale Electricity," MIT Center for Energy and Environmental Policy Research (February 1998): 6, 21.

Ironically, the only beneficiaries, other than the IPPs and power marketers, from deregulation turned out to be the customers of the municipal utilities. Municipal utilities implemented hiring freezes, layoffs, rate hikes, and paid off debts in anticipation of entering the competitive market.[48] Thus their customers benefited from competition without exposure to the market.

Vesting contracts (long-term purchase contracts with divested generation) were discouraged by the CPUC, which was not willing to guarantee that the costs of energy purchased under vesting contracts would be fully recovered. The reluctance of the CPUC to guarantee recovery of costs from vesting contracts may have been due in part to the early optimism about the growth of the retail market. If retail competitors took a large volume of sales away from the IOUs, the vesting contracts could have become stranded assets.[49]

As soon as the market opened, all consumers were eligible to switch to alternative retail providers. There was considerable optimism about the prospects for retail competition. The CPUC launched an $80 million public information campaign to inform consumers that they would be able to choose a new supplier when the market opened. However, only a small fraction of consumers chose new suppliers. Several factors created difficulties for potential new entrants. The mandated discounts meant competitive service providers could only undercut the incumbent if they were willing to sell power for very thin margins. The opportunity to "shop" was primarily attractive to industrial customers, who were the strongest proponents of retail competition.[50]

Some pointed out that there were numerous design flaws that would lead to problems once the wholesale markets began to operate. The excess capacity situation that contributed to the pressures for reform

---

[48] Jennifer Lake, Leah Pease, Ginny Case, and Jennifer Sutton-Hetzel, "Energy Crisis in California: Options for the Future," *Pepperdine School of Public Policy* (March 27, 2001): 24–25.

[49] Carl Blumstein, L.S. Friedman, and R.J. Green, "The History of Electricity Restructuring in California," at 18.

[50] See Paul L. Joskow, "California's Electricity Crisis," HEPG, September 28, 2001, 28. Ironically, Enron was one of the first to abandon the residential retail market. The company spent $10 million in marketing and advertising. However, it was able to round up only 30,000 customers out of 8 million residential accounts in the state. Kenneth Howe, "Enron Out of Home Electricity Market," *SF Chronicle*, April 23, 1998, at http://www.sfgate.com/cgibin/article.cgi?f=/c/a/1998/04/23/BU50228.DTL (last visited June 12, 2012).

in 1993 gradually disappeared as electricity demand grew and no new generating capacity was completed during the four-year period of uncertainty over the shape of the new market. A number of academic articles pointed out serious potential problems, some specifically related to the California market, others more generally with regard to the Western interconnection.[51] In the rush to open the market, these concerns were generally ignored.

---

[51] Severin Borenstein, James Bushnell, Edward Kahn, and Steven Stoft, "Market Power in California Electricity Markets," *Utilities Policy* 5 (July–October 1995): 219–36; Severin Borenstein and James Bushnell, "An Empirical Analysis of the Potential for Market Power in California's Electricity Industry," POWER (December 1998); Steven Stoft, "Analysis of the California WEPEX Applications to FERC," LBNL-39445 (October 1996).

15

Darkness, Darkness

The new markets began operation on April 1, 1998. This was three months behind the original start date, but it had not proved possible to create the necessary computer systems in time. As it was, the markets started before all the final systems were in place, and some temporary patches were needed to keep things going. Within a few months significant problems began to emerge as a result of wholesale market design flaws and suppliers' ability to exploit them. Flaws were identified in the congestion management system, with the local reliability contracts, the protocols for planning and investment in transmission, with the real-time balancing markets, in the ancillary services markets, and in other areas. Within the first two years of operation, CAISO filed thirty major revisions to its protocols with the FERC. The CalPX filed for numerous changes in its operating protocols as well. The complex governance arrangements, with all the major interest groups represented on the Boards of the CalPX and CAISO, made agreement on reforms very difficult.[1]

One problem that was noted by the market-monitoring group was the unusual quantity of resources that normally bid into the CalPX market at a zero price (price taker). Nuclear units, QFs, and run-of-the-river hydro were bid at $0/MWh to ensure their selection in the auction process. These resources typically accounted for approximately 20,000 MW of

[1] The Commission recognized that it was unable to address many issues raised by the parties in connection with the ISO's filings in view of the short time available prior to the Grid Operations Date. *Pacific Gas and Electric Company, et al.*, 81 FERC ¶ 61,320 (1997). On July 15, 1998, the ISO submitted a clarification matrix listing 680 outstanding issues. As of April 1999, there were still more than 120 remaining issues. *California Independent System Operator Corporation*, 87 FERC ¶ 61,102 (1999).

capacity. At lower demand levels, these resources set the market-clearing price at zero. On the demand side, the CalPX was dominated by the three big utilities that represented about 95 percent of the load in the day-ahead energy market.[2]

While there was plenty of capacity on paper in the California market, ownership of the gas-fired thermal units that set the price during high-priced periods was concentrated in a few companies. AES/Williams had 17 percent of the 24,029 MW in competitive fossil capacity, Reliant had 15 percent, Mirant 14 percent, Duke and Dynegy each had 12 percent, and Calpine had 4 percent.[3] Other companies owned fossil capacity, but most of this was under QF contracts. Some market brokers, such as Enron, sometimes controlled total generation comparable to these actual generating companies. The initial market-monitoring report noted that thermal generation bidding behavior suggested that resources were being strategically bid or withheld.[4]

The first major flaw was observed in the ancillary service markets. FERC had not given authority for market-based rates in the ancillary service markets, and so all the bids were based on cost. This made some participants unwilling to offer their plant in the CAISO's markets, as the market-based prices in the CalPX were higher. Many of the plants with RMR contracts knew that the CAISO would have to call these contracts if the units were not offered voluntarily. The RMR contracts promised much higher payments than the cost-based CAISO markets, and so the CAISO was frequently short of offers.[5] In the summer of 1998, FERC granted market-based rates to numerous generation plants in southern California. FERC stated that replacement reserve was not an ancillary service and sellers did not need authorization from FERC to sell at market rates.[6] However, FERC authorized the CAISO to reject

---

[2] Market Monitoring Committee of the California Power Exchange, "Report on Market Issues in the California Power Exchange Energy Markets," prepared for the Federal Energy Regulatory Commission (August 17, 1998): 9–10 (*Report on Market Issues*). The committee included Alvin Klevorick, Chair, Roger Bohn, and Charles Stalon.

[3] Severin Borenstein, James B. Bushnell, and Frank A. Wolak, "Measuring Market Inefficiencies in California's Restructured Wholesale Electricity Market," *American Economic Review* 92 (December 2002): 1380.

[4] *Report on Market Issues*, at 17–19.

[5] CAISO, Market Surveillance Unit, *Preliminary Report On the Operation of the Ancillary Services Markets of the California Independent System Operator (ISO)* (August 19, 1998): 13–14, 23, 31. The Market Surveillance Committee (MSC) was Frank Wolak (Chair), Robert Nordhaus, and Carl Shapiro.

[6] *AES Redondo Beach, L.L.C. et al.*, 83 FERC ¶ 61,358 (1998); *Long Beach Generation, L.L.C. et al.*, 84 FERC ¶ 61,011 (1998); *Ocean Vista Power Generation, L.L.C. et al.*, 84 FERC ¶ 61,013 (1998); *Williams Energy Services Company*, 84 FERC ¶ 61,072 (1998);

any bids to provide ancillary services whenever the CAISO believed those bids were higher than appropriate.[7]

The CAISO was required to buy a fixed amount of each type of reserve and could not substitute reserves of a higher quality (faster response) available at a lower price for lower-quality reserves. Since CAISO purchased the high-quality regulation and responsive reserves first, these markets often cleared at relatively low prices. As the amount of available capacity declined, the market-clearing price would rise, particularly in the replacement reserves market. The CAISO developed the Rational Buyer procedure to correct the perverse situation where lower-quality ancillary services cleared at higher prices than higher-quality services. Under the Rational Buyer procedure, the CAISO could substitute purchases of higher-quality services for higher-priced lower-quality services to reduce total AS procurement costs.[8]

On March 1, 1999, the ISO filed Phase I of its comprehensive redesign of the Ancillary Services markets. CAISO proposed to extend its authority to reject bids in the real-time imbalance energy market and allocated ancillary service obligations to Scheduling Coordinators based on their metered demand rather than their scheduled demand.[9] Loads gamed the system by deliberately underbidding demand, reducing their ancillary service cost allocation that was based on submitted schedules instead of actual load. The loads would then pay the lower real-time market price for excess purchases above their schedules. A utility could receive both the benefit of lower purchase costs and higher payments to its RMR units (because of higher real-time demand). To discourage the use of uninstructed deviations, the ISO charged replacement reserve costs to participants on unscheduled overconsumption and under-generation.[10]

Duke Energy Oakland, L.L.C. et al., 84 FERC ¶ 61,186 (1998). FERC rejected a request by CAISO to apply time-differentiated market power analysis. CAISO was concerned that in a thin market, market power could be exercised for a considerable number of hours. *AES Redondo Beach, L.L.C. et al.*, 83 FERC ¶ 61,358, 62,448 (1998).

[7] See *AES Redondo Beach, L.L.C. et al.*, 84 FERC ¶ 61,046 (1998), *order on reh'g*, 85 FERC ¶ 61,123 (1998), *order on further reh'g*, 87 FERC ¶ 61,208 (1999), *order on further reh'g*, 88 FERC ¶ 61,096 (1999), *order on further reh'g*, 90 FERC ¶ 61,148 (2000).

[8] CAISO, Market Surveillance Unit, "Annual Report on Market Issues and Performance" (June 1999): 3–6; *AES Redondo Beach, L.L.C. et al.*, 87 FERC ¶ 61,028 (1999), *order on reh'g,*, 88 FERC ¶ 61,096 (1999), *order on reh'g*, 90 FERC ¶ 61,036 (2000).

[9] *California Independent System Operator Corporation*, 86 FERC ¶ 61,122 (1999).

[10] CAISO, Market Surveillance Unit, "Preliminary Report On the Operation of the Ancillary Services Markets," 35; CAISO, Market Surveillance Unit, "Annual Report on Market Issues and Performance" (June 1999): 3–5.

In preoperational testing, CAISO had determined that its energy-balancing software was defective. Therefore, CAISO proposed a temporary bid price cap, to remain in effect until the software was corrected. The Commission, on May 28, 1998, conditionally accepted a CAISO proposal to cap bids for energy imbalance service until the ISO corrected the balancing energy software.[11] Following two weeks of dramatic price spikes, CAISO on July 17 imposed a price cap of $500 in all the ancillary services markets. While prices fell from their pre-cap highs, they frequently reached the new cap. On July 24, CAISO lowered the cap to $250/MWh.[12] FERC allowed the remaining generators to receive market-based rates on October 28, eliminating incentives to avoid the CAISO markets.[13]

Despite these start-up problems, competitive wholesale market prices for power were reasonably close to pre-reform projections, averaging $30/MWh between April 1998 and April 2000. These prices were consistent with a study that had been performed for the CEC in 1996.[14] In 1998, the CEC had forecast an average market-clearing price of $26.5/MWh in 2000, low enough to allow the full recovery of stranded costs before the deadline. In February 2000, the CEC had observed rising prices for natural gas, and raised their forecast, but only to $28.5/MWh.[15] In March 2000, the CEC projected prices gradually declining from an average of $31/MWh after 2001 due to new power plants coming online.[16]

However, another analysis done by the CEC in the summer of 1999 should have raised red flags. Based on forecasts of expected load growth, the staff concluded that less generation would be available from the Southwest for export to California in the coming years. The state would become more dependent on imports from the Northwest to meet summer peak loads until new merchant plants came online. In the early 1990s, there

[11] *California Independent System Operator Corporation*, 83 FERC ¶ 61,209 (1998).

[12] Laura Brien, "Why the Ancillary Services Markets in California Don't Work and What to Do About Them," NERA (February 7, 1999): 9; CAISO, Market Surveillance Unit, "Preliminary Report On the Operation of the Ancillary Services Markets of the California Independent System Operator (ISO)" (August 19, 1998): 15.

[13] *AES Redondo Beach, L.L.C. et al.*, 85 FERC ¶ 61,123 (1998); Carl Blumstein, L.S. Friedman, and R.J. Green, "The History of Electricity Restructuring in California," CSEM (August 2002): 19.

[14] LCG Consulting, "Modeling Competitive Energy Markets in California: An Analysis of Restructuring," for the CEC (October 11, 1996): 3–25.

[15] Richard D. Cudahy, "Whither Deregulation: A Look at the Portents," *58 N.Y.U. Annual Survey of American Law* 155, 174 (2001).

[16] CEC, "Market Clearing Prices under Alternative Resource Scenarios, 2000–2010" (February 2000): 4–10.

was a considerable surplus of generating capacity in California, but during the time of transition (1994–1998), no one had an obligation to provide capacity. Once rules were defined, developers quickly applied for permits to build new power plants, only to confront a time-consuming environmental review process and community opposition. The first of these new plants would not be online until the summer of 2001.[17] As of mid-2001, only 1,400 MW of new capacity was online, although an additional 500 MW of peaker capacity went online in the fall.[18] California finally took action in 2000 and 2001 to expedite permitting of new generation facilities.[19]

Warnings about tight western electricity supplies also came from ICF Kaiser, a consulting firm. They speculated that price spikes would be more likely to occur in the summer of 2000 because hydro availability for the summer of 1999 was greater than normal.[20] The second report of the market-monitoring committee for the CalPX also noted the potential for extreme price spikes. The utilities recognized that the real-time price was capped at $250/MWh, so they reduced their day-ahead demand as the CalPX price approached this level, and purchased additional power in the real-time balancing market. If there were no price cap in the real-time market, prices could rise to $2,500/MWh, the software-imposed CalPX price cap.[21]

Continued low prices in the CalPX, the CTC mechanism, and the promised future pass-through of spot prices into retail rates fed utility complacency. Given California's unfortunate experience with long-term QF power purchase agreements, the CPUC was reluctant to allow the utilities to buy power on long-term contracts. The utilities were betting that either prices would stay low – the general expectation – or, if they rose, the CPUC would allow them to raise rates. In both cases, with the CPUC providing no safe harbor, it seemed less risky than signing

[17] Paul L. Joskow, "California's Electricity Crisis," HEPG (September 28, 2001): 24–25.

[18] James L. Sweeney, *The California Electricity Crisis* (Palo Alto, CA, Hoover Institute Press, 2002): 101–03.

[19] A California assembly bill authorized issuance of temporary permits to expedite siting of new electric generation facilities. A.B. 970, 1999- 2000 Leg. Sess. (Cal. 2000). An executive order provided for the CEC to expedite the licensing process for new electricity-generating facilities. See Exec. Order No. D-26–01 (Cal. February 8, 2001).

[20] "High Temperatures & Electricity Demand: An Assessment of Supply Adequacy in California," CEC Staff (July 1999): 3–6.

[21] Market Monitoring Committee of the California Power Exchange, "Second Report on Market Issues in the California Power Exchange Energy Markets," prepared for FERC (March 19, 1999): 47–49.

long-term contracts. In the worst-case scenario, they could face bankruptcy by the regulated entity, but high prices would benefit unregulated electricity generation affiliates. Bankruptcy law limited total potential losses to the value of the regulated affiliate. As long as the utility parent could avoid liability for its regulated affiliates' debts, it would balance that risk against the reward higher prices brought its unregulated electricity supply affiliates. Once a regulated utility is bankrupt, the regulator has no choice but to raise retail rates or risk supply interruptions.

In August 1999, the ISO Board of Governors passed a resolution that raised purchase price caps on the ISO ancillary services and real-time energy markets from $250 to $750/MWh, with the provision that the Board would reduce the cap to $500 if it determined that the markets were not workably competitive. In September 1999, CAISO management filed Amendment 21 to the ISO Tariff to implement the policy adopted by the Board, asking for a one-year extension of price cap authority, which FERC approved in November.[22]

In March 2000, the CAISO Department of Market Analysis recommended a price cap of $750/MWh for the summer of 2000. While the markets were workably competitive during most hours, there was clearly a potential for market power during peak load hours. Historical prices suggested that market power was most significant when CAISO system loads exceeded 40 GW. In these hours, suppliers run little or no risk of not being called, and thus there was no constraint on how high they can bid. The CAISO concluded that the risk of exercise of market power had to be weighed against the need to attract imports.[23] A lack of price-responsive retail demand for energy was identified as one of the main factors inhibiting the competitiveness of the California market. The reason given was that most of the end-use consumers were under a retail rate freeze.[24] In response, several new load response programs were developed for the summer of 2000, which allowed SCE and PG&E to bid up to 1,000 MWh of price-responsive demand into the CalPX day-ahead market. These proposals were approved by FERC in June.[25]

---

[22] CAISO, Department of Market Analysis, "Price Cap Policy For Summer 2000" (March 2000): 8; *California Independent System Operator Corporation*, 89 FERC ¶ 61,169 (1999).

[23] CAISO, Department of Market Analysis, "Price Cap Policy for Summer 2000," 2–4, 10, 18.

[24] CAISO, Market Surveillance Committee, "Report on the Redesign of California Real time Energy and Ancillary Services Markets" (October 18, 1999).

[25] CAISO, Department of Market Analysis, "Price Cap Policy for Summer 2000," 32–37; *California Independent System Operator Corporation*, 91 FERC ¶ 61,256 (2000).

SDG&E, the smallest of the utilities, completed its stranded cost recovery in June 1999, after which the utility was allowed to pass through changes in wholesale purchase costs. When wholesale prices increased in 2000, PG&E and SCE began losing money on each kWh sold. PG&E began shifting purchases from the CalPX market to the CAISO real-time market, using CalPX bid curves designed to clear at quantities well below its load requirements.[26] If utilities under-schedule load, reducing CalPX prices, the economically rational response from generators is either to offer power at what they anticipate the "true" clearing price to be (which would look like economic withholding) or to withdraw supplies from the day-ahead market and offer them only in real time. For out-of-state suppliers in California, it was impossible to secure firm transmission in advance to sell power in the real-time market. A generator could offer the power in the day-ahead market, but also bid "pseudo" load into that market, overscheduling load. When that load failed to materialize in real time, the overbidding entity found itself with excess power and firm transmission rights, allowing that power to be released to the real-time market.[27]

Some electricity markets explicitly permit this behavior by both loads and generators through virtual bidding. This allows market participants to arbitrage between the day-ahead and real-time markets, but to work efficiently, a multi-settlement market system is required, where the ISO runs both markets using similar models. In this case, the two markets are dispatched with the same transmission and reliability constraints, with some exceptions owing to intraday adjustments and the requirements of real-time market clearing and reliability. In California there was no specific mechanism for virtual bidding, and only entities that had an in-state obligation to serve load were permitted to submit schedules to CAISO.

Late in the spring of 2000, the California's new electricity market began to collapse. In May, the average CalPX price was $50/MWh, higher than any previous month. Prices reached the CAISO's $750/MWh price cap in the real-time or ancillary service markets twenty-three times. In June, wholesale prices averaged $132/MWh.[28] High temperatures and

---

[26] Severin Borenstein, James Bushnell, Christopher R. Knittel, and Catherine Wolfram, "Inefficiencies and Market Power in Financial Arbitrage: A Study of California's Electricity Markets," *Journal of Industrial Economics* 56 (2008): 367–71; *San Diego Gas & Electric et al.*, 93 FERC ¶ 61,121 at 61,359–62 (2000).

[27] Ezra Hausman and Richard Tabors, "The Role of Demand Underscheduling in the California Energy Crisis," proceedings of the 37th Hawaii International Conference on System Sciences – 2004, 6.

[28] CAISO Department of Market Analysis, "Report of California Energy Market Issues and Performance: May–June 2000" (August 10, 2000): 13.

generation outages led CAISO to declare system emergencies thirty-nine times between May and August. High prices were also experienced at trading hubs throughout the Western Interconnection. Price caps created incentives for California suppliers to sell their electricity out of state. In the final week of June 2000, utilities in the Pacific Northwest outbid California for electricity, paying as much as $1,400/MWh.[29]

As of mid-2000, the utilities could have reduced the impact of wholesale price increases if they had been able to enter long-term contracts to purchase electricity at fixed prices. These contracts were being offered to the utilities. In June and July, several generators offered to sell significant amounts of capacity with opening offer prices of about $50/MWh. Both PG&E and SCE made requests of the CPUC and appealed to Governor Gray Davis to allow them to enter such contracts. The initial response was negative. On June 22, 2000, the CPUC decided, in a narrowly split vote, to allow the utilities to buy power outside the CAISO and the CalPX markets. However, the California legislature subsequently overrode the decision, requesting that the CPUC demonstrate that allowing utilities to purchase energy was in the public interest, a demonstration that the CPUC never provided. In August, once prices had jumped sharply, the CPUC filed an order allowing the utilities to enter into limited numbers of bilateral contracts. Even then, long-term purchases needed preapproval or face an after-the-fact reasonableness review, whereas purchases from the CalPX were considered per se reasonable. Utilities faced the prospect of being severely penalized if, retrospectively, their long-term contracting decisions turned out to be economically unattractive, but they could not expect to be rewarded if their decisions turned out to be prudent.[30]

On June 28, 2000, the CAISO board, at a specially called meeting, approved a motion that instructed the CAISO management to reduce the maximum purchase price from $750 to $500 per MWh, effective July 1, 2000, through October 15, 2000. FERC accepted the purchase cap but not the board's directive that generators must bid their capacity into the ISO markets when system load exceeded 38,000 MW. Any requirement to sell to the ISO in conjunction with a maximum purchase price would establish a ceiling on the price a seller could charge. Such a market change required a filing under section 205 of the FPA, including sixty

[29] Sweeney, *The California Electricity Crisis*, 131–32.
[30] Id., 135.

days' advance notice, and could not be implemented prior to Commission approval.[31]

On August 2, 2000, SDG&E filed a complaint pursuant to Rule 206 asking the Commission for an emergency order setting $250/MWh bid caps for energy or ancillary services sold into the markets operated by CAISO and the CalPX. FERC denied SDG&E's requested bid caps. However, FERC initiated proceedings pursuant to section 206 of the FPA to investigate the rates and charges, and whether the tariffs and bylaws of the CAISO and CalPX were adversely affecting the operation of wholesale electric power markets in California.[32] Since SDG&E had recovered its stranded costs, its retail rates were allowed to rise in step with wholesale prices, and all of San Diego felt the impact of rates doubling.[33] The FERC held a hearing in San Diego in the fall of 2000, at which CPUC commissioners pleaded for a reversion to what they thought of as "just and reasonable" rates based on cost.[34] In September, the California legislature reestablished retail price controls in San Diego. The price control regime, slated to continue through December 2003, was made retroactive from June 1, 2000. The legislation limited San Diego residential customers' rates to 6.5 cents per kWh. The retail rate cap deferred payment of the total amount due to the utility with interest until 2003.[35]

In the autumn of 2000, prices did not fall as expected. In 1998 and 1999, natural gas prices were relatively stable, averaging about $2.70/MMBtu. In January 2000, natural gas prices began a steady rise from $2/MMBtu to $4 by June and $6 by September. The price of gas fell back slightly until the beginning of November and then a spectacular leap began. In December, the price averaged $19/MMBtu and is reported to have spiked above $50. When natural gas prices rose above $25/MMBtu, the cost for many natural gas–fired plants exceeded the $250/MWh price cap and these plants could not sell into the market without losing money.[36]

California imports 85 percent of its natural gas through four pipelines, from the Rocky Mountain States and Canada. One of the largest pipelines

[31] *Morgan Stanley Capital Group Inc. v. CAISO*, 92 FERC ¶ 61,112 (2000).
[32] *San Diego Gas & Electric et al.*, 92 FERC ¶ 61,112 (2000).
[33] Paul L. Joskow, "California's Electricity Crisis," 24–25.
[34] "Federalism at Work," *Public Utility Fortnightly* (November 1, 2000): 4, 6.
[35] Sweeney, *The California Electricity Crisis*, 142; *San Diego Gas & Electric*, 93 FERC ¶ 61,121, 61,353 (2000).
[36] *Staff Report to the Federal Energy Regulatory Commission on Western Markets and the Causes of the Summer 2000 Price Abnormalities – Part 1* (November 1, 2000): 3–21.

is owned by El Paso Natural Gas Company (EPNG), a subsidiary of El Paso Corporation. The El Paso pipeline and another owned by Transwestern carry gas from the San Juan basin in Northwest New Mexico to the southern California border. The PG&E and Kern River pipelines bring Canadian and Rocky Mountain gas to California, but their capacity is fully committed under long-term contracts to customers in northern California. Intrastate pipeline capacity between northern and southern California is severely limited. Therefore, short-term supplies of natural gas for southern California can only be obtained on the EPNG and Transwestern pipelines.[37]

An explosion took place in the El Paso pipeline in New Mexico in August 2000, reducing capacity by 1,000 MMcf/day (rated capacity was 3,290 MMcf/day) for two weeks, and left it with only 85 percent of rated capacity for five months (because it allegedly could not be shut down for repairs to return it to full capacity). In 1993, the CPUC separated storage from other gas services. When the gas-fired power plants were sold to new owners, they were less willing to pay for storage, since they had to recover those costs from the sale of electricity instead of through the rate base. Gas in storage in November 2000 for industrial and power plant users in southern California had declined by almost 90 percent below previous levels, partially because of drawdowns resulting from the interruption of the EPNG pipeline. When FERC removed all price caps for short-term sales of gas pipeline capacity in the spring of 2000, the stage was set for winter shortages and price spikes.[38]

Another input to electricity generation that had an unanticipated price increase was pollution permits. NO_x emissions in southern California are controlled under Clean Air Act. In 1993, the South Coast Air Quality Management District, which covers the Los Angeles basin, instituted the Regional Clean Air Incentives Market. The program required emitters of NO_x and SO_x to acquire enough permits to match their actual emissions each year. Each permit is valid in one particular year and allows one pound of NO_x emissions. The prices for the first ten months of 2000 increased from $2.15/lb of NO_x in 1999 to an average of about $22.5/lb. Old gas-fired turbines may emit up to four pounds of NO_x per MWh.

---

[37] Staff of the Federal Energy Regulatory Commission, *Final Report on Price Manipulation in Western Markets*, Docket No. PA02-2-000 (March 2003): I-13.

[38] William Marcus and Jan Hamrin, "How We Got Into the California Energy Crisis," 4–5; FERC Staff, *Final Report on Price Manipulation in Western Markets*, Docket No. PA02-2-000, (March 2003): I-14–16, fn 26.

This increased the marginal cost of these units by $82/MWh.[39] There was a sharp increase in permit prices to a peak of more than $50/lb in January and February 2001, shortly after the introduction of the soft price cap. In some months 90 percent of permit purchases were from three electricity wholesalers. While monopsony power is usually exercised to lower the price, in this case it may have been used to raise NO_x permit prices, both increasing the value of allocated permits and raising the price of electricity that could be passed through to consumers.[40]

On August 22, 2000, the CalPX proposed to FERC that it be allowed to change from implicit price caps to bid caps. It proposed to impose $350/MWh maximum bids for the day-ahead and the day of markets, the sum of the $250 price cap on CAISO purchases of imbalance energy plus a $100/MWh estimate of the CAISO payment for replacement reserves. The CPUC, the Oversight Board, PG&E, and SCE supported the filing. On September 14, the CAISO proposed to FERC to extend CAISO purchase price cap authority beyond November 2000. The CPUC also filed a motion for interim relief on October 19, proposing that FERC require certain generators and marketers to offer specified amounts of capacity under forward contracts at FERC-approved cost-based rates. The following day, the CAISO submitted a proposed offer of settlement to impose a $100/MWh price cap, and charges against load and generation for not adhering to forward scheduling requirements.[41]

The incentive to move transactions to the CAISO imbalance market was so strong that by November 2000, as much as 30 percent of electricity was bought and sold on the imbalance market. The CAISO price caps kept CalPX prices at or below $250/MWh as loads refused to pay more. This created incentives for California suppliers to sell their electricity out of state.[42]

On November 1, FERC issued an Order Proposing Remedies for California Wholesale Electric Markets. FERC concluded that the requirement

---

[39] Sweeney, *The California Electricity Crisis*, 122–23.

[40] Mark Jacobsen and Azeem Shaikh, "Electricity Regulation in California and Input Market Distortions" (January 30, 2004): 7–10. By 2001, the recognition that the electricity crisis required relaxation of emission rules finally sunk in. Mirant and Duke Energy negotiated Compliance and Mitigation Agreements to relax temporarily running hour limitations in order to permit units to continue to produce power during CAISO emergencies. Mirant paid a mitigation fee of $10/lb of NO_x emitted from the excess operations. *San Diego Gas & Electric et al.*, 96 FERC ¶ 61,117, 61,446 (2001).

[41] *San Diego Gas & Electric et al.*, 93 FERC ¶ 61,121, 61,355–56 (2000).

[42] Sweeney, *The California Electricity Crisis*, 131–32.

for the IOUs to sell all of their generation into and buy all of their requirements from the CalPX was a significant factor contributing to rates that were unjust and unreasonable. The IOUs would be free to access whatever wholesale markets were suited to meeting the needs of their retail customers. FERC proposed a penalty charge for schedule deviations, while suppliers in the real-time market would receive either a capacity payment for replacement reserves or energy payments, but not both.[43]

FERC denied the CalPX request for price control authority and announced that it was removing the CAISO price cap authority in sixty days. In the interim, it froze the CAISO price cap at $250/MWh. At the end of the sixty days, the CAISO and CalPX auctions would switch to a "soft price cap" system that would limit market-clearing prices to $150/MWh. Market participants could submit verified cost-based bids higher than $150/MWh, which would be paid "as bid," but they would not set the market-clearing price. For natural gas–fired plants within the CAISO Control Area, costs would be estimated based on heat rates, spot market gas prices, and, where applicable, NO_x emission rates and permit costs. For imports, costs were estimated based on daily spot market gas prices and an average 12,000 Btu/kWh heat rate, plus the smaller of 10 percent of operating costs or $25/MWh. The price for natural gas was taken from Gas Daily, a market index weighted heavily toward the self-reported costs of large gas purchasers. FERC imposed a twenty-four-month potential refund obligation on sellers into the CalPX and CAISO markets, permitting the agency to impose retroactive penalties.[44]

The Market Surveillance Committee criticized the FERC Order as at best ineffectual, with the potential to worsen the crisis. The soft cap that applied only to sales to the CAISO and CalPX allowed sellers to evade the cap by diverting sales to uncapped markets. The Order was likely to exacerbate supply problems in California because of uncertainty as to how the Commission's refund policy would be carried out. In times of tight supply margins in the WSCC, generators and marketers would sell into markets that were not subject to a refund condition. The underscheduling penalty encouraged generators to raise their bids in the CalPX to match the implicit price in the CAISO market (cap plus penalty).[45]

[43] *San Diego Gas & Electric et al.*, 93 FERC ¶ 61,121, 61,360–62 (2000).
[44] *San Diego Gas & Electric et al.*, 93 FERC ¶ 61,121, 61,367–69 (2000).
[45] CAISO, Market Surveillance Committee, "Analysis of 'Order Proposing Remedies for California Wholesale Electric Markets (Issued November 1, 2000)'" (December 1, 2000): 2–3.

Before the end of the sixty days, the CAISO markets were on the edge of collapse. The CAISO was forced to declare Stage 2 electrical emergencies for four days in a row and saw no end to the shortage. Blackouts were imminent. On December 1, 2000, Governor Davis outlined his plan to reform the California market. He requested that the Commission impose bid caps in the $100/MW range for the next thirty-six months. Davis's plan called for overcoming environmental restrictions to permit the construction and operation of new power plants. Davis agreed with FERC that the existing CalPX and CAISO stakeholder boards must be replaced with independent boards.[46] On December 8, 2000, Terry Winter, chief executive officer of the CAISO, asked FERC to allow the CAISO to replace its $250/MWh price cap with a soft price cap system set at $250/MWh. The FERC agreed immediately, and California was then able to purchase electricity to avoid blackouts.[47]

The December 15, 2000 FERC order immediately implemented the two major elements of the November order: the elimination of the "must-sell" (in the CalPX) requirement for generation owned by the utility companies; and the imposition of a soft cap on market prices. Enforcement was to be based on an after-the-fact review of sales made above the price cap.[48] The impact of FERC's order on the CalPX was severe. Since most of the nonutility generators had already shifted their sales to the real-time market, the end of utility sales in the CalPX reduced the CalPX's volume nearly to zero. Once there were no longer any transactions on the CalPX, that institution had no way of raising money to pay its costs. At the end of January 2001, the CalPX suspended trading in its markets and commenced wrapping up its operations. It filed for protection under Chapter 11 of the Bankruptcy Code on March 9, 2001.

Despite a worsening situation, the CPUC continued to require the IOUs to purchase power on the spot market and to discourage long-term contracting for power. Although FERC stated that five-year contracts for supply at an average price of or below $74/MWh could be deemed prudent, the CPUC issued a decision on December 21, 2000, reaffirming its position that reasonableness review of bilateral forward contracts continued to be necessary.[49]

---

[46] *San Diego Gas & Electric et al.*, 93 FERC ¶ 61,924, 61,991 (2000).
[47] *California Independent System Operator Corporation*, 93 FERC ¶ 61,239 (2000).
[48] *California Independent System Operator Corporation*, 93 FERC ¶ 61,239 (2000).
[49] *San Diego Gas & Electric et al.*, 93 FERC ¶ 61,924, 61,993–95 (2000); *Order Proposing Clarifications And Modifications of D.00–08–023 And D.00–09–075, and Establishing*

By the fall of 2000, the price squeeze, stemming from the freeze on retail rates, was hitting the electric utilities with tremendous force. They were required to sell electricity to their customers at an average energy price of about $65/MWh (plus another $60/MWh for delivery services), yet the wholesale price of electricity ranged from $150/MWh to $1,000/MWh for half of the electricity they were selling, and almost a quarter of their remaining purchases were under high-priced QF contracts. It was becoming clear that the utilities were likely to become incapable of paying for electricity in a timely manner, if at all. By December, some suppliers had run up against their credit limits and stopped selling electricity to California utilities.[50]

On December 20, 2000, Standard & Poor's warned that utilities would not be able to finance wholesale power purchases without clear and definitive action from California's regulators to ensure that costs could be repaid. Absent such actions, there would be a downgrade of credit ratings of the regulated utilities to "deeply speculative" levels. On January 4, the CPUC agreed to allow SCE and PG&E to raise rates by a mere 1 cent/KWh ($10/MWh). The increase was far too small to begin to compensate for average wholesale costs exceeding $100/MWh. Moreover, the CPUC made it clear that the rate increase would be a temporary surcharge, in effect for ninety days and subject to refund. To keep buying electricity, both PG&E and SCE used their available cash and credit to pay for the massive financial shortfalls. PG&E's costs exceeded its revenues by roughly $1 billion per month. By the end of the first quarter of 2001, its cumulative shortfall amounted to about $9 billion. SCE incurred liabilities and indebtedness totaling approximately $6 billion from procuring electricity.[51]

Prudency Standards for Forward Electricity Contracts, Cal. Pub. Util. Comm'n Decision 00-12-065 (December 21, 2000).

[50] After PG&E and Edison defaulted on debts owed to the markets, a generator told CAISO that, absent an order from the DOE, it would not respond to emergency dispatch instructions and believed that CAISO's power to issue such instructions at all was void if the generator did not receive prior assurances that a creditworthy counterparty would pay for the energy. CAISO filed suit in February 2001, asking the U.S. District Court for an injunction requiring the generator to comply with emergency dispatch instructions. The court issued a temporary restraining order, followed by a preliminary injunction, at which point the generator appealed. The Ninth Circuit issued a preliminary ruling, questioning whether any entity other than FERC could enforce the terms and conditions of the CAISO Tariff. "Commentary by the California Independent System Operator Corporation on the CPUC Staff Investigative Report on Wholesale Electric Generation" (October 25, 2002): 8.

[51] Sweeney, *The California Electricity Crisis*, 173–74.

CAISO stated that a reduction in the credit ratings of SCE and PG&E would result in these entities no longer meeting the creditworthiness requirements of the ISO tariff and would preclude them from scheduling transactions. CAISO asked for temporary authority to waive these requirements. FERC accepted the CAISO proposal, but only to the extent that it applied to SCE's and PG&E's ability to access their own transmission facilities to deliver their resources to their load. FERC held that the CAISO and CalPX could not relax creditworthiness provisions to shift financial risks to suppliers that sell into the California market.[52]

In January 2001, SCE and PG&E defaulted on hundreds of millions of dollars of obligations to the CalPX for December and January purchases. On January 18, 2001, following the downgrading of PG&E and SCE's debt ratings to "junk" status, CalPX suspended trading privileges for the two IOUs. On February 1, 2001, PG&E announced that it could pay only $161 million of the somewhat more than $1 billion due for November CAISO energy purchases and December QF electricity deliveries. Since there was a two-month lag between delivery of power and final settlement of payments, generators had begun to shift sales away from the markets in anticipation of nonpayment. Unit outages were relatively stable during the summer of 2000, averaging about 2,500 MW of capacity out during June–August. Reported outages rose rapidly in the fall to average more than 10,000 MW out during the November–March period of the winter of 2000–01. More than 6,000 MW of cogeneration, small thermal, and renewable capacity that was under contract to the utilities was idled by the suspension in payments.[53]

On January 11, 2001, a powerful winter storm hit California. Ocean swells threatened to clog the cooling system of the 2,200 MW Diablo Canyon nuclear plant operated by PG&E along the central coast. As a preventive measure, its operations were reduced to 20 percent of capacity, prompting CAISO to declare a Stage 3 emergency, because reserves fell below 1.5 percent. Blackouts were averted by importing additional power from the Northwest and by interrupting power to customers served under interruptible rates. The total number of hours for which interruptible customers could be curtailed over the entire year was exhausted in a few weeks. On January 17 and 18, the state was short by 500 MW and 1,000 MW of capacity, respectively. CAISO had to impose rolling blackouts in

[52] *California Independent System Operator Corporation*, 94 FERC ¶ 61,132 (2000), *reh'g denied*, 95 FERC ¶ 61,026 (2001).

[53] Sweeney, *The California Electricity Crisis*, 173–74.

northern California that affected about 380,000 customers. Over the next four days there were seven hours of curtailments, as surplus generation in southern California was unavailable due to constraints on Path 15.[54]

The CAISO Board of Governors became paralyzed at this point, as stakeholders began to shift from cooperative interaction toward championing their own economic interests. As the CAISO struggled to make changes to its rules and tariffs in order to respond to price spikes, many of the Board members began to take the positions of their corporate or advocacy group. Major changes could not achieve a majority vote, paralyzing the CAISO management.[55]

High prices were not confined to California; they were being felt all over the western United States. For the year 2000 as a whole, CalPX prices averaged $91/MWh, compared with $29/MWh in 1999. To the east of California, at the Palo Verde hub, 2000 prices averaged $115/MWh, compared with $31/MWh in 1999. In the northwest, at the Mid-Columbia hub, 2000 prices averaged $139/MWh, compared with $18/MWh in 1999. A review of forward price curves derived from NYMEX forward monthly contracts for deliveries to the California-Oregon border and Palo Verde indicates that the market did not anticipate the price explosion.[56]

On January 17, 2001, Governor Davis issued a Proclamation that a "state of emergency" existed within California.[57] Panicked state lawmakers and the governor drafted emergency legislation under which the California Department of Water Resources (CDWR), a state agency, would temporarily take over the utilities' duty to buy power for all their customers. The bill (SB 7x) passed the Senate on Thursday night, January 18, and was signed by the governor on Friday.[58] The legislature passed Assembly Bill 1 of the 2001–02 First Extraordinary Session (AB 1X), on February 1, 2001, pursuant to which the state took over power procurement. The utilities would sell the electricity on behalf of the state and reimburse the CDWR. The cost of wholesale power purchases would be borne initially by the state treasury, financed through long-term revenue bonds. Repayment of interest and principal of these bonds would

---

[54] Ahmad Faruqui, Hung-po Chao, Vic Niemeyer, Jeremy Platt, and Karl Stahlkopf, "Analyzing California's Power Crisis," *The Energy Journal* 22 (2001): 37.

[55] Vantage Consulting, "Operational Audit of the California Independent System Operator," for FERC (January 25, 2002): 26.

[56] Faruqui, Chao, Niemeyer, Platt, and Stahlkopf, "Analyzing California's Power Crisis," 38.

[57] Proclamation, Cal. Gov. (January 17, 2001).

[58] *See* S.B. 7 and A.B. 1, 2001–02 Legis., 1st Ex. Sess. (Cal.).

be obtained from a surcharge on retail electricity prices.[59] The CDWR became the dominant buyer of electricity in California, spending an average of $50 million per day, to supply about one-third of the electricity used by the customers of the three big utilities.

By the end of January 2001, Governor Davis had replaced the CAISO stakeholder board with a new five-person board, three of whom were closely associated with the Davis administration. The reaction of the industry was that the CAISO was no longer independent and that all actions of the CAISO were directed and/or approved by the governor's office.[60] The Clinton administration tried to broker a deal with Governor Davis in January. Larry Summers suggested that long-term contracts could be obtained at just under $70/MWh if environmental regulations were temporarily loosened. This would require a retail rate hike of a cent or two per kWh to allow the utilities to buy this power under the current price cap. Davis rejected both the price hike and the environmental waiver and insisted on price caps.[61]

During the Clinton administration, the Department of Energy had issued orders, which were enforced in court, requiring generators (who were worried about collecting their bills) to continue supplying the California market. But the Bush administration, which took over in January 2001, announced that it would shortly discontinue these orders.[62] On January 23, the DOE extended for two weeks an emergency federal order directing electricity producers to sell to SCE and PG&E, even though they were not creditworthy. In doing so, however, Energy Secretary Spencer Abraham warned that there would probably be no further extensions.[63]

President Bush took a firm free-market stance, refusing to impose any price controls, ostensibly because these would only exacerbate the presumed shortage of power plants in California.[64] In announcing the effort

---

[59] Sweeney, *The California Electricity Crisis*, 178–80.

[60] Vantage Consulting, "Operational Audit of the California Independent System Operator," 30–36; Timothy P. Duane, "Regulation's Rationale: Learning from the California Energy Crisis," *Yale Journal on Regulation* 17 (2002): 528, fn. 186.

[61] Kurt Eichenwald, *Conspiracy of Fools* (New York, Broadway Books, 2005), 408–12.

[62] Joseph Kahn, "Bush Adds 2 Weeks to Orders Ensuring California Power," *New York Times*, January 24, 2001, A1.

[63] Sweeney, *The California Electricity Crisis*, 180.

[64] See Joseph Kahn, "Administration Leaves Power Crisis in California's Hands," *New York Times*, January 23, 2001, at http://www.nytimes.com/2001/01/23/business/admini-stration-leaves-power-crisis-in-california-s-hands.html?pagewanted=all&src=pm (last visited June 12, 2012); Ken Silverstein, "California Lawsuits: Williams Deal Could Produce Cascading Effect," UtiliPoint Issue Alert (November 15, 2002).

to develop his energy policy, Bush said, "It looks like they're making progress in California and we're pleased, because the situation is going to be best remedied in California, by Californians."[65] At an energy policy round table convened by the Western Governors' Association in Portland, Oregon, on February 2, 2001, eight western governors (three Democrats and five Republicans) called on the administration to establish temporary price restraints on wholesale electricity prices until the energy markets could be returned to normal functioning. Secretary Abraham rejected the plea.[66]

Energy supplies remained tight as smaller California-based independent energy companies demanded payment to continue their operations. A second set of rolling blackouts hit California on March 19, 2001, affecting southern California for the first time. Blackouts ended after two days when public officials moved to ensure that smaller power producers were paid. The CAISO attributed a Stage 2 emergency in April to a number of factors, including 3,000 MW of generation from QFs that was unavailable because of continuing financial concerns. The CPUC's March 27 Order, revising the avoided cost price formula, was directly responsible for most of the QFs being taken offline.[67]

Governor Davis started a process of negotiating with the utilities, offering to purchase electricity transmission facilities, some generating facilities, and other assets. The state legislature and the governor took the view that for the utilities to get financial relief from the controls imposed by the state, they would be required to sell significant proportions of their physical assets to California. There was, in addition, a plan – never implemented – for the state to buy the hydroelectric plants belonging to the utilities.[68] By late March and early April, there had been little real progress in the negotiations. However, with much fanfare, Governor Davis announced in a live address on April 5 that he would provide funds to restore the utilities to financial stability – if they agreed to provide

---

[65] White House, "Remarks by the President at Energy Policy Meeting" (January 29, 2001) at http://georgewbush-whitehouse.archives.gov/news/releases/20010129-1.html (last visited November 16, 2014).

[66] Sam Verhovek, "Energy Secretary Rejects Request to Cap Electricity Price," *New York Times* (February 3, 2001), at http://www.nytimes.com/2001/02/03/us/energy-secretary-rejects-request-to-cap-electricity-price.html?pagewanted=all&src=pm (last visited June 12, 2012).

[67] *San Diego Gas & Electric et al.*, 95 FERC ¶ 61,116, 61,788 (2001).

[68] See Vincent Schodolski, "California Floats Plan to Buy Some Power Plants," *Chicago Tribune*, January 24, 2001, 1, at http://articles.chicagotribune.com/2001-01-24/news/0101240054_1_energy-crisis-hydroelectric-system-power-crisis (last visited June 12, 2012).

low-cost regulated power to the state for ten years, sell their transmission systems to the state, and dismissed lawsuits seeking to recover their losses. PG&E declared bankruptcy the next day.[69]

In response to generator filings, the FERC on April 6, 2001, ordered the CAISO to take steps to ensure that suppliers of power were paid. For transactions involving third-party suppliers, CDWR served as the counterparty. Contrary to the CAISO's interpretation, the February 14 Order did not exempt transactions from the requirement to have a creditworthy buyer in place. FERC made it clear it did not want continuation of overreliance on the real-time market by use of emergency dispatch instructions to serve load. The real-time market was supplying approximately 15 percent of load, far higher than FERC's stated goal of limiting the amount of load supplied in the real-time market to no more than 5 percent.[70]

On April 26, 2001, FERC issued an order that substantially revised the FERC's approach to mitigating unjust and unreasonable prices. The order created bid caps based on heat rates and fuel costs. FERC required that, as a condition of selling into the CAISO markets, all sellers must abide by a must-offer obligation and the price mitigation plan. All available generation (not scheduled or committed to bilateral agreements) must be offered in the real-time market. FERC required price mitigation for all generators in California during periods of reserve deficiency, defined as emergency situations beginning at Stage 1 (i.e., when reserves are 7.5 percent or less). CAISO would use heat rates to calculate a marginal cost for each generator by using a proxy for the gas costs, emission cost, and a $2 adder for operation and maintenance expenses. A generator may submit a bid greater than that calculated through the proxy and be paid as bid above the market price, subject to refund and justification.[71]

---

[69] Sweeney, *The California Electricity Crisis*, 185–86; Laura Holson, "Deal Struck with Utility, California Governor Says," *New York Times*, April 10, 2001, at http://www .nytimes.com/2001/04/10/us/deal-struck-with-utility-california-governor-says.html (last visited June 12, 2012); V. Dion Haynes, "California Reaches Deal to Aid Utility," *Chicago Tribune*, April 10, 2001, at http://articles.chicagotribune.com/2001-04-10/ news/0104100274_1_pacific-gas-and-electric-power-purchases-southern-california-edison (last visited June 12, 2012).

[70] *California Independent System Operator Corporation et al.*, 95 FERC ¶ 61,026, *reh'g denied*, 95 FERC ¶ 61,391, *reh'g denied*, 96 FERC ¶ 61,267 (2001).

[71] *San Diego Gas & Electric Co. et al.*, 95 FERC ¶ 61,115, *order on reh'g*, 95 FERC ¶ 61,418 (2001). The formula was first developed to calculate refunds due to generation bids above marginal cost during Stage 3 emergencies. *San Diego Gas & Electric*, 94 FERC ¶ 61,245 (2001). The Commission developed a proxy market-clearing price of $273/MWh during the hours in January 2001, in which an ISO-declared Stage 3 emergency was in effect. This value was based on a hypothetical CT with a heat rate of

The order specifically prohibited certain types of strategic bidding as a condition of market-based rate authority. Bids that vary with unit output in a way unrelated to the known performance characteristics of the unit, such as a "hockey stick" bid where the last megawatts from a unit are bid at an excessively high price, were prohibited. Similarly, bidding a single unit in a portfolio at an excessively high level, without any apparent cost basis, was also prohibited. Bids that vary over time in a manner unrelated to change in the unit's performance or input costs or other acceptable factors were also prohibited.[72]

In May, Ken Lay tried to marshal his political influence to save deregulation. Lay hosted a private ninety-minute meeting in a conference room at the Peninsula Hotel in Beverly Hills with Arnold Schwarzenegger, Richard Riordan (mayor of Los Angeles), Michael Milken, and other luminaries to drum up support for his solution to California's energy crisis. His prescription called for more rate increases, an end to state and federal investigations, and less regulation. Enron circulated a position paper stating that ratepayers should bear responsibility for the billions in debt incurred by the state's public utilities, and that investigations of power price manipulation and political rhetoric were making matters worse.[73] As Vice President Cheney was crafting the administration's energy policy, Ken Lay presented him with a three-page, eight-point list of priorities for open power markets, including an admonition that the administration should reject any attempt to reregulate wholesale power markets with price caps or other controls. The day after this meeting, Cheney criticized FERC for implementing short-term price caps.[74]

18,073 Btu/kWh, based on the weighted average of the least efficient gas turbines for the three investor-owned utilities. The variable cost of this hypothetical CT was based on a natural gas price of \$12.50/MMBtu, average January NO_x allowance costs of \$22.50/lb, an average NO_x emissions rate of 2 lbs/MWh, and variable O&M costs of \$2/MWh. *Id.* at 61,862–63.

72 *San Diego Gas & Electric et al.*, 95 FERC ¶ 61,115 (2001), at 61,260.
73 Christian Berthelsen and Scott Winokur, "Enron's Secret Bid to Save Deregulation/PRIVATE MEETING: Chairman Pitches his Plan to Prominent Californians," *San Francisco Chronicle*, May 26, 2001, at http://www.sfgate.com/cgi-bin/article.cgi?f=/c/a/2001/05/26/MN209410.DTL (last visited June 12, 2012).
74 Toby Eckert, "Bush, Davis on Collision Course; President, Cheney Firm: No Price Caps," *San Diego Union-Tribune*, May 27, 2001, at http://legacy.utsandiego.com/news/reports/power/archives/20010527-9999_1n27power.html (last visited June 12, 2012); George Skelton, "Price Caps Don't Fit in Cheney's Head for Figures," *Los Angeles Times*, April 19, 2001, at http://articles.latimes.com/2001/apr/19/news/mn-52942 (last visited June 12, 2012); Doyle McManus and Richard Simon, "Cheney Rejects Price Caps, Aid for Calif. Power Crisis," *Los Angeles Times*, May 5, 2001, at http://articles.latimes.com/2001/may/05/news/mn-59651 (last visited June 12, 2012).

On May 15, the CPUC announced that retail rate increases would be granted to all the utilities. Amid warnings by the State Treasurer that the state intervention to purchase electricity was decimating the budget, the CPUC finally agreed to raise the average retail electricity price 3 cents/KWh, or $30/MWh. The CPUC adopted an inclining block rate structure, with households that use low amounts of energy paying prices slightly lower than the delivered cost of power while those using larger amounts paid almost twice the cost for consumption above the initial tier. In order to finance the power purchases of the CDWR, the CPUC approved an additional 1.46 cent per kWh rate increase that became effective October 1, 2001.[75]

The outlook for the summer of 2001 had been dire, with the Department of Energy predicting California residents were likely to experience 113 hours of rolling outages, with an average size of approximately 1,900 MW. This included the expected impact of demand relief and interruptible load programs. In the pessimistic scenario, the expected number of hours of outages could increase to 479 hours.[76] Surprisingly, and defying all predictions, in June 2001, electricity prices in California began to decline. The wholesale price paid for electricity reached a maximum monthly average in December 2000 and stayed high through May 2001. By June, electricity prices in the west had declined sharply, with CAISO citing peak daytime purchase costs of less than $100/MWh and off-peak power purchases of less than $20/MWh. During the week ending June 9, prices for peak power at western trading hubs fell below $55/MWh from a high of about $170/MWh earlier in the week. The sharp decrease in wholesale electricity prices had not generally been anticipated. On May 4, the price for electricity to be delivered in August was $550/MWh. By July 16, futures prices had declined below $100/MWh. In addition, prices for western forward contracts declined dramatically, with year 2002 forward transaction prices falling from $127 to $68/MWh, and 2003 forward contracts from $60 to $41/MWh.[77]

---

[75] See "California Panel Spells Out Rise in Rates for Electricity," *New York Times*, May 16, 2001, at http://www.nytimes.com/2001/05/16/us/california-panel-spells-out-rise-in-rates-for-electricity.html (last visited June 12, 2012); Linda Cohen, Stephen Peck, Paroma Sanyal, and Carl Weinberg, "Retrospective Report on California's Electricity Crisis," California Energy Commission, PIER Project Report, CEC-500–2006–021 (January 2004): 57.

[76] DOE, Office of Policy, *The Impact of Wholesale Electricity Price Controls on California Summer Reliability* (Washington, DC, June 2001): v.

[77] *San Diego Gas & Electric Co. et al.*, 95 FERC ¶ 61,418, 62,546 (2001); Sweeney, *The California Electricity Crisis*, 142.

A cooler-than-expected summer, declining natural gas prices, and the combination of regulatory measures taking effect can be credited with the end of the crisis. In May and June 2001, California gas prices fell from around $12/MMBtu to $5/MMBtu and to $2–$3/MMBtu by September. The consequence of the gas price drop was a very substantial drop in operating costs for gas-fired generators and, under the FERC formula, lower price caps. Long-term contracts removed the incentives for strategic bidding. Regulatory scrutiny of plant outages reduced any tendency of generators to keep their plants offline and strikingly reduced outage rates were reported. There were two more Stage 2 emergencies on two hot days in early July and then no more emergencies for the remainder of 2001.

Several other factors contributed to the end of the crisis. During the energy crisis, Governor Davis introduced a variety of energy efficiency and peak demand reduction measures. These included the "20/20 plan," retail rate increases, rebate programs, public awareness campaigns, and updated energy efficiency standards. Two new energy efficiency bills, Assembly Bill (AB) 29X and Senate Bill (SB) 5X, were signed into law. The "20/20 plan" encouraged residential customers of the Californian IOUs to reduce their monthly consumption of electric power by 20 percent from their consumption in 2000 by providing a 20 percent rate reduction for those consumers who met this goal. The "20/20 plan" was introduced in the summer of 2001 and was repeated in 2002. One-third of eligible consumers qualified for the rebate.[78] State (and federal) buildings enforced stringent conservation codes. Retail rate increases fell disproportionately on larger users, discouraging growth in consumption. While all IOU customers with electricity demand over 500 kW already had time-of-use rates, 23,000 customers with demand over 200 kW were also required to switch to time-of-use rates.[79] There was a campaign of exhortation by the governor and by all sorts of lesser personages. During the summer of 2001, Californians reduced electricity usage by 6 percent and average monthly peak demand by 8 percent, compared to the summer of 2000 (although 2 percent of this reduction was due to milder weather). Without the reduction in demand, *ceteris paribus*, there would have been

[78] Edie Lau, "3 Million Due Power Rebate," *Sacramento Bee*, August 3, 2001, A1 (reporting rebates to millions of customers for reducing electric consumption by more than 20% from the same month one year earlier).

[79] Linda Cohen, Stephen Peck, Paroma Sanyal, and Carl Weinberg, "Retrospective Report on California's Electricity Crisis," CEC, PIER Project Report, CEC-500–2006–021 (January 2004): 57–58.

between 50 and 160 hours of Stage 3 emergencies during the summer of 2001.[80]

Despite the ending of the western electricity crisis, FERC extended the price mitigation plan to all of the western states. Power marketers were required to bid as price takers. Sellers that owned generation could not submit bids during reserve deficiencies that were higher than their marginal cost of generation based on spot gas prices plus variable O&M costs. FERC instructed bidders to invoice the CAISO directly for the cost of emissions permits. This eliminated the temptation to game permit prices to increase the wholesale market price. For spot market electricity sales, the price cap was set at 85 percent of the highest CAISO price during the hours when the last Stage 1 was in effect. This maximum clearing price remained in place until the next Stage 1 was declared and a new price was set. FERC added a 10 percent premium to cover the risk of nonpayment in California. This price mitigation mechanism terminated on September 30, 2002.[81]

A conflict between the generators, the CAISO, and CDWR over power payments was not resolved until 2002. CDWR claimed that the CAISO had insisted on billing the utilities, which were no longer creditworthy, instead of communicating to its marketing branch billing data required to disburse public funds. FERC ordered that CDWR assume responsibility for purchases by the CAISO, and the CAISO was obligated under its Tariff to invoice, collect payments from, and distribute payments to CDWR, as the Scheduling Coordinator for all transactions made on behalf of CDWR. FERC also made it clear that CDWR must accept and pay the rates set by FERC.[82] FERC rejected any role for the state in determining just and reasonable prices in interstate commerce of electricity. FERC also made it clear that the CAISO could not unilaterally net purchases and sales for CDWR.[83]

---

[80] Charles Goldman, Joseph Eto, and Galen Barbose, "California Customer Load Reductions during the Electricity Crisis: Did They Help to Keep the Lights On?" LBNL-49733 (2002); Emily Bartholomew, Robert Van Buskirk, and Chris Marnay, "Conservation in California during the Summer of 2001," LBNL-51477 (September 2002): 15–16.

[81] *San Diego Gas & Electric Co. et al.*, 95 FERC ¶ 61,418, 62,548, 62,564 (2001). The O&M adder was increased from $2/MWh to $6/MWh based on the seventeen-year average of actual nonfuel O&M expenses for oil- and gas-fired steam plants. *Id.* at 62,562–63.

[82] *California Independent System Operator Corporation et al.*, 97 FERC ¶ 61,151 (2001).

[83] *California Independent System Operator Corporation et al.*, 98 FERC ¶ 61,355, 62,430–31, 62,434 (2002).

In September 2001, the CPUC terminated retail competition, thus bringing to a close California's dalliance with restructuring.[84] Small customers were uninterested in switching, and marketers soon abandoned that market segment. Marketers serving larger customers had been unable to get them to pay extra to buy price protection products, such as guaranteed fixed prices. When the market went haywire, companies that had signed customers to such products returned them to the incumbent utilities and paid the penalty for breach of contract. One of the leading marketers, PG&E Energy Services, exited the business after three years of losses.[85]

S. David Freeman, who was general manager of the Los Angeles Department of Water and Power, the largest municipal power utility in the country, was named energy advisor to Governor Davis. The Department of Water and Power had opted out of deregulation and sailed smoothly through the California storm, selling power to the deregulated power pool at very advantageous prices.[86] Freeman set to work negotiating long-term electric supply contracts on behalf of the state.[87] The CDWR had been purchasing up to 200,000 MWh of electricity each day. Because California lacked creditworthy buyers, the department became the market. The department initially had to purchase much of this power from market-savvy sellers, without an experienced, skilled staff needed to perform at this level. An amendment to AB 1X authorized the department to issue up to $13.4 billion in bonds to pay the costs of the power-purchasing program, to be repaid by revenues from the sale of electrical power. From January 2001 through September 2001, the department spent nearly $10.7 billion, purchasing nearly 30 percent of the electricity consumed in the state. The CPUC then ordered the utilities to collect charges from retail customers and remit these fees to the CDWR.[88]

---

[84] Joskow, "California's Electricity Crisis," 4.

[85] Faruqui, Chao, Niemeyer, Platt, and Stahlkopf, "Analyzing California's Power Crisis," 44.

[86] See Barbara Whitaker, "Los Angeles Gains Attention and Money with Its Own Power," *New York Times*, December 22, 2000, at http://www.nytimes.com/2000/12/22/us/los-angeles-gains-attention-and-money-with-its-own-power.html (last visited June 12, 2012).

[87] Devra Ruth Bachrach, "Comparing the Risk Profiles of Renewable and Natural Gas Electricity Contracts: A Summary of the California Department of Water Resources Contracts" (MS Thesis, University of California at Berkeley, May 2002): 6–7 (*DWR Contracts*).

[88] California State Auditor, "California Energy Markets: Pressures Have Eased, but Cost Risks Remain" (December 2001): 5, 11, 15–16.

During the peak of the crisis, the standard belief was that the summer of 2001 would be even worse than December and January had been, since summer is California's period of peak electricity use. This encouraged the CDWR to purchase a portfolio of longer-term contracts at prices below spot prices and future prices. Future prices did not start declining until May, by which time many of the contracts had been signed. So while it is easy to criticize these contracts in hindsight, given the information at the time, they were prudent. The initial portfolio objectives focused on long-term contracting for three to ten years. CDWR purchased an average of 7,000 MW through 2010, with 10,000 MW during peak periods, in a series of twenty-nine long-term contracts. The department's portfolio of power contracts, in its peak year of 2004, exceeded 12,000 MW. Roughly 5,800 MW of this capacity was expected to be supplied from new units scheduled to come online before 2004. The prices averaged more than $90/MWh in 2002, declining to $79/MWh in 2003 and $61/MWh for the 2006–2010 period. The CDWR contracts were initially expected to cost about $42.6 billion over ten years, before many were renegotiated.[89]

Both the CDWR and the generators had incentives to sign long-term contracts. The CDWR was under intense political and financial pressure to sign contracts quickly, to slow the state's expenditures on electricity, to stabilize the market, and to prevent further blackouts. At the same time, since the CDWR had become the single monopsony buyer of electricity in the market, sellers had an incentive to contract with the CDWR. Sellers, however, knew the CDWR would need to contract with most of them to meet the state's needs. The generators were also unsure of the state's commitment to stand by the contracts. The CDWR was understaffed for the task. In addition, it was alleged that some of the consultants working for the CDWR had conflicts of interest that may have led to contracts that were more favorable to the sellers.[90]

Of the fifty-six contracts signed in 2001, thirteen were renegotiated, and the state claimed that it saved $5 billion in the process. Williams Companies was accused of withholding power supplies and for charging the state for electricity it did not deliver. As part of the settlement, the state agreed to drop all criminal charges. In exchange, Williams trimmed $1.4 billion from the contract and paid the state $150 million over eight

[89] California State Auditor, "California Energy Markets: Pressures Have Eased, but Cost Risks Remain," 34–39, 75.

[90] Nancy Vogel, "Electricity Buyer for State Fined for Lapse," *Los Angeles Times*, March 8, 2002, at http://articles.latimes.com/2002/mar/08/local/me-fines8 (last visited June 12, 2012).

years. Calpine, which held the largest contract, lopped $3 billion off a $10-billion agreement. Companies that agreed to new terms included Whitewater Energy, Calpeak, GWF, Colton Power, and PG&E Trading. The price of the remaining contracts remained between $62.50/MWh and $87/MWh, with the bulk of savings coming from eliminating "take or pay" provisions.[91]

The California market meltdown was the product of a "perfect storm" – a combination of drought, emission controls, capacity shortfalls, and a natural gas pipeline accident. But it was also the product of hasty implementation, poor market design, politics, mismanagement, and malfeasance in both the electricity and natural gas markets. California would be both an object lesson in how not to build markets and the jolt to the status quo that snapped FERC out of complacency and into developing the capability to conduct meaningful market oversight.

[91] Ken Silverstein, "California Lawsuits: Williams Deal Could Produce Cascading Effect," *UtiliPoint*, November 15, 2002.

16

California and Market Power

The controversy over the exercise of market power in California illustrated the complexity of identifying and quantifying the existence and impact of such behavior. California became an experiment for testing various theories of price formation, market power, and market manipulation.

There were three different issues involved in determining the existence and extent of market power in California during this period: (1) the extent and impact of market power in the natural gas market, a key input into the electricity market; (2) the extent to which generators were bidding above full marginal cost and exercising market power; and (3) the extent to which generators were withholding capacity and creating shortages that required the CAISO to pay above bid caps to obtain power to ensure reliability. These were interlinked, as higher natural gas prices raised the level of competitive bids, while removing capacity from the market drove up prices by requiring acceptance of higher price bids.

Determining the existence of market power requires more sophisticated analysis than merely comparing the cost of production to the market price. An observed price may reflect factors that would cause it to differ from production costs yet still be efficient. First, transmission lines might be congested, so that the optimal dispatch will result in price exceeding marginal production cost. Marginal costs are hard to determine at units' maximum output, where a boiler and/or turbine may be pushed past its normal operating limits with a corresponding increase in the probability (and thus expected cost, which includes both the cost of repair and lost revenue) of component failure. Energy-constrained plants, which include hydroelectric capacity and plants with limited pollution rights, should be dispatched and priced in a way that reflects the opportunity cost of constrained production.

One of the problems in monitoring the extent of market power is determining the real marginal costs of generators. The primary determinant of costs for gas-fired units, which often set the market price, was the cost of natural gas combined with the heat rate of the unit. A typical method used in studies of market power was to use reported gas prices. However, this method can miss surcharges for smaller spot purchases, depending on contractual arrangements between generators and gas suppliers. Operating and maintenance costs are usually generic adders that do not account for different vintages of generation units. Purchase of environmental permits for NO_x often employed the average price of permits and ignored the operational constraints placed on generation units. If there is a limited number of permits, use of a permit entails a lost opportunity cost later in the year. A generation unit faces a risk of mechanical failure each time it starts up, which requires both fixing the unit and the loss of net revenue if this event occurs during high price periods. A generator may have an additional costs related to start-ups and shutdowns (cycling), owing to higher heat rates. A generator, when it faces markets that are not co-optimized, has to design a bid to account for potential lost revenue if acceptance in one market precludes participation in a more lucrative market.

Studies have found empirical evidence that firms in the California market exercised market power, in the sense of raising prices above marginal cost. Borenstein, Bushnell, and Wolak simulated a perfectly competitive market from 1998 to 2000 and found high price-cost margins during the high-demand summer months, with the margins becoming very large in 2000, primarily because of the increased reliance on California generation, which provided in-state generators the opportunity to exercise market power.[1] Joskow and Kahn devised two empirical methods using publicly available data. One method constructed competitive benchmark prices to predict what market prices would be in the absence of withholding behavior. They admitted that incomplete data and the complexity of the market forced them to make assumptions and simplifications that may skew the benchmark price in comparison to observed prices. They found that actual prices in June, July, and August 2000 were higher than

---

[1] Severin Borenstein, James B. Bushnell, and Frank A. Wolak, "Measuring Market Inefficiencies in California's Restructured Wholesale Electricity Market," *American Economic Review* 92 (December 2002): 1376–1405.

the benchmark prices by 90 percent, 56 percent, and 36 percent, respectively (Borenstein et al. found a markup in those months of 63 percent, 50 percent, and 56 percent). The second method looked for direct evidence of capacity withholding by examining summer hours in which the market price was higher than certain threshold levels. They found a significant "output gap" that could not be explained by the need for ancillary services or by transmission congestion.[2]

Harvey and Hogan responded with a paper that raised numerous questions about the methodology used to estimate market power and capacity withholding. Their role as consultants for defendants in the FERC proceedings and associated lawsuits was to cast reasonable doubt on the allegations of withholding and market manipulation and to frame estimates of damages as speculative, and they did a masterful job. They pointed out that Joskow and Kahn's analysis inadequately addressed environmental constraints on unit operation, did not take into account outages of units that lacked economic incentives to withhold, and failed to account for congestion and capacity used to provide ancillary services and to distinguish between the effects of withholding and imperfect foresight. They noted that generators' decisions to bid higher than "marginal costs" were influenced by one-part bidding, strategies to hedge outage risk, and limited generation times caused by environmental constraints.[3]

One-part bidding excludes start-up costs, minimum-load costs, and operating parameters such as minimum downtimes and run times from bids. Generators design one-part bids to ensure recovery of these costs. The expected run time for the unit determines the period over which these costs can be recovered. So generators will use a higher bid premium (above variable cost) for peaking units compared to shoulder and base load units. Higher heat rates due to start-up and no-load consumption would also impact NO_x emissions and costs. A number of California generating plants were subject to annual restrictions on their hours of operation or their annual capacity factor in order to limit NO_x emissions. Plants subject to such restrictions that reached their limits in 2000 accounted for roughly 4,000–5,000 MW of capacity.[4] If the owners of these plants expected that

---

[2] Paul Joskow and Edward Kahn, "A Quantitative Analysis of Pricing Behavior in California's Wholesale Electricity Market During Summer 2000," NBER Working Paper 8157 (March 2001).

[3] Scott Harvey and William Hogan, "On the Exercise of Market Power Through Strategic Withholding in California," LECG (April 24, 2001): 7–10.

[4] Harvey and Hogan, "On the Exercise of Market Power Through Strategic Withholding in California," 18.

these plants would reach their annual operating limits, then a firm would include in its bids a premium that reflected the opportunity cost of running out of power during higher-priced hours at the end of the year.

Joskow and Kahn responded by adjusting their analysis to account for some of Harvey and Hogan's criticisms. The result of these changes was to increase the gap between the market price and their benchmark analysis for May through September 2000.[5] Joskow and Kahn also reviewed the forced outage data and found that it exceeded historical performance in the aggregate for the generation owned by NUGs. They also found that Duke Energy, which appears to have been fully contracted in forward markets for 90 percent of its potential output, behaved differently from Reliant, Dynegy, and AES/Williams. Duke reported much lower forced outage rates than claimed by other firms, rates below similar plants elsewhere in the United States. They also showed that a number of lower-cost units, owned by AES/Williams, Reliant, or Dynegy, did not run on numerous days in June 2000, despite the absence of environmental constraints on their operations. They extended this analysis through September 2000 and found a similar pattern, that Duke was the only one of the four NUGs that did not have a substantial output gap.[6]

Harvey and Hogan responded by pointing out that simulation models cannot establish an accurate benchmark price to be used to identify market power. It is a commonplace experience with optimization models, such as GE MAPS, that they tend to over-optimize compared to actual experience. Optimizing simulations that assume away details like contingency-constrained networks or dynamic limits are likely to underestimate further the prices that would be generated in a market with no market power.[7] They had a valid point, especially with reference to inefficient markets that fail to optimize between day-ahead, real-time, and ancillary service markets, and which do not accept three-part bids. Price spikes resulting from ramping constraints and poor modeling of ramp rates are common in less sophisticated markets. Harvey and Hogan followed up with a study that attempted to replicate Joskow and Kahn's analysis and test for the sensitivity of key assumptions. They found that

---

[5] Paul Joskow and Edward Kahn, "Identifying the Exercise of Market Power: Refining the Estimates" mimeo, July 5, 2001, 4.

[6] Joskow and Kahn, "Identifying the Exercise of Market Power," 5–6, 25–26; Paul Joskow and Edward Kahn, "A Quantitative Analysis of Pricing Behavior in California's Wholesale Electricity Market During Summer 2000," *Energy Journal* 23 (2002): 23.

[7] Scott Harvey and William Hogan, "Identifying the Exercise of Market Power In California," LECG (December 28, 2001): 8, fn. 19.

there could have been an exercise of market power, but the price gap could also be due to the choice of assumptions.[8]

After the soft cap was implemented in December 2000, withholding to influence the market price was no longer a feasible strategy, because bids above $150/MWh would no longer set that price. Instead, the focus shifted toward fraudulent reporting of generation costs to justify bids above the soft cap to receive excess compensation. The bulk of nonutility supply was offered at prices above the soft bid cap threshold. One reason was the spike in natural gas prices in December 2000, combined with the spike in NO_x credit prices. However, by January 2001, the impact of both of these factors had been mitigated. CAISO estimated that potential refunds for the two months could be as high as $562 million, with two-thirds from inflated prices for imports, which averaged $576/MWh in December 2000 and $372/MWh in January 2001.[9]

Some studies suggest that high prices in California stemmed from a dynamic pricing game, not tacit collusion. Exercising market power does not require active collusion. Repeated interaction could have led to increased prices through a dynamic pricing game, where actors predict what the competition will do and incorporate that prediction into their profit-maximizing offers (generating what are called Cournot prices). Overt collusion involves a formal, explicit agreement and is clearly illegal. Tacit or implicit collusion consists of seemingly independent but parallel actions among competing firms to achieve higher prices and profits without an agreement to collude. One way to test for the presence of collusion is to compare prices that would have occurred if the actors independently pursued a profit-maximizing pricing game, as compared to those prices that occur when actors signal each other to encourage cooperative actions to raise prices. Studies support the conclusion of a pricing game.[10] Another study added a more subtle observation, that firms followed noncooperative Cournot pricing in very low and very high

---

[8] Scott Harvey and William Hogan, "Market Power and Market Simulations," LECG (July 16, 2002): 10–11.

[9] CAISO, Department of Market Analysis, "Report on Real Time Supply Costs Above Single Price Auction Threshold: December 8, 2000–January 31, 2001" (February 28, 2001).

[10] Frank Wolak, "Measuring Unilateral Market Power in Wholesale Electricity Markets: The California Market, 1998–2000," *American Economic Review* (May 2003): 425–30; Frank A. Wolak, "Using Restructured Electricity Supply Industries to Understand Oligopoly Industry Outcomes," *Utilities Policy* 18 (2010): 241–42; Steven Puller, "Pricing and Firm Conduct in California's Deregulated Electricity Market," *Review of Economics and Statistics* 89 (February 2007): 83–85.

demand hours, but seemed to engage in collusive behavior during intermediate demand hours. Because this study used the data furnished during
the litigation that followed after the California electricity crisis, it is more
reliable than earlier studies that depended on public data. Confirming
the observation that forward contracting reduces incentives to collude,
Duke and AES withheld far smaller amounts of capacity than did Dynegy,
Mirant, and Reliant.[11]

Tacit collusion is facilitated by repeated interactions, current information on rivals' behavior, and barriers to entry. The California market
consisted of five large firms and a competitive fringe that interacted daily
in a market where rivals' costs were nearly common knowledge. Power
plants were subject to environmental regulations that made operating
characteristics part of the public record. Because many of the plants were
recently divested, firms had good estimates of the fixed and variable costs
of rivals' operations. The Web site of the western transmission grid coordinator posted real-time generation data for almost all plants until October 2000. The ISO released with a one-day lag each plant's generation that
was sold into the real-time market. Several electronic trading exchanges
provided electricity traders with information on bilateral trades. Firms
observed the ISO's forecast of demand before bidding and observed the
ex post realization of demand immediately after the market cleared.[12]
Underlying market conditions created the potential for restricting output
and increasing prices through a variety of oligopoly pricing games.

While withholding by firms was blamed by some for rolling blackouts and high prices, the truth was more complex. It is hard to argue
that rotating outages were caused by an absolute shortage of generating capacity. Only one of the system's outages occurred when demand
was above 40,000 MW and that outage was caused by transmission constraints, not a shortage of generating capacity. Seven outages occurred
when demand was less than 35,000 MW. The problem was that existing
capacity was not available. Peak demand in 2000 was 2,000 MW below
the 1999 peak, about equal to the decline in hydroelectric imports.[13]

---

[11] Nauman Ilias and Robert Reynolds, "Changing Conduct with Changing Demand: Evidence of Coordination among Suppliers of Electricity in California in 2000," Brattle
Group (2007).

[12] Steven Puller, "Pricing and Firm Conduct in California's Deregulated Electricity Market," 77.

[13] Susan L. Pope, "California Electricity Price Spikes: An Update on the Facts," Harvard
Electricity Policy Group (December 9, 2002): 5. Drought conditions in the Pacific North-
west during 2000 reduced hydroelectric production available for export to California.
The overall impact was a reduction in net imports to California of 2,200 MW.

Historically, between 1,000 MW and 6,000 MW average daily generating capacity would normally be offline in a month. However, in the period between October 2000 and May 2001, a monthly average of 12,000 MW generating capacity was offline, reaching a peak of 15,000 MW in April 2001. The majority of capacity was reportedly offline for repairs or maintenance. In late 2000, some plants had used up their NO_x emissions quotas for the year and were precluded from further production.[14]

One problem was that the CAISO was restricted to real-time purchases and sales of electricity. "Real-time" had been interpreted as during the hour the electricity is needed. Therefore, the CAISO tariff precluded it from acquiring electricity to meet emergency conditions earlier than that hour. This restriction was in effect even when CAISO personnel were confident ahead of time that the electricity would be needed. Organizations other than the CAISO could make contractual commitments to purchase electricity well in advance of the time it would be used. Thus, when electricity supplies were short throughout the western states, the CAISO would be the last entity to be able to acquire supplies to avoid energy emergencies. That restriction increased the likelihood that the blackouts would be concentrated in California.[15]

The substantial decline in nuclear output during the first half of 2001 reflected the impact of the shutdown of Unit 3 of the San Onofre Nuclear Generating Station from January 2001 to June 2001. The shortage caused by the Unit 3 outage was compounded by the refueling outage of Diablo Canyon Nuclear Unit 2 at the end of April 2001. Both nuclear units came back online at the same point at the beginning of June 2001. When SCE and PG&E were unable to pay their bills, QF output fell. QF output dropped by 1,100 MW in April 2001 and 700 MW in May 2001 from the previous year. To compensate, other units had to run at levels above their historical utilization. Output stayed significantly above previous levels throughout the fall of 2000, when maintenance outages typically occur.[16]

However, this does not preclude withholding of capacity, since most of these units normally operated at low capacity factors, and it is cycling

---

[14] A generator noted in early 2001 that a CT located in the San Francisco area had run through half of its allowed hours of operation by the end of January. HEPG, "Twenty-Fourth Plenary Session: Moving Towards Markets in the Face of Surprises and Mistakes," Coronado Island Marriott Resort, San Diego, California (February 1–2, 2001): 2.

[15] Sweeney, *The California Electricity Crisis*, 169.

[16] Pope, *California Electricity Price Spikes: An Update on the Facts*, 7–12.

a unit on and off, more than how many hours the unit has been operating, that increases the probability of failure for a generation unit. The units were divested in 1998, and it is unlikely that buyers would have failed to conduct due diligence inspections, identified major maintenance, and then failed to schedule that work in 1999, a year of low prices in which scheduling major unit overhauls would have small opportunity costs. So while a higher failure rate could be expected over the 2000–01 period, one would not expect that failure rate to be significantly higher than normal, because owners had a strong financial interest in keeping these units operational during a period of high prices.

The evidence of market manipulation by Enron was extensive, involving numerous strategies to game the California markets.[17] The question was whether these strategies constituted illegal behavior, and what remedies could be applied to gain recompense for ratepayers. The high visibility of Enron's activities diverted attention from behavior that was far more costly to ratepayers, though less colorful and comprehensible to the media. Of the more than $10 billion that the CAISO calculated as unjust and unreasonable wholesale electricity prices over the period from June 2000 to June 2001, the strategies outlined in the Enron memos at most accounted for $500 million.[18] FERC staff reached a similar conclusion, noting that the Enron strategies had little overall impact on market prices.[19]

FERC's Enron Report outlined evidence of concerted action among Enron and some of its competitors, designed to influence prices in the California energy market. The vast majority of the evidence concerning manipulation of electric markets involved Enron's West Coast trading

---

[17] On Monday, May 6, 2002, Enron's Washington, DC counsel provided the Commission with three internal memoranda, two of which date from December 2000, that describe certain trading strategies employed by Enron's traders in the west. The Commission made these documents publicly available on the Web site for Docket No. PA02-2-000 within hours of receiving them. These are the infamous "Enron Memos." FERC Enron Report at 85. The first memo, dated December 6, 2000, and sent to Enron's outside counsel, was titled, "Traders' Strategies in the California Wholesale Power Markets/ISO Sanctions." The memo included descriptions of strategies referred to as "inc-ing," "Death Star," "Load Shift," "Get Shorty," "Wheel Out," "Fat Boy," and "Ricochet." The two other memos followed up on the subject of the original memo.

[18] "California Monitor Calls Market Gaming Ubiquitous But 'Irrelevant' to Consumer Protection," *Foster Electric Report* (May 22, 2002): 1.

[19] Staff of the Federal Energy Regulatory Commission, *Initial Report on Company-Specific Separate Proceedings and Generic Reevaluations; Published Natural Gas Price Data; and Enron Trading Strategies*, Docket No. PA02-2-000 (August 2002): 91–94 (*Enron Report*).

operations. Enron's West Desk consisted of 100 trading and support personnel stationed at Portland General Electric, Enron's utility subsidiary in Portland, Oregon.[20] Enron personnel were caught on tape arranging for out-of-state plants to go offline.[21]

Enron's load-shifting strategy involved the receipt of interzonal congestion payments by submitting artificial schedules. Enron would artificially create congestion in California's southern zone by over-scheduling in the southern zone and under-scheduling by a corresponding amount in the northern zone. By creating this imbalance, Enron forced the CAISO to find additional transmission capacity (flowing from north to south). Load was thus shifted from north to south, and Enron was paid congestion rents. However, while Enron was able to increase the amount and duration of congestion, it was unsuccessful in its attempts to increase the price it was paid for congestion. Nor could Enron's strategy affect real-time prices, for those were determined only after corrections had been made to Enron's load forecasts.[22]

"Fat Boy" was a mechanism by which a scheduling coordinator could artificially increase load on the schedule it submitted to CAISO. Enron's physical presence in California included the power from the generation assets that Portland General Electric regularly exported to California. During 2000, Enron routinely over-scheduled load by 500 to 1,000 MW. This strategy "guaranteed" a sale and allowed them to schedule transmission in advance. The strategy was designed to counter the monopsony strategy deployed by PG&E to drive down CalPX prices by under scheduling load. The Fat Boy strategy alleviated the under-scheduling problem by supplying the CAISO with "phantom" load. Many out-of-state generators engaged in this practice, but Enron became most famous by giving it a nickname. FERC concluded that over-scheduling endeavors were a legitimate response to under-scheduling by PG&E and did not represent market manipulation. The strategy involved substantial risk for Enron and was more akin to arbitrage than a market power exercise. Enron was

---

[20] McCullough Research, "Reading Enron's Scheme Accounting Materials," June 12, 2004, at http://www.mresearch.com/pdfs/89.pdf (last visited November 16, 2014).

[21] Timothy Egan, "Tapes Show Enron Arranged Plant Shutdown," *New York Times*, February 4, 2005, at http://www.nytimes.com/2005/02/04/national/04energy.html?_r=0 (last visited June 15, 2012).

[22] Darren Bush and Carrie Mayne, "In (Reluctant) Defense of Enron: Why Bad Regulation Is to Blame for California's Power Woes (or Why Antitrust Law Fails to Protect Against Market Power When the Market Rules Encourage Its Use)," 83 *Oregon Law Review* 207, 266–68 (2004).

essentially wagering that more load would be needed to be served than CAISO was anticipating.[23]

Enron also engaged in strategies called "exports of California Power" and "Ricochet." The exports of California power strategy involved buying energy at the CalPX for export outside of California. This strategy was implemented during the time in which California wholesale prices were capped, while the rest of the WECC faced uncapped wholesale rates. The Ricochet trading strategy involved purchasing power from the day-ahead market and exporting it out of the state. The energy was then resold to CAISO in the real-time market or an out-of-market sale. Buying power in California and selling it out of the market, and then selling power back to California did not have an impact until November 2000. These strategies were used to circumvent soft caps until June 2001. Comparing the quantities from this period to the previous nine months suggests that the actual market impact and motives were relatively benign.[24]

Enron took advantage of flaws in California's congestion management software to receive payment for reducing congestion without ever having to move a single megawatt. "Death Star" referred to the strategy of scheduling energy in the opposite direction of a congestion point, providing counterflow. However, no energy was ever moved, because the counterflow was typically provided against another Enron transaction moving in the direction of the congestion. The moves canceled each other out, except that Enron received a congestion payment. Enron earned only $484,000 attributable to the "Death Star" strategy. Other companies obtained about $11.7 million in counterflow revenues over the 1998–2001 period.[25]

The "Get Shorty" trading strategy was designed to take advantage of flaws in the ancillary services market. Enron would bid to provide ancillary services in the day-ahead market and then cover in the real-time market. This strategy permitted Enron to sell ancillary services at

[23] Severin Borenstein, James Bushnell, Christopher R. Knittel, and Catherine Wolfram, "Inefficiencies and Market Power in Financial Arbitrage: A Study of California's Electricity Markets," *Journal of Industrial Economics* 56 (2008): 371–73; FERC Staff, *Enron Report*, 102–04; CAISO, Department of Market Analysis, "Analysis of Trading and Scheduling Strategies Described in Enron Memos" (October 4, 2002): 2; Bush and Mayne, "In (Reluctant) Defense of Enron," 270–72.

[24] FERC Staff, *Enron Report*, 102–04; CAISO, Department of Market Analysis, "Enron Memos," 4–5, 29; CAISO, Department of Market Analysis, "Supplemental Analysis of Trading and Scheduling Strategies Described in Enron Memos," 24–25.

[25] CAISO, Department of Market Analysis, "Enron Memos," 9; FERC Staff, *Enron Report*, 106–09.

a high price and purchase them at a low price. Enron sought payment for a firm ancillary service even though it had not incurred the costs to line up resources to provide the service. If called upon by the ISO, Enron's strategy was to go to the real-time market to fulfill its obligation. Under the ISO rules, Enron was required to line up resources (and thus to have incurred costs) prior to bidding in the day-ahead market. Enron's strategy did nothing to impact the California crisis. The bad conduct was misinformation, not the exercise of market power.[26]

While Enron became the whipping boy for market manipulation, when FERC finally got around to a close examination of the California electricity crisis, it would turn out that withholding of generation, strategic bidding, and the artificial escalation of natural gas prices were the big culprits. While many of these actions were exempt from antitrust action and were sheltered to some extent under traditional FERC rate regulation, they constituted violations of market rules that had been agreed on by market participants. FERC would not only use this "hook" to garnish ill-gotten gains but make it the mechanism for ensuring that market-based rates were just and reasonable.

---

[26] Bush and Mayne, "In (Reluctant) Defense of Enron," 274–75; FERC Staff, *Enron Report*, 109–10.

17

FERC and Market Power in California

The lasting impact of the California crisis was to create the political will to develop the institutional capability at FERC to perform market analysis and monitor market power. FERC's reaction to the California price spikes was tardy, partially due to the consistent opposition of then Chairman Curt Hébert, who repeatedly expressed his preference for market forces to provide a solution.[1] Once FERC did act, by imposing price caps and mitigation measures, and by initiating investigations and refund proceedings, it found itself embroiled in one of the most complex pieces of litigation in FERC's history.[2]

The Commission that had to deal with the California crisis was more divided than the group that presided over the development of Order 888. Commissioner Santa and Chairman Moler were replaced in June 1997 by Curt Hébert and Linda Key Breathitt. Hébert was first appointed to FERC in 1997 by President Clinton, at the request of Senate Majority Leader Trent Lott (R-Miss.).[3] Commissioner Breathitt came to the

---

[1] See his concurrences in *San Diego Gas & Electric Company*, 92 FERC ¶ 61,172 (2000); *San Diego Gas & Electric Company*, 93 FERC ¶ 61,121 (2000); *San Diego Gas & Electric Company*, 93 FERC ¶ 61,294 (2000).

[2] *San Diego Gas & Electric Company*, 95 FERC ¶ 61,115 (2001) (Western Markets Investigation Order); *San Diego Gas & Electric Company*, 95 FERC ¶ 61,418 (2001) (California Mitigation Order); *San Diego Gas & Electric Company*, 96 FERC ¶ 61,120 (Evidentiary Hearing Order); *San Diego Gas & Electric Company*, 97 FERC ¶ 61,275 (2001) (Mitigation and Refund Clarification Order); *Public Utilities Commission of the State of California*, 99 FERC ¶ 61,087 (2002) (Long-Term Contracts Hearing).

[3] Hébert had a law degree from the Mississippi College School of Law and served on the Mississippi Public Service Commission and in the Mississippi House of Representatives. Southern Company had been a major campaign contributor to Senator Lott. Hébert was

286

Commission after four years on the Kentucky Public Service Commission, including two years as chairwoman.[4] Vicky Bailey left the Commission in January 2000, and James Hoecker in January 2001, but they would not be replaced until Pat Wood and Nora Mead Brownell joined in June 2001. The addition of Wood prompted Hébert to leave in August 2001. Brownell served four years on the Pennsylvania PUC, where she supported retail competition but also had a strong pro-consumer record on electricity, telecommunications, and water issues. Brownell was appointed by Governor Tom Ridge, whose strong ties to Bush helped pave the way for her selection to FERC.[5]

The Commission's tardy and initially ineffectual response to the California crisis can be explained by three factors. First, the intransigence of Governor Davis alienated the Commission, even before Hébert became chairman. Second, the Bush administration had no desire to help resolve an economic crisis in the largest Democratic Party stronghold, and the backwash of the crisis helped elect a Republican governor. Third, Chairman Hébert had ties with Entergy, and his mentor, Senator Lott, with Southern Company, which were opponents of open access and deregulation. Chairman Hébert's support of markets in California seemed to reflect a tactical decision rather than an ideological preference. The California meltdown supported efforts to restrain the spread of deregulation.

The first FERC report on the western energy crisis effectively whitewashed considerations of the exercise of market power. The main observations from the study are summarized below:

- November 2000 was the coldest November nationwide since 1911, with the coldest temperatures in the west and northwest.
- California was under frequent emergency conditions of varying severity during November and December, and was often unable to supply normal winter exports to the northwest region. The California emergency events are correlated with the high prices in the northwest.
- Low water levels, precipitation, and stream flows limited the energy available from hydropower generation.

---

appointed in 1997 to fill the remaining term of Donald Santa. He was reappointed to a full term at the bequest of Lott. *Restructuring Today*, March 9, 1999.

[4] Breathitt was the daughter of former Kentucky governor, Edward Breathitt, and had a bachelor's degree from the University of Kentucky. *National Journal* (June 23, 2001): 2020.

[5] Brownell has a bachelor's degree from Syracuse University. *National Journal* (June 23, 2001): 2020.

- Natural gas price increases and limits on pipeline capacity and storage levels contributed to the pressure on power prices.
- Most of the variation in power prices can be explained by temperature, precipitation, or stream flow levels, as well as tight supply and demand.[6]

On November 29, 2000, consumer attorney Mike Aguirre filed suit in San Diego Superior Court on behalf of a single ratepayer against sixteen power generators. Three similar suits were filed by San Diego County Water Districts. These suits alleged violations of federal antitrust law (Sherman Act section 1) prohibiting unreasonable restraints of trade. State legislators subsequently joined these suits. Initial removal to federal court and motions to dismiss based on federal preemption were denied.[7]

On July 25, 2001, FERC issued an order establishing the scope of and methodology for calculating refunds related to transactions in the spot markets operated by the CAISO and the CalPX during the period from October 2, 2000 through June 20, 2001.[8] The order also established an evidentiary hearing proceeding in order to develop further the factual record so that refunds may be calculated. Initial attempts to facilitate settlement negotiations were thwarted by Governor Davis's insistence that he would not budge from the $8.9 billion claimed by California for the period from May 1, 2000 through May 31, 2001. In response to the $8.9 billion claim, several sellers into the California market made offers contingent upon reaching a global settlement of all issues. These offers totaled $704 million.[9] In addition, the Commission established another proceeding before an administrative law judge (ALJ) to explore whether there may have been unjust and unreasonable charges for spot market sales in the Pacific Northwest from December 25, 2000 through June 20, 2001, and the calculation of any refunds associated with such charges.[10]

The Commission had set October 2, 2000 as an effective date for refunds on sales in the spot markets of the CAISO and the CalPX. FERC concluded that FPA section 206 did not permit the Commission to require

[6] *Staff Report to the Federal Energy Regulatory Commission on Northwest Power Markets in November and December 2000* (February 1, 2001): 2–3.

[7] Robert C. Fellmeth, "Plunging Into Darkness: Energy Deregulation Collides with Scarcity," 33 *Loyola University Chicago Law Journal*, 833, 837 (2002); *Hendricks v. Dynegy Power Mktg., Inc.*, 160 F. Supp. 2d 1155 (S.D. Cal. 2001).

[8] *San Diego Gas & Electric Company*, 96 FERC ¶ 61,120 (2001).

[9] *San Diego Gas & Electric Company*, 93 FERC ¶ 63,007, 65,038–39 (2001).

[10] *See San Diego Gas & Electric Company*, 96 FERC ¶ 61,120, 61,520 (2001).

refunds prior to a date sixty days after the filing of a complaint or the initiation of a Commission investigation. That refund authority can be expanded where sellers have charged a rate other than the filed rate or where an appellate court has found that the Commission committed legal error, but those exceptions did not apply in this situation.[11]

There is no precise legal formulation for setting a just and reasonable rate and no precise bright line for when a rate becomes unjust and unreasonable. The Commission may rely on market-based prices in lieu of cost-of-service regulation to assure a "just and reasonable" result when there is a competitive market.[12] The Commission's authority to rely on competitive pricing, combined with the filed rate doctrine, left the issue of remedies in legal limbo, because case law had not dealt with the validity of market-based rates when it is discovered ex post that markets were indeed not competitive.

The filed rate doctrine has several applications, the most important of which is its use as a defense against antitrust and other claims. The doctrine was developed in the nineteenth century as part of a program to regulate the exercise of monopoly power by the railroads.[13] During that period, railroad companies often charged substantially higher rates on noncompetitive routes, granted secret discounts to preferred shippers, and overcharged competitors of preferred customers. These concerns, among others, led to the passage of the Interstate Commerce Act in 1887. Under the Commerce Act, a carrier could charge a shipper only those rates incorporated in a tariff that the carrier had filed with the Interstate Commerce Commission. The requirement that carriers collect only the rate they filed, or that a regulatory commission established, became commonly referred to as the filed rate doctrine.[14]

The Supreme Court held that the filed rate is the only legal rate. The filed rate doctrine preserves the agency's primary jurisdiction over reasonableness of rates.[15] Not only do the courts lack authority to impose a

---

[11] *San Diego Gas & Electric Company,* 93 FERC ¶ 61,121, 61,370 (2000); *San Diego Gas & Electric Company,* 96 FERC ¶ 61,120, 65,504 (2001).

[12] *Elizabethtown Gas Co. v. FERC,* 10 F.3d 866, 870 (D.C. Cir. 1993).

[13] *Maislin Industries, U.S., Inc. v. Primary Steel, Inc.,* 497 U.S. 116, 138 (1990) (Stevens, J., dissenting).

[14] *Maislin Industries, U.S., Inc. v. Primary Steel, Inc.,* 497 U.S. 116, 127–30 (1990).

[15] *Montana-Dakota Utils. Co. v. Northwestern Pub. Serv. Co.,* 341 U.S. 246, 251 (1951); *City of Cleveland v. FPC,* 525 F.2d 845, 854 (1976). The filed rate doctrine extends beyond rates to any allocation of power that affects rates. *Nantahala Power & Light Co. v. Thornburg,* 476 US 953, 967 (1986).

different rate than the one approved by the Commission, but the Commission itself has no power to alter a rate retroactively or order reparations.[16] In the context of a filed rate that sets a specific price for a sale of goods or services, precedent holds that antitrust damages are unavailable as a remedy.[17] The only remedy is to seek redress at the administrative agency.

When the FPA was written, market-based rates for wholesale electricity were not envisioned, and the concept of a filed rate meant a rate that proscribed the terms of electricity sales. The statute does not dictate or even indicate how the Commission is to establish rates. The filed rate and retroactive ratemaking doctrines would appear to apply equally to cost-based and market-based rates.[18] The use of market-based tariffs was first approved in the natural gas context,[19] then as applied to wholesale sellers of electricity. However, approval of such tariffs was conditioned on the existence of a competitive market.[20] In a competitive market, where neither the buyer nor the seller has significant market power, it is rational to assume that the terms of their voluntary exchange are reasonable.[21]

With respect to the FPA, the filed rate doctrine rests on two provisions: section 205(c), which requires utilities to file rate schedules with the Commission; and section 206(a), which allows the Commission to fix rates and charges, but only prospectively.[22] FERC, unlike the ICC, has no statutory authority to make a utility pay damages or reparations on the grounds that the filed rate was unjust and unreasonable, illegal, or contrary to public policy. When Congress passed the FPA in 1935, it excluded a provision (section 213) that would have allowed the

---

[16] *Arkansas La. Gas Co. v. Hall*, 453 U.S. 571, 577–78 (1981).

[17] *Keogh v. Chicago & Northwestern Ry. Co.*, 260 U.S. 156, 163 (1922) (finding no cause of action under Antitrust Act); *see also Square D Co. v. Niagara Frontier Tariff Bureau, Inc.*, 476 U.S. 409, 424 (1986) ("If there is to be an overruling of the Keogh rule, it must come from Congress, rather than from this Court.").

[18] *See Texas Commercial Energy v. TXU Energy, Inc.*, 413 F. 3d 503, 510 (5th Cir 2005) (PUCT's oversight over the market is sufficient to conclude that the BES energy rates are "filed" within the meaning of the filed rate doctrine.); *Pub. Util. Dist. No. 1 of Snohomish County v. Dynegy Power Marketing, Inc.*, 384 F.3d 756, 762 (9th Cir. 2004) (FERC approved tariffs that governed the California wholesale electricity markets. Therefore, if the prices in those markets were not just and reasonable or if the defendants sold electricity in violation of the filed tariffs, Snohomish's only option is to seek a remedy before FERC.).

[19] *See Elizabethtown Gas Co. v. FERC*, 10 F.3d 866, 870 (D.C. Cir. 1993).

[20] *See Louisiana Energy and Power Authority v. FERC*, 141 F.3d 364, 365 (D.C. Cir. 1998).

[21] *Tejas Power Corp. v. FERC*, 908 F.2d 998, 1004 (D.C. Cir. 1990).

[22] *Towns of Concord, Norwood and Wellesley v. FERC*, 955 F.2d 67, 71–72 (D.C. Cir. 1992).

Commission, upon complaint, to order due reparation, with interest, for unreasonable or excessive charges. Section 213 was included as a standard utility law provision borrowed from the Interstate Commerce Act. This provision was eliminated from the final bill while in committee.[23] Courts have concluded that this exclusion showed that Congress intended that the Commission only have the authority to grant relief in a section 206 proceeding prospectively from the date of its order.[24] The courts have consistently held that under the FPA, the Commission does not have authority to order retroactive rate decreases.[25] However, this limitation does not extend to cases in which there is adequate notice that resolution of some specific issue may cause a later adjustment to the rate.[26]

In 1988, the Regulatory Fairness Act amended § 206 of the FPA to permit limited retroactive refund authority. As amended, FPA section 206 restricts the Commission's authority to establish a refund effective date to no earlier than sixty days after the date that a complaint is filed or the Commission initiates an investigation. The FPA gave the Commission the authority to make an existing rate subject to refund for a period of up to fifteen months from the refund effective date.[27]

Even if the FTC and Justice Department had not been constrained from action by the filed rate doctrine, a good deal of the behavior that led to high prices was legal. Strategic bidding, absent collusion, is not an antitrust violation.[28] Bidding to charge prices in excess of those that would prevail in a competitive market is not unlawful under the antitrust laws because "more than monopoly power is necessary to make the charging of a noncompetitive price unlawful."[29] As long as each actor lacks market power, and does not actively collude with other sellers, it can engage in Cournot or other strategic behavior with impunity unless such behavior is specifically prohibited by FERC rules.

---

[23] *San Diego Gas & Electric Company et al.*, 93 FERC ¶ 61,121, 61,378 (2000).

[24] *See, e.g., City of Bethany v. FERC*, 727 F.2d 1131 (D.C. Cir. 1984), *cert. denied*, 469 U.S. 917 (1984).

[25] *See FPC v. Sierra Pacific Power Co.*, 350 U.S. 348, 353 (1956); *Public Service Co. of New Hampshire v. FERC*, 600 F.2d 944, 957 n. 51 (D.C. Cir. 1979), *cert. denied*, 444 U.S. 990 (1979); *City of Piqua v. FERC*, 610 F.2d 950, 954 (D.C. Cir. 1979).

[26] *Natural Gas Clearinghouse v. FERC*, 965 F.2d 1066, 1075 (D.C. Cir. 1992).

[27] *San Diego Gas & Electric Company et al.*, 93 FERC ¶ 61,121, 61,379 (2000).

[28] However, it has become an important component of merger analysis. Jonathan B. Baker, "Why Did the Antitrust Agencies Embrace Unilateral Effects," 12 *George Mason Law Review* 31 (2003).

[29] *Berkey Photo, Inc. v. Eastman Kodak Co.*, 603 F.2d 263, 297 (2nd Cir. 1979).

Each new generator was subject to review by FERC to determine if it could exercise market power in California as part of the approval process for the right to charge market-based rates. These determinations were based on a formula that generally resulted in approval if a generator controlled 20 percent or less of the market.[30] This methodology ignored the ability of generators to increase prices during periods of peak demand. Nor did the analysis take into account transmission constraints, which often manifested during times of peak demand.[31]

Traditional utilities and power marketers who engage in market-based rate transactions were required to file quarterly reports summarizing transactions to satisfy the filing requirements of § 205(c).[32] Even though FERC described these quarterly reports as "necessary" for FERC to monitor energy markets adequately, FERC did not know – or simply chose to ignore – that dozens of generators were not filing the required information, especially the requirement to report transaction-specific data.[33]

Order 889 required transmission owners to post information about prices and availability of their transmission capacity and services on the OASIS system. Save for a few OASIS sites, it was nearly impossible for anyone to use OASIS to obtain pertinent data for overseeing transmission market behavior. NERC refused access by FERC staff to real-time data on physical electric generation and transmission supply and demand because its members did not want FERC staff to have the data. It is impossible to assess whether players have market power without information on generation and transmission availability in real or near-real time.[34]

---

[30] See *Public Service Company of Indiana*, 51 FERC ¶ 61,367, 62,205 (1990), *order on reh'g*, 52 FERC ¶ 61,260 (1990), *order granting clarification & modifying order*, 53 FERC ¶ 61,131 (1990), *dismissed, Northern Indiana Public Service Company v. FERC*, 954 F.2d 736 (D.C. Cir. 1992); *Louisville Gas and Electric Company*, 62 FERC 61,016 at 61,146.

[31] In 1999, a FERC commissioner admitted that applying the more complex, but still inadequate, merger analysis tests for market power to market-based rates was totally unacceptable to the industry. Peter Fox-Penner and Romkaew Broehm, "Deregulated Electricity Pricing in the U.S.: Dramatic New Rules from the FERC," Brattle Group, April 25, 2004, at http://www.brattle.com/_documents/UploadLibrary/ArticleReport2314.pdf (last visited August 17, 2011). These comments illustrate two disturbing trends: FERC was not concerned about abuse of market-based rates; and industry actors had excessive influence over the Commission.

[32] *Power Co. of America, L.P. v. FERC*, 245 F.3d 839, 846 (D.C. Cir. 2001).

[33] *Enron Power Marketing Inc.*, 65 FERC ¶ 61,305 (1993); *Revised Public Utility Filing Requirements*, 99 FERC ¶ 61,107 (2002); *State of California, ex rel. Bill Lockyer et al.*, 99 FERC ¶ 61,247, 62,066 (2002), *rehearing denied*, 100 FERC ¶ 61,295 (2002).

[34] Ron Rattey, "Open Memorandum to FERC Staff," June 2, 2000.

FERC issued a NOPR on Revised Public Utility Filing Requirements in July 2001, recognizing that technology permitted, and market monitoring required, information to be made available to market participants on a near-real-time basis.[35] Order 2001 was issued in April 2002, as part of a review of information and reporting requirements the Commission was undertaking to enhance the efficiency of market rules and industry compliance with them.[36]

FERC did not address the issue of lax reporting until its May 31, 2002 order responding to the complaint from Bill Lockyer, Attorney General of the State of California, alleging that generators and marketers failed to file their rates as required by section 205(c) of the Federal Power Act. The Commission denied a request to aggregate data in quarterly reports because such data did not provide sufficient disclosure to the public and would prevent customers from detecting improper conduct. The Commission directed all marketers and other public utility sellers that made short-term sales at market-based rates into California markets since October 2, 2000 to file new quarterly transaction reports showing non-aggregated data for sales.[37]

Prompted by Enron's declaration of Chapter 11 bankruptcy on December 2, 2001, allegations were made that Enron, through its affiliates, used its market position to distort electricity and natural gas markets in the west. Enron's filing for bankruptcy coincided with a substantial decline in spot prices, suggesting that Enron may have manipulated prices prior to its bankruptcy.[38] The Commission, on February 13, 2002, directed staff to undertake a fact-finding investigation into whether any entity

---

[35] *Revised Public Utility Filing Requirements, NOPR*, FERC Stats. & Regs. ¶ 34,554 (2001), 66 FR 40929 (August 6, 2001).

[36] *Revised Public Utility Filing Requirements*, Order No. 2001, FERC Stats. & Regs. ¶ 31,127 (2002), 67 FR 31043 (2002), *reh'g denied*, Order No. 2001-A, 100 FERC ¶ 61,074, *reconsideration and clarification denied*, Order No. 2001-B, 100 FERC ¶ 61,342, *order directing filings*, Order No. 2001-C, 101 FERC ¶ 61,314 (2002), *order directing filings*, Order No. 2001-D, 102 FERC ¶ 61,334 (2003), *order refining filing requirements*, Order No. 2001-E, 105 FERC ¶ 61,352 (2003), *clarification order*, Order No. 2001-F, 106 FERC ¶ 61,060 (2004).

[37] *State of California, ex rel. Bill Lockyer et al.*, 99 FERC ¶ 61,247, 62,065–66 (2002).

[38] "FERC Orders Formal Investigations Into 'Possible Misconduct' by Three Enron Affiliates, Avista Corp. and El Paso Electric during California's Energy Crisis," *Foster Electric Report* (August 21, 2002): 1; "PJM Corrects Interface Pricing after Discovering Market Gaming in June and July," *Foster Electric Report* (August 21, 2002): 7; "Avista Energy Pays CFTC $2M to Settle Allegations of Market Manipulation," *Power Markets Week* (August 27, 2001): 1.

manipulated short-term prices in electric energy or natural gas markets in the west for the period from January 1, 2000 onward.[39]

On February 25, 2002, the CPUC and the California Electricity Oversight Board (CEOB) filed two separate complaints against a group of sellers of energy under long-term contracts with the CDWR, alleging that the respondents obtained the prices, terms, and conditions in the contracts through the exercise of market power, in violation of the FPA. The complaints sought to modify more than thirty contracts entered into in 2001.[40]

Pressure on FERC increased with the release of a GAO report, in June 2002, criticizing the Commission for not revising its regulatory and oversight responsibilities to adequately respond to the transition to competitive energy markets. The study found that without effective regulatory oversight, models, and methodology, the Commission could not assure that markets are producing prices that are "just and reasonable." Further, the GAO study noted that the Commission had limited legal authority to impose penalties if it found that companies had manipulated markets. The report blasted a two-year reorganization effort called "FERC First," initiated in 1997 by former chairman Hoecker, as ineffectual. The two-year, $20-million project combined the agency's staff responsible for natural gas and electricity regulation into a new Office of Markets, Tariffs and Rates. Despite new responsibilities, staff declined by 20 percent between 1993 and 2001. The agency did not have enough people who could analyze market information. Frequent changes in FERC's leadership were another contributing factor as FERC had four different chairpersons over five years. Ironically, while the California problem was a "wake-up call" for the agency, it also delayed the agency's efforts to establish an effective market oversight program by diverting substantial management attention and resources.[41]

One problem facing the Commission was the sheer flood of information it would need to monitor to detect malfeasance in natural gas and electricity markets. FERC had more than fifty active information

[39] *Fact-Finding Investigation of Potential Manipulation of Electric and Natural Gas Prices*, 98 FERC ¶ 61,165, 61,614 (2002). A number of formal section 206 complaints were pending before the Commission concerning the justness and reasonableness of prices in long-term sales contracts in the west.

[40] *Public Utilities Commission of the State of California et al.*, 99 FERC ¶ 61,087, 61,377 (2002), *order on reh'g*, 100 FERC ¶ 61,098 (2002).

[41] General Accounting Office, *Energy Markets: Concerted Actions Needed by FERC to Confront Challenges That Impede Effective Oversight* (June 2002): 4–8, 13, 38.

collection and reporting requirements for the energy companies it regulated, and received about 33,600 industry responses annually. Data feeds from the organized electricity markets, industry trading platforms and information services, and financial markets such as NYMEX required data management and storage capabilities. Obtaining information on the names and other details of parties trading in "exempt" commercial markets such as the UBS-Warburg, Dynegydirect, and ICE required that FERC managed another tranche of data.[42]

Chairman Wood said he agreed largely with the conclusions of the GAO report. But Wood pointed out that the report focused on a time period prior to his arrival at the Commission. Wood said that when he arrived at FERC in the summer of 2001, he found that FERC had been working on the infrastructure and the market structure and rules needed for competitive markets, but was doing little in the way of effective market oversight. As a result, he revised the strategic plan to provide a balanced approach that covers all three factors. In January 2002, FERC launched a new Office of Market Oversight and Investigation (OMOI),[43] to be operational in August. Wood made it clear that with the advent of the OMOI unit's investigations, FERC could be expected to hold regular market surveillance briefings.[44]

FERC issued its initial report on market manipulation in August 2002. The staff recommended that the Commission initiate company-specific separate proceedings of the Enron companies, El Paso Gas, and Avista. Staff questioned the validity of published natural gas pricing data and their application to calculating the mitigated market-clearing price in the California refund proceeding. Trade publications reporting spot and forward prices for both electric and natural gas products did not employ statistically valid sampling procedures or a formal verification procedure. A number of energy companies allegedly engaged in manipulation of the natural gas prices found in various natural gas price index publications. The four major sources of information involved in setting the spot market prices at the critical California natural gas delivery points were *Gas Daily*, *Inside FERC*, *Daily Gas Price Index*, and EnronOnLine. The first three

---

[42] GAO, *Energy Markets: Concerted Actions Needed by FERC*, 38–40.
[43] A similar entity, the Market Oversight Division, or MOD, was created in August 2000 when Chairman Wood was leading the electric industry restructuring activities at the Public Utility Commission of Texas.
[44] General Accounting Office, *Energy Markets: Concerted Actions Needed by FERC*, 35–36, 84–85.

sources were trade publications, which were independent from any of the energy and trading companies.[45]

EnronOnLine was a significant source of price discovery and formation and quickly became a major source of market information for traders at different firms. Enron was in a unique position to manipulate the data on EnronOnLine. There was strong evidence that the trading on EnronOnLine involved market manipulation, including "wash trades." Such trades typically involved a sale of gas from a seller to a purchaser followed by a sale back to the same seller from the purchaser to increase reported prices. An Enron affiliate was always one of the parties to the transaction, and Enron affiliates were sometimes on both sides of a transaction. Staff recommended that the Commission require that all market-based rate tariffs include a specific prohibition against the deliberate submission of false information or the omission of material information. Staff also recommended that market-based rate tariffs include standard provisions to permit the Commission to impose penalties on violators.[46]

The CPUC released a report on wholesale generation during the California crisis in September 2002. The report claimed that there was clear evidence of withholding of generation from the market. They examined thirty-two days where the CAISO had called for interruptions or blackouts. On all but two of those days, generators reported that at least 5,000 MW, or 30 percent of their total capacity, was out of service. Specific examples cited of generators ignoring or otherwise refusing to follow CAISO commands during events was far more damning evidence, but there was no estimation of the magnitude of those actions, or whether prices were impacted by this behavior.[47] CAISO confirmed that some of these behaviors occurred. CAISO encountered circumstances where generators refused to run, citing lack of operating personnel, or argued with CAISO operators over the prices at which they would run. However, the

[45] Federal Energy Regulatory Commission, *Initial Report on Company-Specific Separate Proceedings and Generic Reevaluations; Published Natural Gas Price Data; and Enron Trading Strategies*, Docket No. PA02-2-000 (August 2002)(*Enron Report*). FERC staff members were aided by consulting firms Aspen Systems and Analysis Group/Economics. Members of Analysis Group active in this investigation include Edward Kahn and Michael Quinn. Other outside consultants include Hendrik Bessembinder, Robert Pindyck, and Chester Spatt.

[46] FERC, *Enron Report*, 3–6.

[47] CPUC, "Report on Wholesale Electricity Generation Investigation" (September 2002): 45–46, 51–55. However, a serious weakness of this analysis was that Duke had significant unused capacity on many of those days, yet lacked any motive for withholding, as it had forward-contracted 90% of its capacity.

CAISO cast doubt on the validity of the outage and withholding analysis conducted by the CPUC.[48]

FERC's final report on Market Manipulation was issued in March 2003. A key conclusion of the report was that markets for natural gas and electricity in California were inextricably linked, and that dysfunctions in each fed off one another during the crisis. Dysfunctions in the natural gas market appear to stem, at least in part, from efforts to manipulate price indices compiled by trade publications. Staff concluded that large-volume, rapid-fire trading substantially increased natural gas prices in California. Prices in the California spot markets were affected by economic withholding and inflated bidding, violating the anti-gaming provisions of the CAISO and CalPX tariffs. Staff recommended the Commission initiate proceedings to require guilty companies to disgorge profits associated with these tariff violations. This disgorgement would affect activities beginning January 1, 2000 through June 21, 2001, and not just those during the October 2, 2000 through the June 21, 2001 refund period. These disgorgements would be in addition to the refunds resulting from the California Refund Proceeding. The dysfunctional spot market for electricity also influenced forward prices. The influence was greatest for contracts with one- to two-year terms. Staff concluded that EnronOnLine was a key enabler of wash trading. Enron manipulated thinly traded physical markets to profit in financial markets, garnering $500 million in 2000 and 2001. Profits in financial instruments allowed Enron to sustain trading losses in physical trading. The report recommended that the Commission prohibit the use of one-to-many trading platforms such as EnronOnLine and explicitly prohibit wash trading.[49]

Two specific activities – trading in anomalous patterns at Topock, a major delivery point at the junction of El Paso's interstate pipeline and Southern California Gas's intrastate pipeline; and false reporting of market transactions to publications for compilation in price indices – reflected deliberate conduct to manipulate natural gas market outcomes. Topock was the only widely visible spot gas price for imports into southern California. Reliant Energy Services had a netting agreement with Enron that encouraged churning when Reliant was a net buyer. The market would see the change in the prices at which Enron would offer to buy and sell gas

---

[48] "Commentary by the California Independent System Operator Corporation on the CPUC Staff Investigative Report on Wholesale Electric Generation" (October 25, 2002): 3, 3–6.

[49] Staff of the Federal Energy Regulatory Commission, *Final Report on Price Manipulation in Western Markets*, Docket No. PA02-2-000 (March 2003).

without knowing that only one trader was causing the change. Because the published indexes report a midpoint (or an average) price for a day's trading, the churning activity would bias the reported price even if it did not affect closing prices. The highest published price in NGI's Daily Gas Price Index plus a 50 percent adder set the imbalance penalties for SoCalGas transportation customers, increasing the premium paid by customers to avoid imbalance penalties, especially when supplies were short. Reliant shielded itself from these spot prices increases through its agreement with Enron and coordinated with its financial traders to exploit price spikes.[50]

Reported natural gas spot prices were also manipulated by false reports to trade journals. Five companies (Dynegy, AEP, Williams, CMS, and El Paso) admitted that their employees provided false data. On December 2, 2002, the Office of the U.S. Attorney General in Houston indicted a former vice president of El Paso Energy on charges of false reporting and wire fraud in connection with his reporting of false trades to *Inside FERC*. On December 18, 2002, the CFTC imposed a $5 million penalty against Dynegy Marketing and Trade. In its order, the CFTC determined that from 2000 through June 2002, Dynegy knowingly reported false natural gas price and volume information in an attempt to skew gas indices relative to various trading hubs. Motivations for the false reports included attempts to benefit traders' own positions or that of their trading desk, and to offset the inaccurate data other companies were reporting. In addition, data was simply inaccurate.[51]

El Paso Natural Gas was also a key contributor to natural gas price escalation in southern California. EPNG, El Paso's regulated subsidiary, withheld substantial amounts of transportation capacity under its physical control, in part by running its pipeline at less than its maximum approved operating pressure in violation of FERC rules. EPNG diverted substantial available pipeline capacity away from the southern California border in violation of contractual obligations, and El Paso Merchant Energy, El Paso's marketing arm, systematically restricted natural gas transportation capacity to the southern California border by refusing to "release" pipeline capacity for the use of other shippers. In early 2000, El Paso purchased the All American Pipeline (now called Line 2000). Line 2000 was an oil pipeline providing service from Texas to southern

---

[50] FERC Staff, *Final Report on Price Manipulation*, Ch II.
[51] FERC Staff, *Final Report on Price Manipulation*, Ch III.

California, but was capable of conversion to natural gas. El Paso delayed conversion of the pipeline, blocking an increase in natural gas deliveries. In June 2003, the attorney general brokered a settlement that called for El Paso to pay approximately $1.7 billion. El Paso also agreed to extensive structural relief, ensuring that it could not continue to manipulate natural gas supplies in California.[52]

The California market power proceeding involved a cast of industry experts testifying for parties.[53] Many of these experts had also been involved in advising ISOs, FERC, and state regulators on market design and operation, and wrote articles in journals proposing solutions to perceived market problems. Some of the prices that prevailed in California during the time period between May 2000 and December 2001 were market prices to the extent that, given input costs, they were determined by the competitive, independent, profit-maximizing decisions of many different firms, based on the market rules in place at the time.[54] While some prices above marginal cost could be explained by uncoordinated strategic bidding, there was overwhelming evidence that both input prices and market prices were influenced by collusive behavior.

FERC supported staff's contention that the CAISO's Market Monitoring and Information Protocol (MMIP) put market participants on notice. A key function of the MMIP was to ensure that the markets operated by the CAISO were free from abusive conduct. The CAISO tariff, through the MMIP, defines gaming as "taking unfair advantage of the rules and procedures set forth in the CalPX or CAISO tariffs, Protocols or Activity

---

[52] Attorney General Bill Lockyer, State of California, "Attorney General's Energy White Paper: A Law Enforcement Perspective on the California Energy Crisis," 60–61.

[53] Professor Cramton (University of Maryland) testified for Duke Power, Robert Earle (Charles River Associates) for El Paso Electric Co., Dr. William H. Hieronymus (Charles River) for Dynegy and Williams Energy, Dr. Richard Tabors (Tabors Caramanis & Associates) for Dynegy and Powerex, Professor Arthur De Vany (UCLA) for Coral Power and Sempra, Cliff W. Hamal (LECG) for Reliant Energy, Dr. Scott Harvey and Professor William Hogan (LECG) for Mirant, Dr. Charles J. Cicchetti (Pacific Economics Group) for Avista Energy, BP Energy, IDACORP Energy L.P., Puget Sound Energy, TransAlta Energy Marketing, and TransCanada Energy.

Dr. Peter Fox-Penner, Dr. Phillip Hanser (Brattle Group), Dr. Robert Reynolds (Competition Economics), Michael Harris (Econ One Research), and Dr. Carolyn A. Berry testified for the California Parties (Attorney General of the State of California, the California Public Utilities Commission, the Electricity Oversight Board, Southern California Edison, and Pacific Gas and Electric).

[54] San Diego Gas & Electric Company, Dockets Nos EL00–95–075, EL00–98–063, Rebuttal Addendum of Behalf of Duke Energy, Dr. Peter Cramton, "Assessment of Submissions by California Parties" (Mach 20, 2003).

Rules . . . to the detriment of the efficiency of, and of consumers in, the CAISO Markets." Market participants could not reasonably argue that they were not on notice that conduct such as the "Gaming Practices" would be a violation of the CAISO and CalPX tariffs.[55] This provided an end run around the retroactive refund restrictions of the FPA, since market rates had not been "just and reasonable."

The Commission determined that some of these alleged gaming practices violated the MMIP. Included in the practices were "Ricochet" or "Megawatt Laundering," which took advantage of the price differentials that existed between the day-ahead or day-of markets and out-of-market sales in the real-time market; false scheduling of load or counterflow energy to receive congestion payments; ancillary service manipulation, collectively referred to as "Get Shorty," which included selling ancillary services in the day-ahead market without the required resources; Double Selling, or selling ancillary services in the day-ahead market from resources that were initially available but later sold as energy; and selling Non-Firm Energy as Firm Energy. FERC ordered a trial-type evidentiary proceeding to be held before an ALJ, to examine whether specific market participants engaged in gaming practices.[56]

Parallel with the California gaming proceeding, FERC launched an investigation of gaming in western electricity markets. In the Western Markets Report, FERC staff compared the input costs attributable to specific generators (primarily natural gas prices) with the spot market clearing prices for the period from May 1, 2000 to October 2, 2000. Staff concluded that the bid prices for this period appeared to have been excessively elevated solely for the purpose of raising prices, and that, as such, these bidding practices constituted a violation of the MMIP. Staff also concluded that bids at the $250 level during August and September reflected an appropriate scarcity premium above marginal costs. FERC found that the MMIP prohibits noncompetitive bidding, thus market participants cannot reasonably argue that they were not on notice that the bidding behavior outlined here would be in violation of the CAISO and CalPX tariffs' prohibition against anomalous bidding behavior. FERC required that all such unjust profits for the period from May 1, 2000 to October 2, 2000 be disgorged in their entirety, and would consider

[55] *American Electric Power Service et al.*, 103 FERC ¶ 61,345 at P 8, *reh'g denied*, 106 FERC ¶ 61,020 (2003).
[56] *American Electric Power Service et al.*, 103 FERC ¶ 61,345 at PP 37–55, 71 (2003).

additional nonmonetary remedies such as revocation of market-based rate authority.[57]

The Commission adopted many of the presiding judge's proposed findings of fact, issued on December 12, 2002 by the presiding ALJ in the California refund proceeding. The Commission had directed the presiding ALJ to certify findings of fact with respect to application of a method to determine the mitigated price in each hour of the refund period, the amount of refunds owed by each supplier, and the amount owed to each supplier by the CAISO, the three IOUs, and the state of California. The Commission also directed the CAISO to provide the ALJ with a recreation of mitigated prices for every hour from October 2, 2000 through June 20, 2001. The CAISO calculated that for the refund period from October 2, 2000 through June 20, 2001, suppliers owe the CAISO and CalPX a refund of $1.8 billion. The ALJ determined that the suppliers were owed approximately $3 billion, or $1.2 billion after refunds.[58]

In June 2003, FERC set for hearing the long-term contracts entered in by the CDWR before June 20, 2001. A coalition of California governmental agencies submitted a report detailing producers' widespread market gaming and manipulation to the FERC on March 3, 2003, asking the Commission to order the industry to refund California consumers more than $7.5 billion, in addition to the state's overall claim of approximately $9 billion. The CPUC and CEOB sought the extraordinary remedy of contract modification. The Commission's long-standing policy, consistent with a substantial body of Supreme Court precedent, has been to recognize the sanctity of contracts. The Commission has deviated from that policy only in extreme circumstances.[59]

---

[57] *Investigation of Anomalous Bidding Behavior and Practices in the Western Markets,* 103 FERC ¶ 61,345 (2003).

[58] See *San Diego Gas & Electric Company et al.,* 101 FERC ¶ 63,026 (2002); See *San Diego Gas & Electric Company et al.,* 102 FERC ¶ 61,317 at PP 2–3 (2002), *order on reh'g,* 105 FERC ¶ 61,066 (2003).

[59] The *Mobile-Sierra* doctrine, based on two cases decided on the same day in 1956, addressed the authority of the Commission to modify rates set bilaterally by contract rather than unilaterally by tariff. In *United Gas Pipe Line Co. v. Mobile Gas Service Corp.,* 350 U.S. 332 (1956), the Court rejected a natural gas utility's argument that the Natural Gas Act's requirement that it file all new rates with the Commission authorized it to abrogate a lawful contract with a purchaser simply by filing a new tariff. The filing requirement is merely a *precondition* to changing a rate, not an *authorization* to change rates in violation of a lawful contract (i.e., a contract that sets a just and reasonable rate). See *id.,* at 339–44. In *FPC v. Sierra Pacific Power Co.,* 350 U.S. 348, 352–53 (1956), the Court applied *Mobile* to the analogous provisions of the FPA, concluding that the

The hearing was limited to the question of whether the dysfunctional California spot markets adversely affected the long-term bilateral markets, and if so, whether modification of any individual contract at issue was warranted.[60] In June 2003, FERC ruled that the *Mobile Sierra* "public interest" standard governed these contracts, and that the complainants did not met their burden of proof under the "public interest" standard to justify the modification or abrogation of the contracts.[61]

The Ninth Circuit, in September 2004, reaffirmed the legitimacy of market-based rates, but concluded that FERC was negligent in its responsibilities to monitor the behavior of market participants and ensure that markets were competitive. Market-based rates required the lack of market power, coupled with strict reporting requirements, to ensure that the rate is "just and reasonable" and that markets are not subject to manipulation. If the ability to monitor the market, or gauge the "just and reasonable" nature of the rates, is eliminated, then there is no effective federal regulation. The FPA cannot be construed to immunize those who

complaining utility could not supersede a contract rate simply by filing a new tariff. The Court held that the public utility may agree by contract to a rate affording less than a fair return, and the sole concern of the Commission would be whether the rate is so low as to adversely affect the public interest. *Id.*, at 354–55. Parties can contract out of the *Mobile-Sierra* presumption by specifying in their contracts that a new rate filed with the Commission would supersede the contract rate. *United Gas Pipe Line Co. v. Memphis Light, Gas and Water Div.*, 358 U.S. 103, 110–13 (1958).

The Commission began to refer to the two modes of review – one with the *Mobile-Sierra* presumption and the other without – as the public interest standard and the just and reasonable standard. The term "public interest standard" refers to the differing *application* of that just and reasonable standard to contract rates. *Morgan Stanley v. PUD No. 1 of Snohomish County*, 128 S.Ct. 2733, 2740 (2008). *Sierra* was grounded in the notion that sophisticated businesses enjoying presumptively equal bargaining power could be expected to negotiate a "just and reasonable" rate. Therefore, the Commission can declare a contract not to be just and reasonable only when the contract rate seriously harms the consuming public. FERC has ample authority to set aside a contract where there is unfair dealing at the contract formation stage, such as fraud or duress. But the mere fact that the market is imperfect, or even chaotic, is no reason to undermine the stabilizing force of contracts. *Id.* at 2746–47. However, if it is clear that one party to a contract engaged in such extensive unlawful market manipulation as to alter the playing field for contract negotiations, the Commission should not presume that the contract is just and reasonable. FERC may only abrogate a contract on these grounds, with a finding of a causal connection between unlawful activity and the contract rate. *Id.* at 2750–51.

60 *Public Utilities Commission of the State of California et al.*, 99 FERC ¶ 61,087, 61,383 (2002).

61 *Public Utilities Commission of the State of California et al.*, 103 FERC ¶ 61,354, at P3 (2003), *reh'g denied*, 105 FERC ¶ 61,182, (2003), *aff'd Morgan Stanley v PUD No. 1 of Snohomish County*, 128 S.Ct. 2733 (2008).

overcharge and manipulate markets in violation of the FPA. Under such circumstances, there is no filed tariff in place at all. The Court agreed with California that FERC improperly concluded that retroactive refunds were not legally available and remanded the refund issue to FERC.[62]

FERC responded by construing the Ninth Circuit's intent to apply to only the narrow issue of whether any seller that violated the quarterly reporting requirement failed to disclose an increased market share sufficient to give it the ability to exercise market power and thus cause its market-based rates to be unjust and unreasonable.[63] The Commission's market-based rate program presumed that, so long as a seller lacks, or has adequately mitigated, market power, it is unable to significantly influence prices in the market.[64] Since the Commission had already conducted a parallel proceeding to include behavior that violated the MMIP, it did not want to open another series of hearings that would have little practical import for the refund proceedings. FERC encouraged parties to reach settlements instead of resorting to litigation to settle the various proceeding arising out of the California energy crisis. Fair and reasonable settlements, rather than costly, protracted Commission and court litigation, were the most effective and efficient way to bring closure to the numerous proceedings. By June 2006, the Commission had accepted twenty-four settlements in various dockets, with more than $6.3 billion in refunds or other compensation to market participants.[65]

It was a clever strategic decision to focus on violation of market rules rather than whether market-based rates were just and reasonable. Trying to determine whether a market is sufficiently competitive that market-based rates are just and reasonable, as I've noted, is a complex undertaking, since all markets are imperfect to some degree. Focusing on whether market participants have violated market rules against gaming and

---

[62] *California, ex rel. Lockyer v. FERC*, 383 F.3d 1006, 1013, 1015–18 (9th Cir. 2004), cert. denied, *Coral Power, L.L.C. v. Cal. ex rel. Brown*, 551 U.S. 1140 (2007).

[63] *State of California, ex rel. Bill Lockyer v. British Columbia Power Exchange Corp.*, 122 FERC ¶ 61,260 at PP 28–32 (2008), *clarified*, 123 FERC 61,042 (2008), *order on reh'g*, 125 FERC ¶ 61,016 (2008).

[64] *See, e.g., Consumers Energy Co. v. FERC*, 367 F.3d 915, 923 (D.C. Cir. 2004) ("The Commission approves applications to sell electric energy at market-based rates only if the seller and its affiliates do not have, or adequately have mitigated, market power in the generation and transmission of such energy, and cannot erect other barriers to entry by potential competitors") (citing *Louisiana Energy and Power Authority v. FERC*, 141 F.3d 364, 365 (D.C. Cir. 1998)). *See also Tejas Power Corp. v. FERC*, 908 F.2d 998, 1004 (D.C. Cir. 1990).

[65] *Enron Power Marketing, Inc. et al.*, 115 FERC ¶ 61,376 at P 2 (2006).

strategic behavior simplifies litigation and avoids the refund issue. Since the market participant is on notice by the existence of market rules, the Commission merely has to show a violation of those rules and liability begins from the date of the violation. Complex economic issues may arise in damage calculations, but since the Commission is negotiating from a position of strength, it is easier to cajole violators to accept onerous settlement terms and avoid lengthy legal proceedings.

18

Two Steps Forward, One Step Back

The impact of higher gas prices on electricity markets would stop state deregulation efforts and result in financial distress in the independent power sector and retrenchment among energy traders. Retail competition was based on the same assumption as the IPP boom: cheap natural gas was here to stay, and the new gas-fired generators would permanently reduce the cost of electricity. What became apparent is that fools rush in, whereas wise regulators and investors tread carefully. In states that stayed the course, retail competition did advance, although primarily among larger customers and through demand aggregation, as potential savings were harder to achieve than expected and the barriers to switching by small consumers greater than anticipated. Independent power companies consolidated and reorganized but stayed the course. The rise in gas prices made many of their investments uneconomic; but when an energy company goes bankrupt, the shareholders suffer, but the steel on the ground remains in operation. Energy trading was fueled by dubious accounting methods exploiting the irrational exuberance of an investment bubble, but the underlying value of financial instruments survived the revelations of fraud and misstatements of earnings. Energy traders became better financed and more professional, and shifted from a get-rich perspective to developing a long-term presence as risk managers and liquidity suppliers in energy markets.

State Deregulation and Retail Competition

The serious problems that emerged with the new market and regulatory arrangements in California during the summer of 2000 cast a dark shadow over the electric utility restructuring and retail competition programs. In 2000, a number of states had become disillusioned with deregulation. At least a dozen states began taking a second look at opening their consumer power markets to competition. Some that adopted deregulation schedules considered delaying those timetables or altering the terms of implementation. Other states that already were proceeding cautiously to deregulation, such as North Carolina, Minnesota, and Alabama, slowed the process. California was the horror story, but numerous other states also faced price spikes and lukewarm competition for retail customers. There was growing awareness that deregulation had been oversold to consumers.[1] Arkansas, New Mexico, Oklahoma, and West Virginia decided to delay or postpone retail access, while California suspended its retail access program.[2]

In Massachusetts, a competitive retail market soon emerged for large and medium-sized commercial and industrial (C&I) customers. As of June 2002, 44 percent of the state's large C&I customer load and 18 percent of the state's medium C&I load were provided by competitive suppliers. However, almost all residential and small C&I customers received standard offer service or default service. The standard offer rate was low enough that competitors could not offer better rates, stifling competition until the standard offer rate was phased out by 2005. By the end of 2010, 13 percent of non-low-income and 8 percent of low-income residential customers were purchasing power from competitive suppliers, along with 25 percent of small C&I, 41 percent of medium C&I, and 77 percent of large C&I customers. Three years later, 18 percent of residential customers were purchasing power from competitive suppliers.[3]

[1] Andrew Caffrey and Russell Gold, "Deregulation Loses Steam In Many States," *Wall Street Journal*, January 25, 2001, A3; Courtney Barry, "Racing to Finish Last; Three States Slow Down the Rush Toward Electricity Competition," *Public Utilities Fortnightly* (April 15, 2001): 44.

[2] Kenneth Rose and Venkata Bujimalla, "2002 Performance Review of Electric Power Markets," National Regulatory Research Institute, conducted for Virginia State Corporation Commission (2002): 7.

[3] Roger Bergstrom, Christi Cao, and Tommie Tolbert, "Key Aspects of Electric Restructuring Supplemental Volume II: the State Summaries 2003 Updates," Florida Public Service Commission, Office of Market Monitoring and Strategic Analysis, July 2003, 31–32; Department of Energy, Energy Information Administration, *Massachusetts Restructuring Active*, April 2007; Electric Consumer Migration, at http://www.mass.gov/eea/grants-and-tech-assistance/guidance-technical-assistance/agencies-and-divisions/doer/electric-customer-migration-data.html (last visited August 17, 2014).

A similar pattern was seen in New York State, where only 6.7 percent of residential customers had switched by the end of 2005, along with 18 percent of smaller C&I and 56 percent of the largest customers. By the end of 2013, 24 percent of residential customers, 35 percent of smaller C&I, and 73 percent of larger customers had switched to competitive suppliers.[4] In New Jersey, only 15 percent of residential customers switched to competitive suppliers, compared to 28 percent of small C&I and 84 percent of larger C&I customers.[5]

Pennsylvania aggressively advertised a choice of new electricity providers and set the benchmark generation rates for traditional utilities at a fairly high level, which spurred consumers to choose new power providers. As a result, about 10 percent of residential and business users switched to other providers.[6] Most of the Pennsylvania utilities were in PJM and bought power out of the same wholesale market. Yet each of them had a different default service price, reflecting the different levels of their regulated retail prices (and stranded costs) prior to restructuring. Utilities with the highest initial switching rates (PECO and Duquesne) served Philadelphia and Pittsburgh and had high regulated retail prices and significant stranded costs prior to the implementation of retail competition. The other utilities in Pennsylvania had relatively low regulated rates prior to restructuring, and this meant there was little or no margin between their capped rates and the wholesale electricity price, stifling retail competition. Over time, as wholesale prices rose and residential margins declined, electricity retailers abandoned residential customers in favor of commercial customers who have lower marketing and overhead costs to serve.[7] By August 2014, 37 percent of residential customers, 46 percent of commercial customers, and 86 percent of industrial customers had switched to a competitive supplier.[8] Customers with higher

---

[4] New York State Public Service Commission, *Electric Retail Access Migration Summary*, at http://www3.dps.ny.gov/W/PSCWeb.nsf/All/441D4686DF065C5585257687006F396 D?OpenDocument (last visited August 17, 2014).

[5] Board of Public Utilities, New Jersey Electric Switching Statistics – April 2014, at http://www.nj.gov/bpu/pdf/energy/edc07.pdf (last visited August 17, 2014).

[6] Neela Banerjee, "A Dwindling Faith In Deregulation; New Ways to Harness Electricity," *New York Times*, September 15, 2000, C1.

[7] Paul Joskow, "The Difficult Transition to Competitive Electricity Markets in the U.S.," CEEPR (May 2003): 38–39.

[8] Pennsylvania Public Utility Commission, *Customers Switching to an Electric Generation Supplier, June 15, 2011*, at http://extranet.papowerswitch.com/stats/PAPowerSwitch-Stats.pdf?/download/PAPowerSwitch-Stats.pdf (last visited August 17, 2014).

usage levels, electric heating, and those living in more urban and more educated communities with higher median household incomes were more likely to switch.[9]

A similar trend was seen in Ohio, where retail competition began in January 2001. In the areas served by subsidiaries of AEP and Dayton Power and Light, utilities with low regulated prices, essentially no customers left the incumbent utility. However, in the areas served by First Energy's subsidiaries (Ohio Edison, The Illuminating Company, and Toledo Edison) there was significant movement of retail customers to electricity retailers. Some of this residential switching reflected municipal aggregation programs that allowed municipalities to purchase power on behalf of customers, accounting for 90 percent of the residential customers served by competition.[10] Switching accelerated the last few years in Ohio, with 50 percent of residential, 85 percent of commercial, and 85 percent of industrial customers using competitive suppliers.[11]

Public Act 286 of 2008 (Act 286), enacted on October 6, 2008, capped retail sales in Michigan at 10 percent of a utility's sales. Commercial and industrial customers accounted for virtually all of the participation in the electric choice programs in 2010.[12]

Illinois enacted legislation extending rate caps for an additional three years, until 2010, in light of procurement auctions by distribution utilities that suggested rate increases of 20–40 percent. Illinois utilities faced downgrades in their credit ratings and claimed the possibility of bankruptcy. A global settlement was ultimately reached under which Illinois utilities collectively provided $1 billion of rate relief to customers, mostly from Exelon Generation, to assist in paying the higher rates that had taken effect in the "transition" to market rates.[13] Illinois basically canceled residential competition, but had a high rate of large C&I

9 Andrew N. Kleit, Anastasia Shcherbakova, and Xu Chen, "Restructuring and the Retail Residential Market for Power in Pennsylvania," Working Paper (October 2011).

10 Paul L. Joskow, *The Difficult Transition to Competitive Electricity Markets in the U.S.,* CEEPR (May 2003): 39–40.

11 Ohio Public Utility Commission, Division of Planning and Analysis, *Summary of Switch Rates from EDUs to CRES Providers in Terms of Customers For the Month Ending March 31, 2011,* at http://www.puco.ohio.gov/puco/index.cfm/industry-information/statistical-reports/electric-customer-choice-switch-rates/#sthash.k1MRp9cI.vt9KtHtF .dpbs (last visited August 17, 2014).

12 Michigan Public Service Commission, *Status of Electric Competition in Michigan: Report for Calendar Year 2010,* February 1, 2011.

13 James Van Nostrand, "Constitutional Limitations on the Ability of States to Rehabilitate Their Failed Electric Utility Restructuring Plans," 31 *Seattle University Law Review* 593, 627–32 (2007).

taking service from retail providers, and good market penetration even among small C&I. More than one-third of the Com Ed load switched to competitive suppliers, and approximately 60 percent of customers with demand higher than 1 MW switched.[14] The Retail Electric Competition Act of 2006 created a new push to encourage retail competition, and in 2010, municipalities and counties were allowed to aggregate electrical load. By 2014, two-thirds of Illinois retail customers were buying power from independent suppliers, although three-quarters of these customers received that power through government aggregators. Three-quarters of large commercial load and 90 percent of industrial load were served by independent suppliers.[15]

In a few states, the combination of aborted restructuring and increases in electricity costs due to fuel costs and higher construction costs led to drastic actions. The Maryland Restructuring Act mandated residential rate cuts ranging from 3 percent to 7.5 percent, with rate caps until 2004 to 2006, depending on the utility. This worked fine until the cost of procuring energy by the utilities rose substantially in 2005, owing to increases in natural gas prices and exacerbated by transmission congestion in PJM East. Electric supply price increases in the competitive 2005–06 procurements increased customer bills by 35–72 percent. Governor Martin O'Malley issued a media release stating that deregulation had failed and that he would support reregulating Maryland's electricity markets.[16] In June 2006, the Maryland General Assembly passed SB 1, which attempted to terminate the terms of the incumbent members of the Maryland PSC. SB 1 would also phase in the rate increase for Baltimore Gas & Electric, limiting the July 1, 2006 rate increase to 15 percent and deferring payment of the rest of the increase over ten years. On June 22, 2006, Governor Ehrlich vetoed the bill. The Maryland Court of Appeals ruled that the state legislature could not dismiss members of the Maryland PSC and nominate its own slate. The Maryland PSC approved an additional 50 percent rate increase for Baltimore Gas & Electric customers.[17]

---

[14] Scott Potter, "After the Freeze: Issues Facing Some State Regulators as Electric Restructuring Transition Periods End," The National Regulatory Research Institute (September 2003): 4.

[15] Illinois Commerce Commission, *Office of Retail Market Development 2014 Annual Report.*

[16] EIA, *Maryland Restructuring Active*, January 2010.

[17] James Van Nostrand, "Constitutional Limitations on the Ability of States to Rehabilitate Their Failed Electric Utility Restructuring Plans," *Seattle University Law Review* 31 (2008): 612–19.

Still, despite all this angst, 25 percent of residential customers, 59 percent of medium C&I, and 88 percent of large C&I were participating in retail choice.[18]

Delaware also experienced rate increases of 59 percent when rate caps expired in May 2006. A 2006 Act spread the increase over two years and provided for payment of deferred electricity costs over a seventeen-month period. In Virginia, with rate caps due to expire in 2011, termination of these caps was accelerated by two years, combined with the elimination of retail choice except for large customers.[19]

Texas has long been touted as the model for retail competition, but this is partially a triumph of perception over reality. The PUCT's price-to-beat rules assured a sufficient margin to encourage entry of REPs serving the small commercial and residential markets, which also meant higher rates for less sophisticated consumers. Affiliated (with the incumbent utility) REPs were required to sell electricity at the price to beat, although they could offer lower rates beginning January 1, 2005 (or earlier if at least 40 percent of smaller customers move to competitors).[20] As of September 2004, about 18 percent of residential customers were taking service from a nonaffiliated retail electric provider. By September 2006, 34 percent of residential customers, and 39 percent of eligible commercial customers accounting for 67 percent of commercial sales, were purchasing power from unaffiliated REPs.[21] Despite a growing gap between competitive prices and the price to beat, residential customers were slow to respond to the opportunity for potential savings. This effect was notable in 2005 when natural gas prices peaked, driving up the price to beat, and affiliated REPs preferred to maintain higher prices and allow market share to erode to reap profits from less sophisticated consumers. In 2010, legacy providers' standard rates were 10–50 percent higher than the lowest competitive offers.[22] As of September 2010, 53 percent of residential and

[18] Maryland Public Service Commission, *Electric Choice Monthly Enrollment Reports*, at http://webapp.psc.state.md.us/intranet/ElectricInfo/enrollmentrpt_new.cfm (last visited August 17, 2014).

[19] Van Nostrand, "Constitutional Limitations on the Ability of States to Rehabilitate Restructuring Plans," at 620–25.

[20] Rulemaking Relating to Price to Beat, Project No. 21409, Order Adopting New § 25.41 (March 21, 2001).

[21] PUCT, *Scope of Competition in Electric Markets in Texas* (January 2005): 9–11; PUCT, *Scope of Competition in Electric Markets in Texas* (January 2007): 65–67.

[22] PUCT, *Scope of Competition in Electric Markets in Texas* (January 2007): 8; PUCT, *Scope of Competition in Electric Markets in Texas* (January 2011): 50. An explanation of consumer inertia may lie in the incumbent enjoying an economically significant brand, and the costs to consumers of searching for and switching to a more competitive REP.

62 percent of commercial and industrial customers had taken advantage of the opportunity to switch to a competitive REP.[23] The share of residential customers supplied by competitive REPs increased to 59 percent in 2012.[24]

Despite nine years of competition, the REPs with large shares of the retail market are affiliates or former affiliates of large electric utility companies. At the start of retail competition, affiliated REPs inherited the customers in the service areas of the utilities from which they were formed. However, only TXU maintained ownership of its retail operations. Direct Energy (a subsidiary of the British firm Centrica) acquired the affiliated REP business of AEP and Reliant Energy (now owned by NRG) the retail business of old Houston Industries. Many of the larger REPs are associated with major out-of-state energy companies. One reason was the requirement for financial liquidity; increases in electricity prices in 2005 led six REPs to cease operations.[25]

The fundamental problem with retail competition is that electricity is a commodity. The only way to compete for retail customers is by price, but this is self-defeating, because even if suppliers have low-cost energy that enables them to undercut the competition, they are absorbing the opportunity cost of not selling at the market price. Unless they can exploit some sort of economies of scale or scope, sacrificing potential profits to gain market share is an irrational strategy. Although a few suppliers tried to develop "green" power, the market for premium-priced socially conscious electricity is confined to a small minority of customers. The quality and reliability of service will be independent of the electricity supplier, because the distribution company handles the actual power delivery. While kilowatts can be differentiated by the time of day, most small customers do not have time-of-day meters and would gain little from time-of-use rates. Because retail consumption is basically nonresponsive to price, retail competition has little impact on efficiency at the wholesale level.[26]

Households in higher-income neighborhoods have a much higher price elasticity of demand and lower switching costs, and exhibit a faster erosion of the brand advantage. Ali Hortacsu, Seyed Madanizadeh, and Steven Puller, "Power to Choose: An Analysis of Consumer Behavior in the Texas Retail Electricity Market," Working Paper (April 2012): 4–5.

[23] PUCT, *Scope of Competition in Electric Markets in Texas* (January 2011): 55–56.
[24] PUCT, *Scope of Competition in Electric Markets in Texas* (January 2013): 20.
[25] PUCT, *Scope of Competition in Electric Markets in Texas* (January 2007): 71.
[26] Steve Isser, "Electricity Deregulation: Kilowatts for Nothing and Your BTUs for Free," *Review of Policy Research* 20 (2004): 217–36; Paul L. Joskow, "Why Do We Need

The primary problem of establishing meaningful retail competition is to provide customers with sufficient incentives to shop between electricity providers and supply incentives for more efficient production. Getting customers to make the initial switch runs up against behavioral and limited rationality considerations that are hard to overcome with the relatively small gains available to most consumers.[27] Experience with retail competition so far has shown that only a small percentage of customers switch from their default supplier each year. Consumers face switching costs when changing their supplier, including search costs (identifying suppliers and comparing offers), learning costs (understanding their new options for supply), and transaction costs (negotiating new contracts). Once a customer has been obtained, there will be some barriers to switching, depending on the transparency of the retail electric market (i.e., cost of search and complexity of contracts). This creates incentives to "purchase" customers from incumbent utilities if the margins are sufficient to cover acquisition costs.[28]

A much larger proportion of load has shifted to new suppliers, as large industrial and commercial customers are willing to switch for small percentage changes in price.[29] This behavior reflects the relative magnitude of potential savings versus the cost of searching for a better price. A residential customer might only realize $20–30 a year from a 5 percent saving on the wholesale component of electricity, while a mid-sized company might save thousands of dollars. A large customer could also save additional money through time-of-day metering and demand management and demand response programs, providing an incentive for a supplier to tailor a product for that customer.

True retail competition will require technological advances in smart meters and automated controls, at prices that make it practical to install equipment in residences, which would allow customers to specify their trade-offs between price and consumption, even to the extent of programming appliances to turn on or off in response to price signals. In turn, this

---

Electricity Retailers? Or You Can Get It Cheaper Wholesale?" Revised Discussion Draft (February 13, 2000).

[27] Timothy J. Brennan, "Consumer Preference Not to Choose: Methodological and Policy Implications," Resources for the Future, Discussion Paper, RFF DP 05-51 (November 2005); Chris M. Wilson and Catherine Waddams Price, "Do Consumers Switch to the Best Supplier?" *Oxford Economic Papers* 62 (2010): 647–68.

[28] Christophe Defeuilley, "Retail Competition in Electricity Markets," *Energy Policy* 37 (2009): 378.

[29] Rose and Bujimalla, *2002 Performance Review of Electric Power Markets*, v.

would allow suppliers to supply energy management services instead of commodity electricity, as well as aggregate customers into packages that could be matched with the appropriate generation portfolios that would minimize the cost of providing electricity.

IPPs and Market Trading: Easy Money Ain't So Easy

The expectation that new gas-fired generation burning cheap gas would undercut conventional electricity generation drove an investment boom in new combined-cycle plants. Competitors for electricity supply contracts included independent power producers (IPPs) such as AES, Calpine, and Reliant Resources; traditional utilities such as Duke Power, Dominion Resources, Consolidated Edison, Electricité de France, and British Energy; gas companies such as Vectren, Centrica, and Gaz de France; and oil majors such as BP Amoco, ExxonMobil, and Shell. The prospect of highly efficient combined-cycle plants supplanting existing base load plants encouraged IPPs to rush into the new markets. By the end of 2000, around 212,000 MW of gas-fired generation capacity additions had reached at least preliminary stages of development, with combined-cycle plants accounting for about 80 percent of this capacity. Between 1997 and 2002, 147,500 MW of new generation capacity was completed, almost all by IPPs.[30]

Project financing often utilized nonrecourse financing, where the loans were securitized by the project and the parent company had limited financial exposure. Project financing traditionally was used to finance the development of mines and oil fields, where the underlying asset could be valued by the lender. Before deregulation, to develop a power plant, an IPP would acquire a site, sign a long-term PPA with a creditworthy counterparty (usually a regulated utility), negotiate contract and fuel supply contracts, and obtain the necessary regulatory approvals from the utility regulatory commission and environmental agencies. The developer would arrange financing based on the net value of the bundle of contracts associated with the asset.

Developers using project finance could leverage a relatively small amount of equity into a massive building campaign, and the relatively short time from development to completion meant upward pressure on the costs of suitable sites, fuel contracts, and construction. During the

---

[30] Paul L. Joskow, "The Difficult Transition to Competitive Electricity Markets in the U.S.," CEEPR (May 2003), table 2.

course of development, financial and contractual commitments to third parties (such as turbine manufacturers, fuel suppliers, ISOs, creditors, and engineering companies) become more irreversible. As sunk costs were incurred, the break-even revenue for the remaining portion of plant development declined, encouraging plan completion if even projected net revenues were lower than expected as of the date of the initial go-ahead decision. Once commitments to turbines were made, site selection and permitting funneled this generation capacity wherever it was economical to build. Timing for obtaining air, water, and local zoning permits vary dramatically from state to state. While the process in New York and California took two to three years or longer, obtaining permits in Texas averaged about one year. Texas approved about fifty new facilities in the 1995–2000 period, compared to only one facility in New York. States such as California and New York had high levels of public involvement, leading to delays from "not in my back yard" (NIMBY) syndrome, and in the case of coal and nuclear plants, "Build Absolutely Nothing Anywhere Near Anything" (BANANA).[31]

Banks convinced themselves that the new IPPs could obtain a predictable stream of revenues from electricity markets, allowing valuation of the generation asset, similar to other resource infrastructure projects. Without long-term contracts to support payment obligations, lenders offered bridge and medium-term loans of two to five years to bring a power plant from construction to initial operation. Once the plant was proven, the expectation was that these loans would be replaced with less expensive permanent financing that more closely matched the life of the project. The physical assets were likely held in a special-purpose entity separate from the balance sheet of the sponsor. These new hybrids further evolved into "portfolio financing," combining multiple projects into a single, cross-collateralized jumbo financing of, typically, $1 billion or more. Companies employed bulk purchasing, cross-utilization of equipment, and sharing of spare parts to allow the lenders to view the portfolio as a single economic unit. Combining several projects saved time and money by allowing utilization of one set of bankers, consultants, and lawyers. There was a perception of a decrease in the overall risk profile through diversification of projects and cross-collateralization. Merchant plant portfolio financings usually required higher equity positions and employed prioritized money flows to the lenders in the case of covenant breaches caused by poor power plant performance, interest rate hikes,

---

[31] EPRI, "Prospects for Boom/Bust in the U.S. Electric Power Industry," at 5–6.

regional overbuild, or other problems. By 2001, the biggest players in the industry were using portfolio financing, including Calpine, Mirant, NRG, Panda, Sithe, PSEG, and Cinergy.[32]

One important driver of the boom-bust cycle in electricity generation was the lag times between the initial decision to go ahead and the realization that overcapacity was inevitable. The development process for greenfield facilities was from three to four years, with turbine acquisition coming first, followed by site construction, beginning about twenty-four months before start-up. There were only three companies worldwide that built the majority of utility scale machines: General Electric, Simmons Westinghouse, and Alstom. Skyrocketing turbine demand created backlogs of three to four years for large turbines, requiring contractual commitments early in the developmental process. At one point, Calpine, Duke, Florida Power & Light, Entergy, and Dynegy locked up 320 turbines, with a capacity of 70,000 MW, out of a worldwide annual production capacity of approximately 400 units. Contracts were generally not readily assignable without permission from the manufacturer, and secondary market sales invalidated warranties.[33]

The merchant generating and trading sector benefited from a "financial bubble" similar to the one supporting telecom and Internet stocks, giving them easy access to cheap capital. Debt issuance (bank and fixed income) was almost $22 billion in 1999, reached $35 billion in 2000, and then $42.7 billion in 2001, before falling to $12.6 billion in 2002 and evaporating in 2003.[34]

Developers ignored the warning signs and not only invested in new capacity but also failed to choose technologies to guard against market risk. Warnings were issued as early as 1999 that project sponsors may face a boom-bust cycle. A combination of new plants and expanded older plants might trigger price declines of as much as 20 percent.[35] However, some analysts were still pushing merchant generation as late as September 2001. A Credit Suisse analyst suggested that Calpine and Mirant would

[32] George Humphrey and Thomas J. Perich, "State of the Art: An Analysis of Portfolio Power Project Financing," *Project Finance* (September 2001).

[33] EPRI, "Prospects for Boom/Bust in the U.S. Electric Power Industry," 5–4, 5–5.

[34] Société Générale, "Investment in Power Generation: A Banker's Perspective," presentation, March 25, 2003, slide 9, at http://www.oecd-nea.org/ndd/investment/session2/deluze.pdf (last visited on January 2, 2012).

[35] Ann Chambers, "Merchant Fever Rising." *Power Engineering*, August 1999, at http://pepei.pennnet.com/display_article/362322/6/ARTCL/none/none/1/Merchant-Fever-Rising (last visited January 2, 2012).

be able to hit their aggressive earnings targets in the next few years.[36] A careful assessment of the potential for a bust cycle (of excess entry) would have resulted in decisions to forego optimal heat rates, predicated on the assumption that new combined-cycle gas units would be competing with base load coal units, and choose turbine designs designed to cycle on and off every day. The new electricity markets provided demand for services such as regulation and spinning reserves, which could be provided by designing combined-cycle plants to compete in these markets when energy spreads were too low to provide net revenues.[37]

Moody's and Standard and Poor's noted the higher risk associated with merchant generation. The rating of a merchant plant would be lower than that of a traditional single-asset independent power producer with the same capital structure and cash flow coverage because of the greater volatility of its cash flows. An investment-grade-rated merchant power plant should have a break-even point, where it fully covers its debt service obligations, between 30 percent and 50 percent below a reasonable market forecast price. Generators that meet base load demand will have relatively more predictable cash flows and higher ratings. Other plants will face greater uncertainty in their dispatch and therefore in their cash flows. The rating agencies used more conservative assumptions concerning fuel inflation and electricity price predictions and the pace of retirement for older units than consulting studies done for banks and developers. Moody's observed that with relatively little capital spending, older plants could be made competitive.[38]

As spark spreads (calculated by converting fuel cost to $/MMBtu, multiplying by the composite heat rate to produce a fuel cost per MWh, and subtracting this from the spot electricity price) declined in 2002, cash flow from many of these projects failed to cover debt service. While a decline in western prices was predictable, a drop in spark spreads in ERCOT (based on a 7,000 Btu/kWh heat rate) from $22–23/MWh in

---

36 Richard Stravos, "Reversal of Fortune? Wall Street Rethinks Merchant Power," *Public Utility Fortnightly* (September 15, 2001), at http://www.pur.com/pubs/3824.cfm (last visited January 3, 2012).

37 Drew Robb, "Ancillary Markets Provide Revenue Opportunity for Under-Utilized Gas Turbines," *Power Engineering* (September 1, 2003), at http://www.power-eng.com/articles/print/volume-107/issue-9/features/ancillary-markets-provide-revenue-opportunity-for-under-utilized-gas-turbines.html (last visited January 6, 2012); Joe Zwers, "Double Duty," *Power Engineering* (February 1, 2005), at http://www.power-eng.com/articles/print/volume-109/issue-2/features/double-duty.html (last visited January 6, 2012).

38 "The Importance of Being Economic: Credit Risks of US Merchant Power Plants," *Moody's Investment Service*, May 1999; Peter Rigby, "Merchant Power: Project Finance Criteria," *Standard and Poor's*, October 1999.

1999–2000 to $12 in 2001 and $6 in 2002 took many developers and banks by surprise.[39] For a 500 MW unit expecting to run 8,000 hours a year, that was a drop from $90 million to $24 million in net revenues. To make matters worse, as natural gas prices rose, these units were no longer competitive in off-peak hours, operated for only twelve-to-sixteen hours per day, and suffered an efficiency penalty from having to cycle on and off each day. This drove net revenues down further.

The end of the stock market bubble, a better understanding by investors of the real economics and market risks associated with building merchant generating plants and trading commodity electricity, accounting improprieties, credit downgrades, refinancing problems, and uncertainties concerning industry restructuring, wholesale market rules, and retail competition decimated the merchant generating and trading sector.[40] What had been an enormous boom turned into an enormous bust. The optimistic assumptions that fueled the merchant energy boom, made in the excitement of a huge market created by deregulation, turned out to be unfounded. The worst-case scenario that these companies and their lenders considered possible but remote became the base-case scenario. The independent power industry built more generation than the market could use. Natural gas prices rose to levels that made gas-fired generation uncompetitive with base load coal plants. Contrary to the assumptions of many market and feasibility studies, retirements of older coal and nuclear plants did not occur. New owners acquired these older plants, invested in upgrades and retrofits, and increased plant efficiencies and availabilities. Electricity generation turned out to be an industry that was susceptible to boom-bust cycles, not unlike the mining and chemical industries.[41]

The equity values of generation and marketing companies fell dramatically between 2000 and 2003. Short on cash, independent producers postponed or canceled many proposed plants. Investment in new power lines also lagged. About 125,000 MW of new power projects that had been announced prior to 2001 were canceled.[42] Bankers, once burned, put more stringent conditions on financing merchant generation.

---

[39] Société Générale, "Investment in Power Generation: A Banker's Perspective," at slide 10.

[40] Paul Joskow, "The Difficult Transition to Competitive Electricity Markets in the U.S.," 22–23.

[41] Peter Rigby, "Energy Merchant Turmoil," *Standard and Poor's*, March 2004.

[42] Alex Berenson, "Power Giants Have Trouble Raising Cash For Plants," *New York Times*, May 16, 2002 at http://www.nytimes.com/2002/05/16/business/enron-s-many-strands-energy-market-power-giants-have-trouble-raising-cash-for.html?ref=dynegyinc (last visited September 21, 2011).

During the boom, project finance for a new merchant plant would have 70 percent nonrecourse debt and 30 percent equity. Companies that were highly leveraged, had opaque accounting, or were overly aggressive saw funding dry up. The only projects that could attract debt with high levels of leverage were those with contracts that ensured adequate cash flow for debt service.[43]

Smart investors waited to buy rather than rushed to build, exploiting secondary markets in discounted generation assets as low energy prices put pressure on net revenues. Transactions of new natural gas power plants in 2003/2004 were completed at discounted prices. The Duke Southeast 5,300 MW gas-fired portfolio sale transacted at an average price of $89/kW, compared to an original investment cost of between $300 and $600/kW just three to four years prior.[44] During the 2003–2004 period, at least twenty-five financial groups purchased assets accounting for close to 40,000 MW of capacity at an average price of $365/kW. Asset sellers were primarily the nonregulated merchant arms of investor-owned utilities (35,000 of the 60,000 MWs sold) and distressed merchant generators. Purchasers included energy traders such as Goldman Sachs, J.P. Morgan, Merrill Lynch, Louis Dreyfess, and Bank of America; private equity firms such as Blackstone, Carlyle, Kohlberg Kravis Roberts, and Texas Pacific Group; and industry-focused investors, including Delta, ArcLight, Complete Energy, LS Power, and Rockland Capital.[45]

Toward the end of the decade, the prospect of capacity shortages engendered a new wave of investment in generation. However, the irrational exuberance of the early years of the IPP boom was replaced by cold calculation. Many plants were built on brownfield sites, where costs were lower and NIMBY opposition was muted.[46] A significant amount of construction involved repowering brownfield coal sites with

43 Steve Blankinship, "Where's the Money? Power Project Finance," *Power Engineering* (October 2002), at http://pepei.pennnet.com/display_article/160306/6/ARTCL/none/none/1/Where's-the-Money?:-Power-Project-Finance (last visited January 3, 2012).

44 Shanthi Muthiah, "Generation Asset Valuation: Are We at the Nadir for Gas-Fired Power Plants?" *Electric Light & Power* (November/December 2004), at http://www.elp.com/articles/print/volume-82/issue-7/risk-management/generation-asset-valuation-are-we-at-the-nadir-for-gas-fired-power-plants.html (last visited January 3, 2012).

45 Oliver Wyman, *Enter Stage Left: The New Energy Merchants*, 2006, at http://www.oliverwyman.com/pdf_files/Energy05-New_Energy_Merchants.pdf (last visited January 3, 2012).

46 Brownfield site repowering involves demolishing the existing unit, except for possibly the cooling water system and switchyard, and constructing a new plant. There can be

combined-cycle plants, using the building, transmission interconnection facilities, roads, and other existing infrastructure.[47] The addition of incremental MWs through modernizing existing coal and nuclear units was another alternative to building new plants. When coal units required environmental upgrades, concurrent with the environmental equipment installation, turbine generator modernization could provide incremental capacity at a modest installed cost. Generator upgrades could provide incremental capacity at costs of $900 to $1,500/kW. Upgrading existing nuclear assets was another inexpensive source of new capacity. More than forty uprates and extended uprates were approved by the NRC, expanding nuclear capacity by 3,000 to 4,000 MW. This capacity was available at much lower and predictable capital costs than building new nuclear plants could offer.[48]

Companies building new gas-fired plants demanded greater operational flexibility than many project developers sought in the 1990s. New plants, especially in competitive markets, need to meet requirements to supply ancillary services (e.g., ten-minute and thirty-minute ramp times, clutches on combustion turbines), to be eligible to obtain revenues from these markets. When developers bought combined-cycle plants in the past, their pro forma typically was based on running 8,000 hours a year. Today, operators must cycle their gas plants, reflecting low electricity prices in off hours due to excess coal, nuclear, and wind capacity in many regions. New combined-cycle plants are equipped with supplemental firing (for meeting peak demand conditions) and designed for daily cycling and weekend shutdown. Combustion turbines have been engineered to approach full power within ten minutes after starting up, making them a

---

savings in the permitting process, transmission access, and avoidance of political opposition. Plants can also be repowered by replacing an existing boiler with a combustion turbine and a heat recovery steam generator. See William Stenzel, Dale Sopocy, and Stanley Pace, "Repowering Existing Fossil Steam Plants," at http://soapp.epri.com/papers/ Repowering_Fossil_Plants.pdf (last visited January 3, 2012). Generation companies are aware of the value of brownfield sites: "In addition to reduced costs for developing new generation at existing sites because of our ownership of the land and our ownership of and/or access to infrastructure, regulators frequently prefer that new generation be added at existing sites (brownfield development) rather than at new sites (greenfield development)." GenOn Energy, *Form 10-K, 2011*, 6.

[47] Steve Blankinship, "A Different Kind of Boom," *Power Engineering* (October 2007), at http://pepei.pennnet.com/display_article/309145/6/ARTCL/none/none/1/Cover-Feature:- A-Different-Kind-of-Boom (last visited January 3, 2012).

[48] David Walsh, "Back to Basics in Tough Times," *Power Engineering* (June 2009), at http://www.power-eng.com/articles/print/volume-113/issue-6/departments/peak-load/ back-to-basics-in-tough-times.html (last visited January 3, 2012).

stand-alone solution in regions with high wind, which will be purchasing more fast-start reserves.[49]

Enron's role as power marketer and energy trader was exactly what a deregulated electricity market needed had the company focused on building a legitimate trading and arbitrage business. Enron bought and sold futures contracts and helped make a market in electricity. It was estimated that Enron controlled about one-quarter of the country's energy trading.[50] Instruments such as weather derivatives, introduced in 1997, helped buyers and sellers of electricity hedge risk. Close to 5,000 weather contracts with a total exposure of $7.5 billion were transacted between October 1997 and April 2001.[51]

The downfall of Enron affected just about everyone with a connection to the energy business, from power producers to end-users to Wall Street analysts. In response to the Enron crash, credit-rating agencies raised the credit standards for generators and traders. This forced energy concerns to rebalance their debt-to-asset ratios, reduce debt, and cut back investments. Wall Street realized the business of trading power might be riskier than investors and analysts previously thought. Energy merchants all too often lacked the level of market risk management, liquidity management, and internal controls of sophisticated traders in the securities markets. The crisis at Enron exposed a flaw in the business model of energy-trading companies. Most companies can survive if their debt ratings are lowered below investment grade, although they will have higher borrowing costs. The threat of ratings cuts pushed Enron into bankruptcy, because the company's partners were unwilling to trade with it without an investment-grade credit rating. Once Moody's and its peers lowered their ratings, Enron collapsed.[52]

Steps taken by many companies in the merchant energy sector since the end of 2001 were insufficient to restore investor confidence. Deregulation contributed to increased business risks within most operating segments.

---

[49] Steve Blankinship, "A Different Kind of Boom."

[50] Kurt Eichenwald, "Enron's Collapse: Audacious Climb to Success Ended in a Dizzying Plunge," *New York Times*, January 13, 2002, A1.

[51] Magali Delmas and Yesim Tokat, "Deregulation, Governance Structures, and Efficiency: The U.S. Electric Utility Sector," *Strategic Management Journal* 26 (2005): 444, fn. 3.

[52] Alex Berenson, "Deal Is Over But Not Dynegy's Troubles," *New York Times*, November 30, 2001, at http://www.nytimes.com/2001/11/30/business/enron-s-collapse-the-suitor-deal-is-over-but-not-dynegy-s-troubles.html?ref=dynegyinc (last visited September 21, 2011); Kenneth W. Betz, "Energy Industry Short-Circuited by 'Enronitis' Epidemic; Energy Industry Forced to Rebuild Credibility," *Energy User News*, July 1, 2002.

From a ratings standpoint, increased business risk requires a commensurate increase in financial strength. The lack of regulatory oversight of trading activity and opaque accounting were not conducive to maintaining counterparty confidence. Energy trading may lack investment-grade characteristics unless it is ancillary to a more stable core business that generates strong sustainable cash flow.[53]

The shares of energy traders were driven down as several, including Reliant, Dynegy, and CMS Energy, acknowledged that they engaged in round-trip trades of electricity. The transactions, known as wash trades or round trips in the industry, involve swapping large blocks of energy in trades that essentially cancel each other out. Such transactions were used to inflate trading volumes but were generally not considered illegal unless they led to misleading claims about a company's finances.[54] The collapse of Enron caused investors to take a hard look at the accounting practices and heavy debt loads carried by other big power producers. They discovered that the companies had used a variety of accounting gimmicks to make their balance sheets look healthier and their sales and profits seem larger than was really the case. The practices appear to have stemmed from the companies' desire to persuade investors to finance expansion. Changes in Financial Accounting Standards Board rules made energy trading less valuable from a "fool the market" perspective. The new rules required that energy-trading revenues be reported "net" rather than "gross." This limited revenues to fees and margins rather than the entire amount of the contract, drastically reducing companies' gross revenues and thus apparent size. Twelve energy merchant firms lost 86 percent of their market capitalization between May 1, 2001 and July 23, 2002 – a combined $222 billion. Dynegy, Williams, El Paso, and others sold off billions of dollars of hard assets to remain afloat, and Calpine, Mirant, NRG, and Dynegy ended up in bankruptcy. Williams Company was downgraded twice in July 2002 and could not issue commercial paper, float bonds, or sell new shares of stock. The company instead borrowed $900 million from Lehman Brothers and Berkshire Hathaway, pledging

---

[53] "Moody's Calls for Merchant Energy Trading Restructuring," *Foster Natural Gas Report* (June 6, 2002): 7.

[54] Danny Hakim, "CMS Energy Declines on Report of S.E.C. Inquiry," *New York Times*, May 14, 2002, at http://www.nytimes.com/2002/05/14/business/cms-energy-declines-on-report-of-sec-inquiry.html?ref=dynegyinc (last visited September 21, 2011); David Barboza, "Energy Trades Echoed in Broadband Market," *New York Times*, May 17, 2002, at http://www.nytimes.com/2002/05/17/business/energy-trades-echoed-in-broadband-market.html?ref=dynegyinc (last visited September 21, 2011).

gas reserves as collateral. A total of $90 billion in medium-term debt in the electricity sector had to be refinanced over a four-year period.[55]

The shakeout showed investors, regulators, and analysts the true face of an industry that had insisted Enron was a rogue. Many of the companies were badly run and cash-poor, despite their hefty paper profits. Repeatedly, investors heard energy industry executives swear that their companies did not engage in murky accounting, faulty economic modeling, or controversial trading, only to have events contradict them. Power trading became consolidated among fewer companies, with assets and energy businesses to provide cash flow and counterparty confidence. Companies such as Duke Energy and American Electric Power, and investment banks that already traded power, such Goldman Sachs, Morgan Stanley, and UBS Warburg, took on a larger role, as did companies like Electricité de France, by purchasing trading firms. Hedge funds also set up energy-trading desks to take advantage of the volatility in electricity markets.[56] The result was a more financially stable, sophisticated group of financial traders. The downside was that many of these companies saw the industry only in terms of financial trades, and committed the same excesses the financial industry demonstrated in other markets.[57]

---

[55] Jacqueline Lang Weaver, "Can Energy Markets Be Trusted? The Effect of the Rise and Fall of Enron on Energy Markets," *Houston Business and Tax Law Journal* 4 (2004): 92, fn. 297, 109–10.

[56] Neela Banerjee, "Bottom Still Far Off for Energy Traders," *New York Times*, July 25, 2002, at http://www.nytimes.com/2002/07/25/business/bottom-still-far-off-for-energy-traders.html?ref=dynegyinc (last visited September 21, 2011).

[57] A number of financial companies have been the subjects of FERC investigations into market manipulation. See *Deutsche Bank Energy Trading*, 142 FERC 61,056 (2013) (Order Approving Stipulation and Consent Decree); *J.P. Morgan Ventures Energy Corporation* 142 FERC 61,190 (2012) (Order Suspending Market Based Rate Authority); *In Re Make-Whole Payments and Related Bidding Strategies*, 144 FERC 61,068 (2013); *Constellation Energy Commodities*, 145 FERC 61,062 (2013) (Order Approving Stipulation and Consent Agreement).

19

FERC Cracks the Whip

Order 2000 picked up on the voluntary guidelines offered for ISO formation in Order 888. Although FERC's stated objective was for all transmission-owning entities in the nation, including nonpublic utility entities, to place their transmission facilities under the control of RTOs, FERC refrained from ordering participation, preferring to avoid challenges to its authority. Although most utilities filed on time, the Commission rejected all of the initial filings on various pretexts, including inadequate scope, lack of independence in governance, and failure to provide sufficient detail. Over the next two years, various proposed RTOs would refile, and the Commission would hold a series of meetings attempting to garner support for RTOs, specifically proposals to merge various groups and existing ISOs. Part of the problem was that the Commission overreached, with a series of orders issued in July 2001, directing the establishment of single RTOs for the northeast and southeast regions and suggested just two more RTOs (one for the midwest and one for the west) would be adequate for the rest of the country (except Texas and Florida).[1] It was not until December 2001, when FERC approved the MISO RTO proposal, that a RTO was approved.[2] In addition to MISO, the Commission provisionally approved other

---

[1] *PJM Interconnection, L.L.C.*, 96 FERC ¶ 61,061 (2001); *New York Independent System Operator, Inc.*, 96 FERC ¶ 61,059 (2001); *Bangor Hydro-Electric Company et al.*, 96 FERC ¶ 61,063 (2001); *Southern Company Services, Inc.*, 96 FERC ¶ 61,064 (2001); *GridSouth Transco, LLC et al.*, 96 FERC ¶ 61,067 (2001); *Avista Corporation et al.*, 96 FERC ¶ 61,058 (2001).
[2] *Midwest Independent Transmission System Operator, Inc.*, 97 FERC ¶ 61,326 (2001).

RTOs[3] and authorized operation of Independent Transmission Companies that operate under an RTO umbrella.[4]

Enron officials faulted Chairman Hébert and his unwillingness to push vertically integrated companies to deal openly with transmission access issues. Hébert claimed that Kenneth Lay suggested to him that Hébert 's future tenure as FERC chair would depend on his support for Enron's proposals to deregulate the electricity industry. Hébert said that Lay prodded him to back a national push for retail competition in the energy business and a faster pace in opening up access to the electricity transmission grid. Lay said he told the chairman that the final decision on his future was going to be the president's. Hébert was replaced by Pat Wood shortly after Hébert made public his claim about Enron's pressure.[5]

Lay had an unusual opportunity to make his case about candidates in writing and in person to Clay Johnson, the White House personnel chief. He presented a list of eight recommended candidates, including Pat Wood and Nora Brownell. Senior Bush administration officials said they welcomed Lay's input but did not always embrace it. For example, President Bush backed away from curbing carbon dioxide emissions, an effort supported by Enron, which had looked to trade emission rights as part of its energy business. The two most important advisers in deciding on nominees for the Commission were Andrew Lundquist, the director of Vice President Cheney's energy task force, and Pat Wood. When the White House filled the two Republican slots on the federal agency, Wood was the first choice. Senator Lott and Hébert had both been told that Hébert could remain chairman until the administration's nominees were confirmed by the full Senate, and remain a commissioner until the end of his term, which expired in 2004.[6]

---

3 *See GridSouth Transco, LLC*, 94 FERC ¶ 61,273 (2001); *GridFlorida, LLC*, 94 FERC ¶ 61,363 (2001); and *PJM Interconnection, LLC*, 96 FERC ¶ 61,061 (2001).

4 *See TRANSLink Transmission Company, L.L.C. et al.*, 99 FERC ¶ 61,106 (2002) (authorizing operation of an ITC within the Midwest ISO); *Alliance Companies et al.*, 99 FERC ¶ 61,105 (2002).

5 Timothy P. Duane, "Regulation's Rationale: Learning from the California Energy Crisis," *Yale Journal on Regulation* 17 (2002): 493, fn. 80; Lowell German and Jeff Garth, "Power Trader Tied to Bush Finds Washington All Ears," *New York Times*, May 25, 2001, at http://greenspun.com/bboard/q-and-a-fetch-msg.tcl?msg_id=005JrT (last visited July 15, 2011).

6 German and Garth, "Power Trader Tied to Bush Finds Washington All Ears"; Mary Gordon, "Enron Chair Gave List of Favored Names to White House," *Associated Press*, February 1, 2002, at http://www.corpwatch.org/article.php?id=1549 (last visited June 23, 2011).

The George W. Bush administration relied exclusively on the advice of energy companies – many of which donated large sums of money to the Republican Party – in formulating its controversial energy strategy. Energy Secretary Spencer Abraham met more than 100 representatives of energy industry companies and corporate associations from January to May 2001. The meetings were related to the administration's energy task force, chaired by Vice President Cheney, which released its energy strategy in May. Abraham did not meet any representatives of environmental or consumer advocacy groups. A coalition of nearly thirty environmental groups asked to meet the energy secretary in February to discuss energy policy, but officials declined the request, citing Abraham's "busy schedule." Cheney and President Bush refused repeated requests to hand over any documents relating to the task force. The plan included the construction of 1,300 coal-fired power plants, increased oil exploration, including in pristine and protected areas, and reduced environmental regulations for the energy industry.[7]

However, while energy interests were united against environmental regulation, they were divided when it came to electricity restructuring. Despite his strong support from the administration, Pat Wood's attempt to encourage deregulation and the development of electricity markets would be thwarted primarily by utilities and associated politicians from Republican-dominated states in the south and the west. Resistance to FERC's RTO proposal was led by two major multistate holding companies, Southern Company and Entergy, as well as most western states and the Florida and Carolina utilities. They were joined by many of the PUCs in their service areas, because of fears that low-cost power would be exported from those regions.

Humbled by the difficulties of gaining support for RTOs, and chastened by the California experience, FERC turned to market standardization as the next step toward competitive wholesale electricity markets. FERC had success with Order 888's pro forma tariff, which simplified the establishment of open-access tariffs by providing utilities with a generic blueprint that limited their discretion. Standardizing market designs for

---

[7] Daniell Knight, "Documents Show Bush Energy Plan Fuelled by Industry," *Inter Press Service*, March 28, 2002, at http://www.corpwatch.org/article.php?id=1549 (last visited June 23, 2011). Eighteen of the individuals and companies that met Abraham had contributed a total of more than $16 million to the Republican Party since 1999. Among them were Enron, ChevronTexaco, ExxonMobil, British Petroleum, EEI, the Nuclear Energy Institute, and the Independent Petroleum Association of America.

RTOs could also provide a number of benefits, including reducing seams between RTOs.

On July 31, 2002, FERC issued its Standard Market Design (SMD) NOPR.[8] FERC's objective in this rulemaking initiative was to establish a standardized transmission service and wholesale electric market design. FERC proposed an open and transparent spot market design. FERC proposed to exercise jurisdiction over the transmission component of bundled retail transactions and to modify the existing pro forma transmission tariff to include a single flexible transmission service (Network Access Service) that applied consistent transmission rules for all transmission customers. The Commission also proposed that all transmission owners and operators that did not join an RTO must contract with an independent entity to operate their transmission facilities. An Independent Transmission Provider would have no financial interest in any market participant in the region in which it provides transmission services.[9]

SMD relied on bilateral contracts between buyers and sellers to ensure resource adequacy. Short-term spot markets were intended to complement bilateral procurement. Independent Transmission Providers should operate markets for energy and for the procurement of certain ancillary services in conjunction with markets for transmission service. These markets would be bid-based, security-constrained spot markets operating a day ahead of real-time operations and in real time. A market-based LMP transmission congestion management system provided a mechanism for efficiently allocating scarce transmission capacity, while also sending proper price signals to encourage development of transmission, generation, and demand response infrastructure. Efficient spot markets would provide information to help customers negotiate bilateral contracts.[10]

FERC included a market-monitoring and market power mitigation plan in its SMD proposal. Market power mitigation would rely on a combination of methods to protect against the exercise of market power by preventing sellers from withholding economical supplies from the market, while permitting prices to reflect true scarcity. FERC proposed a resource adequacy requirement to ensure adequate electric generating,

---

[8] "Remedying Undue Discrimination through Open Access Transmission Service and Standard Electricity Market Design," FERC SR ¶ 32,563 (2002) (SMD NOPR).

[9] SMD NOPR at PP 3–8.

[10] SMD NOPR at P 10.

transmission, and demand response infrastructure. An RTO or other regional entity must forecast the region's future resource needs and assess the plans of LSEs to meet those needs. Each LSE would be required to meet its share of required resources through a combination of generation and demand reduction.[11]

SMD also established FERC's policy rationale for transmission pricing. The Commission historically permitted transmission providers to assess an access charge, in the form of a load ratio share charge or a per-kW per-month charge, on all transactions taking place on the transmission provider's system. For a single transmission utility, these charges usually take the form of a "postage stamp" rate (the same charge for all customers) and, for an ISO or RTO, a "license plate" rate (a different charge based on the revenue requirement of the transmission owner where the transaction sinks). FERC proposed that transmission owners recover costs through an access charge assessed to LSEs, based on their respective shares of the system's peak load (their load ratio shares, similar to ERCOT). The goal was to eliminate rate pancaking, which raises the cost for generators to compete for customers.[12]

FERC's pricing policy for transmission network upgrades, whether for reliability or economic reasons, traditionally favored "rolled in" pricing, where all users pay an administratively determined share of new facilities. This policy was based on the rationale that the transmission grid is a single piece of equipment. If a transmission expansion supports region-wide reliability, all ratepayers should pay the costs of the expansion. Conversely, interconnection facilities that only help a generator access the grid should be directly assigned to the interconnecting generator. However, upgrades that provide both economic and reliability benefits are difficult to finance. FERC would apply a default pricing policy, rolling in on a region-wide basis high-voltage network upgrades and allocating the cost of lower-voltage expansions where the facilities will be located.[13]

SMD engendered a widespread backlash, from consumer groups to state utility commissions. House Resolution 6, submitted in Congress in 2003, would have imposed an outright moratorium on FERC's ability to promulgate SMD. Utilities opposed to SMD succeeded in having their senators and representatives include language in proposed national energy

---

[11] SMD NOPR at PP 13–14.
[12] SMD NOPR at PP 167–70.
[13] SMD NOPR at PP 191–200.

legislation that would have delayed adoption of SMD by several years.[14] In July 2005, FERC terminated the SMD proceedings.[15]

While FERC was unable to formally impose uniformity across regions, a series of rulemakings and decisions built upon Order 888 and Order 2000 to move utilities outside RTOs in that direction. SMD became a template for an incremental approach to developing uniformity across transmission providers. A series of generation interconnection rulemakings established FERC policy for financing both interconnections and transmission upgrades. Order 2003 established large generation interconnection standards,[16] while Order 2006 dealt with small generation interconnection standards.[17] In Order 2003, the Commission found that it was just and reasonable for interconnection customers to pay for Interconnection Facilities but not for Network Upgrades. Network Upgrades should be funded initially by the interconnection customer (unless the Transmission Provider elects to fund them), but the customer is entitled to a refund as credits against all payments for transmission services, with the full amount to be refunded with interest within five years.[18] The rule also standardized procedures for applying and handling requests for transmission system upgrades.

FERC responded to its experience with California and the western market by conditioning market-based rate authority on acceptance of

[14] Mark Hegedus, "Points Well-Taken: Comments on Professor Peter Carstensen's Paper 'Creating Workably Competitive Wholesale Markets in Energy," 1 *Environmental & Energy Law & Policy Journal* 145, 147 (2006); Joel Eisen, "Regulatory Linearity, Commerce Clause Brinksmanship, and Retrenchment in Electric Utility Deregulation," 40 *Wake Forest LR* 545, 554–55 (2005).

[15] *Remedying Undue Discrimination through Open Access Transmission Service and Standard Electricity Market Design*, Order Terminating Proceeding, 112 FERC ¶ 61,073 (2005). Given the continuing development of voluntary RTOs and ISOs and the initiation of proceedings to consider revisions to the Order 888 pro forma tariff, the Commission concluded that the SMD NOPR had been overtaken by events.

[16] *Standardization of Generator Interconnection Agreements and Procedures*, Order No. 2003, FERC Stats. & Regs. ¶ 31,146 (2003), 68 FR 49845 (August 19, 2003), *order on reh'g*, Order No. 2003-A, FERC Stats. & Regs. ¶ 31,160 (2004), 69 FR 15932 (March 26, 2004), *order on reh'g*, Order No. 2003-B, FERC Stats. & Regs. ¶ 31,171 (2004), 70 FR 265 (January 4, 2005), *order on reh'g*, Order No. 2003-C, FERC Stats. & Regs. ¶ 31,190 (2005), 70 FR 37,661 (June 30, 2005), *aff'd sub nom. National Association of Regulatory Utility Commissioners v. FERC*, 475 F.3d 1277 (D.C. Cir. 2007).

[17] *Standardization of Small Generator Interconnection Agreements and Procedures*, Order No. 2006, FERC Stats. & Regs. ¶ 31,180 (2005), 70 FR 34100 (June 13, 2005), *order on reh'g*, Order No. 2006-A, FERC Stats. & Regs. ¶ 31,196 (2005), 70 FR 71760 (November 30, 2005), *order on clarification*, Order No. 2006-B, 116 FERC ¶ 61,046 (2006).

[18] Order 2003 at PP 21–22.

open-ended refund authority in an order issued November 20, 2001. All market-based rate tariffs and authorizations would be revised to include the following provision: "As a condition of obtaining and retaining market-based rate authority, the seller is prohibited from engaging in anticompetitive behavior or the exercise of market power. The seller's market-based rate authority is subject to refunds or other remedies as may be appropriate to address any anticompetitive behavior or exercise of market power." Violation of this provision would constitute a violation of a tariff or rate schedule on file under FPA section 205, and the Commission would have the authority to address potential anticompetitive behavior or exercise of market power through the imposition of refunds or other remedies.[19] Inserting this provision put the company that applied for market-based rates on notice that anticompetitive behavior could subject that firm to refunds and penalties. The filed rate doctrine does not extend to cases in which there is adequate notice that resolution of some specific issue may cause a later adjustment to the rate.[20]

The Commission updated its 2001 market-based rate authority rule in light of the findings of the various market manipulation proceedings. To provide clarification concerning prohibited behavior, the Commission proposed to identify the transactions and practices that would be prohibited under market-based rates. FERC also proposed modifying natural gas market blanket certificates to contain many of these standards. Should a seller be found to have engaged in the transactions or behavior prohibited under the proposed market behavior rules, it would be subject to disgorgement of unjust profits and appropriate nonmonetary remedies such as revocation of seller's market-based rate authority.[21] The six proposed rules were as follows:

Market Behavior Rule # 1: Unit Operation. Seller will operate and schedule generating facilities, undertake maintenance, declare outages, and commit or otherwise bid supply in a manner that complies with the rules and regulations of the applicable power market.

Market Behavior Rule # 2: Market Manipulation. Actions or transactions without a legitimate business purpose, which manipulate or attempt to manipulate market prices, market conditions, or market

[19] *Investigation of Terms and Conditions of Public Utility Market-Based Rate Authorizations,* 97 FERC ¶ 61,220, 61,976 (2001).
[20] *Natural Gas Clearinghouse v. FERC,* 965 F.2d 1066, 1075 (D.C. Cir. 1992).
[21] *Investigation of Terms and Conditions of Public Utility Market-Based Rate Authorizations,* 103 FERC ¶ 61,349 at P 6 (2003).

rules for electric energy, or result in market prices that do not reflect the legitimate forces of supply and demand, are prohibited.

Market Behavior Rule #3: Communications. Seller will provide complete, accurate, and factual information, and not submit false or misleading information, or omit material information, in any communications with the Commission, market monitors, RTOs, ISOs, or similar entities.

Market Behavior Rule # 4: Reporting. To the extent Seller engages in reporting of transactions to publishers of electricity or natural gas price indices, Seller shall provide complete, accurate, and factual information to any such publisher.

Market Behavior Rule #5: Record Retention. Seller will retain data and information necessary for the reconstruction of energy or energy products prices it charges for a period of three years.

Market Behavior Rule #6: Related Tariffs. Seller shall not violate or collude with another party in actions that violate the Seller's code of conduct or Order 889 standards of conduct.[22]

In the final Market Based Rate order, some of these conditions were changed. Market Rule #1 was revised to clarify that the "rules and regulations" to which the rule refers apply only to "Commission-approved" rules and regulations, and that the rule will not impose a must-offer requirement on sellers. Must-offer requirements limit the ability to withhold resources from the market, and are a requirement for participation in the capacity markets of some ISOs. Market Rule #2a was added, prohibiting wash trades. Market Rule #2b prohibited trades predicated on submitting false information to transmission providers (such as inaccurate load or generation data or scheduling nonfirm service or products sold as firm). Market Rule #2c prohibited transactions in which an entity creates artificial congestion and then purports to relieve such artificial congestion. Market Rule #3 only applies to communications with the Commission and entities subject to its jurisdiction (i.e., not deception with regard to counterparties).[23]

The principal remedy in complaint proceedings brought before the Commission to enforce the Market Behavior Rules was the disgorgement of the seller's unjust profits. However, a market participant request for

---

[22] *Investigation of Terms and Conditions of Public Utility Market-Based Rate Authorizations,* 103 FERC ¶ 61,349 at PP 17–36 (2003).

[23] *Public Utility Market-Based Rate Authorizations,* 105 FERC ¶ 61,218, at PP 52, 64, 76, 108 (2003).

disgorgement relief must be made no later than ninety days after the end of the calendar quarter in which the violation is alleged to have occurred, or ninety days after the market participant should have known of the behavior. The Commission would also be subject to a ninety-day deadline, triggered by communication with FERC enforcement staff.[24]

The Commission also acted to prevent a repeat of the manipulation of price indices, which had occurred in the California natural gas market. In April 2003, the Commission's staff held a technical conference with the staff of the CFTC to explore price formation issues with respect to natural gas, as well as a second conference in June with the NARUC and the CFTC staff. In July 2003, the Commission issued a policy statement on natural gas and electricity price indices. The statement included the conditions under which the Commission will give industry participants safe-harbor protection for good-faith reporting of transactions data.[25] This policy statement was adopted by the Market Behavior Rules Order as well as the Blanket Sales Certificates Order.[26] A November 2004 Order reviewed the submissions of ten price index developers and concluded they had substantially met standards for publishing price indices.[27]

FERC discarded its traditional hub-and-spoke analysis, in use since the early 1980s (which focused on whether a seller had a market share of 20 percent or less in a particular market) for evaluating market-based rate applications, and adopted a new "supply margin assessment" (SMA) screen for use on an interim basis. An applicant is considered pivotal if its capacity exceeds the market's surplus of capacity above peak demand – the market's supply margin. The supply margin threshold identifies whether the applicant is a must-run supplier needed to meet peak load in the control area. To prevent physical withholding, an applicant who fails

---

[24] *Public Utility Market-Based Rate Authorizations*, 105 FERC ¶ 61,218, at PP 146–48 (2003).

[25] *Policy Statement on Natural Gas and Electric Price Indices*, 104 FERC ¶ 61,121, PP 1–8 (2003).

[26] *Order Amending Market-Based Rate Tariffs and Authorizations*, 105 FERC ¶ 61,218 (2003), *reh'g denied* 107 FERC ¶ 61,175 (2004), and Order No. 644, *Amendment to Blanket Sales Certificates*, FERC Stats. & Regs. ¶ 31,153 (2003), *reh'g denied* 107 FERC ¶ 61,174 (2004).

[27] *Price Discovery in Natural Gas and Electric Markets*, Order Regarding Future Monitoring of Voluntary Price Formation, Use of Price Indices in Jurisdictional Tariffs, and Closing Certain Tariff Dockets, 109 FERC ¶ 61,184, PP 35–39 (2004). This finding was confirmed by a GAO study in 2005. GAO, *Natural Gas and Electricity Markets: Federal Government Actions to Improve Private Price Indices and Stakeholder Reaction*, Report to the Ranking Minority Member, Committee on Energy and Natural Resources, U.S. Senate (December 2005).

the SMA screen must offer uncommitted capacity for spot market sales in the relevant market. To prevent economic withholding, uncommitted capacity will be priced under a split-the-savings formula, which was the traditional cost-based ratemaking model used for spot market energy sales.[28]

Subsequently, in the face of sharp criticism, FERC agreed to postpone the implementation of the SMA screen. The Commission asked staff to prepare a paper identifying possible modifications or alternatives to both the SMA and price mitigation measures.[29] The Commission abandoned the SMA and adopted two interim indicative screens for assessing generation market power, a pivotal supplier analysis based on the control area's annual peak demand and a market share analysis applied on a seasonal basis.[30] Both the pivotal supplier analysis and market share analysis would consider native load obligations and other commitments of the applicant. If an applicant passed both screens, there would be a rebuttable presumption that the applicant did not possess market power in generation. However, intervenors could present evidence to rebut the presumption of no market power. On the other hand, if an applicant failed either screen, this would create a rebuttable presumption that market power exists. The applicant may then propose a more robust market power study, file a mitigation proposal, or adopt default cost-based rates.[31]

The pivotal supply analysis screen first determines total supply: the amount of uncommitted capacity in the market plus the uncommitted supplies that can be imported. Imported supplies are limited by simultaneous transmission import capability. The applicant's uncommitted capacity equals the total capacity of generation owned or controlled, less operating reserves, native load commitments, and long-term firm sales. The market's net uncommitted supply is determined by subtracting the total load from the total uncommitted supply. If the applicant's uncommitted capacity is equal to or greater than the net uncommitted supply, then the applicant fails the pivotal supplier analysis.[32]

---

[28] *AEP Power Marketing, Inc. et al.*, 97 FERC ¶ 61,219, 61,969–71 (2001).

[29] *AEP Power Marketing, Inc. et al.*, 107 FERC ¶ 61,018 at P 3 (2004), *order on reh'g*, 108 FERC ¶ 61,026 (2004).

[30] The Commission also imitated a rulemaking proceeding to determine if the interim market power screens should be modified or changed. *Market-Based Rates for Public Utilities*, 107 FERC ¶ 61,019 (2004).

[31] *AEP Power Marketing, Inc. et al.*, 107 FERC ¶ 61,018 at PP 36–39 (2004).

[32] *AEP Power Marketing, Inc. et al.*, 107 FERC ¶ 61,018 at PP 73–99 (2004).

The wholesale market share analysis measures, for each of the four seasons, whether an applicant has a dominant position in the market. Market share is determined by the applicant's share of net available uncommitted supply in each season. Planned outages for each season are included in the calculation. An applicant with a market share of 20 percent or more in the relevant market for any season will have a rebuttable presumption of market power. The Commission based its decision to continue using a market share screen on the economic literature regarding oligopoly, specifically the Stackelberg model. Given that demand elasticity is extremely small in electricity markets, a conservative approach was required in order to ensure competitive outcomes for customers.[33]

An applicant failing one of the initial screens must present an analysis using the Delivered Price Test, used to analyze the effect on competition in merger proceedings.[34] Under the Delivered Price Test, applicants must calculate the market concentration using the HHI. A showing of an HHI less than 2500 (highly concentrated) in the relevant market for all season/load conditions for applicants that are not pivotal and do not possess more than a 20 percent market share would create a presumption of a lack of market power. An applicant with a market share greater than 20 percent could argue that it would be unlikely to possess market power in an unconcentrated market (HHI less than 1000).[35]

The Commission finalized the market-based rate rules with Order 697, issued in June 2007. The Commission adopted the market share screen and the pivotal supplier screen. Sellers that fail either screen will have full opportunity to present evidence demonstrating that they do not have market power.[36] FERC rejected suggestions to substitute the HHI for the market share screen. The HHI provides information on the ability of sellers to exercise market power through coordinated behavior, while the

---

[33] *AEP Power Marketing, Inc. et al.*, 107 FERC ¶ 61,018 at PP 100–04 (2004).

[34] The delivered price test was described in *Revised Filing Requirements Under Part 33 of the Commission's Regulations*, Order No. 642, FERC Stats. & Regs., 31,111 (2000), 65 FR 70983 (November 28, 2000), §33.3(c)(4).

[35] *AEP Power Marketing, Inc. et al.*, 107 FERC ¶ 61,018 at PP 110–11 (2004).

[36] *Market-Based Rates for Wholesale Sales of Electric Energy, Capacity and Ancillary Services by Public Utilities*, Order No. 697, FERC Stats. & Regs. ¶ 31,252 at PP 13–16 (2007), 72 FR 39,904 (July 20, 2007), *clarified*, 121 FERC ¶ 61,260 (2007), *order on reh'g*, Order No. 697-A, FERC Stats. & Regs. ¶ 31,268 (2008), *clarified*, 124 FERC ¶ 61,055 (2008), *order on reh'g*, Order No. 697-B, FERC Stats. & Regs. ¶ 31,285 (2008), *order on reh'g*, Order No. 697-C, FERC Stats. & Regs. ¶ 31,291 (2009), *order on reh'g and clarification*, Order No. 697-D, FERC Stats. & Regs. ¶ 31,305 (2010), *aff'd sub nom. Montana Consumer Counsel v. FERC*, 659 F.3d 910 (9th Cir. 2011).

market share screen provides information on a particular seller's ability to exercise market power unilaterally. The merger guidelines take existing market power as a given and only attempt to prevent mergers that substantially increase market power.[37] Market-based rates provide an applicant the authority to exercise its existing market power, and therefore must be more stringent than the merger guidelines.

The Commission considered the strategic bidding literature and theoretical models demonstrating that market participants who pass market power screens may be able to elevate prices in auction markets through non-collusive strategic bidding, withholding, and gaming tactics. These theoretical models require consideration of numerous assumptions and hypothetical future behavior that would make them difficult to implement as reliable tools to assess whether a seller has market power.[38] The Commission speculated that its Anti-Manipulation Rule prohibits this type of behavior,[39] but failed to examine closely whether non-collusive behavior and other tactics such as signaling would violate the Anti-Manipulation Rule or be easy to detect or prove in a proceeding under the Rule.

The Commission continued the policy under which an OATT is deemed to mitigate a seller's transmission market power. However, OATT violations that result in restraints on competition may subject the seller to revocation of its market-based rate authority or other remedies such as disgorgement of profits or civil penalties. The Commission created a rebuttable presumption that all affiliates of a transmission provider should lose their market-based rate authority in each market in which their affiliated transmission provider loses its market-based rate authority as a result of an OATT violation. The Commission adopted a rebuttable presumption that ownership or control of intrastate natural gas transportation, storage or distribution facilities, sites for generation capacity

---

[37] The Merger Guidelines were used to evaluate the likely potential competitive effect of a merger. Since the concern was with the increase in concentration, the change in the HHI was used as a measure of that increase, and the post-market HHI was a measure of the competitiveness of the market. DOJ and FTC, *Horizontal Merger Guidelines*, 1.51 General Standards, April 2, 1992. In August 2010, new horizontal guidelines were issued that applied more lenient definitions. Moderately concentrated markets were those with HHI between 1500 and 2500, and highly concentrated markets were those with HHI > 2500. DOJ and FTC, *Horizontal Merger Guidelines*, 5.3 Market Concentration, August 19, 2010.

[38] Order 697, P 58.

[39] *Prohibition of Energy Market Manipulation*, Order No. 670, FERC Stats. & Regs. ¶ 31,202 (2006), 71 FR 4244 (January 26, 2006), *reh'g denied*, 114 FERC ¶ 61,300 (2006).

development, and transportation of coal supplies do not allow a seller to raise entry barriers.[40]

The Commission also moved to preempt conflicts over market-based rate contracts for wholesale sales of electric energy by public utilities. A contested issue in cases that had come before FERC was the applicable standard of review, the "just and reasonable" standard of FPA ratemaking or the "public interest" standard of review under the *Mobile-Sierra* doctrine. The Commission proposed language that parties would be required to include in their electric power sales contracts if they intend that the Commission apply the "public interest" standard of review to their contract. If parties to a market-based power sales contract do not include this exact language in their contract, the Commission would construe the omission as demonstrating the intent of the parties to allow a just and reasonable standard of review.[41]

While FERC abandoned its RTO and SMD programs, the *New PJM Companies*[42] demonstrated FERC's willingness to take on state governments to promote the expansion of existing RTOs. When AEP proposed to join PJM to fulfill one of the conditions of its merger with CSW,[43] Kentucky and Virginia attempted to prevent AEP from transferring control. Virginia amended its Restructuring Act to preclude Virginia's incumbent electric utilities from transferring control of their transmission facilities to RTOs before July 2004, and thereafter only with the prior approval of the Virginia State Corporation Commission.[44] The Virginia Commission recommended suspension of the mandate to transfer transmission assets as long as necessary to provide a clear view of the transformed industry. The Kentucky Public Service Commission denied AEP's request to transfer control of its Kentucky transmission facilities to PJM based on a requirement of specific and immediate benefits. FERC used its authority under PURPA 205(a) to approve integration where it would "obtain economical utilization of facilities and resources." The Commission concluded that it was appropriate to use its authority to override the objections of

---

[40] Order No. 697, PP 21–22.

[41] *Standard of Review for Proposed Changes to Market-Based Rate Contracts for Wholesale Sales of Electric Energy by Public Utilities*, FERC SR ¶ 32,562 (2002), 67 FR 51516 (August 8, 2002), PP 1–3.

[42] *The New PJM Companies et al.*, 105 FERC ¶ 61,251 (2003), *Opinion on Initial Decision and Order on reh'g*, 107 FERC ¶ 61,271 (2004), *Order on reh'g and compliance*, 108 ¶ 61,140 (2004).

[43] *American Electric Power Service Corp.*, 103 FERC ¶ 61,008 at 61,025 (2003).

[44] The *New PJM Companies*, 104 FERC ¶ 61,274 (2003) at P4.

the Kentucky and Virginia commissions and to permit AEP to complete its integration into PJM. The Commission found that Kentucky and Virginia had no proper grounds for prohibiting this action.[45] A number of northern and midwestern states (including Michigan, Indiana, Illinois, Pennsylvania, and New Jersey) supported FERC and called for regional coordination to take place without delay. In March 2004, a FERC ALJ found that there was an impressive array of expert testimony as to the benefits of the planned integration of AEP into PJM. The ALJ noted that while PURPA did not allow FERC to mandate coordination, it did grant FERC authority to prevent states from "blocking or frustrating coordination efforts." In June 2004, FERC affirmed the ALJ's decision.[46]

FERC did not want to overstep its authority and attempt to order IOUs to open up their markets, nor did it want to passively accept resistance by IOUs and state regulatory commission to efforts to open up the grid. So it carefully walked a tightrope, strengthening the legal basis for market-based rates, encouraging the expansion of ISOs and RTOs and their assumption of additional responsibilities, and providing pressure to open up the grids of integrated utilities to third-party generators and marketers. Without a clear congressional mandate, and unsure of the limits of its authority, FERC was careful not to trigger court decisions that might require a step backward.

---

[45] *The New PJM Companies*, 105 FERC ¶ 61,251, PP 114–26.
[46] *The New PJM Companies*, 107 FERC ¶ 61,271 (2004) at PP 32–35, 41–44.

20

The Energy Policy Act of 2005

Ironically, Vice President Cheney's manipulations to favor campaign contributors and energy insiders in the development of the National Energy Report proved counterproductive to the administration's energy goals. His solicitation of campaign contributors from the energy industry as advisors, demands for secrecy, and blackballing of public interest and environmental groups triggered intense media scrutiny.[1] Cheney made it more difficult to pass provisions through Congress by raising the salience of energy issues and creating the presumption that provisions in proposed bills were merely giveaways to special interests. However, while

---

[1] Judy Pasternak, "Bush's Energy Plan Bares Industry Clout," *Los Angeles Times*, August 26, 2001, at http://articles.latimes.com/2001/aug/26/news/mn-38530 (last visited March 26, 2012); Joseph Kahn, "Enron's Many Strands: The Energy Task Force; Enron Won Some and Lost Some in White House Energy Report," *New York Times*, February 1, 2002, at http://www.nytimes.com/2002/02/01/business/enron-s-many-strands-energy-task-force-enron-won-some-lost-some-white-house.html (last visited March 26, 2012); Don Van Natta Jr., "Agency Files Suit for Cheney Papers on Energy Policy," *New York Times*, February 23, 2002, http://www.nytimes.com/2002/02/23/business/agency-files-suit-for-cheney-papers-on-energy-policy.html (last visited March 26, 2012); Don Van Natta Jr. and Neela Banerjee, "Top G.O.P. Donors in Energy Industry Met Cheney Panel," *New York Times*, March 1, 2002, at http://www.nytimes.com/2002/03/01/us/top-gop-donors-in-energy-industry-met-cheney-panel.html (last visited March 26, 2012); Don Van Natta Jr. and Neela Banerjee, "Bush Energy Paper Followed Industry Push," *New York Times*, March 27, 2002, at http://www.nytimes.com/2002/03/27/us/bush-energy-paper-followed-industry-push.html (last visited March 26, 2012); Don Van Natta Jr. and Neela Banerjee, "Review Shows Energy Industry's Recommendations to Bush Ended Up Being National Policy," *New York Times*, March 28, 2002, at http://www.nytimes.com/2002/03/28/us/review-shows-energy-industry-s-recommendations-bush-ended-up-being-national.html (last visited March 26, 2012); Michael Abramowitz and Steven Mufson, "Papers Detail Industry's Role in Cheney's Energy Report," *Washington Post*, July 18, 2007, A1.

the Bush administration failed to achieve most of its goals, an unintended by-product of its actions would be to strengthen FERC's authority over the reliability of the electric grid.

Cheney threw oil on the political fire by his atavistic comments that the Bush administration's energy strategy would aim mainly to increase supply of fossil fuels rather than limit demand. Cheney dismissed as 1970s-era thinking the notion that "we could simply conserve or ration our way out" of what he called an energy crisis. The only solution was a government-backed push to find new domestic sources of oil and gas, and an all-out drive to build power plants. Cheney indicated that the administration would put some emphasis on energy efficiency, especially new technologies, but he would oppose any measure based on the premise that people should "do more with less." The budget President Bush submitted to Congress in early April sharply reduced spending by the DOE on research and development for energy efficiency and renewable energy technologies.[2] "You can summarize the president's energy policy as real men dig, drill and burn," said Philip E. Clapp, president of the National Environmental Trust, "and conservation is for wimps."[3] When oil prices fell in the summer of 2001, and the California electricity crisis abated, Cheney resorted to the "Energy Independence" slogan to justify the administration's energy policies. President Bush began to talk about "warning signs" of a crisis, even if supply shortages no longer seemed acute.[4]

The Bush energy plan quickly drew the ire of congressional Democrats, who derided it as a giveaway to his campaign contributors from the energy industries.[5] In a major legislative victory for the White House, the House

[2] Joseph Kahn, "Cheney Promotes Increasing Supply as Energy Policy," *New York Times*, May 1, 2001, at http://www.nytimes.com/2001/05/01/us/cheney-promotes-increasing-supply-as-energy-policy.html (last visited March 26, 2012); Joseph Kahn, "Energy Efficiency Programs Set for Bush Budget Cuts," *New York Times*, April 5, 2001, at http://www.nytimes.com/2001/04/05/us/energy-efficiency-programs-set-for-bush-budget-cuts.html (last visited March 26, 2012).

[3] Richard Berke, "Ideas & Trends: Power Politics; Looking to Win the Energy Issue," *New York Times*, May 20, 2001, at http://www.nytimes.com/2001/05/20/weekinreview/ideas-trends-power-politics-looking-to-win-the-energy-issue.html (last visited March 26, 2012).

[4] Joseph Kahn, "Cheney on the Road, Seeks Support for Energy Program," *New York Times*, July 17, 2001, at http://www.nytimes.com/2001/07/17/us/cheney-on-the-road-seeks-support-for-energy-program.html (last visited March 26, 2012).

[5] Philip Shenon, "Battle Lines in Congress Are Quickly Drawn by Republicans and Democrats," *New York Times*, May 18, 2001, at http://www.nytimes.com/2001/05/18/us/energy-plan-legislative-agenda-battle-lines-congress-are-quickly-drawn.html (last visited March 26, 2012).

voted in August 2001 to allow drilling in the Alaska National Wildlife Reserve (ANWR) shortly before it passed an energy bill that preserved major parts of President Bush's energy plan. Republicans acknowledged that they had put off the more complex issues, including electricity deregulation, the renewal of liability insurance for nuclear power plants, and the overhaul of electricity grids. The legislation included $33.5 billion in subsidies, with the bulk of these tax breaks and credits ($27 billion) to traditional energy producers. President Bush urged the Senate to pass an energy bill that would allow drilling for oil in ANWR, casting the issue as a matter of national security. Critics of drilling in Alaska argue that, by the government's own estimate, opening ANWR would not yield oil for at least seven years.[6]

With the Republicans in control of Congress after the 2002 elections, energy industry lobbyists were confident that their campaign contributions would pay off in friendly legislation. Energy companies had a wish list of tax incentives to promote exploration and expansion, subsidies to develop new technologies, build a natural-gas pipeline in Alaska, and limit the liability of the nuclear power industry. Energy companies were united in their desire to constrain the EPA. Privately, White House officials were concerned that Republicans in Congress and their business allies might be inclined to overreach, making the president appear to be a captive of the energy industry.[7] The Republicans ran into a roadblock in the Senate, where the House bill met a quick death. Supporters of the bill in the Senate attempted to capitalize on the midwestern blackout to combine electricity provisions with other initiatives. The Senate passed a stripped-down bill, which included PUCHA repeal, ethanol requirements, a renewable portfolio standard, and a lesser package of energy subsidies and incentives.[8] The two chambers were unable to come to an agreement before the elections, and the bill died.

---

[6] Lizette Alvarez, "Bush's Energy Bill Is Passed in House in a G.O.P. Triumph," *New York Times*, August 2, 2001, at http://www.nytimes.com/2001/08/02/us/bush-s-energy-bill-is-passed-in-house-in-a-gop-triumph.html (last visited March 26, 2012); Katharine Seelye, "Bush Promotes Energy Bill as Security Issue," *New York Times*, October 12, 2001, at http://www.nytimes.com/2001/10/12/politics/12ENER.html (last visited March 26, 2012).

[7] Katharine Seelye, "Industry Seeking Rewards from G.O.P.-Led Congress," *New York Times*, December 3, 2002, at http://www.nytimes.com/2002/12/03/politics/03ENVI.html (last visited March 26, 2012).

[8] David E. Rosenbaum, "Senate Passes an Energy Bill Called Flawed by Both Sides," *New York Times*, April 26, 2002, at http://www.nytimes.com/2002/04/26/us/senate-passes-an-energy-bill-called-flawed-by-both-sides.html (last visited March 26, 2012).

The omnibus Energy Policy Act of 2003 included electricity provisions such as incentive-based transmission rate treatments, siting of interstate electrical transmission facilities, and open-access transmission by unregulated transmitting utilities. The bill created a statutory mechanism for electric reliability standards incorporating Electric Reliability Organizations, subject to FERC review. The bill also repealed PUHCA. It was sponsored by Representative Billy Tauzin (R-LA), chairman of the Energy and Commerce Committee. The bill included a provision to open drilling in the ANWR and aggressively promoted new domestic energy production through tax breaks for industry and other incentives. The House passed the measure in April, by a vote of 247 to 175.[9] The Senate measure became so bogged down that Republican leaders agreed to pass the Senate energy bill from the previous year, when the Democrats were in charge, to get something to the conference committee. Serious disagreement remained over the requirement for utilities to participate in regional power organizations. Many southern and western lawmakers opposed that approach. To move the Senate energy measure, the leadership agreed to requests from lawmakers seeking a lengthy delay in FERC's SMD.[10]

The primary opponent of SMD, and electricity markets in general, was the Southern Company. The Southern Company had been Enron's main challenger for influence in Washington, DC. Dwight Evans, executive vice president of the Southern Company, said that FERC had tried to "design systems that meet what Enron needs." The company nurtured a loose coalition of southeast lawmakers, including the Senate minority leader, Trent Lott, in support of its view that the states should decide the pace and scope of energy deregulation. Southern strongly opposed efforts to diminish the power of local regulators to supervise electricity pricing, production, and transmission. Between 1999 and 2001, the utility's seven political action committees spent more than $1 million – more than any other energy company – in supporting members of Congress. Southern subsidiaries were the top energy contributors to politicians in Mississippi

---

[9] Carol Hulse, "Advocates of Arctic Drilling Buoyed as House Passes Bill," *New York Times*, April 13, 2003, at http://www.nytimes.com/2003/04/12/politics/12ENER.html (last visited March 26, 2012).

[10] Carl Hulse, "Energy Bill Gives Way to Old One in the Senate," *New York Times*, August 1, 2003, at http://www.nytimes.com/2003/08/01/us/energy-bill-gives-way-to-old-one-in-the-senate.html (last visited March 26, 2012); Carl Hulse, "After 2 Years, Energy Bill Is Getting New Urgency in Congress," *New York Times*, August 16, 2003, at http://www.nytimes.com/2003/08/16/national/16CONG.html (last visited March 26, 2012).

and Georgia, and ranked third in Florida. Southern also had a lineup of high-powered lobbyists, including Haley Barbour and C. Boyden Gray, George H.W. Bush's White House counsel. Marc Racicot, a close friend of the president, had lobbied for the company in the past.[11]

House Republicans and the Bush administration wanted to grant the federal government the power of eminent domain to establish corridors for high-capacity interstate power lines. Republican senators from the west had resisted such new federal powers in the past. The House bill would enable FERC to approve power line routes that had been blocked or delayed by a state if the agency found the new lines would significantly ease congestion along the power grid. Companies building the high-voltage lines would be able to exercise eminent domain to acquire rights-of-way if they compensated landowners. The Senate bill did not allow for such intervention. The National Governors Association, environmental groups, and other organizations representing state and local officials whose powers might be usurped opposed the proposal. But the blackout softened opposition from lawmakers. Tauzin said giving the federal government authority to settle power line disputes would encourage needed investment in transmission systems. He compared it to federal authority for routing natural gas pipelines.[12]

The Bush administration attempted to smooth over House-Senate differences, with Dick Cheney personally urging lawmakers to find a solution. The negotiations remained bogged down in a fight over the taxation of corn-based ethanol.[13] A House-Senate conference committee approved the bill after Republicans defeated a series of Democratic efforts to win changes. The approval by the committee ended almost three years of Congressional wrangling over energy policy.[14]

---

[11] Joseph Kahn and Jeff Gerth, "Enron's Collapse: The Politics; Collapse May Reshape the Battlefield of Deregulation," *New York Times*, December 4, 2001; Laura Cohen, "Southern: The New Power in Power," *Bloomberg Businessweek*, June 3, 2002, at http://www.businessweek.com/magazine/content/02_22/b3785092.htm, (last visited March 26, 2012).

[12] Carl Hulse, "Provision in Energy Bill Brings Unease in G.O.P.," *New York Times*, September 16, 2003, at http://www.nytimes.com/2003/09/16/politics/16ENER.html (last visited March 26, 2012).

[13] Carl Hulse, "Administration Steps Up Energy Bill Efforts," *New York Times*, October 31, 2003, at http://www.nytimes.com/2003/10/31/us/administration-steps-up-energy-bill-efforts.html (last visited March 26, 2012).

[14] Carl Hulse, "Negotiators Make Deal on $30 Billion Energy Bill," *New York Times*, November 18, 2003, at http://www.nytimes.com/2003/11/18/us/negotiators-make-deal-on-30-billion-energy-bill.html (last visited March 26, 2012).

The bill passed the House by a 246–180 vote on November 18, 2003, but attempts to railroad it through the Senate backfired. By introducing the energy and Medicare bills at the last minute and thus limiting debate just before the winter adjournment, the Republican congressional leaders had hoped to push the measures through a weary Congress. Forty members of the Senate succeeded in blocking the energy bill. Too many senators discovered objectionable details in the bill that had not come to light earlier. Senator McCain said that the more closely the members examined the bill, the more unsavory it became.[15] The straw that broke the camel's back was the refusal of Tom DeLay to budge on immunity from liability for refineries making the gasoline additive MTBE. That was part of a deal with midwestern congressmen to expand the use of ethanol as an additive. So the log rolled over the bill.[16]

Senate Republican tried again in 2004, cutting the "goodies" incorporated in the bill by more than half and eliminating legal immunity to MTBE producers. The savings would be achieved by reducing tax breaks for oil and gas companies and eliminating a new energy efficiency program for federal buildings, among other changes. The legislation still included a program to double the use of corn-based ethanol as a gasoline additive, as well as incentives to boost domestic oil and gas production, promote alternative energy sources, and provide loan guarantees for a new natural gas pipeline from Alaska. Leaders in the House dismissed the new plan, particularly the lack of legal protection for makers of MTBE.[17]

The House barely passed an energy bill in 2005, with the MTBE provision surviving by only six votes. The House also rejected an effort to retain state and local control over where to put terminals for importing liquefied natural gas. The House bill would allow drilling in the ANWR. The legislation was more than 1,000 pages long and touched on almost

---

[15] David Firestone, "Congressional Memo; 11th-Hour Bills Irk Lawmakers Left in the Dark," *New York Times*, November 23, 2003, at http://www.nytimes.com/2003/11/22/us/congressional-memo-11th-hour-bills-irk-lawmakers-left-in-the-dark.html (last visited March 26, 2012).

[16] Carl Hulse, "A Final Push in Congress: Energy Bill; Even with Bush's Support, Wide-Ranging Legislation May Have Been Sunk by Excess," *New York Times*, November 26, 2003, at http://www.nytimes.com/2003/11/26/us/final-push-congress-energy-bill-even-with-bush-s-support-wide-ranging.html (last visited March 26, 2012).

[17] Carl Hulse, "Senators Try to Squeeze Slimmer Energy Bill through Congress after Defeat Last Year," *New York Times*, February 11, 2004, at http://www.nytimes.com/2004/02/11/us/senators-try-squeeze-slimmer-energy-bill-through-congress-after-defeat-last-year.html (last visited March 26, 2012).

every aspect of energy production and use. It gave a federal board new authority to force improvements in the power grid to avert blackouts.[18] Heading toward a collision with the House and the White House, the Senate put an environmentally friendly stamp on its energy legislation. In an effort to strengthen their hand in looming negotiations with the House, senators voted 52–48 to require power companies to use more renewable electricity. At the same time, the Finance Committee approved a $14 billion tax incentive package that rewarded alternative fuels and energy efficiency. Lawmakers acknowledged that the tax package, which provided tax breaks for alternative power, hybrid vehicles, and energy-efficient appliances and home construction, was purposefully written to provide a sharp contrast with the House version, where the weight was on tax breaks for fossil fuel industries.[19]

House and Senate negotiators came to agreement on broad energy legislation at the end of July, after four years of wrangling. Lawmakers agreed to a significant new requirement to add corn-based ethanol to the gasoline supply and to build support for the measure from farm state lawmakers, and they killed two major provisions aimed at curbing consumption. MTBE immunity was dropped from the bill, as well as a House proposal to relax some clean air standards. House members rejected an effort to require utilities to use more renewable energy. The tax package did include a substantial emphasis on credits for energy efficiency.[20] On August 8, 2005, President Bush signed the Energy Policy Act of 2005 (EPAct 2005).[21]

Title XII authorizes FERC to certify a national electric reliability organization (ERO) to enforce mandatory reliability standards for the bulk power system. The ERO will develop and enforce reliability standards for the bulk power system, including cybersecurity protection, and will have jurisdiction over any regional entities, and all users, owners, and operators of the bulk power system. All ERO standards will be approved by

---

[18] Carl Hulse, "House Votes to Approve Broad Energy Legislation," *New York Times*, April 22, 2005, at http://www.nytimes.com/2005/04/22/politics/22energy.html?sq=& st=nyt%22=&scp=35&r=0 (last visited March 26, 2012).

[19] Carl Hulse, "Senate Makes Environment the Focus of Energy Bill," *New York Times*, June 17, 2005, at http://www.nytimes.com/2005/06/17/politics/17energy.html?sq=& st=nyt%22=&scp=11 (last visited March 26, 2012).

[20] Carl Hulse, "Provisions to Curb Oil Use Fall Out of Energy Bill," *New York Times*, July 26, 2005, at http://www.nytimes.com/2005/07/26/politics/26energy.html?pagewanted= print (last visited March 26, 2012).

[21] *Energy Policy Act of 2005*, Pub. L. No.1 09–58, tit. 12, 119 Stat. 594. Incorporated into the Federal Power Act as 16 U.S.C. 8240.

FERC. The Commission may approve a proposed reliability standard if it determines that the standard is just, reasonable, not unduly discriminatory, and in the public interest. The Commission shall give due weight to the technical expertise of the ERO but shall not defer with respect to the effect of a standard on competition. In turn, the ERO shall provide a similar presumption to proposals from RTOs. The ERO can impose penalties on a user, owner, or operator of a bulk power system that violates any FERC-approved reliability standard. FERC can also order compliance with a reliability standard and impose penalties. This provision did not give an ERO or FERC authorization to order construction of additional generation or transmission capacity.[22]

EPAct 2005 repealed the PURPA's mandatory purchase requirement if FERC finds that a competitive electricity market exists and a QF has adequate access to wholesale markets.[23] The law required electric utilities and REPs to offer customers real-time, interruptible, and critical peak pricing rates, and for DOE to work with states, utilities and other energy providers to address barriers to the adoption of demand response.[24]

EPAct 2005 repealed PUHCA, allowing utilities to rationalize the structure of their multistate subsidiaries. FERC and state regulatory bodies must be given access to utility books and records.[25] FERC retained its power to require that jurisdictional rates are just and reasonable, including the ability to deny the pass-through of costs, to prevent cross-subsidization. FERC and state commissions retained authority over the inclusion in rates of any costs of an activity performed by, or good and service procured from, an associated company.[26] FERC's authority over utility transactions was limited to transactions with a value of $10 million (formerly $50,000), which still covered practically every merger, acquisition, and affiliate transaction of importance.[27]

The Act also provided the Commission more authority over electricity markets. FERC was required to facilitate price transparency in markets, the integrity of those markets, fair competition, and the protection of consumers. The Commission was granted oversight authority over data provided by industry data publishers and providers of trade-processing

---

[22] *Energy Policy Act of 2005*, § 1211.
[23] *Energy Policy Act of 2005*, § 1253.
[24] *Energy Policy Act of 2005*, § 1252.
[25] *Energy Policy Act of 2005*, § 1263, § 1264, § 1265.
[26] *Energy Policy Act of 2005*, § 1267.
[27] *Energy Policy Act of 2005*, § 1289.

services. No entity shall fraudulently report any information relating to the price of electricity sold at wholesale or the availability of transmission capacity to a federal agency.[28]

Price transparency was combined with increased authority over market manipulation, as the law explicitly prohibited any manipulative or deceptive device or contrivance in contravention of Commission rules.[29] The anti-manipulation clauses specifically referenced section 10(b) of the Securities Exchange Act to define "manipulative or deceptive device or contrivance." SEC Rule 10b-5 implemented section 10(b) of the Exchange Act, and a significant body of legal precedent related to both section 10(b) and Rule 10b-5 has been developed. The Commission modeled its proposed regulations on Rule 10b-5.[30] The responsibility for preventing market manipulation had resided in the SEC with the authority conferred by Rule 10b-5,[31] and the CFTC, with the authority granted under the Commodity Exchange Act.[32] However, the CFTC successfully prosecuted only one case under its "artificial price" standard in thirty-five years.[33] SEC Rule 10b-5 applied only to securities, not commodities or financial derivatives.

Penalties for violations of the FPA Commission rules and orders were stiffened. The fine for a violation of the FPA or the Natural Gas Act was increased from $5,000 to $1 million and the criminal penalty increased from two to five years of imprisonment. Penalties for violations of Commission rules governing electricity were increased from $10,000 to $1 million.[34]

---

[28] *Energy Policy Act of 2005*, § 1281, § 1282.

[29] *Energy Policy Act of 2005*, § 1283.

[30] *Prohibition of Energy Market Manipulation*, 113 FERC ¶ 61,067 at P2 (2005), 70 FR 61930 (October 20, 2005).

[31] 17 CFR § 240.10b-5 (2011).

[32] 7 U.S.C. § 13b (2011).

[33] Shaun Ledgerwood and Dan Harris, "A Comparison of Anti-Manipulation Rules in U.S. and EU Electricity and Natural Gas Markets: A Proposal for a Common Standard," 33 *Energy Law Journal* 1, 4 fn. 6 (2012). The one successful prosecution was *DiPlacido v. CFTC*, 364 F. App'x 657 (2d Cir. 2009), *cert. denied*, 130 S. Ct. 1883 (2010), where the defendant was found to have manipulated settlement prices for electricity futures contracts. The Appeals Court accepted the CFTC's four-pronged test for manipulation: (1) that the accused had the ability to influence market prices; (2) that [he] specifically intended to do so; (3) that artificial prices existed; and (4) that the accused caused the artificial prices. *Id.*

[34] *Energy Policy Act of 2005*, § 1284. The NGA was also amended by inserting a similar clause.

The new market manipulation regulations, adopted on January 19, 2006, in Order 670,[35] were placed in a new Part 1c of the Commission's general regulations. If any entity engages in manipulation and the conduct is found to be "in connection with" a jurisdictional transaction, the entity is subject to the Commission's anti-manipulation authority. The Commission interpreted "any entity" to include any person or form of organization, regardless of its legal status, function, or activities, including nonjurisdictional utilities and governmental agencies. The Commission also found that its authority extended to both purchases and sales and the transportation of natural gas and electricity. However, the offense must affect or be connected with a jurisdictional transaction.[36] FERC rescinded Market Behavior Rule 2 (the anti-manipulation rule) and Rule 6 (anti-collusion rule) to avoid a conflict between regulatory requirements with differing standards of proof.[37] The other four Market Behavior Rules were removed from market-based rate tariffs and codified in FERC regulations.[38]

The expansion of FERC and CFTC authority, which accelerated due both to a major trading fiasco and the financial collapse, would raise issues of overlapping jurisdiction. While the power marketer shakeout reduced the incidents of scandalous behavior, the Amaranth affair, which occurred contemporaneous with the mortgage security meltdown, renewed calls for more vigorous regulation of energy derivatives. Amaranth Advisors was a hedge fund that collapsed in September 2006 after making titanic bets on natural gas. Most of Amaranth's trading occurred on NYMEX. But when the NYMEX ordered the fund to reduce its natural gas futures position, Amaranth substituted private natural gas swaps trading on the ICE.[39]

---

[35] *Prohibition of Energy Market Manipulation*, Order No. 670, FERC Stats. & Regs. ¶ 31,202 (2006), 71 FR 4244 (January 26, 2006), *reh'g denied*, 114 FERC ¶ 61,300 (2006).

[36] Order 670 at PP 16–22.

[37] *Investigation of Terms and Conditions of Public Utility Market Rates-Based Rate Authorizations*, 114 FERC ¶ 61,165 at P21, *reh'g denied*, 115 FERC ¶ 61,053 (2006). Market Rule 2 employed "foreseeability," but the new Part 1c followed SEC precedent that manipulation requires a showing of *scienter*, that is, an intent to deceive, manipulate, or defraud. *Id.* at nt 32.

[38] *Conditions for Public Utility Market-Based Rate Authorization Holders*, Order No. 674, 114 FERC ¶ 61,163 (2006), 71 FR 9695 (February 27, 2006).

[39] Amaranth Advisors LLC lost $4.9 billion in natural gas futures trading and was forced to close their hedge fund. Amaranth had amassed very large positions on both the NYMEX and the ICE in natural gas futures, swaps, and options. In September 2006, the natural gas futures market behaved entirely differently than it had historically, and a risky but reasonable strategy had catastrophic results for the fund. However, the

The result were provisions in the 2008 farm bill that provided the CFTC with authority over "price discovery contract," extending its authority to electronic trading facilities such as ICE with regard to natural gas and electricity derivatives.[40]

The passage of the Dodd-Frank Act[41] in 2010 extended the CFTC's authority over energy derivatives. Title VII of the Dodd-Frank Act deals with the OTC derivatives markets, and eliminates the exclusions and exemptions for energy derivatives from CFTC regulation. The Dodd-Frank Act brings all "swaps" under the jurisdiction of the CFTC and all "securities-based swaps" under the jurisdiction of the SEC. While physical forward contracts are exempt from CFTC regulation, commodity options are considered by CFTC to be "swaps." The modifications of the Commodities and Exchange Act make it unclear who has jurisdiction over instruments such as financial transmission rights (FTRs).[42] In February 2012, the RTOs/ISOs filed a petition with the CFTC for exemption from all provisions of the Commodities and Exchange Act, other than the antifraud and anti-manipulation provisions, for electricity products and services offered pursuant to their approved tariffs or protocols. The CFTC issued an exemption for RTO products in March 2013.[43] The

firm also took such large cumulative positions that it created liquidity risks, that is, they could not sell without adversely changing the price. Ludwig Chincarini, "A Case Study on Risk Management: Lessons from the Collapse of Amaranth Advisors L.L.C.," *Journal of Applied Finance* (Spring/Summer 2008): 1–23. Both FERC and the CFTC filed enforcement actions for manipulation based on the firm's behavior. Shaun Ledgerwood and Dan Harris, "A Comparison of Anti-Manipulation Rules in U.S. and EU Electricity and Natural Gas Markets: A Proposal for a Common Standard," 33 *Energy Law Journal* 1, 10 (2012).

[40] Section 13,201 of the *Food, Conservation, and Energy Act of 2008*, Pub. L. No. 110–234, 122 Stat. 923.

[41] Dodd-Frank Wall Street Reform and Consumer Protection Act, Pub. L. No. 111–203, 124 Stat. 1376 (2010).

[42] FTRs entitle the holder to receive the value of congestion on a contract path, providing a hedge against congestion costs.

[43] Lisa Dowden, Stephen Pearson, and Melissa Birchard, "Update on CFTC Actions under Dodd-Frank as They Affect the Electric Power Industry," Prepared for APPA 2011 Legal Conference (November 9, 2011); Terence Healey, Joseph Williams, and Paul Pantano, Jr., "Energy Commodities: The Netherworld between FERC and CFTC Jurisdiction," *Futures & Derivatives Law Report* 33 (February 2013); Commodity Futures Trading Commission, RIN 3038-AE02, *Final Order in Response to a Petition From Certain Independent System Operators and Regional Transmission Organizations to Exempt Specified Transactions Authorized by a Tariff or Protocol Approved by the Federal Energy Regulatory Commission or the Public Utility Commission of Texas From Certain Provisions of the Commodity Exchange Act Pursuant to the Authority Provided in Section 4(c)(6) of the Act*, March 28, 2013.

two agencies finally executed Memorandum of Understandings concerning potential overlaps of jurisdiction and information sharing in January 2014.

EPAct 2005 required the Secretary of Energy within a year of enactment and every three years thereafter to conduct a study of electric transmission congestion. The Secretary may designate any geographic area experiencing electric energy transmission capacity constraints or congestion as a national interest electric transmission corridor (NIETC). FERC may, after notice and hearing, issue permits for the construction of electric transmission facilities in a NIETC if the Commission finds that a state commission has withheld approval for more than 1 year or conditioned its approval in such a manner to discourage or limit the transmission's facility capability of relieving the constraint. Approval of the permit grants the holder the right of eminent domain. EPAct 2005 called for DOE to act as the lead agency for coordinating federal authorizations and environmental reviews for transmission.[44]

EPAct 2005 required FERC to establish incentive-based (including performance-based) rate treatments for transmission to promote capital investment in transmission facilities by providing a return on equity that attracts new investment (including related transmission technologies). The Commission shall also provide incentives to each utility that joins a RTO. However, all rates approved under these rules were subject to the traditional just and reasonable and nondiscrimination requirements of sections 205 and 206.[45]

One impact of EPAct 2005 was to institutionalize the priority of native load and existing firm transmission rights in LMP-based electricity markets, complicating any attempt to use FTRs to finance transmission and assign congestion costs. LSEs that hold firm transmission rights for the output of generation facilities or purchased energy to provide electric service to end-users or to a distribution utility were entitled to FTRs to the extent required to meet the service obligation of the LSE. The Commission was required to facilitate the planning and expansion of transmission facilities to meet the reasonable needs of LSEs to satisfy their service obligations, and enable LSEs to secure firm transmission rights (or equivalent tradable or financial rights) on a long-term basis for power supplies.[46]

---

[44] *Energy Policy Act of 2005*, § 1221.
[45] *Energy Policy Act of 2005*, § 1241.
[46] *Energy Policy Act of 2005*, § 1233.

The Commission responded to the passage of EPAct 2005 and its grant of additional authority and enhanced penalties for violation of FERC rules by reexamining its landmark Order 888. While Order 2000 had promoted membership in RTOs, there was still about a third of the nation's capacity and customers that were under the control of vertically integrated or unregulated utilities. Transmission customers complained that even in RTO markets there were instances when comparable transmission service was not provided to all customers, particularly in the area of transmission planning. In September 2005, the Commission issued a Notice of Inquiry to seek comments on whether reforms were needed to the Order 888 pro forma OATT and to the OATTs of public utilities.[47] FERC also asked for comments on NERC's Long-Term AFC/ATC Task Force Report and the advisability of developing an industry-wide standard for ATC and associated calculations.[48]

The Commission was concerned that the pro forma OATT could not fully remedy undue discrimination because transmission providers retained both the incentive and the ability to discriminate against third parties. The lag in investment in new transmission had resulted in inadequate infrastructure causing chronic transmission congestion. EPAct 2005 provided the Commission with tools to encourage new infrastructure and to improve the effectiveness of existing infrastructure. FERC proposed to achieve these goals by increasing the clarity and transparency of the rules applicable to the planning and use of the transmission system.[49]

The final rule, Order 890,[50] was issued in February 2007. The Commission rulemaking engendered a large volume of responses, reflecting the economic importance of opening the grid to both new entrants and the desire of incumbents to protect their markets. The Commission received more than 4,000 pages of initial and reply comments on the NOI, 5,700 pages of initial and reply comments in response to the NOPR, and an

---

[47] *Preventing Undue Discrimination and Preference in Transmission Services*, Notice of Inquiry, 112 FERC ¶ 61,299 (2005).

[48] *Information Requirements for Available Transfer Capability*, Notice of Inquiry, 111 FERC ¶ 61,274 (2005).

[49] *Preventing Undue Discrimination and Preference in Transmission Service*, NOPR, FERC Stats. & Regs. ¶ 32,603 at PP 3–4 (2006), 71 FR 32,636 (June 6, 2006).

[50] *Preventing Undue Discrimination and Preference in Transmission Service*, Order No. 890, FERC Stats. & Regs. ¶ 31,241 (2007), 72 FR 12266 (March 15, 2007), *order on reh'g*, Order No. 890-A, FERC Stats. & Regs. ¶ 31,261 (2007), 73 FR 2984 (January 16, 2008), *order on reh'g*, Order No. 890-B, 123 FERC ¶ 61,299 (2008), *order on reh'g and clarification*, Order No. 890-C, 126 FERC ¶ 61,228 (2009), *order on clarification*, Order No. 890-D, 129 FERC ¶ 61,126 (2009).

additional 750 pages in response to a Notice of Request for Supplemental Comments.[51] The Commission based the order on its broad remedial authority to limit opportunities for undue discrimination and the need to ensure open, transparent, and nondiscriminatory access to transmission service. Relying on precedents set in *Associated Gas Distributors*,[52] *TAPSG*,[53] and *National Fuel*,[54] the Commission concluded it had both the duty and authority to modify the OATT to eliminate potential as well as actual discrimination in transmission.[55]

Order 890 eliminated the wide discretion that transmission providers had in calculating ATC. The calculation of ATC determines whether transmission customers can access alternative power supplies. ATC calculation methodologies model the transmission system to establish TTC, expressed in terms of contract paths or flowgates, and then reduce that figure by existing transmission commitments, a margin that recognizes uncertainties with transfer capability, and a margin for meeting generation reliability criteria. These calculation methodologies were based on physical characteristics of the transmission system, historical modeling practices, and data related to system conditions. Utilities manipulated the ATC calculation to prevent third-party generators from competing for customers. The Commission found that the potential for undue discrimination stemmed from the ability of transmission providers to calculate ATC for different customers using different sets of assumptions and methodologies. The Commission therefore required public utilities, working through the NERC, to develop consistent methodologies for ATC calculation and to publish those methodologies to increase transparency.[56]

FERC had relied on functional separation for a decade, through a series of orders establishing standards of conduct that required the

[51] Order 890, at P 24. Parties claiming discrimination included Constellation, APPA, EPSA, East Texas Cooperatives, NRG, Occidental, TDU Systems, Williams, Entegra, and the National Rural Electric Cooperative Association, i.e., power marketers and their potential customers. Those claiming a lack of evidence of discrimination included EEI, Duke, Entergy, Progress Energy, and Southern. RTO members such as Exelon wanted the Commission to hold the transmission providers outside RTOs to the same standard of nondiscrimination that exists within those organizations. *Id*. at PP 27–38.

[52] *Associated Gas Distributors v. FERC*, 824 F.2d 981 (D.C. Cir. 1987).

[53] *Transmission Access Policy Study Group v. FERC*, 225 F.3d 667 (D.C. Cir. 2000), *aff'd sub nom. New York v. FERC*, 535 U.S. 1 (2002).

[54] *National Fuel Gas Supply Corp. v. FERC*, 468 F.3d 831 (D.C. Cir. 2006).

[55] Order 890 at PP 42–43.

[56] Order 890 at PP 207–13.

separation of the utilities' transmission system operations and wholesale marketing functions. Employees engaged in transmission functions must operate separately from employees of energy affiliates and marketing affiliates. Transmission providers were prohibited from allowing employees of their energy and marketing affiliates to obtain access to transmission or customer information, except via OASIS.[57] The Commission relied on cooperation with state agencies and the efforts of its Office of Enforcement to ensure that the separation of functions was fully implemented.[58] Left unmentioned was that structural separation would trigger a political and legal firestorm, as it would force divestiture by utilities with substantial political influence. By imposing onerous requirements on vertical utilities, the Commission provided incentives for voluntary divestiture.

The Commission also took a politically cautious tack toward the issue of opening up the transmission systems of unregulated utilities. In EPAct 2005, Congress authorized, but did not require, the Commission to order these utilities to provide transmission services under a new section 211 A of the FPA. The language permits the Commission to order a nonpublic utility to provide "open access" transmission service. The Commission chose to retain Order 888's reciprocity provisions that applied only to unregulated utilities that utilized regulated transmission. The Commission

---

[57] The rules were first established in Order No. 889. The Standards of Conduct rules were later replaced by a broader set of rules adopted in Order 2004, which were subsequently vacated in part by the DC Court of Appeals with respect to natural gas companies. See *Standards of Conduct for Transmission Providers*, Order No. 2004, FERC Stats. & Regs. ¶ 31,155 (2003), 68 FR 69134 (Dec. 11, 2003), *order on reh'g*, Order No. 2004-A, FERC Stats. & Regs. ¶ 31,161 (2004), 69 FR 23562 (April 29, 2004), *order on reh'g*, Order No. 2004-B, FERC Stats. & Regs. ¶ 31,166 (2004), 69 FR 48371 (August 10, 2004), *order on reh'g*, Order No. 2004-C, FERC Stats. & Regs. ¶ 31,172 (2005), 70 FR 284 (January 4, 2005), *order on reh'g*, Order No. 2004-D, 110 FERC ¶ 61,320 (2005), *vacated and remanded as it applies to natural gas pipelines sub nom. Nat'l Fuel Gas Supply Corporation v. FERC*, 468 F.3d 831 (D.C. Cir. 2006). The Commission issued an interim rule consistent with the Court's decision and initiated a new rulemaking. See *Standards of Conduct for Transmission Providers*, Order No. 690, FERC Stats. & Regs. ¶ 31,327 (2007), 72 FR 2427 (January 19, 2007); *Standards of Conduct for Transmission Providers*, Notice of Proposed Rulemaking, FERC Stats. & Regs. ¶ 32,611 (2007), 72 FR 3958 (January 29, 2007), *Standards of Conduct for Transmission Providers*, Order No. 717, FERC Stats. & Regs. ¶ 31,280 (2008), 73 FR 63,796 (October 27, 2008), *order on reh'g*, Order No. 717-A, FERC Stats. & Regs. ¶ 31,297 (2009), 74 FR 54,463 (October 22, 2009), *order on reh'g*, Order No. 717-B, 129 FERC ¶ 61,123 (2009), 74 FR 60,153 (November 20, 2009), *order on reh'g*, Order No. 717-C, 131 FERC ¶ 61,045 (2010), 75 FR 20,909 (April 22, 2010), *order on reh'g*, Order No. 717-D, 135 FERC ¶ 61,017 (2011).

[58] Order 890, PP 122–23.

proposed to apply section 211A authority on a case-by-case basis. The Commission also stated its expectation that unregulated transmission providers would participate in regional planning processes.[59]

The Commission realized that it could not rely on the self-interest of transmission providers to expand the grid in a nondiscriminatory manner. Transmission providers have an incentive to expand the grid to meet their state-imposed obligations to serve, but may have a disincentive to remedy transmission congestion when doing so reduces the value of their generation or permits new entry in their area. The lack of coordination, openness, and transparency results in opportunities for undue discrimination in transmission planning. New section 217 of the FPA required the Commission to exercise its jurisdiction in a manner that facilitated the planning and expansion of transmission facilities to meet the reasonable needs of LSEs. A more transparent and coordinated regional planning process would further this mandate and support the DOE's responsibilities under section 1221 to study transmission congestion.[60]

Each public utility transmission provider was required to submit, as part of its compliance filing, a proposal for a coordinated and regional planning process that complied with eight planning principles: coordination, openness, transparency, information exchange, comparability, dispute resolution, regional participation, and congestion studies. The Commission expected nonpublic utility transmission providers to participate in the proposed planning processes, given that effective regional planning cannot occur without the participation of all transmission providers, owners, and customers. Transmission customers and stakeholders must be able to participate in each transmission owner's planning process. RTOs and ISOs must indicate how transmission owners within their footprint will comply with the planning requirements.[61]

The Commission included a cost allocation principle in Order 890, narrowly tailored to apply to only to projects that do not fit under the existing structure, such as regional projects involving several transmission owners or economic projects. The principle balanced three considerations: cost causation and beneficiaries; adequate incentives to construct new transmission; and whether the proposal is supported by state authorities and participants across the region. A cost allocation proposal that has broad support across a region is more likely to avoid regulatory

[59] Order 890, PP 164–66.
[60] Order 890, PP 418–25.
[61] Order 890, PP 435–48.

problems with siting. As a general matter, the beneficiaries of any project should agree to support the costs of such projects. However, it was necessary to have the flexibility to overcome free-rider problems, as customers who do not agree to support a particular project may still receive benefits from it.[62]

Transmission providers used more stringent evaluation of transmission availability to serve long-term firm transmission service requests in a manner that was not comparable with the method they used to evaluate their own transmission. Planning redispatch involves a determination of whether generation redispatch can be used to maintain firm service. Conditional firm service involves a determination of whether there are limited conditions or hours under which firm service can be curtailed. The primary purpose of conditional firm service is to address the "all or nothing" problem associated long-term point-to-point service. A request for firm service could be denied because firm service was unavailable for a few hours of the year. Both techniques were used by transmission providers to serve native load, so they should also be made available to transmission customers in order to avoid undue discrimination. Redispatch and conditional firm options were interim measures to be deployed until transmission systems were upgraded to meet the transmission service request.[63]

The Commission imposed an obligation that transmission providers post redispatch cost information associated with redispatch services that must be provided under the pro forma OATT. When a transmission provider provided reliability or planning redispatch, the associated cost information was provided only to the customer receiving the service. The Commission also directed transmission providers to post redispatch costs for resolving transmission constraints so that customers had information to guide requests for studies of congested transmission facilities as part of transmission planning.[64]

The Commission put additional pressure on integrated transmission operators by requiring posting of performance metrics related to requests for firm and nonfirm transmission capacity. Section 19 of the pro forma OATT provided deadlines for issuing system impact study agreements and facilities studies agreements. Performance metrics must be calculated separately for affiliates' and non-affiliates' requests in order to identify

[62] Order 890, PP 557–61.
[63] Order 890, PP 911–29.
[64] Order 890, PP 1157–64.

when transmission providers are processing requests on a discriminatory basis. The Commission also tightened the reporting requirements concerning termination or redesignation of network resources to make firm third-party sales. The Commission wanted to ensure that there was sufficient lead time so that the appropriate set of network resources were included in the ATC calculation (i.e., so other parties would know there was additional transmission capacity available for transactions).[65]

The Commission struggled with balancing third-party sales, reliability considerations, and preventing network customers (who pay for the transmission system through load share allocation of costs) from making excessive claims on transmission capacity. A network customer's designated network resources were limited to designated load, nonfirm sales, losses, and sales under a reserve-sharing agreement. The transmission provider or a network customer was prohibited from using a designated resource for third-party sales that did not fall within one of the specified categories. The intent was to prevent excessive transmission capacity to be set aside and made unavailable to others seeking transmission service.[66]

The Commission strengthened compliance and enforcement efforts, starting with a staff audit program for compliance with OATT requirements, including operational audits. The Commission would address OATT violations on a case-by-case basis and impose civil penalties when warranted. OATT violators would be expected to disgorge unjust profits. The Commission proposed that if it revoked the market-based rate authority of a transmission provider within a particular market due to a significant OATT violation, each affiliate of the transmission provider would also have its market-based rate authority revoked in that market.[67]

[65] Order 890, PP 1296–1309, 1557–89.
[66] Order 890-B, PP 234–41.
[67] Order 890, PP 1715–48.

21

Wired

The continued difficulty of building out a "national grid" became a major issue, first because of increased congestion and barriers to entry into electricity markets, then because of the adoption of renewable portfolio standards by numerous states. The majority of new transmission that was built during the last decade or is currently under construction was either in-state or in RTOs. Between 2000 and mid-2007, only fourteen interstate high-voltage transmission lines, with a total length of 668 miles, were built.[1] While the pace of transmission building has picked up since then, most projects are relatively short, low-voltage lines for local reliability. There are relatively few high-voltage, multistate lines planned outside of the western United States. The CREZ lines in Texas are intrastate and primarily bring wind-generated power from West Texas to urban centers.[2] Although EEI projected that large interstate projects would account for two-thirds of spending over the near future, many of these interstate projects were speculative, and some fell prey to delays and failure to obtain the necessary regulatory approvals.[3]

---

[1] Stan Kaplan, "Electric Power Transmission: Background and Policy Issues," Congressional Research Service (April 14, 2009): 15.
[2] "NERC-Wide Transmission Additions, Upgrades, and Retirements," in NERC, *Long-Term Reliability Assessment*, 2007–2011.
[3] EEI, "Transmission Projects: At A Glance" (March 2011): x. ITC's Green Power Express is a $10–12 billion dollar project that exists only as a concept. The Potomac-Appalachian Transmission Highline (PATH), a joint venture with AEP and Allegheny Energy, Inc. to build a 765 kV transmission line extending from West Virginia to Maryland, was suspended in February 2011. EEI, "Transmission Projects: At a Glance" (March 2011): 19.

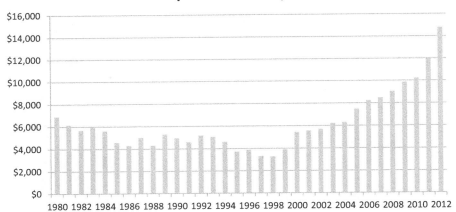

FIGURE 21.1. Transmission Investment. *Source: EEI Statistical Yearbook, 2006,*
Table 9.1: Construction Expenditures for Transmission and Distribution; *EEI*
Actual and Planned Transmission Investment 2007–2016 (September 2013).

Between 1978 and 1982, transmission capacity increased slightly faster
than did summer peak demand. However, during the subsequent two
decades, utilities added transmission capacity at a much lower rate than
the growth in electricity demand. Average annual investment fell in the
1980s and by 1993–1994 hit a low of $2.5 billion. Although total trans-
mission investment reversed its decline in 1999, it failed to keep pace with
peak demand growth until recently. Annual investments begun to climb
during the last decade, reaching $5.8 billion annually in 2005 and rising
to $11.1 billion in 2011.[4]

The lack of new investment in transmission facilities, combined with
new patterns of electricity flows, resulted in an increase in congestion costs
and TLR events. The number of times system operators in the Eastern
Interconnection called for Level 2 (which requires operators to freeze
transactions at current levels) or higher-level TLRs increased from about
500 in 1998 and 1999 to almost 2,000 in 2003. A survey of transmission
congestion in the six operating ISOs found that congestion costs from

[4] Electricity Advisory Committee, "Keeping the Lights On in a New World" (January
2009): 16; Eric Hirst, "U.S. Transmission Capacity: Present Status and Future Prospects,"
prepared for the EEI and DOE (August 2004): 7; EEI, "Transmission Projects: At a
Glance" (March 2013): iii.

1999 to 2002 totaled approximately \$4.8 billion. Congestion costs in PJM ranged from 6 percent to 10 percent of total billings.[5]

Despite the various measures taken to expedite the building of new transmission, the traditional problems of NIMBY and state parochialism remain significant barriers. Opposition is especially intense in the western states, where the long distances between resources and loads require massive transmission projects traversing the western landscape. The corridors of transmission lines could be hundreds of yards wide and thousands of miles long with transmission towers that rise up to 185 feet into the air. Local residents complain that such projects ruin the rural character of their communities only to export wind energy to California and other populated areas. Construction of transmission corridors on federal public lands faces environmental restrictions such as roadless areas and protection of endangered species. In Wyoming and Idaho, opposition to the use of eminent domain has emerged. These conflicts are not aligned along traditional partisan and ideological divides. Citizens seeking to protect the rural character and scenic beauty of their community find themselves aligned with property rights advocates in opposition to transmission projects. They may find themselves at odds with ranchers who want to collect income from wind turbines on their property.[6]

The U.S. electric grid infrastructure consists of about 3,000 consumer-serving entities and 500 transmission owners. The high-voltage transmission network in the United States comprises nearly 170,000 circuit miles of transmission lines at voltages 230 kV and above, and almost 400,000 circuit miles over 100 kV.[7] Until the mid-1990s, the U.S. electricity industry was dominated by vertically integrated utilities. These utilities, because they owned generation and transmission, could optimize investments across both kinds of assets. Utilities routinely scheduled generation day-ahead and redispatched generating units in real time to prevent congestion. Utilities had good data on customer loads and behavior, simplifying the task of forecasting short- and long-run load profiles. Since each utility was the primary investor in new generation, the timing, types, and locations of new generation and retirement of

[5] Eric Hirst, "U.S. Transmission Capacity: Present Status and Future Prospects," at 7–8; *PJM State of the Markets Report 2005* (April 2006).

[6] Sandra K. Davis, "Rewiring Electricity Transmission Policy," Paper Presented at the 2011 Western Political Science Association Conference, April 21–23, 2011.

[7] North American Electric Reliability Corporation, *2008 Long-Term Reliability Assessment: 2008–2017* (October 2008); *2011 Long-Term Reliability Assessment: 2008–2017* (November 2011).

existing units occurred at the discretion of the utility (subject to regulatory oversight). Under the integrated monopoly structure, planning and investment in generation and transmission, as well as operating procedures were often coordinated through an integrated resource planning process.

With the advent of deregulation, generation investment and location are driven by market prices and incentives. The transmission system is often operated by independent transmission organizations that do not own the transmission assets. The primary drivers for transmission upgrades and expansions are reliability considerations and the economic value of new transmission capacity. However, because the operating and investment decisions by generation companies are market driven, valuation of transmission expansion projects must also anticipate the impact of such investments on market prices and power flows.

The ISOs/RTOs no longer have access to much of the information available to integrated utilities. System operators have limited information on the details of retail loads, such as the types of end-use equipment in place and trends and patterns in electricity use. LSEs that have such information may be reluctant to share information with the system operator. Congestion management has become part of the dispatch process and is susceptible to gaming as well as conflict over assignment of costs. The separation of generation from transmission can lead to investment decisions in both sectors that are socially suboptimal. The quantity and complexity of wholesale electricity commerce has exploded over the last decades, from short-term arbitragers exploiting small but predictable differences in prices to large power flows that previously were blocked by lack of transmission capacity, congestion costs, or regulatory barriers. Transactions today can span several control areas, and ownership of the power may change hands several times between injection and the point of withdrawal. Interconnection queues are crowded with projects that will never be built, filed by companies reserving their position in the queue through a small option payment, signaling competitors of potential excess capacity, thus discouraging entry. This complexity makes it difficult for system operators to project transmission flows in future years.[8]

Transmission planning for utility systems is still done primarily with reliability in mind. Solving the first contingency problem for tens of

---

[8] Eric Hirst and Brendan Kirby, "Transmission Planning and the Need for New Capacity," in DOE, *National Transmission Grid Study: Issue Papers* (May 2002): D-6–D-7.

thousands of pieces of equipment in actual power systems is computationally burdensome, and the optimal transmission-planning problem is very difficult to solve. Transmission-planning studies consider multiple scenarios involving peak demand, new investments, and contingencies. The scenarios run by utility transmission planners are used to determine which investments improve system reliability. The transmission-planning process becomes a heuristic or (at best) local optimization problem.[9]

System operators use forecasting models to identify bottlenecks, reliability requirements, and economic upgrades (opportunities to reduce congestion and reduce prices). These models include load forecasting models and market models that project future prices, flows, and generation. There are numerous software packages available for electricity market analysis and transmission planning, but they are essentially "black boxes" that have not been scrutinized by independent third parties for accuracy. The two main tools used for planning are production cost programs and resource planning models. MISO uses the Ventyx product PROMOD as their production cost model. PJM uses GE-MAPS for reserve requirements studies, and ISO-NE and NYISO use Siemens's Power System Simulator for reliability studies. Other production cost models include ABB's Gridview, Argonne's GTMAX, Power-Cost's GenTrader, Henwood's PROSYM, and LCG's UPLAN. MISO uses an EPRI product called EGEAS as their resource-planning model. Other resource-planning models include Ventyx's Strategist and Power-World Simulator. Plexos can be used for both production costing and resource planning. Most of these tools were developed in the 1970s and 1980s.[10]

A key element in planning, because of its impact on cost allocation, is determining whether a transmission upgrade is required for reliability, or is justified by its economic benefits. Reliability projects tend to be socialized, while the cost of economic projects is often assigned to those transmission customers who benefit from the project. Another issue is the trade-off between economies of scale and current needs. It is more cost effective to overbuild in anticipation of future loads (and to increase

[9] Seth Blumsack, "Network Topologies and Transmission Investment Under Electric-Industry Restructuring" (Ph.D. Diss., Carnegie Mellon University, 2006): 9–10, 21.

[10] http://home.eng.iastate.edu/~jdm/ee552/NationalModelingTools.pdf (last visited March 25, 2012); KEMA Consulting, "Analysis and Selection of Analytical Tools to Assess National-Interest Transmission Bottlenecks," for the Department of Energy (March 2003); various vendor Web sites.

the capacity of the system as a whole), both because cost per MW-mile declines substantially[11] and because it is easier to fight one regulatory battle to obtain a sufficiently wide easement for future expansion than having to expand the corridor to upgrade or site a new transmission line in the future. However, if the line is allocated on an economic basis, the current beneficiaries will be overcharged while future beneficiaries will free-ride.

Actual power flows in an electrical network generally diverge from intended delivery paths, or contract paths. Because electricity flows are difficult to trace, it is difficult to define and manage transmission usage. Parallel flows, or loop flows, lead to misalignment between private costs and social costs. The inability to account for externalities due to parallel flows was responsible for the increased use of TLRs. However, TLRs are an awkward solution, requiring ad hoc adjustments. A market-based solution to this externality problem is to issue a set of well-defined transmission rights that internalize these effects.[12] The complications involved in assigning and establishing physical transmission rights led to a shift toward pure financial rights, usually determined as the right to the revenues from congestion on a contract path. FTRs were also politically important as a means to buy off the opposition to LMP markets of cooperatives and municipals by giving them sufficient transmission rights to assure they could access their power plants without incurring large congestion fees.

Congestion pricing and FTRs, or congestion revenue rights, entitle the holder to receive the value of congestion as established by the difference between locational prices of the two nodes that comprise the contract path. Faster computers allowed solution of LMP models in real time, and thus determine nodal prices. The solution produced by these SCED models approximates the efficient solution for optimal dispatch, and congestion costs reflect the marginal value of relaxing a transmission constraint. FTRs provide hedges for market actors against unexpected

---

[11] Installing a 500 kV line instead of a 345 kV line will reduce costs per MW-mile by 40%, but require expanding the corridor width from 125 to 175 feet. This may complicate the approval process, as a wider corridor and higher towers will engender more opposition at regulatory hearings. There is also the problem that a 500 kV line may have a capacity up to 2,000 MW, which could make it the largest contingency on many systems, requiring an increase in operating reserves. Eric Hirst and Brendan Kirby, "Transmission Planning and the Need for New Capacity," in Department of Energy, *National Transmission Grid Study: Issue Papers* (May 2002): D-19.

[12] Hung-po Chao, Stephen Peck, Shmuel Oren, and Robert Wilson, "Flow-Based Transmission Rights and Congestion Management," *Electricity Journal* (October 2000): 38–39.

congestion costs, but they are far from a perfect instrument, as auction clearing prices for FTRs differ significantly and systematically from the realized congestion revenues that determine the payoffs of these rights.[13] While this scheme had been championed by academic economists,[14] in the real world the ability of LMP prices and FTRs to provide the incentives necessary for efficient grid investment turned out to be illusionary.

The appeal of rewarding transmission investment with FTRs is based on the assumption of an idealized world of perfect competition. In this model, marginal investments are always possible and their cost is linear, and any investor can upgrade any line. FTRs reward their holders with a revenue stream equal to the difference in nodal prices at the FTR's source and sink nodes times the quantity of FTRs held (zero except when there is congestion). The congestion rent that would be earned by a marginal upgrade of a transmission path equals the value of the upgrade in reducing congestion costs associated with that investment.[15]

It is difficult to put much faith in the extension of conclusions derived from highly stylized models with a handful of nodes, a couple transmission lines, and actors to electricity markets that often have hundreds or thousands of nodes, a dense network of transmission lines at different voltages, a wide variety of generators with portfolios of plants with different technical characteristics and cost structures, and shifting and fluctuating loads. The simple model of competitive transmission assumes away increasing returns to scale, sunk cost or asset specificity issues,

---

[13] Shi-Jie Deng, Shmuel Oren, and Sakis Meliopoulos, "The Inherent Inefficiency of the Point-to-Point Congestion Revenue Right Auction," Proceeding of the 37th Hawaiian International Conference on System Sciences, 2004; Lester Hadsell and Hany A. Shawky, "Efficiency and Profit in the NYISO Transmission Congestion Contract Market," *Electricity Journal* 30 (November 2009): 1–11.

[14] William Hogan, "Contract Networks for Electric Power Transmission," *Journal of Regulatory Economics* 4(3)(1992): 211–42; William Hogan, "Electric Transmission: A New Model for Old Principles," *The Electricity Journal* (March 1993): 18–29; James Bushnell and Stephen Stoft, "Electric Grid Investment Under a Contract Network Regime," *Journal of Regulatory Economics* 10 (1996): 61–79; Hung-Po Chao and Stephen Peck, "A Market Mechanism for Electric Power Transmission," *Journal of Regulatory Economics* 10 (1996): 25–59; James Bushnell and Stephen Stoft, "Improving Private Incentives for Electric Grid Investment," *Resource and Energy Economics* 19 (1997): 85–108. However, see Shmuel S. Oren et al., "Nodal Prices and Transmission Rights: A Critical Appraisal," *The Electricity Journal* (April 1995): 24–35 and Paul Joskow and Jean Tirole, "Transmission Rights and Market Power on Electric Power Networks," *RAND Journal of Economics* 31 (2000): 450–87.

[15] Steven Stoft, "Problems of Transmission Investment in a Deregulated Power Market," in François Lévêque, ed., *Competitive Electricity Markets and Sustainability* (Cheltenham, Edward Elgar, 2006): 112.

public-good aspects of reliability, network externalities, the stochastic nature of transmission constraints (if a tree falls on a transmission line, someone is sure to get an earful), market power, and incomplete future markets. Incorporating more realistic attributes of transmission networks leads to the conclusion that significant inefficiencies may result from reliance on the merchant transmission investment framework.[16]

There are two classes of transmission investments: deepening investments and de novo transmission lines. Deepening investments increase capacity, reliability, and control of existing lines through the addition of capacitor banks, phase shifters, new communications and relay equipment. Many transmission lines are built with room to build additional lines on the towers, taking advantage of the preexisting right of way to provide the opportunity to increase capacity at relatively low cost. These investments are physically intertwined with the incumbent transmission owner's facilities and would be difficult to open to competition.[17] New transmission lines can be built by merchant transmission, but an investor faces significant investment risk if revenue must be recovered through market mechanisms. Grid expansions and variations in generation and load over time can have a huge impact on congestion revenues, making an investment in a transmission line funded by FTRs a risky undertaking. Lumpy investments in transmission face a similar problem as generators building within a small load pocket. In both cases, the new facility could reduce or eliminate the congestion, which provides revenue, and shifting positive cash flows far into the future raises the risk associated with the investment. The uncertainty surrounding future revenues from congestion increases risk for merchant transmission, almost ensuring underinvestment by private actors.[18]

The one exception seems to be DC lines into highly congested regions, where upgrading the AC system is an expensive and protracted process. Successful merchant projects include TransEnergie's Cross Sound

---

[16] Paul Joskow and Jean Tirole, "Merchant Transmission Investment," *Journal of Industrial Economics* 53 (June 2005): 235.

[17] Joskow and Tirole, "Merchant Transmission Investment," at 238–39.

[18] One suggestion is to utilize a regulated two-part tariff. Under this scheme, a merchant would receive congestion revenues plus/minus the change in fixed fees caused by the merchant investment. The authors admit there are many unresolved issues, such as how to practically characterize the piecewise cost functions, incorporate changes in topology, and address the global optimality properties of the incentives. William Hogan, Juan Rosellón, and Ingo Vogelsang, "Toward a Combined Merchant-Regulatory Mechanism for Electricity Transmission Expansion," *Journal of Regulatory Economics* 38 (2010): 140–41.

Cable,[19] Neptune's Electric Transmission System,[20] and the Trans Bay Cable.[21] Since the DC line will only impact the AC grid at the two points where it interconnects, capacity on the line can be sold without reference to loop flows or other interactions with the AC grid. AC lines and new generation are difficult to construct in highly urbanized and congested load pockets, so the investor has a higher probability of receiving a substantial portion of congestion revenues (explicit allocation of FTRs is not required, as auctioning off the line's capacity will cause revenues from the sale of transmission capacity to approach potential congestion revenues) over an extended period of time.[22]

The emergence of independent transmission companies has had little impact on the transmission-planning paradigm, as these companies work within the regulated transmission paradigm. The American Transmission Company was formed in 2001 by a group of private and municipal utilities and cooperatives to own and operate their transmission systems. Its service area is primarily the Michigan's Upper Peninsula and eastern Wisconsin. The companies that transferred their assets to American Transmission are the owners of the corporation.[23] The International Transmission Company (ITC) is a more entrepreneurial firm, originally founded by Detroit Edison, which sold the company along with its transmission assets to Kohlberg Kravis Roberts and Trimaran Capital Partners in 2003. ITC acquired Michigan Electric Transmission Company in 2006

---

[19] TransEnergie is the U.S. transmission development subsidiary of a division of Hydro-Quebec. The Cross Sound Cable is a 26-mile undersea high-voltage, bidirectional DC cable underneath the Long Island Sound. *TransEnergie U.S.*, 91 FERC ¶ 61,230 (2000).

[20] Neptune Regional Transmission System, LLC developed and owns and operates the Neptune Project, a 65-mile, 660 MW undersea and underground DC transmission line that extends from Sayreville, New Jersey, to Nassau County on Long Island. Neptune operates under a long-term agreement with the Long Island Power Authority, which selected Neptune RTS to build and operate the project in a competitive solicitation in 2004. http://neptunerts.com/ (last visited June 21, 2012).

[21] The Trans Bay Cable is a 53-mile, 400 MW DC submarine transmission line from Pittsburg, CA, to San Francisco. "Pattern Energy Announces Completion of the Trans Bay Cable Project Under San Francisco Bay," *PR Newswire*, November 29, 2010, at http://www.prnewswire.com/news-releases/pattern-energy-announces-completion-of-the-trans-bay-cable-project-under-san-francisco-bay-110965414.html (last visited June 21, 2012).

[22] Merchant investments in the United States and in Europe typically derive revenues from long-term contractual arrangements with regulated entities rather than from spot market arbitrage between locational price differentials. Stephen Littlechild, "Merchant and Regulated Transmission: Theory, Evidence and Policy," *Journal of Regulatory Economics* 42 (2012): 309–10.

[23] http://www.atcllc.com/A1.shtml (last visited March 24, 2012).

and the transmission assets of Interstate Power and Light in Iowa, Illinois, Minnesota, and Missouri in 2007. ITC is developing new facilities in SPP and in December 2011 announced a plan for Entergy to divest its transmission assets, which would then merge with ITC. However, that proposed transaction was terminated in December 2013.[24] ITC's business model is to maintain a lean corporate structure and rely on subcontractors for construction and maintenance. While ITC is rapidly expanding, it is doing so as a regulated utility company, and its projects are financed though FERC approved transmission rates.

The permitting of transmission facilities is highly fragmented among federal government, states, and local authorities. The siting of extra-high-voltage (EHV) transmission projects often involves multiple entities with varied processes. Each local, state, and federal agency typically has its own permitting rules and processes, which are rarely consistent with each other. The participation of a wide spectrum of interested parties, and the nature of interstate EHV transmission crossing jurisdictional boundaries, complicates and impedes the planning, approval, and permitting processes. This can further delay the already lengthy siting process, add to the cost of transmission projects, and increase the financial risk to a transmission developer.[25]

In most states, the siting process is embedded in the state's utility statutes, and usually requires a showing of need or necessity (which implies that the investment is "useful"), usually determined by reference to in-state requirements. Many state siting statutes balance the need for transmission lines against health, safety, and environmental impacts. States vary greatly in the mechanisms used to approve transmission-siting proposals, with the authority to site resting with individual local governments, state environmental regulators, or state public utility commissions.

---

[24] http://investor.itc-holdings.com/releases.cfm?Year=&ReleasesType=Financial,%20International%20Transmission&PageNum=2 (last visited August 18, 2014).

[25] Electricity Advisory Committee, "Keeping the Lights On in a New World" (January 2009): 49. American Electric Power's 765-kV project between West Virginia and Virginia was proposed in 1990, and rerouted in 1997 because of objections by both states and the U.S. Forest Service. West Virginia approved the new route in 1998, but the route was modified in Virginia, with approval for the change finally obtained in 2001. The new route was reapproved by West Virginia in 2002, and the U.S. Forest Service issued a special use permit in 2003. Construction started in April 2004 and the line was energized in June 2006. See http://www.aep.com/about/transmission/Wyoming-Jacksons_Ferry.aspx (last visited on March 26, 2012); David H. Meyer and Richard Sedano, "Transmission Siting and Permitting," Department of Energy, *National Transmission Grid Study: Issue Papers* (May 2002): E-9.

The regulatory commission is usually the body that approves the siting of new transmission lines, typically after conducting a contested case, in which various parties present evidence and witnesses are cross-examined in a quasi-litigation proceeding. Since commissions are political bodies, they are sensitive to the objections of public-interest advocates and politically connected individuals whose land may be impacted by a proposed project. The commission will rarely give weight to benefits accruing to other states.[26]

The cost of new transmission facilities is generally included in the rate base of the utility building the facilities, or when transmission is financed through charges – the revenue requirement. While revenues derived from other users of transmission may be credited against the revenue requirement, the full risk of the revenue responsibility for the line is generally borne by native load customers. This makes the allocation of costs a critical component of obtaining siting approval for a proposed new transmission line. It is highly improbable that a state will approve a line being built by a jurisdictional utility if the costs, or the residual revenue risks, are to be borne by local consumers while the benefits are largely extra-jurisdictional.[27]

For many landowners, transmission lines represent undesirable land uses and thus generate NIMBY opposition. NIMBY can be viewed as a risk-averse strategy. Most NIMBYs are homeowners, and homeowners cannot insure their major (and often only) asset against devaluation by neighborhood effects.[28] In the case of transmission, this extends to rural landowners who have property values based on scenic views or potential residential value. (However, ranchers often welcome wind turbines and transmission when they can receive some income. By negotiating location of these facilities away from living quarters, they ameliorate negative impacts, and as I was told by a rancher in West Texas, "the cows like the shade.") Where major transmission projects encroach on higher-income suburban or high-value exurban regions, opposition

[26] Hoang Dang, "New Power, Few New Lines: A Need For a Federal Solution," 17 *Journal of Land Use & Environmental Law* 327, 336–37 (2002). See also Ahira Ostrow, "Process Preemption in Federal Siting Regimes," 48 *Harvard Journal on Legislation* 289, 298–300 (2011).

[27] Ashley Brown and Jim Rossi, "Siting Transmission Lines in a Changed Milieu: Evolving Notions of the 'Public Interest' in Balancing State and Regional Considerations," 81 *University of Colorado Law Review* 705, 709–11 (2010).

[28] William Fischel, "Why Are There NIMBYs?" *Land Economics* 77 (February 2001): 144–52.

becomes intense (since the residents have financial resources, sophistication, and often political connections). Sophisticated opponents hire expert witnesses who attack transmission projects on need and environmental safety. The equity issue is usually framed as "they're building the line so that they can sell power to someone else."[29]

The regulatory process also allows competitors, both by direct intervention and through support of NIMBY advocates and environmental groups, to hinder projects. For example, northeast utilities, primarily based in Connecticut (with customers in Massachusetts and New Hampshire), owned an older, competing transmission line that ran parallel to the proposed Cross-Sound cable. Northeast utilities favored updating its line over approving the Cross-Sound line. Connecticut's attorney general, backed by environmental interest groups and northeast utilities, threatened litigation if the Cross-Sound line was allowed to go live.[30]

DOE issued its national grid report in 2002. The DOE report identified numerous congested paths in both the eastern and western interchanges. DOE found substantial congestion in the midwest and upper midwest, and from the mid-Atlantic to the northeast. DOE also identified congested pathways in the WECC, mostly into California. DOE analyzed the implications of eliminating pancaked rates (where users pay each utility a fee) and found that this could provide benefits exceeding $1 billion per year. Postage stamp rates would increase electricity trades but also transmission congestion between regions as a result of the increased loading of interregional transmission facilities.[31]

DOE was circumspect when it came to recommendations concerning siting of new transmission facilities, deferring to the politics of federalism while recognizing the need for FERC to be the final arbiter for the siting of interstate transmission. Federal regulators should actively support and defer to state and regional siting and permitting processes, but FERC must have the authority to ensure that the public interest is served and that national interest transmission bottlenecks are addressed. FERC

[29] Robert Wasserstrom, Neil Palmer and Susan Reider, "Trouble on the Line. Deregulation Fuels Public Opposition to Transmission Lines," Terra Group (Houston 1996).

[30] Jim Rossi, "Transmission Siting in Deregulated Wholesale Power Markets: Re-imagining the Role of Courts in Resolving Federal-State Siting Impasses," 15 *Duke Environmental Law & Policy Forum* 315, 317–19 (2005).

[31] DOE, *National Transmission Grid Study* (May 2002): 11–26. The Energy Information Administration had to model constraints directly because the National Energy Model was too aggregated to capture limits on electricity trade because of power flow limitations. Robert Eynon, Thomas Leckey, and Douglas Hale, "The Electric Transmission Network: A Multi-Region Analysis," in EIA, *Issues in Midterm Analysis and Forecasting, 2000.*

must be able to grant designated entities the right of eminent domain to acquire property for rights of way.[32] The recommendations to improve transmission siting, among other measures, became caught up in energy politics.

The supporters of increased federal authority over siting during the four years leading up to the passage of EPAct 2005 included industry groups such as the EEI and APPA. These organizations contended that the reform of siting procedures was necessary not only to ensure reliable, low-cost electricity but for national security as well. Groups opposing the bill's provisions included the Western Governors Association, the National Conference of State Legislatures, NARUC, the National Association of Towns and Townships, the National Association of State Utility Consumer Advocates, and other state and local organizations. Those groups felt that the current methods for siting approval were successfully adapting to the new regional markets and that no changes were needed.[33]

While the passage of EPAct 2005 seemed to have resolved the issue in favor of federal siting authority, at least where the need was greatest, events soon proved otherwise. DOE issued its first congestion report in 2006, as mandated by EPAct 2005.[34] The Department identified two critical congestion areas: the Atlantic coastal area from metropolitan New York southward through Northern Virginia; and Southern California. In the northeast, the two key constrained paths were into Eastern PJM and into New York City. Congestion areas of concern included New England, Phoenix-Tucson, the Seattle-Portland corridor, and the San Francisco Bay Area. Conditional congestion areas, where significant congestion would result if large amounts of new generation resources were to be developed, were almost exclusively in the western states, where potential resources are located far from load centers.[35] Based on the findings of the 2006 study, and subsequent study and input, the Department issued a report and order designating two NIETC in October 2007: the Mid-Atlantic Area NIETC and the Southwest Area NIETC.[36]

---

[32] DOE, *National Transmission Grid Study*, 53.

[33] Steven J. Eagle, "Securing a Reliable Electricity Grid: A New Era in Transmission Siting Regulation?" George Mason University School of Law, Law and Economics Working Paper Series, 05–31 (September 13, 2005): 9–10.

[34] § 1221(a).

[35] DOE, *National Electric Transmission Congestion Study* (August 2006): 39–57.

[36] DOE, [Docket No. 2007–OE–01, Mid-Atlantic Area National Interest Electric Transmission Corridor; Docket No. 2007–OE–02, Southwest Area National Interest Electric Transmission Corridor], *National Electric Transmission Congestion Report*, 72 FR 56992, October 5, 2007.

FERC was granted DOE's lead agency responsibilities for the purpose of coordinating all applicable federal authorizations and preparing a single environmental review document for a designated NIETC. While DOE would conduct a pre-application process for federal authorizations, the Commission would administer a pre-filing process to facilitate participation from interested parties.[37] The applicant must describe alternatives to the project, including alternatives other than new transmission lines, and compare their environmental impacts. Once the application is filed, intervenors can file comments. The Commission will issue a draft environmental document that will also be subject to a comment period. Finally, the Commission will issue an order addressing the issues raised in the proceeding.[38]

The Commission has the authority to issue permits to construct or modify electric transmission facilities under FPA section 216(b) if it finds that a state lacks the authority to approve the facilities; the applicant is not eligible to apply for siting approval in that state, approval is withheld for more than a year after an application is filed; or approval is conditioned in a manner to make the transmission facility economically infeasible. Before issuing a permit, the Commission must find that the proposed facility will be used for the transmission of electricity in interstate commerce, will significantly reduce congestion, and will maximize the transmission capabilities of existing structures. An exception to FERC authority occurs if a state is a party to an interstate compact establishing a regional transmission-siting agency (with three contiguous states) unless the members of the compact are in disagreement and the DOE secretary makes certain findings.[39]

The Commission defined "withholding approval" to include denial of a transmission project application.[40] This did not eliminate the state commission's discretion, as it could still condition approval on reasonable accommodations that did not make the project infeasible. The Commission's interpretation kept a state commission from blocking a priority

---

[37] *Regulations for Filing Applications for Permits to Site Interstate Electric Transmission Facilities*, Notice of Proposed Rulemaking, FERC Stats. & Regs. ¶ 32,605 at PP 6–7 (2006), 71 FR 36258 (June 26, 2006). Effective May 16, 2006, the Secretary delegated paragraphs (2), (3), (4)(A)–(B), and (5) of FPA section 216(h) to the Commission.

[38] Order 689, PP 47–49, 74–89, 120–93.

[39] 16 U.S.C. 824p.

[40] *Regulations for Filing Applications for Permits to Site Interstate Electric Transmission Facilities*, Order No. 689, FERC Stats. & Regs. ¶ 31,234 at PP 25–31 (2006), 71 FR 69,440 (December 1, 2006), *reh'g denied*, 119 FERC ¶ 61,154 (2007).

interstate transmission line in order to pander to local sensibilities. The Fourth Circuit reversed, finding that phrase "withheld approval for more than 1 year" does not give FERC jurisdiction when a state commission denies a permit application in a NIETC.[41] Judge Traxler, in his dissent, pointed out that the purpose of the legislation was to provide FERC the authority to ensure that a state does not frustrate the goal of significantly reducing transmission congestion in a national-interest corridor. The notion that Congress would have been willing to allow FERC to override states when they thwart this goal by granting permits subject to unreasonable conditions but not when states thwart the same goal by denying the permits made no sense.[42]

In the 111th Congress, multiple bills were introduced to expand federal authority over the siting of interstate transmission lines to provide access to renewable energy. The Waxman-Markey Bill, known for creating a carbon cap-and-trade system, also included a provision to allow FERC to preempt state action if a state failed to approve or rejected a transmission line within a year after application. A bill sponsored by Senate Majority Leader Harry Reid (D-NV) would expand FERC's backstop authority to enable transmission from renewable energy zones.[43] Prior to the decision in *Piedmont*, renewable energy was scarcely mentioned, certainly not by the Cheney task force that originally recommended federal authority over transmission siting. The court, litigants, and policymakers had focused on reliability and economic efficiency.[44]

In February 2011, the Ninth Circuit Court of Appeals ruled that DOE failed to properly consult with the affected states in conducting the congestion study and failed to undertake any environmental study for its NIETC designation as required by NEPA. The court vacated the congestion study and NIETC designations and remanded the cases to the DOE.[45] In September 2011, the DOE issued a proposal whereby it would delegate to FERC the authority to conduct congestion studies and designate NIETCs. FERC would invite state participation in proceedings on corridor applications, and in NIETC designations would perform a full NEPA

---

[41] *Piedmont Environmental Council v. FERC*, 558 F. 3d 304, 313–314 (4th Cir 2009), cert. denied, *Edison Elec. Inst. v. Piedmont Envtl. Council*, 130 S. Ct. 1138 (2010).

[42] *Piedmont Environmental Council*, 558 F. 3d 304, 322–324.

[43] Jim Rossi, "The Trojan Horse of Electric Power Transmission Line Siting Authority," 39 *Environmental Law* 1015, 1037–39 (2009).

[44] Michael Dorsi, "Piedmont Environmental Council v. FERC," 34 *Harvard Environmental Law Review* 593, 597–98 (2010).

[45] *California Wilderness Coalition v. Dept. of Energy*, 631 F. 3d 1072 (9th Cir 2011).

analysis, thus responding to the court's concerns.[46] Senator Jeff Bingaman (D-NM), a principal drafter of EPAct 2005, objected to transferring the congestion study and corridor designation authority to FERC. DOE Secretary Steven Chu then announced that the agencies would work together to prepare transmission congestion studies for proposed NIETCs.[47]

While FERC was working with the DOE to expedite construction of crucial interstate transmission lines, the agency had become concerned with the limitations of the conventional transmission-planning process. The lack of regional transmission planning may result in the failure to identify the facilities best suited to meet regional needs. Planning should take into account new public policy requirements established by state or federal laws or regulations, such as renewable portfolio standards, energy efficiency or demand response goals, and economic development policies. The Order 890 transmission-planning requirements might not be just and reasonable if they did not address the need for greater coordination in interregional transmission planning. Existing methods for allocating the costs of new transmission might not be just and reasonable if they inhibited the development of efficient, cost-effective transmission facilities.[48]

FERC staff convened three regional technical conferences in September 2009 to assess existing transmission-planning processes. A NOPR was then issued in June 2010, engendering 5,700 pages of comments. The NOPR comments reflected the split between state and incumbent utilities and "outsiders" who wanted new transmission, primarily to access renewable energy for state RPS markets, but also in some cases as a business opportunity to build transmission. A more interesting split occurred between state commissions and ISOs/RTOs. MISO, the New York Public Service Commission, the Ohio Commission, and WECC argued that existing transmission-planning processes were adequate to achieve the

---

46 *Proposed Siting Delegation to FERC*, at http://www.congestion09.anl.gov/news/index .cfm#ferc (last visited April 10, 2012); *FERC Staff Preliminary and Conceptual Transmission Siting Proposal*, at http://www.congestion09.anl.gov/documents/docs/ Transmission%20Siting%20Narrative%20Draft%20(Clean%208%2026%2011).pdf (last visited April 10, 2012).

47 "Bingaman Opposes US DOE Delegation of Corridor Authority to FERC," *Platts*, September 12, 2011, at http://www.platts.com/RSSFeedDetailedNews/RSSFeed/ ElectricPower/6468308 (last visited April 10, 2012); DOE and FERC Joint Public Statement on Back Stop Siting, October 11, 2011, at http://energy.gov/articles/doe-and-ferc-joint-public-statement-backstop- siting (last visited on April 10, 2012).

48 *Transmission Planning and Cost Allocation by Transmission Owning and Operating Public Utilities*, Notice of Proposed Rulemaking, FERC Stats. & Regs. ¶ 32,660, PP 32–41 (2010), 75 FR 37884 (June 30, 2010).

Commission's stated goals. SPP suggested that the Commission add to the OATT a pro forma seams agreement that included joint collaborative planning and cost allocation across planning regions. The Organization of MISO States argued against the right of first refusal by incumbent transmission owners because it discouraged investment by merchant and independent transmission developers. Eastern PJM governors recommended that the Commission incorporate state and federal public policy objectives (i.e., renewable energy) into the transmission-planning process.[49] What is clear is that the politics of transmission siting had become highly convoluted.

Order 1000 extended the Order 890 planning principles by requiring each public utility transmission provider to coordinate with interconnected systems to ensure that transmission plans used consistent assumptions and data and were simultaneously feasible. The Commission required the development and implementation of procedures for the joint evaluation by neighboring transmission-planning regions of potential interregional transmission facilities.

Transmission plans should identify system enhancements that could relieve congestion or integrate new resources.[50] Each public utility transmission provider would participate in a regional transmission-planning process that satisfies the Order 890 transmission planning principles: (1) coordination; (2) openness; (3) transparency; (4) information exchange; (5) comparability; (6) dispute resolution; and (7) economic planning studies. Public utility transmission providers were to establish procedures for identifying transmission needs driven by public policy requirements. However, failure to comply with a public policy requirement established under state law would not be a violation of its OATT.[51]

The Commission was making an end run around the FPA with its planning requirements. "Section 202(a) requires that the interconnection and coordination, i.e., the coordinated operation, of facilities be voluntary. That section does not mention planning, and nothing in it can be read as impliedly establishing limits on the Commission's jurisdiction

---

[49] Id. at PP 17–24.

[50] *Transmission Planning and Cost Allocation by Transmission Owning and Operating Public Utilities*, Order No. 1000, FERC Stats. & Regs. ¶ 31,323, at PP 70–71, 207–13, 345–50, 373–404, 454–58 (2011), 76 FR 49482 (August 11, 2011); *Order on reh'g*, Order No. 1000-A, 139 FERC ¶ 61,132 (2012), 77 FR 32184 (May 31, 2012); *order on reh'g*, Order No. 1000-B, 141 FERC ¶ 61,044 (2012); *aff'd, South Carolina Public Service Authority v. FERC*, ___ F.3d___ (DC Cir. 2014).

[51] Order 1000 at P 118.

with respect to transmission planning."[52] The Commission focused on ensuring that there was a fair regional transmission-planning *process*. An open, regional transmission-planning process, by broadening the scope of the proceeding and involving numerous actors, would bring political pressure on utilities, and their associated state regulatory commissions, to pursue transmission solutions that did more than reinforce the status quo. The Commission required that each regional transmission-planning process consider and evaluate non-transmission solutions and identify cost-effective transmission facilities. Ensuring access to the models and data used in the regional transmission-planning process would allow stakeholders to determine if their needs were being addressed in a more efficient manner. The Commission was careful to avoid imposing obligations to build or obtain commitments to construct transmission facilities in the regional transmission plan. In a similar fashion, FERC avoided defining the scope of a planning region, other than to affirm that an individual public utility transmission provider cannot, by itself, satisfy the regional transmission-planning requirements of Order 890 or Order 2000.[53]

Order 1000 also required the removal from Commission-jurisdictional tariffs and agreements provisions that grant a federal right of first refusal to construct transmission facilities to incumbent utilities for purposes of cost allocation. The rule applies only to transmission facilities that are evaluated at the regional level and selected in the regional transmission plan for purposes of cost allocation. The right of an incumbent transmission provider to build, own, and recover costs for upgrades to its own transmission facilities was unaffected by the rule.[54] This clause was another example of FERC's subtle campaign to open up regions controlled by vertically integrated utilities. The right of first refusal allowed the incumbent to propose the bare minimum in regional transmission upgrades to block more comprehensive schemes that would expand the grid to permit access to competing sources of supply.

The Commission had begun using transmission rate incentives to encourage new investment in transmission before the enactment of EPAct 2005. The Commission approved rates for merchant transmission facilities with all capacity initially allocated through a fair, nondiscriminatory and transparent open season process. Operational control of the

[52] Order 1000 at P 100.
[53] Order 1000 at PP 113, 146–50, 159–60.
[54] Order 1000, at PP 225–29.

facilities would be turned over to an RTO and service would be provided under the OATT of the RTO.[55] The Commission also used incentives to support the formation of RTOs and the divestiture of transmission assets by vertical utilities after the issuance of Order 2000. FERC permitted a 50-basis-point adder to the return on equity midpoint for use by all participating MISO transmission-owning utilities, and left open the possibility of additional upward adjustments based on the level of operational independence.[56] In 2003, the Commission proposed to provide generic incentives to transmission owners that participate in RTOs and independent transmission companies under RTOs. Any entity that transfers operational control of transmission facilities to a Commission-approved RTO would qualify for an incentive adder on its return on equity for all transferred facilities. Independent transmission companies that participate in RTOs and meet the independent ownership requirement would qualify for an additional incentive. The Commission also proposed a generic incentive for investment in new transmission facilities pursuant to an RTO planning process. FERC was especially interested in encouraging investment in new technologies that could be installed relatively quickly, equipment that allowed greater control of energy flows, and sophisticated monitoring and communication equipment.[57]

EPAct 2005 added a new section 219 to the FPA, which provided a legislate mandate for FERC to continue its incentive-based (including performance-based) rate treatments for transmission.[58] In response to EPAct 2005, FERC closed its Proposed Pricing Policy proceeding and initiated a rulemaking to implement the provisions of the new bill. Order 679, issued in July 2006, provided that investments in transmission infrastructure that ensured reliability or lowered the cost of delivered power by

[55] *Proposed Pricing Policy for Efficient Operation and Expansion of Transmission Grid*, 102 FERC ¶ 61,032, PP 9–10 (2003). See *TransEnergie U.S., Ltd.*, 91 FERC ¶ 61,230, *order on compliance filings*, 91 FERC ¶ 61,347 and 93 FERC ¶ 61,289 (2000); *Neptune Regional Transmission System, LLC*, 96 FERC ¶ 61,147, *order on reh'g*, 96 FERC ¶ 61,326 (2001), *order on motion for clarification*, 98 FERC ¶ 61,140 (2002).

[56] *Midwest Independent Transmission System, Operator, Inc.*, 100 FERC ¶ 61,292, 62,315 (2002), *reh'g denied*, 102 FERC ¶ 61,143 (2003). The ruling was remanded by the DC Court of Appeals, because FERC failed to give notice of its policy to provide an adder to the return on equity. *Public Service Commission of the Commonwealth of Kentucky v. FERC*, 397 F.3d 1004, 1011–13 (D.C. Cir. 2005). The Commission then revoked the incentive adder, but invited MISO or the transmission operators to make a filing to include an incentive adder. *Midwest Independent Transmission System, Operator, Inc.*, 111 FERC ¶ 61,355, at P 1 (2005).

[57] *Proposed Pricing Policy*, 102 FERC ¶ 61,032, at PP 27–32 (2003).

[58] EPAct 2005 § 1241.

reducing transmission congestion would be eligible for incentive-based rate treatments.[59]

The Commission retained a great deal of flexibility in applying rate incentives. The Commission interpreted the incentive mandate narrowly, rejecting separate rate-based incentives for renewable energy projects. The Commission would determine the level of the return on equity on a case-by-case basis. Large new interstate transmission projects that reduce congestion or increase reliability were more likely to receive favorable incentives relative to routine investments made to comply with reliability standards. Where the risks or challenges faced by a new investment were substantial, the Commission may grant a return on equity at the top end of the zone of reasonableness.[60] The Commission allowed public utilities, where appropriate, the ability to include 100 percent of prudently incurred transmission-related construction work in progress in the rate base. This provided up-front regulatory certainty, rate stability, and improved cash flow for applicants. The Commission also allowed accelerated depreciation for new transmission facilities. The Commission proposed allowing recovery of 100 percent of the prudently incurred costs of transmission facilities canceled or abandoned due to factors beyond the control of the public utility, including rejection by siting authorities. The Commission also created a rebuttable presumption of eligibility for incentives for projects that result from a regional planning process that is acceptable to the Commission.[61] In the Final Rule, the Commission stated that it would authorize, when justified, an incentive-based rate treatment for public utilities that join and/or continue to be a member of an ISO or RTO. These utilities would be eligible to apply to recover costs associated with joining the Transmission Organization.[62]

While the Commission's policies were successful in promoting expansion of the transmission grid, outside of a few regions like SPP, it was still difficult to obtain approval for interstate transmission. Congress was unwilling to provide the authority to allow FERC to rationalize

---

[59] *Promoting Transmission Investment through Pricing Reform*, Order No. 679, FERC Stats. & Regs. ¶ 31,222 at P 34 (2006), 71 FR 43,294 (July 31, 2006), *order on reh'g*, Order No. 679-A, FERC Stats. & Regs. ¶ 31,236 (2007), 72 FR 1152 (January 10, 2007), *order on reh'g*, 119 FERC ¶ 61,062 (2007).

[60] Order 679-A, at PP 52–56, 67, 93–94.

[61] Order 679, at P 58, 115–22, 147–54, 163–67; Order 679-A at PP 27, 48.

[62] Order 679, PP 326–31. This reversed the policy adopted in *Southern California Edison Co.*, 114 FERC ¶ 61,018, at P 16 (2005). Note that both the SCE decision and Order 679 were approved by the same trio of commissioners: Joseph Kelliher, Nora Brownell, and Suedeen Kelly.

the national grid, so the agency was forced to resort to applying subtle pressure to reticent IOUs who did not want to make it easier for potential competitors to access their service area. The *Piedmont* Court threw up an additional barrier by effectively providing a veto to states that did not want transmission, whether to protect their electricity cost advantage or to placate landowners and environmental groups. Unfortunately, neither the Republicans supporting access to fossil fuel generators nor the Democrats pushing for opening the grid to renewable energy understood that strengthening the electric grid was good public policy on its own merits, and failed to develop a consensus in favor of policies that served the national interest. Both the transmission-siting controversies and the transmission cost allocation fight reflected the triumph of parochial interests over the common good.

22

Paying the Piper

An issue almost as vexing as siting of transmission was the allocation of costs of new and existing transmission. In the "good old days," cost allocation was fairly simple as most transmission lines were limited to a single state, and the political issues revolved around allocating costs to different customer groups within a utility's service area. Transmission costs were a small fraction of total costs, so they were usually just rolled into fixed costs, and marginal transmission losses, allocation of new investment to peak load, and other economic issues were ignored. As long as demand was growing, overbuilding transmission provided long-term savings because of economies of scale in construction.

The lack of accepted region-wide cost allocation methodologies can complicate and delay the planning and approval of interstate projects, creating a higher level of uncertainty and risk for investors. Large-scale high-voltage transmission generally provides benefits across wide areas, spanning jurisdictional boundaries. Attempting to assign costs for these types of projects is often met with resistance, causing delays. State utility regulators representing retail consumers want to ensure that transmission projects do not result in costs that exceed the local benefits.

The premise that traditionally governed cost allocation was that customers should bear transmission costs according to the benefits that customers derive from the associated investment. Under the FPA, a rate design must be nondiscriminatory and non-preferential as well as being just and reasonable.[1] Section 205(b) proscribes "any *unreasonable* difference in rates" and any "*undue* preference or advantage." If a rate design

[1] *Electricity Consumers Resource Council v. FERC*, 747 F.2d 1511, 1515 (D.C. Cir. 1984).

has different effects on charges for similar services to similar customers, the utility bears the burden of justifying these different effects.[2] FERC's responsibility under section 205 is to ensure just and reasonable rates for both native load customers and for third parties.[3] Utility customers should normally be charged rates that fairly track the costs for which they are responsible.[4] FERC relied on two principles to guide transmission rate design: native load customers of the utility providing the transmission service should be held harmless; and in providing firm transmission service to a third party, the utility should charge the lowest cost-based rate.[5] In general, the courts deferred to the Commission's judgment on rate design.[6]

FERC favored rolled-in cost allocation for the rate to be charged by an integrated transmission system. A utility determines its transmission costs per unit of electricity by dividing the total annual costs of constructing and maintaining its entire transmission network by the load, or the amount of power on the network, at certain peak periods. Each customer is then charged a "postage stamp" rate for its share of peak demand. However, a high degree of coordination involving frequent exchanges of power between adjoining utilities, even when streamlined and facilitated by a computerized broker system, does not necessarily make them an integrated system. If a transmission system is not integrated, a rate set on the basis of rolled-in costs would require some ratepayers to bear the costs of facilities from which they derive no benefit.[7] The Commission began to modify its historic, rolled-in embedded cost pricing policy in the early 1990s. Under the revised policy, when a utility added new capacity to relieve a transmission constraint, the Commission allowed the utility the option of charging the higher of an embedded cost rate (calculated to include the rolled-in costs of the added facilities) *or* a rate based on the incremental cost of expansion.[8]

---

[2] *Alabama Elec. Co-op., Inc. v. FERC*, 684 F.2d 20, 27–29 (D.C. Cir. 1982).

[3] *Texas Power Co. v. FERC*, 908 F.2d 998, 1003 (D.C. Cir. 1990).

[4] *Town of Norwood v. FERC*, 962 F.2d 20, 25 (D.C. Cir. 1992).

[5] *Pennsylvania Electric Co v. FERC*, 11 F.3d 207, 209–10 (D.C. Cir. 1993).

[6] *Town of Norwood v FERC*, 962 F.2d 20, 22 (D.C. Cir. 1992) (Issues of rate design are fairly technical and, insofar as they are not technical, involve policy judgments that lie at the core of the regulatory mission. Not surprisingly, therefore, our review is deferential.).

[7] *City of Holyoke v FERC*, 954 F.2d 740, 742 (1992); *Fort Pierce Util. Auth. v. FERC*, 730 F.2d 778, 782–85 (D.C. Cir. 1984). The transmission network may include radial links if a reasonable argument can be made that those links provide benefits to the transmission system or will do so in the future. *Public Serv. Co. of Ind. v. FERC*, 575 F. 2d 1204, 1217–18 (7th Cir 1978).

[8] *Inquiry Concerning the Commission's Pricing Policy for Transmission Services Provided by Public Utilities Under the Federal Power Act*, Notice of technical conference and request for comments, FERC SR ¶ 35,024, 35,163 (1993), 58 FR 36400 (July 7, 1993).

The Commission provided general guidance on cost allocation in Order 890. The Commission attempted to balance three factors: (1) whether a cost allocation proposal fairly assigns costs among participants; (2) whether a cost allocation proposal provides adequate incentives to construct new transmission; and (3) whether the proposal is generally supported by state authorities and participants across the region. In the past, different regions attempted to address free-rider problems (where customers who do not agree to support a project may receive substantial benefits from it) in a variety of ways, such as by assigning transmission rights to project developers[9] or spreading a portion of the cost of high-voltage projects broadly across customers. The Commission maintained that regional solutions that garner the support of stakeholders, including state authorities, were preferable.[10]

The limits of the Commission's authority to rationalize transmission in an RTO were delineated by the Court of Appeals in *Illinois Commerce Commission*.[11] The presiding ALJ found that PJM's rate design – a license plate rate design where each utility charged for transmission service based on the costs of its transmission facilities – was unjust and unreasonable, because customers paid different rates for access to the regional transmission grid. The ALJ's decision followed *Alabama Power*[12] on finding that existing facilities provide general benefits, such as increased access to generation and reliability benefits, to all PJM zones. The Commission reversed the ALJ's determination and held that the license plate rate design remained just and reasonable because it reflected that these facilities were built principally to support load within the individual transmission owners' zones, and continued to serve those loads. Proposed alternative rate designs presented unacceptable cost shifts among the transmission owners and created adverse incentives toward joining or remaining in PJM.[13] However, the Commission found that the existing methodology for allocating the costs of new facilities within PJM was no longer just and reasonable because it allocated costs to beneficiaries without providing any ex ante certainty. PJM was required to develop a "beneficiary pays"

9 *See California Independent System Operator Corporation*, 102 FERC ¶ 61,278 (2003) (provide congestion revenues, wheeling revenues, and FTR auction revenues to entities other than Participating Transmission Owners, if any such entities fund transmission facility upgrades on the CAISO-Controlled Grid), *reh'g denied and clarification*, 104 FERC ¶ 61,127 (2003), *rejecting compliance filing*, 109 FERC ¶ 61,098 (2004).
10 Order 890 at PP 560–61.
11 *Illinois Commerce Comm'n v. FERC*, 576 F.3d 470 (7th Cir. 2009).
12 *Alabama Power Co. et al. v. FERC*, 993 F.2d 1557 (D.C. Cir. 1993).
13 *PJM Interconnection, L.L.C.*, 119 FERC ¶ 61,063 at PP 17–20, 48–60 (2007), *reh'g denied*, 122 FERC ¶ 61,082 (2008).

methodology to be set forth in its tariff. An RTO can allocate costs using a well-defined modeling approach that identifies beneficiaries based on specific criteria or metrics (e.g., the alleviation of reliability violations or reductions in production costs or locational prices). Alternatively, an RTO can provide ex ante certainty by allocating costs using a fixed, postage stamp allocation of high-voltage facilities, or a RTO can use a combination of these approaches. The Commission sent development of a methodology to allocate costs of lower-voltage lines back to the stakeholders, but accepted PJM's proposal to adopt a postage stamp rate to recover the costs of EHV transmission facilities.[14]

The Seventh Circuit accepted the license plate pricing of transmission below 500 kV but rejected postage stamp pricing for the 500 kV lines. One reason for the court's rejection of the Commission's arguments was circumstantial, while the other was a perception that the Commission made only a perfunctory argument. It was a difficult argument to make because of the odd shape of PJM at the time of the lawsuit. Exelon's service area around Chicago was almost completely isolated from the rest of PJM at that time and derived almost no benefits from expansion of the PJM transmission backbone. It would have been much easier to show benefits to the western portion of PJM after the addition of FirstEnergy's Ohio subsidiaries to PJM in 2011. Using a cutoff of 500 kV instead of 345 kV also skewed the cost/benefit calculation against Exelon's Com Ed subsidiary (but in favor of Exelon's PECO subsidiary).[15] However, PJM failed to meet a minimal evidentiary standard:

We do not suggest that the Commission has to calculate benefits to the last penny, or for that matter to the last million or ten million or perhaps hundred million dollars.... If it cannot quantify the benefits to the midwestern utilities from new 500 kV lines in the East, even though it does so for 345 kV lines, but it has an articulable and plausible reason to believe that the benefits are at least roughly commensurate with those utilities' share of total electricity sales in PJM's region, then fine; the Commission can approve PJM's proposed pricing scheme on that basis. For that matter it can presume that new transmission lines benefit the entire network by reducing the likelihood or severity of outages. But it cannot use the presumption to avoid the duty of "comparing the costs assessed against a party to the burdens imposed or benefits drawn by that party ... " (citations omitted)[16]

The Commission responded to the remand by establishing paper hearing procedures to allow parties to supplement the record. PJM was required to supply information on projects that had been approved through PJM's

[14] *PJM Interconnection, L.L.C.*, 119 FERC ¶ 61,063 at PP 38–47, 65–66 (2007).
[15] *Illinois Commerce Comm'n v. FERC*, 576 F.3d 470, 474–75 (7th Cir. 2009).
[16] *Illinois Commerce Comm'n v. FERC*, 576 F.3d 470, 477.

Regional Transmission Expansion Plan process, as well as details on PJM's cost allocation methodology. PJM was also instructed to provide information on anticipated reliability requirements addressed by the expansion plan, and whether an upgrade addresses broader reliability concerns.[17] The costs of new facilities that operate at or above 500 kV (Regional Facilities), as well as lower-voltage facilities that supported these new Regional Facilities, were allocated on a region-wide basis. The costs of other facilities were allocated based on a "beneficiary pays" approach. The Commission accepted the filing, subject to refund, pending further proceedings on remand.[18]

The Commission read the Seventh Circuit decision as consistent with the cost causation precedent of other courts. Neither the Seventh Circuit decision nor the DC Circuit decisions on which it relied required a comparison of costs and benefits for each customer or utility zone. FERC found that the system-wide benefits of higher-voltage facilities were significant and inured to all members of PJM. The Commission found that using a static model had limitations that rendered it unjust and unreasonable for allocating the costs of PJM's EHV transmission facilities. The model failed to account for the fact that a high voltage upgrade will resolve multiple constraints in multiple areas, and for changes in usage and flow direction over time, given the forty years or longer life span for transmission facilities. The Commission pointed to generalized benefits of PJM membership, hypothetical reliability benefits, and integration of renewables as additional benefits accruing to western PJM utilities.[19] The Seventh Circuit responded by pointing out that cost causation required a legitimate attempt to determine costs, not some vague allusion to potential future benefits.[20]

A similar decision in MISO came to a slightly different result. The MISO transmission expansion cost allocation formula gradually evolved over a period of five years. The Commission encouraged MISO to work with stakeholders to develop a permanent pricing policy based on the Organization of MISO States' principle of payment for upgrades by

[17] *PJM Interconnection, L.L.C.*, 130 FERC ¶ 61,052 at PP 38–47 (2010).
[18] *PJM Interconnection, L.L.C.*, 138 FERC ¶ 61,118 at P 2–5, 14 (2012).
[19] *PJM Interconnection, L.L.C.*, 138 FERC ¶ 61,230 at P 37–125 (2012).
[20] *Illinois Commerce Comm'n v. FERC*, – F.3d –, (7th Cir. 2014), slip opinion. "So some of the benefits of the new high-voltage transmission facilities will indeed 'radiate' to the western utilities, as the Commission said, but 'some' is not a number and does not enable even a ballpark estimate of the benefits of the new transmission lines to the western utilities."

parties that cause and benefit from the upgrades.[21] MISO proposed an allocation formula for Baseline Reliability Projects 345 kV and higher. Twenty percent of project costs would be allocated on a system-wide basis and the remaining project cost allocated subregionally (potentially across several affected pricing zones), based on the effects of a given facility's outage on transmission facilities in each pricing zone. For projects below 345 kV, 100 percent of the costs were allocated to customers in pricing zones.[22] Alternatives to the 20 percent were explored, but it became apparent that if the percentage was higher or lower, the compromise would fall apart. The Commission initially rejected the high-voltage regional cost-sharing formula. However, the Commission accepted the formula on rehearing, after a technical conference.[23]

In July 2010, MISO proposed to establish a new category of transmission projects designated as Multi Value Projects. The proposal was the result of more than nineteen months of MISO stakeholder and task force discussions. To qualify as an multi-value project, one of three criteria must be fulfilled: (1) a project must be developed through the transmission expansion planning process to improve reliability or fulfill public policy mandates; (2) a project must provide multiple types of economic value with a net benefit across multiple pricing zones; or (3) it must address a projected violation of a NERC standard and provide economic value across multiple pricing zones. Filing parties proposed that the costs of the multi-value projects be allocated to all load in, and exports from, MISO on a postage-stamp basis, based on system usage rather than peak demand. The Commission accepted the filing, conditioned on a compliance filing that multi-value projects will be reviewed on a portfolio basis, the rate is not imposed on transactions to the PJM region, and the multi-value usage charge reflects grandfathered service.[24]

The proposal attempted to meet the *Illinois Commerce Commission* requirement that the costs allocated to a beneficiary were roughly commensurate with the benefits expected to accrue to that entity. The

---

[21] *Midwest Independent Transmission System Operator, Inc.*, 108 FERC ¶ 61,027 at P 38 (2004), *order on reh'g*, 109 FERC ¶ 61,085 (2004).

[22] *Midwest Independent Transmission System Operator, Inc.*, 114 FERC ¶ 61,106 at P 28 (2006), *order on reh'g*, 117 FERC ¶ 61,241 (2006), *order on reh'g and clarification*, 118 FERC ¶ 61,208 (2007).

[23] *Midwest Independent Transmission System Operator, Inc.*, 117 FERC ¶ 61,241 at PP 62–65 (2006).

[24] *Midwest Independent Transmission System Operator, Inc.*, 133 FERC ¶ 61,221 at PP 2–4 (2010); *Midwest Independent Transmission System Operator, Inc.*, 137 FERC ¶ 61,074 at P 2–13 (2011).

Commission found that the eligibility criteria would require that each project have regional benefits, and that the portfolio approach to project selection ensures that those benefits would be widely spread around MISO. The Commission accepted the argument that during off-peak hours more opportunity exists to use generation in one region to serve load in another, providing a significant portion of multi-value project benefits. Thus a usage-based cost allocation methodology was consistent with cost causation principles. This reflected the reality that policy-mandated renewable wind resource generation tends to peak in the morning hours. The Seventh Circuit accepted the MISO cost-sharing plan, although it remanded for further analysis by the Commission as to what, if any, limitation on export pricing to PJM by MISO is justified.[25]

SPP had been authorized as an RTO as of October 1, 2004, and in the order approving RTO status, the Commission directed SPP to develop and file a transmission cost allocation plan. SPP filed its cost allocation plan in February 2005. Costs for significant Base Plan upgrades are allocated one-third to the region on a postage stamp basis and the remaining two-thirds to zones based on each zone's share of the incremental benefits. Economic upgrades that would defer or displace the need for a Base Plan upgrade may be compensated for that portion of their costs.[26] The one-third/two-third split was administratively easy to implement and minimized litigation by avoiding the need to evaluate each project individually to determine the portion that should be regionally shared. The Commission accepted the one-third/two-thirds cost allocation without modification. The proposal was supported by the Regional State Committee.[27] Total SPP system usage was 66 percent zonal to service native load, so that one-third of the transmission system usage reflects regional needs.[28]

The Regional State Committee worked with SPP and its stakeholders for two years to develop cost allocation procedures for economic

---

[25] *Midwest Independent Transmission System Operator, Inc.*, 133 FERC ¶ 61,221 at PP 54–55, 200–38, 383–89 (2010); *Midwest Independent Transmission System Operator, Inc.*, 137 FERC ¶ 61,074 at PP 28–29, 112–50, 253–61 (2011); *aff'd and remanded*, *Illinois Commerce Com'n v. FERC*, 721 F. 3d 764 (7th Cir 2013).

[26] *Southwest Power Pool, Inc.*, 111 FERC ¶ 61,118, at PP 8–10 (2005), *order on reh'g*, 112 FERC ¶ 61,319 (2005).

[27] The Regional State Committee provides state regulatory agency input on regional matters related to the development and operation of bulk electric transmission and is comprised of retail regulatory commissioners from agencies in Arkansas, Kansas, Missouri, New Mexico, Oklahoma, and Texas.

[28] *Southwest Power Pool, Inc.*, 111 FERC ¶ 61,118, at PP 15, 31–35 (2005).

upgrades. In an August 2008 filing, SPP submitted a balanced portfolio process, which the Commission accepted in October. SPP would
evaluate a portfolio of economic upgrades, each of which must include
a 345 kV or higher facility, rather than evaluate the benefits of individual projects. A portfolio not only must exhibit overall positive net
present value over a ten-year period but also be "balanced," providing
net benefits for each zone. The benefits component includes changes in
production costs attributable to the portfolio. Benefits such as reductions in system losses, improvements to capacity margin and operating
reserve requirements, increased competition in wholesale markets, reliability enhancement, and critical infrastructure benefits were excluded
due to lack of metrics, but may be added in the future. A reallocation
mechanism allows an unbalanced portfolio to include economic upgrades
below the 345 kV level to increase the benefits to deficient zones. SPP
may transfer zonal revenue requirements from a deficient zone to balance a portfolio (i.e., SPP proposed to institutionalize Kaldor-Hicks side
payments).[29]

SPP and its stakeholders then went back to the drawing board for
another fifteen months to reform SPP's cost allocation mechanisms and
transmission-planning processes. SPP proposed to adopt the Highway/
Byway Methodology in 2010. SPP stated that owing to the realities of an
integrated network and Commission policies such as Order 890, transmission system planning in SPP had evolved to a region-wide approach.
A region-wide approach takes into account not only reliability issues
but also congestion reduction and state and federal policy goals such as
increased use of renewable energy resources. Integration of the western
and eastern portions of the SPP grid would enable wind resources in the
west to serve load centers in the east. The costs of Base Plan facilities operating at 300 kV would be allocated 100 percent across the SPP region
on a postage stamp basis, and the costs of facilities operating at lower
voltages allocated one-third on a postage stamp basis and two-thirds to
the zone in which the facilities are located. The Commission accepted
SPP's Highway/Byway Methodology, noting that EHV facilities provide
benefits that are difficult to quantify. Users of an integrated system change
over time, and the availability of the system is itself a benefit to the users
as a whole.[30]

[29] *Southwest Power Pool, Inc.*, 125 FERC ¶ 61,054, at PP 2–8 (2008), *reh'g denied*, 127
FERC ¶ 61,271 (2009).
[30] *Southwest Power Pool, Inc.*, 131 FERC ¶ 61,252, at PP 6–12, 21–31, 62–89 (2010).

The Commission formalized its new cost allocation policies in Order 1000. The Commission required each public utility transmission provider have in its OATT a method, or set of methods, for allocating the costs of new transmission facilities selected in the regional transmission plan and the costs of new interregional transmission facilities. The OATTs of all public utility transmission providers in a region must include the same cost allocation method or methods adopted by the region.[31]

Transmission providers were required to satisfy six regional cost allocation principles:

1. The costs of a new interregional facility must be allocated to each transmission-planning region that is roughly commensurate with the estimated benefits of that facility. However, the Commission did not prescribe a particular definition of "benefits" or "beneficiaries."
2. A transmission-planning region that receives no benefit from an interregional transmission facility, either at present or in a likely future scenario, must not be involuntarily allocated the costs of that facility. Transmission providers may propose a portfolio cost allocation method that considers the benefits and costs of a group of facilities.
3. A benefit-cost threshold ratio used to determine whether a facility qualifies for interregional cost allocation may not exceed 1.25, unless Commission approves a higher ratio.
4. Costs allocated for an interregional facility must be assigned only to regions in which the facility is located.
5. The cost allocation method and data must be transparent, with adequate documentation. The method or methods for determining benefits and beneficiaries must balance being pragmatic and implementable with being accurate and unbiased.
6. Cost allocation methods may distinguish among transmission facilities associated with maintaining reliability, addressing economic considerations, and achieving public policy requirements. Each cost allocation method must be set out and explained in detail.[32]

In the event of a failure to reach an agreement on a cost allocation method or methods, the Commission will use the record in the relevant proceeding as a basis to develop a cost allocation method. Public utility transmission providers must document in their compliance filings the steps they have

---

[31] Order 1000 at PP 482, 550–52.
[32] Order 1000 at PP 622–93.

taken to reach consensus on a cost allocation method, and provide the necessary information for the Commission to make a determination.[33]

The planning process dovetailed with FERC's ruling on long-term financial transmission rights. FERC proposed that long-term FTRs be made available with terms (and/or rights to renewal) that were sufficient to meet the needs of LSEs to satisfy a service obligation. Additionally, transmission organizations would be required to award long-term FTRs to market participants that request and support an expansion or upgrade to the transmission system in accordance with the prevailing rules for cost allocation. In the event that a transmission organization cannot accommodate all requests for long-term FTRs, a preference must be given to LSEs with long-term power supply arrangements used to meet service obligations.[34] The FTR rule allowed the transmission organization to place reasonable limits on the total amount of capacity it will offer as long-term rights. LSEs would have no guarantee that they will be able to obtain all the FTRs requested. Once long-term rights are awarded to a LSE, however, they must be fully funded over their entire term.[35]

FERC believed that Congress's intent was to provide long-term firm transmission service to LSEs and that LSEs in general should be "first in line" for transmission rights when existing capacity is limited, regardless of their contractual arrangements with suppliers. Transmission organizations must provide the opportunity for market participants to obtain long-term FTRs by supporting an expansion or upgrade of grid transfer capability. This enables LSEs to obtain long-term rights that they may have requested but not received due to infeasibility.[36] LSEs that are obligated to pay the embedded costs of the transmission system should be able to receive an equitable share of long-term FTRs without having to submit a competitive bid for those rights. Historically, the cost of constructing and maintaining the grid has largely been borne by LSEs on an equitable basis without regard to the term of their power supply arrangements. It is for this reason that each LSE is entitled to an equitable allocation of the FTRs that are supported by existing capacity. A preference for LSEs with

---

[33] Order 1000 at P 607.

[34] *Long-Term Firm Transmission Rights in Organized Electricity Markets*, NOPR, FERC Stats. & Regs. ¶ 32,598 at P 42 (2006), 71 FR 6693 (February 9, 2006).

[35] *Long-Term Firm Transmission Rights in Organized Electricity Markets*, Order No. 681, FERC Stats. & Regs. ¶ 31,226, at P 18 (2006), 71 FR 43,564 (August 1, 2006), *reh'g denied*, Order No. 681-A, 117 FERC ¶ 61,201 (2006); *reh'g and clarification*, Order No. 681-B, 117 FERC ¶ 61,201 (2009).

[36] Order No. 681, PP 19–23.

long-term supply arrangements only applied when a transmission system may temporarily not have enough capacity to provide simultaneously feasible, long-term FTRs to all load serving entities.[37]

Given the full funding requirement, appropriate planning for long-term firm transmission rights was essential to ensure that other market participants were not faced with excessive charges to cover revenue shortfalls. Accordingly, the transmission organization must include, along with upgrades needed for system reliability, upgrades needed to support long-term firm transmission rights in its base plan for system expansion.[38] The combination of the requirements for full funding of long-term FTRs and the requirement to plan transmission expansion to maintain the feasibility of long-term FTRs created a bias in RTO transmission planning toward overexpansion. Overbuilding transmission would not only support the feasibility of long-term FTRs; it would reduce the funding requirement for FTRs (by reducing congestion) and shift costs from uplift to support FTRs to payments for new wires.

FERC progressed on the cost allocation and FTR issues in a manner similar to what it did with transmission planning: two steps forward, one step back. Cost allocation is the flip side of planning; because these tend to be parallel processes, a menu of transmission projects are considered, but the allocation of costs will help determine support for various options. State mandates for renewable energy added another level of complexity, since the lowest-cost resource – wind – was rarely located near load centers. FTRs provided another lever for FERC to encourage grid expansion, as the lack of capacity to support FTRs provided the grounds to reject plans that ignored the need to increase transmission capacity. However, FTRs also illustrated the importance of the "real" Coase theorem: the initial allocation of property rights creates inertia against change, and it is not a simple matter to engineer side payments to move to a pareto optimal solution. In electricity markets, congestion is fluid, and every change – whether loads shifting with regional development, new generators at new sites or new investments in transmission – impacts the value of congestion rights as well as existing assets.

[37] Order No. 681-A, at PP 68–70.
[38] Order No. 681, at PP 453–57.

23

Leave the Lights On

A key issue that has yet to be resolved in market design is ensuring reliability. Reliability consists of two components: system security and resource adequacy. Security refers to the system's ability to withstand contingencies, a possible or actual breakdown of some physical component of the power system that results in the loss to the system of the power produced by a generator. A contingency leaves the system unbalanced, with demand greater than supply; consequently, system frequency and voltage begin to drop, and unless they are restored in a very short period, the system can experience cascading blackouts and collapse. Operating reserves are required to be maintained at a level sufficient to enable the system operators to manage very short-term disturbances and to rebalance the system quickly following a contingency to maintain system security. For day-ahead planning and real-time operation, utilities are required by NERC and regional-reliability-council rules to maintain minimum levels of operating reserves, typically 4–8 percent of the projected daily peak (normally based on the size of the largest potential contingency within the regional reliability council).

Resource adequacy refers to maintaining a sufficient supply of available generation capacity to maintain system security under all but the most extreme circumstances. In effect, resource adequacy requires planning generation and transmission investment so as to meet projected peak energy demand plus sufficient operating reserves to preserve system security. Although transmission and generation are both substitutes and complements, generation capacity requirements are usually determined in the context of a given transmission system (demand responsive load can be employed as an imperfect substitute for capacity).

Scarcity conditions are triggered when system operators find that they have an operating reserve deficiency that cannot be satisfied by buying more energy or operating reserves through ordinary market mechanisms. This in turn typically triggers the system operator's implementation of a set of actions to reduce demand or augment supply using out-of-market instruments. Only as a last resort – and very infrequently – has it been necessary to implement rolling blackouts.

At times, electricity systems can be the victim of cascading events that can result in blackouts over a wide region for a sustained duration. These events are usually not the result of generation shortages per se; rather, they often stem from transmission failures, operator error, severe weather, or unexpected demand during shoulder periods of the year when units are offline. There are a wide variety of triggering events including earthquakes, tornados, hurricanes or tropical storms, ice storms, lightning, wind or rainstorms, other cold weather, fire, fuel shortages, human error, and mechanical failure.[1]

The transmission operator or balancing authority has the authority to shed load rather than risk an uncontrolled failure. The operators of large-scale electrical power systems must be constantly alert to possibilities of a system failure. Rolling brownouts or local blackouts often signify that the operators are taking remedial measures to ensure that a local failure does not cascade. Thus, measures to mitigate the occurrence of cascading blackouts could increase the frequency of local blackouts and brownouts.[2] Under frequency load (UFL) shedding is triggered when the frequency drops below a threshold. In most regions, UFL is triggered when the frequency drops below 59 Hz (in ERCOT, the trigger is set at 59.7 Hz for LaaRs). Power system controlled islanding (or separation) is considered as the last line of defense. It stops cascading outages by separating the whole system into several predefined islands, which are simple to restore. This strategy confines the disturbance to a local area.[3]

At steady state, the operating power system should have the capability of tolerating the loss of any one element in the system (this is the NERC "N-1" standard), such as a generator, transmission line, or transformer.

[1]   Paul Hines, Jay Apt, and Sarosh Talukdar, "Large Blackouts in North America: Historical Trends and Policy Implications," CEIC Working Paper 09–01 (2009): 8.
[2]   José Delgado, "The Blackout of 2003 and Its Connection to Open Access," in U.S.-Canada Power System Outage Task Force, *Recommendation 12: The Relationship between Competitive Power Markets and Grid Reliability* (July 2006): 45–46.
[3]   Vijay Vittal et al., "Detection, Prevention and Mitigation of Cascading Events: Adaptive Islanding with Selective Under-Frequency Load Shedding, Final Project Report, Part III," Power Systems Engineering Research Center (2008): 3–5.

If a key transmission line is damaged, severe power imbalances will occur at both the sending and receiving ends. Since voltage magnitudes at buses and active power flows on transmission lines are closely related to power angles, out-of-step swings will occur without timely control actions. Protective relay devices are installed across the system to protect generators, transmission lines, and transformers from damage during fault conditions. During unstable swings, voltage magnitudes at buses and power flows on branches oscillate severely. Once a severe swing is initiated, cascading outages are likely to occur, because when lines are tripped when they experience a violation of relay settings, the cascading events progress across the electrical system. False tripping of protective relays is the main problem leading to cascading outages.[4]

Despite automation of transmission operations and exponential increases in computing power over the last two decades, cascading failures are probably inevitable. The enormous number of components in the system, each of which has unique discrete and continuous dynamic properties and is geographically dispersed, makes it impractical to implement solutions that require extensive monitoring and control. Large blackouts can involve cascades of tens to hundreds of events. Determining all the possible combinations of cascading failures that could lead to blackouts is computationally unfeasible. Since attention is focused on mitigating foreseeable causes of failure, blackouts tend to involve unexpected combinations of events. Combinations of several of types of failures and interactions can typically occur in large blackouts, including cascading overloads, failures of protection equipment, transient instability, forced outages, reactive power problems and voltage collapse, and software, communication, and operational errors and mistakes.[5]

There has not been an increase or decrease in significant blackout events (>300 MW of power lost), excluding extraordinary circumstances such as earthquakes and hurricanes, since 1984, despite improvements in communication and control technologies. Blackout frequency increases substantially during the late summer and midwinter months, corresponding to the occurrence of severe storms. Blackouts peak during midafternoon hours, reflecting both weather-related events and perhaps the result

---

[4] Id.
[5] IEEE PES CAMS Task Force, "Initial Review of Methods for Cascading Failure Analysis in Electric Power Transmission Systems," IEEE Power Engineering Society General Meeting, Pittsburgh, PA (July 2008): 1; Paul Hines, "A Decentralized Approach to Reducing the Social Costs of Cascading Failures," (Ph.D. diss., Carnegie Mellon University, August 2007): 127–28.

of power networks being more stressed.[6] While many events began with failures in transmission lines, several of the cascading failures began with failures at substations (often resulting from problems with metering transformers that hang off of substation bus conductors). Substation failures are particularly likely to result in a cascading failure because they result in multiple transmission line outages surrounding the substation.[7]

The most famous cascading failure was the Northeast Blackout of 1965. Thirty million customers lost power when a backup protective relay opened a 230 kV line taking power from Niagara Falls to the Toronto area on November 9, 1965. When the flows redistributed to the remaining four lines, they tripped out and the resultant power swings resulted in a cascading outage, moving from upstate New York to New England, which blacked out much of the northeast. The blackout lasted as long as thirteen hours in some parts of New York City.[8]

Joseph Swidler, then chairman of the FPC, responding to a request from President Johnson, set up investigative teams to look into the prevention of future blackouts.[9] In July 1967, the FPC issued a three-volume report on preventing large-scale blackouts and proposed an Electric Power Reliability Act. Lew White, the new chairman of the FPC, favored expanding the FPC's authority over transmission facilities. The FPC proposed creating a council, consisting of regional organizations funded by member utilities, to coordinate planning, construction, and operation of power systems and to exchange information between utilities. The bill, the U.S. Electric Power Reliability Act of 1967, was opposed by private utilities but generally supported by public power. Private utilities did not want federal intervention in power system planning, construction, and operations, or to be required to interconnect with other utilities. As a result, they established the National Electric Reliability Council (NERC)[10] in June 1968 and adopted many of the FPC proposals, but

---

[6] Hines, Apt, and Talukdar, "Large Blackouts in North America: Historical Trends and Policy Implications," 14–21.

[7] Hines, "A Decentralized Approach to Reducing the Social Costs of Cascading Failures," 30.

[8] David Nye, *When the Lights When Out: A History of Blackouts in America* (Cambridge, MA, MIT Press, 2010): 85–86.

[9] Jack Casazza and Frank Delea, Understanding Electric Power Systems: An Overview of Technology, the Marketplace and Government Regulation, Second Edition (Hoboken, NJ, IEEE Press and John Wiley & Sons, 2010): 9.

[10] NERC changed its name to the North American Electric Reliability Council in recognition of Canada's participation, but maintained the same acronym. It was later renamed to North American Electric Reliability Corporation with the same acronym.

relied on voluntary cooperation rather than mandatory standards. The utilities voluntarily formed regional reliability councils that were represented on NERC.[11]

On July 13, 1977, nine million people in the New York City area lost power for an entire day. The separation and total collapse of the Con Ed system began when two 345 kV lines on a common tower in northern Westchester were struck by lightning and tripped out. The outage could have been avoided if Con Ed's circuit breakers and grounding system had been properly maintained. The Indian Point nuclear power plant automatically shut down. At first the system coped with the emergency by bringing in additional power, but less than twenty minutes later lightning struck again and short-circuited two additional 345 kV lines. Another 345 kV line tripped, after excess load caused it to sag to a tree, resulting in a fault that caused the line to open. Under-frequency load shedding unloaded cable circuits and actually raised the system voltage, causing 844 MW of generation to be dropped from the system. Con Ed's control room succumbed to confusion and panic, and operator mistakes ensured a total collapse of the system. A combination of human error and poor design prevented measures that could have allowed the Con Ed system to recover with only short-term rolling brownouts.[12]

The December 22, 1982 West Coast Blackout, which affected more than five million people, began when high winds caused a 500 kV transmission tower to topple into a parallel 500 kV line tower, and both lines were lost. The collapse of these two lines caused three additional towers to fail on each line, and took down two 230 kV lines crossing under the 500 kV rights of way. The loss of the 500 kV lines activated a remedial action scheme to separate the western interconnection into two pre-engineered islands and trip generation in the Pacific Northwest in order to minimize customer outages and speed up restoration. However, delayed implementation of the remedial action scheme caused the interconnection to separate into four islands. Generator tripping and separation schemes operated slowly or did not operate as planned, and a backup separation scheme also failed to operate. Operators struggled to

---

[11] Hyunsoo Park, "The Social Structure of Large Scale Blackouts: Changing Environment, Institutional Imbalance, and Unresponsive Organizations," (Ph.D. Diss., Rutgers University, October 2010): 175–79.

[12] Nye, *When the Lights When Out*, 118–19; R.G. Farmer and E.H. Allen, "Power System Dynamic Performance Advancement From History of North American Blackouts," IEEE PSCE (2006): 295.

assess the extent of the disturbance and what corrective action should be taken due to poor data handling and displays.[13]

Gradually, both government and industry actors began to perceive a need for tighter reliability standards. In 1992, the NERC Board of Trustees stated that conformance to NERC and regional reliability policies, criteria, and guides should be mandatory to ensure reliability. The next year, NERC published "NERC 2000," a four-part action plan, which recommended policies for interconnected systems operation: planning reliable bulk electric systems; mandatory compliance with NERC policies, criteria, and guides; and a process for addressing violations.[14] However, it seemed that progress was predicated on blackouts; large-scale events were the trigger for new steps to improve standards.

On August 10, 1996, 7.5 million customers in various western states experienced blackouts of up to nine hours. Higher-than-normal temperature in the northwest, in conjunction with heavy line loading, resulted in increased line sag. In the hours before the outage, two 500 kV lines in the Portland area were forced out of service as a result of inadequate maintenance leading to tree contact. Bonneville Power Administration operators failed to send warning signals to other WSCC operators at dispatch centers for ninety minutes after the two major lines went out of service. Heavy load on another transmission line caused it to sag close to a tree and flash over. Thirteen generators tripped sequentially because of an exciter protection malfunction. As frequency decayed and intertie load fell below schedules, automatic generation control and governors caused an increase in generation. Power surged to the east then south through Idaho, Utah, Colorado, Arizona, New Mexico, Nevada, and southern California, separating the system into four islands. As a result, fifteen large thermal and nuclear generating units shut down in California and the southwest.[15]

In the wake of the 1996 Pacific Northwest blackout, a 1997 NERC report suggested a new organization that would have oversight authority and be separate from the ten regional reliability councils in governance and funding. The federal government's role would be limited to review

[13] US-Canada Power System Outage Task Force, *Final Report on the August 14, 2003 Blackout in the United States and Canada: Causes and Recommendations* (April 2004): 105.

[14] http://www.nerc.com/page.php?cid=1|7|11.

[15] Park, "The Social Structure of Large Scale Blackouts," 229–31; Farmer and Allen, "Power System Dynamic Performance Advancement From History of North American Blackouts," 296–97.

and approval of standards and procedures. In its interim report in July 1997, the Electric System Reliability Task Force of the DOE suggested that system operators should be independent of commercial interests in electricity markets. In 1998, the Task Force supported assigning oversight authority to FERC. NERC requested that the DOE support a transition from voluntary reliability standards to mandatory and enforceable standards, responding to the political pressures created by the California crisis while maintaining NERC's independence.[16]

NERC responded with new guidelines that eventually led to stiffer reliability standards. NERC and its Regional Reliability Councils developed system operating and planning standards based on seven key concepts:[17]

- balance power generation and demand continuously;
- balance reactive power supply and demand to maintain scheduled voltages;
- monitor flows over transmission lines and other facilities to ensure that thermal (heating) limits are not exceeded;
- keep the system in a stable condition;
- operate the system so that it remains in a reliable condition even if a contingency occurs, such as the loss of a key generator or transmission facility;
- plan, design, and maintain the system to operate reliably;
- prepare for emergencies.

However, because NERC was controlled by utility executives and funded by member utilities, it had limited autonomy. Member utilities preferred to adopt reliability standards that did not impinge on their control of system operation. NERC lacked the authority to reorganize loosely coordinated practices among utilities and their dispatch control centers. NERC standards were minimum requirements that could be made more stringent by regional bodies, but the regions varied in their willingness to implement reliability standards. The NERC compliance program and region-based auditing process was neither comprehensive nor aggressive enough to assess the capability of all control areas. Regional councils' efforts to audit for compliance with reliability requirements varied significantly. There was no mechanism to ensure that an entity found to be deficient in an audit would remedy the deficiency.[18]

---

[16] Park, "The Social Structure of Large Scale Blackouts," 225–27.
[17] *Final Report on the August 14, 2003 Blackout*, 6–10.
[18] *Final Report on the August 14, 2003 Blackout*, 20–21.

Because of the diversity of more than 140 control centers, utilities had to operate with technically different control systems that were often the product of local conditions. MISO had thirty-seven different control areas spread over four Regional Reliability Councils, and PJM had nine control areas spread over three Regional Reliability Councils.[19] This resulted in different normal and emergency ratings for 345 kV transmission lines among the control centers in the ECAR and MAAC reliability regions, which came to light after the 2003 blackout.[20]

MISO was the triumph of optimism over reality. The MISO proposal was different from previous ISOs addressed by the Commission, as MISO was not a traditional control area operator carrying out both transmission and generation control functions. The numerous separate control areas in the ECAR and MAIN reliability regions were a legacy of the historical structure of vertically integrated utilities. The public utilities that formed MISO had limited experience in coordinating the operation of their respective transmission systems. FERC shared the concern raised by the Illinois Commission regarding coordination between the ISO and the various reliability councils. FERC simply glossed over its own concerns and allowed the formation of a market that exceeded the abilities of the new RTO to administer and control. FERC vaguely referenced that measures might be adopted to address any problems identified, but other than the development of emergency procedures, it proscribed no remedial measures to be taken before initiation of market operations.[21] When the Operating Committee of NERC approved MISO's Security Plan in July 2001, FERC shifted its focus to other issues.[22]

On August 14, 2003, the largest electrical power failure in the U.S. history occurred in the northeastern region, with a loss of more than 60,000 MW of load affecting 50 million people. The mixture of several small contingencies resulted in a massive power failure. The blackout started in the Cleveland-Akron area. One of FirstEnergy's coal-fired units tripped when its operator sought to increase the unit's reactive power output, and the unit's protection system detected a failure. Around this time, the failure to trim trees resulted in a Dayton Power & Light transmission

---

[19] *Final Report on the August 14, 2003 Blackout*, 14.

[20] Park, "The Social Structure of Large Scale Blackouts," 216–18.

[21] *Midwest Independent Transmission System Operator, Inc.*, 84 FERC ¶ 61,231, 62,155–60 (1998).

[22] *Midwest Independent Transmission System Operator, Inc.*, 97 FERC ¶ 61,326, 62,508 (2001).

line tripping from a tree flashover. MISO's state estimator was unable to assess system conditions for three hours, owing to a combination of human error and the loss of this line. This meant that MISO could not determine that other transmission lines would overload if FirstEnergy lost a major transmission line, and could not issue appropriate warnings and operational instructions. At the same time, FirstEnergy's computer system lost its alarm function, and thus the FirstEnergy operators did not recognize transmission line trips. The increased flows on other lines caused three lines to sag into a tree and trip in the Cleveland area, as a result of failure to properly trim vegetation around the lines. Lines continued to trip as operators failed to take measure to relieve load, due to lack of training and a failure to communicate the extent of the outages. The collapse of FirstEnergy's transmission system induced power surges along Lake Erie, as power was shunted through Michigan and New York-Ontario transmission lines, tripping off additional lines and power plants. The lines from New York to PJM tripped, leaving the northeast isolated from the rest of the Eastern Interconnection.[23]

Deregulation has been blamed for the events leading up to the 2003 Blackout, but in retrospect, the impact of deregulation was at best indirect, increasing flows between utilities that increase the potential of cascading events due to incompetence at a single utility. It has been claimed that deregulation caused a reduction in expenses for maintenance of power system facilities (including but not limited to tree trimming).[24] Failure to trim vegetation properly was an ongoing problem before deregulation could have had substantive impacts on maintenance. The transmission operations of the major utilities remained regulated, and under cost-of-service regulation there was no incentive to reduce these expenditures, other than pressure from regulatory bodies (often motivated by political pressure from consumer groups and industrial customers). The exception was where integrated utilities faced rate freezes or caps, squeezing the entire organization. There seems to be no correlation between deregulation and blackout events. However, exposing utilities to penalties for violations of planning standards can reduce power system

---

[23] Janusz Bialek, "Recent Blackouts in US and Continental Europe: Is Liberalisation to Blame?" Cambridge Working Papers in Economics, CWPE 0407 (January 16, 2004): 2–7; *Final Report on the August 14, 2003 Blackout*, 45–93.

[24] Jack Casazza, Frank Delea, and George Loehr, "Contributions of the Restructuring of the Electric Power Industry to the August 14, 2003 Blackout," Working Paper (August 2005): 11.

disturbances.[25] So it seems even in the age of deregulation, stringent reliability regulation is required for system reliability.

The diffusion of authority in electricity markets may have encouraged complacency in utilities with regard to manning and training personnel for local control areas. The motivation for automating operation and control processes was to increase operational efficiency and achieve enhanced performance at lower cost. SCADA allowed the remote operation of switches to reconfigure the system topology, along with increased monitoring of circuit data, and more information and greater precision of knowledge about the system status. However, new operators using SCADA systems failed to develop an experience-based mental map of the system, and automated systems became so complex and demanding in their operation that they were no longer transparent in real time.[26] The stagnation of the industry in the 1980s and 1990s resulted in a brain drain via retirement, which was acerbated by the staffing demands of the new ISOs/RTOs.[27] The result was systems that worked better in normal conditions but set up inexperienced operators for failure when things went wrong.

Solutions that worked reasonably well in the world of monopolistic and vertically integrated utilities were insufficient in an environment where flows between utilities, and reliance on reserves outside of utilities' traditional service areas, played a more prominent role. Within a short time after open-access tariffs were enacted, the number and size of wholesale transactions boomed. Transmission service was sold mostly on a contract-path, point-to-point basis. The resulting loop flows soon made it very difficult for control area operators to control their systems and created congestion and reliability problems. Many portions of the network that had been deemed adequate through 1996 by NERC regional councils soon became marginally adequate. Control room operators were facing system emergency conditions that they had seldom seen before the implementation of FERC Order 888.[28]

[25] Park, "The Social Structure of Large Scale Blackouts," 157–59.

[26] Alexandra von Meier, "Occupational Cultures as a Challenge to Technological Innovation," *IEEE Transactions* (1999): 101–14.

[27] Dennis Ray and Bill Snyder, "Strategies to Address the Problem of Exiting Expertise in the Electric Power Industry," Proceedings of the 39th Hawaii International Conference on System Sciences, 2006.

[28] Bialek, "Recent Blackouts in US and Continental Europe: Is Liberalisation to Blame?" 15–17; Jose Delgado, "The Blackout of 2003 and Its Connection to Open Access," in U.S.-Canada Power System Outage Task Force, *Recommendation 12: The Relationship between Competitive Power Markets and Grid Reliability* (July 2006): 45–46.

The blackout report suggested NERC lacked a well-defined control area audit process that addressed all control area responsibilities. Control area audits had generally not been conducted with sufficient regularity, and compliance with audit results was not mandatory. ECAR did not conduct adequate review or analyses of FirstEnergy's voltage criteria, reactive power management practices, and operating needs, or it might have discovered that FirstEnergy did not have an adequate automatic undervoltage load-shedding program in the Cleveland-Akron area. The report recommended congressional action to enact reliability legislation.[29]

The Electricity Modernization Act of 2005 was included as Title XII in the Energy Policy Act of 2005.[30] Subtitle A amended Part II of the FPA, adding section 215, Electric Reliability. Section 215 provides for a system of mandatory, enforceable reliability standards to be developed by the electric reliability organization (ERO), subject to Commission review and approval. Section 215(b) provided that the Commission should have jurisdiction over the certified ERO, any regional entities, and all users, owners, and operators of the bulk power system. Section 215(d) required the ERO to file each reliability standard, subject to Commission review and approval. Section 215(e) provides the ERO with the authority to impose a penalty for a violation of a reliability standard approved by the Commission. Penalties are subject to review by the Commission, on its own motion or upon application. The Commission can also order compliance with reliability standards and impose penalties for violations. The Commission can authorize the ERO to delegate authority to develop standards to regional entities if the regional entity is governed by an independent board. Section 215 (i) restricts development and enforcement of reliability standards to the bulk power system. The definition of bulk power system – "electric energy from generation facilities needed to maintain transmission system reliability" – brought generators under the purview of FERC. However, the Commission was not authorized to order the construction of additional generation or transmission capacity.[31]

On February 3, 2006, the Commission issued Order 672.[32] The Commission established general principles for determining whether a

---

[29] *Final Report on the August 14, 2003 Blackout*, 19–22, 140.
[30] Energy Policy Act of 2005, Pub.L. No. 109–58.
[31] EPAct 2005, § 1211.
[32] *Rules Concerning Certification of the Electric Reliability Organization; and Procedures for the Establishment, Approval, and Enforcement of Electric Reliability Standards*, Order No. 672, FERC Stats. & Regs. ¶ 31,204 (2006), 71 FR 8,662 (February 17, 2006).

proposed reliability standard was acceptable. The proposed standard may not extend beyond reliable operation of facilities necessary for operating an interconnected electric energy transmission network. The proposed standard must be designed to achieve a specified reliability goal and must contain a technically sound means to achieve this goal. The proposed standard should be clear and unambiguous, including the range of possible penalties for noncompliance. Development of a standard through the ERO's stakeholder process is no guarantee that it will not have a discriminatory impact or negative effect on competition. The Commission will give special attention to the effect of a proposed standard on competition. The Commission will also consider environmental and social goals in its review of proposed standards. A proposed standard should be designed to apply throughout the interconnected North American power system. The Final Rule permitted regional differences in a reliability standard, in particular for more stringent standards. The Commission will determine, after consulting with both the state and the ERO, if there is an inconsistency between the reliability standard and state action, including the PUCT. If there is an inconsistency, the reliability standard is controlling under the statute.[33]

The Commission certified NERC as the ERO in July 2006.[34] In March 2007, FERC approved 83 of a 107 proposed reliability standards, six of the eight proposed regional differences, and the Glossary of Terms Used in Reliability Standards. FERC, however, required the ERO to submit significant improvements to fifty-six of the approved reliability standards to reflect the recommendations of the 2003 Blackout Report.[35] In April, FERC approved NERC's pro forma delegation agreement, to be used by NERC and the regional entities to monitor, assess, and enforce compliance with NERC's reliability standards. The Commission also approved each of the agreements through which NERC delegated responsibility to the eight regional entities to audit, investigate, and otherwise ensure compliance with NERC's reliability standards.[36] On June 18, 2007,

---

[33] Order No. 672, at PP 41–44, 321–38, 831–32.

[34] *North American Electric Reliability Corp.*, 116 FERC ¶ 61,062 (2006), *order on reh'g and compliance*, 117 FERC ¶ 61,126 (2006), *order on compliance*, 118 FERC ¶ 61,030, *order on compliance*, 118 FERC ¶ 61,190, *order on reh'g*, 119 FERC ¶ 61,046 (2007).

[35] *Mandatory Reliability Standards for the Bulk-Power System*, Order No. 693, FERC Stats. & Regs. ¶ 31,242, *order on reh'g*, Order No. 693-A, 120 FERC ¶ 61,053 (2007).

[36] *North American Electric Reliability Council*, 119 FERC ¶ 61,060 (2007) at P 4. The ten original NERC reliability councils were reorganized into eight North American Electric Reliability Corporation Regions.

compliance with approved NERC reliability standards became mandatory in the United States.[37]

The new reliability standards built on both previous NERC practice and the recommendations of the 2003 Blackout Report. Currently, there are fourteen categories of standards, reflecting different operational and planning considerations. The two key contributors to the 2003 Blackout were human error and failure to conduct preventative maintenance. NERC established standards for personnel performance and training to improve operator response in emergency situations. Failure to manage tree growth around power lines was a reoccurring problem in major blackouts. The facilities maintenance standards improved vegetation management, and outages due to vegetation have been reduced substantially since 2010.[38] One important impact of mandatory NERC standards is that it is easier for utilities to justify reliability-related expenditures in rate cases, encouraging them to increase spending on reliability knowing they are likely to receive full recovery of those costs.

A special reliability topic that has increased in importance in recent years is the threat of terrorist attacks and/or cybersecurity issues. In a sense, a terrorist attack is similar to a contingency due to weather or earthquake, except that a sophisticated terrorist can target attacks where the grid is most vulnerable, instead of striking at random.[39] An IRA

FRCC   Florida Reliability Coordinating Council
MRO   Midwest Reliability Organization
NPCC   Northeast Power Coordinating Council
RFC   ReliabilityFirst Corporation
SERC   SERC Reliability Corporation
SPP   Southwest Power Pool, RE
TRE   Texas Regional Entity
WECC   Western Electricity Coordinating Council

[37] http://www.nerc.com/page.php?cid=1|7|11.

[38] NERC, *2013 Annual Report* (February 2014): 13–14. During the 2004–2010 period, there were sixty-three reported grow-in outages. In the three subsequent years, only one grow-in outage has occurred.

[39] However, the issue had arisen well before then. U.S. Congress, Office of Technology Assessment, *Physical Vulnerability of Electric System to Natural Disasters and Sabotage*, OTA-E-453 (Washington, DC: U.S. GPO, June 1990).

> Sabotage could cause the most devastating blackouts because many key facilities can be targeted. Substations present the greatest concern. The transmission lines themselves are even easier to disrupt because they can be attacked anywhere along the line, but they are also much easier to repair.... Virtually any region would suffer major, extended blackouts if more than three key substations were destroyed.

Id. at 4.

attempt in 1996 to blow up the four electricity substations that supply London with much of its electricity was thwarted by the police and intelligence services, but had it succeeded, it would have wrecked electricity supplies to the southeast of England for many months.[40] However, other than a well-organized attack by unknown assailants at a substation in San Jose,[41] there have been no physical attempts at sabotaging the grid. Rather, the typical incident is some fool firing at a substation for entertainment, stealing copper, or doing some malicious damage to the site. In Texas, shooting up equipment was so prevalent that utility operators put up metal bull's-eyes on their poles so people are shooting the targets rather than the distribution transformers.[42]

Cyber attacks may present a more serious threat. The Nuclear Regulatory Commission confirmed that in January 2003, the Microsoft SQL Server worm known as "Slammer" infected a private computer network at the Davis-Besse nuclear power plant in Oak Harbor, Ohio, and disabled a safety monitoring system for nearly five hours. Fortunately the plant was offline at the time. In November 2009, *60 Minutes* aired a piece confirming rumors of break-ins to the Brazilian energy system in 2005 and 2007. In January 2008, the Central Intelligence Agency reported

---

[40] Warren Hoge, "British Convicts 6 of Plot to Black Out London," *New York Times*, July 3, 1997, at http://www.nytimes.com/1997/07/03/world/britain-convicts-6-of-plot-to-black-out-london.html (last visited August 21, 2014).

[41] The attack took about an hour, beginning with cutting the AT&T fiber-optic telecommunications cables in an underground vault near the substation. Gunmen opened fire on a substation adjacent to the Metcalf Energy Center. Shooting for nineteen minutes, they surgically knocked out seventeen transformers. The shooters appear to have aimed at the transformers' oil-filled cooling systems. Riddled with bullet holes, the transformers leaked 52,000 gallons of oil, then overheated. It took utility workers twenty-seven days to make repairs and bring the substation back to life. Rebecca Smith, "Assault on California Power Station Raises Alarm on Potential for Terrorism," *Wall Street Journal Online*, February 5, 2014, at http://online.wsj.com/news/articles/SB10001424052702304851104579359141941621778 (last visited August 21, 2014). PG&E intends to spend $100 million over the next three years to improve security at an unspecified number of substations and was considering asking for a rate increase to finance these measures. Work at substations is expected to include opaque fences to obscure the sites, as well as improved lighting, upgraded cameras, altering or removing trees and vegetation near substations, and other measures. George Avalos, "PG&E Upgrading Substation Security after San Jose Sniper Attack," *Oakland Tribune*, June 18, 2014, at http://www.mercurynews.com/business/ci_25988091/pg-e-expects-begin-metcalf-substation-security-upgrades?source=pkg (last visited August 21, 2014).

[42] "Utilities Installing Bull's-eyes at Substations to Combat Frequent Attacks," *SNL*, July 31, 2014, at http://www.snl.com/InteractiveX/Article.aspx?cdid=A-28785732-11815 (last visited August 21, 2014).

knowledge of disruptions, or threatened disruptions, by hackers of the power supplies for four cities.[43]

The security of cyber and communication networks is essential for the reliable operation of the grid. Existing control systems, originally designed for use with proprietary, stand-alone communication networks, were connected to the Internet without added technologies to ensure their security. Any telecommunication link that is even partly outside the control of the organization that owns and operates power plants, SCADA systems, or energy management systems represents a potential threat to the larger transmission grid. Strong centralized control, which is essential for reliable operations, requires multiple, high-data-rate, two-way communication links, a powerful central computing facility, and an elaborate operation control center, all of which are vulnerable during serious system stresses or power disruptions.[44]

There are a number of problems that will make it difficult to secure the power grid. There is a large fixed investment in control systems and software that was built before cybersecurity was a consideration, and it will be difficult to design it to be both connected (required for centralized control and monitoring) and secure. Utilities lack the incentive to invest past the point of corporate liability, which is unlikely to include the damages from a coordinated series of attacks. When NERC Cyber Asset Identification standards included black-start generators, plant managers removed black-start capability from units to avoid paying for NERC compliance. Some transmission operators were removing connectivity from their networks, thereby escaping NERC regulations, while leaving other serial communications into their networks vulnerable.[45] State regulators will be reluctant to make these investments because they would be asking local ratepayers to "insure" other states from the potential damage of coordinated attacks. FERC has authority to require measures to increase reliability at the transmission level, but less so for distribution.

FERC has used its authority under EPAct 2005 to encourage NERC to establish standards for protection of physical infrastructure and cybersecurity. Order 761 approved modified Critical Infrastructure Protection Reliability Standards, for the identification and protection of "Critical

---

[43] Ross Anderson and Shailendra Fuloria, "Security Economics and Critical National Infrastructure," in *Economics of Information Security and Privacy*, Tyler Moore, David Pym, Christos Ioannidis, eds. (New York, Springer, 2010): 56–57.

[44] S. Massoud Amin, "Securing the Electricity Grid," *The Bridge* 40 (2010): 13–20.

[45] Anderson and Fuloria, "Security Economics and Critical National Infrastructure," 60.

Cyber Assets" that are associated with "Critical Assets" to support the reliable operation of the Bulk-Power System.

FERC and NERC developed a number of standards for both protection of physical infrastructure and cyber security. In January 2008, the Commission approved the eight Critical Infrastructure Protection Reliability Standards submitted by NERC, with some changes.[46] Numerous commentators wanted the flexibility to make security decisions based on the utility's business concerns. The Commission rejected the concept of "reasonable business judgment" as a guide for determining what constituted appropriate compliance. The Commission also rejected language permitting an entity not to take actions specified in the Requirement if they documented an acceptance of risk. While the Commission accepted a role for economic feasibility, especially given the prevalence of legacy technologies, it did not want utilities putting cost minimization ahead of grid security.[47] The Commission approved Versions 2 and 3 of the Critical Infrastructure Protection Reliability Standards, each version including changes to some of the directives in Order No. 706.[48] Approval of Version 4 was issued as Order 761 in April 2012,[49] and Version 5 was approved in November 2013.[50] Over time, the NERC standards incorporated elements of the National Institute of Standards and Technology Risk Management Framework for categorizing and applying security controls. Development of these standards will continue to be an ongoing process, as a better understanding of system vulnerabilities evolves along with changes in information and communication technologies.

FERC also directed NERC to develop reliability standards that will require entities to demonstrate that they have taken steps to address

---

[46] *Mandatory Reliability Standards for Critical Infrastructure Protection*, Order No. 706, 122 FERC ¶ 61,040, *denying reh'g and granting clarification*, Order No. 706-A, 123 FERC ¶ 61,174 (2008), *order on clarification*, Order No. 706-B, 126 FERC ¶ 61,229 (2009), *order denying clarification*, Order No. 706-C, 127 FERC ¶ 61,273 (2009).

[47] Order 706, PP 107, 132–38, 150–56.

[48] *North American Electric Reliability Corp.*, 128 FERC ¶ 61,291 (2009), *order denying reh'g and granting clarification*, 129 FERC ¶ 61,236 (2009) (approving Version 2 of the CIP Reliability Standards); *North American Electric Reliability Corp.*, 130 FERC ¶ 61,271 (2010) (approving Version 3 of the CIP Reliability Standards).

[49] *Version 4 Critical Infrastructure Protection Reliability Standards*, Order No. 761, Final Rule, 77 Fed. Reg. 24,594 (April 25, 2012), 139 FERC ¶ 61,058 (2012), *order denying reh'g*, 140 FERC ¶ 61,109 (2012).

[50] *Version 5 Critical Infrastructure Protection Reliability Standards*, Order No. 791, Final Rule, 145 FERC ¶ 61,160 (2013), *denying reh'g and granting clarification*, 146 FERC ¶ 61,188 (2014).

physical security risks and vulnerabilities. The standards should require owners or operators of a bulk power system to perform a risk assessment of their systems to identify "critical facilities," the ones that, if rendered inoperable or damaged, could have a critical impact on operations. In the second step, the reliability standards should require owners or operators of critical facilities to evaluate the potential threats and vulnerabilities to those identified facilities. Reliability standards should require owners or operators of critical facilities to develop and implement a security plan designed to protect against attacks. Procedures to ensure confidential treatment of sensitive information that might aid such an attack were also part of the Commission's instructions to NERC.[51]

A NERC exercise in 2014 revealed that a severe attack on both cyber and physical assets could have significant second- and third-order impacts. Some entities reported that the cyber attack conditions degraded physical security surveillance assets. Utilities need to consider the dependencies of physical security monitoring processes on cyber systems. Hardwiring some communications and retaining the option of manual response will improve redundancy. Another issue will be the quick, cost-effective replacement of transformers and other expensive equipment. While there are programs such as NERC's Spare Equipment Database, the Edison Electric Institute's Spare Transformer Equipment Program, and the DHS Recovery Transformer program, participation adds another element of expense.[52]

One approach that can improve security and reliability, but at a substantial cost, would be to build more redundancy into the grid at all levels. Traditionally, utilities attempted to exploit economics of scale in transmission and generation, and to a lesser extent, distribution. This meant large power plants, feeding high-voltage lines, often with multiple transmission lines through the same right of way and on the same towers, and centralized substations feeding lower-voltage lines. The result is large contingencies, high-value targets for terrorists, and limited robustness. While gas-fired generation led to smaller generation units, they were often bunched in generation centers to be serviced by high-voltage transmission. Dispersing generation, building more transmission at relatively lower voltage, and feeding more substations and distribution voltage

---

[51] *Reliability Standards for Physical Security Measures*, 146 FERC ¶ 61,166 (2014) at PP 6–10.
[52] NERC, *Grid Security Exercise (GridEx II): After-Action Report*, March 2014.

lines would result in a system with fewer "key" targets and more redundancy that would be more difficult to take down, but this would probably require higher capital and operating costs. As electricity generation becomes dependent on natural gas, security may require extending protection to the gas pipeline system.

24

How Much Is Too Much?

While EPAct 2005 and FERC's subsequent measures to establish NERC as the ERO and to put teeth into NERC enforcement of reliability standards dealt with the issue of system security, resource adequacy proved to be another complicated issue to address.

Brownouts and rolling blackouts are far more frequent than cascading failures, and are more commonly associated with generation capacity shortfalls. As early as September 23, 1970, the northeast experienced brownouts during an early-fall heat wave. In 1988, Seattle suffered a three-day blackout during a heat wave that caused millions of dollars in losses. During 1989, utilities resorted to rolling blackouts in Houston, Tampa, and Jacksonville, selectively cutting off groups of customers in rotation through their service areas. In the summer of 1998, rolling blackouts were necessary in Colorado and Chicago. The following summer, 100,000 Chicagoans suffered a blackout on July 30 – the hottest day of the year.[1] During the first 150 days of 2001, Californians experienced thirty-eight rolling blackouts. The rolling blackouts experienced in California were the result of deliberate actions taken by the control area operator to shed loads in a controlled manner to respond to the problem of inadequate operating reserves.[2]

Generally, brownouts and rolling blackouts are a sign of resource scarcity, insufficient generation capacity to provide enough energy and

[1] David Nye, *When the Lights When Out: A History of Blackouts in America* (Cambridge, MA, MIT Press, 2010): 140, 148, 151.
[2] U.S.-Canada Power System Outage Task Force, *Recommendation 12: The Relationship between Competitive Power Markets and Grid Reliability* (July 2006): 7.

operating reserves to meet unexpected spikes in demand and/or contingencies. Market prices during scarcity periods, while often not as high as wished by generators, are generally substantially above marginal cost and should elicit sufficient bids if generators are acting as competitive price takers and not engaged in strategic behavior. A key problem is maintaining sufficient capacity to meet demand, not just the peak demand in the summer (or winter in areas with cold weather and electric heating), but also unexpected demand spikes during shoulder periods when many generation units are offline for maintenance. The second problem to be solved is ensuring sufficient ramping capacity to follow unexpected shifts and changes in load, and in recent years, the output of renewable resources.

Minor loss of power events occur constantly on a distribution grid, affecting small groups of customers for limited time periods. The larger the event, the greater the economic costs and also the political consequences. A major blackout or even extended rolling blackouts and brownouts can prompt an avalanche of phone calls and unpleasant meetings for state regulatory commissioners. The pain is then transmitted downstream to ISO and utility CEOs. Regulatory commissioners soon learned that a small incremental increase in rates from excess capacity is hard to monitor and rarely prompted complaints, but the lights going out engendered rapid and disagreeable consequences.

Resource adequacy standards were set so as to limit the number and duration of instances in which load would exceed available capacity. Traditionally, integrated utilities were required by regulators to maintain a reserve margin cushion, usually 15–18 percent of peak demand. These reserve margins were set to meet a "one day in 10 years" resource adequacy criterion, under which curtailments of firm load due to inadequate capacity should occur no more than once every ten years. The origination of the 1-in-10 metric is somewhat vague, although there are multiple references to it starting with articles by Calabrese from the 1940s.[3] This is an arbitrary limit, set without regard to the value of lost load (VoLL), the average social cost of shedding load (in $/MWh).

VoLL calculations are uncertain because they vary according to different customers, require heroic assumptions about how customers value

[3] G. Calabrese, "Determination of Reserve Capacity by the Probability Method," *Transactions of the American Institute of Electrical Engineers* 69 (January 1950): 1681–89, cited in Kevin Carden, Nick Wintermantel, and Johannes Pfeifenberger, "The Economics of Resource Adequacy Planning: Why Reserve Margins Are Not Just About Keeping the Lights On," National Regulatory Research Institute (April 2011): 2.

security of supply, and aggregate heterogeneous customers to provide a value per MWh of lost load. Customers with very high levels of VoLL (server farms, delicate manufacturing processes, etc.) will self-insure by paying for installing on-site backup generation and/or uninterruptible power supply systems using batteries or flywheels. They are concerned with the typical lost load event, which is localized and of limited duration – for example, when a squirrel commits self-immolation by short-circuiting a transformer. The cost of lost load will be a function of the duration and scope of a blackout: a few minutes may be a minor inconvenience, a few hours can result in significant costs, a day or longer across an entire urban region can result in major social disruptions.

Little empirical work has been undertaken to quantify the economic value provided by reserve margins based on the 1-in-10 standard or to confirm that this standard reasonably balances the trade-off between the economic value of reliability and the cost of carrying target reserve margins. If you compare the cost of "excess capacity" with the expected value of avoiding curtailments, determined by the product of VoLL and the expected quantity of lost load, the standard seems excessive.[4] The once-in-ten-years criterion is not as conservative as it seems at first glance. Reserve margin explicitly addresses the peak day rolling blackout or brownout that occurs because of a lack of operating capacity. It provides a sufficient margin that if a transmission line fails, taking some generators offline, or a large generator is out of service, there is sufficient generation available to avoid involuntary load curtailments to preserve system reliability. However, having sufficient generation to avoid failure on that peak day also provides the system with a larger margin on days when failures usually occur: off-peak periods with unexpected demand and units offline due to maintenance, or catastrophic weather events.

New modeling techniques have begun to address the resource adequacy question directly by asking what margin would be required to provide different levels of reliability. Reliability modeling involves simulating potential scenarios, using thousands of "runs" to ensure incorporation of low-probability extreme system conditions. The three key variables are weather, load forecast errors, and generator outages. Reliability models simulate random generator failure using Monte Carlo methods in which variables are modeled as probability distributions, and each run extracts

[4] James F. Wilson, "Reconsidering Resource Adequacy, Part 1: Has the One-day-in-10 years Criterion Outlived Its Usefulness?" *Public Utilities Fortnightly* (April 2010): 33–34.

a value for each relevant variable. This analysis is typically done with a bulk power reliability-planning tool that can run thousands of hourly scenarios[5] (which requires gross simplifications of the electrical system and market behavior to get useful results in a meaningful time frame and at a reasonable cost[6]).

The results of reliability modeling will be biased toward lower levels of reserve margins because they will fail to incorporate all the possible causes of system failure.[7] Some of these potential events will occur independently of most reasonable reserve margin values (such as the failure of multiple transmission lines); others are more likely to be mitigated if there is excess capacity. Many studies treat generation capacity as if it was homogenous, yet from the vantage point of recovering from contingencies, the quantity and type of operating reserves, and the ability of offline units to ramp up, are as important as the total available capacity.

Implementing a one-day-in-ten-years standard also requires defining whether the standard is 2.4 hours per year or one major event in ten years. Moreover, the 1-in-10 standard also does not generally define the magnitude or duration of the firm load shed. Target reserve margins can vary by 8 percentage points based simply on different approaches to the selection of input variables. Even when there is no actual load shed, there are benefits from avoiding costs from calling interruptible loads, dispatching high-cost emergency resources, and emergency purchases from neighboring systems. In this case, the option value of excess capacity, with respect to providing a lower-cost option than other measures short of load shedding, should be considered. When the full range of reliability-related impacts and costs is quantified, the 1-in-10 standard may result in target reserve margins that are too low from a cost-effectiveness perspective.[8]

---

[5] Carden, Wintermantel, and Pfeifenberger, "The Economics of Resource Adequacy Planning," 4.

[6] NERC has generally adopted the probabilistic model methodology for resource adequacy planning. Load-generation-transmission simulation software is used for computing forward-looking probabilistic metrics. Random outages for all generation units are modeled as random variables as opposed to de-rating the unit's capacity. The transmission modeling method incorporates major transmission constraints, limitations, and issues such as deliverability of resources and imports of supplemental resources. NERC, "Generation & Transmission Reliability Planning Models Task Force Final Report on Methodology and Metrics" (December 8, 2010).

[7] Frank A. Felder, "Incorporating Resource Dynamics to Determine Generation Adequacy Levels in Restructured Bulk Power Systems," *KIEE International Transactions on PE* 4 (2004): 100–05.

[8] Carden, Wintermantel, and Pfeifenberger, "The Economics of Resource Adequacy Planning," 8–9, 17.

Once the desired level of reserve margins is set, the question is what mechanism should be used to ensure that level of resource adequacy. For an integrated utility, under the jurisdiction of a state utility commission, the commission usually determines the required margin, and the utility responds to the regulatory commission's dictates. The utility will have some flexibility in how it meets that target, balancing the need to justify investments in rate proceedings with operational requirements of an integrated, primarily self-sufficient system.

The problem becomes far more complex in electricity markets. If load is incapable of sufficient response to peak prices in the very short run to balance supply and demand, electricity markets will need to maintain excess capacity to meet a desired level of reliability. The conventional wisdom is that a lack of real-time metering and billing results in little price-responsive behavior, and thus price does not act to ration limited electricity supplies among customers. However, customer behavior suggests that requiring or subsidizing real-time metering will not solve the demand-side problem. Large, sophisticated customers, especially those in energy-intensive industries, generally engage in demand management, especially as the cost of energy management systems has declined and their flexibility improved. However, many large customers have loads that are expensive to curtail on short notice, as the opportunity cost of stopping revenue-producing business activities far exceeds the cost of paying a high electricity price for a few hours.[9] In practice, many customers facing mandatory hourly prices have contracted with third parties to hedge against price volatility rather than attempt to respond to prices. Smaller customers, even when smart meters are installed, face large opportunity costs to respond quickly to prices.[10] Although many smart meters include electronic shut-off switches, these are not designed to be used to rapidly curtail loads, as their purpose is to reduce the cost of switching customers on and off.

As technology improves, and the cost of control equipment declines, demand will become more responsive to price, but the speed at which

---

[9] See Jay Zarnikau and Ian Hallett, "Aggregate Industrial Energy Consumer Response to Wholesale Prices in the Restructured Texas Electricity Market," *Energy Economics* 20 (2008): 1798–1808.

[10] There are large economies of scale associated with controlling demand. At the residential level, the typical peak demand may be 4 kW, so a 25% reduction saves a kWh over a peak hour, which means that even at $10,000/MWh prices, the savings would be only $10 for that hour. As price became more responsive and price spikes were reduced, the value of potential savings would also be reduced.

reliability incidents occur caution against dependence on demand responding to scarcity prices to ensure reliability. Some demand response products such as LaaRs allow the purchaser of demand response to require curtailment, or even directly control customer demand.[11] Most demand response programs require substantial lead times (thirty minutes to two hours), because loads have costs to curtail, unlike generators whose business is producing energy, loads produce services *with* energy, and opportunity costs of curtailment can be extremely high in the very short-run.

Even if consumers were more price-responsive, there would be a free-rider problem, in the sense that the market price would not include a premium for the value of reliability at risk. During periods of scarcity, the probability of system failure increases because it is more vulnerable to contingencies cascading into blackouts. In an electricity market that clears, the price during periods of scarcity will reflect only the cost of the marginal generation unit, and not the increased risk faced by all customers due to an increased probability of a reliability event. Ironically, the increased opportunities to exercise market power, which occur during scarcity periods, may cause prices to rise to their "efficient" level.

There are three basic options for maintaining sufficient capacity reserves in electricity markets: energy prices, capacity payments (whether administrative through rates or through a capacity market), and/or purchasing greater quantities of ancillary services. These three alternatives will have different impacts on the composition of the generation fleet. Scarcity prices during periods of real capacity shortage (only a few hours per year) favor baseload over peaker units relative to a capacity payment. Baseload units will receive more net revenues per kW for the hours of scarcity pricing and are also more likely to be "in the money" during those price spikes. A capacity payment is more likely to incentivize the building (or maintaining in operation) of peaking units. However, a capacity payment will also subsidize units that are unable to respond quickly enough to support reliability during contingencies, whereas energy prices reward generators who supply energy when required by the market.[12] Larger

---

[11] Comverge sells the ability to cycle residential and business customer HVAC systems during periods of high demand, and can respond relatively quickly. Other DR providers have some automated capability, but most DR suppliers are not willing to grant the DR vendor direct control over their loads. EnerNOC has the ability to dispatch emergency generation in some cases on customer sites.

[12] Peter Cramton and Steven Stoft, "A Capacity Market That Makes Sense," *Electricity Journal* 18 (August–September 2005): 46–48.

ancillary service procurements will favor technologies, such as combustion turbines and combined-cycle plants that provide operational flexibility. Since payments for ancillary services are only made for hours in which units are available to the system operator, they are a direct payment for reliability augmenting resources. Increasing purchases of reserves will push energy prices upward (by reducing supply in the energy market).

It may be hard to raise energy prices high enough over an extended period to provide a peaker unit with enough revenue to enter a market. In the short run, inelastic demand raises the real possibility that strategic bidding will result in prices well above marginal cost, transferring income from consumers to existing generators. Generators bidding into the market face a vertical demand curve, and absent some constraints on bids, electricity prices could rise to extreme levels. This also applies to operating reserves if the system operator must comply with reliability criteria at all costs. Extreme price spikes may not encourage investment since entry is predicated on expectations of future prices, not current revenues. If an entrant does not believe market power will continue to be exercised once additional capacity has entered the market, it will refrain from building new generation. An investor may also be wary of whether regulators will permit high prices to continue indefinitely in the face of political pressure. Bid caps can limit the exercise of market power.[13] However, these bid caps will further reduce the incentives for building new generation.

One alternative to providing higher energy prices without condoning the exercise of market power is to tie price increases to reserve shortages through administrative scarcity prices. Involuntary curtailments are averted by the system operator through dispatch of reserves. When resource scarcity leads to deployment of reserves, energy prices would be augmented with a prorated portion of the reserve capacity payments.[14] For example, if non-spinning reserves are paid $10/MW-hr to be available but are dispatched for only eighty-seven hours a year, the cost per hour of dispatch would be $1,000/MWh, plus incremental costs. By pricing energy at approximately the "true" cost of non-spinning reserves, the excess funds collected by the system operator could be rebated against uplift charges while sending a scarcity price signal to the market.

[13] Even the most expensive generation units have marginal costs of only a few hundred dollars per MWh, although the marginal costs of the last few MWs of generation can be extremely high due to opportunity costs, such as a higher probability of mechanical failure from running generation units above their rated capacity.

[14] Shmuel S. Oren, "Ensuring Generation Adequacy in Competitive Electricity Market," University of California Energy Institute, WP 007 (June 2003).

However, this would create a temptation for generators to withhold resources to force the operator to employ reserves, triggering price spikes.

Using reserves to set scarcity prices, instead of some estimate of VoLL, has certain attractive properties, as setting prices to VoLL, to provide a proxy for the value of avoiding curtailments, has some serious difficulties. The value of VoLL is both contentious, with a wide variance of estimates, and misleading, since if a curtailment market existed, there would be increasing quantities offered as prices rose. By tying scarcity prices to "cascading" reserve deployments, the system operator can approximate a hypothetical VoLL curve. As capacity becomes scarce, higher-value reserves are deployed and prices increase in lockstep with increased scarcity. Buying larger quantities of reserves will trigger reserve calls more often (since there will be less capacity available to supply energy), reducing the scarcity price (since the cost of reserves will be spread over more hours, the capacity cost to be recovered per hour declines) but triggering it more frequently.

In the long run, a capacity payment system designed to yield the same level of system reliability as a pure energy market, or one that also funds generators partially through operating reserve payments, should acquire the same quantity of generator investment with the same overall cost to consumers. Capacity charges have been on the order of 15–20 percent of total electricity costs.[15] In long-run equilibrium, this capacity payment will be collected explicitly or implicitly (without a capacity market, it would be reflected in the higher energy prices required to induce investment and/or higher operating reserves costs). Thus payments to capacity and reserves, by providing the revenues suppressed by price caps, should result in the same net revenue to the marginal generator in long-run equilibrium. In practice, different structures of payments will result in a somewhat different mix of generation technology because net payments to different types of generators will differ.

Concerns about the adequacy of net revenues to maintain resource adequacy have been raised since the electricity markets opened. Due to low natural gas prices and over-investment at the dawn of deregulation, the net revenue earned by marginal generators was far below the carrying cost of a new combustion turbine. Older conventional steam plants were

---

[15] The four-year average for PJM from 2009 to 2012 for wholesale electricity costs breaks down as follows: 72% energy charges, 17% capacity, 7% transmission, and 4% for ancillary services and PJM administrative fees. Calculated from data in Monitoring Analytics, LLC, *State of the Market Report For PJM, Volume 2, Detailed Analysis* (March 14, 2013): 15, table 1–9.

pushed higher up in the merit order and provided operating reserves during tight supply situations. The scarcity rents were not high enough to compensate for the costs of keeping these plants in operation, and absent an additional source of revenues, they would eventually be mothballed or retired.[16]

The realization that net revenues were insufficient to incentivize new investment or maintain existing generators in operation led FERC to support capacity markets and other mechanisms to maintain resource adequacy. The seven electricity markets have relied on a variety of mechanisms. ISO-NE, NYISO, and PJM have resorted to capacity markets that have evolved over time to include capacity demand curves and forward markets. MISO – and CAISO since its meltdown – has relied on state-mandated reserve margins. ERCOT is an energy-only market, while SPP is currently developing a capacity mechanism.

The three northeast ISOs employed installed capacity (ICAP) obligations in connection with administered capacity markets to maintain desired capacity levels.[17] These ICAP requirements evolved out of the commitments imposed on LSEs as integrated members of tight power pools. They set the penalty for a capacity shortfall at the cost of a new combustion turbine. With deregulation, and reorganization of the power pools into ISOs, these commitments were replaced by obligations to buy capacity from generators sufficient to cover the LSE's expected annual peak plus a reserve margin. These installed capability (or capacity) requirements were met through purchases in annual, seasonal, or monthly auctions administered by the ISOs or through bilateral contracts with generators. The ISOs required generators who sold capacity to accept commitments to bid their generation into the market, or at least make it available to be recalled when required by the ISO. ICAP eligibility began to resemble a call option on the generation of a unit, with the strike price set by the market.

The key issues in designing ICAP markets were the level of required capacity, the penalty for under-purchasing ICAP, and the structure of the ICAP auction. PJM and New England set ICAP penalties equal to the

---

[16] Paul L. Joskow, "The Difficult Transition to Competitive Electricity Markets in the U.S.," CEEPR (May 2003): 61–67; Potomac Economics, *New York ISO 2004 State of the Market Report*, July 2005.

[17] *New York Independent System Operator, Inc.*, 96 FERC ¶ 61,251 (2001); *PJM Interconnection, LLC*, 86 FERC ¶ 61,017, 61,042, 61,044 (1999); *ISO New England, Inc. et al.*, 91 FERC ¶ 61, 311, 62080 (2000), *order on reh'g and compliance filings*, 95 FERC ¶ 61,384 (2001).

cost of a new CT, while New York raised its penalty up to three times the cost of a new CT. The period over which the penalty is imposed is significant because it determines the magnitude of the penalty. As the ISOs realized that generation outside of constrained regions could not contribute to reliability inside the constraints, they designed deliverability tests to create locational capacity markets reflecting these constraints. A deliverability test for ICAP requires resources to be capable of delivering their power to the LSE at times of peak load (when constraints tend to be binding).

The initial ICAP markets demonstrated "all or nothing" behavior, with prices during surplus periods trending toward zero, while when capacity supplies approached the market requirement, generators would bid the maximum price, confident that most of their bid quantities would clear and they would set the market price at the cap. This resulted in the worst of all worlds, market manipulation and insufficient revenues to encourage new investment. As problems mounted, each capacity market evolved into more sophisticated structures.

In the NYISO, the market had been bifurcated because of transmission constraints into New York City and Long Island. The New York State Reliability Council set the Installed Capacity Requirement to 118 percent of expected peak demand. In addition to the statewide minimum requirement, New York City and Long Island have locational ICAP requirements of 80 percent and 95 percent of their peak load levels, respectively, which must be met with resources located within those areas. FERC had previously accepted a Con Ed proposal to cap ICAP at $105/kW-year in New York City. Con Ed was concerned that the requirement that 80 percent of installed capacity be in-city meant there would be little competition to discipline the price of installed capacity.[18]

On March 21, 2003, NYISO filed a proposal to use a Demand Curve for ICAP in a monthly auction. A capacity demand curve, by gradually adjusting capacity prices as the level of capacity changes over time, provides more predictable capacity market prices. Estimating a capacity demand curve combines two ad hoc procedures, the traditional estimation of an "optimal" level of capacity, and the parameters of the capacity demand curve. The general procedure is to set the capacity price at the optimal quantity of capacity to the net revenue requirement (adjusted for revenues from energy and ancillary service markets) of a new combustion turbine, since it is desirable for a new unit to earn zero economic

---

[18] *Consolidated Edison Company of New York, Inc.*, 84 FERC ¶ 61,287 (1998).

profit when there is sufficient capacity. This is usually referred to as the cost of new entry (CONE). The high-capacity price is usually set at some multiple of the CONE value. In New York, the price was set equal to the net CONE for each area (Long Island, New York City, and the rest of New York state) at a capacity level of 118 percent of peak load. The price gradually fell to $0 at 132 percent of peak load and rose for levels of capacity below 118 percent of peak load to a maximum of twice the net CONE.[19] The annualized capital costs of new generation, determined by a consultant and adjusted for net revenues, were $72/kW-year for upstate New York, $128/kW-year for New York City, and $105/kW-year for Long Island.[20] The amount of generation in the interconnection process increased after the ICAP Demand Curves became effective in May 2003, but tapered off due to proposed high-voltage lines into New York. The threat of additional imports discouraged building generation in such a high-cost region.[21]

PJM began setting weekly capacity requirements in 1956, and they became an ICAP annual requirement in 1974. A capacity deficiency rate based on the annualized cost of a combustion turbine was established as a penalty. The method was used from 1974 to 1998 and modified in 1999 to a daily obligation.[22] PJM's Reliability Assurance Agreement was established to ensure that adequate capacity resources were planned and made available. All LSEs within the PJM control area are parties to the agreement.[23] Each LSE must install or contract for capacity resources or obtain capacity sufficient to satisfy its daily capacity obligation. PJM established an auction market for capacity credits to meet the generation capacity obligation. The PJM capacity market initially operated on a daily or a monthly basis, but this was changed to a seasonal basis because of problems with frequent delisting of generation capacity.[24] LSEs typically satisfied approximately 95 percent of their capacity obligations through

---

[19] *New York Independent System Operator, Inc.*, 103 FERC ¶ 61,201 (2003) at PP 2–8.
[20] *New York Independent System Operator, Inc.*, 111FERC ¶ 61,117 at PP 17 (2005), *reh'g denied*, 112 FERC ¶ 61,283 (2005).
[21] NYISO, *Annual Report in Docket Nos. ER01–3001-, ER03–647-* (December 20, 2011): 48.
[22] Marty Bhavaraju, Benhamin Hobbs, and Ming-Che Hu, "PJM Reliability Pricing Model – A Summary and Dynamic Analysis," IEEE 2007.
[23] *Pennsylvania-New Jersey-Maryland Interconnection et al.*, 81 FERC ¶ 61,257 (1997), *order on clarification*, 82 FERC ¶ 61,008 (1998), *order on reh'g*, 92 FERC ¶ 61,282 (2000).
[24] *PJM Interconnection, LLC*, 95 FERC ¶ 61,330, 62,175, 62,178–79 (2001), *reh'g. denied*, 96 FERC ¶ 61,206 (2001).

self-supply and bilateral contracts.[25] PJM set the annual Installed Reserve Margin at 15 percent of peak capacity.

In the first years of the PJM markets, the PJM region experienced a boom in new plant construction, but a spike in announced retirements of older, marginally economic units reflected insufficient generator revenues. High rates of generation retirements and transmission constraints meant the eastern region of PJM faced violations of reliability criteria in the near future. PJM concluded that it would need to have locational requirements to provide incentives for new generation investment in areas affected by transmission "deliverability" constraints.[26]

PJM proposed the Reliability Pricing Model (RPM), a new capacity market construct, incorporating forward procurement of capacity. The Commission accepted the general concepts, such as Locational Deliverability Areas, a downward-sloping demand curve and the participation of demand response in the capacity auction, but asked for clarification of key issues.[27] PJM resubmitted its RPM proposal after settlement negotiations. The Commission accepted the settlement, with a few changes, in December 2006.[28] Three breakpoints determined the shape of the demand curve, the Installed Reserve Margin minus 3 percent (price set at 150 percent of net CONE), the Reserve Margin plus 1 percent (net CONE), and the Reserve Margin plus 5 percent (20 percent of net CONE). The capacity auction would be conducted three years in advance of the delivery year, with incremental auctions held between the initial auction and the delivery year. Generating capacity not yet built could be offered based on its projected net costs. The settlement provided for demand resources to receive the capacity auction clearing price.[29] The RPM settlement includes a "minimum offer price rule" for review of offers from net capacity buyers to prevent capacity buyers from attempting to manipulate the auction.[30]

---

[25] *PJM Interconnection, LLC*, 95 FERC ¶ 61,175 (2001).

[26] *PJM Interconnection, L.L.C.*, Docket Nos. ER05-148-000 and EL05-1410-000 (August 31, 2005): 5–7.

[27] *PJM Interconnection, L.L.C.*, 115 FERC ¶ 61,079 (2006) at PP 51–52, 68–72, 84–86, 103–04.

[28] *PJM Interconnection, L.L.C.*, 117 FERC ¶ 61,331 (2006) at PP 5–6, *reh'g and clarification*, 119 FERC ¶ 61,318 (2007), *reh'g denied*, 121 FERC ¶ 61,173 (2007).

[29] *PJM Interconnection, L.L.C.*, 117 FERC ¶ 61,331 (2006) at PP 24–31.

[30] *PJM Interconnection, L.L.C.*, 122 FERC ¶ 61,264 (2007) at PP 11–15. For purposes of determining CONE, PJM was divided into three areas: Area 1, centered in New Jersey; Area 2, centered in Maryland; and Area 3 that covers the Midwest and Virginia portions of PJM.

Estimates of CONE became a contentious issue since they set the auction price. In January 2008, in response to rapidly escalating costs of construction,[31] PJM proposed to increase CONE values 40–50 percent.[32] A report commissioned by PJM in response to a FERC directive, along with a report by the PJM market monitor, supported a higher CONE value. FERC accepted an increase in the CONE value of 70 percent, reflecting higher costs of new generation, and the Handy Whitman construction cost index was chosen to adjust future CONE values.[33] Demand response resources were required to bid into the auctions to receive capacity payments. Energy efficiency resources could participate in the RPM market and would be compensated for each year the resource provider submitted updated measurement and verification data to PJM.[34]

The impact of excess capacity in PJM kept capacity auction prices below net CONE. Prices were higher in the mid-Atlantic region until the 2014–15 auction when the expectation that new transmission would remove constraints into this area caused bids to converge with the rest of PJM. Increased penetration of DSM resources combined with decreases in load forecasts exerted substantial downward pressure on capacity prices. Despite low capacity prices, 4,847 MW of new generation has cleared the auctions since 2007.[35] This suggests a phenomenon seen in other markets – an upward sloping supply curve for new generation.

NEPOOL had an ICAP requirement since 1990. Until 1998, LSEs who failed to satisfy their ICAP requirements were assessed an administratively determined charge ($105/kW-year). In 1998, the charge was replaced by the requirement for deficient LSEs to purchase ICAP capacity through an auction market. As in PJM, the market-clearing ICAP price was at or near

---

[31] Marc W. Chupka and Gregory Basheda, the Brattle Group, "Rising Utility Construction Costs: Sources and Impacts," The Edison Foundation, September 2007; "Construction Costs for New Power Plants Continue to Escalate: IHS CERA Power Capital Costs Index," May 30, 2008.

[32] *PJM Interconnection, L.L.C.*, 123 FERC ¶ 61,015 (2008) at PP 4–6, 28–30.

[33] Johannes Pfeifenberger et al., "Review of PJM's Reliability Pricing Model (RPM)," Brattle Group for PJM Interconnection LLC (June 30, 2008); *PJM Interconnection, L.L.C.*, 124 FERC ¶ 61,272 (2008) at PP 44–46; *PJM Interconnection, L.L.C.*, 126 FERC ¶ 61,275, PP 24, 36 (2009), *order on reh'g, PJM Interconnection, L.L.C.*, 128 FERC ¶ 61,157 (2009); *PJM Interconnection, L.L.C.*, 131 FERC ¶ 61,168 (2010) at PP 14–18.

[34] *PJM Interconnection, L.L.C.*, 126 FERC ¶ 61,275 (2009) at PP 66–70, 83–84, 121–22, 130–39.

[35] Johannes Pfeifenberger et al., "Second Performance Assessment of PJM's Reliability Pricing Model," Prepared for PJM Interconnection, L.L.C by the Brattle Group (August 26, 2011): 13–18.

$0 per kW except for a dramatic spike in January 2000. The Commission agreed that elimination of the ICAP auction market was appropriate and required the ISO to revert to administratively determined sanctions for failure to meet the existing ICAP requirement.[36] When the ISO proposed an ICAP deficiency charge of $0.17/kW month, the average clearing price in the ICAP auction market in 1999, the Commission rejected this ploy, pointing out that the ISO stated that it desired to induce the building of generation in New England. The Commission required that the ISO reinstitute the original NEPOOL administrative charge.[37]

The First Circuit Court of Appeals found that FERC's failure to discuss in any detail the extensive affidavit filings by objectors was unacceptable. The First Circuit went out of its way to side with the Commission's conclusion, noting that most of the utilities served by ISO-NE were net buyers and had incentives to object to a capacity charge. Given the impact of any widespread power shortage, FERC had every reason to want effective enforcement of reserve requirements, even if enforcement came at a high price. However, although an agency's expert judgments are entitled to deference, there must be some semblance of serious discussion to provide a judgment worthy of deference. The Court remanded for further explanation.[38]

The ISO-NE countered with a new ICAP proposal. The proposal capped energy bids of ICAP sellers at $1,000/MW and imposed a revised ICAP deficiency charge equivalent to the PJM ICAP deficiency charge, based on the cost of a new peaking unit. The Commission found that basing the ICAP deficiency charge on the net cost of a new peaking unit was appropriate.[39]

In early 2003, several units located in southwest Connecticut filed with FERC for approval of RMR contracts. The southwest Connecticut region had a history of underinvestment in transmission and generation. FERC directed ISO-NE to develop a market-based mechanism that implemented locational or deliverability requirements in the resource adequacy market. ISO-NE filed a locational installed capacity market proposal on March 1, 2004. Previously, an LSE could obtain resources anywhere in

---

36 *ISO New England, Inc.*, 91 FERC ¶ 61, 311, at 62,080–81 (2000), *order on reh'g and compliance filings*, 95 FERC ¶ 61,384 (2001).

37 *ISO New England, Inc.*, 91 FERC ¶ 61, 290, at 61,973–74 (2000), *order on reh'g*, 94 FERC ¶ 61, 237 (2001).

38 *Central Maine Power Co. v FERC*, 252 F.3d 34 (1st Cir. 2001).

39 *ISO New England, Inc.*, 96 FERC ¶ 61,234, at 61,943–44 (2001), *order on reh'g*, 97 FERC ¶ 61,212 (2001), *order on reh'g*, 98 FERC ¶ 61,103 (2002).

the NEPOOL control area to meet its ICAP requirement, even if energy from those resources could not be physically delivered to that load. ISO-NE's LICAP proposal imposed separate ICAP requirements for each of four regions: Maine, Connecticut, northeastern Massachusetts/Boston, and the remainder of New England. The price of capacity would be determined monthly using a demand curve for each region. The proposed ISO-NE demand curve set the ICAP price to the net CONE at the quantity equal to the average surplus capacity, 19.5 percent above the expected peak demand. The demand curve was intended to ensure that capacity levels fell below this minimum in only about 15 percent of years. The Commission agreed with the idea of ICAP regions and the use of a demand curve.[40]

Political pressure was brought on the Commission to kill LICAP. In the Energy Policy Act of 2005, Congress noted the New England governors' concerns that the LICAP proposal would not provide adequate capacity or reliability while imposing high costs on consumers.[41] The Commission, responding to this pressure, appointed a settlement judge to guide the process of developing an alternative proposal.[42] The Settlement Agreement provided for the implementation of a Forward Capacity Market (FCM). The Settlement Agreement was the end-product of a series of more than thirty formal settlement conferences that occurred over a four-month period. One hundred and fifteen parties participated in the settlement proceedings.[43]

The FCM established annual auctions for capacity. Forward Capacity Auctions would procure capacity three-plus years ahead of the commitment period, providing a planning period for new entry and allow potential new capacity to compete in the auctions. New capacity may select a commitment period of up to five years, in one-year increments, to facilitate financing. The capacity auctions were designed as descending clock auctions. In such an auction, the administrator announces a starting price. With subsequent rounds prices decline until supply and demand match. The starting price for the auction was two times the CONE, initially $7.50/kW-month. Subsequent to the first auction, CONEs would

---

[40] *Devon Power LLC, et al.*, 103 FERC ¶ 61,240 (2004) at P 9–13, 28–32; *Prepared Direct Testimony of Steven E. Stoft on Behalf of ISO New England Inc.*, Docket No. ER03–563–030 (August 31, 2004).

[41] Pub. L. No. 109–58, § 1236, 119 Stat. 961 (2005).

[42] *Devon Power LLC*, 113 FERC ¶ 61,075 (2005) at P 5, 10–14.

[43] *Devon Power LLC*, 115 FERC ¶ 61,340 (2006), at PP 15–16, *reh'g denied*, 117 FERC 61,133 (2006).

be determined based on preceding CONEs and the clearing price of the previous auction. Until there were three successful auctions, the price for existing capacity would be set within a range of $4.50 to $10.50/kW-month. Separate capacity zones would be established for each yearly auction when the ISO determines in advance that transmission constraints are likely to bind.[44]

The Maine Public Utilities Commission and the attorneys general of Connecticut and Massachusetts petitioned for review after the Commission denied rehearing of its order approving the FCM settlement.[45] The DC Circuit Court objected to Section 4.C of the settlement agreement, which provided that the transition payments and the final prices from the Forward Market auctions would be reviewed under the *Mobile-Sierra*[46] "public interest" standard rather than the "just and reasonable" standard. The crux of the *Mobile-Sierra* doctrine was that it applied to voluntary agreements between parties. The Court concluded that FERC lacked the authority to approve a settlement agreement that applies the public interest standard to rate challenges brought by non-contracting third parties.[47] While the DC Court made a legalistic argument, its decision also made sense from a public policy perspective. If the FCM were a reasonable, workable construct, then it would withstand challenges under the "just and reasonable" standard. The Commission in essence took this stand in their remand order.[48]

The issue became more complicated when the Supreme Court gave its ruling in *Morgan Stanley*,[49] clarifying the "public interest" versus "just and reasonable" dichotomy. There is only one statutory standard for assessing wholesale electricity rates, whether set by contract or tariff, the just-and-reasonable standard. Parties to a contract have presumptively equal bargaining power, thus they can be expected to negotiate a just

---

[44] *Devon Power LLC*, 115 FERC ¶ 61,340 (2006) at PP 16–20, 123.

[45] *Maine PUC v. FERC*, 520 F.3d 464, 470–76 (D.C. Cir. 2008).

[46] *United Gas Pipe Line Co. v. Mobile Gas Serv. Corp.*, 350 U.S. 332; *FPC v. Sierra Pac. Power Co.*, 350 U.S. 348, 355 (1956).

[47] *Maine PUC v. FERC*, 520 F.3d 464, 477–78 (D.C. Cir. 2008).

[48] *Devon Power LLC*, 126 FERC ¶ 61,027 (2009).

> In taking this action, we emphasize that the Commission found the Settlement Agreement, a contested settlement, to be just and reasonable based on a voluminous record. Non-parties to this settlement will have a high burden should they seek to modify the settlement in the future under a just and reasonable standard.

Id. at P 6.

[49] *Morgan Stanley Capital Group Inc. v. Public Utility District No. 1 of Snohomish County*, 128 S.Ct. 2733, 554 U.S. 527 (2008).

and reasonable rate between the two of them. Therefore, only when the contract rate seriously harms the consuming public may the Commission declare it not to be just and reasonable.[50] In light of that decision, the Supreme Court took *certiorari* to answer whether *Mobile-Sierra's* public-interest standard applies when a contract rate is challenged by a third party.[51] The *Mobile-Sierra* presumption does not depend on the identity of the complainant who seeks FERC investigation. A presumption applicable to contracting parties only, and inoperative as to consumers, advocacy groups and state utility commissions, could scarcely provide the stability *Mobile-Sierra* aimed to secure. When FERC presumes that a contract rate resulting from fair, arm's-length negotiations is just and reasonable, this presumption also applies to non-contracting parties.[52]

The DC Court, after expressing some bewilderment as to the exact intent of the Supreme Court, concerning the distinction between "just and reasonable" and "just and reasonable" under the *Mobile-Sierra* rule, determined that FERC never articulated in its orders a rationale for its decision to approve a *Mobile-Sierra* clause outside the contract context. FERC must explain why the rates are entitled to *Mobile-Sierra* treatment.[53]

FERC noted that the capacity auction results and transition payments apply to all suppliers and purchasers of capacity within the ISO-NE market, not just to the settling parties, and the rates set by the forward capacity auctions represent tariff, not contract, rates. Nonetheless, the Commission found that it was appropriate to exercise its discretion to apply a more rigorous application of the "just and reasonable" standard of review to the Settlement as an overall package that advanced the interests of all market participants. In circumstances outside the context of the type of "contract rates" addressed in *Morgan Stanley*, if it is unjust and unreasonable to lock in a more stringent application of the just and reasonable standard, then the Commission has the discretion not to impose that more stringent standard of review.[54]

Capacity prices in New England gradually rose due to a transition price mechanism, but the transition prices seemed to be vindicated by the first auction, for 2010–11, which resulted in an auction price above

[50] *Morgan Stanley*, 128 S.Ct. 2733, 2745–46.
[51] *NRG Power Mktg., LLC v Maine Public Utilities Commission*, 130 S.Ct. 693, 698 (2010).
[52] *NRG Power Mktg., LLC*, 130 S.Ct. 693, 700–01.
[53] *Maine PUC v. FERC*, 625 F.3d 754, 759–60 (D.C. Cir. 2010).
[54] *Devon Power LLC*, 134 FERC ¶ 61,208 (2011) at P 12–14, 24.

the transition price. As in PJM, the participation of demand resources put downward pressure on future capacity prices. By the third auction, the price was set at the floor price, which continued through the fourth and fifth auctions. Imports also had a sizeable impact, but by the fourth auction, for 2013–14, the availability of additional imports was beginning to run against transfer capability restraints.[55]

MISO began initial operations of its market on April 1, 2005. MISO's Transmission and Energy Markets Tariff (TEMT) delineated MISO's Day 2 operations in its fifteen-state region. The Day 2 operations included day-ahead and real-time energy markets and a FTR market for transmission capacity.[56] The MISO market covers multiple reliability organizations (MAIN, MAPP, and ECAR), including some Canadian provinces, and has both open retail access and vertically integrated states. This would make negotiating a resource adequacy mechanism extremely difficult. Resource Adequacy Requirements were based on the current reliability mechanisms of the states and the Regional Reliability Organizations within the midwest ISO. Market participants must comply with the appropriate state or regional reliability requirements where their load is served. In the event of a conflict between state and regional reliability requirements, market participants would fully comply with the state's requirements and then regional reliability requirements that are feasible. If there were no reliability standards in place MISO proposed a default annual reserve margin of 12 percent.[57]

A December 2007 MISO proposal contained mandatory requirements for any market participant serving load in MISO to have sufficient planning resources, including generation capacity and demand response. MISO proposed to manage resource adequacy through financial settlement/enforcement provisions that were still under development.[58] The Commission made it clear that a role for state authorities cannot undercut the Commission's authority to review resource adequacy and reserve margins. In situations where one party's resource adequacy decisions can cause adverse reliability and costs impacts on other participants in

[55] ISO New England Inc., *2010 Annual Markets Report*, p. 107; ISO New England, *Forward Capacity Market Result Reports*, various years.

[56] *Midwest Independent Transmission System Operator, Inc.*, 108 FERC ¶ 61,163, *order on reh'g*, 109 FERC ¶ 61,157 (2004), *order on reh'g*, 111 FERC ¶ 61,043 (2005).

[57] *Midwest Independent Transmission System Operator, Inc.*, 108 FERC ¶ 61,163 (2004) at PP 388–422.

[58] *Midwest Independent Transmission System Operator, Inc.*, 122 FERC ¶ 61,283 (2008) at PP 11–12.

a regionally operated system, it is appropriate for FERC to consider resource adequacy in determining whether rates are just and reasonable. States have the authority to set their own reserve margins as long as they are not inconsistent with any reliability standard approved by the Commission. Given this caveat, the Commission approved the overall construct under which states can set differing reserve margins within MISO.[59]

MISO's resource adequacy program was premised on LSEs meeting their planning reserve requirements primarily through bilateral contracting. A minimum margin requirement and financial charges assessed to deficient LSEs, in combination with scarcity pricing, created long-term incentives to obtain adequate capacity via bilateral contracts. Without a minimum margin requirement, states that did not require their utilities to maintain sufficient capacity could benefit from the investment in states that imposed more prudent policies. A voluntary auction provided LSEs a means to procure remaining capacity obligations in a spot market. This mechanism was consistent with a market predominantly composed of traditional, vertically integrated utilities. It was supported by the states in the MISO footprint that opposed the centralized capacity markets found in other eastern regional transmission organizations.[60] The results of the voluntary auction reflected the problems of the ICAP markets in the northeast. After a one-month spike in July 2009, the price collapsed close to zero.[61] This was due to excess capacity in MISO, a situation that should persist as long as states impose margin requirements on utilities equal to or greater than the MISO resource adequacy margins.

California in 2000 was a good example of the negative effects of having insufficient resources to reliably serve load. The shortages of 2000 stemmed from a combination of drought, market manipulation, poor market design and bad policy. The failure of the CPUC to encourage additional transmission to reduce the impact of transmission constraints between northern and southern California was a contributing factor, as was the combination of NIMBY and environmental constraints on the siting of new generation. However, a resource adequacy requirement modeled after the northeast RTOs would probably have made little difference. During the previous two years, owing to abundant hydropower

---

[59] *Midwest Independent Transmission System Operator, Inc.*, 122 FERC ¶ 61,283 (2008) at PP 52–63.
[60] *Midwest Independent Transmission System Operator, Inc.*, 127 FERC ¶ 61,054 (2009) at PP 24–31.
[61] VCA Summary, various years.

imports and mild weather, California experienced low energy prices, and had a resource adequacy mechanism been in place, capacity prices probably would have been insufficient to engender more new capacity than actually came online in 2000 and 2001. California serves as an example why scarcity pricing and short-run capacity markets are unlikely to be able to respond to severe capacity shortages in time to alleviate extreme economic hardships to consumers.

On October 29, 2001, the CPUC opened a proceeding to establish operating procedures and ratemaking mechanisms for the three major private utilities, PG&E, SDG&E, and SCE (whose customers account for approximately 80 percent of California's electricity usage), to resume full procurement responsibilities by January 1, 2003.[62] The CDWR power purchase contracts were allocated to each utility, requirements for the procurement of renewable resources were assigned, and cost recovery mechanisms were established. The CPUC emphasized that the utilities should take into account the regulatory preference that resource adequacy be met first through cost-effective energy efficiency programs, other demand reduction programs, and renewable resources. The CPUC adopted a planning reserve margin for LSEs of 15–17 percent to be met by January 1, 2008. The utilities were to forward-contract 90 percent of their summer peaking needs (loads plus planning reserves) a year in advance and were restricted to purchasing no more than 5 percent of their energy needs from the spot market.[63]

The CPUC instituted a rulemaking for Electric Utility Resource Planning in April 2004.[64] The CPUC quickly discovered that in the absence of a LMP market that automatically assigned congestion costs that

---

[62] *Order Instituting Rulemaking to Establish Policies and Cost Recovery Mechanisms for Generation Procurement and Renewable Resource Development*, Rulemaking (R.) 01–10–024, issued October 29, 2001 (Generation Procurement Proceeding).

[63] Generation Procurement Proceeding, *Interim Opinion*, Decision 04–01–50, January 22, 2004.

[64] Public Utilities Commission of the State of California, *Order Instituting Rulemaking to Promote Policy and Program Coordination and Integration in Electric Utility Resource Planning*, Docket # R. 04–04–003, April 1, 2004 (Resource Adequacy Proceeding). The proceeding was the successor to the *Generation Procurement Proceeding*. The Rulemaking was guided by the statewide Energy Action Plan (EAP) adopted in 2003 by CPUC, the California Energy Commission (CEC) and the California Consumer Power and Conservation Financing Authority. The Resource Adequacy proceeding also took into account a number of other proceedings, including Demand Response, R.02–06–001, Distributed Generation, R.04–03–017, Energy Efficiency, R.01–08–028, Renewable Portfolio Standards and the Transmission Assessment Process, R.04–01–026 and Transmission Planning, I.00–11–001. Nothing is ever simple in California.

there was a conflict between LSE cost minimization and system reliability. The CAISO informed SCE and the director of the CPUC's Energy Division of reliability related concerns due, in part, to scheduling of resources that were not deliverable to load. The CPUC ruled that a utility-scheduling practice or procurement plan that focused solely on least-cost energy, without regard to deliverability, was not in compliance with prior decisions.[65]

In an April 28, 2004 letter to CPUC President Peevey, Governor Schwarzenegger indicated that the phase-in date for resource adequacy of 2008 was too slow. The CPUC responded by moving the date to achieve full implementation of the 15–17 percent reserve margin up to June 1, 2006. LSEs were to acquire a mix of resources capable of satisfying the reserve margin for the hours for each month that their loads were within 10 percent of their maximum contribution to the monthly system peak. Different resources could be used for different hours and months. The CPUC monitored the terms and prices of contracts to ensure that they were reasonable.[66] The CPUC authorized the utilities to enter into short-term, mid-term, and long-term contracts for power. The utilities were directed to procure the maximum feasible amount of renewable energy, and to employ a "GHG adder" when evaluating energy bids to internalize the cost of GHG emissions.[67] In September 2005, the California legislature enacted AB 380, which required the CPUC, in consultation with the CAISO, to establish resource adequacy requirements for all LSEs within the CPUC's jurisdiction. AB 380 required publicly owned utilities to procure adequate resources to meet their peak demands and planning and operating reserves.[68]

Concurrent with CPUC efforts to ensure sufficient capacity for reliability, CAISO had initiated a market redesign effort in response to FERC orders. In January 2000, the Commission directed the CAISO to design a comprehensive replacement market.[69] On May 1, 2002 the CAISO

---

[65] Resource Adequacy Proceeding, *Interim Opinion Regarding Electricity Reliability Issues*, Decision 04–07–028, July 8, 2004.

[66] Resource Adequacy Proceeding, *Interim Opinion Regarding Resource Adequacy*, Decision 04–10–035, October 28, 2004.

[67] Resource Adequacy Proceeding, *Opinion Adopting Pacific Gas and Electric Company, Southern California Edison Company and San Diego Gas & Electric Company's Long-Term Procurement Plans*, Decision 04–12–048, December 28, 2004.

[68] Resource Adequacy Proceeding, *Opinion on Resource Adequacy Requirements*, Decision 05–10–042, October 27, 2005.

[69] *California Independent System Operator Corp.*, 90 FERC ¶ 61,006, *reh'g denied*, 91 FERC ¶ 61,026 (2000).

submitted Comprehensive Market Design 2002, and a revised version in July 2003. The proposal included a day-ahead and hour-ahead market, with a Residual Unit Commitment procedure in both markets. CAISO proposed to co-optimize energy and ancillary services and to use LMP. CAISO also proposed market power mitigation elements including must-offer obligations in real-time and forward markets, continuation of the $250/MWh bid cap, Automatic Mitigation Procedures, and local market power mitigation.[70] By 2005, Market Design 2002 had morphed into the Market Redesign and Technology Upgrade Proposal. Market participants would submit schedules and bids for energy and ancillary services through a CAISO-certified Scheduling Coordinator. Load aggregation zones would be established for load scheduling, bidding, and settlement purposes.[71]

The Market Redesign Tariff proposed that LSEs within the CAISO control area would have system resource adequacy requirements based on a 15 percent reserve margin requirement. LSEs would also have local capacity requirements to ensure that the CAISO has sufficient resources in the appropriate locations to operate the transmission system. LSEs subject to the CPUC's jurisdiction will be subject to the requirements established by the CPUC. FERC found that while it lacked regulatory oversight over federal and state power agencies, these agencies must comply with resource adequacy requirements as a condition for participating in the CAISO market. In effect, FERC established an "if you play, you must pay" rule for participation in electricity markets. FERC balked at allowing CAISO to set a reserve requirement for LSEs. However, if a local regulatory authority failed to implement a reserve margin, then the CAISO should implement the 15 percent default reserve margin. LSEs within the CAISO control area benefit from the reliable supply of energy at just and reasonable prices, so it is not unreasonable to require that all LSEs accept resource adequacy obligations. An LSE should not be able to free-ride to the detriment of their customers and grid reliability as a whole.[72]

---

[70] *California Independent System Operator Corporation*, 105 FERC ¶ 61,240, at PP 1–17 (2003). The Commission issued various guidance orders, *California Independent System Operator Corp.*, 107 FERC ¶ 61,274 (2004); *California Independent System Operator Corporation*, 108 FERC ¶ 61,254 (2004), *reh'g denied*, *California Independent System Operator Corporation*, 110 FERC ¶ 61,041 (2005).

[71] *California Independent System Operator Corp.*, 112 FERC ¶ 61,013, at PP 10–14 (2005).

[72] *California Independent System Operator Corp.*, 116 FERC ¶ 61,274, at PP 1094, 1112–19, 1137–43, 1153–55 (2006).

Along with mechanisms to ensure long-term resource adequacy, the Commission also turned to scarcity pricing to support short-term system security by encouraging price response demand. A side benefit was the increased revenues to generators when a region was experiencing frequent capacity shortages. The Commission found that existing market rules might not accurately reflect the value of energy during periods of true scarcity (i.e., when there is a shortage of operating reserves). Being able to see the proper price signals in all hours, especially during periods of scarcity, will allow loads to contract with generators and demand response resources to mitigate the risk and to avoid the associated scarcity prices. Furthermore, loads will have the incentive to invest in technologies to avoid paying scarcity prices and to provide ancillary services. Scarcity pricing should provide appropriate price signals for resources bidding in reserve markets, and thereby ensure short-term reliability. Such price signals would encourage entry by generators, investment in new technology, and more participation in demand response programs.[73]

The Commission identified four authorized approaches. As operating reserves grow short (FERC preferred "shortage pricing" to the term "scarcity pricing"), or an emergency condition arises, market rules should operate to: (1) increase demand bid caps above the current level; (2) increase both demand bid caps and supply prices above the current level; (3) establish a demand curve for operating reserves for the purpose of raising prices in a previously agreed-on way; or (4) set the market-clearing price for supply and demand response resources equal to the payment made to participants in an emergency demand response program. In addition to these four authorized approaches, the Commission permitted RTOs and ISOs to propose their own alternative approaches.[74]

NYISO's existing shortage pricing regimes satisfied Order 719. NYISO was the first ISO/RTO to use ancillary services demand curves to incorporate scarcity pricing provisions. In 2005, NYISO implemented demand curves for operating reserves and regulation service to establish real-time energy clearing prices during operating reserve shortages. The demand curves allow energy prices to rise in response to shortage conditions and their performance is reviewed annually by the Independent Market

---

[73] *Wholesale Competition in Regions with Organized Electric Markets*, Order 719, FERC Stats. & Regs. ¶ 32,628 at PP 192–94, 202–03 (2008), 73 FR 12576 (March 7, 2008); *order on reh'g*, Order No. 719-A, FERC Stats. & Regs. ¶ 31,292 (2009), 74 FR 37776 (July 29, 2009), *order denying reh'g and clarification*, Order No. 719-B, 129 FERC ¶ 61,252 (2009).

[74] Order No. 719, at PP 208, 235.

Advisor through the State of the Market Report. The ancillary services demand curves have a proven record of allowing market-clearing prices to rise while also preserving reliability and preventing market power abuses.[75]

ISO-NE had also implemented a real-time market that co-optimized the dispatch of resources to provide both energy and reserves in October 2006, as part of Phase II of the Ancillary Services Market project. When there is a reserve shortage, the clearing prices were derived from administratively determined Reserve Constraint Penalty Factors. The Penalty Factors values are intended to reflect the maximum price that would be paid to redispatch the system to create Operating Reserves, comparable to the maximum prices allowed under the reserve market demand curves used by the NYISO.[76]

PJM submitted a compliance filing in June 2010 to bring its reserves pricing under the Order 719 scarcity pricing mandate. PJM proposed to require: simultaneous dispatch of energy and reserves (including in the price of reserves opportunity costs associated with foregone profits in the energy market); establish an $850/MWh reserve price cap (triggered first by overall reserve shortages and then doubled when triggered again by shortages of synchronized reserves) and a $2,700 aggregated price cap for the energy and reserve markets; and permit the prices of reserves to reflect shortages in the event of voltage reduction or load shedding. PJM proposed to establish a demand curve for operating reserves and implement monitoring mechanisms.[77]

MISO incorporated a scarcity curve mechanism into its ancillary service market proposal. MISO proposed to manage system and zone reserve shortages through both emergency actions and scarcity pricing. In the event capacity is available to meet demand but does not relieve operating reserve shortages, scarcity pricing will be invoked through the use of demand curves, up to $1,100/MWh and, if the response is still insufficient, $3,500/MWh. The $3,500/MWh cap for reserve offers during the most critical stage of a shortage represented an estimate of VoLL.[78]

[75] *New York Independent System Operator, Inc.*, 129 FERC ¶ 61,164 at PP 46, 50 (2009).

[76] *New England Power Pool and ISO New England, Inc.*, 115 FERC ¶ 61,175 at PP 6–7, 90 (2006); *reh'g denied*, 115 FERC ¶ 61,106 (2006).

[77] *PJM Interconnection, L.L.C.*, 139 FERC ¶ 61,057 at PP 5, 15–20 (2012).

[78] *Midwest Independent Transmission System Operator, Inc.*, 119 FERC ¶ 61,311 (2007) at PP 50–54, 61–65, *order on reh'g*, 120 FERC ¶ 61,202 (2007); *Midwest Independent Transmission System Operator, Inc.*, 122 FERC ¶ 61,172 (2008) at PP 212–14.

The CAISO also incorporated a Scarcity Reserve Pricing Mechanism in the new market, responding to the Commission's dictates in Order 719. CAISO's proposed Scarcity Pricing Mechanism applied when supply was insufficient to meet any of CAISO's ancillary service procurement requirements within a service region or subregion. The scarcity demand curves cleared the ancillary services market with administratively determined prices. The price for a higher-quality ancillary service that can substitute for another ancillary service would always be higher than the price for a lower-quality ancillary service.[79]

The Texas market ignored the developments in the rest of the country, preferring to follow its own vision of a pure market solution. Resource adequacy issues were discussed but never really resolved during the debates over restructuring the ERCOT market. The debate over resource adequacy in the ERCOT Market began in earnest with a July 2001 workshop.[80] The PUCT followed up with a request for comments on whether there should be a minimum reserve margin, how that margin should be determined, and what mechanism should be used to maintain that margin.[81] In January 2002, the PUCT converted the investigatory project to a rulemaking project. Five workshops were held, most of which focused on determining an appropriate structure for a reserve margin mechanism. Meanwhile, the ERCOT Technical Advisory Committee, with Board approval, maintained a minimum reserve margin of 12.5 percent.[82]

The explosion in merchant plant construction as the zonal market was opening led to excessive capacity and reserve margins well above the 12.5 percent ERCOT target level. The PUCT staff concluded that even with conservative assumptions, reserve margins would still be higher than 20 percent by 2008. In July 2003, the proceeding was put on hold and rescheduled. The proceeding was further delayed into 2005 because of a lack of urgency.[83]

---

[79] *California Independent System Operator Corp.*, 131 FERC ¶ 61,280, at PP 1–10 (2009); *California Independent System Operator Corp.*, 133 FERC ¶ 61,113 (2010).

[80] *Petition of the Electric Reliability Council of Texas for Approval of the ERCOT Protocols*, Docket No. 23220_238, April 11, 2001, p. 40; Docket No. 23220, Order on Rehearing, June 4, 2001, p. 41.

[81] Request for Comments, *PUC Investigation of the Need for Planning Reserve Margin Requirements*, Project No. 24255_7, July 23, 2001.

[82] Staff Memorandum, *PUC Investigation of the Need for Planning Reserve Margin Requirements*, Project No. 24255_96, August 27, 2004, p. 2.

[83] Market Oversight Division, Memorandum, *PUC Investigation of the Need for Planning Reserve Margin Requirements*, Project No. 24255_71, June 16, 2003; Market

In April 2005, Dr. Eric Schubert, a Commission staff economist, submitted a white paper describing an energy-only market design based on the Australian National Energy Market.[84] The northeast electricity markets with a low offer cap ($1,000) and capacity payments were contrasted with Australia, with a very high offer cap but no capacity market. It was claimed that the high offer caps in Australia had increased bilateral contracting between buyers and sellers, which resulted in lower average spot market prices. A higher offer cap would provide incentives for LSEs to cover risk through bilateral contracts, which in turn would increase supply. The potential for higher price spikes could provide owners of generation with strong incentives to physically withhold units from the spot market to increase prices for their remaining fleet. For an energy-only resource adequacy mechanism to work efficiently, the market would need widespread participation of demand-side resources to undermine this gaming strategy.[85]

While the issue remained unresolved, ERCOT modified its calculation of reserve margins. The new methodology, combined with load growth, meant that the large reserve margin cushion predicted earlier in the decade had evaporated, creating a sense of urgency to resolve the resource adequacy issue.[86] In August 2005, the PUCT chose an energy-only market as an alternative to establishing a formal capacity market. The PUCT concluded that capacity markets represented additional regulation, and preferred a market approach to providing incentives for investment. The resource adequacy mechanism was based on the Australian market, adjusted to the ERCOT market. The PUCT contended that the necessary infrastructure for price-responsive demand was in place or soon would be implemented. Advanced metering should give customers access to more discrete information on their consumption and result in time-of-use pricing for customers. Demand-side response could act as a shock absorber

Oversight Division, Memorandum, *Rulemaking Proceeding on Wholesale Market Design Issues in the Electric Reliability Council of Texas*, Project No. 26376, July 2, 2003, p. 6; Staff Memorandum, *PUC Investigation of the Need for Planning Reserve Margin Requirements*, Project No. 24255_96, August 27, 2004.

[84] Project 24255_98, Staff White Paper on an Energy-Only Resource Adequacy Mechanism, April 11, 2005 ("Energy-Only White Paper").

[85] "Energy-Only White Paper" at 5–6, 14–17.

[86] ERCOT, Notice of Revisions to the Reserve Market Calculation, Activities Related to the Projected, *ERCOT Reserve Margin and the Methodology For Calculating the ERCOT Reserve Margin*, Project No. 30715_4, July 12, 2005; Wholesale Market Oversight, Memorandum of Consolidation, *Rulemaking on Wholesale Electric Market Power and Resource Adequacy in the ERCOT Power Region*, Project No. 31972_3.

for boom-and-bust investment cycles and price-responsive demand would curb high prices. Loads could arrange multiple-year contracts, to protect them from high spot market prices.[87]

The rule set the peaker net margin at a $175,000/MW threshold, allowing recovery of more than twice the annualized fixed costs of a new gas-fired peaking unit. When the net margin threshold is reached, the high system-wide offer cap is replaced by the low system-wide offer cap. The resource adequacy cycle would then restart at the beginning of the next calendar year, reinstating the high cap.[88] The low cap was set as the greater of $500/MWh or fifty times the Houston Ship Channel gas price index, expressed as dollars per MWh. Beginning March 1, 2007, the high cap was set at $1,500/MWh, increasing to $2,250/MWh in 2008 and to $3,000/MWh two months after the nodal market opened. To encourage investment, ERCOT was to publish projections of load and existing and planned generation, and projected assessments of system adequacy.[89]

The PUCT implicitly provided a "license to engage in strategic bidding" to smaller generators. Entities owning less than 5 percent of installed capacity were deemed not to have ERCOT-wide market power, providing broad latitude in their bidding strategies.[90] In effect, the Commission was fudging the problem of providing scarcity prices without generators bidding at least part of their capacity at prices well above marginal cost. The rule gave carte blanche to smaller generators, who might still control thousands of MWs of generation (5 percent of ERCOT market capacity is currently about 4,000 MW), to engage in strategic bidding to raise prices.[91]

The combination of declining reserve margins and impending environmental regulations caused the PUCT to open a new resource adequacy proceeding. Due to the recession, in 2010, the projected summer margin

[87] *Rulemaking on Wholesale Electric Market Power and Resource Adequacy in the ERCOT Power Region*, Project No. 31972_78, Order Adopting Amendment to §25.502, New §25.504, and New §25.502, As Approved at the August 10, 2006 Open Meeting, August 24, 2006, (*Resource Adequacy Order*), 6, 42, 54–60.

[88] *Resource Adequacy Order*, 73–75, 121. The PNM equals the estimate of net revenue given by the sum of the market price minus ten times the Houston Ship Channel gas price index over all intervals when this value is > 0.

[89] P.U.C. SUBST. R. 25.505.

[90] *Resource Adequacy Order*, 89–93.

[91] Mark Watson, "Texas 'Small Fish' Rule Bad for ERCOT, Stakeholders Say: Analysis," *Platts*, December 3, 2013, at http://www.platts.com/news-feature/2013/electricpower/ercot/index (last visited August 25, 2014).

was 21.4 percent, and margins were not expected to fall to the minimum requirement until at least 2015.[92] However, this cushion for the new nodal market, which began operation in December 2010, soon evaporated. A winter freeze resulted in power interruptions in February 2011, while a record-hot summer stressed the system, resulting in two emergencies in August 2011. A falling reserve margin, and a reserve margin requirement that rose to 13.75 percent, created a sense of crisis.[93]

The governor's office and the PUCT were well aware of large, untapped reserves of reasonably cost-energy-efficiency measures, but despite stated concerns about reserve margins took no steps to increase the funding of the PUCT's energy efficiency programs. The legislature, in Senate Bill 1125, passed in May 2011, did increase the energy efficiency goal to 30 percent of the growth of residential and commercial loads, but this will have little impact on ERCOT reserve margins in the near future.[94]

The problems in Texas stemmed from three factors: retirement of older units, misplaced faith in the Australian model, and the failure of price-responsive demand to develop despite the widespread installation of smart meters. More than 12,300 megawatts of older gas generation retired since the beginning of the ERCOT competitive market in 2002, and 4,284 MW was placed in "mothball" status (though ERCOT jawboning and high prices brought nearly 2,000 MW back online in the summer of 2012[95]). Almost all of these plants were fifty years or older, inefficient units with high heat rates and operations and maintenance costs.[96] Modeling results revealed that only two-thirds of costs of a new generator would be recovered in the Australian market. To achieve 100

---

[92] ERCOT, "Report on the Capacity, Demand, and Reserves in the ERCOT Region," May 2010.

[93] ERCOT, "2010 ERCOT Target Reserve Margin Study," November 1, 2010.

[94] Itron, "Assessment of the Feasible and Achievable Levels of Electricity Savings from Investor Owned Utilities in Texas: 2009–2018," December 23, 2008, submitted in *Study of the Potential For Energy Efficiency Measures, Under PURA § 39.905*, Project 35266_15. The goal is based on a rolling average of the previous five years of load growth, so that the higher goal will not have an appreciable impact until 2014 or 2015. And since it applies only to residential and commercial loads of public utilities, only about 60% of ERCOT's load will be impacted.

[95] ERCOT, "Generation Reserves Remain Tight For Summer; ERCOT Expects Calls for Energy Conservation," May 1, 2012, http://www.ercot.com/news/press_releases/show/510 (last visited July 5, 2012).

[96] PUCT, *Summary of Changes to Generation Capacity (MW) in Texas By Status and Resource Type* (updated December 30, 2011), at www.puc.state.tx.us/industry/maps/elecmaps/gen_tables.xls.

percent cost recovery, the market price cap would need to double. Forward prices in the Australian market were also insufficient to finance a new peaker plant.[97] There is almost no price-responsive demand in Texas, despite a $3,000 bid cap and smart meters. There is a group of energy-intensive large industrials, primarily refineries and petrochemical companies who have highly sophisticated energy management systems and participate in ancillary service markets as LaaRs.[98] When there is an excess of LaaRs, some of this demand response capacity bids into the emergency demand response program. There is strong evidence that even industrial customers, who have stronger incentives to respond to price (economies of scale in monitoring and demand response capability), do not generally respond to price signals on an hourly or shorter basis.[99] When large customers respond to price signals, it is more likely in response to transmission pricing (transmission costs are allocated over the average of the customer's demand during the four monthly peaks in the summer) when they can plan to curtail hours or a day in advance (peak demand almost always occurs between 4 PM and 6 PM).[100] Smart meters may provide the data to make it feasible to compensate customers for responding to price signals, but they do not provide the incentives to encourage them to do so.

The PUCT and ERCOT took a number of steps to correct market pricing and increase revenues to generators, including imposing offer floors for responsive reserve service and non-spinning reserves, increasing responsive reserves by 500 MW and decreasing non-spinning reserves procured and establishing an offer floor for units committed through RUC. The PUCT temporarily raised the high cap to $4,500/MWh starting August 1, 2012, to $5,000/MWh in 2013, then rising to $9,000/MWh in

[97] Paul Simshauser, "Vertical Integration, Credit Ratings and Retail Price Settings in Energy-only Markets: Navigating the Resource Adequacy Problem," 38 *Energy Policy* 7429–36 (2010).

[98] Note that participating in markets such as responsive reserves as a LaaR *discourages* price response because the entity must maintain sufficient demand to be able to drop its load by its bid within ten minutes.

[99] Jay Zarnikau and Ian Hallett, "Aggregate Industrial Energy Consumer Response to Wholesale Prices in the Restructured Texas Electricity Market," 30 *Energy Economics* 1805, 1805–07 (2008).

[100] There is limited demand response capacity outside of the LaaRs and emergency programs. The majority of demand responsive customers can't respond to real-time prices (many require as long as an hour to respond). About 223 MW of transmission price peak load shedding capability and 119 MW total of direct load control curtailable load was reported in ERCOT, with most of the latter in a legacy Austin Energy program. ERCOT, "Load Response Survey, Interim Update," September 28, 2007.

2015.[101] Low gas prices and mild weather limited the impact of the rule changes on the ERCOT market price in 2013. The year 2014 saw a price spike during a cool winter but experienced lower summer prices as mild weather resulted in higher-than-expected capacity margins.[102]

The results of the Texas experiment will not be known for a few years, until the state experiences extreme weather and the operational and political viability of the energy only market is tested. As California showed, mild weather can disguise the flaws of a dysfunctional market. The FERC model (capacity markets plus scarcity pricing) is more likely to be robust, but determining whether it is a more cost-effective resource adequacy mechanism will require a sufficiently long period to account for investment cycling and climate variability. This, of course, is no comfort to policymakers who have to make decisions today.

[101] Project No. 37897_104, *PUC Proceeding Relating to Resource and Reserve Adequacy and Shortage Pricing*, Order Adopting New 25.508 As Approved at the June 28, 2012, Open Meeting, July 3, 2012.

[102] Beth Garza, "Item 5: IMM Report," ERCOT Board of Directors meeting, August 12, 2014; ERCOT Energy and Demand Report, 2014.

25

From Small Things Big Things One Day Come

The parallel EPA rulemakings on Cross-State Air Pollution Rule (CSAPR), replacing the CAIR, and the Mercury and Air Toxics Standards (MATS), raised concern among electricity regulators that it could force the retirement of plants needed for reliability. However, the EPA rulemakings were not an example of arbitrary government interference in the economy, as cost-benefit analysis overwhelming supported stronger controls on SO_2, NO_x, and smaller particulate matter ($PM_{2.5}$). Coal plants were responsible for about 58 percent of SO_2 emissions, 46 percent of Hg emissions, 11 percent of NO_x emissions, and about 4 percent of particulates.[1]

CAIR was issued on March 10, 2005, to address ozone nonattainment and attain the NAAQS for $PM_{2.5}$ by reducing small particulate and ozone precursors, SO_2 and NO_x. CAIR created three separate compliance programs: an Annual NO_x program, an Ozone Season NO_x program, and an Annual SO_2 program. Each of the three programs uses a two-phased approach, with declining emission caps in each phase. The first phase began in 2009 for the NO_x Annual and NO_x Ozone Season programs, and started in 2010 for the SO_2 Annual program. The rule also established a second phase for all three programs beginning in 2015. Similar to the NO_x SIP Call, CAIR gave affected states' NO_x emission budgets and the flexibility to reduce emissions using a strategy that best suited their circumstances, including regional cap and trade programs. Twenty-eight states and the District of Columbia chose to be part of the

---

[1] David Farnsworth, "Preparing for EPA Regulations: Working to Ensure Reliable and Affordable Environmental Compliance," Regulatory Assistance Project (July 2011): 4.

435

EPA-administered regional CAIR trading programs. Monitoring and reporting for the NO_x programs began in 2008; monitoring and reporting for SO_2 began in 2009.[2]

North Carolina and some electric utility companies challenged the CAIR program, and on July 11, 2008, the D.C. Circuit issued a ruling vacating CAIR in its entirety.[3] The D.C. Court found that EPA's apportionment decisions had nothing to do with each state's "significant contribution" to downwind pollution because overall emissions were reduced through the cap-and-trade program and didn't focus on individual state's emissions. The EPA must promulgate a rule that achieves something measurable toward the goal of prohibiting sources within one state from contributing to nonattainment in other states. The court required EPA to identify and mitigate upwind states that interfere with downwind maintenance of ambient air quality, but failed to provide any guidance as to what constitutes sufficient downwind interference. EPA's notion of an "equitable governmental approach to attainment" is not among the objectives of section 110. The Court also rejected EPA's allocation of NO_x emission budgets between states, because EPA could not make one state's significant contribution depend on another state's cost of eliminating emissions. The court also rejected EPA's effort to "harmonize" CAIR's regulation of SO_2 with the existing program for trading SO_2 emissions allowances under Title IV of the CAA.[4] EPA and other parties requested a rehearing, and on December 23, 2008, the court revised its decision and remanded CAIR to EPA without *vacatur* (keeping CAIR in effect until an alternative acceptable to the court can be implemented).[5]

The CSAPR replaced the CAIR. Section 110(a)(2)(D)(i)(I) of the CAA requires the elimination of upwind state emissions that significantly contribute to nonattainment in another state. EPA employed a state-specific methodology for identifying the necessary emission reductions required if a state's contribution to downwind emissions exceeded EPA-determined thresholds. The EPA found that emissions of SO_2 and NO_x in twenty-seven eastern, midwestern, and southern states contribute significantly to nonattainment or interfere with maintenance in one or more downwind states. EPA also proposed Federal Implementation Plans to implement the emission reductions. EPA would regulate these sources through a

---

[2] EPA, *Clean Air Markets: Highlights*, http://www.epa.gov/airmarkets/progress/NBP_4 .html (last visited May 23, 2011).
[3] *North Carolina v. EPA*, 531 F.3d 896 (D.C. Cir. 2008).
[4] *North Carolina v. EPA*, 531 F.3d 896, 907, 910–11, 917–22.
[5] *North Carolina v. EPA*, 550 F.3d 1176 (D.C. Cir. 2008).

program that used state-specific budgets and allowed intrastate and limited interstate trading. EPA required that all significant contribution to nonattainment and interference with maintenance with respect to the $PM_{2.5}$ NAAQS be eliminated by 2014.[6]

The final rule was promulgated in August 2011. The rule required emission reductions related to interstate transport of fine particles in twenty-three states. The rule employed air-quality-assured trading programs to ensure that the necessary reductions would occur within every covered state, substantially similar to the preferred trading remedy structure presented in the proposal. The first phase of Transport Rule compliance commenced January 1, 2012 for SO_2 and annual NO_x reductions, and May 1, 2012 for ozone-season NO_x reductions. The second phase of Transport Rule reductions commenced January 1, 2014.[7] The EPA issued a new final rule in June 2012. The revised rule targeted specific revisions to state budgets and new unit set-asides to accommodate generation facilities needed for reliability.[8]

However, all this work was negated when the D.C. Circuit vacated the CSAPR on August 21, 2012. The Court found that the EPA's Transport Rule exceeds the agency's statutory authority in two independent respects. The EPA required upwind states to reduce emissions by more than their own significant contributions to a downwind state's nonattainment. Second, when EPA quantified states' obligations, it did not allow the states the initial opportunity to implement the required reductions with respect to sources within their borders. Instead, EPA set forth Federal Implementation Plans to implement those obligations. By doing so, EPA departed from its consistent prior approach and violated the Act. EPA must continue administering CAIR pending the promulgation of a valid replacement.[9]

---

[6] EPA, *Federal Implementation Plans to Reduce Interstate Transport of Fine Particulate Matter and Ozone*, 75 FR 45210, 45213–15, August 2, 2010.

[7] EPA, *Federal Implementation Plans: Interstate Transport of Fine Particulate Matter and Ozone and Correction of SIP Approvals, Final Rule*, 76 FR 48208 (August 8, 2011). Benefits range from $110 billion to $250 billion, using a 7% real discount rate. The benefits result primarily from 13,000 to 34,000 fewer $PM_{2.5}$ and ozone-related premature mortalities. Retail electricity prices were projected to increase by an average of 1.3% in 2012 and 0.8% in 2014 with the final Transport Rule. About 4.8 GW of coal-fired capacity was projected to be uneconomic to maintain. EPA, *Regulatory Impact Analysis for the Federal Implementation Plans to Reduce Interstate Transport of Fine Particulate Matter and Ozone in 27 States; Correction of SIP Approvals for 22 States* (June 2011): 11–17.

[8] EPA, *Revisions to Federal Implementation Plans to Reduce Interstate Transport of Fine Particulate Matter and Ozone*, 77 FR 34830, 34838–42 (June 12, 2012).

[9] *EME Homer City Generation v EPA*, 696 F.3d 7 (DC Cir 2012).

EPA also promulgated the Clean Air Mercury Rule at the same time it was issuing CAIR.[10] The Mercury Rule replaced the mercury maximum achievable control technology standard, applicable to hazardous air pollutants.[11] If EPA had not exempted power plants from the mercury standards, this would have called for a 90 percent reduction in mercury emissions from all affected power plants by 2008, a much greater reduction than under the Mercury Rule.[12] On February 9, 2008, the D.C. Circuit Court vacated the 2005 Mercury Rule.[13] In response, EPA proposed requiring the mercury technology standard for all coal- and oil-fired generation units.[14]

The final Mercury and Air Toxics Standards (MATS) rule was issued in February, 2012. EPA received more than 900,000 comments on the proposed rule, substantially more than for any other regulatory proposal.[15] The technology required to reduce mercury emissions will also reduce emissions of certain $PM_{2.5}$ precursors such as SO_2. EPA estimated that the final rule would yield annual benefits of \$33–\$81 billion with annualized costs of compliance at \$9.6 billion. The great majority of the benefits are attributable to reduced mortality thanks to reducing $PM_{2.5}$ below the level of the NAAQS set in 2006. The benefits from reductions in mercury emissions are expected to be trivial. About 4.7 GW coal-fired capacity – predominantly smaller and less frequently used generating units – was projected by EPA to become uneconomic to maintain.[16] EPA explicitly

[10] EPA, *Standards of Performance for New and Existing Stationary Sources: Electric Utility Steam Generating Units (CAMR)*, 70 FR 28,606 (May 18, 2005).

[11] 42 U.S.C. § 7612(b) (2006).

[12] Brian H. Potts, "Trading Grandfathered Air – A New, Simpler Approach," *Harvard Environmental Law Review* 31 (2007), 115, 128, fn. 103.

[13] *State of New Jersey v. EPA*, 517 F.3d 574, 583 (D.C. Cir. 2008), *cert. denied*, 129 S. Ct. 1308, *cert. dismissed*, 129 S. Ct. 1313 (2009).

[14] EPA, *National Emission Standards for Hazardous Air Pollutants from Coal and Oil-Fired Electric Utility Steam Generating Units and Standards of Performance for Fossil-Fuel-Fired Electric Utility, Industrial-Commercial-Institutional, and Small Industrial-Commercial-Institutional Steam Generating Units, Proposed Rule*, 76 FR 24976 (May 3, 2011).

[15] EPA, *National Emission Standards for Hazardous Air Pollutants from Coal and Oil-Fired Electric Utility Steam Generating Units and Standards of Performance for Fossil-Fuel-Fired Electric Utility, Industrial-Commercial-Institutional, and Small Industrial-Commercial-Institutional Steam Generating Units, Final Rule*, 77 FR 9304, 9305–6, February 16, 2012, *aff'd*, *White Stallion Energy Center, LLC v. EPA*, 748 F. 3d 1222 (DC Cir. 2014).

[16] EPA, *Regulatory Impact Analysis for the Final Mercury and Air Toxics Standards*, EPA-452/R-11-011, December 2011, ES-4–ES-13. Of the coal-fired power plants that currently lack pollution control technology, 40% are more than fifty years old and 80% are smaller than 200 MW. BernsteinResearch, "U.S. Utilities: Coal-Fired Generation Is Squeezed in the Vice of EPA Regulation: Who Wins and Who Loses?" (October 2010): 2.

stated that a motivation behind the rule was to encourage retirement of the grandfathered high-polluting units that were initially exempted from the CAA on Congress's assumption that their useful life was near an end.[17]

These two rulemakings were a boon for the energy consulting industry, as more than a dozen studies were performed to provide ammunition for regulatory filings, protests, and political maneuvering. Initial projections of expected retirements caused by the new EPA rules varied, from 15–20 GW on the low end to as high as 60–70 GW on the high end.[18] Since many of these studies were conducted based on worse-case scenarios of what EPA might do, before the final rules were issued, they exaggerated the impacts of the rules.[19] These forecasts are generally made using large complex models that rely on assumptions about how electricity markets behave, future economic conditions, fuels costs, alternative generating resources, the costs of environmental compliance, and many other variables. These models can be easily manipulated by adjusting assumptions to shift results toward those desired by clients.[20] So it is not surprising that consultants hired by utilities with coal plants that would be impacted tend to find greater consequences from implementation of EPA rules. The split was not just between environmentalists and electricity generators, but between coal-dependent generators like Southern Company and Luminant and utilities that had substantial natural gas, nuclear, or new coal

---

[17] EPA, *National Emission Standards for Hazardous Air Pollutants from Coal and Oil-Fired Electric Utility Steam Generating Units and Standards of Performance for Fossil-Fuel-Fired Electric Utility, Industrial-Commercial-Institutional, and Small Industrial-Commercial-Institutional Steam Generating Units*, Proposed Rule, 76 FR 24976, 23980 May 3, 2011 (MATS Proposed Rule).

[18] ICF, "Coal-Fired Electric Generation Unit Retirement Analysis," Presented to the INGAA, May 18, 2010; NERA, "Potential Impacts of EPA Air, Coal Combustion Residuals, and Cooling Water Regulations," prepared for American Coalition for Clean Coal Electricity, September, 2011; Credit Suisse, "Growth From Subtraction; Impact of EPA Rules on Power Markets," September 23, 2010; FBR Capital Markets, "Coal Retirements in Perspective – Quantifying the Upcoming EPA Rules," December 13, 2010; Charles River Associates, "A Reliability Assessment of EPA's Proposed Transport Rule and Forthcoming Utility MACT," prepared for Exelon Corporation, December 16, 2010; The Brattle Group, "Potential Coal Plant Retirements under Emerging Environmental Regulations," August 10, 2011; MJ Bradley & Associates and Analysis Group, "Ensuring a Clean, Modern Electric Generating Fleet While Maintaining Electric System Reliability," prepared for the Clean Energy Group, November 2011; DOE, "Resource Adequacy Implications of Forthcoming EPA Air Quality Regulations," December 2011.

[19] Bipartisan Policy Center, "Environmental Regulation and Electric System Reliability" (2011).

[20] Susan F. Tierney and Charles Cicchetti, "The Results in Context: A Peer Review of EEI's "Potential Impacts of Environmental Regulation on the U.S. Generation Fleet," Analysis Group (May 2011); James Staudt, "Assumptions That Lead to Overestimation of the Cost of Regulations," Andover Technology Partners (October 31, 2011).

plants that had installed modern control equipment. The latter group did not want polluting coal plants to suppress electricity prices by delaying implementation of the EPA rules.

Many of the retirements attributed to the EPA rules would have occurred in any case, due to the shrinking gap between coal and natural gas prices. Rising exports have supported coal prices while excessive drilling due to shale gas lease provisions resulted in a glut of natural gas and downward pressure on gas prices. The result was to shrink net revenue margins for coal plants. Companies announced plans to retire older coal-fired power plants, blaming EPA rules when many of these high-cost plants already been idled or were scheduled to be retired.[21]

The key reliability issue turned out to be the time required to retrofit coal-fired units that could be economically operated with more stringent environmental controls. A large number of units installing pollution control equipment may need more than the three years provided under the MATS rule. Not only may some projects take as long as five years, but requiring numerous coal plants to make similar environmental investments at the same time would strain the resources of the limited skill labor force and companies capable of making these retrofits.[22] This created a regulatory dilemma: while some petitioners were sincere in their desire to comply with the new rules, others merely wanted to delay implementation as long as possible to maximize the value of their "right to pollute" before retiring these units. Allowing a plant to avoid controls for an additional year or two gave coal-fired generators a competitive advantage in economic dispatch relative to cleaner plants. The parasitic loads associated with environmental control equipment increased the marginal cost of generation.[23] A joint filing by five ISOs/RTOs requested a narrowly drawn reliability "safety valve" granting a retiring generator an extension to implement reliability solutions to replace the resource.[24]

[21] Susan F. Tierney, "Why Coal Plants Retire: Power Market Fundamental as of 2012," Analysis Group (February 16, 2012): 10–12.

[22] EEI, "Comments," *MATS Proposed Rule*, Docket Nos. EPA-HQ-OAR-209–0234; EPA-HQ-OAR-2011–0044 (August 3, 2011).

[23] John Hanger, "Reliability-Only Dispatch: Protecting Lives & Human Health While Ensuring System Reliability," Clean Air Task Force (2011): 11–12. Note that this report was sponsored by Exelon and Constellation Energy.

[24] "Joint Comments of the Electric Reliability Council of Texas (ERCOT), The Midwest Independent Transmission System Operator (MISO), The New York Independent System Operator (NYISO), PJM Interconnection, L.L.C. (PJM), and the Southwest Power Pool (SPP)," *MATS Proposed Rule*, Docket Nos. EPA-HQ-OAR-2009–0234; EPA-HQ-OAR-2011–0044; FRL-9286–1 (August 4, 2011).

Under Section 112(i)(3) of the CAA, affected sources must be compliant with MATS within three years, with an extension of up to one year available in certain cases. An EPA Policy Memorandum contemplated requests for electric generating units that may affect reliability due to deactivation or delays related to the installation of controls.[25] FERC staff proposed that each administrative order request should be filed with the Commission as an informational filing and include the same information submitted to the EPA. The Commission's review would be based on whether there might be a violation of a Commission-approved reliability standard.[26]

Doubts about the effectiveness of emission regulatory instruments have been raised regularly since the 1980s. CAA Amendment provisions were primarily source-specific but did not impose national emission caps until the 1990 acid rain trading program. New Source Review raised the cost of new coal power plants relative to existing plants, effectively creating a financial incentive for firms to keep old plants operating rather than to build new ones. The CAA Amendments also generated unintended incentives for the development of emission control technology. Flue gas desulfurization innovations up until 1990 tended to reduce the cost of scrubbing without significantly improving effectiveness. Only after 1990, with the creation of a tradable permits market for SO_2 was there a shift toward innovations that enhanced the removal efficiency of scrubbers. Although some of the EPA regulations initially had a perverse effect, technological forcing eventually resulted in overall emission reductions. Emissions fell after 1970, partly because of oil price shocks but primarily because of indirect effects from the introduction of the CAA Amendments.[27] The new wave of EPA regulations will finally euthanize the godfathered coal plants and continue the long-term trend of improved air quality.

The cumulative impact of these regulations also meant that the EPA's new greenhouse gas regulations would have a limited impact in the short term. Following the Supreme Court's decision in *Massachusetts*,[28] which

---

[25] *The Environmental Protection Agency's Enforcement Response Policy for Use of Clean Air Act Section 113(a) Administrative Orders in Relation to Electric Reliability and the Mercury and Air Toxics Standard*, December 16, 2011, at http://www.epa.gov/mats/pdfs/EnforcementResponsePolicyforCAA113.pdf (last visited March 15, 2012).

[26] FERC Staff, "White Paper on the Commission's Role Regarding Environmental Protection Agency's Mercury and Air Toxics Standards" (January 30, 2012).

[27] Ross McKitrick, "Why Did US Air Pollution Decline after 1970?" *Empirical Economics* 33 (2007): 491–513.

[28] *Massachusetts v. EPA*, 549 U.S. 497 (2007).

clarified that greenhouse gases are an "air pollutant" subject to regulation under the CAA, the EPA issued an Endangerment Finding, in which it determined that greenhouse gases may "reasonably be anticipated to endanger public health or welfare." The EPA also determined that the CAA requires major stationary sources of greenhouse gases to obtain construction and operating permits. Under EPA's view, the PSD and Title V permitting requirements applied to all stationary sources with the potential to emit 100 tons per year of CO_2 under Title V, and 100 or 250 tons per year under the PSD program. But because regulation of all such sources would result in overwhelming permitting burdens, EPA issued the Timing and Tailoring Rules, in which it determined that only the largest stationary sources would initially be subject to permitting requirements.[29] The Supreme Court found that EPA exceeded its statutory authority when it interpreted the CAA to require PSD and Title V permitting for stationary sources based on their greenhouse gas emissions. EPA may, however, continue to treat greenhouse gases as a pollutant for purposes of requiring best available technology for sources otherwise subject to PSD review.[30]

The EPA's "Clean Power Plan" proposed a state-centric framework for regulating greenhouse gas emissions from existing power plants. Every state will have to submit a plan by 2016 that charts a path to a 30 percent GHG emission reduction in 2030 relative to a 2005 baseline through a combination of state regulations imposing efficiency improvements, shifts in energy generation toward nuclear or renewables (or from coal toward natural gas), and demand-side efficiency programs. However, the final rules will not be issued until 2015, followed by the inevitable rounds of litigation as it works its way through the court system. Meanwhile, current EPA rules and the natural gas glut will shut down the most inefficient coal plants while discouraging investment in new coal plants, obtaining many of the benefits (given the 2005 baseline was just before the great recession) expected under the Clean Power Plan.

---

[29] *Coalition for Responsible Regulation v. EPA*, 684 F. 3d 102, 113 (D.C. Cir 2012).
[30] *Utility Air Regulatory Group v. EPA*, 573 U.S. _ (2014).

26

Blinded by the Light

There has been a continuing controversy over whether deregulation has delivered the promised benefits or a fraud was perpetrated by a cabal of industrial customers, opportunistic utilities, and independent power producers and marketers. There are bad studies on both sides of the issue, from public power attacks on deregulation to conservative think tanks blindly praising the "successful" implementation of electricity markets. Too many studies were sponsored by self-interest parties that coincidently resulted in findings that reflected the sponsors' interests.[1] Obviously, these parties were not interested in paying for a study that resulted in findings that contradicted their economic interests. A similar effect applied to

---

[1] See, for example, a study by Global Energy Decisions claims to independently have determined that consumers realized $15.1 billion in value from wholesale electric competition in the 1999–2003 study period. These "savings" consisted primarily of "accounting savings," the operational savings were reductions in nuclear plant refueling outage time and improvement in coal plant heat rates and O&M cost, with no underlying analysis of the source of these improvements. The report was sponsored by BP Energy, Constellation Energy, Exelon Corporation, Mirant, NRG Energy, Inc., PSEG, Reliant Energy, Shell Trading Gas and Power, Williams and Suez Energy North America. The Electric Power Supply Association served as project manager on behalf of the sponsors. Global Energy Decisions, "Putting Competitive Power Markets to the Test, The Benefits of Competition in America's Electric Grid: Cost Savings and Operating Efficiencies" (July 2005): RS-1, fn. 2. Similarly, a Brattle study that found efficiency gains was sponsored by COMPETE. James Reitzes, Peter Fox-Penner, Adam Schumacher, and Daniel Gaynor, "Generation Cost Savings from Day 1 and Day 2 RTO Market Designs," The Brattle Group (October 1, 2009). The COMPETE Coalition lists 602 electricity stakeholders, but since membership is free, these names conceal the real contributors and controlling interests of the coalition.

studies purporting to show the benefits of RTOs, conducted or commissioned by RTOs.

One problem with a plethora of studies on restructuring and the new electricity markets is that many of them simply had not allowed enough time to pass to make a meaningful judgment. Utility investments are long-lived, and path dependence is an important factor when accounting for relative efficiency.[2] Since the value of relative generation investments is highly reliant on both the cost of fuels and the cost of money during the period the investment is made, after-the-fact analyses "demonstrating" inefficient patterns of investment can be misleading. The timing of technology emergence also can skew these studies: for example, combined-cycle technology did not really mature until the late 1990s.

Different sources of efficiency will have different relationships to deregulation. Allocative efficiency shifts production to more efficient generators, while production efficiencies stem from improved operation (fewer inputs per unit of output) at existing facilities. Investment-related efficiencies are derived from replacing less efficient plants with new technologies, or improving average efficiency as the generation mix is weighted toward new power plants. Managerial efficiencies are related to production efficiencies but occur at a higher level of aggregation – for example, exploiting economics of scale or scope to provide services at lower cost across a utility. Some studies confuse efficiency and income transfers: if a divested generation company has to pay a higher cost for capital because the market perceives greater risk to the company, increased costs reflect a shift of risk from ratepayers to stockholders and bondholders but do not imply decreased efficiency.

The available data is often highly aggregated. This means that econometric studies often garner insights on efficiencies from crude proxies for trading and operations. While EPA has data on individual plant performance, this data is both limited and less than 100 percent reliable. There

---

[2] This can create numerous problems for studies that attempt to use production frontier analyses to compare relative efficiency. There is an identification problem; the more "inefficient" utilities may reflect rational decisions under regulation that led to higher costs, or incompetence, or both. Lock-in is a serious problem for utilities; once the decision is made to build a power plant, even if it is relatively inefficient, its cost of operation may be lower than the all-in cost of a new technology. Predicting future demand is difficult at best, and the track record of economic forecasters does not inspire confidence. Transmission lines are built given current and expected generation and demand locations and may cause existing generation to operate in an "inefficient" manner due to congestion as economic development shifts geographically over time.

can be timing and technological issues, as plant performance depends on maintenance schedules, ambient temperatures, fuel quality, and other factors for which data is usually not available. Plants may have a portfolio of vintages among their turbines, which means even plant-level modeling may obscure differences that would lead to different levels of dispatch and operation. Fuel prices are often estimated from aggregated data, which ignores differences in contract terms and transportation cost from trading hubs. A large-volume base load unit with steady, predictable demand can negotiate better terms than a peaking plant that makes intermittent demands on a gas pipeline.

Various studies employed different levels of disaggregation, different dependent variables, and different econometric and simulation techniques. Determining an improvement in efficiency or changes in price requires a baseline or counterfactual from which to measure that difference. A review of studies revealed wide disparities in methodologies, dependent variables, level of aggregation, and simulation techniques.[3]

One problem in determining the impact of deregulation is to separate the impact of the development of power pools from the effect of the establishment of formal electricity markets. A study compared a sample of municipal and cooperatives utilities in the northeast with similar utilities in the southeast over the 1990–2004 period. Implementation of coordinated markets reduced average residential rates from $0.50 to $1.80 per MWh.[4] The estimated rate savings are the net benefits of coordination, but can only partially be attributed to RTOs, since these areas operated as increasingly tight power pools over this period. A natural experiment, when AEP's utilities joined PJM, suggests there were substantial gains from participation in a market owing to shifting output between generation units. Output rose at low-cost midwestern power plants in 2004, after the utilities joined PJM, and declined at high-cost eastern power plants, to the point of creating eastbound congestion in 98 percent of all hours after October 1, 2004.[5]

---

[3] John Kwoka, "Restructuring the U.S. Electric Power Sector: A Review of Recent Studies," *Review of Industrial Organization* 32 (2008): 165–96.

[4] Scott Harvey, Bruce McConihe, and Susan Pope, *Analysis of the Impact of Coordinated Electricity Markets on Consumer Electricity Charges*, LECG (November 20, 2006).

[5] Eric Mansur and Matthew White, "Market Organization and Efficiency in Electricity Markets" (June 30, 2009): 22–25. See also Andrew Kleit and James Reitzes, "The Effectiveness of FERC's Transmission Policy: Is Transmission Used Efficiently and When Is It Scarce?" *Journal of Regulatory Economics* 34 (2008): 1–26.

Both regulated and unregulated firms had to adjust to a transition from vertical integration to restructured markets, and reallocate resources, from changes in generation investment to using labor more efficiently in deregulated environments because of increased competition. Wires companies had to adjust to shifts in generation capacity, operation, and location. These reorganizations may lead to lower productive efficiency in the short run. Deregulation actually had a negative effect on efficiency during the 1998–2001 transitory period. One factor was that this was a period of extensive consolidation, and electric utilities in the process of merging with other utilities or independent power producers were less efficient.[6] Mandatory divestiture also impacted efficiency, as those firms forced to divest experienced higher distribution costs, but those firms that voluntarily divested were self-selected and did not experience cost increases.[7]

The impact of deregulation on operating efficiency, at least initially, seems to have been exaggerated, at least with respect to fossil fuel plants. A study of fossil-fuel-fired plants used data from the EPA's Continuous Emissions Monitoring System, which collects hourly data on emissions, fuel consumption, and gross power production, allowed direct comparison of unit efficiency under different ownership and regulatory regimes. Heat rates declined by roughly 2 percent at divested plants. Similar, though slightly smaller, improvements were seen at utility-owned plants in states that imposed rate freezes during the same time period. Efficiency improvements in divested plants were dominated by the gains made at plants that were transferred to unregulated affiliates of the selling utility.[8] A study of 950 plants from 1996 to 2006 suggested that investor-owned plants in states with market restructuring are about 13.5 percent more efficient than similar plants located in states without restructuring. Municipality-owned plants in states with market restructuring are about 12 percent more efficient than plants located in states without restructuring. Efficiency gains stemmed from internal organizational and technological changes within the plant and were not caused by the

[6] Magali Delmas and Yesim Tokat, "Deregulation, Governance Structures, and Efficiency: The U.S. Electric Utility Sector," *Strategic Management Journal* 26 (2005): 456.

[7] Sanem I. Sergici, *Three Essays on U.S. Electricity Restructuring* (Ph.D. Diss., Northeastern University, January 2008): 32–33.

[8] James Bushnell and Catherine Wolfram, "Ownership Change, Incentives and Plant Efficiency: Divestiture of U.S. Electric Generation Plants," Working Paper (March 2005): 22.

attrition of inefficient plants from the sample over time. Efficiency gains were most prominent for coal-fired plants.[9]

Employment in the electricity industry declined substantially, from more than 550,000 in 1990 to 400,000 in 2005. At least post-1997, the major cuts in the industry were driven by employment reductions at power plants. Restructuring was partially responsible for the decline, as regulated power plants operating in states that passed restructuring legislation reduced the number of employees and the level of nonfuel operating expenses by more than other privately and municipally owned power plants. Adoption of automated monitoring technology beginning in the late 1980s was also a factor in the declining employment rates. Plants in states that eventually restructured had higher intensities of employees and nonfuel operating expenses, while municipal and cooperative plants tended to be younger and much smaller, providing fewer opportunities for operating efficiencies.[10]

The most striking results of restructuring and potential competition were on the operating efficiency of nuclear power plants. A study of nuclear plants from 1992 to 1998 found a 9.1 percent increase in capacity factor for plants in states that restructured and a 5.7 percent increase in soon to be restructured states. Plants in restructured states were more likely to invest in upgrades.[11] However, there was a self-selection bias, because restructuring was more likely in states with higher costs, and those were often the states where utilities had problems constructing and operating nuclear plants. Divestiture, not deregulation, accounted for this improved performance. Deregulation was accompanied by substantial market consolidation; today, three companies control one-third of U.S. nuclear capacity. Plants in states about to liberalize their electricity market underwent maintenance outages in preparation for that event, exaggerating the improvement in efficiency after deregulation.[12] During this period, all nuclear plants increased their efficiency, probably

[9] J. Dean Craig and Scott Savage, "Market Restructuring, Competition and the Efficiency of Electricity Generation: Plant-level Evidence from the United States 1996 to 2006," *The Energy Journal* 34 (2013): 1–31.

[10] Kira M. Fabrizio, Nancy L. Rose, and Catherine Wolfram, "Do Markets Reduce Costs? Assessing the Impact of Regulatory Restructuring on U.S. Electric Generation Efficiency," *American Economic Review* 97 (September 2007): 1250–77.

[11] Fan Zhang, "Does Electricity Restructuring Work? Evidence from the U.S. Nuclear Energy Industry," *Journal of Industrial Economics* 55 (September 2007): 397–418.

[12] Christophe Munster, "Divestiture and Operating Efficiency of U.S. Nuclear Power Plants" (MS Thesis, Humboldt University, January 2011): 81–84.

due to learning curve effects, but the divested plants were the least efficient plants. Divestiture and consolidation are associated with a 10 percent increase in operating efficiency, achieved primarily by reducing the frequency and, more importantly, the duration of reactor outages. Efficiency gains were experienced broadly across reactors of different types, manufacturers, and vintages.[13]

A second problem is understanding the impact of deregulation. In many states, deregulation was coupled with stranded cost recovery, which in effect had ratepayers pay the cost of retiring inefficient units before their book value had been recovered. State regulatory commissions could have achieved some of these efficiency improvements simply by allowing their regulated utilities to recover the book value of retired units as regulatory assets given a showing of overall cost efficiencies from replacing inefficient units with new combined-cycle technologies. However, absent deregulation, one might suspect that the opposition of consumer groups would make this a politically perilous regulatory strategy.

In the wake of the California crisis, economists generally lost their faith that deregulation would automatically lead to beneficial results for consumers. Various papers noted the existence of market power in U.S. electricity markets other than California, including PJM,[14] ISO-New England,[15] New York ISO,[16] and Texas.[17] However, the warning signs were available before the American markets began operation, as the British experience provided plenty of evidence of the potential for the exercise of market power.[18] Problems with market power in electricity

---

[13] Lucas Davis and Catherine Wolfram, "Deregulation, Consolidation, and Efficiency: Evidence from U.S. Nuclear Power," EI @ Haas Working Paper 217 (August 2011).

[14] Erin T. Mansur, "Upstream Competition and Vertical Integration in Electricity Markets," 50 *Journal of Law and Economics* 125 (February 2007).

[15] James B. Bushnell and Celeste Saravia, "An Empirical Assessment of the Competitiveness of the New England Electricity Market," CSEM working paper no. 101 (2002).

[16] Celeste Saravia, "Speculative Trading and Market Performance: The Effect of Arbitrageurs on Efficiency and Market Power in the New York Electricity Market," CSEM working paper no. 121 (2003).

[17] Ali Hortacsu and Steven Puller, "Understanding Strategic Bidding in Multi-Unit Auctions: a Case Study of the Texas Electricity Spot Market," *Rand Journal of Economics* 39 (Spring 2008): 86–114; "PUCT Staff Inquiry into Allegations Made by Texas Commercial Energy regarding ERCOT Market Manipulation," Project No. 27937 (January 28, 2004). Also available at: https://www.puc.state.tx.us/industry/electric/reports/ERCOT_annual_reports/Default.aspx.

[18] Richard J. Green and David Newbery, "Competition in the British Electricity Spot Market," *Journal of Political Economy* 100 (October 1992): 929–53; Nils-Henrik Morch von der Fehr and David Harbord, "Spot Market Competition in the UK Electricity Industry," *Economic Journal* 103 (May 1993): 531–46; Frank Wolak and Robert Patrick,

markets had been postulated, and even observed in the 1990s, but these studies were generally glossed over in the rush to deregulation.[19]

Electricity markets are susceptible to the exercise of market power by suppliers under a number of different circumstances. In the short run, inelastic demand, combined with a market supply curve that becomes steep as generation capacity is deployed, creates conditions when withholding relatively small amounts of capacity can result in large price jumps. In electricity markets, while there are circumstances where physical withholding may occur, "economic" withholding is more common, with firms bidding units at prohibitively high prices to remove them from the market. Electricity supply curves may have large discrete jumps where technology changes (coal to natural gas, natural-gas-fired combined cycles to combustion turbine plants), or when the next unit is an older, less efficient vintage of the same technology. Market actors can model the bid stack and know when they can influence a jump in price by strategically withholding relatively small quantities of capacity. System reliability requires that supply and demand are continuously balanced over a very short period, while many generator units require from thirty minutes to a few hours to ramp up to full capacity. So market power can be exercised for short periods because of ramp constraints and longer periods when only a few generators are available to meet peak demand.

This situation can persist for years, as new supply depends on both the expectation that high prices will continue and the availability of sites for new plants. Incumbent generating companies in a market may have a stranglehold on brownfield sites that can be quickly developed, either because they inherited them from the integrated utility or because they purchased the sites for internal expansion and to curtail entry by potential competitors. Developing greenfield sites is more expensive and time consuming, and transmission and interconnection facilities must be planned and built. Brownfield sites are more likely to be located near load centers because they are usually where the integrated utility built power plants to serve its load. Building new power plants near urban centers is difficult

"The Impact of Market Rules and Market Structure on the Price Determination Process in the England and Wales Electricity Market," *POWER* Working Paper PWP-047, (February, 1997).

[19] Aleksandr Rudkevich, Max Duckworth, and Richard Rosen, "Modeling Electricity Pricing in a Deregulated Generation Industry: The Potential for Oligopoly Pricing in a Poolco," *Energy Journal* 19 (1998): 19–48; Severin Borenstein and James Bushnell, "An Empirical Analysis of the Potential for Market Power in Californnia's Electricity Industry," *Journal of Industrial Economics* 47 (September 1999): 285–323.

because of the NIMBY phenomenon. This allows incumbents to deter entry, since they can threaten to enter at a lower cost than a potential competitor.[20]

There is no consensus about how to model market power in electricity markets. One group of economists argues that the Cournot model is an appropriate framework for analyzing the potential for market power.[21] In a traditional Cournot model, firms decide how much output to sell in each time period, using their expectations of the output decisions of the other suppliers in the market. Each supplier submits bids to maximize its profits given its marginal cost curve, its expectations about market demand, and its expectations of the supply curves of the other bidders. Each bidder sets its bid at the point where the gain from bidding a little bit higher exactly balances the loss from the quantity that will go unsold as a result of the higher bid. The spread between the optimal bid and marginal cost increases with the quantity that the bidder is supplying and the extent to which the supply of the other bidders is less responsive to price. This incentive to bid above marginal cost is not the result of coordinated action. Each bidder independently selects its bid to maximize profits based on its estimate of the residual demand curve (demand at each price after all other firms bid at that price) it faces.[22] Under Cournot competition, the market price will approach marginal cost with numerous bidders, but during periods with few bidders it can rise substantially, with the limit being the monopoly price when only one pivotal unit supplies the last increment of demand.

Another approach is the supply function equilibrium (SFE) of Klemperer and Meyer. They model an oligopoly facing uncertain demand in which each firm chooses as its strategy a "supply function" relating its quantity to its price. In the absence of uncertainty, there are multiple

---

[20] Dennis Carlton, "Why Barriers to Entry Are Barriers to Understanding," *American Economic Review* 94 (May 2004): 466–70; B. Curtis Eaton and Richard Lipsey, "Exit Barriers are Entry Barriers: the Durability of Capital as a Barrier to Entry," *Bell Journal of Economics* (Autumn 1980): 721–29; Robert Pindyck, "Sunk Costs and Risk-Based Barriers to Entry," working paper (February 13, 2009).

[21] Severin Borenstein, James Bushnell, and Frank A. Wolak, "Measuring Market Inefficiencies in California's Restructured Wholesale Electricity Market," *American Economic Review* 92 (2002): 1376–1405; Severin Borenstein, James Bushnell, Edward Kahn, and Steven Stoft, "Market Power in California Electricity Markets," *Utilities Policy* 5 (1995): 219–36.

[22] Peter Cramton, "Competitive Bidding Behavior in Uniform-Price Auction Markets," *Proceedings of the Hawaii International Conference on System Sciences* (January 2004): 5–6.

equilibriums in supply functions, but uncertainty forces each firm's supply function to be optimal against a range of possible residual demand curves. Firms' equilibrium supply functions are steeper with steep marginal cost curves, fewer firms, and demand uncertainty that is greater at higher prices. The steeper the supply functions, the more closely competition resembles the Cournot model. This is consistent with the behavior of thermal plants, which typically bid up to ten segments per unit, depending on market rules. These units often bid their last increments of capacity at high marginal costs. While this can be a strategy to induce high peak prices, it also reflects the reality that some thermal units at the edge of their operating capacity face higher probabilities of failure, and thus much higher opportunity costs. During periods of low demand, firms have relatively flat supply curves, and price is close to the competitive solution; during periods of high demand and peak pricing, prices converge with the results suggested by the Cournot oligopoly model.[23]

However, a serious question, which has not been resolved, is what exactly constitutes market power in an electricity market.[24] In most markets, sellers have some ability to raise price, owing to differing technology, product differentiation, a finite number of suppliers, consumer ignorance and inertia, the persuasive power of marketing, or differing consumer tastes. The strict requirements of perfect competition, including atomistic firms with no ability to raise price, is an abstraction almost never realized in the real world. Workable competition accepts some level of market power as the norm in most markets.[25]

The D.C. Circuit concluded that "while the Commission can obviously use a definition of workably competitive that allows for occasional exercises of market power, the presence of workable competition would suggest that many, perhaps most, possibly all, of the bids triggering mitigation will be due not to market power but to temporary scarcity." The

---

[23] Paul Klemperer and Margaret Meyer, "Supply Function Equilibria in Oligopoly under Uncertainty," *Econometrica* 57 (1989): 1243–77. Richard J. Green and David Newbery, "Competition in the British Electricity Spot Market," *Journal of Political Economy* 100 (October 1992): 929–53 applied the SFE framework to model the British electricity market.

[24] As Harry First points out, the answer to this question differs substantially if you are an economist or a judge. See Harry First, "'Market Power': Why Are We Asking? A Comment on 'Electricity and Market Power'," 1 *Environmental & Energy Law & Policy Journal* 43, 44–48 (2006).

[25] Alan J. Meese, "Reframing Antitrust in Light of Scientific Revolution: Accounting for Transaction Costs in Rule of Reason Analysis," 62 *Hastings Law Journal* 457, 466–84 (December 2010).

court noted the difficulty of distinguishing between bid increments due to scarcity and ones due to market power. The Court inferred that in conditions of workable competition the application of a "conduct" test based on production cost would catch scarcity-based bid hikes.[26]

Many studies used the difference between the prices that would exist under all firms bidding their short-run marginal costs (SRMC) and actual prices as the measure for market power. No rational firm would bid its SRMC, as measured by these studies (which usually use heat rate, fuel prices, and some estimate of variable costs), because at this price it could make no profit but would have to bear the risks of starting up and operation, which should be included in marginal cost. Generation units incur costs, as well as the risk of catastrophic failure (turbine blade failure, etc.) each time they start up. A rational bidder would offer its supply at a price between its fully loaded SRMC and the estimated cost of the next more expensive resource. So we would expect actual prices, especially those in a market with sophisticated dispatch (i.e., that takes into account factors ignored or glossed over by the models used to estimate market power), to exceed ideal prices by some appreciable margin. The question becomes what is an acceptable "mark-up" in electricity markets.[27]

The issue then becomes defining both the baseline price (often a moving target because of changes in input prices and shifts in technology over time) from which the exercise of market power above a *de minimis* level is considered an abuse of market power. Determining the magnitude of a price increase that would result in violation of "just and reasonable" prices is complicated in electricity markets. While there are numerous attempts to define market power, the general consensus revolves around ability to maintain price above competitive levels for a sustained period of time.[28] In the case of electricity markets, there may be long periods when no market power is exercised, some intermediate periods when some market power is exercised, and a few hundred hours when prices can potentially be well above competitive levels.

---

[26] *Edison Mission Energy, Inc. v. FERC*, 394 F.3d 964, 968 (D.C. Cir 2005).

[27] Eric Mansur estimated the extent to which prices in PJM had been raised above the level provided by the cost minimization solution subject to production constraints. He found that market power raised prices 3–8%, compared to estimates of 13–21% given by static models of market power. Eric Mansur, "Measuring Welfare in Restructured Electricity Markets," NBER Working Paper No. 13509 (October 2007).

[28] James D. Reitzes et al., "Review of PJM's Market Power Mitigation Practices in Comparison to Other Organized Electricity Markets," The Brattle Group for PJM Interconnection, LLC (September 14, 2007): 16–17.

A simple example illustrates the various ways the exercise of market power in an electricity market could result in a significant increase in average costs to consumers. The FTC/DOJ merger guidelines use the 5 percent threshold for a significant price increase.[29] Assume a market where the average load is 30,000 MWh and the average price is $40/MWh. Annual wholesale power costs (excluding ancillary services, congestion, and administrative and other costs) would be a little more than $10 billion. So a 5 percent increase in generator revenue/customer cost would be about $526 million. This threshold could be reached by raising prices by a large amount over a few hours (the highest price hours will usually be those with the highest load) or by smaller amounts over 500 to 1,000 hours. As market power is extended to more hours, the magnitude of the price increase required to reach the significant market power threshold declines. An increase of a few percent or a few dollars per MWh above marginal cost in bids is going to be harder to detect than bids that substantially exceed the expected marginal cost for a peaking generator. This would allow various intermediate and peaking generation units to bid above their marginal cost and easily avoid the screening test.[30]

Market concentration often increases in the upper part of the supply curve. For example, in PJM in 2002, the average HHI for base load generation was 1402, for intermediate units it was 2000, and for peaking units it was 4744.[31] Even with the expansion of PJM, in 2010, the respective HHIs were 1235, 1619, and 6139.[32] As the HHI rises, the potential for strategic bidding also increases; as the number of participants bidding the next generation unit declines, each remaining generator faces a steeper residual demand curve.[33] Since it is the peaking units, and to a lesser extent intermediate units, that determine the highest prices in the market,

---

[29] U.S. Department of Justice and the Federal Trade Commission, *Horizontal Merger Guidelines*, August 19, 2010, p. 10.

[30] The composition of the market portfolios of participants can have a significant impact on the exercise of market power, since a generator with limited base load capacity has a smaller incentive to raise market prices and a larger incentive to ensure that its units are "in the money" at all times. Diversified firms have incentives to use their high-cost plants to increase market prices and profits from their base load plants, but may not have enough price-setting capacity to do so. See Albert Banal-Estañol and Augusto Rupérez Micola, "Composition of Electricity Generation Portfolios, Pivotal Dynamics, and Market Prices," *Management Science* 55 (November 2009): 1813.

[31] PJM Market Monitoring Unit, *2002 State of the Market* (March 5, 2003): 24.

[32] Monitoring Analytics, LLC, *2010 State of the Market Report for PJM, Volume 2: Detailed Analysis* (March 10, 2011): 39.

[33] Paul Twomey, Richard Green, Karsten Neuhoff, and David Newbery, "A Review of the Monitoring of Market Power," *The Journal of Energy Literature* 11 (2005): 21–22.

even if overall concentration in the market is limited, there is substantial potential for large price increases for a few hours. This is reflected in estimates of markups over marginal cost for real time prices in PJM, which were highest for July 2010 peak hours, averaging $11.72/MWh. Markups also increased with the market price, reflecting the markup on higher-priced generation units, reaching $41.66 when the market price exceeded $160/MWh. However, markups on day-ahead bids, even in peak hours, were minimal.[34]

The combination of wholesale electricity deregulation and patchwork retail competition resulted in a variety of market structures, from the traditional vertical utilities, to Texas with competitive wholesale markets and partial retail competition (municipalities and cooperatives remained integrated), to MISO and PJM with a mix of deregulated wholesale electricity and some states in various stages of retail competition. This had significant impacts on competition and market power, as it meant markets were obtaining supplies from companies with varied incentives to exercise market power. In PJM, PECO and Pennsylvania Power and Light became large net sellers, with incentives to exercise oligopoly power, after restructuring of the Pennsylvania retail electricity market. The two firms reduced output by approximately 13 percent relative to the other firms after the market was restructured, and behaved in a manner consistent with profit maximization for the Cournot-Nash equilibrium. Other firms in PJM, which were nearly perfectly vertically integrated, did not set high prices.[35]

The ISOs/RTOs gradually improved their market-monitoring and mitigation practices, while FERC went through its own learning process. FERC allowed generators to use market power mitigation programs overseen by RTOs as a safe harbor if they fail FERC's market power screens. Applicants may accept the presumption of market power and go directly to mitigation.[36] An entity in an ISO/RTO may point to ISO/RTO spot

---

[34] Monitoring Analytics, LLC, *2010 State of the Market Report for PJM, Volume 2: Detailed Analysis*, at 51–54.

[35] Erin Mansur, "Upstream Competition and Vertical Integration in Electricity Markets," 50 *Journal of Law and Economics* 125 (2007). Vertical integration has been seen as a barrier to the exercise of market power in other markets as well. James Bushnell, Erin Mansur, and Celeste Saravia, "Vertical Arrangements, Market Structure, and Competition: An Analysis of Restructured US Electricity Markets," *American Economic Review* 98 (2008): 237–66.

[36] *AEP Power Marketing, Inc.*, 107 FERC ¶ 61,018 at PP 38–39, *order on reh'g, AEP Power Marketing, Inc.*, 108 FERC ¶ 61,026 (2004).

market mitigation as adequately mitigating market power. The Commission determined, on a case-by-case basis, whether the ISO/RTO mitigation was adequate or if additional cost-based default price mitigation should be imposed.[37]

A number of RTOs have implemented structural screens based on the concept of pivotal suppliers, following the example of FERC. A pivotal supplier is a seller whose output must be purchased in order to satisfy demand. The pivotal supplier test identifies whether one or several suppliers have the ability to substantially raise market prices. It is a more useful test than focusing on the size of the largest suppliers or the HHI because it allows direct identification of the potential to exercise market power. The three jointly pivotal supplier or 3JPS tests used by PJM reflect the reality that when a small number of suppliers are pivotal, implicit collusion becomes more likely. Although no single supplier can withhold enough capacity to set prices, there are so few suppliers that each will incorporate the others' expected behavior when making bids, and jointly may bid their few remaining generators far above marginal cost.

Electricity markets often permit parties to offer virtual generation and bid virtual load, which are financial bids that do not involve actual physical quantities. This practice has been criticized as encouraging speculation, but evidence supports the contention that these virtual bids and offers improve the operation of markets and reduce the exercise of market power. Before virtual bidding was permitted in the NYISO, day-ahead prices were significantly greater than the average real-time price, consistent with a model of price discrimination between buyers in the two markets. Generators in exporting zones withhold power to prevent transmission congestion in the day-ahead market in order to sell power at a higher price. Once those sales are locked in, the exporter can sell additional quantities in real time without reducing day-ahead prices. The result was to increase real-time transmission costs. Once virtual bidding was added to the market, the margins of the firms in exporting zones decreased.[38]

In general, the studies from industry and consultants have found large price savings (or other consumer benefits) from restructuring, whereas studies from academic researchers have found no evidence linking

---

[37] *AEP Power Marketing, Inc.,* 108 FERC ¶ 61,026 at PP 174–82.

[38] Celeste Saravia, "Speculative Trading and Market Performance: The Effect of Arbitrageurs on Efficiency and Market Power in the New York Electricity Market," Center for the Study of Energy Markets, CSEM WP 121 (November 2003).

electricity restructuring with lower retail electric rates.[39] As with some industry-sponsored studies purporting to find efficiency, many of the studies finding deleterious impacts seem biased and often poorly designed.[40]

Restructuring typically involved provision for stranded cost recovery and initial rate reductions, followed by rate freezes. By 2005, sixteen states were in various stages of deregulation, with some rate freezes expiring and others still in effect. In some states these rate restriction varied between utilities.[41] Initial rate reductions ranged from 3 percent to 20 percent, ensuring immediate gains to consumers. Freezes extended from two to ten years. When costs rose with natural gas prices, some regulators responded by allowing utilities to book costs that exceeded revenues from the frozen rates. These deferred balances could then be charged to ratepayers as soon as the rate freeze expired. The effect was to keep retail prices below their equilibrium level until the expiration of the freeze, at which time those prices would jump substantially.[42]

Stranded costs raise a difficult issue in determining the impact of deregulation on price. These are legitimate costs because they reflect financing of capital assets (and some mandated social programs) under regulation. These costs were imbedded in pre-deregulation prices as the return on book value, but were then accelerated (but usually financed through securitization, not as part of the utility's rate base). So while wholesale generation prices post-deregulation did not reflect these sunk costs, retail prices included these costs. The regulatory treatment of these costs after deregulation could impact retail prices in both directions.

An interesting question is whether the excessive investment in capacity following deregulation should be considered a benefit of deregulation

---

[39] Mark L. Fagan, "Measuring and Explaining Electricity Price Changes in Restructured States," Regulatory Policy Program Working Paper RPP-2006–02, John F. Kennedy School of Government, Harvard University (2006).

[40] See Edward Bodmer, "The Electric Honeypot: The Profitability of Deregulated Electric Generation Companies," for the APPA (January 2007); Edward Bodmer, "The Deregulation Penalty: Losses for Consumers and Gains for Sellers," a report to the APPA (August 2009). A critique of this work is found in Jonathan A Lesser, "Bad Economics, by Any Other Name, is Still Bad: APPA's Analysis of Wholesale Electric Competition is Flawed," Briefing Paper No. 2009–08–01 (August 2009). Note, however, that Lesser's report was sponsored by the Electric Power Supply Association. McCullough Research has also published a number of reports on electricity markets that have been magnets for criticism.

[41] Kenneth Rose and Karl Meeusen, "2006 Performance Review of Electric Power Markets," Conducted for the Virginia State Corporations Commission (August 27, 2006).

[42] John Kwoka, "Restructuring the U.S. Electric Power Sector: A Review of Recent Studies," *Review of Industrial Organization* 32 (2008): 169.

or just an episode of irrational exuberance. Obviously, over-investment in combined-cycle units, based on faulty forecasts of future natural gas prices, results in inefficient investment. However, this sort of mistake is normal behavior in all markets, including regulated markets, where utilities often made inefficient investments based on faulty projections of electricity demand. Studies conducted in mid-decade would ascribe lower prices to deregulation rather than to a simple miscalculation. By the end of the decade, this generation surplus was exhausted, and one impact of the IPP boom fallout was to raise the cost of new generation through higher financing costs.

While there is evidence for some efficiency gains, primarily from improved operation of nuclear plants transferred to more competent managers and increased output from lower-cost base load plants due to economic dispatch and gains from trade, these gains did not necessarily flow through to consumers. If deregulation and operation of electricity markets based on bids rather than marginal costs result in the exercise of market power, both the efficiency gains and additional revenue can be transferred to generators without reducing prices paid by consumers.

A study that focused on price-cost markups found that utilities that divested themselves of generation and had their service territory opened up to retail competition saw their prices rise. Retail competition is associated with higher price-cost markups, while the combination of RTO membership and retail competition is associated with lower price-cost markups. The reallocation of risks and rewards suggests that firms in the electricity market will demand higher profits in return for shouldering more of the risk of bad investments or management practices. However, this may also indicate the existence of market power by producers.[43]

Texas, as the most competitive state at the retail level, gives evidence that retail prices reflect wholesale prices with little impact from retail competition. Commercial electricity prices generally increased more in the areas opened to competition than in the areas of Texas that did not introduce customer choice, due to the rise in natural gas prices in the years retail competition was introduced. Some IOUs not affected by retail choice experienced various rate freezes, accounting for some of the gap.[44]

---

[43] Seth Blumsack, Lester Lave, and Jay Apt, "Electricity Prices and Costs Under Regulation and Restructuring," Carnegie Mellon Electricity Industry Center Working Paper CEIC-08–03 (May 2008): 23–25.

[44] Jay Zarnikau, Marilyn Fox, and Paul Smolen, "Trends in Prices to Commercial Energy Consumers in the Competitive Texas Electricity Market," *Energy Policy* 35 (2007): 4332–39.

The effects of competitive markets depend on the structure of retail competition. In states with relatively high participation rates by consumers, and competitive retail providers purchasing from the wholesale market competing with incumbent retail providers, competition has eventually lowered rates. In states where the standard offer price is provided by entities obtaining power through a competitive bidding process, there seems little benefit from competition.[45]

There is a real question whether any net benefits have been received by consumers from retail competition, at least in the short and medium runs. In states where consumers purchasing from competitive providers have received lower prices, this may simply reflect incumbent price discrimination, masking a larger margin from consumers who exhibit inertia. It is uncertain whether retail competition has resulted in lower wholesale prices, and if so, whether those savings have been passed through to consumers or have been dissipated through investments in marketing and excessive risk taking and profits by REPs. States where supplies for standard offer pricing were obtained from competitive bidding may have provided the same pressure on wholesale markets as did REP purchasers. There simply is not enough evidence at this time to determine if retail competition had any impact on wholesale markets.

---

[45] Mine Yucel and Adam Swadley, "Did Residential Electricity Rates Fall After Retail Competition? A Dynamic Panel Analysis," Federal Reserve Bank of Dallas Working Paper 1105 (May 2011).

Conclusion

Electricity restructuring has been a far more convoluted process than is generally acknowledged. Electricity restructuring is the proper term, because even in regions where both wholesale and retail markets were "deregulated," there is plenty of regulation, market rules to prevent the exercise of market power and delineate participation in electricity markets, reliability rules to ensure the security of the grid, and rules governing the behavior of retail electric providers. There are other regulations in place to encourage energy efficiency and expansion of the use of renewable energy, environmental regulations on power plants and the siting of transmission lines, etc. And in most areas, "deregulation" has been only partially accomplished, with a mixture of integrated utilities, independent power producers, and publicly owned utilities.

Regulated electricity companies were not the abysmal performers that many of the proponents of deregulation claimed. The two biggest factors in higher electricity prices were poor performance of nuclear power and overpriced QF contracts. Nuclear power was an example of management hubris. While some utilities were prudent in insisting on turnkey or fixed-cost contracts, and built the capabilities to manage the new technology, too many utilities bought the hype of the nuclear power vendors. However, we have seen similar foolishness in deregulated markets, such as the behavior that lead to the fiscal crisis of 2007.[1] The spasm of over-investment that accompanied deregulation in many markets was also a

---

[1] Andrew W. Lo, "Reading about the Financial Crisis: A Twenty-One-Book Review," *Journal of Economic Literature* 50 (2012): 151–78.

waste of resources that had long-term consequences, driving up the cost of financing merchant power after the boom. QF contracts were independent of market structure as a government-mandated subsidy, and had little correlation with utility management competence.

This is not to deny that there were real efficiency gains from restructuring, rather that these improvements in efficiency were incremental, and some of these improvements in resource allocation were achieved through pooling and more stringent regulation. Gains from trade could have been achieved with existing market structures by providing vertically integrated utilities with incentives to make efficiency-enhancing trades. Investment in transmission across traditional boundaries improved allocative efficiency. Additional gains were achieved by establishment of regional electricity markets, postage stamp transmission pricing, and SCED. LMP pricing provided better signals to the market for locating generation (and to regulators concerning generation expansion) and provided efficiencies from better congestion management.

If there is one lesson to be learned from the last few decades of electricity restructuring, it is that with complex interlinked systems like the electric grid, incremental change is more effective than radical restructuring. Incremental change has received a bad name because of the illusion in economics and management decision science that large complex problems can be modeled and solved. This is impossible to do in the real world. Muddling through is a way of implementing a global plan (say, a new electricity market structure), by accepting that such plans are inherently flawed. The optimal strategy may be to implement incrementally a global plan while retaining the option to change course as new information becomes available. The rush to build and implement a market in California not only illustrates the pitfalls of a comprehensive approach to change but also, through its exposure of institutional weakness at the FERC, shows how secondary actors can be overwhelmed by "big steps."

The gradual evolution from reliability regions to strong power pools to ISO's allowed the building of effective institutions, by permitting staff to develop expertise and providing staff with time to learn how to integrate numerous control areas under their authority. The least effective ISOs were the ones such as MISO, which were hastily cobbled together and governed numerous entities that had limited experience interacting with peers. It also helps to have excess capacity during the change in regimes as a buffer against policy errors. Texas benefited both from a deliberate effort to expand transmission in anticipation of deregulation and an investment boom that bought years to develop a resource adequacy mechanism. The Northeast ISOs made their share of mistakes but had more robust structures that allowed them to learn and evolve without serious mishaps.

The second lesson is "don't drink the Kool-Aid." The claims of dramatic cost savings and improvements from deregulation proved to be so much hype and hot air. Building effective markets has turned out to be a trial-and-error process all over the world, and most of the successful markets have evolved over time. Efficiency gains from competition are driven by long-term dynamics, but transition costs and transaction costs (including the cost of building the institutions to operate electricity markets) are incurred early in the process.

The third lesson is that most of the potential gains from restructuring are created by the development of competitive wholesale markets combined with stronger regulation of transmission. These go hand in hand, because wholesale competition requires opening transmission to third-party transactions. The ideal solution is separation of generation and wires; the second-best solution is transferring control of the wires to an independent transmission operator such as a RTO or Transco; the third-best solution is heavy-handed regulation to enforce functional separation. But electricity markets are vulnerable to the exercise of market power, and there is no efficient market solution to the "missing money" problem. Rational regulation is required to preserve these efficiency gains and prevent investment in rent-seeking activities designed to transfer revenues from consumers to generators and power marketers.

Retail competition has been grossly overrated. In the one market where it has been a "success," Texas, market penetration was forced through regulatory action, and a large proportion of residential and small commercial customers have not taken advantage of lower prices. Nor has there been any evidence of widespread innovation or an increase in price responsiveness. Many of the REPs in Texas buy power at fixed prices from large generators, then turn around and sell it to consumers with a markup, simply replacing the sales force of the formerly integrated utilities. In fact, it is becoming clear that the vision of an electricity market that would be self-regulating, with customers reacting to price as in most markets, is decades away, if it ever emerges. This vision will require technology advancements that sufficiently reduce the cost of automating control of residential electricity consumption (sensors, controls, software) to make it feasible to provide value-added services to residential customers. Lowering costs means moving from hard-wired systems that require truck rolls and "ownership" of customers (through regulatory fiat or long-term contracts) to wireless communication systems employing embedded controls in appliances and HVAC systems.

When it comes to industrial and large commercial customers, competition – and especially regulatory requirements for time of use pricing – has accelerated some technological innovation. However, many customers have contracted their way out of the uncertainty posed by dynamic pricing. As the cost of demand management decreases, and companies become more educated about the benefits of managing energy costs, there will be an increase in both price-responsive load and resources available as demand-response resources. But this has proven to be an incremental process, evolutionary, not revolutionary.

One wonders if electricity deregulation would have triumphed had the claims in the 1990s reflected reality. Maybe it required bogus promises of huge consumer savings to push politicians toward a policy that would provide long-term benefits, though often with short-run costs such as increased price volatility, large transition costs, and the occasional market meltdown. Overcoming lock-in and institutional inertia required bringing political pressure to bear on legislators and regulators, and it is difficult to maintain sustained pressure to force continual incremental movement from the status quo. Legislation tends to come in spasms of activity, followed by political exhaustion. The three major pieces of congressional legislation that resulted in the restructuring of the electricity industry – National Energy Act of 1978, EPAct 1992, and EPAct 2005 – all were omnibus bills that tried to balance and log roll across the energy industries. A similar pattern was seen with the Clean Air Act, with an initial bill in 1970, amendments in 1977 and 1990, and legislative gridlock preventing rationalization or adjustment for more than two decades. In both cases, legislation was honeycombed with inconsistencies caused by the need to compromise to get a bill passed.

Yet in the end, despite the rush to deregulation, the reality has been gradual evolution, led by FERC. Regulatory agencies have to work within the confines of the often ambiguous mandates provided by legislation. FERC was mandated to open up electricity markets to competition without the authority to override state regulators when it came to transmission, generation, and retail sales. I'm not sure FERC has always known where it was going, but if you look at FERC policies over the last three decades, there has been steady progress toward integrated markets employing LMP pricing, multi-settlement markets with a financially binding day-ahead market, scarcity pricing based on reserve demand curves, and capacity markets that provide additional revenues for generators in return for constraints on the exercise of market power. All seven markets have converged to this design. Even though Texas has resisted implementing a formal capacity mechanism, it has resorted to an ad hoc market collusion mechanism with revenue-related price caps to attempt to provide generators with the equivalent of capacity payments.

In the regions where integrated utilities employed their political power to thwart regional integration, FERC has gradually tightened the screws, increasing the regulatory burden and shifting the burden of proof to the integrated utility to show they are not engaged in discriminatory practices. The decision by Entergy to join MISO after a decade of prevarication suggests this strategy is having an effect. The holdouts have been reduced to the southeast utilities and WECC.

Muddling through may not be the ideal solution for social engineers or academic economists, who draw up plans for optimal market and regulatory structures, then criticize politicians and special interests when the real world diverges from their vision. However, regulators and policymakers must deal with numerous vested interests, consumer advocates, environmentalists, politicians, corporate lobbyists, and other parties pursuing their own vision of the ideal solution, engaging in turf wars or protecting their piece of the pie. While slicing the Gordian knot of political inertia is tempting, patiently unraveling its strands is often the better strategy.

References

Cases

Alabama Elec. Co-op., Inc. v. FERC, 684 F.2d 20 (D.C. Cir. 1982).

Alabama Power Co. v. Costle, 636 F.2d 323 (D.C. Cir. 1979).

Alabama Power Co. et al. v. FERC, 993 F.2d 1557 (D.C. Cir. 1993).

American Lung Assoc. v. Browner, 884 F.Supp. 345 (DCD Az. 1994).

Arkansas La. Gas Co. v. Hall, 453 U.S. 571 (1981).

Associated Gas Distributors v. FERC, 824 F.2d 981, 998 (D.C. Cir. 1987).

Berkey Photo, Inc. v. Eastman Kodak Co., 603 F.2d 263 (2nd Cir. 1979).

California, ex rel. Lockyer v. FERC, 383 F.3d 1006 (9th Cir. 2004), *cert. denied*, Coral Power, L.L.C. v. Cal. ex rel. Brown, 551 U.S. 1140 (2007).

California Wilderness Coalition v. Dept. of Energy, 631 F. 3d 1072 (9th Cir 2011).

Central Iowa Power Coop v. FERC, 606 F.2d 1156 (DC Cir 1979).

Central Maine Power Co. v. FERC, 252 F.3d 34 (1st Cir. 2001).

Chevron U.S.A., Inc. v. Natural Resources Defense Council, 467 U.S. 837 (1984).

City of Bethany v. FERC, 727 F.2d 1131 (D.C. Cir. 1984), *cert. denied*, 469 U.S. 917 (1984).

City of Cleveland v. FPC, 525 F.2d 845 (1976).

City of Holyoke v. FERC, 954 F.2d 740 (1992).

City of Holyoke Gas & Elec. Dept. v. SEC, 972 F. 2d 358 (DC Cir 1992).

City of Huntingburg v. FPC, 498 F.2d 778 (D.C. Cir. 1974).

City of Piqua v. FERC, 610 F.2d 950 (D.C. Cir. 1979).

Consumers Energy Co. v. FERC, 367 F.3d 915 (D.C. Cir. 2004).

DiPlacido v. CFTC, 364 F. App'x 657 (2d Cir. 2009), *cert. denied*, 130 S. Ct. 1883 (2010).

Duquesne Light Co. v. Barasch et al., 488 U.S. 299 (1989).

Edison Mission Energy, Inc. v. FERC, 394 F.3d 964 (D.C. Cir 2005).

Electricity Consumers Resource Council v. FERC, 747 F.2d 1511 (D.C. Cir. 1984).

Elizabethtown Gas Co. v. FERC, 10 F.3d 866 (D.C. Cir. 1993).

Environmental Action Inc., et al. v. FERC, 939 F.2d 1057 (D.C. Cir. 1991).

Environmental Defense v. Duke Energy Corporation, 127 S. Ct. 1423 (2007).

Farmers Union Central Exchange, Inc., 734 F.2d 1486 (D.C. Cir. 1984), *cert. denied*, 469 U.S. 1034 (1984).

Fort Pierce Util. Auth. v. FERC, 730 F.2d 778 (D.C. Cir. 1984).

FPC v. Hope Natural Gas Co., 320 U.S. 591 (1944).

FPC v. Natural Gas Pipeline Co. et al., 315 U.S. 575 (1942).

FPC v. Sierra Pacific Power Co., 350 U.S. 348 (1956).

Hendricks v. Dynegy Power Mktg., Inc., 160 F. Supp. 2d 1155 (S.D. Cal. 2001).

Illinois Commerce Comm'n v. FERC, 576 F.3d 470 (7th Cir. 2009).

Illinois Commerce Com'n v. FERC, 721 F. 3d 764 (7th Cir. 2013).

Illinois Commerce Com'n v. FERC, –F.3d – (7th Cir. 2014).

Jacobellis v. Ohio, 378 U.S. 184, 197 (1964).

Jersey Cent. Power & Light Co. v. FERC, 810 F. 2d 1168 (DC Cir 1988).

Keogh v. Chicago & Northwestern Ry. Co., 260 U.S. 156 (1922).

Lead Indus. Ass'n v. EPA, 647 F.2d 1130 (D.C. Cir.), *cert. denied*, 449 U.S. 1042 (1980).

Louisiana Energy and Power Authority v. FERC, 141 F.3d 364 (D.C. Cir. 1998).

Maine PUC v. FERC, 520 F.3d 464 (D.C. Cir. 2008).

Maine PUC v. FERC, 625 F.3d 754 (D.C. Cir. 2010).

Maislin Industries, U.S., Inc. v. Primary Steel, Inc., 497 U.S. 116 (1990).

Market Street Railway Co. v. Railroad Commission of California et al., 324 U.S. 548 (1945).

MCI Telecommunications Corp. v. AT&T Co., 512 U.S. 218 (1994).

Mississippi Power and Light Co. v. Mississippi, 487 U.S. 354 (1988).

Mobil Oil Corp. v. FPC et al., 417 U.S. 283 (1974).

Montana-Dakota Utils. Co. v. Northwestern Pub. Serv. Co., 341 U.S. 246 (1951).

Morgan Stanley v. PUD No. 1 of Snohomish County, 128 S.Ct. 2733 (2008).

Nantahala Power & Light v. Thornburg, 476 U.S. 953 (1986).

National Fuel Gas Supply Corp. v. FERC, 468 F.3d 831 (D.C. Cir. 2006).

National Resources Defense Council v. EPA, 489 F.2d 390 (5th Cir. 1974).

Natural Gas Clearinghouse v. FERC, 965 F.2d 1066 (D.C. Cir. 1992).

New England Power Generators Ass'n v. FERC, 707 F. 3d 364 (D.C. Cir. 2013).

New York v. EPA, 443 F.3d 880 (DC Cir 2006), *cert. denied*, 127 S. Ct. 2127 (2007).

New York et al. v. FERC, 531 U.S. 1 (2002).

New York Elec. & Gas Corp. v. FERC, 638 F.2d 388 (2d Cir. 1980), *cert. denied*, 454 U.S. 821.

North Carolina v. EPA, 531 F.3d 896 (D.C. Cir. 2008).

North Carolina v. EPA, 550 F.3d 1176 (D.C. Cir. 2008).

Northeast Utilities v. FERC, 993 F.2d 937 (1st Cir. 1993).

Northern Indiana Public Service Company v. FERC, 954 F.2d 736 (D.C. Cir. 1992).

NRG Power Mktg., LLC v. Maine Public Utilities Commission, 130 S.Ct. 693 (2010).

Otter Tail Power Co. v. United States, 410 U.S. 366 (1973).

Pacific Power & Light Co. v. FPC, 111 F.2d 1014 (9th Cir. 1940).

Pennsylvania Electric Co v. FERC, 11 F.3d 207 (D.C. Cir. 1993).

Piedmont Environmental Council v. FERC, 558 F. 3d 304 (4th Cir 2009), *cert. denied, Edison Elec. Inst. v. Piedmont Envtl. Council*, 130 S. Ct. 1138 (2010).

Power Co. of America, L.P. v. FERC, 245 F.3d 839 (D.C. Cir. 2001).

Public Serv. Co. of Ind. v. FERC, 575 F. 2d 1204 (7th Cir 1978).

Public Service Co. of New Hampshire v. FERC, 600 F.2d 944 (D.C. Cir. 1979), *cert. denied*, 444 U.S. 990 (1979).

Public Service Co. of New Hampshire v. Patch, 167 F. 3d 15 (1st Cir. 1998).

Pub. Util. Comm'n of Rhode Island v. Attleboro Steam & Electric Co., 273 U.S. 83 (1927).

Public Utility District No. 1 of Snohomish County v. Dynegy Power Marketing, Inc., 384 F.3d 756 (9th Cir. 2004).

Public Utility District No. 1 of Snohomish County v. FERC, 272 F.3d 607 (D.C. Cir. 2001).

Sierra Club v. Ruckelshaus, 344 F. Supp. 253 (DC Cir. 1972), *atf'd per curiam sub nom. Fri v. Sierra Club*, 412 U.S. 541 (1973).

South Carolina Public Service Authority v. FERC, – F.3d – (DC Cir 2014).

Square D Co. v. Niagara Frontier Tariff Bureau, Inc., 476 U.S. 409 (1986).

State of New Jersey v. EPA, 517 F.3d 574 (D.C. Cir. 2008), *cert. denied*, 129 S. Ct. 1308 (2009).

Steere Tank Lines, Inc. v. Interstate Commerce Commission, 703 F.2nd 927 (5th Cir. 1983).

Tampa Elec. Co. v. Garcia, 767 So. 2d 428 (Fla. 2000).

Tejas Power Corp. v. FERC, 908 F.2d 998 (D.C. Cir. 1990).

Texas Commercial Energy v. TXU Energy, Inc., 413 F.3d 503 (5th Cir. 2005).

Texas Power Co. v. FERC, 908 F.2d 998 (D.C. Cir. 1990).

Town of Norwood v. FERC, 962 F.2d 20 (D.C. Cir. 1992).

Town of Norwood, Mass. v. New England Power Co., 202 F.3d 408 (1st Cir. 2000).

Towns of Concord, Norwood and Wellesley v. FERC, 955 F.2d 67 (D.C. Cir. 1992).

Transmission Access Policy Study Group v. FERC, 225 F.3d 667 (D.C. Cir. 2000).

Union Elec. Co. v. EPA, 427 U.S. 246, 257 (1976).

United Gas Pipe Line Co. v. Memphis Light, Gas and Water Div., 358 U.S. 103 (1958).

United Gas Pipe Line Co. v. Mobile Gas Service Corp., 350 U.S. 332 (1956).

United States v. Grinnell Corp., 384 U.S. 563 (1966).

United States v. City of Painesville, 644 F.2d 1186 (6th Cir. 1981), *cert. denied*, 454 U.S. 894 (1981).

Utilimax.com, Inc. v. PPL Energy Plus, LLC, 378 F.3d 303 (3rd Cir. 2004).

Utility Users League v. FPC, 394 F. 2d 16 (7th Cir. 1968), *cert. denied*, 393 U.S. 953 (1968).

Verizon Commc'ns Inc. v. Law Offices of Curtis V. Trinko, LLP, 540 U.S. 398 (2004).

Wah Chang v. Duke Energy Trading and Marketing, LLC, 507 F.3d 1222 (9th Cir. 2007).

Whitman v. American Trucking, 531 U. S. 457 (2001).
Wisconsin Electric Power Co. v. Reilly, 893 F.2d 901 (7th Cir. 1990).

Books and Articles

Ackerman, Bruce A. and William T. Hassler, "Beyond the New Deal: Coal and the Clean Air Act," 89 *Yale Law Journal* 1466 (1980).

Ackerman, Frank, et al., "Grandfathering and Coal Plant Emissions: the Cost of Cleaning up the Clean Air Act," *Energy Policy* 27 (1999): 92–40.

Adams, Aster, "Impact of Deregulation on Cost Efficiency, Financial Performance and Shareholder Wealth of Electric Utilities in the United States" (Ph.D. Diss., Vanderbilt University, December 2008).

Adib, Parviz and Jay Zarnikau, "Texas: The Most Robust Competitive Market in North America," in Fereidoon P. Sioshansi and Wolfgang Pfaffenberger, eds., *Electricity Market Reform: An International Perspective* (Holland, Elsevier, 2006).

Adler, Jonathan H., "Fables of the Cuyahoga: Reconstructing a History of Environmental Protection," 14 *Fordham Environmental Law Journal* 89 (2002).

Agnone, Jon, "Amplifying Public Opinion: The Policy Impact of the U.S. Environmental Movement," *Social Forces* 85 (June 2007): 1593–1620.

Akerlof, George, "The Market for 'Lemons': Quality Uncertainty and the Market Mechanism," *Quarterly Journal of Economics* (1970): 488–500.

Alexander, Barbara R., *Part One: An Analysis of Residential Energy Markets in Georgia, Massachusetts, Ohio, New York and Texas*, at http://neaap.ncat.org/experts/PartOnePDF.pdf (last visited June 17, 2011).

Allison, Gary D., "Imprudent Power Construction Projects: The Malaise of Traditional Public Utility Policies," 13 *Hofstra Law Review* 507 (1985).

Alvarado, Fernando and Rajesh Rajaraman, "The Best Game in Town: NERC's TLR Rules," IEEE Winter Meeting, Tutorial on Game Theory, 1999.

American Economic Association, "American Economic Association Adopts Extensions to Principles for Author Disclosure of Conflict of Interest," press release, January 5, 2012, at https://www.aeaweb.org/PDF_files/PR/AEA_Adopts_Extensions_to_Principles_for_Author_Disclosure_01-05-12.pdf (last visited November 19, 2014).

American Gas Foundation, Public Policy and Real Energy Efficiency: Assessing the Effects of Federal Policies on Energy Consumption and the Environment, prepared for the American Gas Foundation by GARDAnalytics (October 2005).

Anderson, John, "The Competitive Sourcing of Retail Electricity: An Idea Whose Time Has (Finally) Come," Utility Director's Workshop, Williamsburg, VA, September 10, 1993.

Ando, Amy W. and Karen L. Palmer, "Getting on the Map: The Political Economy of State-Level Electricity Restructuring," Resources for the Future, 8–19-REV, May 1998.

Andrews Richard N.L., *Managing the Environment, Managing Ourselves: A History of American Environmental Policy* (New Haven, Yale University Press, 1999).

Arciniegas, Ismael, Chris Barrett, and Achla Marathe, "Assessing the Efficiency of US Electricity Markets," *Utilities Policy* 11 (2003): 75–86.

Arocena, Pablo, David Saal, and Tim Coelli, "Measuring Economies of Horizontal and Vertical Integration in the US Electric Power Industry: How Costly Is Unbundling?" Working Paper RP 0917, Aston Business School, June 2009.

Arthur, W. Brian, "Competing Technologies, Increasing Returns, and Lock-In By Historical Events," *Economic Journal* 99 (1989): 116–31.

Atwood, James R., "Antitrust, Joint Ventures, and Electric Utility Restructuring: RTGS and POOLCOS," 64 *Antitrust Law Journal* 323 (Winter 1996).

Auffhammer, Maximilian and Alan Sanstad, "Energy Efficiency in the Residential and Commercial Sectors," *Resources for the Future*, Background Paper (January, 2011).

Averch, Harvey and Leland L. Johnson, "Behavior of the Firm Under Regulatory Constraint," *American Economic Review* 52 (December 1962): 1053–69.

Bachman, John, "Will the Circle Be Unbroken: A History of the U.S. National Ambient Air Quality Standards," *Journal of the Air & Waste Management Association* 57 (June 2007): 652–97.

Bachrach, Devra Ruth, "Comparing the Risk Profiles of Renewable and Natural Gas Electricity Contracts: A Summary of the California Department of Water Resources Contracts" (MS Thesis, University of California at Berkeley, May 2002).

Bailey, Elizabeth E., "Contestability and the Design of Regulatory and Antitrust Policy," *American Economic Review* 71 (May 1981): 178–83.

Bailey, Elizabeth E. and William J. Baumol, "Deregulation and the Theory of Contestable Markets," 1 *Yale Journal on Regulation* 111 (1984).

Bailey, Elizabeth M., "The Geographic Expanse of the Market for Wholesale Electricity," Working paper, Massachusetts Institute of Technology (February 1998).

Baldick, Ross, "Computing the Electricity Market Equilibrium: Uses of Market Equilibrium Models," IEEE, Power Systems Conference and Exposition (2006).

Bamberger, Kenneth and Peter Strauss, "Chevron's Two Steps," 95 *Virginia Law Review* 611 (2009).

Banal-Estañol, Albert and Augusto Rupérez Micola, "Composition of Electricity Generation Portfolios, Pivotal Dynamics, and Market Prices," *Management Science* 55 (November 2009): 1813–31.

Barnett, A.H., Keith A. Reutter, and Henry Thompson, "The First Step in Restructuring the US Electric Industry," *Energy Economics* 27 (2005): 225–235.

Bartholomew, Emily S., Robert Van Buskirk, and Chris Marnay, *Conservation in California During the Summer of 2001*, LBNL-51477 (September 2002).

Baumol, William J., J.C. Panzer and R.P. Willig, *Contestable Markets and the Theory of Industry Structure* (San Diego, Harcourt Brace Jovanovich, 1982).

Baumol, William J. and J. Gregory Sidak, "Stranded Costs," 18 *Harvard Journal of Law & Public Policy* 837 (Summer 1995).

Becker, Gary, "Irrational Behavior and Economic Theory," *Journal of Political Economy* 70 (February 1962): 1–13.

Becker, Gary, "A Theory of Competition Among Pressure Groups for Political Influence," *Quarterly Journal of Economics* 98 (August 1983): 371–400.

Becker-Blease, John, Lawrence Goldberg, and Fred Kaen, "Post Deregulation Restructuring of the Electric Power Industry: Value Creation or Value Destruction?" Working Paper, February 26, 2004.

Beermann, Jack, "The Turn Toward Congress in Administrative Law," 89 *Boston University Law Review* 727 (2009).

Bennett, Andrew and Colin Elman, "Complex Causal Relations and Case Study Methods; the Example of Path Dependence," *Political Analysis* 14 (2006): 250–67.

Bergek, Anna, et al., "Technological Capabilities and Late Shakeouts: Industrial Dynamics in the Advanced Gas Turbine Industry, 1987–2002," *Industrial and Corporate Change* 17 (2008): 335–92.

Bergstrom, Roger, Christi Cao, and Tommie Tolbert, *Key Aspects of Electric Restructuring Supplemental Volume II: the State Summaries 2003 Updates*, Florida Public Service Commission, July 2003.

BernsteinResearch, "U.S. Utilities: Coal-Fired Generation is Squeezed in the Vice of EPA Regulation; Who Wins and Who Loses?" (October 2010).

BernsteinResearch, "U.S. Utilities: Can Texas Comply With the Cross-State Air Pollution Rule? Yes, If Existing Scrubbers Are Turned On" (July 20, 2011).

Berry, William W., "The Case for Competition in the Electric Utility Industry," *Public Utilities Fortnightly* 110 (September 1982): 12–20.

Besanko, David, Julia D'Souza, and S. Ramu Thiagarajan, "The Effect of Wholesale Market Deregulation on Shareholder Wealth in the Electric Power Industry," 44 *Journal of Law and Economics* 65 (April 2001).

Bhavaraju, Marty, Benhamin Hobbs, and Ming-Che Hu, "PJM Reliability Pricing Model – A Summary and Dynamic Analysis," *IEEE* (2007).

Bialek, Janusz, "Recent Blackouts in US and Continental Europe: Is Liberalisation to Blame?" Cambridge Working Papers in Economics, CWPE 0407 (January 16, 2004).

Blacconiere, Walter G., Marilyn F. Johnson, and Mark S. Johnson, "Market Valuation and Deregulation of Electric Utilities," *Journal of Accounting and Economics*, 29 (2000): 231–60.

Black, Bernard S. and Richard J. Pierce, Jr., "The Choice Between Markets and Central Planning in Regulating the U.S. Electricity Industry," 93 *Columbia Law Review* 1339 (1993).

Blair, Peter, "The Role of Analytical Models: Issues and Frontiers," EMF WP 10.2 (March 1991).

Blumsack, Seth, "Network Topologies and Transmission Investment Under Electric-Industry Restructuring," (Ph.D Diss., Carnegie Mellon University, 2006).

Blumsack, Seth, Lester Lave, and Jay Apt, "Electricity Prices and Costs Under Regulation and Restructuring," CEIC-08–03 (May 2008).

Blumstein, Carl, L.S. Friedman, and R.J. Green, "The History of Electricity Restructuring in California," CSEM (August 2002).

Blumstein, Carl, Charles Goldman, and Galen Barbose, "Who Should Administer Energy-Efficiency Programs?" Lawrence Berkeley National Laboratory (August 2003).

Bodmer, Edward, "The Electric Honeypot: The Profitability of Deregulated Electric Generation Companies," for the APPA (January 2007).

Bodmer, Edward, "The Deregulation Penalty: Losses for Consumers and Gains for Sellers," a report to the APPA (August 2009).

Bohn, Roger B., Richard U. Tabors, Bennett W. Golub, and Fred C. Schweppe, "Deregulating the Electric Utility Industry," MIT Energy Laboratory Technical Report (January 1982).

Bonardi, Jean-Philippe, Guy Holburn, and Richard Vanden Bergh, "Nonmarket Strategy Performance: Evidence From U.S. Electric Utilities," *Academy of Management Journal* 49 (2006): 1209–28.

Bonbright, James C., *Principles of Public Utility Rates* (New York, Columbia University Press, 1961).

Borenstein, Severin, James Bushnell, Edward Kahn, and Steven Stoft, "Market Power in California Electricity Markets," *Utilities Policy* 5 (July/October 1995): 219–236.

Borenstein, Severin, James Bushnell, Edward Kahn, and Steven Stoft, "An Empirical Analysis of the Potential for Market Power in California's Electricity Industry," POWER (December 1998).

Borenstein, Severin, James Bushnell, Christopher R. Knittel, and Catherine Wolfram, "Inefficiencies and Market Power in Financial Arbitrage: A Study of California's Electricity Markets," Working Paper (September 24, 2006).

Borenstein, Severin, James Bushnell, and Steven Stoft, "The Competitive Effects of Transmission Capacity in a Deregulated Electricity Market," *Rand Journal of Economics* 31 (Summer 2000): 294–325.

Borenstein, Severin, James Bushnell, and Frank A. Wolak, "Measuring Market Inefficiencies in California's Restructured Wholesale Electricity Market," *American Economic Review* 92 (December 2002): 1376–1405.

Bosso, Christopher J. and Deborah Lynn Guber, "Maintaining Presence: Environmental Advocacy and the Permanent Campaign," in N.J. Vig and M.E. Kraft, eds., *Environmental Policy: New Directions for the Twenty First Century* (Washington DC, CQ Press, 2006).

Bouknight, Jr., J.A. and David Raskin, "Planning for Wholesale Customer Loads in a Competitive Environment: The Obligation to Provide Wholesale Service under the Federal Power Act," 8 *Energy Law Journal* 237 (1987).

Bradley Jr., Robert L., "The Origins of Political Electricity: Market Failure or Political Opportunism?" 17 *Energy Law Journal* 59 (1996).

Bratton, William, "Does Corporate Law Protect the Interest of Shareholders and Other Stakeholders? Enron and the Dark Side of Shareholder Value," 76 *Tulane Law Review* 1275 (June 2002).

Brennan, Timothy J., "Consumer Preference Not to Choose: Methodological and Policy Implications," Resources For the Future, RFF DP 05–51 (November 2005).

Bressman, Lisa, "Procedures as Politics in Administrative Law," 107 *Columbia Law Review* 1749 (2007).

Bressman, Lisa and Michael Vandenbergh, "Inside the Administrative State: A Critical Look at the Practice of Presidential Control," 105 *Michigan Law Review* 47 (2006).

Brien, Laura, "Why the Ancillary Services Markets in California Don't Work and What to Do About Them," NERA, February 7, 1999.

Brown, Ashley and Jim Rossi, "Siting Transmission Lines in a Changed Milieu: Evolving Notions of the 'Public Interest' in Balancing State and Regional Considerations," 81 *University of Colorado Law Review* 705 (2010).

Bryce, Robert, *Pipe Dreams: Greed, Ego and the Death of Enron* (New York, PublicAffairs, 2002).

Bryner, Gary C., *Blue Skies, Green Politics, The Clean Air Act of 1990* (Washington, DC, CQ Press 1995).

Buchmann, Alan and Robert Tongren, "Nonunanimous Settlements of Public Utility Rate Cases: A Response," 113 *Yale Journal on Regulation* 337 (Winter 1996).

Burns, Robert E., et al., *The Prudent Investment Test in the 1980s* (Columbus, National Regulatory Research Institute, April 1985).

Burtraw, Dallas and Karen Palmer, "The Paparazzi Take a Look at a Living Legend: The SO2 Cap-and-Trade Program for Power Plants in the United States," Resources For the Future, DP03–15 (April 2003).

Burtraw, Dallas, et al., "The Costs and Benefits of Reducing Acid Rain," Resources For the Future, Discussion Paper 97–31-REV (September 1997).

Burtraw, Dallas, et al., "Price Discovery in Emissions Permit Auctions," Resources For the Future, DP 10–32 (June 2010).

Bush, Darren and Carrie Mayne, "In (Reluctant) Defense of Enron: Why Bad Regulation Is to Blame for California's Power Woes (or Why Antitrust Law Fails to Protect Against Market Power When the Market Rules Encourage Its Use)," 83 *Oregon Law Review* 207 (2004).

Bushnell, James and Carl Blumstein, "A Reader's Guide to the Blue Book: Issues in California's Electric Industry Restructuring and Regulatory Reform," POWER (June 1994).

Bushnell, James, Erin Mansur, and Celeste Saravia, "Vertical Arrangements, Market Structure, and Competition: An Analysis of Restructured US Electricity Markets," *American Economic Review* 98 (2008): 237–66.

Bushnell, James and Celeste Saravia, "An Empirical Assessment of the Competitiveness of the New England Electricity Market," Center for the Study of Energy Markets, WP 101 (2002).

Bushnell, James and Stephen Stoft, "Electric Grid Investment Under a Contract Network Regime," *Journal of Regulatory Economics* 10 (1996): 61–79.

Bushnell, James and Stephen Stoft, "Improving Private Incentives for Electric Grid Investment," *Resource and Energy Economics* 19 (1997): 85–108.

Bushnell, James and Catherine Wolfram, "Ownership Change, Incentives and Plant Efficiency: Divestiture of U.S. Electric Generation Plants," Working Paper (March 2005).

Bushnell, James and Catherine Wolfram, "The Guy at the Controls: Labor Quality and Power Plant Efficiency," Center for the Study of Energy Markets, WP 121 (July 2007).

CAISO, Department of Market Analysis, "Price Cap Policy for Summer 2000" (March 2000).

CAISO, Department of Market Analysis, "Report of California Energy Market Issues and Performance: May–June 2000" (August 10, 2000).

CAISO, Department of Market Analysis, "Report on Real Time Supply Costs above Single Price Auction Threshold: December 8, 2000 – January 31, 2001" (February 28, 2001).

CAISO, Department of Market Analysis, "Analysis of Trading and Scheduling Strategies Described in Enron Memos" (October 4, 2002).

CAISO, Market Surveillance Unit, "Preliminary Report On the Operation of the Ancillary Services Markets of the California Independent System Operator (ISO)" (August 19, 1998).

CAISO, "Annual Report on Market Issues and Performance" (June 1999).

CAISO Market Surveillance Committee, "Report on the Redesign of California Real time Energy and Ancillary Services Markets" (October 18, 1999).

CAISO Market Surveillance Committee, "Analysis of 'Order Proposing Remedies for California Wholesale Electric Markets (Issued November 1, 2000)," (December 1, 2000).

California Energy Commission, "High Temperatures & Electricity Demand: An Assessment of Supply Adequacy in California," Staff Report (July 1999).

California Energy Commission, "Market Clearing Prices Under Alternative Resource Scenarios, 2000–2010," Staff Report (February 2000).

California State Auditor, "California Energy Markets: Pressures Have Eased, but Cost Risks Remain," Report #2001-009, Sacramento, CA (December 2001).

CalPX Market Monitoring Committee, "Report on Market Issues in the California Power Exchange Energy Markets," Prepared for FERC, August 17, 1998.

CalPX Market Monitoring Committee, "Second Report on Market Issues in the California Power Exchange Energy Markets," Prepared for FERC, March 19, 1999.

Caplan, Bryan, "From Friedman to Whittman: The Transformation of Chicago Political Economy," *Economic Journal Watch* 2 (April 2005): 1–21.

Carden, Kevin, Nick Wintermantel, and Johannes Pfeifenberger, *The Economics of Resource Adequacy Planning: Why Reserve Margins Are Not Just About Keeping the Lights On* (Columbus, National Regulatory Research Institute, 2011).

Carlton, Dennis, "Why Barriers to Entry are Barriers to Understanding," *American Economic Review* 94 (May 2004): 466–70.

Carlton, Dennis and Jeffrey Perloff, *Modern Industrial Organization* (Glenview, Scott Foresman/Little Brown, 1990).

Casazza, Jack and Frank Delea, *Understanding Electric Power Systems: An Overview of Technology, the Marketplace and Government Regulation*, 2nd Ed. (Hoboken, John Wiley & Sons, 2010).

Casazza, Jack, Frank Delea, and George Loehr, "Contributions of the Restructuring of the Electric Power Industry to the August 14, 2003 Blackout," in US-Canada Power System Outage Task Force, Final Report on the August 14, 2003 Blackout in the United States and Canada: Causes and Recommendations, Recommendation 12: The Relationship between Competitive Power Markets and Grid Reliability (July 2006).

Cavanagh, Ralph, "Least-Cost Planning Imperatives for Electric Utilities and Their Regulators," 5 *Harvard Environmental Law Review* 299 (1988).

Cavanagh, Sheila, Robert Hahn, and Robert Stavins, "National Environmental Policy During the Clinton Years," Resources for the Future, Discussion Paper 01–38, September 2001.

CBO, *Promoting Efficiency in the Electricity Sector* (Washington, DC, GPO, 1982).

CBO, *Electric Utilities: Deregulation and Stranded Costs* (Washington, DC, GPO, 1998).

Celebi, Metin, "Potential Coal Plant Retirements Under Emerging Environmental Regulations," The Brattle Group, presentation to MREA, St. Cloud, Minnesota, August 10, 2011.

Celebi, Metin, "Potential Coal Plant Retirements: 2012 Update," The Brattle Group, Discussion Paper, October 2012.

Chao, Hung-po, Shmuel Oren, and Robert Wilson, "Restructured Electricity Markets: Reevaluation of Vertical Integration and Unbundling," in Fereidoon P. Sioshansi, ed., *Competitive Electricity Markets: Design, Implementation, Performance* (Amsterdam, Elsevier, 2008).

Chao, Hung-Po and Stephen Peck, "A Market Mechanism for Electric Power Transmission," *Journal of Regulatory Economics* 10 (1996): 25–59.

Chao, Hung-po, Stephen Peck, Shmuel Oren, and Robert Wilson, "Flow-Based Transmission Rights and Congestion Management," *Electricity Journal* (October 2000): 38–58.

Chase, David L., "Combined-Cycle Development Evolution and Future," GE Power Systems GER-4206 (April 2001).

Chen, Jim, "The Death of the Regulatory Compact: Adjusting Prices and Expectations in the Law of Regulated Industries," 67 *Ohio State Law Journal* 1265 (2006).

Cheney, Dick, et al., *National Energy Policy: Report of the National Energy Policy Development Group* (Washington, DC, GPO, 2001).

Chestnut, Lauraine and David Mills, "A Fresh Look at the Benefits and Costs of the US Acid Rain Program," *Journal of Environmental Management* 77 (2005): 252–66.

Chincarini, Ludwig, "A Case Study on Risk Management: Lessons from the Collapse of Amaranth Advisors L.L.C.," *Journal of Applied Finance* (Spring/Summer 2008): 1–23.

Christensen, Laurits R. and William Greene, "Economies of Scale in U.S. Electric Power Generation," *Journal of Political Economy* 84 (1976): 655–76.

Chupka, Marc W. and Gregory Basheda, "Rising Utility Construction Costs: Sources and Impacts," Brattle Group for the Edison Foundation (September 2007).

Clark, John Maurice, "Toward a Concept of Workable Competition," *American Economic Review* 30 (1940): 241–56.

Coglianese, Cary, "Social Movements, Law, and Society: Institutionalization of the Environmental Movement," 150 *University of Pennsylvania Law Review* 85 (2001).

Coglianese, Gary, "Presidential Control of Administrative Agencies: A Debate Over Law or Politics?" 12 *Journal of Constitutional Law* 637 (2010).

Cohen, Armond and Steven Kihm, "The Political Economy of Retail Wheeling, or How Not to Refight the Last War," *Electricity Journal* (April 1994): 49–61.

Cohen, Linda, Stephen Peck, Paroma Sanyal, and Carl Weinberg, "Retrospective Report on California's Electricity Crisis," CEC, PIER Report, CEC-500-2006-021 (January 2004).

Cohen, Matthew, "Efficiency and Competition in the Electric Power Industry," 88 *Yale Law Journal* 1511 (1979).

Cohen, Richard E., *Washington at Work: Back Rooms and Clean Air*, 2nd ed. (Boston, Allyn and Bacon, 1995).

Colton, Roger, "Excess Capacity: A Case Study in Ratemaking Theory and Application," 20 *Tulsa Law Journal* 402 (1984).

Comnes, G.A., T.N. Belden, and E.P. Kahn, "The Price of Electricity from Private Power Producers, Stage II: Expansion of Sample and Preliminary Statistical Analysis," Lawrence Berkeley National Laboratory, LBL-36054 (February 1995).

Conley II, Joe Greene, "Environmentalism Contained: A History of Corporate Response to the New Environmentalism" (Ph.D. Diss, Princeton University, November 2006).

Costello, Kenneth W., Robert E. Burns, and Youssef Hegazy, "Overview of Issues Relating to the Retail Wheeling of Electricity," National Regulatory Research Institute, NRRI 94–09 (May 1994).

Cowan, Robin, "Nuclear Power Reactors: A Study in Technological Lock-in," *Journal of Economic History* 50 (September 1990): 541–67.

CPUC, "California's Electric Services Industry: Perspectives on the Past, Strategies for the Future" (February 1993) ("Yellow Book").

CPUC, "Order Instituting Rulemaking on the Commission's Proposed Policies Governing Restructuring California's Electric Services Industry and Reforming Regulation; Order Instituting Rulemaking and Order Instituting Investigation" (April 20, 1994) ("Blue Book").

CRA, "A Reliability Assessment of EPA's Proposed Transport Rule and Forthcoming Utility MACT," prepared for Exelon Corporation (December 16, 2010).

Craig, J. Dean and Scott Savage, "Market Restructuring, Competition and the Efficiency of Electricity Generation: Plant-level Evidence from the United States 1996 to 2006," *The Energy Journal* 34 (2013): 1–31.

Crain, Andrew, "Ford, Carter, and Deregulation in the 1970s," *Journal on Telecommunications & High Technology Law* 5 (2007): 413–47.

Cramton, Peter, "Assessment of Submissions by California Parties," Rebuttal Addendum of Behalf of Duke Energy, San Diego Gas & Electric Company, Dockets Nos EL00–95–075, EL00–98–063, March 20, 2003.

Cramton, Peter, "Competitive Bidding Behavior in Uniform-Price Auction Markets," Proceedings of the Hawaii International Conference on System Sciences (January 2004).

Cramton, Peter and Steven Stoft, "A Capacity Market That Makes Sense," *Electricity Journal* 18 (August/September 2005): 43–54.

Cramton, Peter and Robert Wilson, "A Review of ISO New England's Proposed Market Rules," Exhibit A, ISO-NE filing (September 9, 1998).

Credit Suisse, "Growth From Subtraction; Impact of EPA Rules on Power Markets" (September 23, 2010).

Criddle, Evan, "Chevron's Consensus," 88 *Boston University Law Review* 1271 (2009).

Cudahy, Richard D., "Whither Deregulation: A Look at the Portents," 58 *N.Y.U. Annual Survey of American Law* 155 (2001).

Cudahy, Richard and William Henderson, "From Insull to Enron: Corporate (Re)Regulation After the Rise and Fall of Two Energy Icons," 26 *Energy Law Journal* 35 (2005).

Culp, Christopher and Steve Hanke, "Empire of the Sun: An Economic Interpretation of Enron's Energy Business," *Policy Analysis* 470 (February 20, 2003): 1–19.

Daly, Herman E., *Toward a Steady-State Economy* (San Francisco, W.H. Freeman, 1973).

Dang, Hoang, "New Power, Few New Lines: A Need For a Federal Solution," 17 *Journal of Land Use and Environmental Law* 327 (2002).

David, Paul, "Clio and the Economics of QWERTY," *American Economic Review* 75 (May 1985): 332–37.

David, Paul, "Why Are Institutions the 'Carriers of History': Path Dependence and the Evolution of Conventions, Organizations and Institutions," *Structural Change and Economic Dynamics* 5 (1994): 205–20.

Davis, Lucas and Catherine Wolfram, "Deregulation, Consolidation, and Efficiency: Evidence from U.S. Nuclear Power," EI @ Haas Working Paper 217 (August 2011).

Davis, Sandra K., "Rewiring Electricity Transmission Policy," Paper Presented at the 2011 WPSA conference (April 21–23, 2011).

Davis, Steven, Cheryl Grim and John Haltiwanger, "Productivity Dispersion and Input Prices: the Case of Electricity," U.S. Bureau of the Census, CES 08–33 (September 2008).

Davis, Steven, Cheryl Grim, John Haltiwanger, and Mary Streitwieser, "Electricity Pricing to U.S. Manufacturing Plants, 1963–2000" (April 22, 2009).

De Long, J. Bradford and Kevin Lang, "Are All Economic Hypotheses False?" *Journal of Political Economy* 100 (1992): 1257–72.

Defeuilley, Christophe, "Retail Competition in Electricity Markets," *Energy Policy* 37 (2009): 378.

Delgado, Jose, "The Blackout of 2003 and its Connection to Open Access," in *U.S.-Canada Power System Outage Task Force*, Recommendation 12: The Relationship between Competitive Power Markets and Grid Reliability (July 2006).

Delmas, Magali and Yesim Tokat, "Deregulation, Governance Structures, and Efficiency: The U.S. Electric Utility Sector," *Strategic Management Journal* 26 (2005): 441–60.

Demsetz, Harold, "Why Regulate Utilities," 11 *Journal of Law and Economics* 55 (April 1968).

DeMocker, James, Judith Greenwald and Paul Schwengel, "Extended Lifetimes for Coal-fired Power Plants: Effect Upon Air Quality," *Public Utilities Fortnightly* 177 (March 20, 1986).

Deng, Shi-Jie, Shmuel Oren, and Sakis Meliopoulos, "The Inherent Inefficiency of the Point-to-Point Congestion Revenue Right Auction," Proceeding of the 37th Hawaiian International Conference on System Sciences (2004).

Dennis, Jeffery S., "Federalism, Electric Industry Restructuring, and the Dormant Commerce Clause: Tampa Electric Co. v. Garcia and State Restrictions on the Development of Merchant Power Plants," 43 *Natural Resources Journal* 615 (Spring 2003).

Derman, Emanuel and Paul Wilmott, "The Financial Modelers' Manifesto" (January 7, 2009).

Derthick, Martha and Paul J. Quirk, *The Politics of Deregulation* (Washington, DC, Brookings Institution Press, 1985).

Dobson, Ian et al., "Electric Power Transfer Capability: Concepts, Applications, Sensitivity and Uncertainty," Power Systems Engineering Research Center (November 2001).

DOE, Electricity Advisory Committee, *Keeping the Lights On in a New World* (Washington, DC, January 2009).

DOE, Office of Policy Planning and Analysis, "Integration of Electric Power: A Framework for Analysis, A Draft Discussion Paper, Phase 2 Report," prepared by MIT, September 1982.

DOE, Office of Policy Planning and Analysis, "The Impact of Wholesale Electricity Price Controls on California Summer Reliability," June 2001.

DOE, Office of Policy Planning and Analysis, *National Transmission Grid Study* (May 2002).

DOE, Office of Policy Planning and Analysis, "The Value of Economic Dispatch; A Report to Congress Pursuant to Section 1234 of the Energy Policy Act of 2005" (November 7, 2005).

DOE, Office of Policy Planning and Analysis, *National Electric Transmission Congestion Study* (August 2006).

DOE, Office of Policy Planning and Analysis, "National Electric Transmission Congestion Report" (October 5, 2007).

DOE, Office of Policy Planning and Analysis, "Resource Adequacy Implications of Forthcoming EPA Air Quality Regulations" (December 2011).

DOJ and FTC, *Horizontal Merger Guidelines*, April 2, 1992, 57 FR 41552 (1992).

DOJ and FTC, *Horizontal Merger Guidelines* (August 19, 2010).

Domagalski, John L., Agustin J. Ros, and Philip R. O'Connor, "Another Look at What's Driving Utility Stock Prices," *Public Utilities Fortnightly* 135 (January 15, 1997): 42–45.

Dorsi, Michael, "Piedmont Environmental Council v. FERC," 34 *Harvard Environmental Law Review* 593 (2010).

Doucet, Joseph and Stephen Littlechild, "Negotiated Settlements: The Development of Economic and Legal Thinking," CWPE 0622 and EPRG 0604 (September 2006).

Doucouliagos, Chris and T.D. Stanley, "Theory Competition and Selectivity: Are All Economic Facts Greatly Exaggerated?" *Journal of Economic Surveys* 27 (2012): 316–39.

Dowden, Lisa, Stephen Pearson, and Melissa Birchard, "Update on CFTC Actions under Dodd-Frank as They Affect the Electric Power Industry," Prepared for APPA 2011 Legal Conference (November 9, 2011).

D'Souza, Julia and John Jacob, "Electric Utility Stranded Costs: Valuation and Disclosure Issues," *Journal of Accounting Research* 39 (2001): 495–512.

Duane, Timothy P., "Regulation's Rationale: Learning from the California Energy Crisis," 19 *Yale Journal on Regulation* 471 (2002).

Eagle, Steven J., "Securing a Reliable Electricity Grid: A New Era in Transmission Siting Regulation?" George Mason University School of Law (September 13, 2005).

Earley, Wilbur C., "FERC Regulation of Bulk Power Coordination Transactions," FERC Working Paper (July 1984).

Eaton, B. Curtis and Richard Lipsey, "Exit Barriers Are Entry Barriers: The Durability of Capital as a Barrier to Entry," *Bell Journal of Economics* 11 (Autumn 1980): 721–29.

Eaton, Jade Alice, "Recent United States Department of Justice Actions in the Electric Utility Industry," 9 *Connecticut Journal of International Law* 857 (Summer 1994).

Economic Report of the President, 2012 (Washington, DC, GPO, 2012).

EEI, "Deregulation of Electric Utilities: A Survey of Major Concepts and Issues" (July 1981).

EEI, *Statistical Yearbook of the Electric Utility Industry 1982* (Washington, DC, 1983).

EEI, "Transmission Projects: At a Glance" (March 2011).

EEI, "New Source Review: a History" (2001).

Ehrlich, Paul, *The Population Bomb* (New York, Ballantine, 1968).

EIA, *The Changing Structure of the Electric Power Industry 1970–1991* (Washington, DC, GPO, 1993).

EIA, *Financial Statistics of Major U.S. Investor-Owned Electric Utilities 1992* (Washington, DC, GPO, 1993).

EIA, *Electric Power Annual 1992* (Washington, DC, GPO, 1994).

EIA, *Financial Impacts of Nonutility Power Purchases on Investor-Owned Electric Utilities* (Washington, DC, GPO, 1994).

EIA, *The Effects of Title IV of the Clean Air Act Amendments of 1990 on Electric Utilities: An Update* (Washington, DC, GPO, 1997).

EIA, *State Energy Price and Expenditure Report* (Washington, DC, GPO, 1995).

EIA, *The Changing Structure of the Electric Power Industry: An Update* (Washington, DC, GPO, 1996).

EIA, *Electricity Prices in a Competitive Environment: Marginal Cost Pricing of Generation Services and Financial Status of Electric Utilities* (Washington, DC, GPO, 1997).

EIA, *The Changing Structure of the Electric Power Industry 1999: Mergers and Other Corporate Combinations* (Washington, DC, GPO, 1999).

EIA, *Annual Energy Review*, various years.

Eichenwald, Kurt, *Conspiracy of Fools: A True Story* (New York, Random House, 2005).

Eisen, Joel, "Regulatory Linearity, Commerce Clause Brinksmanship, and Retrenchment in Electric Utility Deregulation," 40 *Wake Forest Law Review* 545 (2005).

Ellerman, Denny and Florence Dubroeucq, "Sources of Emission Reductions: Evidence for US SO_2 Emissions 1985–2002," Cambridge Working Papers in Economics, CWPE 0429 (2004).

Ellerman, Denny and Juan-Pablo Montero, "The Declining Trend in Sulfur Dioxide Emissions: Implications for Allowance Prices," *Journal of Environmental Economics and Management* 36 (1998): 26–45.

Elliott, James D., "Electric Utility Regulation Reform in New York: Economic Competitiveness at the Expense of the Environment?" 13 *Pace Environmental Law Review* 281 (1995).

Emmons III, William, "Franklin D. Roosevelt, Electric Utilities, and the Power of Competition," *Journal of Economic History* 53 (1993): 880–907.

Energy Policy Project of the Ford Foundation, *A Time to Choose: America's Energy Future* (Cambridge, MA, Ballinger, 1974).

England, Richard W. and Eric P. Mitchell, "Federal Regulation and Environmental Impact of the U.S. Nuclear Power Industry, 1974–1984," 30 *Natural Resources Journal* 537 (1990).

EPA, "New Source Review: Report to the President" (June 2002).

EPA, "Wisconsin Electric Power Company (WEPCO) Clean Air Act Civil Settlement" (April 2003).

EPA, "Allowance Markets Assessment: A Closer Look at the Two Biggest Price Changes in the Federal SO_2 and NO_X Allowance Markets," White Paper (April 23, 2009).

EPA, "Acid Rain and Related Programs; 2009 Emission, Compliance, and Market Analyses" (September 2010).

EPA, "NOx Reductions Under Phase II of the Acid Rain Program," at http://www.epa.gov/airmarkets/progsregs/arp/reductions.html (last visited May 23, 2011).

EPRI, "Prospects for Boom/Bust in the U.S. Electric Power Industry" (December 2000).

EPRI, "Power System Dynamics Tutorial" (July 2009).

Eto, Joseph, "The Past, Present, and Future of U.S. Utility Demand-Side Management Programs," Lawrence Berkeley National Laboratory, LBNL-39931 (December 1996).

Eubanks II, William S., "The Clean Air Act's New Source Review Program: Beneficial to Public Health or Merely a Smoke-And-Mirrors Scheme?" 29 *Journal of Land, Resources & Environmental Law* 361 (2009).

Evans, David A., et al., "Modeling the Effects of Changes in New Source Review on National SO2 and NOX Emissions from Electricity-Generating Units," Resources for the Future, DP 07–01 (March 2007).

Evans, Joanne and Richard Green, "Why Did British Electricity Prices Fall after 1998?" Working Paper (July 2005).

Eynon, Robert, Thomas Leckey, and Douglas Hale, "The Electric Transmission Network: A Multi-Region Analysis," in EIA, *Issues in Midterm Analysis and Forecasting*, 2000.

Fabrizio, Kira M., Nancy L. Rose, and Catherine Wolfram, "Do Markets Reduce Costs? Assessing the Impact of Regulatory Restructuring on U.S. Electric Generation Efficiency," *American Economic Review* 97 (September, 2007): 1250–77.

Fagan, Mark L., "Measuring and Explaining Electricity Price Changes in Restructured States," Regulatory Policy Program Working Paper RPP-2006-02, Harvard (2006).

Fairman, James F. and John C. Scott, "Transmission, Power Pools, and Competition in the Electric Utility Industry," 28 *Hastings Law Journal* 1159 (May 1977).

Fanelli, Daniele, "Negative Results are Disappearing from Most Disciplines and Countries," *Scientometrics* 90 (2012): 891–904.

Fanelli, Daniele, "Positive' Results Increase Down the Hierarchy of the Sciences," *PLoS One* 5 (April 2010).

Farmer, R.G. and E.H. Allen, "Power System Dynamic Performance Advancement From History of North American Blackouts," IEEE PSCE (2006).

Farrell, Joseph and Paul Klemperer, "Coordination and Lock-In: Competition with Switching Costs and Network Effects," in Mark Armstrong and Robert Porter, eds., *Handbook of Industrial Organization, Volume 3* (Amsterdam, North-Holland, 2007): 1967–2143.

Faruqui, Ahmad, Hung-po Chao, Vic Niemeyer, Jeremy Platt, and Karl Stahlkopf, "Analyzing California's Power Crisis," *The Energy Journal* 22 (2001): 29–52.

FBR Capital Markets, "Coal Retirements in Perspective – Quantifying the Upcoming EPA Rules" (December 13, 2010).

Felder, Frank A., "Incorporating Resource Dynamics to Determine Generation Adequacy Levels in Restructured Bulk Power Systems," *KIEE International Transactions on PE* 4 (2004): 100–05.

Fellmeth, Robert C., "Plunging into Darkness: Energy Deregulation Collides with Scarcity," 33 *Loyola University Chicago Law Journal* 833 (2002).

FERC, "Regulating Independent Power Producers: A Policy Analysis" (October 13, 1987).

FERC, Office of Electric Power Regulation, "Power Pooling in the United States" (December 1981).

FERC, Staff, "Report on the Causes of Wholesale Electric Pricing Abnormalities in the Midwest during June 1998" (September 22, 1998).

FERC, Staff, "Investigation of Bulk Power Markets: ERCOT (Texas)" (November 1, 2000).

FERC, Staff, "Report to the Federal Energy Regulatory Commission on Northwest Power Markets in November and December 2000" (February 1, 2001).

FERC, Staff, "Report to the Federal Energy Regulatory Commission on Western Markets and the Causes of the Summer 2000 Price Abnormalities – Part 1" (November 1, 2000).

FERC, Staff, "Initial Report on Company-Specific Separate Proceedings and Generic Reevaluations; Published Natural Gas Price Data; and Enron Trading Strategies," Docket No. PA02-2-000 (August 2002).

FERC, Staff, "Final Report on Price Manipulation in Western Markets," Docket No. PA02-2-000 (March 2003).

First, Harry, "Regulated Deregulation: The New York Experience in Electric Utility Deregulation," 33 *Loyola University Chicago Law Journal* 911 (Summer 2002).

Fischel, William, "Why Are There NIMBYs?" *Land Economics* 77 (February 2001): 144–52.

Fisher, Alan, Frederick Johnson, and Robert Lande, "Price Effects of Horizontal Mergers," 77 *California Law Review* 777 (1989).

FitchRatings, "Corporates: Energy Future Holdings Corp" (April 27, 2009).

Fleisher, Jared, "ERCOT's Jurisdictional Status: A Legal History and Contemporary Appraisal," 3 *Texas Journal of Oil, Gas, and Energy Law* 1 (2008).

Flowers, Marilyn, "Rent Seeking and Rent Dissipation: A Critical View," *Cato Journal* 7 (Fall 1987): 431–40.

Fox, Loren, *Enron: The Rise and Fall* (Hoboken, John Wiley & Sons, 2003).

Frank, Sue and Gregory Lewis, "Government Employees: Working Hard or Hardly Working," *American Review of Public Administration* 34 (March 2004): 36–51.

Frayer, Julia, Amr Ibrahim, Serkan Bahceci, and Sanela Pecenkovic, "A Comparative Analysis of Actual Locational Marginal Prices in the PJM Market and Estimated Short-Run Marginal Costs: 2003–2006" (January 31, 2007).

Fremeth, Adam and Guy Holburn, "Information Asymmetries and Regulatory Decision Costs: Evidence From Electric Utility Rate Reviews 1980–2000," *Journal of Law, Economics and Organization* 28 (Spring 2012): 127–62.

Gabaix, Xavier and David Laibson, "Shrouded Attributes, Consumer Myopia, and Information Suppression in Competitive Markets," *Quarterly Journal of Economics* 121 (May 2006): 505–40.

GAO, "Electric Powerplant Cancellations and Delays," Report to the Congress (December 8, 1980).

GAO, "Electricity Supply: The Effect of Competitive Power Purchases Are Not Yet Certain" (August 23, 1990).

GAO, *Older Plants' Impact on Reliability and Air Quality* (Washington, DC, GPO, 1990).

GAO, *Electricity Supply: Regulating Utility Holding Companies in a Changing Electric Industry* (Washington, DC, GPO, 1992).

GAO, "No Evidence That Communications Between the FERC Chairman and the Chairman of Enron Corporation Violated Criminal Statutes or Ethics Regulations," letter to Senator Joseph I. Lieberman, GAO-01-1020R (April 16, 2001).

GAO, *Energy Markets: Concerted Actions Needed by FERC to Confront Challenges That Impede Effective Oversight* (Washington, DC, GPO, 2002).

Geller, Howard and Sophie Attali, *The Experience With Energy Efficiency Policies and Programmes in IEA Countries* (Paris, International Energy Agency, 2005).

Gerber, Alan and Neil Malhotra, "Do Statistical Reporting Standards Affect What Is Published? Publication Bias in Two Leading Political Science Journals," *Quarterly Journal of Political Science* 3 (2008): 313–26.

Gerking, Shelby and Stephen Hamilton, "What Explains the Increased Utilization of Powder River Basin Coal in Electric Power Generation," *American Journal of Agricultural Economics* 90 (November 2008): 933–50.

Gifford, Daniel, "The New Deal Regulatory Model: A History of Criticisms and Refinements," 68 *Minnesota Law Review* 299 (1993).

Gilbert, Richard, Edward Kahn, and Matthew White, "Coordination in the Wholesale Market: Where Does It Work?" *Electricity Journal* 6 (October 1993): 51–59.

Gillan, Stuart L. and John D. Martin, *"Financial Engineering, Corporate Governance, and the Collapse of Enron,"* University of Delaware College of Business and Economics, Center for Corporate Governance (2002).

Gilligan, Donald D., "Energy Efficiency Program Planning Workbook," US DOE, EERE (December 2002).

Gillingham, Kenneth, Richard G. Newell, and Karen Palmer, "Retrospective Examination of Demand-Side Energy Efficiency Policies," Resources For the Future, DP 04–19 REV (September 2004).

Gilsdorf, Keith, "Vertical Integration Efficiencies and Electric Utilities: A Cost Complementarity Perspective," *Quarterly Review of Economics and Finance* 34 (Fall 1994): 261–82.

Glicksman, Robert and Christopher H. Schroeder, "EPA and the Courts: Twenty Years of Law and Politics," 54 *Law and Contemporary Problems* 249 (1991).

Global Energy Decisions, "Putting Competitive Power Markets to the Test, The Benefits of Competition in America's Electric Grid: Cost Savings and Operating Efficiencies" (July 2005).

Goldman, Charles, Joseph Eto, and Galen Barbose, "California Customer Load Reductions during the Electricity Crisis: Did They Help to Keep the Lights On?" Lawrence Berkeley National Laboratory, LBNL-49733 (2002).

Graham, John, Paul Noe, and Elizabeth Branch, "Managing the Regulatory State: The Experience of the Bush Administration," 33 *Fordham Urban Law Journal* 101 (2006).

Grainer, John and Stan Lee, "Identification, Definition and Evaluation of Potential Impacts Facing the U.S. Electric Utility Industry Over the Next Decade," Report for Los Alamos National Laboratory, LA-SUB – 94–83 (November 26, 1994).

Granovetter, Mark and Patrick McGuire, "The Making of an Industry: Electricity in the United States," in Michel Callon, ed., *The Laws of the Markets* (London, Blackwell Publishers, 1988).

Green, Richard and David Newbery, "Competition in the British Electricity Spot Market," *Journal of Political Economy* 100 (1992): 929–53.

Grossback, Lawrence, Sean Nicholson-Crotty, and David Peterson, "Ideology and Learning in Policy Diffusion," *American Politics Research* 31 (2003): 1–25.

Guber, Deborah Lynn, "Up and Down With Ecology Revisited: The Stability of Public Attitudes Towards Environmental Spending, 1973–1998," 33rd Annual Meeting of the Northeast Political Science Association, Philadelphia, Pennsylvania (November 8–10, 2001).

Guber, Deborah Lynn, "Voting Preferences and the Environment in the American Electorate," *Society and Natural Resources* (2001): 455–69.

Hadsell, Lester and Hany A. Shawky, "Efficiency and Profit in the NYISO Transmission Congestion Contract Market," *Electricity Journal* 30 (November 2009): 1–11.

Hamilton, Walton, "Affectation with Public Interest," 39 *Yale Law Journal* 1089 (1930).

Hanger, John, "Reliability-Only Dispatch: Protecting Lives & Human Health While Ensuring System Reliability," Clean Air Task Force (2011).

Harvey, Scott and William Hogan, "On the Exercise of Market Power Through Strategic Withholding In California," LECG (April 24, 2001).

Harvey, Scott and William Hogan, "Identifying the Exercise of Market Power In California," LECG (December 28, 2001).

Harvey, Scott and William Hogan, "Market Power and Market Simulations," LECG (July 17, 2002).

Harvey, Scott, Bruce McConihe, and Susan Pope, "Analysis of the Impact of Coordinated Electricity Markets on Consumer Electricity Charges," LECG (November 20, 2006).

Hathaway, Oona, "Path Dependence in the Law: The Course and Pattern of Legal Change in a Common Law System," 86 *Iowa Law Review* 101 (2001).

Hausman, Catherine, "Corporate Incentives and Nuclear Safety," EI @ Hass Working Paper 223R (November 2011).

Hausman, Ezra and Richard Tabors, "The Role of Demand Underscheduling in the California Energy Crisis," Proceedings of the 37th Hawaii International Conference on System Sciences (2004).

Hausman, William J. and John L. Neufeld, "The Structure and Profitability of the US Electric Utility Industry at the Turn of the Century," *Business History* 32 (1990): 225–43.

Hausman, William J. and John L. Neufeld, "The Market for Capital and the Origins of State Regulation of Electric Utilities in the United States," *Journal of Economic History* 62 (December 2002): 1050–73.

Hausman, William J. and John L. Neufeld, "The Economics of Electricity Networks and the Evolution of the U.S. Electric Utility Industry, 1882–1935," *Business and Economic History On-line* 2 (2004): 1–26.

Hayashi, Paul M., James Yeoung-Jia Goo, and William Chamberlain, "Vertical Economies: The Case of U.S. Electric Utility Industry, 1983–87," *Southern Economic Journal* 63 (1997): 710.

Hegedus, Mark, "Points Well-Taken: Comments on Professor Peter Carstensen's Paper 'Creating Workably Competitive Wholesale Markets in Energy," 1 *Environmental & Energy Law & Policy Journal* 145 (2006).

Henderson, J. Stephen, "Cost Estimation for Vertically Integrated Firms: The Cost of Electricity," in M.A. Crew, ed., *Analyzing the Impact of Regulatory Change in Public Utilities* (Lexington, Lexington Books, 1984).

Hendry, David, "Applied Econometrics Without Sinning," *Journal of Economic Surveys* 16 (2002): 591–604.

Heutel, Garth, "Plant Vintages, Grandfathering, and Environmental Policy," *Journal of Environmental Economics and Management* 61 (2011): 36–51.

Hey, Sonia and Edward Rubin, "A Centurial History of Technological Change and Learning Curves for Pulverized Coal-Fired Utility Boilers," *Energy* 32 (2007): 1996–2005.

Hillstrom, Kevin, *U.S. Environmental Policy and Politics: A Documentary History* (Washington, DC, CQ Press, 2010).

Hines, James, "Three Sides of Harberger Triangles," *Journal of Economic Perspectives* 13 (Spring 1999): 167–88.

Hines, Paul, A Decentralized Approach to Reducing the Social Costs of Cascading Failures, (Ph.D. Diss., Carnegie Mellon, August 2007).

Hines, Paul, Jay Apt, and Sarosh Talukdar, "Large Blackouts in North America: Historical Trends and Policy Implications," CEIC Working Paper 09–01 (2009).

Hirsh, Richard F., *Power Loss: The Origins of Deregulation and Restructuring in the American Electric Utility System* (Cambridge, MA, MIT Press, 1999).

Hirst, Eric, "U.S. Transmission Capacity: Present Status and Future Prospects," prepared for the EEI and DOE (August 2004).

Hirst, Eric and Brendan Kirby, "Unbundling Generation and Transmission Services for Competitive Electricity Markets," Oak Ridge National Laboratory for NRRI (January 1998).

Hirst, Eric and Brendan Kirby, "Transmission Planning and the Need for New Capacity," in DOE, *National Transmission Grid Study: Issue Papers* (May 2002).

Hogan, William, "Contract Networks for Electric Power Transmission," *Journal of Regulatory Economics* 4 (1992): 211–42.

Hogan, William, "Electric Transmission: A New Model for Old Principles," *Electricity Journal* 6 (March 1993): 18–29.

Hogan, William, "A Wholesale Pool Spot Market Must Be Administered by the Independent System Operator: Avoiding the Separation Fallacy," *Electricity Journal* 8 (December 1995): 26–37.

Hogan, William, "Getting the Prices Right in PJM: Analysis and Summary: April 1998 through March 1999," *The First Anniversary of Full Locational Pricing*, John F. Kennedy School of Government, Harvard University (1999).

Hogan, William, "Electricity Market Restructuring: Reforms of Reforms," paper presented at the 20th Annual Conference, Center for Research in Regulated Industries (May 25, 2001).

Hogan, William, Juan Rosellón, and Ingo Vogelsang, "Toward a Combined Merchant-Regulatory Mechanism for Electricity Transmission Expansion," *Journal of Regulatory Economics* 38 (2010): 113–43.

Hoover, Kevin and Stephen Perez, "Three Attitudes Toward Data Mining," *Journal of Economic Methodology* 7 (2000): 195–210.

Hortacsu, Ali, Seyed Madanizadeh, and Steven Puller, "Power to Choose: An Analysis of Choice Frictions in the Residential Electricity Market," Working Paper (April 2012).

Hortacsu, Ali and Steven Puller, "Understanding Strategic Bidding in Multi-Unit Auctions: A Case Study of the Texas Electricity Spot Market," *Rand Journal of Economics* 39 (Spring 2008): 86–114.

Hovenkamp, Herbert, "Regulatory Conflict in the Gilded Age: Federalism and the Railroad Problem," 97 *Yale Law Journal* 1017 (1988).

Howarth, Richard B., "Against High Interest Rates," Rensselaer Polytechnic Institute, Department of Economics, Working Paper No. 0404 (March 2004).

Howes, John, "The Politics of Electric Power Deregulation," *Regulation* (Winter 1992): 17–20.

Hsu, Shi-Ling, "The Real Problem With New Source Review," 36 *Environmental Law Reporter* 10095 (2006).

Hubbell, Bryan, Richard Crune, Dale Evars, and Jeff Cohen, "Regulation and Progress under the 1990 Clean Air Act Amendments," *Review of Environmental Economics and Policy* 4 (2010): 122–38.

Huettner, David A. and John H. Landon, "Electric Utilities: Scale Economies and Diseconomies." *Southern Economic Journal* 44 (1977): 883–912.

Humphrey, George and Thomas J. Perich, "State of the Art: An Analysis of Portfolio Power Project Financing," *Project Finance Magazine – Power Report Supplement* (September 2001).

Hyman, Leonard, "A Financial Postmortem: Ten Years of Electricity Restructuring," *Public Utilities Fortnightly* (November 15, 2003): 10–15.

ICF, "Coal-Fired Electric Generation Unit Retirement Analysis," Presented to the INGAA (May 18, 2010).

IEEE PES CAMS Task Force, "Initial Review of Methods for Cascading Failure Analysis in Electric Power Transmission Systems," IEEE Power Engineering Society General Meeting, Pittsburgh, PA (July 2008).

Investor Responsibility Research Center, "Survey of Non-Utility Electric Power Producers," OTA (July 11, 1984).

Ishii, Jun, "Technology Adoption and Regulatory Regimes: Gas Turbine Electricity Generators from 1980 to 2001," CSEM WP 128 (March 2004).

Ishii, Jun, "From Investor-owned Utility to Independent Power Producer," CSEM, WP 108 (January 2006).

Isser, Steve, *The Economics and Politics of the United States Oil Industry, 1920–1990: Profits, Populism, and Petroleum* (New York, Garland Publishing, 1996).

Isser, Steve, "Electricity Deregulation: Kilowatts for Nothing and Your BTUs for Free," *Review of Policy Research* 20 (2004): 217–36.

Itron, "Assessment of the Feasible and Achievable Levels of Electricity Savings from Investor Owned Utilities in Texas: 2009–2018," submitted to the PUCT (December 23, 2008).

Jaber, Makram B., "Utility Settlements in New Source Review Lawsuits," 18 *Natural Resources & Environment* 22 (Winter 2004).

Jacobsen, Grant, "Do Economic Conditions Influence Environmental Policy? Evidence from the U.S. Senate," *Economic Letters* 120 (2013): 167–70.

Jacobsen, Mark and Azeem Shaikh, "Electricity Regulation in California and Input Market Distortions," Stanford Institute for Economic Policy Research, SIEPR Discussion Paper 03-1 (2004).

Jacobson, Charles, "Expecting the Unexpected: Networks, Markets, and the Failure of Electric Utility Restructuring in California," *Business and Economic History On-line* 2 (2004): 1–41.

Jandik, Tomas and Anil Makhija, "Can Diversification Create Value? Evidence from the Electric Utility Industry," *Financial Management* 34 (Spring 2005): 61–93.

Johns, Stephen M., "Ossification's Demise? An Empirical Analysis of EPA Rulemaking from 2001–2005," 38 *Environmental Law* 467 (2008).

Johnson, Erik, "Changing Issue Representation among Major United States Environmental Movement Organizations," *Rural Sociology* 71 (March 2006): 132–54.

Jones, P.M.S. and G. Woite, "Cost of Nuclear and Conventional Baseload Electricity Generation," *IAEA Bulletin* 3 (1990): 18–23.

Joskow, Paul L., The Determination of the Allowed Rate of Return in a Formal Regulatory Hearing," *Bell Journal of Economics* 3 (1972): 632–44.

Joskow, Paul L., "Pricing Decisions of Regulated Firms: A Behavioral Approach." *Bell Journal of Economics* 4 (Spring 1973): 118–140.

Joskow, Paul L., "Regulatory Failure, Regulatory Reform, and Structural Change in the Electrical Power Industry," *Brookings Papers: Microeconomics* (1989): 125–208.

Joskow, Paul L., "Why Do We Need Electricity Retailers? Or You Can Get It Cheaper Wholesale?" Revised Discussion Draft (February 13, 2000).

Joskow, Paul L., "California's Electricity Crisis," Harvard Energy Policy Group (September 28, 2001).

Joskow, Paul L., "The Difficult Transition to Competitive Electricity Markets in the U.S.," CEEPR (May 2003).

Joskow, Paul L., "Regulation and Deregulation after 25 Years: Lessons Learned for Research in Industrial Organization," *Review of Industrial Organization* 26 (2005): 169–93.

Joskow, Paul L., "Regulation of Natural Monopoly," in Mitchell Polinsky and Steven Shavell, eds., *Handbook of Law and Economics*, Volume 2 (Amsterdam, Elsevier, 2007): 1227–1348.

Joskow, Paul and Edward Kahn, "Identifying the Exercise of Market Power: Refining the Estimates" Mimeo (July 5, 2001).

Joskow, Paul and Edward Kahn, "A Quantitative Analysis of Pricing Behavior in California's Wholesale Electricity Market during Summer 2000," *Energy Journal* 23 (2002): 1–35.

Joskow, Paul and Nancy Rose, "The Effects of Technological Change, Experience, and Environmental Regulation on the Construction Cost of Coal-Burning Generating Units," *Rand Journal of Economics* 16 (Spring 1985): 1–17.

Joskow, Paul and Richard Schmalansee, *Markets for Power: An Analysis of Electrical Utility Deregulation* (Cambridge, MA, MIT Press, 1983).

Joskow, Paul and Richard Schmalansee, "The Political Economy of Market-Based Environmental Policy: The U.S. Acid Rain Program," *Journal of Law and Economics* 41 (April 1998): 37–83.

Joskow, Paul and Jean Tirole, "Transmission Rights and Market Power on Electric Power Networks," *RAND Journal of Economics* 31 (2000): 450–87.

Joskow, Paul and Jean Tirole, "Merchant Transmission Investment," *Journal of Industrial Economics* 53 (June 2005): 233–64.

Kahn, Alfred, *The Economics of Regulation: Principles and Institutions* (Hoboken, John Wiley & Sons, 1970).

Kahn, Edward, Steven Stoft, Chris Marnay, and Douglas Berman, "Contracts For Dispatchable Power: Economic Implications for the Competitive Bidding Market," LBNL (October 1990).

Kahn, Matthew and Matthew Kotchen, "Environmental Concern and the Business Cycle: The Chilling Effect of Recession," NBER, Working Paper 16241 (July 2010).

Kalt, Joseph and Mark Zupan. "Capture and Ideology in the Economic Theory of Politics." *American Economic Review* 74 (June 1984): 279–300.

Kandel, Eugene, Konstantin Kosenko, Randall Morck, and Yishay Yafeh, "Business Groups in the United States: A Revised History of Corporate Ownership, Pyramids and Regulation, 1930–1950," NBER Working Paper 19691 (December 2013).

Kaplan, Stan, "Electric Power Transmission: Background and Policy Issues," Congressional Research Service (April 14, 2009).

Kaserman, David L. and John W. Mayo, "The Measurement of Vertical Economies and the Efficient Structure of the Electric Utility Industry," *Journal of Industrial Economics* 39 (September 1991): 483–502.

Kehoe, Timothy J., T.N. Srinivasan and John Whalley, eds., *Frontiers in Applied General Equilibrium Modeling* (Cambridge, Cambridge University Press, 2005).

Kelley, Sean, Christo Leventis, and Arthur Weiss, "The Failure of Risk Management: A New Perspective on the California Electricity Market," Northwest University Research Paper (May 2001).

KEMA Consulting, "Analysis and Selection of Analytical Tools to Assess National-Interest Transmission Bottlenecks," for DOE, (March 2003).

Ketzback, Thor, "The Evolution of Offsets and the Dawn of Emissions Trading Markets" (LLM Thesis, DePaul College of Law, May 1997).

Kim, E. Han, Adair Morse, and Luigi Zingales, "What Has Mattered to Economics Since 1970," *Journal of Economic Perspectives* 20 (Fall 2006): 189–202.

Klein, Joel I., "Making the Transition from Regulation to Competition: Thinking About Merger Policy During the Process of Electric Power Restructuring," FERC Distinguished Speaker Series (January 21, 1998).

Kleit, Andrew and James Reitzes, "The Effectiveness of FERC's Transmission Policy: Is Transmission Used Efficiently and When Is It Scarce?" *Journal of Regulatory Economics* 34 (2008): 1–26.

Kleit, Andrew, Anastasia Shcherbakova, and Xu Chen, "Restructuring and the Retail Residential Market for Power in Pennsylvania," *Energy Policy* 46 (2012): 443–51.

Klemperer, Paul and Margaret Meyer, "Supply Function Equilibria in Oligopoly under Uncertainty," *Econometrica* 57 (1989): 1243–77.

Knittel, Christopher, "The Adoption of State Electricity Regulation: The Role Of Interest Groups," *Journal of Industrial Economics* 54 (206): 201–22.

Kramer, Bruce M., "The 1970 Clean Air Amendments: Federalism in Action or Inaction," 6 *Texas Tech Law Review* 47 (1974).

Kreps, David, *Game Theory and Economic Modeling* (Oxford, Oxford University Press, 1990).

Kreuger, Anne, "The Political Economy of the Rent-Seeking Society," *American Economic Review* 64 (June 1974): 291–303.

Kushler, Martin, Dan York, and Patti Witte, "Five Years In: An Examination of the First Half-Decade of Public Benefits Energy Efficiency Policies," ACEEE (April 2004).

Kwoka, John, "Restructuring the U.S. Electric Power Sector: A Review of Recent Studies," *Review of Industrial Organization* 32 (2008): 165–96.

Kwoka, John, Sanem Ozturk, and Michael Pollitt, "Divestiture Policy and Operating Efficiency in U.S. Electric Power Distribution," EPRG Working Paper 0819 (July 2008).

Kwoka, John and Michael Pollitt, "Industry Restructuring, Mergers, and Efficiency: Evidence from Electric Power," CWPE (April 2007).

Ladd, Everett and Karlyn Bowman, "Public Opinion on the Environment," *Resources* 123 (1996): 5–7.

Laband, David and Robert Tollison, "Dry Holes in Economic Research," *Kyklos* 56 (2003): 161–74.

Lake, Jennifer, Leah Pease, Ginny Case, and Jennifer Sutton-Hetzel, "Energy Crisis in California: Options for the Future," Pepperdine School of Public Policy (March 27, 2001).

Lamoreaux, Naomi, Daniel Raff, and Peter Temin, "New Economic Approaches to the Study of Business History," *Business and Economic History* 26 (Fall 1997): 57–79.

Lange, Ian and Allen S. Bellas, "The 1990 Clean Air Act and the Implicit Price of Sulfur in Coal," *The B.E. Journal of Economic Analysis & Policy* 7 (2007).

Lash, Joseph, *Dealers and Dreamers: A New Look at the New Deal* (New York, Doubleday, 1988).

Lasser, William, *Benjamin V. Cohen, Architect of the New Deal* (New Haven, Yale University Press, 2002).

Law, Stephen M., "Assessing Evidence for the Averch-Johnson-Wellisz Effect for Regulated Utilities," Atlantic Canada Economics Association Papers and Proceedings (2008).

LCG Consulting, "Modeling Competitive Energy Markets In California: An Analysis of Restructuring," for the CEC (October 11, 1996).

Leamer, Edward, "Let's Take the Con Out of Econometrics," *American Economic Review* 73 (March 1983): 31–43.

Ledgerwood, Shaun and Dan Harris, "A Comparison of Anti-Manipulation Rules in U.S. and EU Electricity and Natural Gas Markets: A Proposal for a Common Standard," 33 *Energy Law Journal* 1 (2012).

Lenard, Thomas, "Getting the Transcos Right," *Electricity Journal* 11 (November 1998): 47–52.

Lesser, Jonathan A., "The Used and Useful Test: Implications for a Restructured Electricity Industry," 23 *Energy Law Journal* 349 (2002).

Lesser, Jonathan A., "Bad Economics, by Any Other Name, is Still Bad: APPA's Analysis of Wholesale Electric Competition is Flawed," Briefing Paper No. 2009-08-01 (August 2009).

Lindblom, Charles, "The Science of 'Muddling Through'," *Public Administration Review* 19 (1959): 79–88.

Lindblom, Charles, "Still Muddling, Not Yet Through," *Public Administration Review* 39 (1979): 517–26.

Lipsey, Richard G., "Reflections on the General Theory of Second Best at Its Golden Jubilee," *International Tax and Public Finance* 14 (2007): 349–64.

Lipsey, Richard G. and Kevin Lancaster, "The General Theory of Second Best," *Review of Economic Studies* 24 (1956): 11–32.

Littlechild, Stephen "Merchant and Regulated Transmission: Theory, Evidence and Policy," *Journal of Regulatory Economics* 42 (2012): 308–35.

Liu, Xin, "The U.S. Environmental Protection Agency: A Historical Perspective on Its Role in Environmental Protection," (Ph.D Diss., Ludwig-Maximilians-Universität, 2010).

Lo, Andrew W. and Mark T. Mueller, "WARNING: Physics Envy May Be Hazardous to Your Wealth!" Sloan School of Management, MIT, unpublished working paper (March 19, 2010).

Lockyer, Bill, "Attorney General's Energy White Paper: A Law Enforcement Perspective on the California Energy Crisis" (April 2004), at http://oag.ca.gov/sites/all/files/agweb/pdfs/publications/energywhitepaper.pdf (last visited November 20, 2014).

Lovins, Amory, "Energy Strategy: The Road Not Taken?" *Foreign Affairs* 55 (October 1976): 65–96.

Lyon, Thomas and John Mayo, "Regulatory Opportunism and Investment Behavior: Evidence From the U.S. Electric Utility Industry," *Rand Journal of Economics* 36 (2005): 628–44.

Macedonia, Jennifer, Joe Kruger, Lourdes Long, and Meghan McGuinness, "Environmental Regulation and Electric System Reliability," Staff Report of the Bipartisan Policy Center, June 2011.

Mahoney, James, "Path Dependence in Historical Sociology," *Theory and Society* 29 (2000): 507–48.

Mahoney, Paul, "The Public Utility Pyramids," 41 *Journal of Legal Studies* 37 (2012).

Mansur, Eric, "Measuring Welfare in Restructured Electricity Markets," NBER Working Paper No. 13509 (October 2007).

Mansur, Eric and Matthew White, "Market Organization and Efficiency in Electricity Markets," Yale School of Management Working Paper (June 30, 2009).

Mansur, Erin, "Upstream Competition and Vertical Integration in Electricity Markets," 50 *Journal of Law and Economics* 125 (February 2007).

McAfee, Preston and John McMillan, "Auctions and Bidding," *Journal of Economic Literature* 25 (June 1987): 699–738.

McAfee, Preston and John McMillan, "Competition and Game Theory," *Journal of Marketing Research* 33 (August 1996): 263–67.

McArthur, John Burritt, "The Irreconcilable Differences Between FERC's Natural Gas and Electricity Stranded Cost Treatments," 46 *Buffalo Law Review* 71 (Winter 1998).

McCabe, Mark J., "Principals, Agents, and the Learning Curve: The Case of Steam-Electric Power Plant Design and Construction," *Journal of Industrial Economics* 44 (December 1996): 360–61.

McChesney, Fred, "Rent Extraction and Rent Creation in the Economic Theory of Regulation," *Journal of Legal Studies* 16 (1987): 101–09.

McClosky, Deirde, "The Good Old Coase Theorem and the Good Old Chicago School: A Comment on Zerbe and Medema," in Steven G. Medema, ed., *Coasean Economics* (Boston, Kluwer, 1992).

McCloskey, Donald, "Does the Past Have Use Economics?" *Journal of Economic History* (1976): 434–61.

McCubbins, Mathew, Rogers Noll, and Barry Weingast, "Administrative Procedures as Instruments of Political Control," *Journal of Law, Economics and Organization* 3 (1987): 243–77.

McCubbins, Mathew, Rogers Noll, and Barry Weingast, "Structure and Process, Politics and Policy: Administrative Arrangements And The Political Control Of Agencies," 75 *Virginia Law Review* 431 (1989).

McCubbins, Mathew and Thomas Schwartz, "Congressional Oversight Overlooked: Police Patrols versus Fire Alarms," *American Journal Political Science* 28 (1984): 165–79.

McCullough, B.D., "Replication Section: Introduction," *Journal of Economic and Social Measurement* 31 (2006): 103–05.

McGraw, Thomas, "Regulation in America: A Review Article," *Business History Review* 49 (1975): 159–83.

McGraw, Thomas, *Prophets of Regulation: Charles Francis Adams, Louis D. Brandeis, James M. Landis, Alfred E. Kahn* (Cambridge, MA, Harvard University Press, 1984).

McKitrick, Ross, "Why Did US Air Pollution Decline after 1970?" *Empirical Economics* 33 (2006): 491–513.

McNerney, James, Jessika Trancik, and J. Doyne Farmer, "Historical Costs of Coal-Fired Electricity and Implications for the Future," *Energy Policy* 39 (2011): 3042–54.

Meadows, Donela H., Dennis L. Meadows, Jorgen Randers, and William W. Behrens III, *The Limits to Growth: A Report for the Club of Rome's Project on the Predicament of Mankind* (New York, Universe Books, 1972).

Meese, Alan J., "Reframing Antitrust in Light of Scientific Revolution: Accounting for Transaction Costs in Rule of Reason Analysis," 62 *Hastings Law Journal* 466 (2010).

Melnick, R. Shep, *Regulation and the Courts: The Case of the Clean Air Act* (Washington, DC, Brookings Institute, 1983).

Merrill, Thomas, "Article III, Agency Adjudication, and the Origins of the Appellate Review Model of Administrative Law," 111 *Columbia Law Review* 939 (June 2011).

Meyer, David H. and Richard Sedano, "Transmission Siting and Permitting," in DOE, *National Transmission Grid Study: Issue Papers* (May 2002).

Meyer, Rolan, "Benchmarking Economies of Vertical Integration in U.S. Electricity Supply: An Application of DEA," Jacobs University Bremen (October 17, 2010).

Meyers, Stephen, James McMahon, and Michael McNeil, "Realized and Prospective Impacts of U.S. Energy Efficiency Standards for Residential Appliances: 2004 Update," LBNL (May 2005).

Miles, Thomas and Cass Sunstein, "The Real World of Arbitrariness Review," 75 *University of Chicago Law Review* 761 (2008).

Milgrom, Paul, "Auctions and Bidding: A Primer," *Journal of Economic Perspectives* 3 (Summer 1989): 3–22.

Milgrom, Paul, "What the Seller Won't Tell You: Persuasion and Disclosure in Markets," *Journal of Economic Perspectives* 22 (Spring 2008): 115–31.

Miller, John, "A Needed Reform of the Organization and Regulation of the Interstate Electric Power Industry," 38 *Fordham Law Review* 635 (1970).

MJ Bradley & Associates and Analysis Group, "Ensuring a Clean, Modern Electric Generating Fleet While Maintaining Electric System Reliability," prepared for the Clean Energy Group (August 2010).

Monitoring Analytics, LLC, *State of the Market Report for PJM* (various years).

Montero, Juan-Pablo, "Voluntary Compliance with Market-Based Environmental Policy: Evidence from the U.S. Acid Rain Program," *Journal of Political Economy* 107 (1999): 999–1005.

Moody's Investment Service, "The Importance of Being Economic: Credit Risks of US Merchant Power Plants" (May 1999).

Mooz, William, "Cost Analysis of Light Water Reactor Power Plants," Rand for the Department of Energy, R-2304-DOE (June 1978).

Morey, Edward R., "Confuser Surplus," *American Economic Review* 74 (March 1984): 163–73.

Munster, Christophe, *Divestiture and Operating Efficiency of U.S. Nuclear Power Plants* (MS Thesis, Humboldt University, January 2011).

Nadel, Steve and David Goldstein, "Appliance and Equipment Efficiency Standards: History, Impacts, Current Status, and Future Directions," ACEEE (1996).

Napolitano, Sam, et al., "The U.S. Acid Rain Program: Key Insights from the Design, Operation, and Assessment of a Cap-and-Trade Program," *Electricity Journal* 20 (2007): 47–58.

Narula, Ram, Martin Massy, and Jyoti Singh, "Design Considerations for Combined Cycle Plants for the Deregulated Market – An EPC Contractor's Perspective," ASME Turbo Expo (2002).

Nash, Jonathan and Richard Revesz, "Grandfathering and Environmental Regulation: the Law and Economics of New Source Review," 101 *Northwestern University Law Review* 1677 (2007).

Nauman, Ilias and Robert Reynolds, "Changing Conduct with Changing Demand: Evidence of Coordination among Suppliers of Electricity in California in 2000," Brattle Group (2007).

Navarro, Peter, "The 1977 Clean Air Act Amendments: Energy, Environmental, Economic, and Distributional Impacts," *Public Policy* 29 (1981): 121–46.

Neal, Larry, "A Shocking View of Economic History," *Journal of Economic History* 60 (June 2000): 317–34.

Nelson, Olof S. and Roger W. Sant, "Two IPP Points of View," *Public Utilities Fortnightly* (June 1, 1993).

Nelson, Robert H., "Environmental Religion: A Theological Critique," 55 *Case Western Reserve Law Review* 51 (2004).

NERA, "Potential Impacts of EPA Air, Coal Combustion Residuals, and Cooling Water Regulations," prepared for American Coalition for Clean Coal Electricity (September 2011).

NERC, "Generation & Transmission Reliability Planning Models Task Force Final Report on Methodology and Metrics" (December 8, 2010), at http://www.nerc.com/comm/PC/Reliability%20Assessment%20Subcommittee%20RAS%20DL/GTRPMTF_Meth_Metrics_Report_final_w%20_PC_approvals_revisions_12%2008%2010.pdf (last visited November 20, 2014).

NERC, *Long-Term Reliability Assessments* (various years).

Newbery, David, "Electricity Liberalisation in Britain: The Quest for a Satisfactory Wholesale Market Design," *Energy Journal* 26 (2005): 43–70.

Noll, Roger G. and Bruce M. Owen, eds., *The Political Economy of Deregulation: Interest Groups in the Regulatory Process* (Washington, DC, AEI, 1983).

North, Douglass, *Institutions, Institutional Change and Economic Performance* (Cambridge, Cambridge University Press, 1990).

North, Douglass, "Economic Performance Though Time," *American Economic Review* 84 (1994): 359–68.

Nostrand, James Van, "Constitutional Limitations on the Ability of States to Rehabilitate Their Failed Electric Utility Restructuring Plans," 31 *Seattle University Law Review* 593 (2008).

Nowell, Clifford and John Tschirhart, "The Public Utility Regulatory Act and Regulatory Behavior," *Journal of Regulatory Economics* 2 (1990): 21–36.

NPS Energy Management, "Alternative Models of Electric Power Deregulation," for EEI (May 1982).

Nwaeze, Emeka, "Public Utility Regulation in the U.S. and Asymmetric Return Responses to Positive and Negative Abnormal Earnings," *Multinational Finance Journal* 2 (1998): 269–93.

Nye, David, *When the Lights When Out: A History of Blackouts in America* (Cambridge, MA, MIT Press, 2010).

O'Donnell, Arthur J., *Soul of the Grid: A Cultural Biography of the California Independent System Operator* (Lincoln, I Universe, 2003).

Office of Technology Assessment, "Electric Power Wheeling and Dealing: Technological Considerations for Increasing Competition," OTA-E-409 (May 1989).

Olsen, Johan, "Garbage Cans, New Institutionalism, and the Study of Politics," *American Political Science Review* 95 (March 2001): 191–98.

Oren, Shmuel S., "Ensuring Generation Adequacy in Competitive Electricity Market," University of California Energy Institute, WP 007 (June 2003).

Oren, Shmuel S., et al., "Nodal Prices and Transmission Rights: A Critical Appraisal," *The Electricity Journal* 8 (April 1995): 24–35.

Ostrow, Ahira, "Process Preemption in Federal Siting Regimes," 48 *Harvard Journal on Legislation* 289 (2011).

Pace, Joe E. and John H. Landon, "Introducing Competition into the Electric Utility Industry: An Economic Appraisal," 3 *Energy Law Journal* 1 (1982).

Page, Scott, "Path Dependence," *Quarterly Journal of Political Science* 1 (2006): 87–115.

Pandey, Sanjay and Edmund Stazyk, "Antecedents and Correlates of Public Service Motivation," in James L. Perry and Annie Hondeghem, eds., *Motivation in Public Management: The Call of Public Service* (Oxford, Oxford University Press, 2008).

Park, Hyunsoo, *The Social Structure of Large Scale Blackouts: Changing Environment, Institutional Imbalance, and Unresponsive Organizations* (Ph.D. Diss., Rutgers University, October 2010).

Pashigian, Peter, "Environmental Regulation: Whose Self-Interests Are Being Protected?" *Economic Inquiry* 23 (October 1985): 551–84.

Peltzman, Sam, "Toward a More General Theory of Regulation," 19 *Journal of Law and Economics* 211 (1976).

Perez-Gonzalez, Francisco, "Organizational Form and Firm Performance: Evidence from the 'Death Sentence' Clause of the Public Utility Act of 1935" (April 2014).

Perino, Grischa, "Price Discrimination Based on Downstream Regulation: Evidence from the Market for SO2 Scrubbers," Centre for Competition Policy, Working Paper 10–9 (July 9, 2010).

Perloff, Jeffrey, Larry Karp, and Amos Golan, *Estimating Market Power and Strategies* (Cambridge, Cambridge University Press, 2007).

Pesendorfer, Wolfgang, "Behavioral Economics Comes of Age: A Review Essay on Advances in Behavioral Economics," *Journal of Economic Literature* 64 (September 2006): 712–21.

Pfeifenberger, Johannes, et al., "Review of PJM's Reliability Pricing Model (RPM)," Brattle Group for PJM (June 30, 2008).

Pfeifenberger, Johannes, et al., "Second Performance Assessment of PJM's Reliability Pricing Model," Prepared for PJM by the Brattle Group (August 26, 2011).

Pierce, Jr., Richard J., "The Regulatory Treatment of Mistakes in Retrospect: Canceled Plants and Excess Capacity," 132 *University of Pennsylvania Law Review* 497 (1984).

Pierce, Jr., Richard J., "A Proposal to Deregulate the Market For Bulk Power," 72 *Virginia Law Review* 1183 (October 1986).

Pierce, Jr., Richard J., "Public Utility Regulatory Takings: Should the Judiciary Attempt To Police the Political Institutions?," 77 *Georgetown Law Journal* 2031 (1989).

Pierson, Paul, "Increasing Returns, Path Dependence, and the Study of Politics," *American Political Science Review* 94 (2000): 251–67.

Pindyck, Robert, "Sunk Costs and Risk-Based Barriers to Entry," NBER Working Paper #14755 (2009).

PJM Market Monitoring Unit, *State of the Market Report* (various years).

Pollitt, G. M., *Ownership and Performance in Electric Utilities: The International Evidence on Privatization and Efficiency* (Oxford, Oxford University Press, 1995).

Polsby, Nelson W., "Where Do You Get Your Ideas?" *PS: Political Science and Politics* 26 (1993): 83–87.

Pope, Susan L., "California Electricity Price Spikes: An Update on the Facts," Harvard Electricity Policy Group (December 12, 2002).

Posner, Richard, "Theories of Economic Regulation," *Bell Journal of Economics* 5 (Autumn 1984): 335–58.

Posner, Richard, "Past-Dependency, Pragmatism, and Critique of History in Adjudication and Legal Scholarship," 67 *University of Chicago Law Review* 573 (2000).

Potomac Economics, *State of the Market Reports*, NYISO, ISO-NE, MISO, ERCOT (various years).

Potter, Scott, "After the Freeze: Issues Facing Some State Regulators as Electric Restructuring Transition Periods End," NRRI (September 2003).

Potts, Brian H., "Trading Grandfathered Air – A New, Simpler Approach," 31 *Harvard Environmental Law Review* 115 (2007).

Powell, Mark R., "The 1987 Revision of the NAAQS for Particulate Matter and the 1993 Decision Not to Revise the NAAQS for Ozone: Two Case Studies in EPA's Use of Science," Resources for the Future, Discussion Paper 97–07 (March 1997).

Priest, George, "The Origins of Utility Regulation and the 'Theories of Regulation' Debate," *Journal of Law and Economics* 36 (1993): 289–323.

Primeaux, Walter J., "The Monopoly Market in Electric Utilities," in Almarin Phillips, ed., *Promoting Competition in Regulated Markets* (Washington, DC, Brookings Institution, 1975).

Provost, Colin, Brian Gerber, and Mark Pickup, "Enforcement Dynamics in Federal Air Pollution Policy," Paper Presented at the Meeting of the European Consortium of Political Research, Pisa, Italy (September 6–8, 2007).

Public Citizen, "Blind Faith: How Deregulation and Enron's Influence over Government Looted Billions from Americans," Public Citizen's Critical Mass Energy and Environment Program (December 2001).

PUCT, *Electricity Pricing in Competitive Retail Markets in Texas*, Legislative Report (March 3, 2006).

PUCT, *The Scope of Competition in the Electric Industry in Texas* (various years).

PUCT, *Scope of Competition in Electric Markets in Texas* (various years).

Puller, Steven, "Pricing and Firm Conduct in California's Deregulated Electricity Market," *Review of Economics and Statistics* 89 (February 2007): 75–87.

Rao, Narasimha and Richard Tabors, "Transmission Markets: Stretching the Rules for Fun and Profit," *Electricity Journal* 13 (June 2000): 20–29.

Ray, Dennis and Bill Snyder, "Strategies to Address the Problem of Exiting Expertise in the Electric Power Industry," Proceedings of the 39th Hawaii International Conference on System Sciences (2006).

Raynolds, Ned and Richard Cowart, "The Contribution of Energy Efficiency to the Reliability of the U.S. Electric System," Alliance to Save Energy White Paper. Washington, DC (2000).

Reitze, Jr., Arnold W., "Overview and Critique: A Century of Air Pollution Control Law: What's Worked; What's Failed; What Might Work," 21 *Environmental Law* 1549 (1991).

Reitze, Jr., Arnold W., "The Legislative History of U.S. Air Pollution Control," 26 *Houston Law Review* 679 (1999).

Reitzes, James, Peter Fox-Penner, Adam Schumacher, and Daniel Gaynor, "Generation Cost Savings From Day 1 and Day 2 RTO Market Designs," Brattle Group, October 1, 2009.

Reitzes, James D., et al., "Review of PJM's Market Power Mitigation Practices in Comparison to Other Organized Electricity Markets," Brattle Group for PJM (September 14, 2007).

Rigby, Peter, "Merchant Power: Project Finance Criteria," *Standard and Poor's* Corporation 1999 Infrastructure Finance: Criteria and Commentary (October 1999).

Rigby, Peter, "Energy Merchant Turmoil," The Energy & Utilities Project (March 2004).

Rose, Kenneth and Venkata Bujimalla, "2002 Performance Review of Electric Power Markets," NRRI, conducted for Virginia State Corporation Commission (August 30, 2002).

Rose, Kenneth and Karl Meeusen, "2006 Performance Review of Electric Power Markets," Conducted for the Virginia State Corporation Commission (August 27, 2006).

Rossi, Jim, "Redeeming Judicial Review: The Hard Look Doctrine and Federal Regulatory Efforts to Restructure the Electricity Utility Industry," 1994 *Wisconsin Law Review* 763 (1994).

Rossi, Jim, "The Electric Deregulation Fiasco: Looking to Regulatory Federalism to Promote a Balance Between Markets and the Provision of Public Goods," 100 *Michigan Law Review* 1768 (2002).

Rossi, Jim, "Transmission Siting in Deregulated Wholesale Power Markets: Reimagining the Role of Courts in Resolving Federal-State Siting Impasses," 15 *Duke Environmental Law & Policy Forum* 315 (2005).

Rossi, Jim, "The Trojan Horse of Electric Power Transmission Line Siting Authority," 39 *Environmental Law* 1015 (2009).

Rubin, Edward, Sonia Yeh, David Hounshell, and Margaret Taylor, "Experience Curves for Power Plant Emission Control Technologies," *International Journal of Energy Technology and Policy* 2 (2004): 52–69.

Rubin, Edward, et al., "Integrated Environmental Modeling of Coal-Fired Power Systems," *Journal of Air & Waste Management Association* 47 (1997): 1180–88.

Rudkevich, Aleksandr, Max Duckworth, and Richard Rosen, "Modeling Electricity Pricing in a Deregulated Generation Industry: The Potential for Oligopoly Pricing in a Poolco," *Energy Journal* 19 (1998): 19–48.

Russell, Christopher, "Efficiency and Innovation In U.S. Manufacturing Energy Use," National Association of Manufacturers, Energy Efficiency Forum, Washington, DC (2005).

Russo, Michael, "Institutions, Exchange Relations, and the Emergence of New Fields: Regulatory Policies and Independent Power Production in America, 1978–1992," *Administrative Science Quarterly*, 46 (2001): 57–86.

Sala-I-Martin, Xavier, "I Just Ran Two Million Regressions," *American Economic Review* 87 (May 2007): 178–83.

Salop, Steven, "Question: What is the Real and Proper Antitrust Welfare Standard? Answer: The True Consumer Welfare Standard," 22 *Loyola Consumer Law Review* 336 (2010).

Salop, Steven and David Scheffman, "Raising Rivals' Cost," *American Economic Review* 73 (May 1983): 267–71.

Sant, Roger, "The Least-Cost Energy Strategy: Minimizing Consumer Costs Through Competition," Energy Productivity Center, Mellon Institute, Arlington, VA (1979).

Santa, Jr., Donald F. and Clifford Sikora, "Open Access and Transition Costs: Will the Electric Industry Transition Track the Natural Gas Industry Restructuring?" 15 *Energy Law Journal* 273 (Spring 1994).

Sanyal, Paroma and Laarni Bulan, "Regulatory Risk, Market Uncertainties, and Firm Financing Choices: Evidence from US Electricity Market Restructuring," *Quarterly Review of Economics and Finance* 51 (2011): 248–68.

Saravia, Celeste, "Speculative Trading and Market Performance: The Effect of Arbitrageurs on Efficiency and Market Power in the New York Electricity Market," CSEM working paper no. 121 (2003).

Scheffman, David and Mary Coleman, "Quantitative Analyses of Potential Competitive Effects From a Merger," 12 *George Mason Law Review* 319 (2003).

Scheiber, Harry, "The Road to Munn: Eminent Domain and the Concept of Public Purpose in the State Courts," *Perspectives in American History* 5 (1971): 329–402.

Schiller, Steven R., Charles A. Goldman, and Brian Henderson, "Public Benefit Charge Funded Performance Contracting Programs – Survey and Guidelines," Lawrence Berkeley National Laboratory (August 2000).

Schmalensee, Richard, *The Control of Natural Monopolies* (Lexington, Lexington Books, 1979).

Schumacher, E.F., *Small is Beautiful: Economics as If People Mattered* (London, Blond and Briggs, 1973).

Schweppe, Fred, Michael Caramanis, Richard Tabors, and Roger Bohn, *Spot Pricing of Electricity* (Boston, Kluwer, 1988).

Sergici, Sanem I., "Three Essays on U.S. Electricity Restructuring" (Ph.D. Diss., Northeastern University, January 2008).

Shabecoff, Philip, *A Fierce Green Fire, The American Environmental Movement*, rev. ed. (Washington, DC, Island Press, 2003).

Shahidehpour, Mohammad and Muwaffaq Alomoush, *Restructured Electrical Power Systems: Operation, Trading, and Volatility* (New York, Marcel Dekker, 1991).

Shiller, Robert, "From Efficient Markets Theory to Behavioral Finance," *Journal of Economic Perspectives* 17 (Winter 2003): 83–104.

Sidak, J. Gregory and Daniel Spulber, *Deregulatory Takings and the Regulatory Contract*, (Cambridge, Cambridge University Press, 1998).

Simshauser, Paul, "Vertical Integration, Credit Ratings and Retail Price Settings in Energy-Only Markets: Navigating the Resource Adequacy Problem," *Energy Policy* 38 (2010): 7427–41.

Sioshansi, Ramteen, Richard O'Neill, and Shmuel S. Oren, "Economic Consequences of Alternative Soution Methods for Centralized Unit Commitment in Day-Ahead Electricity Markets," *IEEE Transactions on Power Systems* 23 (2008): 344–52.

Sissine, Fred, "Energy Efficiency: Budget, Oil Conservation, and Electricity Conservation Issues," Congressional Research Service (August 22, 2005).

Smith, Vernon L., "Regulatory Reform in the Electric Power Industry," *Regulation* 19 (1996): 33–46.

Société Générale, "Investment in Power Generation: A Banker's Perspective," presentation, March 25, 2003, slide 10, at http://www.oecd-nea.org/ndd/investment/session2/deluze.pdf (last visited January 2, 2012).

Sotkiewicz, Paul and Lynne Holt, "Public Utility Commission Regulation and Cost-Effectiveness of Title IV: Lessons for CAIR," *Electricity Journal* 18 (October 2005): 68–80.

Spanos, Aris, "Revisiting Data Mining: 'Hunting' with or without a License," *Journal of Economic Methodology* 7 (2000): 231–64.

Spence, Michael, "Signaling in Retrospect and the Informational Structure of Markets," *American Economic Review* 92 (June 2002): 434–59.

Staudt, James, "Assumptions That Lead to Overestimation of the Cost of Regulations," Andover Technology Partners (October 31, 2011).

Steering Committee of Cities Served by Oncor & The Texas Coalition for Affordable Power, "The Story of ERCOT: The Grid Operator, Power Market & Prices Under Texas Electric Deregulation" (February 2011).

Stigler, George, "The Theory of Economic Regulation," *Bell Journal of Economics* 2 (1971): 3–21.

Stigler, George and Gary Becker, "De Gustibus Non Est Disputandum," *American Economic Review* 67 (March 1977): 76–90.

Stigler, George and Claire Friedland, "What Can Regulators Regulate? The Case of Electricity," 5 *Journal of Law and Economics* 1 (October 1962).

Stobaugh, Robert and Daniel Yergin, eds., *Energy Future: Report of the Energy Project at the Harvard Business School* (New York: Random House, 1979).

Stoft, Steven, "Analysis of the California WEPEX Applications to FERC," Lawrence Berkeley National Laboratory, LBNL-39445 (October 1996).

Stoft, Steven, *Power System Economics: Designing Markets for Electricity* (Piscataway, IEEE Press and John Wiley & Sons, 2002).

Stoft, Steven, "Problems of Transmission Investment in a Deregulated Power Market," in François Lévêque, ed., *Competitive Electricity Markets and Sustainability* (Cheltenham, Edward Elgar Publishing, 2006).

Stout, Mark, "Comparative Power Analysis of the California Electric Utility Industry Deregulation Process" (MS Thesis, University of California at Berkeley, May 25, 1997).

Stravos, Richard, "Reversal of Fortune? Wall Street Rethinks Merchant Power," *Public Utility Fortnightly* 139 (September 15, 2001): 12–23.

Studness, Charles M., "The Big Squeeze: 1992 Electric Utility Financial Results," *Public Utility Fortnightly* (June 1, 1993).

Swartwout, Robert, "Current Utility Regulatory Practice From a Historical Perspective," 32 *Natural Resource Journal* 289 (Spring 1992).

Sweeney, James L., *The California Electricity Crisis* (Palo Alto, Hoover Institute, 2002).

Sweeting, Andrew, "Market Power in the England and Wales Wholesale Electricity," CEEPR WP 04–013 (August 2004).

Swift, Byron, "U.S. Emissions Trading: Myths, Realities, and Opportunities," 20 *Natural Resources & Environment* (Summer 2005): 3–9.

Tabors, Caramanis & Associates and KEMA Consulting, Inc., "Market Restructuring Cost-Benefit Analysis," prepared for ERCOT (November 30, 2004).

Thompson, Herbert G., et al., "Economies of Scale and Vertical Integration in the Investor-Owned Electric Utility Industry," NRRI 96–05 (January 1996).

Thompson, Mozelle, "Deregulation and Competition in the Electricity Industry," Prepared Statement of the Federal Trade Commission, Before The Committee on the Judiciary United States House of Representatives (July 28, 1999).

Thorncraft, S.R., H.R. Outhred, and D.J. Clements, "Heuristics to Assist in Overcoming the Complexity of a Restructured Electricity Industry," IEEE PES General Meeting, Montreal, Canada (June 18–22, 2006).

Tierney, Susan F., "Why Coal Plants Retire: Power Market Fundamental as of 2012," Analysis Group (February 16, 2012).

Tierney, Susan F. and Charles Cicchetti, "The Results in Context: A Peer Review of EEI's 'Potential Impacts of Environmental Regulation on the U.S. Generation Fleet,'" Analysis Group (May 2011).

Tierney, Susan F. and Edward Kahn, "Cost-benefit Analysis of the New York Independent System Operator: The Initial Years," Analysis Group (March 2007).

Tietenberg, Tom, "Cap-and-Trade: The Evolution of an Economic Idea," *Agricultural and Resource Economics Review* 39 (October 2010): 359–67.

Tirole, Jean, *The Theory of Industrial Organization* (Cambridge, MA, MIT Press, 1988).

Tol, Richard and John Weyant, "Energy Economics' Most Influential Papers," *Energy Economics* 28 (2006): 405–09.

Train, Kenneth, *Optimal Regulation: The Economic Theory of Natural Monopoly* (Cambridge, MA, MIT Press, 1991).

Tullock, Gordon, "The Welfare Costs of Tariffs, Monopolies, and Theft," reprinted in James Buchanan, Robert Tollison, and Gordon Tullock, eds., *Toward A Theory of the Rent-Seeking Society* (College Station, Texas A&M Press, 1980).

Twomey, Paul, Richard Green, Karsten Neuhoff, and David Newbery, "A Review of the Monitoring of Market Power," *Journal of Energy Literature* 11 (2005): 3–54.

Unger, Darian and Howard Herzog, "Comparative Study on Energy R&D Performance: Gas Turbine Case Study," MIT Energy Laboratory (August 1998).

US-Canada Power System Outage Task Force, *Final Report on the August 14, 2003 Blackout in the United States and Canada: Causes and Recommendations*, United States Department of Energy and National Resources Canada (April, 2004).

U.S. House of Representatives, Committee on Government Reform, Minority Staff, "How Lax Regulation and Inadequate Oversight Contributed to the Enron Collapse," 107th Congress (February 7, 2002).

Vantage Consulting, "Operational Audit of the California Independent System Operator," for FERC (January 25, 2002).

Vergne, Jean-Philippe and Rodolphe Durand, "The Missing Link between the Theory and Empirics of Path Dependence: Conceptual Clarification, Testability Issue, and Methodological Implications," *Journal of Management Studies* 47 (2010): 736–59.

Vietor, Richard H.K., *Contrived Competition: Regulation and Deregulation in America* (Cambridge, MA, Harvard University Press, 1994).

Vitaliano, Donald and Gregory Stella, "A Frontier Approach to Testing the Averch-Johnson Hypothesis," *International Journal of the Economics of Business* 16 (2009): 347–63.

Vittal, Vijay, et al., "Detection, Prevention and Mitigation of Cascading Events: Adaptive Islanding with Selective Under-Frequency Load Shedding," Final Project Report, Part III, PSERC (2008).

Vogel, David, "The Public-Interest Movement and the American Reform Tradition," *Political Science Quarterly* (Winter 1980–81): 616–27.

von der Fehr, Niles-Henrik M. and David Harbor, "Spot Market Competition in the UK Electricity Industry," *Economic Journal* 103 (1993): 531–46.

von Meier, Alexandra, "Occupational Cultures as a Challenge to Technological Innovation," IEEE Transactions (1999).

Washington International Energy Group, "Natural Gas for Electric Generation: Realizing the Potential," Prepared for the INGAA Foundation, Inc. (May 1994).

Wasserstrom, Robert, Neil Palmer, and Susan Reider, "Trouble on the Line: Deregulation Fuels Public Opposition to Transmission Lines," Terra Group, Houston (1996).

Watkiss, Jeffrey D. and Douglas W. Smith, "The Energy Policy Act of 1992 – A Watershed for Competition in the Wholesale Power Market," 10 *Yale Journal on Regulation* 447 (Summer 1993).

Weaver, Jacqueline Lang, "Can Energy Markets Be Trusted? The Effect of the Rise and Fall of Enron on Energy Markets," *Houston Business and Tax Law Journal* 4 (2004): 1.

Weiss, L.W., "Antitrust in the Electric Power Industry," in Almarin Phillips, ed., *Promoting Competition in Regulated Markets* (Washington, DC, Brookings Institution, 1975).

Wellinghoff, Jon B. and Cynthia K. Mitchell, "A Model for Statewide Integrated Utility Resource Planning," *Public Utilities Fortnightly* 116 (August 8, 1985): 19–26.

White, Eugene, "The Past and Future of Economic History in Economics," *Quarterly Review of Economics and Finance* 36 (1996): 61–72.

White, Mathew W., "Dynamic Efficiency and the Regulated Firm: Empirical Evidence," Unpublished Working Paper (January 2005).

Williamson, Oliver E., "Economies as an Antitrust Defense: The Welfare Trade-offs," *American Economic Review* 58 (1968): 18–36.

Wilson, Chris and Catherine Waddams Price, "Do Consumers Switch to the Best Supplier?" CCP Working Paper No. 07-6 (2007).

Wilson, James F., "Reconsidering Resource Adequacy, Part 1: Has the One-Day-in-10 years Criterion Outlived its Usefulness?" *Public Utilities Fortnightly* (April 2010): 33–39.

Wing, Ian Sue, "Explaining the Declining Energy Intensity of the U.S. Economy," *Resource and Energy Economics* 30 (2008): 21–49.

Wolak, Frank, "Measuring Unilateral Market Power in Wholesale Electricity Markets: The California Market, 1998–2000," *American Economic Review* 93 (May 2003): 425–30.

Wolak, Frank, "Using Restructured Electricity Supply Industries to Understand Oligopoly Industry Outcomes," *Utilities Policy* 18 (2010): 227–46.

Wolak, Frank and Robert Patrick, "The Impact of Market Rules and Market Structure on the Price Determination Process in the England and Wales Electricity Market," POWER (February 1997).

Yandle, Bruce, "Bootleggers and Baptists-The Education of a Regulatory Economist," *Regulation* 7 (May–June 1983): 12–16.

Yatchew, A., "Scale Economies in Electricity Distribution: A Semiparametric Analysis," *Journal of Applied Econometrics* 15 (2000): 187–210.

Yergin, Daniel, *Cold War, Shattered Peace: The Origins of the Cold War and the National Security State* (Boston, Houghton Mifflin 1977).

Yucel, Mine and Adam Swadley, "Did Residential Electricity Rates Fall After Retail Competition? A Dynamic Panel Analysis," Federal Reserve Bank of Dallas (May 2011).

Zarnikau, Jay, Marilyn Fox, and Paul Smolen, "Trends in Prices to Commercial Energy Consumers in the Competitive Texas Electricity Market," *Energy Policy* 35 (2007): 4332–39.

Zarnikau, Jay and Ian Hallett, "Aggregate Industrial Energy Consumer Response to Wholesale Prices in the Restructured Texas Electricity Market," *Energy Economics* 20 (2008): 1798–1808.

Zhang, Fan, "Does Electricity Restructuring Work? Evidence from the U.S. Nuclear Energy Industry," *Journal of Industrial Economics* 55 (September 2007): 397–418.

Index